PAGE
26

ON THE
ROAD

YOUR COMPLETE DESTINATION GUIDE
In-depth reviews, detailed listings
and insider tips

**Naples &
Campania**
p28

**Puglia,
Basilicata &
Calabria**
p91

Sicily
p148

D0067536

PAGE
247

SURVIVAL
GUIDE

VITAL PRACTICAL INFORMATION TO
HELP YOU HAVE A SMOOTH TRIP

Language

Standard Italian is taught and spoken
throughout Italy. Regional dialects are an
important part of identity in many parts of
the country, but you'll have no trouble being
understood anywhere if you stick to standard
Italian, which we've also used in this chapter.
   The sounds used in spoken Italian can
all be found in English. If you read our coloured pronunciation guides as if they were
English, you'll be understood. The stressed
syllables are indicated with italics. Note that
·ai· is pronounced as 'ai' aisle, ·ii· as 'ay'
·oo· as in 'oh', ·ii· as the 'ai' in 'lati', and that
·s· a strong and rolled sound. Keep in mind
that Italian consonants can have a stronger,
emphatic pronunciation – if the consonant
is written as a double letter, it should be
stressed a little stronger; eg some ·ee·

Yes.	Sì.
No.	No.
Excuse me.	Mi scusi. (pol)
	Scusami. (inf)
Sorry.	Mi dispiace.
Please.	Per favore.
Thank you.	Grazie.
You're welcome.	Prego.

How are you?
Come sta/stai? (pol/inf)

Fine. And you?
Bene. E Lei/tu? (pol/inf)

What's your
Come si

THIS EDITION WRITTEN AND RESEARCHED BY

**Cristian Bonetto,
Gregor Clark, Olivia Pozzan**

welcome to Southern Italy

History & Art

Few parts of Europe would dare compare their cultural riches to those of Italy's Mezzogiorno (land of the midday sun). For millennia at the crossroads of civilisations, southern Italy is a World Heritage overachiever, bursting with superlative art and architecture. Let your imagination run wild among the prehistoric *sassi* (cave dwellings) of Matera, or the Disney-like *trulli* (conical dwellings) of the Valle d'Itria. Channel the past at the Greek temples of Segesta and Paestum, or on the haunted streets of Pompeii and Herculaneum. Compare the Byzantine glitter of Sicily's cathedrals to the darkness of Caravaggio's *Flagellazione* in Naples. Then watch the region outdo itself with its idiosyncratic baroque. From Caserta's gilded royal palace to the fantastical facades of Lecce and southeastern Sicily, the south's flood of frescoes, marble and curves will leave you begging for more.

Food, Glorious Food

The lust doesn't stop there. This is the country's culinary soul, home to Italy's best pizza, pasta, mozzarella, vegetables, citrus and seafood. It's like one never-ending feast: bubbling, wood-fired pizza and potent espresso in Naples; long, lazy lunches at vine-framed Pugliese farmhouses; just-caught sardines by lapping waves on a Tyrrhenian island; lavish, luscious pastries in

Volcanic, voluptuous and irrepressibly vivacious, southern Italy is a hypnotic collision of ancient cultures, exotic flavours and hedonistic urges. Welcome to where Europe ends and the rest of the world begins.

(left) Rugged mountains meet the jewel-like sea on the southern coast of Capri (p53)
(below) Spaghetti *alle vongole* (with clams), a Companian speciality (p208)

chintzy Palermo *pasticcerie* (pastry shops). Should you go mushroom hunting in the wilds of Calabria? Taste-test your first red aubergine (eggplant) at an heirloom trattoria in Basilicata? Feast on fresh sea urchin on an Adriatic beach? Or just kick back with a glass of crisp local Falanghina as you debate who has the creamiest buffalo mozzarella – Caserta, Paestum or Foggia? Whatever your choice, be certain that good food and wine will play starring roles in your southern sojourn.

Natural Highs

Mother Nature went into overdrive in the south, creating a thrilling jumble of rugged mountains, fiery volcanoes and glittering coastal grottoes. It's like one giant playground begging to be tackled – at a pace that's fast and furious, or romantic and relaxed. Crank up the heart rate white-water rafting down Calabria's river Lao; scaling Europe's most active volcano, Stromboli; or diving into prehistoric sea caves on Puglia's Promontorio del Gargano. If you need to bring it down a notch, the options are just as enticing, from slow pedalling across Puglia's gentle countryside, or sailing along the Amalfi Coast, to simply stripping down and soaking in Vulcano's healing geothermal mud. The options may be many, but there is one constant – a landscape that is beautiful, diverse and just a little magic.

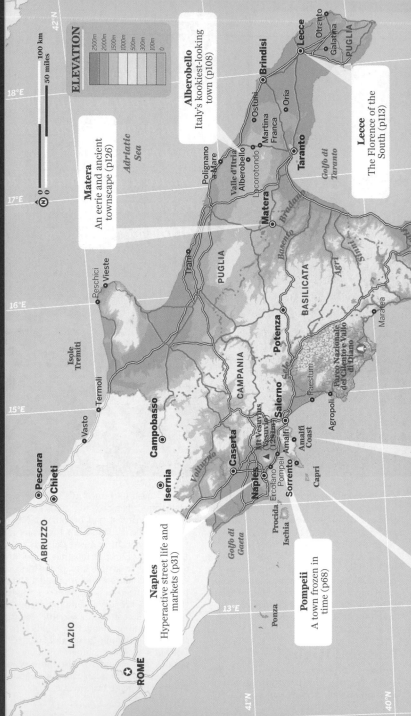

Matera
An eerie and ancient townscape (p126)

Alberobello
Italy's kookiest-looking town (p108)

Lecce
The Florence of the South (p113)

Naples
Hyperactive street life and markets (p31)

Pompeii
A town frozen in time (p68)

ELEVATION

2500m
2000m
1500m
1000m
500m
300m
100m
0

100 km
50 miles

LAZIO

ABRUZZO

CAMPANIA

PUGLIA

BASILICATA

MOLISE

ROME

Pescara
Chieti
Vasto
Termoli
Campobasso
Isernia
Caserta
Naples
Mt Vesuvius (1281m)
Ercolano
Pompei
Sorrento
Amalfi
Amalfi Coast
Capri
Salerno
Paestum
Agropoli
Potenza
Matera
Peschici
Vieste
Trani
Polignano a Mare
Alberobello
Valle d'Itria
Locorotondo
Martina Franca
Ostuni
Oria
Taranto
Brindisi
Lecce
Otranto
Galatina
Maratea

Isole Tremiti

Ponza
Procida
Ischia

Golfo di Gaeta

Adriatic Sea

Golfo di Taranto

Volturno

Sele

Basento

Bradano

Agri

Sinni

Parco Nazionale del Cilento e Vallo di Diano

Volturno

40°N
41°N
42°N

13°E
15°E
16°E
17°E
18°E

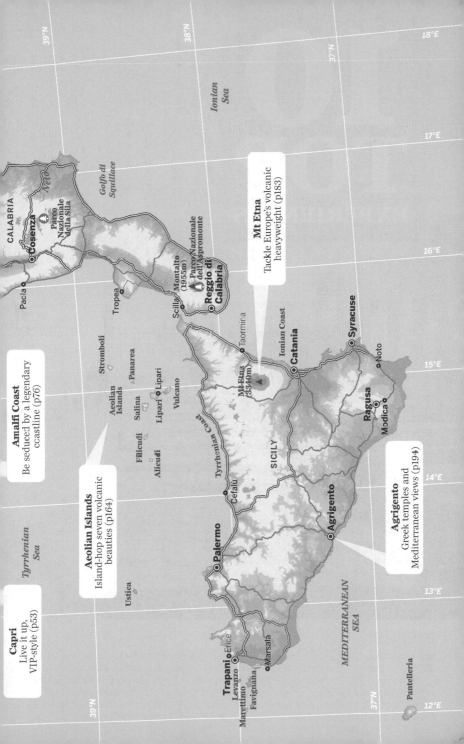

Capri
Live it up,
VIP-style (p53)

Amalfi Coast
Be seduced by a legendary
coastline (p76)

Aeolian Islands
Island-hop seven volcanic
beauties (p164)

Mt Etna
Tackle Europe's volcanic
heavyweight (p183)

Agrigento
Greek temples and
Mediterranean views (p194)

39°N
38°N
37°N
39°N
37°N

18°E
17°E
16°E
15°E
14°E
13°E
12°E

*Ionian
Sea*

*Tyrrhenian
Sea*

*Golfo di
Squillace*

*MEDITERRANEAN
SEA*

CALABRIA
Cosenza
Parco
Nazionale
della Sila
Neto

Paola
Tropea
Scilla
Monte Montalto
(1955m)
Parco
Nazionale
dell'Aspromonte
**Reggio di
Calabria**

Stromboli
Panarea
Aeolian
Islands
Salina
Lipari
Lipari
Vulcano
Filicudi
Alicudi

Tyrrhenian Coast

Cefalù
Ustica

Palermo

Trapani
Erice
Levanzo
Marettimo
Favignana
Marsala

Pantelleria

Taormina
Ionian Coast
Mt Etna
(3340m)
Catania
Syracuse
Noto

SICILY

Ragusa
Modica

Agrigento

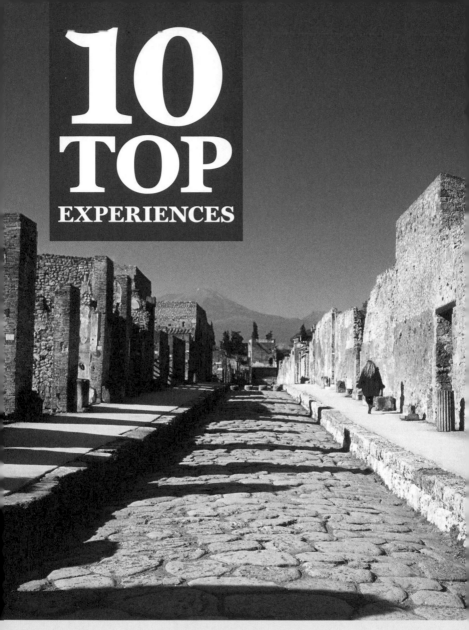

10 TOP EXPERIENCES

Pompeii

1 Nothing piques human curiosity quite like a mass catastrophe, and few have left a mark like Pompeii (p68), a once-thriving Roman town frozen in its death throes for all time. Wander Roman streets, the grassy, column-lined forum, the city brothel, the 5000-seat theatre and the frescoed Villa dei Misteri while you ponder Pliny the Younger's terrifying account of the tragedy: 'Darkness came on again, again ashes, thick and heavy. We got up repeatedly to shake these off; otherwise we would have been buried and crushed by the weight'. Pompeii street and Mt Vesuvius, above

JEAN-BERNARD CARILLET/LONELY PLANET IMAGES ©

Neapolitan Street Life

2 There's nothing like waking up to the sound of a Neapolitan street market, whether it's rough-and-ready Mercato di Porta Nolana (p36) or the city's oldest, La Pignasecca (p37). A feast for the senses, these markets are as much akin to a North African bazaar as a European market: fruit vendors raucously hawking their wares in Neapolitan dialect, swordfish heads casting sidelong glances at you across heaps of silvery sardines on ice, the perfume of crunchy *casareccio* (homestyle) bread, and the cinnamon-laced aroma of *sfogliatelle* (sweetened ricotta pastries). La Pignasecca, left

Temples in Agrigento

3 Few archaeological sites evoke the past like Agrigento's Valle dei Templi (p194). Located on a ridge looking out at the Mediterranean, its stoic, sunbaked temples belonged to Akragas, a once-great city settled by the Greeks. The scars of ancient battle endure in the 5th-century-BC Tempio di Hera, while the Tempio della Concordia's remarkable state of preservation inspired Unesco's own logo. To conjure the ghosts of the past, roam the ruins late in the afternoon, when the crowds have thinned and the wind whistles between the columns. Tempio della Concordia, above

Capri

4 Even the summer hordes can't quite dilute the ethereal magic of Capri (p53). Described as 'one of the magnetic points of the earth' by the writer and painter Alberto Savinio, Italy's most fabled island has been seducing mere mortals for millennia. Emperor Tiberius reputedly threw his lovers off its dizzying cliffs, Grand Tourists waxed lyrical about its electric-blue grotto, and celebrities continue to moor their yachts in its turquoise waters. For a view you won't forget, head to the summit of Monte Solaro (think bath-time boats and sugar-cube houses). View from Monte Solaro, below

Alberobello

DAVID BORLAND/LONELY PLANET IMAGES ©

5 Your imagination will run riot in Alberobello (p108), famed for its kooky, one-of-a-kind architecture. We're talking *trulli* – white-washed circular dwellings with cone-shaped roofs. Looking like they're straight out of a Disney cartoon, these sunbaked dwellings tumble down the slopes like armies of hatted dwarves. You can dine in some of them, and sleep in others. Just don't be surprised if you need to pinch yourself... Was that Snow White? Are you on Earth? Unesco seems to thinks so, bestowing World Heritage status on them in 1996. Conical roofs of *trulli*, left

Aeolian Island-Hopping

6 The Greeks don't have a monopoly on Mediterranean island-hopping. Sicily's Aeolian Islands (p164) might be a little less famous than their Aegean Sea rivals, but they are no less stunning. Mix and match from seven volcanic outcrops, among them thermal hot-spot Vulcano (p168), vine-laced Salina (p169) and lava-oozing Stromboli (p170). But don't just take our word for it. The islands are one of only two Italian natural landscapes on Unesco's World Heritage list (the other being the Dolomites in Italy's north). Pollara beach, Salina, above

Matera

7 The best time to explore Matera (p126) is before it gets up. The town is tinged gold by the morning sun and the scent of the day's first coffee lingers in the air. Matera is an extraordinary place: its World Heritage–listed *sassi* (former cave dwellings) developed from caves that pock a dizzying ravine. In no other place do you come face to face with such powerful images of Italy's lost peasant culture; these cavernous dwellings echo a level of poverty difficult to fathom in a wealthy G8 country. Chiesa di Santa Maria d'Idris, above

Amalfi Coast

8 With its scented lemon groves, flower-strewn cliffsides, tumbling sherbet-hued towns and bobbing fishing boats, the Amalfi Coast still claims the crown as the prettiest coast on the Italian peninsula. Others may argue for Liguria's Cinque Terre or Calabria's Costa Viola, but the Hollywood divas and starry-eyed day trippers say differently. After all, who's to disagree with the likes of Gore Vidal, Truman Capote and Greta Garbo? The stretch from Sorrento (p72) to Positano (p77) is the least developed and most alluring. Positano, below

Baroque Lecce

9 The extravagant architectural character of many Puglian towns is down to the local style of *barocco leccese*. The local stone was so soft, art critic Cesare Brandi claimed 'it can be carved with a penknife'. Local craftsmen vied for ever-greater heights of creativity, crowding facades with swirling vegetal designs, gargoyles and strange zoomorphic figures. Lecce's Basilica di Santa Croce (p113) is the high point of the style, so outrageously busy the Marchese Grimaldi said it made him think a lunatic was having a nightmare. Facade of Basilica di Santa Croce, left

Mt Etna

10 Known to the Greeks as the 'column that holds up the sky', Mt Etna (p183) is Europe's largest volcano and one of the world's most active. It's also the highest mountain south of the Alps. The ancients believed the giant Tifone (Typhoon) lived in its crater and lit up the sky with regular, spectacular pyrotechnics. At 3330m it literally towers above Sicily's Ionian Coast, and since 1987 its slopes have been part of the Parco dell'Etna, an area that encompasses both alpine forests and the forbiddingly black summit.

need to know

Currency
» Euro (€)

Language
» Italian

When to Go

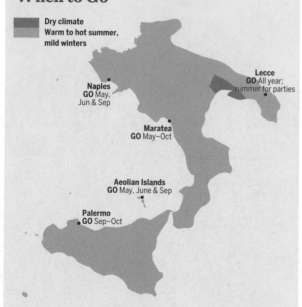

Dry climate
Warm to hot summer, mild winters

Naples
GO May, Jun & Sep

Lecce
GO All year; summer for parties

Maratea
GO May–Oct

Aeolian Islands
GO May, June & Sep

Palermo
GO Sep–Oct

High Season
(Jul–Aug)

» Queues and crowds at big sights, beaches and on the road, especially August

» A good period for cultural events in tourist areas

Shoulder (Apr–Jun & Sep–Oct)

» Good deals on accommodation

» Spring is best for festivals, flowers and local produce

» Autumn is best for warm weather and the grape harvest

Low Season
(Nov–Mar)

» Prices can be 30% lower than high season (except Christmas, New Year and Easter)

» Many sights, hotels and restaurants closed in coastal and mountainous areas

» Christmas feasting and colourful Carnevale

Your Daily Budget

Budget up to
€100

» Dorm bed: €15–25

» Double room in a budget hotel: €50–100

» Meal of pizza and pasta: €15

» Excellent markets and delis for self-catering

Midrange
€100–200

» Double room in a hotel: €80–180

» Lunch and dinner in local restaurants: €25–50

Top end over
€200

» Double room in a four- or five-star hotel: €200–450

» Top restaurant dinner: €50–150

Money

» ATMs at every airport, most train stations and widely available in towns and cities. Credit cards accepted in most hotels and restaurants.

Visas

» Generally not required for stays of up to 90 days (or at all for EU nationals); some nationalities need a Schengen visa (p258).

Mobile (Cell) Phones

» European and Australian phones work, other phones should be set to roaming. Use a local SIM card for cheaper rates on local calls.

Driving

» Drive on the right; steering wheel is on the left side of the car. Be aware that headlights are legally required on all motorways.

Websites

» **Lonely Planet** (www.lonelyplanet. com/italy) Destination information, hotel bookings, traveller forum and more.

» **Trenitalia** (www. trenitalia.com) Italian railways.

» **Agriturismi** (www. agriturismi.it) Guide to farm accommodation.

» **Slow Food** (www. slowfood.com) For the best local producers, restaurants and markets.

» **Enit Italia** (www. italiantourism.com) Italian government tourism website.

» **Italia Kids** (www. italiakids.com) Fantastic family resource.

Exchange Rates

Australia	A$1	€0.73
Canada	C$1	€0.71
Japan	¥100	€0.86
New Zealand	NZ$1	€0.56
Switzerland	Sfr1	€0.82
UK	UK£1	€1.13
US	US$1	€0.69

For current exchange rates see www.xe.com

Important Numbers

To dial listings in this book from outside Italy, dial your international access code, Italy's country code, and then the number (including the '0').

Italy country code	☎39
International access code	☎00
Ambulance	☎118
Police	☎113

Arriving in Southern Italy

» **Aeroporto Capodichino**
Shuttle – To Naples centre every 20 minutes, 6.30am to 11.40pm
Taxi – €19 set fare; 30 minutes

» **Aeroporto Palese**
Shuttle – To Bari centre half hourly, 6am to 10.50pm
Taxi – Around €24; 15 minutes

» **Aeroporto Falcone-Borsellino**
Shuttle – To Palermo centre half hourly, 6.30am to midnight
Train – To Palermo centre hourly, 7.25am to 10pm
Taxis – €35–45 set fare; 30 minutes

Safety in the South

Despite mafia notoriety, southern Italy is not a dangerous place and the biggest threat you face is from faceless pickpockets and bag-snatchers. Leave valuables in your hotel room and never leave them in your car. If carrying a bag or camera, wear the strap across your body and away from the road – moped thieves can swipe a bag and be gone in seconds. Be vigilant for pickpockets in crowded areas, including at train stations and ferry terminals, on buses and in markets (especially those in Naples, Palermo and Catania). Never buy electronics, including mobile phones, from market vendors – one common scam sees the boxes filled with bricks. Always report thefts to the police within 24 hours, and ask for a statement, otherwise your travel insurance company won't pay out.

first time

Everyone needs a helping hand when they visit a country for the first time. There are phrases to learn, customs to get used to and etiquette to understand. The following section will help demystify southern Italy so your first trip goes as smoothly as your fifth.

Language

Unlike many other European countries, English is not widely spoken in Italy. Of course, you can get by in the main tourist centres, but in the countryside and off the tourist track, you'll need to master a few basic phrases. This will improve your experience no end, especially when ordering in restaurants, some of which have no written menu. See the language section of this book (p268) for all the phrases you need to get by.

Booking Ahead

Reserving a room is essential during high season and during key events (such as Easter and Christmas) when demand is usually high. Big-name restaurants and experiences such as an evening at the opera also need to be booked ahead.

Hello	Buongiorno
I would like to book...	Vorrei prenotare...
a single room	una camera singola
a double room	una camera doppia con letto matrimoniale
in the name of...	in nome di...
from... to... (date)	dal... al...
How much is it...?	Quanto costa...?
per night/per person	per la notte/per persona
Thank you very much	Grazie (mille)

What to Wear

Appearances matter in Italy. The concept of *la bella figura* (making a good impression) encapsulates the Italian obsession with looking good. In general, trousers (pants), jeans, shirts and polo shirts for men and skirts or trousers for women will serve you well in the city. Shorts, T-shirts and sandals are fine in summer and at the beach, but long sleeves are required for dining out. Come evening, think smart casual. A light sweater or waterproof jacket is useful in spring and autumn, and sturdy shoes are good for visiting archaeological sites.

What to Pack

» Passport (and a photocopy of it, kept separately)
» Credit cards
» Drivers licence
» Phrasebook
» Travel plug
» Mobile (cell) phone charger
» Sunscreen and sunglasses
» Waterproof jacket
» Comfortable shoes
» A stylish outfit
» Camera
» Money belt
» Earplugs
» A detailed driving map

Checklist

» Check the validity of your passport

» Check airline baggage restrictions

» Organise travel insurance (see p254)

» Make bookings (for sights, entertainment and accommodation)

» Inform your credit/debit card company

» Check if you can use your mobile (cell) phone (see p257)

» Find out what you need to hire a car (see p265)

Etiquette

Italy is a surprisingly formal society; the following tips will help you avoid any awkward moments.

» Greetings
Shake hands and say *buongiorno* (good day) or *buona sera* (good evening) to strangers; kiss both cheeks and say *come stai* (how are you) for friends. Use *lei* (you) in polite company; use *tu* (you) with friends and children. Only use first names if invited.

» Asking for help
Say *mi scusi* (excuse me) to attract attention; use *permesso* (permission) when you want to pass by in a crowded space.

» Religion
Dress modestly (cover shoulders, torso and thighs) and be quiet when visiting religious sites.

» Eating & Drinking
When dining in an Italian home, bring a small gift of *dolci* (sweets) or wine and dress well. Let your host lead when sitting and starting the meal. When dining out, summon the waiter by saying *per favore?* (please?).

» Gestures
Maintain eye contact during conversation.

Tipping

» When to Tip
Tipping is customary in restaurants, optional elsewhere.

» Taxis
Optional, but most people round up to the nearest euro.

» Restaurants
Most restaurants have a *coperto* (cover charge; usually €1 to €2) and a *servizio* (service charge) of 10% to 15%. If service isn't included, a small tip is appropriate.

» Bars
Optional, but most locals leave a tip of €0.10 to €0.20; if drinks are brought to your table, tip as in a restaurant.

Money

Credit and debit cards can be used almost everywhere, with the exception of some rural towns and villages. Visa and MasterCard are among the most widely recognised, but others like Cirrus and Maestro are also well covered. American Express is only accepted by some major chains and big hotels, and few places take Diners Club. Ask if bars and restaurants take cards before you order. Chip-and-pin is the norm for card transactions. ATMs are everywhere, but be aware of transaction fees. Some ATMs in Italy reject foreign cards. If this happens, try a few before assuming the problem is with your card. In theory, you can change travellers cheques at banks and post offices, but some readers have reported problems and hefty commissions, even on cheques denominated in euros. To avoid per-cheque charges get your cheques in large denominations.

if you like...

Food, Glorious Food

Southern Italy's rich soil, produce-packed hillsides and turquoise seas are a giant natural larder, tended by proud farmers and fishermen. In this part of the world, traditions are fiercely protected and eating well is a given. Tuck in!

Pizza Italy's most famous export is best sampled in its spiritual home, Naples (p45).

Buffalo mozzarella Sink your teeth into Italy's silkiest cheese in Campania (p28).

Seafood So fresh it's eaten *crudo* (raw) in Campania (p28), Puglia (p93) and Sicily (p148).

Il Frantoio The eight-course lunches at this working farm are the very definition of slow food (p112).

Markets Lip-smacking produce and electric street life collide at markets like Porta Nolana (p36), Ballarò (p155) and La Pescheria (p177).

Chocolate Cocoa connoisseurs flock to Modica (p192), whose legendary chocolate creations come in flavours like vanilla and cinnamon, and *peperoncino* (hot chilli).

Medieval Towns

Find peace in the hushed alleys of southern Italy's medieval villages. Here, cobbled streets snake up hillsides to sculpted fountains, the scent of *ragù* wafts from shuttered windows and washing hangs like holiday bunting.

Ravello Romantic gardens, heavenly views, and a world-class music festival define this Amalfi Coast jewel (p83).

Taormina It draws the summertime hordes, but with good reason – think twisting streets, secret gardens and a panoramic ancient amphitheatre (p172).

Cefalù Arabesque streets are soaked in sunshine and fringed by lapping waves; the glorious Norman cathedral is a highlight (p162).

Maratea A 13th-century *borgo* (medieval town) with pint-sized piazzas, wriggling alleys and startling views across the Gulf of Policastro (p133).

Puglia From the Valle d'Itria (p107) to the sierras of the Salento (p113), Puglia is sprinkled with biscuit-coloured hilltop towns.

Erice Ancient walls, brooding castles, and views across to Africa make this hilltop town one of Italy's finest (p204).

Baroque Architecture

Innately extravagant, effusive and loud, southern Italy found its soul mate in the baroque architecture of the 17th and 18th centuries. Plunge into a world of outrageous palaces and bling-tastic churches and reconsider the adage 'less is more'.

Val di Noto A valley studded with role-model baroque towns, including best-of-the-lot: Noto (p190).

Lecce This hallucinogenic city is to the baroque what Florence is to the Renaissance (p113).

Palazzo Reale As seen in *Star Wars,* Caserta's royal pad is Italian baroque at its most ambitious (p41).

Certosa di San Martino A who's who of visionary artists contributed to this monastery's jaw-dropping church (p37).

Chiesa e Chiostro di San Gregorio Armeno Obscenely lavish chancels make this a decadent Catholic show-off. (p36).

Catania Designed by Giovanni Vaccarini, the city's Piazza del Duomo is a World Heritage pin-up (p177).

» Interior of the Certosa di San Martino in Naples (p37)

Hiking

Whether you're hankering for a gentle stroll or a hardcore trek, Italy's south delivers the goods. Slip into silent forests in Puglia, Basilicata and Calabria, or come face to face with Mother Nature's wrath in lava-spewing Sicily.

Sentiero degli Dei Hit the 'Path of the Gods' for a refreshingly different take on the stunning Amalfi Coast (p82).

Mt Etna Hike the picturesque slopes of Europe's tallest active volcano (p183).

Stromboli Your reward for this challenging, calf-toning adventure is an explosive volcanic spectacular (p170).

Parco Nazionale del Gargano Explore an enchanted world of Aleppo pines, springtime orchids, roe deer and sacred pilgrimage sites (p102).

Parco Nazionale del Pollino Italy's largest national park is nothing short of breathtaking, crammed with valleys, river canyons, rare flora and ancient mountain communities (p138).

Parco Nazionale del Cilento e Vallo di Diano Dive into deep, rugged forests and two remarkable, ancient grottoes (p89).

Islands & Beaches

Northern Italy would pay a mint for a coastline this alluring. From steamy volcanic beaches and bijou islands to crystal-clear grottoes, the south's offerings are as varied as they are beautiful.

Puglia The region's superlative beaches include Baia dei Turchi (p121) and the cliff-backed beaches of the Gargano (p102).

Aeolian Islands Island-hop Sicily's seven volcanic gems (p164).

Pantelleria This wild, windswept outcrop has a bewitching Arabesque flavour (p203).

Capri Bronzed VIPs and a razzle-dazzle grotto keep this island on the international A-list (p53).

Procida This pastel-hued island is an old favourite with soul-searching artists (p65).

Ischia Bubbling beaches and thermal spas give Ischia a soothing, salubrious air (p59).

Amalfi Coast Tumbling villages and milky-blue waters on Europe's most famous coast (p76).

Maratea With its cooling pines and head-spinning cliffs, this Tyrrhenian jewel gives the Amalfi Coast a run for its money (p133).

Tropea Sugar-soft beaches, piercing sunsets and picture-perfect laneways make this Calabria's coastal 'It' kid (p146).

Mosaics

Southern Italy's cosmopolitan past comes to life in its glorious, sparkling mosaics. Lose yourself in scenes of classical mythology or ponder the glories of Constantinople in exotic Byzantine creations.

Villa Romana del Casale Sicily's top Roman site is home to the finest Roman floor mosaics in existence (p195).

Museo Archeologico Nazionale Feast your eyes on exquisite mosaics from Pompeii and Herculaneum at Naples' world-renowned archaeological museum (p36).

Herculaneum From geometric floors to technicolour walls, these Roman mosaics live on in their original, ill-fated setting (p67).

Cappella Palatina This glittering chapel is the jewel in Palermo's cultural crown (p155).

Monreale Cathedral Lavish 12th-century tile-work brings the Old Testament to life in this Arab-Norman wonder (p162).

Cefalù Duomo The elaborate Byzantine mosaics inside Cefalù's cathedral are Sicily's oldest and best preserved (p163).

Otranto Cathedral Look down for a bizarre, technicolour fusion of the classics, Christianity, and good old fashioned superstition (p121).

month by month

February

Short and accursed is how Italians describe February. It might still be chilly down south, but almond trees start to blossom and Carnevale season brightens things up with confetti, costumes and sugar-dusted treats.

Carnevale

In the period leading up to Ash Wednesday, many southern towns stage pre-Lenten carnivals. One of the most flamboyant is the Carnevale di Acireale (p179; www.carnevalediacireale.it), the elaborate and whimsical floats of which are famous throughout the country.

March

The weather in March is capricious: sunny, rainy and windy all at once. The official start of spring is 21 March, but things only really start to open up for the main season during Easter week.

Settimana Santa

Processions and passion plays mark Easter Holy Week across the south. On Good Friday and the Thursday preceding it, hooded penitents walk through the streets of Sorrento (p72). On Procida (p65), Good Friday sees wooden statues and life-size tableaux carted across the island.

May

The month of roses and early summer produce makes May a perfect time to travel, especially for walkers. The weather is warm but not too hot and prices throughout the south are good value. It's also patron-saint season.

Festa di San Gennaro

As patron-saint days go, Naples' Festa di San Gennaro has a lot riding on it, namely securing the city from volcanic disaster. The faithful gather in the cathedral to see San Gennaro's blood liquefy. If it does, the city is safe. Repeat performances take place on 19 September and 16 December (p42).

Ciclo di Rappresentazioni Classiche

Classical intrigue in an evocative setting, the Festival of Greek Theatre brings of Syracuse's 5th-century-BC amphitheatre to life from mid-May to mid-June, with performances from Italy's acting greats (p188; www.indafondazione.org).

June

The summer season kicks off in June. The temperature cranks up quickly, beach lidos start to open in earnest and some of the big summer festivals commence. There's a national holiday on 2 June, the Anniversary of the Republic.

Ravello Festival

Perched high above the Amalfi Coast, Ravello draws world-renowned artists during its summer-long festival (p83; www.ravellofestival.com). Spanning everything from music and dance to film and art exhibitions, several events take place in the exquisite Villa Rufolo gardens from June to mid-September.

July

School is out and Italians everywhere are heading out of the cities and to the mountains or beaches for their summer holidays. Prices and temperatures rise. The beach is in full swing, but many cities host summer art festivals.

Taormina Arte

Ancient ruins and languid summer nights set a seductive scene for Taormina's arts festival (p174; www.taormina-arte.com). Held between July and August, its programme includes film, theatre, concerts and opera, from both Italy and beyond.

Festival della Valle d'Itria

Between mid-July and early August, the town of Martina Franca sets toes a-tapping with its esteemed music festival (p110; www.festivaldellavalleditria.it). The focus is on classical music and opera, especially obscure pieces and more famous works performed in their original form.

August

August in southern Italy is hot, expensive and crowded. Everyone is on holiday and while it may no longer be true that everything is shut, many businesses and restaurants do close for part of the month.

Ferragosto

After Christmas and Easter, Ferragosto is Italy's biggest holiday. While it now marks the Feast of the Assumption, even the ancient Romans honoured their pagan gods on Feriae Augusti. Naples lets loose with particular fervour.

La Notte della Taranta

Puglia celebrates its hypnotic *pizzica* dance with the Night of the Taranta (p121; www.lanottedellataranta.it), a two-week festival held in tiny Melpignano. Dancing aside, the event also showcases Salento's folk-music traditions.

September

This is a glorious month in the south. As summer wanes into autumn, the grape harvest begins. Adding to the culinary excitement are the many local *sagre* (food festivals), celebrating regional produce and traditions.

Couscous Fest

The Sicilian town of San Vito celebrates multiculturalism and its famous fish couscous at this six-day festival (p201; www.couscousfest.it). Highlights include an international couscous cook-off, cooking workshops from well-known chefs, tastings and live world-music gigs.

November

The advent of winter creeps down the peninsula in November, but there's still plenty going on. Head south for the chestnut harvest, mushroom picking and All Saints Day.

Opera Season

Southern Italy is home to two of the world's great opera houses: Naples' Teatro San Carlo and Palermo's Teatro Massimo. The season traditionally runs from mid-October to March. Book tickets well in advance and don't forget to slick up.

December

The days of alfresco living are at an end. Yet, despite the cooler days and longer nights, looming Christmas festivities warm things up with festive street lights, nativity scenes and Yuletide specialities.

Natale

The weeks preceding Christmas are studded with religious events. Many churches set up nativity scenes known as *presepe*. While Naples (p28) is especially famous for these, you'll find impressive tableaux in many southern towns, including Erice (p204) in Sicily.

itineraries

Whether you've got nine days or 21, these itineraries provide a starting point for the trip of a lifetime. Want more inspiration? Head online to lonelyplanet. com/thorntree to chat with other travellers.

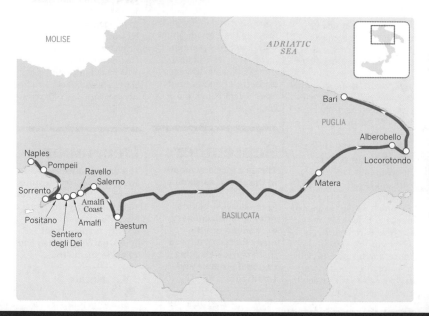

Two Weeks
Southern Overview

Start your sojourn with three days in **Naples**, indulging in its architectural, artistic and culinary riches. On day four, time travel in **Pompeii** before some evening *dolce vita* in buzzing **Sorrento**. Hairpin turns and unforgettable vistas define day five as you hit the enigmatic Amalfi Coast. Spend two romantic nights in **Positano**, from where you can walk some of the breathtaking **Sentiero degli Dei** (Walk of the Gods). Spend another two days in deeply historic **Amalfi** and panoramic **Ravello**, the latter well known for its summer-long arts fest. On day nine, continue east to upbeat **Salerno** to sample the city's fabulous seafood, pastries and street life. Spend day 10 roaming the Greek ruins of **Paestum** before heading east to Basilicata's even older **Matera**. Spend a couple of days exploring the town's extraordinary *sassi* (former cave dwellings) and hiking through the dramatic Matera Gravina gorge. Cap your trip off with two days in Puglia's Valle d'Itria, checking out World Heritage *trulli* (conical abodes) in **Alberobello** and sampling local *vino bianco* (white wine) in **Locorotondo**. From here, it's an easy onward jump to transport hub **Bari**.

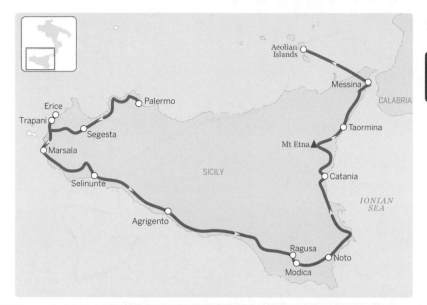

Three Weeks
Best of Sicily

Sicily is sweet, sour, spicy and intriguing. For a taste, fly into **Palermo** and take three days to savour its crumbling, magnificent streets and lip-smacking street food. Dive into the city's souk-like markets and eye-up the East-meets-West exotica of its churches and mosaics. Spend day four roaming the evocative temple and amphitheatre at **Segesta** and continue on to the foodie mecca of **Trapani** to sample its Arabesque cuisine. Come morning, it's time to hop on the funicular to medieval **Erice**, one of Italy's most arresting medieval hilltop towns. Come back down to spend day six sipping sweet local wine in elegant **Marsala** and day seven roaming the Greek ruins of **Selinunte**. More ancient survivors await on day eight as you head to the incredible Valle dei Templi in **Agrigento**, its five Doric structures spectacularly perched on a ridge overlooking the Mediterranean coast. On day nine, shoot southeast to the Val di Noto and spend a couple of days exploring the baroque splendour of its Unesco World Heritage towns, especially **Ragusa**, **Modica** and **Noto**. Modica is also renowned for its chocolate, so prepare for a memorable sugary high. Change gear on days 12 and 13 with a stay in youthful, worldly **Catania**, a city famed for its baroque buildings, market and kicking nightlife. Pumped, head straight up to the crater rim of **Mt Etna** (Europe's highest active volcano) on day 14 before two indulgent days of wining, dining and coastal posing in the chic resort town of **Taormina**. Assuming you manage to pull yourself away, head further northeast to **Messina** to catch a hydrofoil to the **Aeolian Islands**. Here, enjoy five unforgettable days of island-hopping along this bubbling, pyrotechnic volcanic ridge. Luxuriate in thermal mud on Vulcano, catch the Sciara del Fuoco on Stromboli, and work on that must-have southern tan.

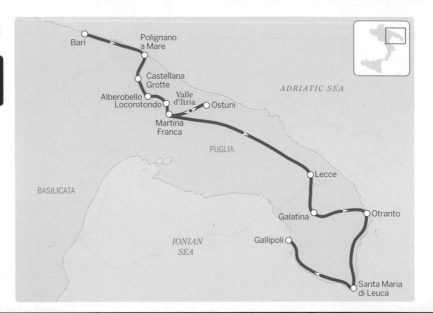

Two Weeks
Puglia

For the majority of visitors to Italy, a trip 'south' means Naples and the Amalfi Coast. What a shame! Puglia, which forms the heel of Lo Stivale ('the Boot'), is one of the country's most underrated regions. To see what you've been missing out on, start in dynamic **Bari**, with its ancient historic centre and huge Romanesque basilica. The latter is home to the relics of San Nicola (aka Father Christmas). After writing your Christmas wish list, strike out south, via **Polignano a Mare**, to the famous **Grotte di Castellana**, Italy's longest network of subterranean caves. From here, a two- to three-day drive south will take you through some of the finest Valle d'Itria towns, including **Alberobello**, with its hobbitlike, Unesco-lauded *trulli* houses, wine-producing **Locorotondo**, beautiful baroque **Martina Franca** and chic, whitewashed **Ostuni**. Just outside Ostuni you'll find Il Frantoio, one of the region's top *masserie* (farmhouses). Consider checking in for a day or two of long, lazy lunches and general bucolic bliss. In Martina Franca, you get just a small taste of what is awaiting you in **Lecce**, otherwise known as the 'Florence of the South' for its operatic architectural ensembles and scholarly bent. Hire a bike and spend at least three or four days here before moving on to **Galatina**, its basilica awash with astounding frescoes. From here, head east to the fortified port of **Otranto**. Hit the sugar-soft, white-sand beaches of the Baia dei Turchi, and then push south along the wild, vertiginous coastline to **Santa Maria di Leuca**, the very tip of the Italian stiletto. Watch the Adriatic and Ionian seas kiss and make up before heading north to the island city of **Gallipoli**. Dive into its elegant old town and savour the flavour of its famous raw sea urchins and octopuses. You've earned it.

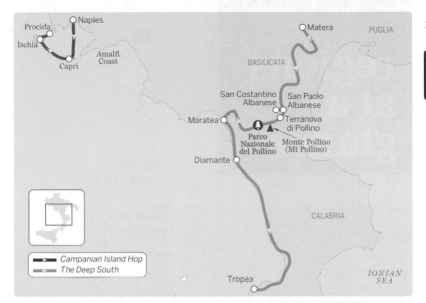

Campanian Island Hop
The Deep South

Nine Days
The Deep South

Start your soul saunter in the cave city of **Matera**. Spend a couple of days exploring its famous *sassi*, as well as the *chiese rupestri* (cave churches) on a hike along the Gravina. From here, continue south to the **Parco Nazionale del Pollino** for a serious nature fix in Italy's largest national park. Base yourself in **Terranova di Pollino** for four days, hiking through pine woods and beech forest to Basilicata's highest peak, Monte Pollino, and dancing to the *zampogne* in the Albanian villages of **San Paolo Albanese** and **San Costantino Albanese**. Don't leave the park without spotting the rare Bosnian pine tree, *pino loricato*. Lungs filled with mountain air, it's time to head west to the gorgeous coastal gem of **Maratea**. Pass a couple of days soothing your muscles in the town's crystalline Tyrrhenian waters, kicking back at local bars and feasting on fresh seafood. From here, head south to Calabria on the SS18 coastal road. If it's September, you might catch a chilli-eating competition in **Diamante**. Otherwise, keep moving until you reach Calabria's most arresting coastal town, **Tropea**, where your journey ends with piercing views and sunsets.

Nine Days
Campanian Island Hop

Three islands stud the Bay of Naples, and each has its own distinct feeling and appeal. Fly into **Naples** and dive into the city's heady jumble of hyperactive street life, castles and art-crammed palaces. On the third day catch a hydrofoil to **Capri**, your first island stop. Amble lazily through the chichi laneways of Capri Town and Anacapri, roam the ruins of an imperial Roman villa, and be rowed into the world's most stunning grotto. On day five catch a ferry west to **Ischia**, the biggest of the bay islands. Spend your three days rambling through luxurious gardens and soaking in the island's famous thermal waters. Sample some of the island's renowned white wine and tuck into its most celebrated dish, *coniglio all'ischitana* (Ischian-style rabbit). If you can manage to pull yourself away, catch a ferry across to tiny **Procida** on day eight for two days of lo-fi bliss. Relive scenes from the film *Il Postino* in pastel-hued Marina Corricella, eat seafood by the beach and take a dive to explore the island's rich marine life.

regions at a glance

Home to fairy-tale destinations like Capri and the Amalfi Coast, not to mention the artistic and architectural riches of Naples, it's not surprising that Campania has traditionally been southern Italy's blockbuster region.

In recent years Puglia and Basilicata have become the darlings of the in-the-know set, famed for their gorgeous beaches, fantastic food, architectural quirks and authentic festivals. While off-the-radar Calabria may lack big-hitter sights and cosmopolitan cities, it's well compensated by its rugged natural beauty, outdoor thrills and spicy rustic grub.

Like Campania, Sicily offers an enviable repertoire of landscapes, from volcanic peaks and vine-laced slopes to milky blue beaches. It's also home to some of Italy's greatest Graeco-Roman ruins, baroque architecture and culinary traditions.

Naples & Campania

Food ✓✓✓
Roman Sites ✓✓✓
Coastline ✓✓✓

Pizza & Pasta

Vying hard for Italy's culinary crown, Campania produces some of Italy's most famous flavours: coffee, pizza, tomatoes, pasta, *sfogliatella* (sweetened ricotta pastry) and a panoply of seafood, eaten every which way you can.

Roman Sites

Sitting beneath Mt Vesuvius, the Neapolitans abide by the motto, carpe diem (seize the day). And why not? All around them, at Pompeii, Ercolano, Cuma and the Campi Flegrei, they have reminders that life is short.

Cliffs & Coves

From the citrus-fringed panoramas of the Amalfi Coast to Ischia's tropical gardens and Capri's dramatic cliffs, the views from this coastline are as famous as the celebrities who holiday here.

p28

25

PLAN YOUR TRIP REGIONS AT A GLANCE

Puglia, Basilicata & Calabria

Beaches ✓✓✓
Nature ✓✓
Food ✓✓✓

Seaside Savvy
Italy's northern shores may have all the drama, but the south has all the sand. Lounge beneath white cliffs in the Gargano, gaze at the violet sunsets in Tropea and spend summer on the golden beaches of Otranto and Gallipoli.

Wild Places
With its crush of spiky mountains, Basilicata and Calabria are where the wild things are. Burst through the clouds in mountaintop Pietrapertosa, pick bergamot in the Aspromonte and take time to swap pleasantries with the locals.

Culture & Cuisine
Puglia has turned its poverty into a fine art, both on and off the plate. Check out the renovated cave dwellings in Matera and then feast on creamy *burrata* (cheese made from mozzarella and cream) and turnip greens in Ostuni and Lecce.

p91

Sicily

Food ✓✓✓
History ✓✓✓
Activities ✓✓✓

Seafood & Sweets
Sicilian cuisine will dazzle seafood lovers and set that sweet tooth on edge. Tuna, sardines, swordfish and shellfish come grilled, fried or seasoned with mint or wild fennel. Desserts, laden with local citrus, ricotta, almonds and pistachios, include Arab-Italian dishes such as *cannoli, cassata* and marzipan fruits.

Cultural Hybrid
A Mediterranean crossroads for centuries, Sicily spoils history buffs with windswept Greek temples and theatres, Roman and Byzantine mosaics, Phoenician statues and sun-bleached Arab-Norman churches.

Volcanoes & Islands
Sicily's hyperactive geology gives outdoor activities a thrilling kick. Pamper weary muscles in bubbling volcanic waters, hike the Aeolian Islands' dramatic coastlines or take in the thrill of the natural fireworks of Stromboli and Etna.

p148

Look out for these icons:

 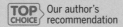 Our author's recommendation

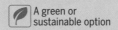 A green or sustainable option

 No payment required

On the Road

Naples & Campania

POPULATION: 5.8 MILLION

Best Places to Eat

» Ristorante Il Buco (p74)
» Lo Scoglio (p76)
» Ristorante Radici (p45)
» Pizzeria Gino Sorbillo (p45)
» President (p71)

Best Places to Stay

» Hotel San Francesco al Monte (p44)
» Hotel Piazza Bellini (p43)
» Hotel Luna Convento (p81)
» Casale Giancesare (p88)
» Hotel La Vigna (p66)

Why Go?

Campania could be a multi–Academy Award winner, scooping everything from Best Cinematography to Best Original Screenplay. Strewn with three millennia worth of temples, castles and palaces, it heaves with legend: Icarus plunged to his death in the Campi Flegrei, sirens lured sailors off Sorrento, and Wagner put quill to paper in lofty Ravello. Campania's cast includes some of Europe's most fabled destinations, from haunting Pompeii to Med-chic Capri. At its heart thumps bad boy Naples, a love-it-or-loathe-it sprawl of operatic *palazzi* (mansions), mouthwatering markets, and art-crammed museums. Home to Italy's top coffee and pizza, it's also one of the country's gastronomic superstars. Beyond its pounding streets lies a wonderland of lush bay islands, faded fishing villages and wild mountains. Welcome to Italy at its nail-biting best.

When to Go
Naples

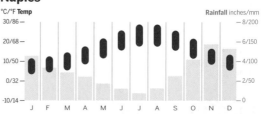

Easter Follow the faithful at Sorrento and Procida's Easter processions.

May Naples celebrates culture with its Maggio dei Monumenti festival.

Sep Hit the coast for warm, languid days without the August crowds.

The Subterranean City

Mysterious shrines, secret passageways, forgotten burial crypts: it might sound like the set of an *Indiana Jones* film, but it's actually what lurks beneath Naples' loud and greasy streets. Subterranean Naples is one of the world's most thrilling urban wonderlands; a silent, mostly undiscovered sprawl of cathedral-like cisterns, pin-sized conduits, catacombs and ancient ruins.

Speleologists (cave specialists) estimate that about 60% of Neapolitans live and work above this network, known in Italian as the *sottosuolo* (underground). Since the end of WWII, some 700 cavities have been discovered, from original Greek-era grottoes, to Paleo-Christian burial chambers and royal Bourbon escape routes. According to the experts, this is simply a prelude, with another 2 million sq m of troglodytic treats to unfurl.

Naples' dedicated caving geeks are quick to tell you that their underworld is one of the largest and oldest on earth. Sure, Paris might claim a catacomb or two, but its subterranean offerings don't come close to this giant's 2500-year history.

And what a history it is. Naples' most famous saint, San Gennaro, was interred in the Catacombe di San Gennaro in the 5th century. A century later, in 536, Belisario and his troops caught Naples by surprise by storming the city through its ancient tunnels. According to legend, Alfonso of Aragon used the same trick in 1442, undermining the city walls by using an underground passageway leading into a tailor's shop and straight into town. Even the city's dreaded Camorra has got in on the act. In 1992 the notorious Stolder clan were busted for running a subterranean drug lab, with escape routes heading straight to the clan boss's pad.

CAMPANIA'S NATURAL WONDERS

» Grotta Azzurra (p53) Nature outdazzles Disney in this magical coastal cave

» Sentiero degli Dei (p82) Experience the Amalfi Coast from a heavenly elevation

» Parco Nazionale del Cilento e Vallo di Diano (p89) A wild and rugged playground begging to be hiked

» Mt Vesuvius (p68) Peer into the crater of this panoramic time bomb

» Solfatara crater (p51) Feel the earth's wrath at this geological freak show

Don't Miss

Naples' Cappella Sansevero is home to the astounding Cristo Velato (Veiled Christ), its marble veil so translucent it baffles to this day.

BEST PLACES TO WHISPER 'TI AMO'

» Villa Cimbrone (p83)
» Palazzo Petrucci (p45)
» Monte Solaro (p55)
» La Conchiglia (p66)

Hold the Prawns

Order a pizza marinara in Naples and you'll get tomato, garlic and olive oil. And the seafood? There is none. The pizza was named after the fishermen who would take it out to sea for lunch.

Resources

» Turismo Regione Campania (www.incampania.it) Up-to-date events, as well as articles and itineraries.

» Italy Traveller (www.italytraveller.com) Luxe hotel listings, themed itineraries and travel ideas.

Naples' Top Museums

» Museo Archeologico Nazionale (p36) A treasure chest of ancient art, propaganda and erotica

» Museo di Capodimonte (p41) From Caravaggio to Warhol, a sprawling palace of masterpieces

» Museo del Novecento, Castel San't Elmo (p37) A stylish ode to Naples' 20th-century art scene

» Museo Nazionale di San Martino (p37) Royal carriages and barges, ambitious nativity scenes and a lavish baroque chapel

» MADRE (p36) Big names of contemporary art

Naples & Campania Highlights

1 Explore Naples' labyrinthine underworld on a **Napoli Sotterranea** (p42) tour

2 Channel the ancients on the streets of **Pompeii** (p68)

3 Be bewitched by Capri's ethereal **Grotta Azzurra** (p53)

4 Lunch by the waves on pastel-hued **Procida** (p66)

5 Treat your senses to a concert at Ravello's dreamy **Villa Rufolo** (p83)

6 Pretend you're royalty at bigger-than-thou **Palazzo Reale** (p52)

7 Whet your appetite at Naples' produce-packed **Mercato di Porta Nolana** (p36)

8 Indulge in a little thermal therapy on **Ischia** (p59)

9 Walk with the gods on the **Amalfi Coast** (p82)

10 Admire Hellenic ingenuity at the World Heritage–listed temples of **Paestum** (p88)

NAPLES

POP 3,079,000

Italy's most misunderstood city is also one of its finest – an exhilarating mess of bombastic baroque churches, bellowing baristas and electrifying street life. Contradiction is the catchphrase here; a place where anarchy, pollution and crime sidle up to mighty museums, lavish palaces and aristocratic tailors.

First stop for many is the Unesco World Heritage–listed *centro storico* (historic city centre). It's here, under the washing lines, that you'll find Naples' arabesque street life – cocky kids playing football in noisy piazzas, overloaded Vespas hurtling through cobbled alleyways and clued-up *casalinghe* (homemakers) bullying market vendors. Once the heart of Roman Neapolis, this intoxicating warren of Dickensian streets groans with ancient churches, citrus-filled cloisters and rough-and-tumble pizzerias.

By the sea the cityscape opens up. Imperious palaces flank show-off squares as Gucci-clad shoppers strut their stuff and lunch in chandeliered cafes. This is Royal Naples, the Naples of the Bourbons that so impressed the 18th-century Grand Tourists.

History

According to legend, traders from Rhodes established the city on the island of Megaris (where Castel dell'Ovo now stands) in about 680 BC. Originally called Parthenope in honour of the siren whose body had earlier washed up there (she drowned herself after failing to seduce Ulysses), it was eventu-

ally incorporated into a new city, Neapolis, founded by Greeks from Cumae (Cuma) in 474 BC. However, within 150 years it was in Roman hands, becoming something of a VIP resort favoured by emperors Pompey, Caesar and Tiberius.

After the fall of the Roman Empire, Naples became a duchy, originally under the Byzantines and later as an independent dukedom, until it was captured in 1139 by the Normans and absorbed into the Kingdom of the Two Sicilies. The Normans, in turn, were replaced by the German Swabians, whose charismatic leader Frederick II injected the city with new institutions, including its university.

The Swabian period came to a violent end with the victory of Charles I of Anjou at the 1266 battle of Benevento. The Angevins did much for Naples, promoting art and culture, building Castel Nuovo and enlarging the port, but they were unable to stop the Spanish Aragons taking the city in 1442. Naples continued to prosper, though. Alfonso I of Aragon, in particular, introduced new laws and encouraged the arts and sciences.

In 1503 Naples was absorbed by Spain, which sent viceroys to rule as virtual dictators. Despite Spain's heavy-handed rule, Naples flourished artistically and acquired much of its splendour. It continued to bloom when the Spanish Bourbons re-established Naples as the capital of the Kingdom of the Two Sicilies in 1734. Aside from a Napoleonic interlude under Joachim Murat (1806–15), the Bourbons remained until unseated by Garibaldi and the Kingdom of Italy in 1860.

NAPLES IN...

Two Days

Kick-start with espresso at **Caffè Mexico** before taking in the frescoes inside **Chiesa del Gesù Nuovo**, the majolica-tiled cloisters of **Basilica di Santa Chiara** and the sculptures inside **Cappella Sansevero**. Lunch at **Pizzeria Gino Sorbillo** before taking the funicular up to Vomero and the **Certosa di San Martino**. When the sun sets, sample an aperitivo at **Nàis** and dine at **Ristorante Radici**. Start day two with a *sfogliatella* (sweetened ricotta pastry) from **Pintauro** before tackling the **Museo Archeologico Nazionale**. Refuel with cheese and wine at **La Stanza del Gusto** then go underground on a **Napoli Sotterranea** tour. Catch an evening sea breeze at **Castel dell'Ovo** before a bite at **Penguin Café**.

Four Days

Spend day three among the ruins at **Pompeii** or **Herculaneum**, dining at **President** before heading back to town for a nightcap at elegant, piazza-side **Intra Moenia**. On day four, grab some picnic provisions at **La Pignasecca** and devour them in leafy **Capodimonte**. Fed, catch Caravaggio's moving *Flagellazione* at the art-crammed **Museo di Capodimonte**, then cap off your stay with a night of encores at the luscious **Teatro San Carlo**.

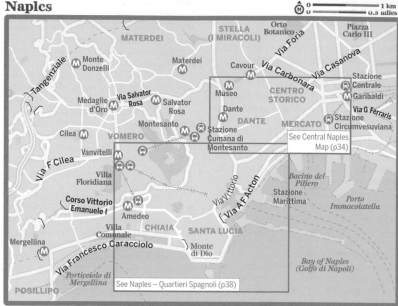

MODERN STRUGGLES & HOPES

Naples was heavily bombed in WWII, and the effects can still be seen on many monuments around the city. Since the war, Campania's capital has continued to suffer. Endemic corruption and the re-emergence of the Camorra have plagued much of the city's postwar resurrection, reaching a nadir in the 1980s after a severe earthquake in 1980.

In 2011, the city's intermittent garbage-disposal crisis flared up again, leading frustrated residents to set fire to uncollected rubbish in the streets.

More encouraging has been the recent inauguration of the poptastic Università metro station (designed by Karim Rashid and the first of four new stations on the nearly completed extension of Linea 1) and the city's upcoming role as host of the Universal Forum of Cultures in 2013.

Sights

CENTRO STORICO

The three east–west *decumani* (main streets) of Naples' historic centre follow the original street plan of ancient Neapolis. Most of the major sights are grouped around the busiest two of these classical thoroughfares; 'Spaccanapoli' (consiting of Via Benedetto Croce, Via San Biagio dei Librai and Via Vicaria

Vecchia) and Via dei Tribunali. North of Via dei Tribunali, Via della Sapienza, Via Anticaglia and Via Santissimi Apostoli make up the quieter third *decumanus*.

Duomo
DUOMO, MUSEUM

(Map p34; ☑081 44 90 97; Via Duomo; ⊗8.30am-1.30pm & 2.30-8pm Mon-Sat, 8.30am-1.30pm & 4.30-8pm Sun) This is Naples' spiritual centrepiece, sitting on the site of earlier churches, themselves preceded by a temple to the god Neptune. Begun by Charles I of Anjou in 1272 and consecrated in 1315, it was largely destroyed by an earthquake in 1456. Copious nips and tucks over the centuries, including the addition of a late-19th-century neo-Gothic facade, have created a melange of styles and influences.

Topping the huge central nave is a gilded coffered ceiling studded with late mannerist art. The high sections of the nave and the transept were decorated by Luca Giordano.

The 17th-century baroque **Cappella di San Gennaro** (Chapel of St Januarius, also known as the Chapel of the Treasury; ⊗8.30am-12.30pm & 4.30-6.30pm Mon-Sat, 8.30am-1pm & 5-7pm Sun) features a fiery painting by Giuseppe Ribera and a bevy of silver busts and bronze statues. Above them, a heavenly dome glows with frescoes by Giovanni Lanfranco. Hidden away behind the altar is a 14th-century silver bust containing the skull of St Januarius and the two phials that hold his miraculous blood. Naples' patron saint was martyred at Pozzuoli in AD 305, and according to legend, his blood liquefied in these phials when his body was transferred back to Naples. For information on the mysterious San Gennaro festival, see p42.

The next chapel eastwards contains an urn with the saint's bones, cupboards full of femurs, tibias and fibulas, and a stash of other grisly relics. Below the high altar is the Renaissance **Cappella Carafa**, also known as the Crypt of San Gennaro.

Halfway down the north aisle and beyond the 17th-century Basilica di Santa Restituta is the fascinating **archaeological zone** (⊙varies am-noon & 4.30-7pm Mon-Sat, 9am-noon Sun), where tunnels burrow into the remains of the site's original Greek and Roman buildings. At the time of research, the archaeological zone was closed for restoration, although the **baptistry** (admission €1.50; ⊙8.30am-12.30pm & 4.30-7pm Mon-Sat, 8.30am-1.30pm Sun), the oldest in western Europe, with remarkably fresh 4th-century mosaics, remained open.

At the *duomo's* southern end, the **Museo del Tesoro di San Gennaro** (⊘081 29 49 80; Via Duomo 149; admission €6; ⊙10am-5pm Thu-Tue) glimmers with gifts made to St Januarius over the centuries, from bronze busts and sumptuous paintings to silver ampullas and a gilded 18th-century sedan chair.

Cappella Sansevero   CHURCH
(Map p34; ⊘081 551 84 70; www.museosansevero. it; Via de Sanctis 19; admission €7; ⊙10am-5.40pm Mon & Wed-Sat, 10am-1.10pm Sun) Don't be fooled by the plain Jane exterior: awaiting inside is some of the city's most sumptuous sculpture, including Corradini's erotically charged, ironically named *Pudicizia* (Modesty). The centrepiece, however, is *Cristo Velato* (Veiled Christ), Giuseppe Sanmartino's jaw-dropping depiction of Jesus covered by a veil so realistic that it's tempting to try and lift it. The air of mystery continues downstairs, where two meticulously preserved human arterial systems are a testament to the bizarre obsession of alchemist Prince Raimondo di Sangro, the man who financed the chapel's 18th-century makeover.

Basilica di Santa Chiara   CHURCH, MUSEUM
(Map p34; ⊘081 551 66 73; www.monasterodi santachiara.eu; Via Benedetto Croce; ⊙7.30am-1pm & 4.30-8pm) What you see today is not the original 14th-century Angevin church but a brilliant re-creation – the original was all but destroyed by Allied bombing in August 1943. The real attraction, however, is the adjacent **nuns' cloisters** (adult/reduced €5/3.50; ⊙9.30am-5.30pm Mon-Sat, 10am-2.30pm Sun, last entry 30min before closing), a long parapet lavished with decorative ceramic tiles depicting scenes of rural life, from hunting to posing peasants. The four internal walls are covered with softly coloured 17th-century frescoes of Franciscan tales. Adjacent to the cloisters, an elegant **museum** of mostly ecclesiastical props also features the excavated ruins of a 1st-century spa complex.

THE DARK PRINCE OF NAPLES

While Naples' history bubbles with tales of miraculous and magical characters, few rev up the rumour mill like Raimondo di Sangro (1710–71). Inventor, scientist, soldier and alchemist, the so-called Prince of Sansevero reputedly imported freemasonry into the Kingdom of Naples, resulting in a temporary excommunication from the Catholic Church.

Yet even a papal rethink couldn't quell the salacious stories surrounding Raimondo, which spanned everything from castrating promising young sopranos to knocking off seven cardinals and making furniture with their skin and bones. According to Italian philosopher Benedetto Croce (1866–1952), who wrote about Di Sangro in his book *Storie e Leggende Napoletane* (Neapolitan Stories and Legends), the alchemist held a Faustian fascination for the masses of the *centro storico* (historic city centre). To them, his supposed knack for the dark arts saw him master everything from replicating the miracle of San Gennaro's blood to reducing marble to dust with a simple touch.

To this day, rumours surround the two perfect anatomical models in the crypt of the Di Sangro funerary chapel, the Cappella Sansevero. Believed to be the preserved bodies of his defunct domestics, some believe that they were far from dead when the Prince got started on the embalming. Tall tale or not, the exact method of preservation still confounds scientists today.

Central Naples

N

400 m
0.2 miles

Museo
Archeologico
Nazionale

To Catacombe di Gennaro (1.6km);
Palazzo Reale di Capodimonte (2.2km);
Museo di Capodimonte (2.2km);
Parco di Capodimonte (2.2km)

To MADRE (50m)

Piazza
Museo
Nazionale

TOLEDO

Via S Tommasi

Via Francesco
Saverio Correra

Via Broggia

Via Santa Maria di Costantinopoli

Via Bellini

Via S Gaudioso

Via Enrico Pessina

Piazza
Dante

Dante

DANTE

Via G Brombeis

Via Port'Alba

Piazza
Dante

Via S Anna dei Lombardi

Via D Lioy

Piazza
Carità

Via Toledo

Via Pignasecca

Via Duomo

Vico Giganti

Via Pisanelli

Via d'Anticaglia

Via Santissimi Apostoli

Via San Paolo

Via del Sole

Via Atri

Via F del Giudice

Piazza
Luigi
Miraglia

Piazza
Bellini

Via San Sebastiano

Via Benedetto Croce

Piazza
del
Gesù Nuovo

Via Santa Chiara

Via San Biagio dei Librai

Chiesa e Scavi
di San Lorenzo
Maggiore

Via San
Gregorio Armeno

Cappella
Sansevero

Piazza San
Domenico
Maggiore

Vico S Nicola al Nilo

Vico S Severino

Via S Nicola
dei Caserti

Via dei Tribunali

Vico della Pace

Via della Zite

Vico Zuroli

Via Vicaria Vecchia

CENTRO
STORICO

Via P Colletta

Via dell'Annunziata

Via Duchesca

Via Mancini

Via Ranieri

Via Carbonara

Via C Muzy

Piazza
Principe
Umberto

Via Firenze

Corso Novara

Stazione
Centrale

Garibaldi

ANM Bus
Information
Kiosk

Piazza
Garibaldi

Intercity & ANM
Bus Station

Corso G Garibaldi

Via Sopramuro

Via C Carmignano

Via G Pica

Via S Cosmo Fuori Porta Nolana

To SITA Bus Stop
(150m)

Stazione
Circumvesuviana

Piazza
Nolana

Via Nolana

Via Lavinaio

Via A de Pace

Vico Barre

Via G Savarese

Via Amerigo Vespucci

Piazza
di G Pepe

Chiesa di
Santa Maria
del Carmine

Piazza del
Mercato

Piazza
Masaniello

Via D Carmine

Via E Cosenz

Vico S Giovanni

Via della Marinella

Via Nuova Marina

MERCATO

Via Sant'Eligio

To SITA Bus
Stop (180m)

Via Duca di
San Donato

Corso Umberto I

Via Duomo

Piazza
Nicola
Amore

Via B Capasso

Vico
Donnaromita

Via G Paladino

Via Mezzocannone

Vico San Geronimo

Largo
Giusso

Corso Umberto I

Via Scialoia

Piazetta
Orefici

See Naples – Quartieri Spagnoli Map (p38)

Via Donnalbina

Via S Biagio dei Librai

Vico dei
Cimbri

Via d'Alagno

Piazza Museo
Filangieri

Via Donnalbina

Museo

Numbered markers
1
2
3
4
5
6
7
8
9
10
11
12
13
14
15
16
17
18
19
20
21
22
23
24
25
26
27
28
29
30

NAPLES & CAMPANIA

Chiesa del Gesù Nuovo CHURCH
(Map p34; ☑081 557 81 11; Piazza del Gesù Nuovo; ☺7am-1pm & 4.15-7.45pm Mon-Sat, 7am-1.45pm Sun) One of Naples' finest Renaissance buildings, this 16th-century church actually sports the 15th-century, pyramid-shaped facade of Palazzo Sanseverino, converted to create the church. Awaiting inside is a lavish 17th-century makeover, with works by a trio of Naples' mightiest baroque artists: Cosimo Fanzago, Luca Giordano and Francesco Solimena.

Puncturing the Piazza del Gesù outside is the soaring **Guglia dell'Immacolata**, an 18th-century obelisk.

Chiesa e Scavi di San Lorenzo Maggiore CHURCH, HISTORICAL SITE
(Map p34; ☑081 211 08 60; Via dei Tribunali 316; church admission free, excavations & museum adult/child €9/6; ☺9.30am-5.30pm Mon-Sat, to 1.30pm Sun) A masterpiece of French Gothic architecture, this late-13th-century church features the 14th-century mosaic-covered tomb of Catherine of Austria. You can also pass through to the cloisters of the neigh-

bouring convent, where the poet Petrarch stayed in 1345.

Beneath the complex are some remarkable *scavi* (excavations) of the original Graeco-Roman city. Stretching the length of the underground area is a road lined with ancient bakeries, wineries and communal laundries.

Basilica di San Paolo Maggiore CHURCH
(Map p34; ☑081 45 40 48; Piazza San Gaetano 76; ☺9am-6pm Mon-Sat, 10am-12.30pm Sun) Across the street on Via dei Tribunali, a grand double staircase leads up to this basilica, the huge gold-stuccoed interior of which features paintings by Massimo Stanzione, as well as frescoes by Francesco Solimena in the exquisite sacristy.

Pio Monte della Misericordia CHURCH, ART GALLERY
(Map p34; ☑081 44 69 44; Via dei Tribunali 253; admission €5; ☺9am-2pm Thu-Tue) Caravaggio's masterpiece *Le sette opere di Misericordia* (The Seven Acts of Mercy) is considered by many to be the most important painting in

Naples. And it's here that you'll see it, hung above the main altar of this small octagonal church. The small 1st-floor art gallery boasts a fine collection of Renaissance and baroque paintings.

MADRE MUSEUM
(Museo d'Arte Contemporanea Donnaregina; off Map p34; ☑081 1931 3016; www.museomadre. it; Via Settembrini 79; admission €7, Mon free; ⊙10.30am-2.30pm Wed-Mon) In a city overwhelmed by the classical, Naples' top contemporary museum makes for a refreshing change. Permanent collection highlights include Jeff Koons' uber-kitsch *Wild Boy and Puppy*, Rebecca Horn's eerie *Spirits* and a perspective-warping installation by Anish Kapoor.

Mercato di Porta Nolana MARKET
(Map p34; ⊙8am-6pm Mon-Sat, to 2pm Sun) A heady spectacle of singsong fishmongers, fragrant bakeries, industrious Chinese traders and contraband cigarette stalls, this street market is Naples at its vociferous, gut-rumbling best. Dive in for anything from buxom tomatoes and mozzarella or golden-fried street snacks to cheap luggage. The market's namesake, **Porta Nolana**, is one of Naples' medieval city gates. Standing at the head of Via Sopramuro, its arch features a bas-relief of Ferdinand I of Aragon on horseback.

Museo Diocesano di Napoli MUSEUM
(Map p34; ☑081 557 13 65; www.museodiocesano napoli.it; Chiesa di Santa Maria Donnaregina Nuova, Largo Donnaregina; admission €6; ⊙9.30am-4.30pm Mon & Wed-Sat, to 2pm Sun) Once a baroque church, the Chiesa di Donnaregina Nuova has reinvented itself as a superb repository of religiously themed art, from Renaissance triptychs and 19th-century wooden sculptures to works from baroque greats like Fabrizio Santafede, Andrea Vaccaro and Luca Giordano.

Chiesa di San Domenico Maggiore CHURCH
(Map p34; ☑081 557 32 04; Piazza San Domenico Maggiore 8a; ⊙8.30am-noon & 4-7pm Mon-Sat, 9am-1pm & 4.30-7.15pm Sun) Backing on to lively Piazza San Domenico Maggiore, this Gothic beauty was completed in 1324 and much favoured by the Angevin nobility. The interior, a cross between baroque and 19th-century neo-Gothic, features some fine 14th-century frescoes by Pietro Cavallini and, in the sacristy, 45 coffins of Aragon princes and other nobles.

Chiesa di Sant'Angelo a Nilo CHURCH
(Map p34; ☑081 420 12 22; Vico Donnaromita 15; ⊙9am-1pm daily plus 4-6pm Mon-Sat) Nudging at the southeast corner of Piazza San Domenico Maggiore is the 14th-century Chiesa di Sant'Angelo a Nilo, home to Cardinal Brancaccio's monumental Renaissance tomb, created by Donatello and others.

Via San Gregorio Armeno STREET, CHURCH
Connecting Spaccanapoli with Via dei Tribunali, the *decumanus maior* (main road) of ancient Neapolis, this narrow street is the heart of the city's *presepe* (nativity scene) obsession, its clutter of shops selling everything from doting donkeys to tongue-in-cheek caricatures of Silvio Berlusconi.

Amidst the kitsch sits the 16th-century **Chiesa e Chiostro di San Gregorio Armeno** (Map p34; ☑081 420 63 85; Via San Gregorio Armeno 44; ⊙9.30am-noon Mon-Sat, to 1pm Sun), a blast of bombastic baroque. Highlights include lavish frescoes by Paolo de Matteis and Luca Giordano.

TOLEDO & QUARTIERI SPAGNOLI
Museo Archeologico Nazionale MUSEUM
(Map p34; ☑081 44 01 66; Piazza Museo Nazionale 19; admission €6.50; ⊙9am-7.30pm Wed-Mon) Head here for one of the world's finest collections of Graeco-Roman artefacts. Originally a cavalry barracks and later the seat of the city's university, the museum was established by the Bourbon king Charles VII in the late 18th century to house the rich collection of antiquities he had inherited from his mother, Elisabetta Farnese, as well as treasures that had been looted from Pompeii and Herculaneum. The museum also contains the Borgia collection of Etruscan and Egyptian relics.

To avoid getting lost in its rambling galleries (numbered in Roman numerals), invest €7.50 in the green quick-guide *National Archaeological Museum of Naples* or, to concentrate on the highlights, €5 for an audioguide in English. It's also worth calling ahead to ensure the galleries you want to see are open, as staff shortages often mean that sections of the museum close for part of the day.

While the basement houses the Borgia collection of Egyptian relics and epigraphs, the ground floor is given over to the **Farnese collection** of Greek and Roman sculpture. The two highlights are the colossal *Toro Farnese* (Farnese Bull) in Room XVI and gigantic *Ercole* (Hercules) in Room XIII. Sculpted in the early 3rd century AD, the *Toro Farnese*, probably a Roman copy of a Greek original, depicts the death of Dirce, Queen of Thebes, who was tied to a bull and torn apart over rocks. The sculpture, carved from a single block, was discovered in Rome in 1545 and restored by Michelangelo before being shipped to Naples in 1787. *Ercole* was discovered in the same Roman excavations. It was found legless, but the Bourbons had his original pins, which turned up at a later dig, fitted.

On the mezzanine floor is a small but stunning collection of **mosaics**, mostly from Pompeii. Of the series taken from the Casa del Fauno at Pompeii, it's the awe-inspiring *La Battaglia di Alessandro Contro Dario* (The Battle of Alexander against Darius) that stands out. Measuring 20 sq metres, it's the best-known depiction of Alexander the Great in existence.

Beyond the mosaics is the **Gabinetto Segreto** (Secret Room), home to the museum's ancient porn. The climax, so to speak, is an intriguing statue of Pan servicing a nanny goat, originally found in Herculaneum. The erotic paintings depicting sexual positions once served as a menu for brothel clients.

On the 1st floor, the vast **Sala Meridiana** contains the *Farnese Atlante,* a statue of Atlas carrying a globe on his shoulders. The rest of the floor is largely devoted to discoveries from Pompeii, Herculaneum, Stabiae and Cuma. Items range from huge murals and frescoes to a pair of gladiator helmets, household items, ceramics and glassware.

La Pignasecca MARKET
(Map p34; Via Pignasecca; ⊙8am-1pm) Slap bang in the lively Quartieri Spagnoli, Naples' oldest street market offers a multi-sensory escapade into a world of wriggling seafood, drool-inducing delis and clued-up *casalinghe*. It's a great place to soak up the city's trademark street life and pick up a few bargains.

VOMERO

Visible from all over Naples, the stunning Certosa di San Martino is the one compelling reason to take the funicular (p50) up to Vomero (*vom*-e-ro), an area of spectacular views, Liberty mansions and middle-class manners.

**Museo Nazionale
di San Martino** MONASTERY, MUSEUM
(Map p38; ☑848 80 02 88; Largo San Martino 5; admission €6; ⊙8.30am-7.30pm Thu-Tue, last entry 6.30pm) The high point (quite literally) of Neapolitan baroque, this stunning charterhouse-turned-museum was founded as a Carthusian monastery in the 14th century. The **Certosa** owes most of its present look to facelifts in the 16th and 17th centuries, the latter by baroque maestro Cosimo Fanzago. The **church** contains a feast of frescoes and paintings by Naples' greatest 17th-century artists: Francesco Solimena, Massimo Stanzione, Giuseppe de Ribera and Battista Caracciolo.

Adjacent to the church, the elegant **Chiostro dei Procuratori** is the smaller of the monastery's two cloisters. A grand corridor on the left leads to the larger **Chiostro Grande**, considered one of Italy's finest. Originally designed by Giovanni Antonio Dosio in the late 16th century and added to by Fanzago, it's a sublime composition of white Tuscan Doric porticoes, camelias and marble statues. The skulls mounted on the balustrade were a light-hearted reminder to the monks of their own mortality.

Just off the Chiostro dei Procuratori, the **Sezione Navale** focuses on the history of the Bourbon navy from 1734 to 1860, and features a small collection of beautiful royal barges.

To the north of the Chiostro Grande, the **Sezione Presepiale** houses a whimsical collection of rare Neapolitan *presepi* (nativity scenes) carved in the 18th and 19th centuries.

The **Quarto del Priore** (Prior's Quarter) in the southern wing houses the bulk of the picture collection, as well as one of the museum's most famous pieces, Pietro Bernini's tender *La Vergine col Bambino e San Giovannino* (Madonna and Child with the Infant John the Baptist).

Castel Sant'Elmo CASTLE, MUSEUM
(Map p38; ☑081 229 44 01; Via Tito Angelini 22; admission €5; ⊙8.30am-7.30pm Wed-Mon, last entry 6.30pm) Commanding spectacular city views, this star-shaped castle was built by the Spanish in 1538. Impressive though it is, the austere castle has seen little real military action. It has, however, seen plenty of prisoners: a long-time jail, its dungeons were used as a military prison until the 1970s.

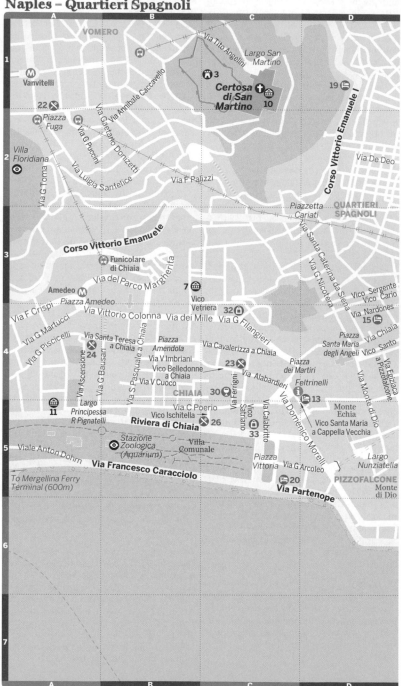

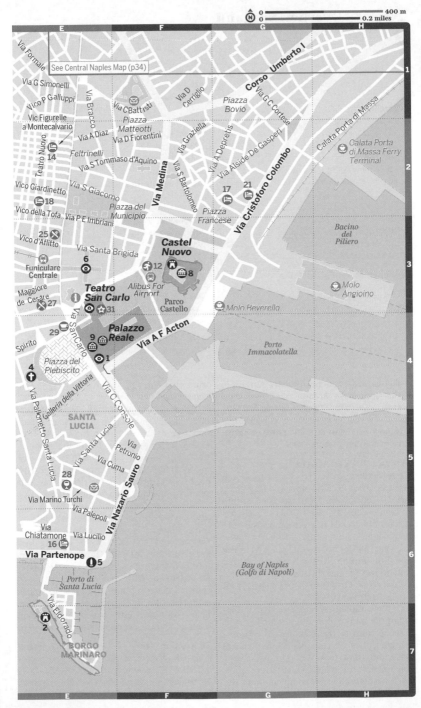

0   400 m
0   0.2 miles

See Central Naples Map (p34)

Via Formale
Via G Simonelli
Vico P Galluppi
Vic Figurelle
a Montecalvario
Via Bracco
Via A Diaz
Teatro Nuovo
14
Feltrinelli
Via S Tommaso d'Aquino
Vico Giardinetto
18
Vico della Tofa
Via P E Imbriani
Via S Giacomo
Via S Giacomo
25
Vico d'Aflitto
6
Funiculare
Centrale
Maggiore
de Cesare
27
Via Santa Brigida
Spirito
29
9
Palazzo
Reale
1
4
Piazza del
Plebiscito
Galleria della Vittoria
SANTA
LUCIA
28
Via Marino Turchi
Via Palepoli
Via
Chiatamone
16
Via Lucilio
Via Partenope
5
Porto di
Santa Lucia
2
BORGO
MARINARO

Via C Battisti
Piazza
Matteotti
Via D Fiorentini
Via D
Cerriglio
Piazza
Bovio
Corso Umberto I
Via G C Cortese
Via Graziella
Via A Depretis
Via Alside De Gasperi
Via Cristoforo Colombo
Via Medina
Via S Bartolomeo
Piazza del
Municipio
17
21
Piazza
Francese
Castel
Nuovo
12
8
Alibus For
Airport
Teatro
San Carlo
31
Parco
Castello
Via A F Acton
Molo Beverella
Via C Console
Via
Petronio
Via Santa Lucia
Via Cuma
Via Nazario Sauro
Via Eldorado

Calata Porta di Massa
Calata Porta
di Massa Ferry
Terminal
Bacino
del
Piliero
Molo
Angioino
Porto
Immacolatella
Bay of Naples
(Golfo di Napoli)

◎ **Top Sights**

Castel Nuovo..F3
Certosa di San Martino C1
Palazzo Reale... E4
Teatro San Carlo................................... E3

◎ **Sights**

1 Biblioteca Nazionale............................. E4
2 Castel dell'Ovo.......................................E7
3 Castel Sant'Elmo...................................C1
4 Chiesa di San Francesco di Paola E4
5 Fontana dell'Immacolatella E6
6 Galleria Umberto I E3
7 ISI Arti Associate B3
8 Museo Civico..F3
9 Museo del Palazzo Reale E4
10 Museo Nazionale di San
    Martino C1
11 Museo Pignatelli A5

⊕ **Activities, Courses & Tours**

12 City Sightseeing Napoli.........................F3

🛏 **Sleeping**

13 B&B Cappella Vecchia 11 .... D4
14 B&B Sui Tetti di Napoli......................... E2
15 Chiaja Hotel de Charme........................ D4

16 Grand Hotel Vesuvio E6
17 Hostel of the Sun G2
18 Hotel Il Convento.................................. E2
19 Hotel San Francesco al Monte D1
20 Parteno... C5
21 Romeo Hotel.. G2

⊗ **Eating**

22 Friggitoria Vomero A1
23 La Focaccia.. C4
24 La Trattoria dell'Oca A4
25 Pintauro E3
26 Ristorante Radici................................... C5
27 Trattoria San Ferdinando E3

◉ **Drinking**

28 Penguin Café..E5
29 Caffè Gambrinus E4
30 Nàis C4

◎ **Entertainment**

Box Office..(see 6)
31 Teatro San Carlo E3

🛍 **Shopping**

32 Mariano Rubinacci C4
33 Marinella C5

The newest resident of Castel Sant'Elmo is the impressive **Museo del Novecento Napoli** (☎081 558 77 08; ⊙9am-6pm Wed-Mon, entry on the hour, every hour), its collection of paintings and sculpture focussing on 20th-century southern Italian art.

SANTA LUCIA & CHIAIA

Castel Nuovo   CASTLE, MUSEUM
(Map p38; ☎081 795 58 77; admission €5; ⊙9am-7pm Mon-Sat) Known locally as the Maschio Angioino (Angevin Keep), this crenellated 13th-century castle is a strapping Neapolitan landmark. Built as part of the city makeover that Charles I of Anjou launched in the late 13th century, it was erected in three years from 1279 and christened the Castrum Novum (New Castle) to distinguish it from the Castel dell'Ovo.

Of the original structure only the Cappella Palatina remains; the rest is the result of renovations by the Aragonese two centuries later, as well as a meticulous restoration effort prior to WWII. The two-storey Renaissance triumphal arch at the entrance, the Torre della Guardia, commemorates the triumphal entry of Alfonso I of Aragon into Naples in 1443.

The walls of the **Cappella Palatina** were once graced by Giotto frescoes, of which only fragments remain on the splays of the Gothic windows. To the left of the cappella, the glass-floored **Sala dell'Armeria** (Armoury Hall) showcases Roman ruins discovered during restoration works on the **Sala dei Baroni** (Hall of the Barons) above.

Nowadays, they all form part of the **Museo Civico** spread across several halls on three floors. The 14th- and 15th-century frescoes and sculptures on the ground floor are of the most interest. The other two floors mostly display paintings, either by Neapolitan artists, or with Naples or Campania as subjects, covering the 17th to the early 20th centuries. Worth looking out for is Guglielmo Monaco's 15th-century bronze door, complete with a cannonball embedded in it.

Teatro San Carlo   THEATRE
(Map p38; ☎box office 081 797 23 31; guided tours 081 553 45 65; www.teatrosancarlo.it; Via San Carlo 98; tours €5; ⊙10am-5.30pm Mon-Sat, call ahead to book). Famed for its perfect acoustics,

Italy's largest opera house was built in 1737, predating its northern rival, Milan's La Scala, by 41 years. Severely damaged by a fire in 1816 it was rebuilt by Antonio Niccolini, the same architect who a few years before had added the facade.

Across Via San Carlo is one of the four entrances to the palatial glass atrium of the **Galleria Umberto I** shopping centre. Opened in 1900 as a twin arcade to the Galleria Vittorio Emanuele II in Milan, it's worth a quick look for its beautiful marble floor and elegant engineering.

Palazzo Reale   PALAZZO, MUSEUM
(Royal Palace; Map p38; ☑081 40 05 47; Piazza Trieste e Trento; admission €4; ☺9am-7pm Thu-Tue) Flanking Piazza del Plebiscito, this former royal residence traces its birth date to around 1600. Revamped in 1841 and extensively damaged during WWII, its monumental double staircase leads to the royal apartments, now home to the **Museo del Palazzo Reale** and its rich collection of baroque and neoclassical furnishings, porcelain, tapestries, statues and paintings. There's also a lavish private theatre, the Teatrino di Corte (1768), and a colossal 18th-century *presepe* in the Cappella Reale (Royal Chapel).

The palace also houses the **Biblioteca Nazionale** (National Library; Map p38; ☑081 781 91 11; ☺8.30am-7.30pm Mon-Fri, to 1.30pm Sat), which includes at least 2000 papyruses discovered at Herculaneum and fragments of a 5th-century Coptic Bible. Bring photo ID.

Chiesa di San Francesco di Paola   CHURCH
(Map p38; ☑081 74 51 33; Piazza del Plebiscito; ☺8.30am-noon & 4-7pm) This church is a neoclassical copy of Rome's Pantheon. A later addition to the colonnade that formed the highlight of Joachim Murat's original piazza (1809), the church was commissioned by Ferdinand I in 1817 to celebrate the restoration of his kingdom after the Napoleonic interlude.

Castel dell'Ovo   CASTLE
(Map p38; ☑081 240 00 55; Borgo Marinaro; admission free; ☺8.30am-7.30pm Mon-Sat, to 1.45pm Sun) Marking the eastern end of the 2.5km *lungomare* (seafront promenade), Naples' oldest castle sits atop the rocky Borgo Marinaro. Built by the Normans in the 12th century, it became a key fortress in the defence of Campania. According to myth, the castle owes its improbable name (Castle of the Egg) to Virgil, who was said to have buried an egg on the site where the castle now

stands, warning that when the egg breaks, the castle (and Naples) will fall.

Nearby, the **Fontana dell'Immacolatella** dates from the 17th century and features statues by Bernini and Naccherini.

ISI Arti Associate   ART GALLERY
(Map p38; ☑081 658 63 81; www.isiartiassociate. net; Vico del Vasto a Chiaia 47; ☺during exhibitions, check website) This hip art space exhibits anything from contemporary painting and photography to sculpture and multimedia installations from Italy and abroad. From September to May, special Friday-night events might include DJ sessions, live music or performance art. There's even an intimate bistro (meals €15, open for lunch Tuesday to Saturday, September to May), serving honest, well-executed dishes at bohemian prices. Check the website for upcoming exhibitions, performances and themed culinary tastings.

Museo Pignatelli   MUSEUM
(Map p38; ☑081 761 23 56; Riviera di Chiaia 200; admission €2; ☺8.30am-1.30pm Wed-Mon) Housed in a neoclassical villa once belonging to the Rothschilds, this chichi museum contains mostly 19th-century furnishings, china and other mildly interesting knick-knacks. A pavilion set in the villa's handsome gardens houses a coach museum, currently closed.

CAPODIMONTE
Palazzo Reale
di Capodimonte   PALAZZO, MUSEUM
On the northern edge of the city, this colossal palace took more than a century to build. It was originally intended as a hunting lodge for Charles VII of Bourbon, but as construction got under way in 1738, the plans got grander and grander. The result was the monumental *palazzo* that since 1759 has housed the art collection that Charles inherited from his mother Elisabetta Farnese.

Museo di Capodimonte
(☑081 749 91 11; www.museo-capodimonte.it; Parco di Capodimonte; admission €7.50; ☺8.30am-7.30pm Tue-Mon, last entry 90min before closing) This museum is spread over three floors and 160 rooms. You'll never see the whole place in one day, but a morning should be enough for an abridged best-of tour.

On the 1st floor you'll find works by Bellini, Botticelli, Caravaggio, Masaccio and Titian. Highlights are numerous, but look out for Masaccio's *Crocifissione* (Crucifixion), Bellini's *Trasfigurazione* (Transfiguration) and Parmigianino's *Antea*.

MAKING THE MOST OF YOUR EURO

If you're planning to blitz the sights, the **Campania artecard** (☎800 600601; www.campaniartecard.it) is an excellent investment. A cumulative ticket that covers museum admission and transport, it comes in various forms. The Naples and Campi Flegrei three-day ticket (adult/ EU citizens 18 to 25 years €16/10) gives free admission to three participating sites, a 50% discount on others and free transport in Naples and the Campi Flegrei. Other options range from €12 to €30 and cover sites as far afield as Pompeii and Paestum. The tickets can be bought at the Stazione Centrale (Central Station) infopoint, participating museums and archaeological sites, online or through the call centre.

Also on the 1st floor, the **royal apartments** are a study in regal excess. The Salottino di Porcellana (Room 51) is an outrageous example of 18th-century chinoiserie, its walls and ceiling crawling with whimsically themed porcelain 'stucco'. Originally created between 1757 and 1759 for the Palazzo Reale in Portici, it was transferred to Capodimonte in 1867.

Upstairs, the 2nd-floor galleries display work by Neapolitan artists from the 13th to the 19th centuries, plus some spectacular 16th-century Belgian tapestries. The piece that many come to Capodimonte to see, Caravaggio's *Flagellazione* (Flagellation; 1607–10), hangs in reverential solitude in Room 78, at the end of a long corridor.

If you have any energy left, the small **gallery of modern art** on the 3rd floor is worth a quick look, if for nothing else than Andy Warhol's poptastic *Mt Vesuvius*.

Parco di Capodimonte

(admission free; ☺9am to 1hr before sunset) Once you're finished in the museum, this adjoining 130-hectare park provides a much-needed breath of fresh air.

Catacombe di San Gennaro   CATACOMB

(☎081 744 37 14; www.catacombedinapoli.it; Via di Capodimonte 13; admission €8; ☺1hr tours every hour 10am-5pm Mon-Sat, to 1pm Sun) The oldest and most famous of Naples' ancient catacombs date to the 2nd century. Spread over two levels and decorated with early Christian frescoes, they contain a mix of tombs, corridors and broad vestibules held up by columns and arches. They were an important pilgrimage site in the 5th century, when St Januarius' body was brought here.

☞ Tours

Napoli Sotterranea   WALKING

(Underground Naples; Map p34; ☎081 29 69 44; www.napolisotterranea.org; Piazza San Gaetano 68; tours €9; ☺tours noon, 2pm & 4pm Mon-Fri, extra tours Thu, Sat & Sun) This outfit runs 1½-hour guided tours of the city's underworld. Visits take you 40m below the city to explore a network of creepy passages and caves. The passages were originally hewn by the Greeks to extract tufa stone used in construction and channel water from Mt Vesuvius. Extended by the Romans, the network of conduits and cisterns was more recently used as air-raid shelters in WWII. Part of the tour takes place by candlelight via extremely narrow passages – not suitable for expanded girths!

City Sightseeing Napoli   BUS

(Map p38; ☎081 551 72 79; www.napoli.city-sightseeing.it; adult/child €22/11) A hop-on, hop-off bus service with four routes across the city. All depart from Piazza del Municipio Parco Castello, and tickets, available on board, are valid for 24 hours for each of the routes. Tour commentaries are provided in English.

✰✰ Festivals & Events

Festa di San Gennaro   RELIGIOUS

Naples' main festival honours St Januarius. On the first Sunday in May and then on 19 September and 16 December, thousands of people gather in the *duomo* to witness the saint's blood liquefy – a miracle believed to save the city from potential disasters. In 1944 the miracle failed and Mt Vesuvius erupted; in 1980 it failed again and the city was struck by an earthquake.

Maggio dei Monumenti   CULTURAL

In May, Naples premier cultural event ensures a month-long menu of exhibitions, concerts, dance performances, guided tours and more.

Napoli Teatro Festival Italia   THEATRE

(www.teatrofestivalitalia.it) Usually in June and July, the Napoli Teatro Festival Italia serves up over three weeks of local and international theatre in venues across the city.

Madonna del Carmine RELIGIOUS

Held on 16 July, Madonna del Carmine culminates in a fabulous fireworks display on Piazza del Carmine.

Neapolis Rock Festival MUSIC

(www.neapolis.it) Southern Italy's top rock fest, it attracts premier international acts in July/August.

Festa di Piedigrotta CULTURAL

(www.festadipiedigrotta.it) In early to mid-September, Naples' Piedigrotta combines folk tunes with floats and fireworks around the Chiesa di Piedigrotta in Mergellina.

🛏 Sleeping

Ranging from funky B&Bs and cheery hostels to luxe seafront piles, slumber options in Naples are varied, plentiful and relatively cheap.

For maximum atmosphere, consider the *centro storico*, where you'll have many of the city's sights on your doorstep.

Seaside Santa Lucia is home to some of the city's most prestigious hotels, and Chiaia is cool and chic. For lofty views and a chilled-out vibe, hit Vomero.

CENTRO STORICO & PORT AREA

Hotel Piazza Bellini BOUTIQUE HOTEL €€

(Map p34; ☑081 45 17 32; www.hotelpiazza bellini.com; Via Costantinopoli 101; s €70-125, d €80-150, tr €100-170; ﹡@🕏) Naples' newest art hotel inhabits a 16th-century *palazzo*, its cool white spaces spiked with original majolica tiles and the work of emerging artists. Rooms offer pared-back cool, with designer fittings, chic bathrooms and mirror frames drawn straight on the wall. Rooms on the 5th and 6th floors feature panoramic balconies.

Romeo Hotel DESIGN HOTEL €€€

(Map p38; ☑081 017 50 01; www.romeohotel.it; Via Cristoforo Colombo 45; r €165-330; ﹡@🕏) Naples' top design hotel combines Artesia stone with A-list art and furniture, a fabulous rooftop restaurant and supersleek spa centre. 'Classic' category rooms are small but luxe, with DeLonghi espresso machines and sleek bathrooms. Up a notch, 'Deluxe' rooms (€225 to €450) offer the same perks but with added space and bay views.

B&B Cerasiello B&B €

(☑081 033 09 77, 338 9264453; www.cerasiello. it; Via Supportico Lopez 20; s €40-60, d €55-80, tr €70-95; ﹡🕏) Technically in the Sanità dis-

trict but a short walk north of the *centro storico*, this gorgeous B&B has four rooms, an enchanting communal terrace, stylish kitchen and an ethno-chic look. Bring €0.10 for the lift.

Costantinopoli 104 BOUTIQUE HOTEL €€€

(Map p34; ☑081 557 10 35; www.costantinopoli 104.it; Via Santa Maria di Costantinopoli 104; s/d/ ste €170/220/250; ﹡@🕏🏊) Sprinkled with books and antiques, Costantinopoli 104 is set in a chic neoclassical villa in the city's bohemian heartland. Although showing a bit of wear in places, rooms remain elegant and clean – those on the 1st floor open on to a sun terrace, while ground-floor rooms face the small, palm-fringed pool. The suites are simply gorgeous.

Hostel of the Sun HOSTEL €

(Map p38; ☑081 420 63 93; www.hostelnapoli. com; Via Melisurgo 15; dm €16-18, s with bathroom €30-35, d with bathroom €60-70; ﹡@🕏) Recently renovated and constantly winning accolades, HOTS is an ultrafriendly hostel near the port. Located on the 7th floor (have €0.05 handy for the lift), it's a bright, sociable place with multicoloured dorms, a cute in-house bar, and, a few floors down, a series of hotel-standard private rooms, two with private bathroom.

Decumani Hotel de Charme BOUTIQUE HOTEL €€

(Map p34; ☑081 551 81 88; www.decumani.it; Via San Giovanni Maggiore Pignatelli 15; s €90-105, d €105-130, deluxe d €130-150; ﹡@🕏) Don't be fooled by the scruffy staircase; this boutique hotel is fresh, elegant and located in the former *palazzo* of Cardinal Sisto Riario Sforza, the last bishop of the Bourbon Kingdom. The simple yet stylish rooms have high ceilings, 19th-century furniture and modern bathrooms. Deluxe rooms have a jacuzzi, and the restored baroque hall hosts cultural soirées.

B&B DiLetto a Napoli B&B €

(Map p34; ☑081 033 09 77, 338 9264453; www. dilettoanapoli.it; Vicolo Sedil Capuano 16; s €35-55, d €50-75, tr €65-90; P﹡🕏) Four rooms with vintage *cotto* (fired clay) floor tiles, organza curtains and artisan decor set a stylish scene at this B&B in a 15th-century *palazzo*. The urbane communal lounge comes with a kitchenette and dining table for convivial noshing and lounging.

TOLEDO & VOMERO

Hotel San Francesco al Monte
LUXURY HOTEL €€€

(Map p38; ☏081 423 91 11; www.hotelsanfran cesco.it; Corso Vittorio Emanuele I 328; s €160-190, d €170-225;) The monks in this 16th-century monastery never had it as good as the hotel's pampered guests. The cells have been converted into stylish rooms, the ancient cloisters house an open-air bar and the barrel-vaulted corridors are cool and atmospheric. Topping it all off is the 7th-floor swimming pool.

B&B Sui Tetti di Napoli
B&B €

(Map p38; ☏081 033 09 77, 338 9264453; www.sui tettidinapoli.net; Vico Figuerelle a Montecalvario 6; s €35-60, d €45-80, tr €60-95;) A block away from Via Toledo, this B&B is more like four apartments atop a thigh-toning stairwell. While two apartments share a terrace, the rooftop option has its own, complete with mesmerising views. All apartments include a kitchenette (the cheapest two share a kitchen); bright, simple furnishings and a homey vibe.

Hotel Il Convento
HOTEL €€

(Map p38; ☏081 40 39 77; www.hotelilconvento. com; Via Speranzella 137a; s €55-90, d €65-160;) Taking its name from the neighbouring convent, this lovely hotel blends antique Tuscan furniture, erudite book collections and candlelit stairs. Rooms are cosy and elegant, with creamy tones, dark woods and patches of 16th-century brickwork. For €80 to €180 you get a room with a private roof garden.

SANTA LUCIA & CHIAIA

Chiaja Hotel de Charme
BOUTIQUE HOTEL €€

(Map p38; ☏081 41 55 55; www.hotelchiaia.it; Via Chiaia 216; s €95-105, d €99-145, superior d €140-165;) Encompassing a former brothel and an aristocratic town house, this refined, peaceful hotel lives up to its name. The look is effortlessly noble – think gilt-framed portraits on pale lemon walls, opulent table lamps and heavy fabrics. Rooms facing pedestrianised shopping strip Via Chiaia come with a jacuzzi.

B&B Cappella Vecchia
B&B €

(Map p38; ☏081 240 51 17; www.cappellavecchia11. it; Vico Santa Maria a Cappella Vecchia 11; s €50-70, d €75-100;) Run by a superhelpful young couple, this B&B has six simple, witty rooms with funky bathrooms and different Neapolitan themes, from *mal'occhio* (evil

cye) to *peperoncino* (chilli). There's a spacious communal area for breakfast, and free internet available 24/7.

Parteno
B&B €€

(Map p38; ☏081 245 20 95; www.parteno.it; Via Partenope 1; s €80-99, d €100-125;) Six chic rooms are exquisitely decorated with period furniture, vintage Neapolitan prints and silk bedding. The azalea room (€130 to €165) steals the show with its seamless view of sea, sky and Capri. Hi-tech touches include satellite TV and free calls to Italian mobile numbers and to landlines in Europe, USA and Canada.

Grand Hotel Vesuvio
LUXURY HOTEL €€€

(Map p38; ☏081 764 00 44; www.vesuvio.it; Via Partenope 45; s €230-370, d €290-450;) Known for bedding legends – past guests include Rita Hayworth and Humphrey Bogart – this five-star heavyweight is a wonderland of dripping chandeliers, period antiques and opulent rooms. Count your lucky stars while drinking a martini at the rooftop restaurant.

✖ Eating

Pizza and pasta are the staples of Neapolitan cuisine. Pizza was created here and nowhere will you eat it better. Seafood is another local speciality and you'll find mussels and clams served in many dishes.

Neapolitan street food is equally brilliant. *Misto di frittura* – courgette flowers, deep-fried potato and eggplant – makes for a great snack, especially if eaten from paper outside a tiny streetside stall.

Many eateries close for two to four weeks in August.

AROUND STAZIONE CENTRALE & MERCATO

Attanasio
STREET FOOD €

(Map p34; Vico Ferrovia 1-4; snacks from €1.10; ⏰6.30am-7.30pm Tue-Sun) This retro pastry peddler makes one mighty *sfogliatella* (sweetened ricotta pastry), not to mention creamy *cannolli siciliani* (pastry shells filled with sweet ricotta) and runny, rummy *babà* (rum-soaked sponge cake). Savoury fiends shouldn't miss the hearty *pasticcino rustico* (savoury bread), stuffed with *provola* (provolone), ricotta and salami.

Da Michele
PIZZERIA €

(Map p34; Via Cesare Sersale 1; pizzas from €4; ⏰Mon-Sat) As hardcore as it gets, Naples' most famous pizzeria takes the no-frills ethos to its extremes. It's dingy and old-fashioned and serves only two types of pizza: *margherita* (tomato, basil and mozzarella) and *marinara* (tomatoes, garlic and oregano). Grab a ticket and join the queue.

CENTRO STORICO

Pizzeria Gino Sorbillo `TOP CHOICE` PIZZERIA €

(Map p34; Via dei Tribunali 32; pizzas from €2.30; ⊘Mon-Sat) The clamouring crowds say it all: Gino Sorbillo is king of the pizza pack. Head in for gigantic, wood-fired perfection, best followed by a velvety *semifreddo;* the chocolate and *torroncino* (almond nougat) combo is divine.

Palazzo Petrucci MODERN ITALIAN €€€

(Map p34; ✆081 552 40 68; www.palazzopetrucci.it, in Italian; Piazza San Domenico Maggiore 4; 5-course degustation menu €50; ⊘Mon-Sat) Progressive Petrucci is a breath of fresh air, exciting palates with mostly successful new-school creations like raw prawn and mozzarella 'lasagne' or poached egg onion soup. Balancing fine-dining elegance and a relaxed air, it's a fine choice if you plan on celebrating something special.

La Stanza del Gusto CHEESE BAR, MODERN ITALIAN €€

(Map p34; ✆081 40 15 78; www.lastanzadelgusto.com, in Italian; Via Costantinopoli 100; lunch special €13, 5-/7-course tasting menu €45/65; ⊘cheese bar 3.30pm-midnight Mon, 11am-midnight Tue-Sat;,restaurant dinner Mon-Sat) Creative and eclectic, the 'Taste Room' is divided into a casual ground-floor 'cheese bar' and a more formal upstairs dining room. Kick back with fabulous wine and rare *formaggi* (cheeses), or taste-test the mod-twist fare (think almond and saffron soup). Servings are small but the food is fab.

Trattoria Mangia e Bevi TRATTORIA €

(Map p34; Via Sedile di Porto 92; meals €10; ⊘lunch Mon-Fri) Everyone from pierced students to bespectacled *professori* squeeze around the lively, communal tables for brilliant home cooking at rock-bottom prices. Scan the daily-changing menu, jot down your choices and brace for gems like juicy *salsiccia di maiale* (pork sausage) and *peperoncino*-spiked *friarielli* (local broccoli).

TOLEDO & VOMERO

Trattoria San Ferdinando TRATTORIA €€

(Map p38; Via Nardones 117; meals €30; ⊘lunch Mon-Sat, dinner Wed-Fri) Hung with theatre posters and playbills, saffron-hued San Ferdinando pulls in well-spoken theatre types

and intellectuals. For a Neapolitan taste trip, ask for a rundown of the day's antipasti and choose your favourites for an *antipasto misto.* Seafood standouts include a delicate *seppia ripieno* (stuffed squid), while the homemade desserts make for a satisfying denouement.

Il Garum TRADITONAL ITALIAN €€

(Map p34; Piazza Monteoliveto 2a; meals €39) In the soft glow of wrought-iron lanterns, regulars tuck into made-with-love gems like rigatoni with shredded zucchini and mussels, and an exquisite grilled calamari stuffed with vegetables, cherry tomatoes and parmesan. All the desserts are made on-site.

Friggitoria Vomero STREET FOOD €

(Map p38; Via Cimarosa 44; snacks from €1; ⊘9.30am-2.30pm & 5-9.30pm Mon-Fri, 9.30am-2.30pm & 5-11pm Sat) The Brits don't have a monopoly on fried food served in paper. Here you'll find piles of crunchy deep-fried eggplants and artichokes, croquets filled with prosciutto and mozzarella, and a whole lot more.

Pintauro PASTRIES & CAKES €

(Map p38; Via Toledo 275; sfogliatelle €2; ⊘8am-2pm & 2.30-8pm Mon-Sat, 9am-2pm Sun Sep-May) Another local institution, the cinnamon-scented Pintauro peddles perfect *sfogliatelle* to shopped-out locals.

SANTA LUCIA & CHIAIA

Ristorante Radici MODERN ITALIAN €€€

(Map p38; ✆081 248 11 00; www.ristoranteradici.it, in Italian; Via Riviera di Chiaia 268; meals €50; ⊘dinner Mon-Sat) Elegant yet warm, Radici offers respite from the tried-and-tested standards on most local menus. Here, prime local produce is revamped in dishes like melt-in-your-mouth *spigola* (European sea bass) patties topped with tomatoes and served in a delicate broth. Book ahead.

La Trattoria dell'Oca TRATTORIA €€

(Map p38; Via Santa Teresa a Chiaia 11; meals €35; ⊘closed dinner Sun Oct-May, closed all day Sun Jun-Sep) Refined yet relaxed, this softly lit trattoria celebrates beautifully cooked classics, which may include *gnocchi al ragú* or a superb *baccalá* (salted cod) cooked with succulent cherry tomatoes, capers and olives.

La Focaccia PIZZA BY SLICE €

(Map p38; Vico Belledonne a Chiaia 31; focaccia from €1.50; ⊘11am-late Mon-Sat, 5pm-late Sun) Head to this funky, no-fuss bolthole for fat focaccia squares stacked with combos like artichokes and *provola,* or eggplant with *pecorino* cheese and smoked ham. Best of all, there isn't a microwave oven in sight.

Drinking

The city's student and alternative drinking scene is around the piazzas and alleyways of the *centro storico.* For a chicer vibe, hit the cobbled lanes of upmarket Chiaia. While some bars operate from 8am, most open from around 6.30pm and close around 2am.

Penguin Café   WINE BAR
(Map p38; Via Santa Lucia 88; ⊘7.30pm-late) Not just a snug wine bar, Penguin sells cinema-themed books, hosts literary events and offers live music Thursday to Saturday. The 100-plus wine list includes six fine drops by the glass, perfectly paired with quality cheeses, *salumi* (charcuterie), salads and a handful of heartier, seasonal dishes.

Caffè Mexico   CAFE
(Map p34; Piazza Dante 86; ⊘7am-8.30pm Mon-Sat) Make a beeline for Naples' best-loved espresso bar, where old-school baristas serve up the city's mightiest espresso. Don't forget to ask for *un bicchiere di acqua, per favore* (a glass of water, please), which you should drink *before* your coffee.

Intra Moenia   CAFE
(Map p34; Piazza Bellini 70) Of the squareside hang-outs on bohemian Piazza Bellini, this cafe-bookshop is our top choice. Favoured by local writers, artists and people who prefer a learned atmosphere with their Negroni, it's the perfect spot to while away an afternoon.

Nàis   BAR
(Map p38; Via Ferrigni 29) Slap bang on *aperitivo* strip Via Ferrigni, Nàis oozes a warm, convivial air with friendly bartenders, comfy suede banquettes and a book-lined shelf. Order a glass of vino, pick at the *aperitivi,* and enjoy the eye-candy crowd.

Caffè Gambrinus   CAFE
(Map p38; Via Chiaia 12) Tourists and over-dressed visitors self-consciously sip coffee and overpriced cocktails at Naples' most venerable cafe. Oscar Wilde and Bill Clinton count among the celebs who have graced its lavish art-nouveau interior.

☆ Entertainment

Options run the gamut from world-class opera and jazz to rock festivals and cavernous clubbing. For cultural listings check www.in

campania.it; for the latest club news check out the free minimag *Zero* (www.zero.eu, in Italian), available from many bars.

You can buy tickets for most cultural events at the box office inside **Feltrinelli** (⊘081 764 21 11; Piazza dei Martiri; ⊘4.30-8pm Mon-Sat).

The month-long **Maggio dei Monumenti** festival in May offers concerts and cultural activities in various museums and monuments around town, most of which are free. From May until September, alfresco concerts are common throughout the city. Tourist offices have details.

Football

Naples' football team Napoli is the third-most supported in the country after Juventus and Milan, and watching them play at the **Stadio San Paolo** (Piazzale Vincenzo Tecchio) is a highly charged rush. The season runs from September to May and you can expect to pay between €20 and €100 for a seat. Tickets can be purchased from **Azzurro Service** (⊘081 593 40 01; www.azzurroservice.net, in Italian; Via Francesco Galeota 19; ⊘9am-1pm & 3.30-7.30pm Mon-Fri, also Sat & Sun on match days) and **Box Office** (Map p38; ⊘081 551 91 88; www.boxoffice napoli.it, in Italian; Galleria Umberto I 17; ⊘9.30am-8.30pm Mon-Fri, 9.30am-1.30pm & 4.30-8pm Sat), as well as from some tobacconsists. Tickets are best booked two weeks in advance; don't forget to take photo ID.

Nightclubs & Live Music

Clubs usually open at 10.30pm or 11pm but don't fill up until after midnight. Many close in summer (July to September), some transferring to out-of-town beach locations. Admission charges vary, but expect to pay between €5 and €30, which may or may not include a drink.

Galleria 19   NIGHTCLUB
(Map p34; www.galleria19.it; Via San Sebastiano 19; ⊘Tue-Sat) Set in a long, cavernous cellar scattered with chesterfields and industrial lamps, this cool and edgy club draws a uni crowd early in the week and 20- and 30-somethings with its Friday electronica sessions and Saturday live-music gigs. Resident mixologist Gianluca Morziello is one of the city's best (order his Cucumber Slumber to understand why).

Kinky Klub   LIVE MUSIC, NIGHTCLUB
(Map p34; www.kinkyjam.com; Vicolo della Quercia 26; ⊘Tue-Sun mid-Sep–mid-Jun) Don't come here expecting latex and leather. Despite

the name, Kinky's speciality is both live and DJ-spun reggae, rocksteady ska and dancehall tunes. Acts span local to global names. Check the website for upcoming gigs.

Arenile Reload LIVE MUSIC, NIGHTCLUB
(www.arenilereload.com, in Italian; Via Coroglio 14, Bagnoli) The biggest of Naples' beachside clubs, head in for poolside cocktails, see-and-be-seen *aperitivo* sessions, live bands and dancing under the stars. The club is a short walk south of Bagnoli station on the Cumana rail line.

Around Midnight LIVE MUSIC
(⏰081 742 32 78; www.aroundmidnight.it, in Italian; Via Bonito 32a; ⏰Tue-Sun Sep-Jun) One of Naples' oldest and most famous jazz clubs, this tiny swinging bolthole features mostly home-grown live gigs, with the occasional blues band putting in a performance. Check the website for the week's line-up.

Theatre
Teatro San Carlo OPERA HOUSE
(Map p38; ⏰081 797 23 31; www.teatrosancarlo.it, Via San Carlo 98; ⏰box office 10am-7pm Tue-Sat, to 3.30pm Sun) One of Italy's premier opera venues, the theatre stages a year-round programme of opera, ballet and concerts, though tickets can be fiendishly difficult to get hold of. For opera, count on at least €50 for a place in the sixth tier and around €140 for a seat in the stalls.

Shopping

Colourful markets, artisan studios and heirloom tailors – shopping in Naples is highly idiosyncratic.

For a gastronomic souvenir, head to **Limonè** (Map p34; Piazza San Gaetano 72), where you can try the organic *limoncello* (lemon liqueur) before buying a bottle. If it goes to your head, grab some lemon pasta as well.

For organic, handmade soaps and beauty products, try **Kiphy** (Map p34; www.kiphy.it, in Italian; Vico San Domenico Maggiore 3), while those after quality, handcrafted nativity-scene figurines shouldn't miss **La Scarabattola** (Map p34; www.lascarabattola.it; Via dei Tribunali 50).

Elegant Chiaia is home to several legendary Neapolitan tailors, including **Mariano Rubinacci** (Map p38; www.marianorubinacci.net; Via Filangieri 26) and **Marinella** (Map p38; www.marinellanapoli.it; Via Riviera di Chiaia 287); the latter's made-to-measure ties once worn by Aristotle Onassis.

ℹ Information

Dangers & Annoyances
Petty crime can be a problem in Naples but with a little common sense you shouldn't have a problem. Leave valuables in your hotel room and never leave bags unattended. Be vigilant for pickpockets in crowded areas and carry bags across your body. Car and motorcycle theft is rife, so think twice before bringing a vehicle into town and never leave anything in your car. Use only marked, registered taxis and ensure the meter is running. Be careful if walking alone late at night, particularly near Stazione Centrale.

Emergency
Police station (⏰081 794 11 11; Via Medina 75) To report a stolen car, call ⏰113.

Internet Access
Navig@ndo (Via Santa Anna di Lombardi 28; per hour €2; ⏰10am-7.30pm Mon-Fri, to 1.30pm Sat)

Internet Resources
I Naples (www.inaples.it) The city's official tourist board site.

Turismo Regione Campania (www.turismoregionecampania.it) Up-to-date events listings, as well as audio clips and itineraries.

Napoli Unplugged (www.napoliunplugged.com) Attractions, up-to-date listings, news, articles and blog entries.

Medical Services
Ospedale Loreto-Mare (⏰081 20 10 33; Via Amerigo Vespucci 26)
Pharmacy (Stazione Centrale; ⏰7am-10pm)

Post
Post office (Piazza Matteotti; ⏰8am-6.30pm Mon-Sat)

Tourist Information
Head to the following tourist bureaus for information and a map of the city.
Tourist Information Office Piazza del Gesù Nuovo 7 (Map p34; ⏰9am-7pm Mon-Sat, to 2pm Sun); Stazione Centrale (Map p34; ⏰9am-8pm Mon-Sat, to 6pm Sun); Via San Carlo 9 (Map p38; ⏰9.30am-1.30pm & 2.30-6.30pm Mon-Sat, 9am-1.30pm Sun)

Travel Agencies
CTS (⏰081 033 19 48; Via Luigi Settembrini 86) Student travel centre.

ℹ Getting There & Away

Air
Capodichino airport (NAP; ⏰081 751 54 71; www.gesac.it), 7km northeast of the city centre, is southern Italy's main airport, linking Naples with most Italian and several major European

cities, as well as New York. Airlines include Alitalia and British Airways, and budget carrier easyJet, the latter's connections including London, Paris (Orly) and Berlin.

Boat

Naples, the bay islands and the Amalfi Coast are served by a comprehensive ferry network. Catch fast ferries and hydrofoils for Capri, Sorrento, Ischia (both Ischia Porto and Forio) and Procida from Molo Beverello in front of Castel Nuovo; hydrofoils for Capri, Ischia and Procida also sail from Mergellina.

Ferries for Sicily, the Aeolian Islands and Sardinia sail from Molo Angioino (right beside Molo Beverello) and neighbouring Calata Porta di Massa. Slow ferries to Ischia and Procida also depart from Calata Porta di Massa.

Ferry services are pared back considerably in the winter, and adverse sea conditions may affect sailing schedules.

The following tables list hydrofoil and ferry destinations from Naples. The fares, unless otherwise stated, are for a one-way, high-season, deck-class single.

Tickets for shorter journeys can be bought at the ticket booths on Molo Beverello and at Mergellina. For longer journeys try the offices of the ferry companies or a travel agent. The following is a list of hydrofoil and ferry companies:

Caremar (☑081 551 38 82; www.caremar.it, in Italian)

Gescab-Alilauro (☑081 497 22 22; www.alilauro.it)

Gescab-Navigazione Libera del Golfo (NLG; ☑081 552 07 63; www.navlib.it, in Italian)

Gescab-SNAV (☑081 428 55 55; www.snav.it)

Medmar (☑081 333 44 11; www.medmar group.it)

Siremar (☑199 118866; www.siremar.it, in Italian)

Tirrenia (☑081 720 11 11; www.tirrenia.it)

Suspended indefinitely at the time of writing, **Metrò del Mare** (☑199 600700; www.metrodel mare.net, in Italian) normally runs summer-only ferry services between Naples and Ercolano, Sorrento, Positano, Amalfi and Salerno, as well as between the main Amalfi Coast towns and from Naples to Pozzuoli and Baia/Bacoli in the Campi Flegrei. Check the website for updates.

Bus

Most national and international buses leave from Piazza Garibaldi.

Regional bus services are operated by numerous companies, the most useful of which is **SITA** (☑089 40 51 45; www.sitabus.it, in Italian). Connections from Naples include the following:

Amalfi (€4, two hours, five daily Monday to Saturday)

Pompeii (€2.80, 30 minutes, half-hourly)

Positano (€4, 2hrs, one daily Monday to Saturday)

Salerno (€4, one hour 10 minutes, every 25 minutes).

You can buy SITA tickets and catch buses either from Porto Immacolatella, near Molo Angioino, or from Via Galileo Ferraris, near Stazione Centrale.

Miccolis (☑081 20 03 80; www.miccolis-spa. it, in Italian) connects Naples to the following destinations:

Taranto (€19, four hours, three daily)

Brindisi (€26.60, five hours)

Lecce (€29, 5½ hours)

HYDROFOILS & HIGH-SPEED FERRIES

DESTINATION (FROM NAPLES – MOLO BEVERELLO)	FERRY COMPANY	PRICE (€)	DURATION (MIN)	DAILY FREQUENCY (HIGH SEASON)
Capri	Caremar	16	50	18
	Gescab-Navigazione Libera del Golfo	17	40	8-12
	Gescab-SNAV	17	45	12
Ischia (Casamicciola Terme & Forio)	Caremar	16	50	5
	Gescab-Alilauro	17	50-65	10
	Gescab-SNAV	16	55	4
Procida	Caremar	13	40	5
	Gescab-SNAV	13	35	4
Sorrento	Gescab-Alilauro	11	35	5
	SNAV	11	35	7

DESTINATION (FROM NAPLES – CALATA PORTA DI MASSA & MOLO ANGIOINO)	COMPANY	PRICE (€)	DURATION (MIN)	FREQUENCY (HIGH SEASON)
Capri	Caremar	9.60	80	3 daily
Ischia	Caremar	11	80	7 daily
	Medmar	11	75	6 daily
Procida	Caremar	9.60	45	7 daily
Aeolian Islands	Siremar	from 50		2 weekly
	Gescab-SNAV (summer only)	from 65		1 daily
Milazzo (Sicily)	Siremar	from 50		2 weekly
Palermo (Sicily)	Gescab-SNAV	from 35		1-2 daily
	Tirrenia	from 45		1 daily
Cagliari (Sardinia)	Tirrenia	from 45		2 weekly

Marino (☎080 311 23 35; www.marinobus.it) runs to the following:

Bari (€19, three hours, three to six daily)
Matera (€19, 4½ hours, two or three daily)

Car & Motorcycle

Naples is on the Autostrada del Sole, the A1 (north to Rome and Milan) and the A3 (south to Salerno and Reggio di Calabria). The A30 skirts Naples to the northeast, while the A16 heads across the Apennines to Bari.

On approaching the city, the motorways meet the Tangenziale di Napoli, a major ring road around the city. The ring road hugs the city's northern fringe, meeting the A1 for Rome in the east, and continuing westwards towards the Campi Flegrei and Pozzuoli.

Train

Naples is southern Italy's main rail hub. Most national trains arrive at or depart from Stazione Centrale or, underneath the main station, Stazione Garibaldi. Some services also stop at Mergellina station. There are up to 42 trains daily to Rome. Travel times and prices vary according to train type chosen. Options to/from Rome are as follows:

Frecciarossa (High Velocity; 2nd class one way €45, 70 minutes)
ES (Eurostar; 2nd class one way €36, 1¾ hours)
IC (InterCity; 2nd class one way €22, two hours)
regionale (slow local; one way €10.50, 2¾ to 3½ hours)

Stazione Circumvesuviana (☎081 772 24 44; www.vesuviana.it; Corso Garibaldi), southwest of Stazione Centrale (follow the signs from the main concourse), connects Naples to Sorrento (€4, 65 minutes, around 40 trains daily). Stops along the way include Ercolano (€2.10, 15 minutes) and Pompeii (€2.80, 35 minutes).

Ferrovia Cumana and **Circumflegrea** (☎800 053939; www.sepsa.it, in Italian), based at Stazione Cumana di Montesanto on Piazza Montesanto, 500m southwest of Piazza Dante, operate services to Pozzuoli (€1.20, 20 minutes, every 25 minutes).

ⓘ Getting Around
To/From the Airport

By public transport you can take either the regular **ANM** (☎800 639525; www.unicocampania. it) bus 3S (€1.20, 45 minutes, every 20 minutes) from Piazza Garibaldi or the **Alibus** (☎800 639525) airport shuttle (€3, 45 minutes, every 20 minutes) from Piazza del Municipio or Piazza Garibaldi.

Official taxi fares to the airport are as follows: €23 from a seafront hotel or from the Mergellina hydrofoil terminal; €19 from Piazza del Municipio; and €15.50 from Stazione Centrale.

Bus

In Naples, buses are operated by the city transport company **ANM** (☎800 639525; www. unicocampania.it). There's no central bus station, but most buses pass through Piazza Garibaldi, the city's chaotic transport hub. To locate your bus stop you'll probably need to ask at the information kiosk in the centre of the square.

Useful bus services:

140 Santa Lucia to Posillipo via Mergellina.

152 From Piazza Garibaldi to Fuorigrotta via Molo Beverello, Piazza Vittoria and Mergellina.

C28 From Piazza Vittoria to Piazza Vanvitelli in Vomero via Via dei Mille.

E1 From Piazza del Gesù, along Via Costantinopoli, to Museo Archeologico Nazionale, Via Tribunali, Via Duomo, Piazza Nicola Amore, along Corso Umberto I and Via Mezzocannone.

N3 A night bus operating from midnight to 4.50am (hourly departures) from Via Brin to Stazione Centrale, Piazza del Municipio, Piazza Dante and Vomero, and then back down to Stazione Centrale and Via Brin.

R1 From Piazza Medaglie d'Oro to Piazza Carità, Piazza Dante and Piazza Bovio.

R2 From Stazione Centrale, along Corso Umberto I, to Piazza Bovio, Piazza del Municipio and Piazza Trieste e Trento.

R4 From Capodimonte down past Via Dante to Piazza Municipio and back again.

Car & Motorcycle

Vehicle theft and anarchic traffic make driving in Naples a bad option.

Officially much of the city centre is closed to nonresident traffic for part of the day. Daily restrictions are in place in the *centro storico*, in the area around Piazza del Municipio and Via Toledo, and in the Chiaia district around Piazza dei Martiri. Hours vary but are typically from 8am to 6.30pm, possibly later.

East of the city centre, there's a 24-hour car park at Via Brin (€1.30 for the first four hours, €7.20 for 24 hours).

If hiring a car, expect to pay around €60 per day for an economy car or a scooter. The major car-hire firms are all represented in Naples.

Avis (☑081 28 40 41; www.avisautonoleggio.it; Corso Novara 5) Also at Capodichino airport.

Hertz (☑081 20 62 28; www.hertz.it; Via Giuseppe Ricciardi 5) Also at Capodichino airport and Mergellina.

Maggiore (☑081 28 78 58; www.maggiore.it; Stazione Centrale) Also at Capodichino airport.

Rent Sprint (☑081 764 13 33; Via Santa Lucia 36) Scooter hire only.

Funicular

Unico Napoli tickets (see boxed text, p52) are valid on the funiculars. Three of Naples' four funicular railways connect the centre with Vomero (the fourth, Funicolare di Mergellina, connects the waterfront at Via Mergellina with Via Manzoni).

Funicolare Centrale Ascends from Via Toledo to Piazza Fuga.

Funicolare di Chiaia From Via del Parco Margherita to Via Domenico Cimarosa.

Funicolare di Montesanto From Piazza Montesanto to Via Raffaele Morghen.

Metro

Naples' **Metropolitana** (☑800 568866; www.metro.na.it) metro system is covered by Unico Napoli tickets (see boxed text, p52).

Line 1 Runs north from Università (Piazza Bovio), stopping at Toledo (projected station opening 2012), Piazza Dante, Museo (for Piazza Cavour and Line 2), Materdei, Salvator Rosa, Cilea, Piazza Vanvitelli, Piazza Medaglie d'Oro and seven stops beyond. In 2012 the line is also expected to connect Università to Garibaldi (Stazione Centrale).

Line 2 Runs from Gianturco, just east of Stazione Centrale, with stops at Piazza Garibaldi (for Stazione Centrale), Piazza Cavour, Montesanto, Piazza Amedeo, Mergellina, Piazza Leopardi, Campi Flegrei, Cavalleggeri d'Aosta, Bagnoli and Pozzuoli.

Taxi

Official taxis are white and have meters. There are taxi stands at most of the city's main piazzas or you can call one of the five taxi cooperatives: **Napoli** (☑081 556 44 44), **Consortaxi** (☑081 22 22), **Cotana** (☑081 570 70 70), **Free** (☑081 551 51 51) or **Partenope** (☑081 556 02 02).

The minimum taxi fare is €4.50, of which €3 is the starting fare. There's also a baffling range of additional charges: €1 for a radio taxi call, €2.50 extra between 10pm and 7am and all day on Sundays, €2.60 to €4 for an airport run and €0.50 per piece of luggage in the boot. Guide dogs for the blind and wheelchairs are carried free of charge.

Always ensure the meter is running.

AROUND NAPLES

Campi Flegrei

Stretching west from Posillipo to the Tyrrhenian Sea, the Campi Flegrei (Phlegraean – or 'Fiery' – Fields) is a pockmarked area of craters, lakes and fumaroles, one of the world's most geologically unstable. Here, archaeological ruins stand in the midst of modern eyesores, and history merges with myth. This is where Greek colonists first settled in Italy – Cuma dates to the 8th century BC.

Before exploring the area it's worth stopping at Pozzuoli's tourist office for updated information on the area's sights and opening times. Also a good idea is the two-day €4 cumulative ticket that covers the archaeological sites of Baia and Cuma.

POZZUOLI

The first town that emerges beyond Naples' dreary western suburbs is Pozzuoli, a workaday place with attractions that are not immediately apparent. However, nose around and you'll find some impressive Roman ruins and a steaming volcanic crater. The town was established by the Greeks around 530 BC and later renamed Puteoli (Little Wells) by the Romans, who turned it into a major port. It was here that St Paul is said to have landed in AD 61 and that screen goddess Sophia Loren spent her childhood.

The **tourist office** (☑081 526 66 39; Piazza G Matteotti 1a; ⊗9am-3.30pm Mon-Fri) is beside the Porta Napoli gate, around 700m downhill from the metro station.

◎ Sights

Anfiteatro Flavio   AMPHITHEATRE
(☑081 526 60 07; Via Terracciano 75; admission €4; ⊗9am to 1hr before sunset Wed-Mon) Head northeast along Via Rosini to the ruins of this 1st-century-BC amphitheatre. Italy's third largest, it could hold over 20,000 spectators and was occasionally flooded for mock naval battles. Head under the main arena and get your head around the complex mechanics involved in hoisting the caged wild beasts up to their waiting victims. In AD 305, seven Christian martyrs, including St Januarius, were thrown to the animals here. They survived only to be beheaded later.

Solfatara Crater   NATURE RESERVE
(☑081 526 23 41; www.solfatara.it; Via Solfatara 161; admission €6; ⊗8.30am to 1hr before sunset) Some 2km up Via Rosini, which becomes Via Solfatara, this was known to the Romans as the Forum Vulcani (home of the god of fire). At the far end of the steaming, malodorous crater are the **Stufe**, in which two ancient grottoes were excavated at the end of the 19th century to create two brick *sudatoria* (sweat rooms). Christened Purgatory and Hell, they both reach temperatures of up to 90°C. To get to the crater, catch any city bus heading uphill from the metro station and ask the driver to let you off at Solfatara.

Tempio di Serapide   HISTORICAL SITE
Despite its name, the Temple of Serapis wasn't a temple at all, but an ancient *macellum* (town market). Named after a statue of the Egyptian god Serapis found here in 1750, its toilets (at either side of the eastern apse) are considered works of ancient ingenuity. Badly damaged over the centuries by bradyseism (the slow upward and downward movement of the earth's crust), the temple is occasionally flooded by sea water. You'll find it just east of the port in a leafy piazza.

BAIA

About 7km southwest of Pozzuoli, Baia was an upmarket Roman holiday resort with a reputation for sex and sin. Today much of the ancient town is underwater, and modern development has left what is effectively a built-up, ugly and uninspiring coastal road.

Between April and October, CYMBA runs glass-bottom boat tours of the underwater ruins of ancient **Baia Sommersa** (☑349 4974183; www.baiasommersa.it; tours €12; ⊗10am, noon & 3pm Sat & Sun). All year round, however, you can admire the elaborate *nymphaeum* (shrine to the water nymph), complete with statues, jewels, coins and decorative pillars dredged up and reassembled in the little-known but worthy **Museo Archeologico dei Campi Flegrei** (☑081 523 37 97; Via Castello; admission €4; ⊗varies, usually 9am to 1hr before sunset Tue-Sun). The 15th-century castle that houses the museum was built by Naples' Aragon rulers as a defence against possible French invasion.

CUMA & LUCRINO

Located 3km northwest of Baia, the quaint town of Cuma was the earliest Greek colony on the Italian mainland. Just to the east, Lucrino is where you'll find a peaceful lake with a sinister mythical past.

The highlight of ancient Cumae's **Acropoli di Cuma** (☑081 854 30 60; Via Montecuma; admission €4; ⊗9am to 1hr before sunset) is the haunting **Antro della Sibilla Cumana** (Cave of the Cuman Sybil). Hollowed out of the tufa bank, its eerie 130m-long trapezoidal tunnel leads to the vaulted chamber where the Sybil was said to pass on messages from Apollo. Virgil writes of Aeneas coming here to seek the oracle, who directs him to Hades (the underworld), entered from nearby Lago d'Averno (Lake Avernus).

❶ Getting There & Away

BOAT There are frequent car and passenger ferries from Pozzuoli to Ischia and Procida. Typical prices are €6.60 to Procida and €7.60 to Ischia – more if you take a hydrofoil.

BUS AMN bus 152 links Naples to Pozzuoli.

TICKETS PLEASE

Tickets for public transport in Naples and the surrounding Campania region are managed by **Unico Campania** (www.unicocampania.it) and sold at stations, ANM booths and tobacconists. There are various tickets, depending on where you plan to travel. The following is a rundown of the various tickets on offer:

» **Unico Napoli** (90 minutes €1.20, 24 hours weekdays/weekends €3.60/€3) Unlimited travel by bus, tram, funicular, metro, Ferrovia Cumana or Circumflegrea.

» **Unico 3T** (72 hours €20) Unlimited travel throughout Campania, including the Alibus, EAV buses to Mt Vesuvius and transport on the islands of Ischia and Procida.

» **Unico Ischia** (90 minutes €1.40, 24 hours €5.40) Unlimited bus travel on Ischia.

» **Unico Capri** (60 minutes €2.40, 24 hours €8.40) Unlimited bus travel on Capri. The 60-minute ticket also allows a single trip on the funicular connecting Marina Grande to Capri Town; the daily ticket allows for two funicular trips.

» **Unico Costiera** (45 minutes €2.40, 90 minutes €3.60; 24 hours €7.20, 72 hours €18) A money-saver if you plan on much travelling by SITA or EAV bus and/or Circumvesuviana train in the Bay of Naples and Amalfi Coast area. The 24- and 72-hour tickets also cover the City Sightseeing tourist bus between Amalfi and Ravello, and Amalfi and Maiori, which runs from April to October.

CAR Take the Tangenziale ring road from Naples and swing off at the Pozzuoli exit. Less swift but more scenic is taking Via Francesco Caracciolo along the Naples waterfront to Posillipo, then on to Pozzuoli.

TRAIN Both the **Ferrovia Cumana** (☑800 001616; www.sepsa.it) and the Naples metro (line 2) serve Pozzuoli. To reach Cuma, take the Ferrovia Cumana train to Fusaro station, walk 150m north to Via Fusaro and jump on a Cuma-bound **EAV bus** (www.eavbus.it, in Italian), which runs roughly every 30 minutes Monday to Saturday and every hour on Sunday. For Baia, jump on a Miseno-bound EAV Bus from the opposite side of the street.

Caserta

POP 78,670

The one compelling reason to stop at this otherwise nondescript town, 22km north of Naples, is to visit the colossal Palazzo Reale. One of the greatest – and last – achievements of Italian baroque architecture, its film credits include *Mission Impossible III* and the interiors of Queen Amidala's royal residence in *Star Wars: Episode 1 – The Phantom Menace* and *Star Wars: Episode 2 – Attack of the Clones*.

Caserta was founded in the 8th century by the Lombards on the site of a Roman emplacement atop Monte Tifata, expanding onto the plains below from the 12th century.

Caserta's **tourist office** (☑0823 32 11 37; www.eptcaserta.it; Corso Trieste; ☺9am-1pm Mon-Fri) is 600m east of the palace.

⊙ Sights

Palazzo Reale   PALAZZO, GARDEN
(Reggia di Caserta; ☑0823 44 80 84; Viale Douhet 22; admission €12; ☺8.30am-7pm Wed-Mon) In 1752 Charles VII of Bourbon ordered a place to rival Versailles; the result was this Unesco-listed palace. Neapolitan Luigi Vanvitelli was commissioned for the job and built a palace bigger than its French rival. With its 1200 rooms, 1790 windows, 34 staircases and a 250m-long facade, it was reputedly the largest building in 18th-century Europe.

You enter by Vanvitelli's immense staircase, a masterpiece of vainglorious baroque, and follow a route through the royal apartments, richly decorated with tapestries, furniture and crystal. Beyond the library is a room containing a vast collection of *presepi* composed of hundreds of hand-carved nativity pieces.

To clear your head afterwards, explore the elegant landscaped **park** (☺8.30am-6pm Jun-Aug, to 5.30pm May & Sep, to 5pm Apr, to 4.30pm Oct, to 4pm Mar, to 2.30pm Nov-Feb). It stretches for some 3km to a waterfall and fountain of Diana and the famous **Giardino Inglese** (English Garden; ☺Wed-Mon) with its intricate pathways, exotic plants, pools and cascades.

The weary can cover the same ground in a pony and trap (from €5), or for €1 you can bring a bike into the park. A picnic is another good idea. Within the palace there's also the **Mostra Terrea Motus** (admission free with palace ticket; ☺9am-6pm Wed-Mon), illustrating the 1980 earthquake that devastated the region.

❶ Getting There & Away

BUS **CTP** (www.ctp.na.it, in Italian) buses connect Caserta with Naples' Piazza Garibaldi (€2.90) about every 20 to 60 minutes between 4.30am and 11.30pm. Some Benevento services also stop in Caserta.

TRAIN The town is on the main train line between Rome (IC €21, around two hours and 30 minutes) and Naples (€3.40, 40 minutes). Both bus and train stations are near the Palazzo Reale entrance. If you're driving, follow signs for the Reggia.

BAY OF NAPLES

Capri

POP 14,050

A stark mass of limestone rock that rises sheerly through impossibly blue water, Capri (*ca*-pri) is the perfect microcosm of Mediterranean appeal – a smooth cocktail of chichi piazzas and cool cafes, Roman ruins and rugged seascapes. It's also a hugely popular day-trip destination and a summer favourite of holidaying VIPs. Inevitably, the two main centres, Capri Town and its uphill rival, Anacapri, are almost entirely given over to tourism and high prices. But explore beyond the designer boutiques and pointedly traditional trattorias and you'll find that Capri's hinterland retains an unspoiled rural charm with grand villas, overgrown vegetable plots, sun-bleached peeling stucco and banks of brilliantly coloured bougainvillea.

◉ Sights

Grotta Azzurra GROTTO
(Blue Grotto; Map p54; admission €11.50; ☺9am to 1hr before sunset) Long known to local fishermen, this stunning sea cave was rediscovered by two Germans, Augustus Kopisch and Ernst Fries, in 1826. Subsequent research, however, revealed that Emperor Tiberius had built a quay in the cave around AD 30, complete with a *nymphaeum*. You can still see the carved Roman landing stage towards the rear of the cave.

Far from being an overblown tourist attraction, the grotto's iridescent blue light is pure magic. It's caused by the refraction of sunlight off the sides of the 1.3m-high entrance, coupled with the reflection off the white sandy bottom.

The easiest way to visit is to take a boat tour from Marina Grande. A return trip will cost €23.50, comprising a return motorboat to the cave, a rowing boat into the cave and admission fee; allow a good hour. The singing 'captains' are included in the price, so don't feel any obligation if they push for a tip.

The grotto is closed if the sea is too choppy, so before embarking check that it's open at the Marina Grande tourist office.

Capri Town TOWN
With its whitewashed stone buildings and tiny car-free streets, Capri Town evokes a film set. In summer its toy-town streets swell with camera-wielding day trippers and the glossy rich. Central to the action is **Piazza Umberto I** (aka the Piazzetta), the showy, open-air salon where tanned tourists pay eye-watering prices to sip at one of four squareside cafes. Nearby, the 17th-century **Chiesa di Santo Stefano** (Map p56; Piazza Umberto I; ☺8am-8pm) has a well-preserved marble floor (taken from Villa Jovis) and a statue of San Costanzo, Capri's patron saint. Beside the northern chapel is a reliquary with a saintly bone that reputedly saved Capri from the plague in the 19th century.

Across the road, **Museo Cerio** (Map p56; ☎081 837 66 81; Piazzetta Cerio 5; adult/reduced €2.50/1; ☺10am-1pm Tue-Sat) harbours a library of books and journals about the island (mostly in Italian) and a collection of locally found fossils.

To the east of the Piazzetta, Via Vittorio Emanuele and its continuation, Via Serena, lead down to the picturesque **Certosa di San Giacomo** (Charterhouse of San Giacomo; Map p56; ☎081 837 62 18; Viale Certosa 40; admission free; ☺9am-2pm Tue-Sun), a 14th-century monastery with two cloisters and some fine 17th-century frescoes in the chapel.

From the *certosa* (charterhouse), Via Matteotti leads down to the colourful **Giardini di Augusto** (Gardens of Augustus; Map p56; ☺dawn-dusk), founded by the Emperor Augustus. The view from the gardens is breathtaking, looking over to the **Isole Faraglioni** (Map p54), three limestone pinnacles that rise vertically out of the sea.

Villa Jovis VILLA
(Jupiter's Villa; Map p54; ☎081 837 06 34; Via Tiberio; admission €2; ☺9am to 1hr before sunset) East of Capri Town, a comfortable 2km walk along Via Tiberio is Villa Jovis (aka Palazzo di Tiberio). Standing 354m above sea level, this was the largest and most sumptuous of the island's 12 Roman villas and Tiberius' main Capri residence. It's not in great nick

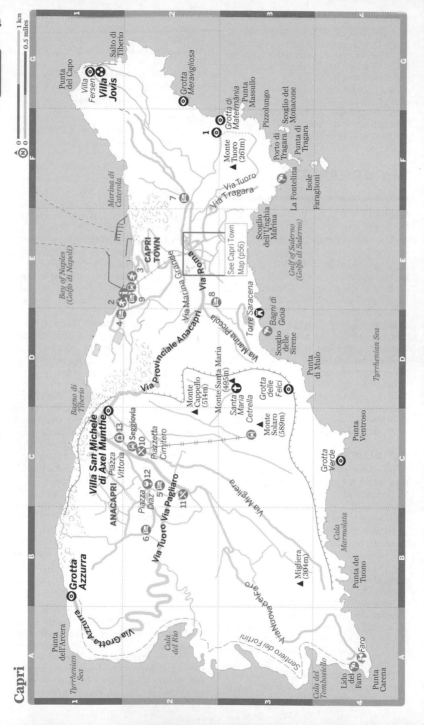

Capri

1 km
0.5 miles

Punta del Capo
Villa Fersen
Villa Jovis
Salto di Tiberio
Grotta Meravigliosa
Grotta di Matermània
Punta Massullo
Pizzolungo
Scoglio del Monacone
Porto di Tragara
Punta di Tragara
La Fontelina
Isole Faraglioni
Monte Tuoro (261m)
Via Tuoro
Via Tragara

Marina di Caterola

Bay of Naples (Golfo di Napoli)

CAPRI TOWN

See Capri Town Map (p56)

Via Roma
Via Marina Grande
Via Provinciale Anacapri
Via Marina Piccola

Torre Saracena
Scoglio dell'Unghia Marina
Gulf of Salerno (Golfo di Salerno)
Bagni di Gioia
Scoglio delle Sirene
Punta di Mulo
Punta Ventroso

Tyrrhenian Sea

Bagno di Tiberio
Villa San Michele di Axel Munthe
Piazza Vittoria
Seggiovia
Piazzetta Cimitero
Monte Cappello (514m)
Monte Santa Maria (495m)
Santa Maria Cetrella
Monte Solaro (589m)
Grotta delle Felci
Grotta Verde

ANACAPRI
Piazza Diaz
Via Tuoro Via Pagliaro

Migliera (304m)

Grotta Azzurra
Punta dell'Arcera
Via Grotta Azzurra
Cala del Rio

Tyrrhenian Sea

Sentiero dei Fortini
Via Nuova del Faro
Via Migliera

Cala del Tombosiello
Lido del Faro
Faro
Punta Carena

Cala Marmolata
Punta del Tuono

today, but the size of the ruins gives an idea of the scale at which Tiberius liked to live. His private rooms, with superb views over to the Punta Campanella, were on the northern and eastern sides of the complex.

The stairway behind the villa leads to the 330m-high **Salto di Tiberio** (Tiberius' Leap), a sheer cliff from where Tiberius had out-of-favour subjects hurled into the sea.

A 1.5km walk from the villa, down Via Tiberio and Via Matermània, is the **Arco Naturale** (Map p54), a huge rock arch formed by the pounding sea.

Villa San Michele di Axel Munthe MUSEUM, GARDEN
(Map p54; ☑081 837 14 01; www.villasanmichele. eu; Via Axel Munthe; admission €6; ⊙9am-6pm May-Sep, 9am-3.30pm Nov-Feb, 9am-4.30pm Mar, 9am-5pm Apr & Oct) A short walk from Anacapri's Piazza Vittoria awaits the former home of self-aggrandising Swedish doctor Axel Munthe. The story behind the villa, built on the ruined site of a Roman villa, is told by Munthe himself in his autobiography *The Story of San Michele* (1929). Other than the collection of Roman sculpture, the villa's best feature is the beautifully preserved gardens and their superb views. If you are here in July or August, you may be able to catch one of the classical concerts that take place in the gardens. Check the website for programme and reservation information.

Beyond the villa, Via Axel Munthe continues to the 800-step stairway leading down to Capri Town. Built in the early 19th century, this was the only link between Anacapri and the rest of the island until the present mountain road was constructed in

the 1950s. Traditionally, the people of Capri and Anacapri have been at loggerheads, and they are always ready to trot out their respective patron saints to ward off the *malocchio* (evil eye) of their rivals.

Seggiovia VIEWPOINT
(Map p54; ☑081 837 14 28; Piazza Vittoria; single/ return €7.50/10; ⊙9.30am-4.30pm Apr-Oct, to 3.30pm Nov-Mar) Hop onto this chairlift and head up to the summit of **Monte Solaro** (589m), Capri's highest point. The views from the top are utterly unforgettable – on a clear day you can see the entire Bay of Naples and the islands of Ischia and Procida.

Faro LIGHTHOUSE
(Map p54) Rising above Punta Carena, Capri's rugged southwesterly point, is Italy's second-tallest and most powerful lighthouse. From Anacapri a bus runs to the Faro every 20 minutes from April to October and every 30 to 40 minutes from November to March.

🏃 **Activities**

Top swimming spots include **La Fontelina** (Map p54), reached along Via Tragara. Access to the private beach will set you back €19 but it's right beside Capri's craggy Faraglioni stacks and one of the few beaches exposed to the sun until late in the day. On the west coast, **Lido del Faro** (Map p54) at Punta Carena is another good option. It costs €20 to access the private beach, complete with swimming pool and a pricey but fabulous restaurant. Otherwise, opt for the neighbouring public beach, and grab a decent bite at snack bar Da Antonio. To get here, catch the bus to Faro and follow the steps down to the beach.

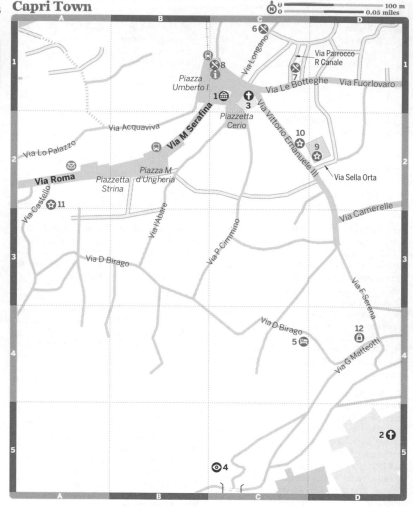

Capri also offers some memorable hiking. Favourite routes link the Arco Naturale with Punta di Tragara, and Monte Solaro with Anacapri. Running along the island's oft-overlooked western coast, the Sentiero dei Fortini (Path of the Small Forts) leads from Punta Carena up to the Grotta Azzurra.

Marina Grande is the hub of Capri's thriving water-sports business.

Sercomar DIVE CENTRE
(Map p54; ☎081 837 87 81; www.caprisub.com, in Italian; Via Colombo 64; ⊙closed Nov) Offers various diving packages, costing from €100 for a single dive to €350 for a four-session beginners' course.

Bagni di Gioia CANOEING
(Map p54; ☎081 837 77 02) You can hire canoes here for €8/14 per hour for a single/double canoe.

Banana Sport BOATING
(Map p54; ☎081 837 51 88, 330 227064; ⊙mid-May–Oct) Operating out of a kiosk to the west of the port, Banana Sport hires out five-person motorised dinghies for €70 to €90 for two hours or €150 to €190 for the day.

Capri Town

🛏 Sleeping

Capri's accommodation is top-heavy, with plenty of four- and five-star hotels but few budget options. Cheaper *pensioni* do exist, but they tend to be at the top of their price bracket. Although there are a growing number of B&Bs, they're rarely much of a saving. As a general rule, the further you go from Capri Town, the less you'll pay. Camping is forbidden.

Always book ahead. Hotel space is at a premium during the summer, and many places close in winter, typically between November and March.

TOP CHOICE Casa Mariantonia   BOUTIQUE HOTEL €€
(Map p54; ✆081 837 29 23; www.casamariantonia .com; Via G Orlandi 80, Anacapri; r €100-260, ste €180-400; ⏸✻🖥🏊) Past guests include Jean-Paul Sartre and Alberto Moravia, so you might just find your own muse by the pool at this gorgeous boutique retreat. Rooms deliver restrained elegance in soothing hues, as well as a private terrace with garden views.

Relais Maresca   HOTEL €€
(Map p54; ✆081 837 96 19; www.relaismaresca. it; Via Marina Grande 284, Marina Grande; r incl breakfast €130-250; ⏱Apr-Oct; ✻🖥) A delightful four-star hotel, this is the top choice in Marina Grande, with acres of gleaming ceramic in turquoise, blue and yellow. There's a range of rooms (and corresponding pric-

es); the best have balconies and sea views. There's also a lovely flower-filled 4th-floor terrace. Minimum two-day stay on weekends in July and August.

Hotel Villa Sarah   HOTEL €€
(Map p54; ✆081 837 78 17; www.villasarahcapri. com; Via Tiberio 3a, Capri Town; s €95-155, d €145-225; ⏱Easter-Oct; ✻🖥) Villa Sarah retains a rustic appeal that so many of the island's hotels have long lost. Surrounded by its own fruit-producing gardens, it has 20 airy rooms, all decorated in classical local style with ceramic tiles and old-fashioned furniture. Best of all, though, is the small swimming pool.

Hotel Bussola   HOTEL €€
(Map p54; ✆081 838 20 10; www.caprihotelbussola .com; Traversa La Vigna 14, Anacapri; s €50-120, d €70-140; ✻@🖥) This hotel has moved up several elegant notches from its days as a hostel-cum-hotel. The sun-filled rooms have luxurious drapes and a blue-and-white colour scheme, while the public spaces are a Pompeii-esque combo of columns, statues and vaulted ceilings. To get here take the bus up to Piazza Vittoria and call for the hotel shuttle service.

Hotel La Tosca   PENSIONE €€
(Map p56; ✆081 837 09 89; www.latoscahotel. com; Via Birago 5, Capri Town; s €50-100, d €75-160; ⏱Apr-Oct; ✻🖥) This charming one-star *pensione* is hidden away down a quiet back lane overlooking the Certosa di San Giacomo and the surrounding mountains. The rooms are plain but comfortable, with cool whitewashed walls and large bathrooms; several have private terraces. The genial owner extends a warm welcome. It's popular, so book ahead!

Belvedere e Tre Re   HOTEL €€
(Map p54; ✆081 837 03 45; www.belvedere -tre-re.com; Via Marina Grande 264, Marina Grande; s €80-120, d 100-140; ⏱Apr-Oct; ✻) Five minutes' walk from the port with superb boat views, this fairly modest two-star hotel offers comfortable rooms, complete with private covered balconies. There's a sun-bronzing terrace on the top floor. Breakfast is an extra €5 per person.

Pensione Guarracino   PENSIONE €€
(Map p54; ✆081 837 71 40; guarracino@capri. it; Via Mulo 13; s €70-85, d €90-130; ✻) A short walk from the centre of Capri Town and within easy striking distance of Marina Pic-

cola, this small, family-run *pensione* has 13 modest rooms, each decked out with a comfy bed, decent shower and independent air-con.

✕ Eating

Traditional food in traditional trattorias is what you'll find on Capri. The island's culinary gift to the world is *insalata caprese*, a salad of fresh tomato, basil and mozzarella bathed in olive oil. Also look out for *caprese* cheese, a cross between mozzarella and ricotta, and *ravioli caprese*, ravioli stuffed with ricotta and herbs.

Many restaurants, like the hotels, close over winter.

TOP CHOICE Pulalli
WINE BAR €€

(Map p56; Piazza Umberto I 4, Capri Town; meals €40; ☺Wed-Mon Easter-Oct) Climb the clocktower steps to the right of Capri Town's tourist office and your reward is a laid-back local hang-out, where fabulous *vino* meets a discerning selection of cheeses, *salumi* and more substantial fare like spaghetti with zucchini flowers. Try for a seat on the terrace or, if you're feeling lucky, the coveted table on its own petite balcony.

Buca di Bacco
TRATTORIA, PIZZERIA €€

(Map p56; Via Longano 35, Capri Town; pizzas €6-15, meals €40; ☺Thu-Tue Mar-Oct) A famous hangout for artists early last century, this hidden Capri Town treasure is now better known for its solid local cooking, bubbling pizzas and amiable staff. The seafood is especially good, as is the window table with dreamy sea views.

Le Arcate
TRADITIONAL ITALIAN €€

(Map p54; Via de Tommaso 24, Anacapri; meals €40) This is the restaurant that the locals recommend – and frequent. An unpretentious place with hanging baskets of ivy and well-aged terracotta tiles, it specialises in delicious *primi* (first courses) and pizzas. A real show-stopper is the *risotto con polpa di granchio, rughetta e scaglie di parmigiano* (risotto with crab meat, rocket and shavings of Parmesan).

Capri Pasta
TAKE AWAY €

(Map p56; Via Parrocco R Canale 12, Capri Town; meals €8; ☺closed Mon) In-the-know locals come here for a cheap, tasty takeaway lunch. The just-cooked soul food might include *parmigiana di melanzana* (eggplant parmigiana) and *friarelle* (local broccoli). The house ravioli is legendary and offered fresh or ready-to-eat in dishes like *ravioli fritti* (fried ravioli) stuffed with Caciotta cheese and marjoram.

Salemeria da Aldo
DELI €

(Map p54; Via Cristoforo Colombo 26, Marina Grande; sandwiches from €3.50) Ignore the restaurant touts and head straight to this honest portside deli, where bespectacled Aldo will make you his legendary *panino alla Caprese* (crusty bread stuffed with silky mozzarella and tomatoes from his own garden). Grab a bottle of Falanghina and you're set for a day at the beach.

Pizzeria Aumm Aumm
PIZZERIA €

(Map p54; Via Caprile 18, Anacapri; pizzas €5-9; ☺dinner Tue-Sun) Usually open until 1am, this is the locals' late-night option, complete with TV screen to capture any soccer goals. The wood-fired pizzas are seriously good, made with only fresh produce.

♟ Drinking & Entertainment

The main evening activity is styling up and hanging out, ideally on Capri Town's Piazzetta. There are few nightclubs to speak of and just a few upmarket taverns. Most places open around 10pm (don't expect a crowd until midnight), charging anywhere between €30 and €40 for admission. Many close between November and Easter.

Caffè Michelangelo
CAFE

(Map p54; Via Orlandi 138, Anacapri) A laid-back cafe good for people-watching.

Anema e Core
LIVE MUSIC, NIGHTCLUB

(Map p56; Via Sella Orta 39e, Capri Town) Celebs head for this self-styled tavern, the island's most famous nightspot.

O Guarracino
LIVE MUSIC

(Map p56; ☎081 837 05 14; Via Castello 7, Capri Town) Somewhat more casual.

Number One
LIVE MUSIC, NIGHTCLUB

(Map p56; Via Vittorio Emanuele III 55, Capri Town) The latest hot spot, it offers live music and a small dance floor.

🔒 Shopping

If you're not in the market for a new Rolex or Prada bag, look out for ceramic work, lemon-scented perfume and *limoncello*. For perfume don't miss **Carthusia I Profumi di Capri** (Map p56; Via F Serena 28) in Capri

Town; for *limoncello* head up to Anacapri and **Limoncello Capri** (Map p54; Via Capodimonte 27).

If you *are* in the market for a new Rolex or Prada bag, head to Via Vittorio Emanuele and Via Camerelle.

❶ Information

Emergency
Police station (☑081 837 42 11; Via Roma 70, Capri Town)

Internet Access
Capri Internet Point (☑081 837 32 83; Piazzetta Cimitero, Anacapri; per hour €2; ⊙9am-9pm Mon-Sat, to 2.30pm Sun May-Oct, shorter hours Nov-Apr) Also sells international newspapers.

Internet Resources
Capri Island (www.capri.net) Excellent website with listings, itineraries and ferry schedules.
Capri Tourism (www.capritourism.com) Official website of Capri's tourist office.

Medical Services
Farmacia Internazionale (Via Roma 45, Capri Town)
Hospital (☑081 838 12 05; Via Provinciale Anacapri 5)

Post
Post office Anacapri (Via de Tommaso 8); Capri Town (Map p56; Via Roma 50)

Tourist information
Tourist office Anacapri (Via Orlandi 59; ⊙9am-3pm Mon-Sat Apr-Sep); Capri Town (Map p56; Piazza Umberto I; ⊙9am-1pm & 4-7.15pm Mon-Sat, to 3pm Sun Apr-Sep, 9.15am-1.15pm & 3-6.15pm Mon-Sat Oct-Mar); Marina Grande (Map p54; ⊙9.15am-1pm & 3-6.15pm Mon-Sat, 9am-3pm Sun Apr-Sep) Each tourist office can provide a free map of the island with town plans of Capri and Anacapri, and a more detailed one for €1. For hotel listings and other useful information, ask for a free copy of *Capri è*.

❶ Getting There & Away

See Naples (p48) and Sorrento (p75) for details of ferries and hydrofoils to the island.

In summer hydrofoils connect with Positano (€17, 30 to 40 minutes) and Ischia (€16.50, one hour).

Note that some companies require you to pay a small supplement for luggage, typically around €2.

❶ Getting Around

The best way to get around Capri is by bus. There's no car-hire service on the island, and between Easter and October you can bring a vehicle to the island only if it's registered outside Italy.

Sippic (☑081 837 04 20) runs regular buses between Capri Town and Marina Grande, Anacapri and Marina Piccola. It also operates buses from Marina Grande to Anacapri and from Marina Piccola to Anacapri.

From Anacapri bus terminal, **Staiano Autotrasporti** (www.staiano-capri.com, in Italian) buses serve the Grotta Azzurra and Faro.

Single tickets cost €1.60 on all routes, as does the funicular that links Marina Grande with Capri Town.

You can hire a scooter from **Ciro dei Motorini** (☑081 837 80 18; Via Marina Grande 55) at Marina Grande. Rates are about €30 per two hours or €65 per 24 hours.

From Marina Grande, a **taxi** (☑in Capri Town 081 837 05 43, in Anacapri 081 837 11 75) costs around €20 to Capri and €25 to Anacapri; from Capri to Anacapri costs about €15.

Ischia
POP 62,030

Sprawling over 46 sq km, Ischia is the biggest and busiest island in the bay. It's a lush concoction of sprawling spa towns, mud-wrapped Germans and ancient booty. Also famous for its thermal waters, it has some fine beaches and spectacular scenery.

Most visitors stay on the touristy north coast, but go inland and you'll find a rural landscape of chestnut forests, dusty farms and earthy hillside towns. On the tranquil south coast, Sant'Angelo is a blissful blend of twisting laneways, cosy harbour and bubbling beaches.

◉ Sights

Castello Aragonese   CASTLE, MUSEUM
(☑081 99 28 34; Rocca del Castello; admission €10; ⊙9am-1 hour before sunset) Ischia's imposing, iconic castle sits on a rocky islet just off Ischia Ponte. A sprawling complex comprising a 14th-century cathedral and several smaller churches, it largely dates to the 1400s, when King Alfonso of Aragon gave an older Angevin fortress a makeover. Inside, the **Museo delle Armi** (Weaponry Museum) has a curious collection of torture tools, kinky illustrations and medieval armoury.

(Continued on page 64)

Ancient Wonders

Colonised by the Greeks and adorned by the Romans, southern Italy is a sun-drenched repository of ancient art and architecture. Delve past Pompeii to discover the region's other treasures, from World Heritage temples and cities to relics of ancient domestic life.

Paestum

1 Great Greek temples never go out of vogue and those at Paestum (p88) are among the greatest outside of Greece. With its oldest structures dating from the 6th century BC, the place makes Rome's Colosseum feel positively modern.

Campi Flegrei

2 The Phlegraean Fields are riddled with ruins. Seek out the Sybil at the Acropoli di Cuma (p51), ponder ancient booty at the Museo Archeologico dei Campi Flegrei (p51) or spare a thought for panicked martyrs at the Anfiteatro Flavio (p51).

Villa Romana del Casale

3 Beverly Hills would've had nothing on this villa (p195), whose luxury knows no ancient equal. Inside lie the world's finest Roman mosaics, their rich colours depicting everything from African wildlife to bikini-clad athletes.

Herculaneum

4 Buried by the same eruption that devastated Pompeii, bite-sized Herculaneum (p66) is even better preserved than its larger nearby rival. This is the place to delve into the details, from advertisements and furniture to quirky mosaics and an ancient security grille.

Greek Sicily

5 Sicily is bursting with Hellenic highlights. Pay tribute to the former ruling Greeks at the temples of Segesta (p205), Selinunte (p200) and Agrigento (p194), or applaud Aeschylus at the fabled Greek theatres of Syracuse (p187) and Taormina (p172).

Clockwise from top left
1. Tempio di Cerere, Paestum **2.** Under the Anfiteatro Flavio, Campi Flegrei **3.** Mosaic in Villa Romana del Casale **4.** Casa di Nettuno e Anfitrite, Herculaneum

Tragedy in Pompeii

24 AUGUST AD 79

8am Buildings including the **Terme Suburbane** 1 and the **foro** 2 are still undergoing repair after an earthquake in AD 63 caused significant damage to the city. Despite violent earth tremors overnight, residents have little idea of the catastrophe that lies ahead.

Midday Peckish locals pour into the **Thermopolium di Vetutius Placidus** 3. The lustful slip into the **Lupanare** 4, and gladiators practise for the evening's planned games at the **anfiteatro** 5. A massive boom heralds the eruption. Shocked onlookers witness a dark cloud of volcanic matter shoot some 14km above the crater.

3pm–5pm Lapilli (burning pumice stone) rains down on Pompeii. Terrified locals begin to flee; others take shelter. Within two hours, the plume is 25km high and the sky has darkened. Roofs collapse under the weight of the debris, burying those inside.

25 AUGUST AD 79

Midnight Mudflows bury the town of Herculaneum. Lapilli and ash continue to rain down on Pompeii, bursting through buildings and suffocating those taking refuge within.

4am–8am Ash and gas avalanches hit Herculaneum. Subsequent surges smother Pompeii, killing all remaining residents, including those in the **Orto dei Fuggiaschi** 6. The volcanic 'blanket' will safeguard frescoed treasures like the **Casa del Menandro** 7 and **Villa dei Misteri** 8 for almost two millennia.

Terme Suburbane
The *laconicum* (sauna), *caldarium* (hot bath) and large, heated swimming pool weren't the only sources of heat here; scan the walls of this suburban bathhouse for some of the city's raunchiest frescoes.

Villa di Diomede

Casa dei Vettii

Casa del Poeta Tragico

Porta Ercolano

Casa del Fauno

Basilica

Tempio di Apollo

Porta Marina

Terme del Foro

Macellum

Teatro Grande

Quadriportico dei Teatri

Porta di Stabia

Teatro Piccolo

Foro
An ancient Times Square of sorts, the forum sits at the intersection of Pompeii's main streets and was closed to traffic in the 1st century AD. The plinths on the southern edge featured statues of the imperial family.

TOP TIPS

» **Visit** in the afternoon
» **Allow** three hours
» **Wear** comfortable shoes and a hat
» **Bring** drinking water
» **Don't** use flash photography

Villa dei Misteri

Home to the world-famous *Dionysiac Frieze* fresco. Other highlights at this villa include *trompe l'oeil* wall decorations In the *cubiculum* (bedroom) and Egyptian-themed artwork in the *tablinum* (reception).

Lupanare

The prostitutes at this brothel were often slaves of Greek or Asian origin. Mattresses once covered the stone beds and the names engraved in the walls are possibly those of the workers and their clients.

Thermopolium di Vetutius Placidus

The counter at this ancient snack bar once held urns filled with hot food. The *lararium* (household shrine) on the back wall depicts Dionysus (the god of wine) and Mercury (the god of profit and commerce).

Eyewitness Account

Pliny the Younger (AD 61–c 112) gives a gripping, first-hand account of the catastrophe in his letters to Tacitus (AD 56–117).

Porta del Vesuvio

Porta di Nola

Casa della Venere in Conchiglia

Porta di Sarno

3

7

6

Grande Palestra

5

Tempio di Iside

Casa del Menandro

This dwelling most likely belonged to the family of Poppaea Sabina, Nero's second wife. A room to the left of the atrium features Trojan War paintings and a polychrome mosaic of pygmies rowing down the Nile.

Orto dei Fuggiaschi

The Garden of the Fugitives showcases the plaster moulds of thirteen locals seeking refuge during Vesuvius' eruption – the largest number of victims found in any one area. The huddled bodies make for a moving scene.

Anfiteatro

Magistrates, local senators and the games' sponsors and organisers enjoyed front-row seating at this veteran amphitheatre, home to gladiatorial battles and the odd riot. The parapet circling the stadium featured paintings of combat, victory celebrations and hunting scenes.

La Mortella
GARDEN

(☎081 98 62 20; www.lamortella.it; Via F Calese 39, Forio; admission €12; ☺9am-7pm Tue, Thu, Sat & Sun Apr-Oct) More than 1000 rare and exotic plants flourish in this veritable Garden of Eden on Ischia's west coast. Designed by Russell Page and inspired by the Moorish gardens of Granada's Alhambra in Spain, they were established by Sir William Walton, the late British composer, and his wife, who made La Mortella their home in 1949. Classical-music concerts are staged on the premises; check the website.

Activities

Unlike Capri, Ischia has some great beaches. From chic Sant'Angelo on the south coast, water taxis reach the sandy **Spiaggia dei Maronti** (€5 one way; ☺Apr-Oct) and the intimate cove of **Il Sorgeto** (€7 one way; ☺Apr-Oct), with its steamy thermal spring. Sorgeto can also be reached on foot down a poorly signposted path from the village of Panza.

Negombo
HOT SPRING, BEACH

(☎081 98 61 52; www.negombo.it; Baia di San Montano, Lacco Ameno; all-day admission €25; ☺8.30am-7pm Apr-Oct) Part spa resort, part botanical wonderland, Negombo's Zen-like thermal pools, hammam, contemporary sculpture and private beach make for a serious day of R&R. There's a decent *tavola calda* (snack bar) and a full range of pampering treatments and massages. Admission charges get cheaper the later in the day you arrive,

Monte Epomeo
HIKE

A strenuous uphill walk from the village of Fontana brings you to the top of Ischia's highest point (788m), with superb views of the Bay of Naples. The little church near the summit is the 15th-century **Cappella di San Nicola di Bari**, which features a pretty majolica floor.

Ischia Diving Center
DIVING

(☎081 98 18 52; www.ischiadiving.net; Via Iasolino 106, Ischia Porto) Offers diving equipment and courses. A single dive will typically cost from €38.

Sleeping

Most hotels close in winter, and prices normally drop considerably among those that stay open.

Albergo Il Monastero
BOUTIQUE HOTEL €€

(☎081 99 24 35; www.albergoilmonastero.it; Castello Aragonese, Ischia Ponte; s €75-90, d €100-170, ste €250-300; ☺Easter-Oct; ❄@☎) For sheer location, it's hard to beat this lofty ex-convent inside the Castello Aragonese. Rooms are small but comfortable, some with vaulted ceilings and all with heavenly views. The spacious two-bedroom suite has been recently renovated, while the terrace restaurant serves tasty Ischian fare with produce from the garden.

Hotel Semiramis
HOTEL €€

(☎081 90 75 11; www.hotelsemiramisischia.it; Spiaggia di Citara, Forio; r €94-142; ☺Apr-Sep; ❄❄❄) This bright, friendly hotel has a tropical-oasis feel, with its central pool surrounded by palms. Rooms, the best of which have distant sea views, are large and beautifully tiled in the traditional yellow-and-turquoise pattern.

Hotel Casa Celestino
HOTEL €€

(☎081 99 92 13; www.casacelestino.it; Via Chiaia di Rose 20, Sant'Angelo; s €70-145, d €100-230; ☺Jan-Oct; ❄) This chic little number is a soothing blend of vibrant furnishings, whitewashed walls and contemporary art. Bedrooms have majolica-tiled floors, modern bathrooms and balconies overlooking the sea. There's a good restaurant across the way.

Camping Mirage
CAMPGROUND €

(☎081 99 05 51; www.campingmirage.it; Via Maronti 37, Spiaggia dei Maronti, Barano d'Ischia; camping 2 people & tent €29.50-36.50; ❄) On Spiaggia dei Maronti is this shady campground with pitches under a panoply of eucalyptus trees. On-site facilities include showers, a laundry, a bar and a restaurant serving great seafood pasta.

Albergo Macrì
HOTEL €

(☎/fax 081 99 26 03; Via Iasolino 78a, Ischia Porto; s €38-46, d €65-78; ❄❄) Down a blind alley near the main port, this place oozes a friendly vibe. While the pine and bamboo furnishings won't snag any design awards, rooms are clean, bright and comfy. All 1st-floor rooms have terraces, and the small downstairs bar serves a mean espresso.

Eating

Seafood aside, Ischia is famed for its rabbit, which is bred on inland farms. Another local speciality is *rucolino* – a green liquorice-flavoured liqueur made from *rucola* (rocket) leaves.

TOP CHOICE **Il Focolare** TRATTORIA €€

(☎081 90 29 44; Via Cretaio 36, Casamicciola Terme; meals €40; ☺lunch Fri-Sun, dinner Mon-Sun, closed Wed Nov-May) Turf upstages surf at this Slow Food favourite, tucked away in the hills above Casamicciola Terme. Complete with crackling fire, it's one of the best spots to sample the island's legendary *coniglio all'ischitana* (claypot-cooked rabbit with garlic, onion, tomatoes, wild thyme and white wine).

Lo Scoglio TRADITIONAL ITALIAN €€

(☎081 99 95 29; Via Cava Ruffano 58, Sant'Angelo; meals €32; ☺Apr-Oct) Jutting out over the sea beside a gorgeous beach cove, Lo Scoglio dishes up brilliant seafood. The ingredients are as fresh as the day's catch, appearing in dishes like mussel soup and grilled sea bass. Sunday lunchtime is a popular weekly event.

Pantera Rosa TRADITIONAL ITALIAN €€€

(Via Porto 53, Ischia Porto; meals €50) Of Ischia Porto's string of harbourside restaurants, the 'Pink Panther' is our choice for good food and genuine, honest service. Tuck into gems like pappardelle pasta with seafood, followed by one of the homemade desserts and a frosty fix of the house *limoncello*.

ℹ Information

Ischia Online (www.ischiaonline.it) Website with hotels, sights, activities and events.

Tourist office (www.infoischia procida.it; Via Sogliuzzo 72, Ischia Porto; ☺9am-2pm & 3-8pm Mon-Sat)

ℹ Getting There & Away

See p48 for details of hydrofoils and ferries to/ from Naples. You can also catch hydrofoils direct to Capri (€15) and Procida (€9).

ℹ Getting Around

There are two principal bus lines: the CS (Circo Sinistra; Left Circle) and CD (Circo Destra; Right Circle), which circle the island in opposite directions, passing through each town and leaving every 30 minutes. Buses pass near all hotels and campgrounds. A single ticket, valid for 90 minutes, costs €1.40, while a 24-hour, multi-use ticket is €4.50. Taxis and microtaxis (scooter-engined three-wheelers) are also available.

Help the island avoid congestion and pollution by not bringing a car. If you want to hire one, there are plenty of firms, including **Fratelli del Franco** (☎081 99 13 34; Via A De Luca 127, Ischia Ponte), which hires out cars (from €30 per day), scooters (€25 to €35) and mountain bikes (around €10 per day). You can't take a rental off the island.

Procida

POP 10,620

Dig out your paintbox: the Bay of Naples' smallest island (and its best-kept secret) is a soulful blend of hidden lemon groves, weathered fishers and pastel-hued houses.

August aside – when beach-bound mainlanders flock to its shores – its narrow sun-bleached streets are the domain of the locals: wiry young boys clutch fishing rods, weary mothers clutch wiry young boys and wizened old seafarers swap tales of malaise.

◉ Sights & Activities

The best way to explore the island – a mere 4 sq km – is on foot or by bike. However, the island's narrow roads can be clogged with cars – one of its few drawbacks.

From panoramic Piazza dei Martiri, the village of **Corricella** tumbles down to its marina in a riot of pinks, yellows and whites. Further south, a steep flight of steps leads down to **Chiaia** beach, one of the island's most beautiful.

All pink, white and blue, little **Marina di Chiaiolella** has a yacht-stocked marina, old-school eateries and a languid disposition. Nearby, the **Lido** is a popular beach.

Castello d'Avalos HISTORICAL BUILDING

Clinging on to Procida's highest point is the crumbling 16th-century former Bourbon hunting lodge and ex-prison.

Abbazia di San Michele Arcangelo MUSEUM

(☎081 896 76 12; Via Terra Murata 89; admission €3; ☺9.45am-12.45pm Mon-Sat year-round, plus 3.30-6pm May-Oct) Next door to Castello d'Avalos, this one-time Benedictine abbey contains a church, a small museum with some arresting paintings, and a honeycomb of catacombs.

Procida Diving Centre DIVE CENTRE

(☎081 896 83 85; www.vacanzeaprocida.it/frame diving01-uk.htm; Via Cristoforo Colombo 6, Marina di Chiaiolella) This outfit runs diving courses and hires out equipment. The price ranges from €45 for a single dive to €130 for a snorkelling course and €350 for more advanced open-water diving.

Blue Dream BOATING

(☎081 896 05 79, 339 572 08 74; www.bluedream charter.com; Via Ottimo 3) You can charter a yacht from Blue Dream, from €70 per person per day (minimum of six people).

✰✰ Festivals & Events

Procession of the Misteri   RELIGIOUS

Good Friday sees a colourful procession of the Misteri. A wooden statue of Christ and the Madonna Addolorata, along with life-sized tableaux of plaster and papier-mâché illustrating events leading to Christ's crucifixion, is carted across the island. Men dress in blue tunics with white hoods, while many of the young girls dress as the Madonna.

🛏 Sleeping

Campgrounds are dotted around the island and open from April/May to September/October. Typical prices are €10 per site plus €10 per person. Reliable places include **La Caravella** (☑081 810 18 38; Via IV Novembre).

TOP CHOICE Hotel La Vigna   BOUTIQUE HOTEL €€
(☑081 896 04 69; www.albergolavigna.it; Via Principessa Margherita 46; s €75-150, d €90-180, ste €140-230; ✽@🕏) A cliff-side, vine-fringed garden and an in-house spa make this 18th-century villa a top choice. Five of the spacious, simply furnished standard rooms offer direct access to the garden. Superior rooms (€110 to €200) feature family-friendly mezzanines, while the suite comes with a bedside jacuzzi.

Casa Giovanni da Procida   B&B €
(☑081 896 03 58; www.casagiovannidaprocida.it; Via Giovanni da Procida 3; d €65-110, tr €90-130; ✆closed Feb; P✽🕏) This chic farmhouse B&B basks in the shade of a centuries-old magnolia tree and has split-level rooms with low-rise beds and contemporary furniture. Bathrooms are small but slick, with funky mosaic tiling and cube basins.

Hotel La Corricella   HOTEL €€
(☑081 896 75 75; www.hotellacorricella.it; Via Marina Corricella 88; s €60-110, d €80-140; ✆mid-Mar–mid-Nov) One bookend to Marina Corricella, La Corricella offers comfy, low-fuss rooms with fans (air-con rooms cost an extra €10 to €20). The terrace offers gorgeous harbour views, the restaurant serves local specialities and there's a boat service to the nearby beach.

✕ Eating

Ristorante Scarabeo   TRADITIONAL ITALIAN €€
(☑081 896 99 18; Via Salette 10; meals €35; ✆daily Jun-Oct, weekends only Dec-Feb & Mar-May, closed Nov) Behind a veritable jungle of lemon trees, Signor Francesco whips up classics like *fritelle di basilico* (fried patties of bread, egg, Parmesan and basil) and *ravioli di provola e melanzana* (ravioli stuffed with *provola* cheese and eggplant). Best of all, it's all yours to devour under a pergola of bulbous lemons.

La Conchiglia   TRADITIONAL ITALIAN €€
(☑081 896 76 02; Via Pizzaco 10; meals €30; ✆lunch Mar-Oct, dinner May–mid-Sep) Topaz waves at your feet, pastel Corricella in the distance – this is what you come to Procida for. Up against the views, the food holds its own with dishes such as *spaghetti alla povera* (spaghetti with *peperoncino,* green peppers, cherry tomatoes and anchovies). To get here, take the steep steps down from Via Pizzaco or book a boat from Corricella.

Gorgonia   TRADITIONAL ITALIAN €
(Via Marina Corricella; meals €24; ✆Mar-Oct) Along unpretentious Marina Corricella, with its old fishing boats, piles of fishing nets and sleek, lazy cats, any restaurant will provide you with a memorable experience. That said, this place peddles particularly fine smoked-seafood dishes, including swordfish and tuna steaks.

ⓘ Information

Procida Holidays (☑081 896 95 94; www.isoladiprocida.it; Via Roma 117; ✆9am-1pm & 4-8pm Mon-Sat Apr-Oct, closed Sat afternoon Nov-Mar) can organise accommodation (single/double from €40/50) and boat trips (about €15 for a two-hour tour), and also has a free map of the island.

ⓘ Getting There & Around

Procida is linked by boat and hydrofoil to Ischia (€9), Pozzuoli (€9) and Naples (see p48).

There is a limited bus service (€1), with four lines radiating out from Marina Grande. Bus L1 connects the port and Marina di Chiaiolella.

Microtaxis can be hired for two to three hours for about €35, depending on your bargaining prowess. Contact **Sport & Company** (Via Roma 137; ✆closed Sun) for bike hire (per day €18).

SOUTH OF NAPLES

Ercolano & Herculaneum

Ercolano is an uninspiring Neapolitan suburb that's home to one of Italy's best-preserved ancient sites – Herculaneum. A superbly conserved Roman fishing town, Herculaneum is smaller and less daunting than Pompeii, allowing you to visit without that nagging itch that you're bound to miss something.

History
In contrast to modern Ercolano, classical Herculaneum was a peaceful fishing and port town of about 4000 inhabitants, and something of a resort for wealthy Romans and Campanians.

Herculaneum's fate paralleled that of nearby Pompeii. Destroyed by an earthquake in AD 63, it was completely submerged in the AD 79 eruption of Mt Vesuvius. However, as it was much closer to the volcano than Pompeii, it drowned in a 16m-thick sea of mud rather than in the lapilli (burning pumice stone) and ash that rained down on Pompeii. This essentially fossilised the town, ensuring that even delicate items, like furniture and clothing, were discovered remarkably well preserved.

The town was rediscovered in 1709, and amateur excavations were carried out intermittently until 1874, with many finds being carted off to Naples to decorate the houses of the well-to-do or to end up in museums. Serious archaeological work began again in 1927 and continues to this day, although with much of the ancient site buried beneath modern Ercolano, it's slow going.

◎ Sights

Ruins of Herculaneum   RUINS
(☑081 732 43 38; Corso Resina 6; adult/EU national under 18yr & over 65yr/EU national 18-25yr €11/free/5.50; ☺8.30am-7.30pm Apr-Oct, to 5pm Nov-Mar) Pompeii may be much larger, but the ruins of Herculaneum are better preserved, offering an unrivalled insight into ancient Roman life.

From the site's main gateway on Corso Resina, head down the wide boulevard, where you'll find the ticket office on the left. Pick up a free map and guide booklet here, and then follow the boulevard right to the actual entrance into the ruins themselves. Here you can hire the useful audioguide (€6.50).

To enter the ruins you pass through what appears to be a moat around the town but is in fact the ancient shoreline. It was here in 1980 that archaeologists discovered some 300 skeletons, the remains of a crowd that had fled to the beach only to be overcome by boiling surge clouds sweeping down from Vesuvius.

As you begin your exploration northeast along Cardo III you'll stumble across **Casa d'Argo** (Argus House), a well-preserved example of a Roman noble family's house, complete with porticoed garden and triclinium (dining area).

Across the street sits the **Casa dello Scheletro** (House of the Skeleton), a modest-sized house with five styles of mosaic flooring and the remnants of an ancient security grille protecting the original skylight.

Across the Decumano Inferiore (one of ancient Herculaneum's main streets), the **Terme Maschili** was the men's section of the **Terme del Foro** (Forum Baths). Note the ancient latrine to the left of the entrance before stepping into the *apodyterium* (changing room). To the left is the *frigidarium* (cold bath), to the right the *tepadarium* (tepid bath), *caldarium* (hot bath) and an exercise area.

At the end of Cardo III, **Decumano Massimo** (Herculaneum's main thoroughfare) is lined with ancient shops and advertising, such as that adorning the wall to the right of the **Casa del Salone Nero**.

Further east along Decumano Massimo, a crucifix found in an upstairs room of the **Casa del Bicentenario** (Bicentenary House) provides possible evidence that there was a Christian presence in pre-Vesuvius Herculaneum.

Turn into Cardo IV from Decumano Massimo and you'll find the **Casa del Bel Cortile** (House of the Beautiful Courtyard), which houses three of the 300 skeletons discovered on the ancient shore in 1980.

Next door, the **Casa di Nettuno e Anfitrite** (House of Neptune and Amphitrite) is named after the extraordinary mosaic in the *nymphaeum*.

Over the road, the **Terme Femminili** was the women's section of the Terme del Foro; note the finely executed floor mosaic of a naked Triton in the *apodyterium*.

Further southwest on Cardo IV, the **Casa dell'Atrio a Mosaico** (House of the Mosaic Atrium; closed for restoration) is an impressive mansion with extensive floor mosaics, including a black-and-white chessboard design in the atrium.

Backtrack up Cardo IV and turn right at Decumano Inferiore. Here you'll find the **Casa del Gran Portale** (House of the Large Portal), the main entrance of which is flanked by elegant brick Corinthian columns. Inside are some well-preserved wall paintings.

Accessible from Cardo V, **Casa dei Cervi** (House of the Deer) is an imposing example of a Roman noble family's house. The two-storey villa, around a central courtyard, contains murals and still-life paintings. In the courtyard is a diminutive pair of marble deer assailed by dogs and an engaging statue of a peeing Hercules.

Marking the site's southernmost tip, the 1st-century-AD **Terme Suburbane** (Suburban Baths; closed for restoration) is one of the best-preserved bath complexes in existence, with deep pools, stucco friezes and bas-reliefs looking down upon marble seats and floors.

Northwest of the ruins, **Villa dei Papiri** was a vast four-storey, 245m-long complex owned by Julius Caesar's father-in-law. At the time of research, the villa was closed for restoration. For updates, contact www.arethusa.net.

MAV

(Museo Archeologico Virtuale; ☏081 1980 6511; www.museomav.com; Via IV Novembre; admission €7.50; ☾9am-5.30pm Tue-Sun) On the main street linking the ruins and the train station, child-friendly MAV is a virtual-reality archaeology museum bringing the region's ruins back to life through holograms and computer-generated video.

ℹ️ Information

You'll find the **tourist office** (Via IV Novembre 82; ☾9am-6pm Mon-Sat) en route from the train station to the ruins, on your right.

ℹ️ Getting There & Away

The best way to get to Ercolano is by Circumvesuviana train (get off at Ercolano-Scavi). Trains run regularly to/from Naples (€2.10), Pompeii (€1.50) and Sorrento (€2.10).

By car take the A3 from Naples, exit at Ercolano Portico and follow the signs to car parks near the site's entrance.

Mt Vesuvius

Towering darkly over Naples and its environs, Mt Vesuvius (Vesuvio; 1281m) is the only active volcano on the European mainland. Since it exploded into history in AD 79, burying Pompeii and Herculaneum and pushing the coastline out several kilometres, it has erupted more than 30 times. The most devastating of these was in 1631, the most recent in 1944. And while there's little

evidence to suggest any imminent activity, observers worry that the current lull is the longest in the past 500 years.

A full-scale eruption would be catastrophic. Some 600,000 people live within 7km of the crater and, despite incentives to relocate, few are willing to go.

Established in 1995, **Parco Nazionale del Vesuvio** (Vesuvius National Park; www.parconazionaledelvesuvio.it) attracts some 400,000 visitors annually. From a car park at the summit, an 860m path leads up to the volcano's **crater** (admission incl tour €8; ☾9am-6pm Jul & Aug, to 5pm Apr-Jun & Sep, to 4pm Mar & Oct, to 3pm Nov-Feb). It's not a strenuous walk, but it's more comfortable in trainers than in sandals or flip-flops. You'd also do well to take sunglasses – useful against swirling ash – and a sweater, as it can be chilly up top, even in summer.

About halfway up the hill, the **Museo dell'Osservatorio Vesuviano** (Museum of the Vesuvian Observatory; ☏081 610 84 83; www.ov.ingv.it; admission free; ☾10am-2pm Sat & Sun) tells the history of 2000 years of Vesuvius-watching.

EAV Bus (☏800 053 939; www.eavbus.it) runs two daily services from Naples to Vesuvius (€14.60 return, 90 minutes), stopping at Piazza Garibaldi at 9.25am and 10.40am. Two return services depart Vesuvius at 12.30pm and 2pm. It also runs eight to 10 daily buses to Vesuvius from Piazza Anfiteatro in Pompeii (€10, one hour). Buses terminate in the crater car park.

By car, exit the A3 at Ercolano Portico and follow signs for the Parco Nazionale del Vesuvio.

Note that when weather conditions are bad the summit path is shut and bus departures are suspended.

Pompeii

POP 25,760

A stark reminder of the malign forces that lie deep inside Vesuvius, Pompeii (Pompei in Italian) is Europe's most compelling archaeological site. Each year about 2.5 million people pour in to wander the ghostly shell of what was once a thriving commercial centre.

Its appeal goes beyond tourism, though. From an archaeological point of view, it's priceless. Much of the value lies in the fact that it wasn't simply blown away by Vesuvius: rather it was buried under a layer of lapilli, as Pliny the Younger describes in his celebrated account of the eruption.

History

The eruption of Vesuvius wasn't the first disaster to strike the Roman port of Pompeii. In AD 63 a massive earthquake hit the city, causing widespread damage and the evacuation of much of the 20,000-strong population. Many had not returned when Vesuvius blew its top on 24 August AD 79, burying the city under a layer of lapilli and killing some 2000 men, women and children.

The origins of Pompeii are uncertain, but it seems likely that it was founded in the 7th century BC by the Campanian Oscans. Over the next seven centuries the city fell to the ancient Greeks and the Samnites before becoming a Roman colony in 80 BC.

After its catastrophic demise, Pompeii receded from the public eye until 1594, when the architect Domenico Fontana stumbled across the ruins while digging a canal. However, short of recording the find, he took no further action.

Exploration proper began in 1748 under the Bourbon king Charles VII and continued into the 19th century. In the early days, many of the more spectacular mosaics were siphoned off to decorate Charles' palace in Portici; thankfully, though, most were subsequently moved up to Naples, where they now sit in the Museo Archeologico Nazionale (p36).

Work continues today and although new discoveries are being made, the emphasis is now on restoring what has already been unearthed rather than raking for new finds. Given the spate of recent government funding cuts, this has been a challenging task, the shock collapse of the Casa dei Gladiatori (House of the Gladiators) in November 2010 bringing to light the challenges faced in protecting this fragile site.

⊙ Sights

Ruins of Pompeii RUINS

(☑081 861 90 03; entrances at Porta Marina & Piazza Anfiteatro; adult/EU national under 18yr & over 65yr/EU national 18yr-25yr €11/free/5.50; ⊗8.30am-7.30pm Apr-Oct, to 5pm Nov-Mar) Of Pompeii's original 66 hectares, 44 have now been excavated. Of course, that doesn't mean that you'll have unhindered access to every inch of the Unesco World Heritage–listed site: you'll come across areas cordoned off for no apparent reason, the odd stray dog and a noticeable lack of clear

signs. Audioguides (€6.50) are a sensible investment, and a good guidebook will help – try the €10 *Pompeii* published by Electa Napoli.

If visiting in summer, note that there's not much shade on-site, so bring a hat and sunscreen. To do justice to the site, allow at least three or four hours, longer if you want to go into detail.

The site's main entrance is at **Porta Marina**, the most impressive of the seven gates that punctuated the ancient town walls. A busy passageway, now as then, it originally connected the town with the nearby harbour. Just outside the wall is the impressive **Terme Suburbane**. Accessible subject to prior booking at www.arethusa.net (click on 'Prenotazioni e Prevendite'), these baths are famed for the risqué frescoes in the *apodyterium,* which include a rare homocrotic scene involving two women.

Immediately on the right as you enter Porta Marina is the 1st-century-BC **Tempio di Venere** (Temple of Venus), formerly one of the town's most opulent temples.

Continuing down Via Marina you come to the **basilica**, the 2nd-century-BC seat of the city's law courts and exchange. Opposite, the **Tempio di Apollo** (Temple of Apollo) is the oldest and most important of Pompeii's religious buildings, dating to the 2nd century BC. The grassy **foro** (forum) adjacent to the temple was the city's main piazza – a huge traffic-free rectangle flanked by limestone columns.

North of the forum stands the **Tempio di Giove** (Temple of Jupiter), with one of two flanking triumphal arches remaining, and the **Granai del Foro** (Forum Granary), now used to store hundreds of amphorae and a number of body casts. These casts were made in the late 19th century by pouring plaster into the hollows left by disintegrated bodies. Nearby, the **macellum** was the city's main meat and fish market.

From the market follow Via degli Augustali until Vicolo del Lupanare. Halfway down this narrow alley is the **Lupanare**, an ancient brothel. A tiny two-storey building with five rooms on each floor, it's lined with some of Pompeii's raunchiest frescoes.

At the end of Via dei Teatri, the green **Foro Triangolare** would originally have overlooked the sea. The main attraction here was, and still is, the 2nd-century-BC **Teatro Grande**, a huge 5000-seat theatre. Behind the stage, the porticoed **Quadriportico dei**

Teatri was initially used for the audience to stroll between acts and later as a barracks for gladiators. Next door, the **Teatro Piccolo**, also known as the Odeion, was once an indoor theatre, while the pre-Roman **Tempio di Iside** (Temple of Isis) was a popular place of cult worship.

Just to the east, Via dell'Anfiteatro (which becomes Vico Meridionale) is where you'll find **Casa del Menandro**. One of Pompeii's grander private homes, its highlights include an elegant peristyle (colonnaded garden) and a striking mosaic floor in the *caldarium*.

Old Pompeii

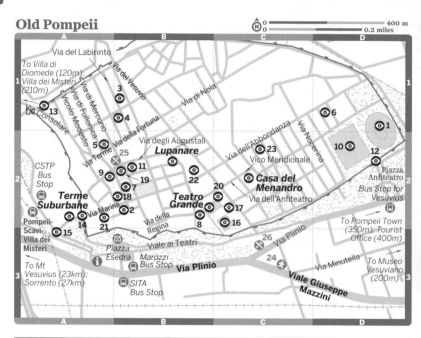

Old Pompeii

Back on Via dell'Abbondanza, the **Terme Stabiane** is a typical 2nd-century-BC bath complex. Entering from the vestibule, bathers would stop off in the vaulted *apodyterium* before passing through to the *tepidarium* and *caldarium*. Further northeast along Via dell'Abbondanza, the **Thermopolium di Vetutius Placidus** is a fine example of a Roman snack bar, while the **Casa della Venere in Conchiglia** (House of the Venus Marina) harbours a lovely peristyle looking on to a small, manicured garden. It's here that you'll find the striking Venus fresco after which the house is named.

Nearby, the grassy **anfiteatro** is the oldest-known Roman amphitheatre in existence. Built in 70 BC, it was at one time capable of holding up to 20,000 bloodthirsty spectators. Over the way, the **Grande Palestra** is an athletics field with an impressive portico and, at its centre, the remains of a swimming pool.

From here, double back along Via dell'Abbondanza and turn right into Via Stabiana to see some of Pompeii's grandest houses. Turn left into Via della Fortuna for the **Casa del Fauno** (House of the Faun), Pompeii's largest private house. Named after the small bronze statue in the *impluvium* (rain tank), it was here that early excavators found Pompeii's greatest mosaics, most of which are now in Naples' Museo Archeologico Nazionale. A couple of blocks away, the **Casa del Poeta Tragico** (House of the Tragic Poet) features the world's first 'beware of the dog' - *cave canem* - warnings. To the north, on Vicolo di Mercurio, the **Casa dei Vettii** is home to a famous depiction of Priapus with his gigantic phallus balanced on a pair of scales.

From here follow the road west and turn right into Via Consolare, which takes you out of the town through **Porta Ercolano**. Continue past **Villa di Diomede**, turn right, and you'll come to the **Villa dei Misteri**, one of the most complete structures left standing in Pompeii. The *Dionysiac Frieze*, the most important fresco still on-site, spans the walls of the large dining room. One of the world's largest ancient paintings, it depicts the initiation of a bride-to-be into the cult of Dionysus, the Greek god of wine.

The **Museo Vesuviano** (☑081 850 72 55; Via Bartolomeo 12; admission free; ☺9am-1pm Mon-Fri), southeast of the excavations, contains an interesting array of artefacts.

Tours

You'll almost certainly be approached by a guide outside the *scavi* ticket office. Authorised guides wear identification tags and you can expect to pay between €100 and €120 for a two-hour tour, whether you're alone or in a group. Reputable tour operators include **Yellow Sudmarine** (☑329 1010 328; www.yellowsudmarine.com), **Torres Travel** (☑081 856 78 02; www.torrestravel.it) and **Pompeii Cast** (☑081 850 49 12; www.pompeiicast.it), all of which offer tours of the ruins, as well as excursions to other regional highlights, including Naples, Capri and the Amalfi Coast.

Sleeping & Eating

There's really no need to stay overnight in Pompeii. The ruins are best visited on a day trip from Naples, Sorrento or Salerno, and once the excavations close for the day, the area around the site becomes decidedly seedy. Most of the restaurants near the ruins are characterless affairs set up for feeding busloads of tourists. Wander down to the modern town and it's a little better, with a few decent restaurants serving excellent local food.

If you'd rather stay at the ruins, the onsite **cafeteria** (Via di Mercurio) peddles the standard choice of panini, pizza slices, salads, hot meals and gelato. You'll find it near the Tempio di Giove.

TOP CHOICE **President** MODERN ITALIAN €€
(☑081 850 72 45; Piazza Schettini 12; meals €40; ☺closed Mon & dinner Sun Nov-Mar, closed 2 weeks Jan) Under dripping chandeliers, regional produce is celebrated in brilliant creations like eggplant *millefoglie* (flaky puff pastry) with Cetara anchovies, mozzarella *filante* (melted mozzarella) and grated *tarallo* (savoury almond biscuit). The degustation menus (€40 to €70) are a gourmand's delight.

Plinio Hostaria OSTERIA, PIZZERIA €€
(Via Plinio 12; pizza €4-12, meal €30) Located 450m west of Piazza Anfiteatro, this homely *osteria* (casual tavern) is one of the better eateries near the ruins. Tuck into decent pizzas, warming lasagna or fresh salads. If the weather is warm, nosh alfresco in the leafy courtyard.

ℹ Information

First-aid post (☑081 535 91 11; Via Colle San Bartolomeo 50)
Police station (☑081 856 35 11; Piazza Porta Marina Inferiore)

Pompeii Sites (www.pompeiisites.org) A comprehensive website covering Pompeii and Herculaneum.

Post office (Piazza Esedra)

Tourist office Pompeii town (⌨081 850 72 55; Via Sacra 1; ⊗8am-3.30pm Mon-Fri, to 1.30pm Sat); Porta Marina (⌨081 536 32 93; www. pompeiturismo.it; Piazza Porta Marina Inferiore 12; ⊗8am-3.45pm Mon-Sat)

❶ Getting There & Away

Frequent Circumvesuviana trains run from Pompeii-Scavi-Villa dei Misteri station to Naples (€2.80, 35 minutes) and Sorrento (€2.10, 30 minutes).

Otherwise, **SITA** (⌨089 40 51 45; www. sitabus.it, in Italian) operates buses half-hourly to/from Naples (€2.80, 30 minutes); and **CSTP** (⌨800 016 659; www.cstp.it, in Italian) bus 4 runs to/from Salerno (€2.10, one hour).

For Rome, **Marozzi** (⌨080 579 01 11; www. marozzivt.it) has one to two daily buses (€16.50, three hours), departing from Piazza Esedra.

For information on getting to/from Vesuvius see p68. Buses to Vesuvius depart from Piazza Anfiteatro.

To get here by car, take the A3 from Naples. Use the Pompeii exit and follow signs to Pompeii Scavi. Car parks (approximately €5 per hour) are clearly marked and vigorously touted.

Sorrento

POP 16,610

On paper, cliff-straddling Sorrento is a place to avoid – a package-holiday centre with few must-see sights, no beach to speak of and a glut of brassy English-style pubs. In reality, it's a strangely appealing place, its laid-back southern Italian charm resisting all attempts to swamp it in souvenir tat and graceless development.

Dating to Greek times and known to Romans as Surrentum, it's ideally situated for exploring the surrounding area: to the west, the best of the peninsula's unspoiled countryside and beyond that the Amalfi Coast; to the north, Pompeii and the archaeological sites; offshore, the fabled island of Capri.

According to Greek legend, it was in Sorrento's waters that the mythical sirens once lived. Sailors of antiquity were powerless to resist the beautiful song of these charming maidens-cum-monsters, who would lure them and their ships to their doom. Homer's Ulysses escaped by having his oarsmen plug their ears with wax and by strapping himself to his ship's mast as he sailed past.

⊙ Sights

Spearing off from Piazza Tasso, Corso Italia (closed to traffic from 7pm to 1am daily during summer, and from 10am to 1pm on Sundays and public holidays) cuts through the *centro storico*, the narrow streets of which throng with tourists on summer evenings. An attractive area, it's thick with loud souvenir stores, cafes, churches and restaurants.

Chiesa di San Francesco   CHURCH
(⌨081 878 12 69; Via San Francesco; ⊗8am-1pm & 2-8pm) The attraction here is not the church but its beautiful medieval cloisters. A harmonious marriage of architectural styles – two sides are lined with 14th-century crossed arches, the other two with round arches supported by octagonal pillars – they are often used to host exhibitions and summer concerts.

Next door, the **Villa Comunale park** (⊗8am-8pm mid-Oct–mid-Apr, to midnight mid-Apr–mid-Oct) commands grand views over the water to Mt Vesuvius.

Museo Correale   MUSEUM
(⌨081 878 18 46; www.museocorreale.com; Via Correale 50; admission €7; ⊗9.30am-1.30pm Wed-Mon) Sorrento's main museum houses a rich collection of 17th- and 19th-century Neapolitan art, Japanese, Chinese and European ceramics, clocks and furniture, as well as Greek and Roman artefacts. The gardens are equally impressive, with heavenly bay views.

Museo Bottega della Tarsia Lignea MUSEUM
(⌨081 877 19 42; Via San Nicola 28; admission €8; ⊗10am-1pm & 3-6.30pm) Further west, the palatial Bottega della Tarsia Lignea showcases some fabulous examples of *intarsio* (marquetry) furniture – a craft Sorrento has been famous for since the 18th century.

Duomo   DUOMO
(⌨081 878 22 48; Corso Italia; ⊗8am-noon & 6-8pm) The gleaming white exterior of Sorrento's spiritual centrepiece gives no hint of its inner exuberance. Of particular note are the marble bishop's throne and the beautiful wooden choir stalls. Outside, the triple-tiered bell tower rests on an archway into which three classical columns have been set.

🏃 Activities

The bad news: Sorrento does not have great beaches. In town the two main swimming spots are **Marina Piccola** and, to the east, **Marina Grande**, although neither is es-

Sorrento

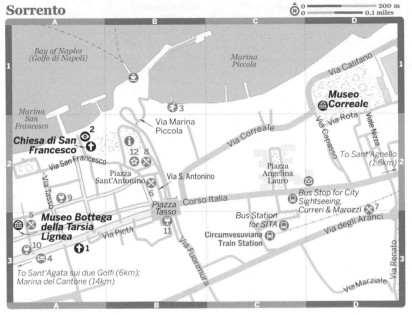

Sorrento

pecially appealing. The good news: **Bagni Regina Giovanna**, a rocky beach set among the ruins of the Roman Villa Pollio Felix, is much nicer. It's possible to walk there (follow Via Capo west for about 2km), but it's quicker to get the SITA bus or the EAV bus (Linea A) for Massalubrense.

To find the best swimming spots, you'll really need a boat. **Sic Sic** (☎081 807 22 83; www.nauticasicsic.com; Via Marina Piccola 43; ☺May-Oct) rents out a variety of boats, starting at around €50 per hour or €150 a day (excluding petrol).

⌖ Tours

City Sightseeing Sorrento   BUS
(☎081 877 47 07; www.sorrento.city-sightseeing. it; adult/6-15yr €12/6) This hop-on, hop-off bus tour covers Sorrento and the surrounding area. Daily departures are at 9.30am, 11.30am, 1.30pm and 3.30pm from Piazza De Curtis (Circumvesuviana station). English-language commentaries are provided, and tickets, available on board, are valid for six hours.

✿ Festivals & Events

The city's patron saint, Sant'Antonino, is remembered on 14 February each year with processions and huge markets. The saint is credited with having saved Sorrento during WWII, when Salerno and Naples were heavily bombed.

Sorrento's **Settimana Santa** Easter processions are famous throughout Italy. There are two main processions: one at midnight on the Thursday preceding Good Friday, the second on Good Friday.

🛏 Sleeping

Most accommodation is in the town centre or clustered along Via Capo, the coastal road west of the centre. Be sure to book early for the summer season.

La Tonnarella   HOTEL €€€

(☎081 878 11 53; www.latonnarella.it; Via Capo 31; d €112-225, ste €300-400; ☺Apr-Oct; P❋@🖥) A dazzling combo of blue-and-yellow majolica tiles, antiques, chandeliers and statues. Most of the classically themed rooms have their own balcony or small terrace, and the hotel has its own private beach (accessible by lift). There's an excellent terrace restaurant to boot. The hotel is located just west of central Sorrento, on Via Capo (the continuation of Via degli Aranci).

Hotel Cristina   HOTEL €€

(☎081 878 35 62; www.hotelcristinasorrento. it; Via Privata Rubinacci 6, Sant'Agnello; s €90-135, d €90-200; ☺Apr-Oct; ❋🖥▨) Perched above Sant'Agnello, Hotel Cristina boasts unrivalled views, best enjoyed from the swimming pool. Elegant rooms fuse inlaid wooden furniture and vintage prints with contemporary touches like Philippe Starck chairs. There's an in-house restaurant and a free shuttle bus to/from Sorrento's Circumvesuviana station, 1.5km to the west.

Casa Astarita   B&B €

(☎081 877 49 06; www.casastarita.com; Corso Italia 67, Sorrento; s €55-100, d €70-115; ❋@) This gem of a B&B is housed in a central, 16th-century building. All six rooms combine original structural elements with flat-screen TVs, fridges and excellent water pressure. Tasteful artwork and antiques complete the eclectic look. Rooms surround a central parlour where breakfast is served on a large rustic table.

Seven Hostel   HOSTEL €

(☎081 878 67 58; www.sevenhostel.com; Via Iommella Grande 99, Sant'Agnello; dm €20-32, s €50-80, d €60-100; ❋@🖥) Seven sexes up 'budget' with its sleek spaces, chic rooftop terraces and weekend live-music gigs. Dorms are spacious and contemporary (some with en-suite bathroom), private rooms small but smart, and the on-site laundry is a welcome bonus. It's 800m north of the Sant'Agnello Circumvesuviana train station, one stop from Sorrento.

Nube d'Argento   CAMPGROUND €

(☎081 878 13 44; www.nubedargento.com; Via Capo 21; camping 2 people, tent & car €25-37, 2-person bungalows €50-85; ☺Mar-Dec; 🖥▨🚿) This inviting campground is an easy 1km drive west of the Sorrento town centre. Pitches and wooden chalet-style bungalows are spread out beneath a canopy of olive trees, and the facilities, including an open-air swimming pool, are excellent.

✕ Eating

A local speciality to look out for is *gnocchi alla sorrentina* (gnocchi baked in tomato sauce with mozzarella).

TOP CHOICE Inn Bufalito   CHEESE BAR €€

(Via Fuoro 21; meals €30; ☺Apr-Oct) A brilliant Slow Food mozzarella bar-restaurant. Head here for sterling local produce – think Sorrento-style cheese fondue, buffalo meat carpaccio and *salsiccia* (local sausage) with broccoli. There are regular cheese tastings, as well as the odd art exhibition or live-music act.

Ristorante Il Buco   GASTRONOMIC €€€

(☎081 878 23 54; Rampa Marina Piccola 5; meals €70, 6-course degustation menu €75-85; ☺Thu-Tue Feb-Dec) Hardly the hole its name suggests, this Michelin-starred restaurant is housed in a former monks' wine cellar. The emphasis is on innovative regional cooking, so expect revived classics such as cheese tartlet with tomato tartare and rucola pesto. Reservations recommended.

La Basilica   MODERN ITALIAN, PIZZERIA €€

(Via S Antonino 12; pizzas €6-11, meals €50; ☺noon-midnight) Elegant without the attitude, barrel-vaulted Basilica serves regional nosh with subtle yet confident twists (think house-made black *scialatielli* pasta with calamari and *pomodorini* or a decadent dark chocolate and whiskey tart). For a cheaper feed, dig into the excellent wood-fired pizzas.

Mondo Bio VEGETARIAN €
(Via degli Aranci 146; snacks €3, pasta from €6.50; ⊙8.30am-8.30pm Mon-Sat) Flying the banner for organic vegetarian food, this bright shop-cum-restaurant serves a limited range of meat-free antipasti, mains and sweets. The menu, chalked up outside, changes daily but might include *zuppa di soia verde* (soybean soup) and *polpette di tofu* (tofu balls).

Drinking

From wood-panelled wine bars to cocktail-centric cafes, you'll find no shortage of drinking dens in Sorrento.

Café Latino CAFE, BAR
(Vico I Fuoro 4a) A romantic choice, this is the place to sit among orange and lemon trees and gaze into your lover's eyes over a chilled cocktail. If you can't drag yourselves away, you can also eat here (meals around €30).

Fauno Bar CAFE, BAR
(Piazza Tasso) This elegant cafe covers half of Piazza Tasso and offers the best people-watching in town. Expect stiff drinks at stiff prices – cocktails start at around €8.50. Snacks and sandwiches are also available (from €7).

Bollicine WINE BAR
(Via dell'Accademia 9; ⊙closed Tue) An unpretentious wine bar with a dark wooden interior and boxes of bottles littered around the place. The wine list includes all the big Italian names and a selection of local labels – the amiable bartender will happily advise you. There's also a menu of rustic dishes, including pizza and homemade salami.

☆ Entertainment

In the summer, concerts are held in the cloisters of Chiesa di San Francesco.

Teatro Tasso LIVE MUSIC, THEATRE
(☑081 807 55 25; www.teatrotasso.com; Piazza Sant'Antonino) Head here for a good old singalong. The southern Italian equivalent of a cockney music hall, it's home to the Sorrento Musical (€25), a sentimental revue of Neapolitan classics such as 'O Sole Mio'. The 75-minute performances start at 9.30pm every evening from Monday to Saturday from Easter to October.

Fauno Notte Club LIVE MUSIC, THEATRE
(☑081 878 10 21; www.faunonotte.it; Piazza Tasso 1) Teatro Tasso's direct competitor offers 'a fantastic journey through history, legends and folklore'. In other words, 500 years of Neapolitan history set to music.

❶ Information

Hospital (☑081 533 11 11; Corso Italia 1)
Police station (☑081 807 53 11; Via Capasso 11)
Post office (Corso Italia 210)
Sorrento Tour (www.sorrentotour.it) Extensive website with tourist and transport information on Sorrento and environs.
Tourist office (Via Luigi De Maio 35; ⊙8.30am-4.15pm Mon-Fri) In the Circolo dei Forestieri (Foreigners' Club). Has printed material and can offer accommodation advice. From May to September, you'll also find information kiosks (open 10am to 1pm and 4pm to 9pm) at the train station, ferry terminal and in the centre of town.

❶ Getting There & Away

Boat

Sorrento is the main jumping-off point for Capri and also has excellent ferry connections to Naples, Ischia and Amalfi coastal resorts. **Alilauro** (☑081 878 14 30; www.alilauro.it) runs up to five daily hydrofoils between Naples and Sorrento (€11, 35 minutes). The slower **Metrò del Mare** (☑199 600700; www.metrodelmare.net) covers the same route but was suspended indefinitely at the time of writing. **Gescab-Linee Marittime Partenope** (☑081 704 19 11; www.consorziolmp.it) runs hydrofoils from Sorrento to Capri from April to November (€15, 20 minutes, 15 daily).

All ferries and hydrofoils depart from the port at Marina Piccola, where you buy your tickets.

Bus

Curreri (☑081 801 54 20; www.curreriviaggi.it) runs six daily services to Sorrento from Naples' Capodichino airport, departing from outside the Arrivals hall and arriving in Piazza Tasso. Buy tickets (€10) for the 75-minute journey on the bus.

SITA (☑089 40 51 45; www.sitabus.it, in Italian) buses serve the Amalfi Coast and Sant'Agata sui due Golfi, leaving from outside the Circumvesuviana train station. Buy tickets at the station bar or from shops bearing the blue SITA sign. Around 30 buses run daily between Sorrento and Amalfi (€2.80, 1¾ hours), looping around Positano (€1.50, one hour). Change at Amalfi for Ravello.

Marozzi (☑080 579 01 11; www.marozzivt.it) operates one to two daily buses to/from Rome (€17.50).

Train

Circumvesuviana (☑081 772 24 44; www.vesuviana.it) trains run every half-hour between Sorrento and Naples (€4), via Pompeii (€2.10) and Ercolano (€2.10).

ⓘ Getting Around

Local bus Line B runs from Piazza Sant'Antonino to the port at Marina Piccola (€1).

Jolly Service & Rent (☏081 877 34 50; www. jollyrent.eu; Via degli Aranci 180) has smart cars from €53 a day and 50cc scooters from €27.

For a taxi, call ☏081 878 22 04.

West of Sorrento

The countryside west of Sorrento is the very essence of southern Italy. Tortuous roads wind their way through hills covered in olive trees and lemon groves, passing through sleepy villages and tiny fishing ports. There are magnificent views at every turn, the best from Sant'Agata sui due Golfi and the high points overlooking Punta Campanella, the westernmost point of the Sorrentine Peninsula.

SANT'AGATA SUI DUE GOLFI

Perched high in the hills above Sorrento, sleepy Sant'Agata sui due Golfi commands spectacular views of the Bay of Naples on one side and the Bay of Salerno on the other (hence its name, Saint Agatha on the two Gulfs). The best viewpoint is the **Deserto** (☏081 878 01 99; Via Deserto; ⏰gardens 7am-7pm, panoramic lookout 5-8pm Apr-Sep, 3-4pm Oct-Mar), a Carmelite convent 1.5km uphill from the village centre. The **convent** (s incl breakfast, lunch & dinner €45) also offers simple, peaceful accommodation for those who find the peace and panorama too hard to leave.

🖉 **Agriturismo Le Tore** (☏081 808 06 37; www.letore.com; Via Pontone 43; s €50-80, d €90-110; ⏰Easter–mid-Nov; ℗) is a working organic farm with eight barnlike rooms and an apartment that sleeps six (€600 to €1000 per week), with dinner available for €25 to €35. A short drive or a long walk from the village, the setting is lovely, a rustic farmhouse hidden among fruit trees and olive groves.

From Sorrento, there's a pretty 3km (approximately one hour) trail up to Sant'Agata. Otherwise, hourly SITA buses leave from the Circumvesuviana train station.

MARINA DEL CANTONE

From Sorrento, follow the coastal road round to **Termini**. Stop a moment to admire the views before continuing on to **Nerano**, from where a beautiful hiking trail leads down to the stunning **Bay of Ieranto**, one of the coast's top swimming spots, and **Marina del**

Cantone. This unassuming village with its small pebble beach is a lovely, tranquil place to stay and a popular diving destination.

Nettuno Diving (☏081 808 10 51; www. sorrentodiving.com; Via Vespucci 39) Padi Dive Resort leads various underwater activities, including snorkelling excursions, beginner courses and cave dives. Adult rates start at €25 for a day-long outing to the Bay of Ieranto.

Set among olive groves by the village entrance, **Villaggio Residence Nettuno** (☏081 808 10 51; www.villaggionettuno.it, www. torreturbolo.com; Via Vespucci 39; camping 2 people, tent & car €15-31, bungalow €35-80, apt €60-250; ⏰Mar-early Nov; ℗ ❄ @ 🛜 🛥) offers tent pitches, bungalows for two to eight people, mobile homes for two to four people, and apartments in a 16th-century tower for two to five people.

The village has a reputation as a gastronomic hot spot and VIPs regularly boat over from Capri to dine here. A favourite is **Lo Scoglio** (☏081 808 10 26; Marina del Cantone; meals €55), which serves superlative seafood tempters like a €30 antipasto of raw seafood and a celestial *spaghetti al riccio* (spaghetti with sea urchins).

SITA runs regular bus services between Sorrento and Marina del Cantone (marked on timetables as Nerano Cantone; €2.10, one hour).

AMALFI COAST

Stretching about 50km along the southern side of the Sorrentine Peninsula, the Amalfi Coast (Costiera Amalfitana) is one of Europe's most breathtaking coastlines. Cliffs terraced with scented lemon groves sheer down into sparkling seas; sherbet-hued villas cling precariously to unforgiving slopes while sea and sky merge in one vast blue horizon.

Yet its stunning topography has not always been a blessing. For centuries after the passing of Amalfi's glory days as a maritime superpower (from the 9th to the 12th centuries), the area was poor and its isolated villages regular victims of foreign incursions, earthquakes and landslides. But it was this very isolation that first drew visitors in the early 1900s, paving the way for the advent of tourism in the latter half of the century. Today the Amalfi Coast is one of Italy's premier tourist destinations, a favourite of cashed-up jet-setters and love-struck couples.

The best time to visit is in spring or early autumn. In summer the coast's single road (SS163) gets very busy and prices are inflated; in winter much of the coast simply shuts down.

ⓘ Getting There & Away

Boat
Boat services to the Amalfi Coast towns are generally limited to the period between April and October.

Gescab-Alicost (☎089 87 14 83; www.alicost.it, in Italian) operates one daily ferry and one daily hydrofoil from Salerno to Amalfi (€7/9), Positano (€11/13) and Capri (€18.50/20) from mid-April to October. Services from Amalfi and Positano to Capri run twice daily. It also runs two daily ferries from Sorrento to Positano (€13) and Amalfi (€14).

TraVelMar (☎089 87 29 50; www.travelmar.it, in Italian) connects Salerno with Amalfi (€7, six daily) and Positano (€11, six daily) from April to October.

Metrò del Mare (☎199 600700; www.metrodelmare.net, in Italian) was suspended indefinitely at the time of writing but normally runs summer services to various Amalfi Coast destinations, including Sorrento, Positano, Amalfi and Salerno.

Bus
SITA (☎089 40 51 45; www.sitabus.it, in Italian) operates a frequent, year-round service along the SS163 between Sorrento and Salerno (€3.30), via Amalfi.

Car & Motorcycle
If driving from the north, exit the A3 autostrada at Vietri sul Mare and follow the SS163 along the coast. From the south leave the A3 at Salerno and head for Vietri sul Mare and the SS163.

Train
From Naples you can take either the Circumvesuviana to Sorrento or a Trenitalia train to Salerno, then continue along the Amalfi Coast, eastwards or westwards, by SITA bus.

Positano

POP 3985

The pearl in the pack, Positano is the coast's most photogenic and expensive town. Its steeply stacked houses are a medley of peaches, pinks and terracottas, and its near-vertical streets (many of which are, in fact, staircases) are lined with voguish shop displays, jewellery stalls, elegant hotels and smart restaurants. Look closely, though, and you'll find reassuring signs of everyday reality – crumbling stucco, streaked paintwork and even, on occasion, a faint whiff of drains.

An early visitor, John Steinbeck wrote in *Harper's Bazaar* in May 1953: 'Positano bites deep. It is a dream place that isn't quite real when you are there and becomes beckoningly real after you have gone.' More than 50 years on, his words still ring true.

◉ Sights

Chiesa di Santa Maria Assunta   CHURCH
(Piazza Flavio Gioia; ☺8am-noon & 4-9pm) The lofty, ceramic-tiled dome of this church is the town's most famous, and pretty much only, major sight. Inside the building, classical lines are broken by pillars topped with gilded Ionic capitals, while winged cherubs peek from above every arch. Above the main altar is a 13th-century Byzantine Black Madonna and Child.

🏃 Activities

Spiaggia Grande   BEACH
Although it's no one's dream beach, with greyish sand covered by legions of brightly coloured umbrellas, the water's clean and the setting *is* memorable. Hiring a chair and umbrella in the fenced-off areas costs around €20 per person per day, but the crowded public areas are free.

Blue Star   BOATING, TOURS
(☎329 622 44 04; www.bluestarpositano.it; Spiaggia Grande; ☺9am-9pm Apr-Nov) Operating out of a kiosk on Spiaggia Grande, Blue Star hires out small motorboats for around €55 per hour and also organises excursions to Capri, the Grotta dello Smeraldo and all along the Amalfi Coast.

L'Uomo e il Mare   BOATING, TOURS
(☎089 81 16 13; www.gennaroesalvatore.it; ☺8am-8pm Easter-Nov) Similar to Blue Star, this outfit operates from a kiosk near the ferry terminal and offers a range of tours, including day trips to Capri (€50, including *prosecco* – sparkling wine – and cakes) and along the Amalfi Coast (€80, including lunch), and a sunset cruise to the Li Galli islands (€30).

🛏 Sleeping

Most hotels are three-star and above and prices are universally high. Cheaper accommodation is more limited and must usually be booked well in advance for summer. Ask at the tourist office about rooms or apartments in private houses.

NAPLES & CAMPANIA AMALFI COAST

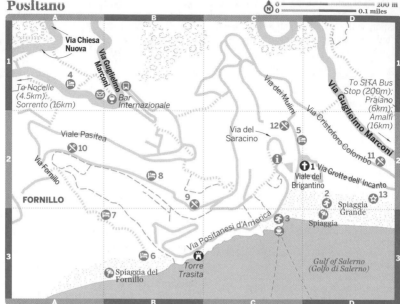

Positano

◎ Sights
1 Chiesa di Santa Maria Assunta D2

◎ Activities, Courses & Tours
2 Blue Star... D2
3 L'Uomo e il Mare................................... C3

◎ Sleeping
4 Hostel Brikette....................................... A1
5 Hotel Palazzo Murat.............................. C2
6 Hotel Ristorante Pupetto...................... B3

7 Pensione Maria Luisa............................ B3
8 Villa Nettuno.. B2

◎ Eating
9 Da Vincenzo... B2
10 Il Saraceno d'Oro A2
11 Ristorante Bruno.................................... D2
12 Ristorante Max C2

◎ Entertainment
13 Music on the Rocks................................ D2

TOP
CHOICE Pensione Maria Luisa PENSIONE €
(☎089 87 50 23; www.pensionemarialuisa.com; Via Fornillo 42; s €50, d €70-85; @🖥) The best budget choice in town, Maria Luisa's rooms and bathrooms have recently been updated with shiny new blue tiles and fittings; those with private terraces are well worth the extra €10 to €15 for the bay view. Other perks include a sunny communal area and a jovial, helpful owner. Payment is by cash only.

Hotel Palazzo Murat LUXURY HOTEL €€€
(☎089 87 51 77; www.palazzomurat.it; Via dei Mulini 23; s €130-315, d €150-370; ⊙late Mar-Oct; ❄@🖥) This upmarket treat is housed in the

palazzo that Gioacchino Murat, Napoleon's brother-in-law and one-time king of Naples, used as his summer residence. Beyond the lush gardens, rooms are traditional, with antiques, original oil paintings and plenty of lavish marble.

Hotel Ristorante Pupetto HOTEL €€
(☎089 87 50 87; www.hotelpupetto.it; Via Fornillo 37; s €90-100, d €130-170; ⊙Apr-Oct; @🖥) Overlooking Spiaggia del Fornillo, this is as close to the beach as you can get without sleeping on a sun-lounge. A bustling, cheerful place, the hotel forms part of a rambling beach complex with a popular terraced restaurant

(meals €25), a nautical-theme bar and sunny, renovated guest rooms with sea views.

Villa Nettuno
PENSIONE €

(☎089 87 54 01; www.villanettunopositano.it; Viale Pasitea 208; s €70, d €80-95; ✳) Hidden behind a barrage of foliage, Villa Nettuno oozes charm. Rooms in the 300-year-old part of the building have heavy rustic decor, frescoed wardrobes and a communal terrace; those in the renovated part are still good value but less interesting. That said, you probably won't be thinking of the furniture as you lie in bed gazing out to sea.

Hostel Brikette
HOSTEL €

(☎089 87 58 57; www.brikette.com; Via Marconi 358; dm €23-25, d €65-85, apt €115-180; ☺late Mar-Nov; @⏇) Not far from the Bar Internazionale bus stop on the coastal road is this bright and cheerful hostel offering the cheapest accommodation in town. There are various options: six- to eight-person dorms (single sex and mixed), double rooms and apartments for two to five people. There are also laundry and left-luggage facilities.

✕ Eating

Most restaurants, bars and trattorias, many of which are unashamedly touristy, close over winter, making a brief reappearance for Christmas and New Year.

TOP CHOICE Da Vincenzo
TRATTORIA €€

(☎089 87 51 28; Viale Pasitea 172-178; meals €40; ☺dinner daily, lunch Wed-Mon Apr-Nov) The best of the town's trattorias, Da Vincenzo has been serving *cucina di territorio* (cuisine of the territory) since 1958. Simple dishes sing with flavour, from fresh fish to a triumphant starter of grilled octopus skewers with fried artichokes.

Ristorante Bruno
TRADITIONAL ITALIAN €€

(Via Colombo 157; meals €40; ☺closed Nov-Jan) Don't let the underwhelming decor fool you – this unassuming restaurant serves superb seafood. Bag a table across the street and enjoy *the* view of Positano while swooning over house specialities like the antipasto of marinated fish with vegetables, orange and Parmesan; for a main course try the grilled fish with a wedge of local lemon.

Ristorante Max
TRADITIONAL ITALIAN €€€

(☎089 87 50 56; Via dei Mulini 22; meals €45; ☺Mar-Nov) Peruse the artwork while choosing your dish at this perennial favourite of 'ladies who lunch'. Eavesdrop over dishes like ravioli with clams and asparagus, and buttery eggplant *melanzana*. Cooking courses are offered in the summer months.

Il Saraceno d'Oro
TRADITIONAL ITALIAN €€

(Viale Pasitea 254; pizzas from €7, meals €35; ☺Mar-Oct) A busy, bustling place, the Saracen's blend of cheery service, uncomplicated food and reasonable prices continues to please the punters. The pizzas are good, the pasta's tasty and the desserts are sticky and sweet. The complimentary end-of-meal glass of *limoncello* makes for a pleasing epilogue.

☆ Entertainment

Generally speaking, Positano's nightlife is genteel, sophisticated and safe.

Music on the Rocks
BAR/CLUB

(www.musicontherocks.it; Via Grotte dell'Incanto 51; ☺Easter-Oct) Carved into the tower at the eastern end of Spiaggia Grande, this uberchic nightclub attracts a good-looking crowd and some of the region's best DJs. Sounds are mainstream house and disco.

❶ Information

La Brezza (☎089 87 58 11; Via del Brigantino 1; per 15min €3; ☺10am-10pm Mar-Nov) Small ceramics shop with internet access.

Police station (☎089 87 50 11; cnr Via Marconi & Viale Pasitea)

Positano (www.positano.com) A slick website with hotel and restaurant listings, itineraries and transport information.

Post office (Via Marconi 318)

Tourist office (www.aziendaturismopositano. it; Via del Saracino 4; ☺8.30am-7.30pm Mon-Sat Apr-Oct, 8.30am-4.30pm Mon-Fri Nov-Mar)

❶ Getting There & Away

Boat

Between April and October, ferries link Positano with Amalfi (€7, seven daily), Sorrento (€9 to €13, six daily), Salerno (€7 to €11, seven daily), and Capri (€15.50, 45 minutes, four daily).

Bus

SITA runs frequent buses to/from Amalfi (€1.50, 40 to 50 minutes) and Sorrento (€1.50, 60 minutes). Buses drop you off at one of two main bus stops: coming from Sorrento and the west, opposite Bar Internazionale; arriving from Amalfi and the east, at the top of Via Colombo. When departing, buy bus tickets at Bar Internazionale or, if headed eastwards, from the tobacconist at the bottom of Via Colombo.

NOCELLE

A tiny, still-isolated mountain village, Nocelle (450m) affords some of the most spectacular views on the entire coast. A world apart from touristy Positano, it's a sleepy, silent place where not much ever happens and none of the few residents would ever want it to.

The easiest way to get here is by local bus from Positano (€1.10, 30 minutes, 17 daily). Hikers tackling the Sentiero degli Dei (see p82) might fancy lunch at the **Ristorante Santa Croce** (Via Nocelle 19; meals €25; ⊙summer) as they pass through.

Getting Around

Getting around Positano is largely a matter of walking. If your knees can handle them, there are dozens of narrow alleys and stairways that make walking relatively easy and joyously traffic-free. Otherwise, an orange bus follows the lower ring road every half-hour, passing along Viale Pasitea, Via Colombo and Via Marconi. Buy your ticket (€1.60) on board or at a *tabaccaio* (tobacconist's shop). It passes by both SITA bus stops.

Praiano & Furore

An ancient fishing village, Praiano has one of the coast's most popular beaches, Marina di Praia. From the SS163 (next to the Hotel Continental), take the steep path that leads down the side of the cliffs to a tiny inlet with a small stretch of coarse sand and deep-blue water.

The **Centro Sub Costiera Amalfitana** (☑089 81 21 48; www.centrosub.it; Via Marina di Praia) runs beginner to expert dives (€80 to €130) exploring the area's coral, marine life and grottoes.

On the coastal road east of Praiano, **Hotel Pensione Continental** (☑089 87 40 84; www.continental.praiano.it; Via Roma 21; camping 2 people, tent & car €35-40, s €45-65, d €70-90, apt per week €500-1500; ⊙camping & rooms Easter-Oct, r & apt year-round) offers the full gamut of accommodation: cool, white rooms with sea views, apartments sleeping up to six people, and 12 tent sites on a series of grassy terraces. From the lowest of these a private staircase leads down to a rocky platform on the sea. Transport is no problem, either, as there's a bus stop just outside the hotel.

A few kilometres further on, **Marina di Furore** sits at the bottom of what's known as the fjord of Furore, a giant cleft that cuts through the Lattari mountains. The main village, however, stands 300m above, in the upper Vallone del Furore. A one-horse place that sees few tourists, it breathes a distinctly rural air despite the colourful murals and unlikely modern sculpture.

To get to upper Furore by car, follow the SS163 and then the SS366 signposted to Agerola; from Positano, it's 15km. Otherwise, regular SITA buses depart from the bus terminus in Amalfi (€1.20, 30 minutes, five times daily).

Amalfi

POP 5340

It is hard to grasp that pretty little Amalfi, with its sun-filled piazzas and small beach, was once a maritime superpower with a population of more than 70,000. For one thing, it's not a big place – you can easily walk from one end to the other in about 20 minutes. For another, there are very few historical buildings of note. The explanation is chilling – most of the old city, and its populace, simply slid into the sea during an earthquake in 1343.

Today, although the resident population is fairly modest, the numbers swell significantly during summer, when day trippers pour in by the coachload.

Just around the headland, neighbouring Atrani is a picturesque tangle of whitewashed alleys and arches centred on a lively, lived-in piazza and popular beach.

Sights

Cattedrale di Sant'Andrea DUOMO, MUSEUM
(☑089 87 10 59; Piazza del Duomo; ⊙9am-6.45pm Apr-Jun, to 7.45pm Jul-Sep, reduced hours off season) Dominating Piazza del Duomo, Amalfi's iconic cathedral makes an imposing sight at the top of its sweeping flight of stairs. The cathedral dates in part from the early 10th century, although its distinctive striped facade has been rebuilt twice, most recently at the end of the 19th century. It's a melange of architectural styles: the two-toned masonry is largely Sicilian Arabic-Norman while the interior is pure baroque. The exquisite **crypt** is home to the reliquary of St Andrew the Apostle. The fresco facing the crypt's altar is by Neapolitan baroque maestro Aniello Falcone. Between 10am and 5pm, entrance to

the cathedral is through the adjacent Chiostro del Paradiso.

To the left of the cathedral's porch, the pint-sized **Chiostro del Paradiso** (☑089 87 13 24; adult/11-17yrs €3/1; ☺9am-6.45pm Apr-Jun, to 7.45pm Jul-Sep, reduced hours off season) was built in 1266 to house the tombs of Amalfi's prominent citizens. From here you enter the **Basilica del Crucifisso**, Amalfi's original 9th-century cathedral, itself built on the remains of an earlier Paleo-Christian temple. It's home to a small, yet fascinating collection of ecclesial treasures, including a jewel-studded, 13th-century Angevin mitre.

Museo della Carta   MUSEUM
(Paper Museum; ☑089 830 45 61; www.museodellacarta.it; Via delle Cartiere; admission €4; ☺10am-6.30pm Apr–mid-Nov, 10am-3pm Tue, Wed & Fri-Sun mid-Nov–Mar) Housed in a 13th-century paper mill (the oldest in Europe), this fascinating museum lovingly preserves the original paper presses, which are still in full working order, as you'll see during the 15-minute guided tour (in English).

Museo Arsenale Amalfi   MUSEUM
(☑089 87 11 70; Largo Cesareo Console 3; admission €2; ☺10am-2pm & 4.30-8.30pm) Amalfi's other museum of note is home to the *Tavole Amalfitane,* an ancient manuscript draft of Amalfi's maritime code, and other historical documents. Harking back to Amalfi's days as a great maritime republic, the museum is housed in the cavernous **Arsenale**, once the town's main shipbuilding depot.

Grotta dello Smeraldo   GROTTO
(admission €5; ☺9am-4pm Mar-Oct, 9am-3pm Nov-Feb) Four kilometres west of Amalfi, Conca dei Marini is home to this haunting cave, named after the eerie emerald colour that emanates from the seawater. SITA buses regularly pass the car park above the cave entrance (from where you take a lift or stairs down to the rowing boats). Alternatively, **Coop Sant'Andrea** (☑089 87 31 90; www.coopsantandrea.it; Lungomare dei Cavalieri 1) runs hourly boats from Amalfi (€14 return) between 9am and 3pm daily from May to October. Allow around one hour for the round trip.

🏊 Activities

For all its seafaring history, Amalfi's main beach is not a particularly appealing swimming spot. If you're intent on a dip, think about hiring a boat. You'll find a number of operators along Lungomare dei Cavalieri, charging about €50 for a couple of hours.

✰✰ Festivals & Events

Every 24 December and 6 January, skin-divers from all over Italy make a pilgrimage to the ceramic *presepe* submerged in the Grotta dello Smeraldo.

The **Regatta of the Four Ancient Maritime Republics**, which rotates between Amalfi, Venice, Pisa and Genoa, is held on the first Sunday in June. Amalfi's turn comes round again in 2013.

🛌 Sleeping

☑TOP CHOICE **Hotel Luna Convento**   HOTEL €€€
(☑089 87 10 02; www.lunahotel.it; Via Pantaleone Comite 33; s €220-280, d €240-300; P✳@☎☒) This former convent was founded by St Francis in 1222. Rooms in the original building are in the former nuns' cells, but there's nothing pokey about the bright tiles, balconies and sea views. The newer wing is equally beguiling, with religious frescoes over the bed (to stop any misbehaving). The cloistered courtyard is magnificent.

Hotel Lidomare   HOTEL €€
(☑089 87 13 32; www.lidomare.it; Largo Duchi Piccolomini 9; s/d €50/120; ✳) This old-fashioned, family-run hotel has real character. The spacious rooms have an air of gentility, with their appealingly haphazard decor, old-fashioned tiles and fine old antiques. Some rooms have jacuzzi bathtubs, others boast sea views.

Hotel Centrale   HOTEL €€
(☑089 87 26 08; www.amalfihotelcentrale.it; Largo Duchi Piccolomini 1; s €60-120, d €70-140; ✳@☎) This is one of the best-value hotels in Amalfi. The entrance is on a tiny little piazza in the *centro storico,* but many rooms actually overlook Piazza del Duomo (24 is a good choice). The bright green and blue tile work gives the place a vibrant, fresh look, and the views from the rooftop terrace are magnificent.

A'Scalinatella Hostel   HOSTEL €
(☑089 87 14 92; www.hostelscalinatella.com; Piazza Umberto I, Atrani; dm €20-25, s €35-50, d €70-90, all incl breakfast) This bare-bones operation, just round the headland in Atrani, has dorms, rooms and apartments scattered across the village. There's also a laundry available.

Rising steeply from the coast, the densely wooded Lattari mountains provide some stunning walking opportunities. An extraordinary network of paths traverses the craggy, precipitous peaks, climbing to remote farmhouses through wild and beautiful valleys. It's tough going, though – long ascents up seemingly endless flights of steps are almost unavoidable.

Probably the best-known walk, the 12km Sentiero degli Dei (Path of the Gods; 5½ to six hours) follows the steep, often rocky paths linking Positano to Praiano. It's a spectacular trail passing through some of the area's least developed countryside. The route is marked by red-and-white stripes daubed on rocks and trees, although some of these have become worn in places and might be difficult to make out. Pick up a map of the walk at local tourist offices, included in a series of three excellent booklets containing the area's most popular hikes, including the equally famed (and lyrically named) *Via degli Incanti* (Trail of Charms) from Amalfi to Positano.

To the west, the tip of the Sorrentine Peninsula is another hiking hot spot. Some 110km of paths criss-cross the area, linking the spectacular coastline with the rural hinterland. These range from tough all-day treks – such as the 14.1km Alta Via dei Monti Lattari from the Fontanelle hills near Positano down to the Punta Campanella – to shorter walks suitable for the family. Tourist offices throughout the area can provide maps detailing the colour-coded routes. With the exception of the Alta Via dei Monti Lattari (marked in red and white), long routes are shown in red on the map; coast-to-coast trails in blue; paths connecting villages in green; and circular routes in yellow.

If you're intent on trying one of the more demanding routes in the region, invest in a detailed map such as the CAI's (Club Alpino Italiano) *Monti Lattari, Peninsola Sorrentina, Costiera Amalfitana: Carta dei Sentieri* (€8) at 1:30,000 scale.

✕ Eating

Ristorante
La Caravella   TRADITIONAL, MODERN ITALIAN €€€
(☑089 87 10 29; www.ristorantelacaravella.it; Via Matteo Camera 12; meals €65, tasting menu €75; ⊙Wed-Mon, closed Nov & early Jan-early Feb) One of the few places in Amalfi where you pay for the food rather than the location, this celebrated dining den serves a mix of simple, soulful classics and regional specialities with a nouvelle twist – think lemon risotto with cooked and raw prawns and grey mullet roe. The 1750-plus wines are an aficionado's dream.

Trattoria Il Mulino   TRATTORIA €€
(Via delle Cartiere 36; pizzas €6, meals €29) A TV-in-the-corner, kids-running-between-the-tables sort of place, this is about as authentic a trattoria as you'll find in Amalfi. The menu features the usual pizzas, pasta and seafood, but the food is tasty and the prices honest. The *scialatiella alla pescatore* (pasta ribbons with prawns, mussels, tomato and parsley) is fabulous.

Pasticceria Pansa   PASTRIES & CAKES €
(Piazza Duomo 40; pastries from €1.50) Compromising waistlines since 1830, this vintage pastry peddler is a must for gluttons. Musttrys include chocolate-dipped candied citrus peels (the fruit is grown at the family's own estate), *torta setteveli* (a multi-layered chocolate and hazelnut cake) and the *limoncello*-laced local *delizia al limone*.

Le Arcate   TRADITIONAL ITALIAN €€
(Largo Orlando Buonocore Atrani; pizzas from €6, meals €40; ⊙closed early Jan–mid-Feb & Mon Sep-Jun) On a sunny day it's hard to beat the dreamy harbourside location. Beyond the sprawl of alfresco tables is a cavernous, stone-lined interior. Pizzas are served at night, while daytime fare includes the house speciality, *scialatielli* pasta with shrimp and zucchini.

Supermercato Decò   SUPERMARKET €
(Salita dei Curiali 6) Picnickers and self-caterers can stock up here.

❶ Information

Amalfi Servizi Express (Piazza dei Dogi 8; internet per 15min €3; ⊙9.30am-1.30pm & 4.30-8pm Mon-Sat, closed Thu evening)

Post office (Corso delle Repubbliche Marinare 31) Next door to the tourist office.

Tourist office (www.amalfitouristoffice.it; Corso delle Repubbliche Marinare 27; ⊙9am-

1pm & 2-6pm Mon-Sat, 9am-1pm Sun, closed Sun Apr, May & Sep, closed Sat & Sun Oct-Mar) Good for bus and ferry timetables.

ⓘ Getting There & Away

Boat

Between April and October there are daily ferry sailings to Salerno (€7, seven daily), Positano (€7, seven daily) and Capri (€17, one daily). There is also a hydrofoil service to Capri (€19, one daily).

Bus

SITA buses run from Piazza Flavio Gioia to Sorrento (€2.80, 1½ hours, around 30 times daily) via Positano (€1.50, 40 minutes), and also to Ravello (€1.20, 25 minutes, every 30 minutes), and Salerno (€2.10, 1¼ hours, hourly). There are only two daily connections to Naples (€4, two to three hours depending on the route), so you're better off catching a bus to Sorrento and then the Circumvesuviana train to Naples. Buy tickets and check schedules at **Bar Il Giardino delle Palme** (Piazza Flavio Gioia), opposite the bus stop.

Ravello

POP 2475

Sitting high in the hills above Amalfi, refined Ravello is a polished town almost entirely dedicated to tourism. Boasting impeccable bohemian credentials – Wagner, DH Lawrence and Virginia Woolf all lounged here – it's today known for its ravishing gardens and stupendous views, the best in the world according to former resident Gore Vidal.

Most people visit on a day trip from Amalfi – a nerve-tingling 7km drive up the Valle del Dragone – although to best enjoy Ravello's romantic otherworldly atmosphere you'll need to stay overnight.

The **tourist office** (www.ravellotime.it; Via Roma 18bis; ☺9.30am-7pm Apr-Oct, to 5pm Nov-Mar) has some general information on the town, plus a handy map with walking trails.

◉ Sights & Activities

Cathedral   DUOMO, MUSEUM

(☺8am-noon & 5.30-8.30pm) Forming the eastern flank of Piazza del Duomo, Ravello's cathedral was originally built in 1086 but has since undergone various facelifts. The facade is 16th century, even if the central bronze door is an 1179 original; the interior is a late-20th-century interpretation of what

the original must once have looked like. The pulpit is particularly striking, supported by six twisting columns set on marble lions and decorated with flamboyant mosaics of peacocks, birds and dancing lions. Note also how the floor is tilted towards the square – a deliberate measure to enhance the perspective effect. To the right of the central nave, stairs lead down to the cathedral **museum** (admission €2; ☺9am-7pm) and its modest collection of religious artefacts.

Villa Rufolo   GARDEN

(☎089 85 76 21; admission €5; ☺9am-sunset) To the south of the cathedral, Villa Rufolo is famous for its romantic 19th-century gardens. Commanding mesmerising views, they are packed with exotic colours, artistically crumbling towers and luxurious blooms. On seeing them in 1880, Wagner wrote that he had found the garden of Klingsor (setting for the second act of his opera *Parsifal*). Today the gardens are used to stage concerts during the town's celebrated festival.

Villa Cimbrone   GARDEN

(☎089 85 74 59; adult/reduced €6/4; ☺9am-sunset) If Villa Rufolo's gardens leave you longing for more, seek out the 20th-century Villa Cimbrone for the vast views from the delightfully ramshackle gardens. The best viewpoint is the Belvedere of Infinity, an awe-inspiring terrace lined with fake classical busts. The villa is some 600m south of Piazza del Duomo.

✦ Festivals & Events

Ravello Festival   CULTURAL

(☎089 85 83 60; www.ravellofestival.com) Between June and mid-September the Ravello Festival turns much of the town centre into a stage. Events ranging from orchestral concerts and chamber music to ballet performances, film screenings and exhibitions are held in various locations.

Ravello Concert Society   MUSIC

(☎089 85 81 49; www.ravelloarts.org) Ravello's program of classical music actually begins in April and continues until late October. Performances are world class, and the two venues of Villa Rufolo and the Convento di Santa Rosa in Conca dei Marini (the latter was closed for restoration at the time of writing) are unforgettable. Tickets can be booked either by fax (☎089 85 82 49) or on the website.

🛌 Sleeping

Agriturismo Monte Brusara   AGRITURISMO €
(☎089 85 74 67; www.montebrusara.com; Via Monte Brusara 32; s €42-45, d €84-90) It's a tough half-hour walk from Ravello's centre, but this authentic mountainside *agriturismo* (farm-stay accommodation) is the real Mc-Coy. It's an ideal spot to escape the crowds and offers three comfortable but basic rooms, fabulous food and some big views. Half-board is also available.

Hotel Villa Amore   PENSIONE €
(☎/fax 089 85 71 35; www.villaamore.it; Via dei Fusco 5; s €50-60, d €75-100; 🕾) This welcoming *pensione* is the best budget choice in town. Tucked away down a quiet lane, it has modest, homey rooms and sparkling bathrooms. All rooms have their own balcony and some have bathtubs. The garden restaurant (meals about €25) is a further plus.

Hotel Toro   HOTEL €€
(☎089 85 72 11; www.hoteltoro.it; Via Roma 16; s/d €85/118; ⊙mid-Apr–Nov; ❄🕾) A hotel since the late 19th century, the Toro is just off Piazza del Duomo, within easy range of the clanging cathedral bells. The not-huge rooms are decked out in traditional style with terracotta or light-marble tiles and soothing cream furnishings. Outside, the walled garden is the perfect place for a sundowner.

🍴 Eating

Cumpà Cosimo   TRADITIONAL ITALIAN, PIZZERIA €€
(☎089 85 71 56; Via Roma 44-46; pizzas €6-12, meals €45) Netta Bottone's rustic cooking is so good that even US celebrity Rosie O'Donnell tried to get her on her show. Netta didn't make it to Hollywood but she still rules the roost at this historic trattoria. Order the *piatto misto* (mixed plate), which may include Ravello's trademark *crespolini* (cheese and prosciutto-stuffed crepes). Evening options include pizza.

Da Salvatore   TRADITIONAL & MODERN ITALIAN €€
(www.salvatoreravello.com; Via della Republicca 2; meals €35; ⊙restaurant lunch & dinner Tue-Sun, pizzeria dinner Thu-Tue, both open daily Aug) Located just before the bus stop and the Garden Hotel, this average-looking nosh spot has an exceptional view, not to mention creative dishes like mixed Gragnano pasta with potato and calamari. In the evening, head in for some of the best wood-fired pizza this side of Naples.

Take Away da Nino   STREET FOOD €
(Viale Parco della Rimembranza 41) Fast food Ravello-style – come here for takeaway pizza and crunchy fried nibbles.

❶ Getting There & Away

SITA operates hourly buses from the eastern side of Piazza Flavio Gioia in Amalfi (€1.20, 25 minutes). By car, turn north about 2km east of Amalfi. Vehicles are not permitted in Ravello's town centre, but there's plenty of space in supervised car parks on the perimeter.

South of Amalfi

FROM AMALFI TO SALERNO

The 26km drive to Salerno, though less exciting than the 16km stretch westwards to Positano, is exhilarating and dotted with a series of small towns, each with their own character and each worth a brief look.

Three and a half kilometres east of Amalfi, or a steep 1km-long walk down from Ravello, **Minori** is a small, workaday town, popular with holidaying Italians. Further along, **Maiori** is the coast's biggest resort, a brassy place full of large seafront hotels, restaurants and beach clubs.

Just beyond **Erchie** and its beautiful beach, **Cetara** is a picturesque tumbledown fishing village with a reputation as a gastronomic highlight. Tuna and anchovies are the local specialities, appearing in various guises at **Al Convento** (☎089 26 10 39; Piazza San Francesco 16; meals €25; ⊙closed Wed Oct–mid-May), a sterling seafood restaurant near the small harbour. For your money, you'll probably not eat better anywhere else on the coast; the *puttanesca con alici fresche* (pasta with fresh anchovies, chilli and garlic) sings with flavour.

Shortly before Salerno, the road passes through **Vietri sul Mare**, the ceramics capital of Campania. Its not-unattractive historic centre is packed to the gills with ceramics shops, the most famous of which is **Ceramica Artistica Solimene** (www.solimene.com; Via Madonna degli Angeli 7; ⊙8am-7pm Mon-Fri, 8am-1.30pm & 4-7pm Sat), a vast factory outlet with an extraordinary glass-and-ceramic facade.

SALERNO
POP 139,700

Upstaged by the glut of postcard-pretty towns along the Amalfi Coast, Campania's second-largest city is actually a pleasant surprise. A decade of civic determination has turned this major port and transport hub into one of southern Italy's most liveable cities, and its small but buzzing *centro storico* is a vibrant mix of medieval churches, tasty trattorias and good-spirited, bar-hopping locals.

Originally an Etruscan and later a Roman colony, Salerno flourished with the arrival of the Normans in the 11th century. Robert Guiscard made it the capital of his dukedom in 1076 and, under his patronage, the Scuola Medica Salernitana was renowned as one of medieval Europe's greatest medical institutes. More recently, it was ravaged by the heavy fighting that followed the 1943 landings of the American 5th Army, just south of the city.

◎ Sights

Cathedral   DUOMO
(☑089 23 13 87; Piazza Alfano; ☺9.30am-6pm Mon-Sat, 1-6pm Sun) Salerno's cathedral is the highlight of the *centro storico*. Built by the Normans under Robert Guiscard in the 11th century and remodelled in the 18th century, it sustained severe damage in the 1980 earthquake. It's dedicated to San Matteo (St Matthew), whose remains were reputedly brought to the city in 954 and now lie beneath the main altar in the exquisite vaulted crypt. In the right-hand apse, the **Cappella delle Crociate** (Chapel of the Crusades) was so named because crusaders' weapons were blessed here. Under the altar stands the tomb of the 11th-century pope Gregory VII.

Scuola Medica Salernitana
Museo Virtuale   MUSEUM
(☑089 257 32 13; www.museovirtualescuola medicasalernitana.it; Via Mercanti 74; donation €1) Slap bang in Salerno's historic centre, this engaging museum deploys 3D and touch-screen technology to explore the teachings and wince-inducing procedures of Salerno's once-famous, now defunct medical institute. Established in the 9th century and surviving 10 centuries, the school was Europe's first and most prestigious centre of medicine.

Castello di Arechi   CASTLE, MUSEUM
(☑089 285 45 33; Via Benedetto Croce; admission €3; ☺9am-7pm Tue-Sun May-Sep, to 5pm Oct-Apr) Salerno's lofty *castello* is spectacularly positioned 263m above the city. Originally a Byzantine fort, it was built by the Lombard duke of Benevento, Arechi II, in the 8th century and subsequently modified by the Normans and Aragonese. Today it houses a permanent collection of ceramics, arms and coins. To get there take bus 19 from Piazza XXIV Maggio in the city centre.

Museo Pinacoteca Provinciale   MUSEUM
(☑089 258 30 73; Via Mercanti 63; admission free; ☺9am-7.45pm Tue-Sun) Facing the Scuola Medica Salernitana Museo Virtuale, this small but interesting art collection dates from the Renaissance right up to the first half of the 19th century.

⌂ Sleeping

Ostello Ave Gratia Plena   HOSTEL €
(☑089 23 47 76; www.ostellodisalerno.it; Via dei Canali; dm/s/d €15/33/47; @☎) Housed in a 16th-century convent, Salerno's HI hostel is right in the heart of the *centro storico*. Inside there's a charming central courtyard and a range of bright rooms, from dorms to doubles with private bathroom. The 2am curfew is for dorms only.

Hotel Plaza   HOTEL €
(☑089 22 44 77; www.plazasalerno.it; Piazza Vittorio Veneto 42; s/d €65/100; ✳@☎) The Plaza is convenient and comfortable, a stone's throw from the train station. It's a friendly place and the decent-size rooms, complete with gleaming bathrooms, are pretty good value for money. Those facing the station have terraces overlooking the city and, beyond, the mountains.

✕ Eating

Head to Via Roma and Via Mercanti in the lively medieval centre, where you'll find everything from traditional, family-run trattorias and gelaterie to wine bars, pubs and restaurants.

La Cucina di Edoardo   TRADITIONAL ITALIAN €
(☑089 296 26 67; Vico della Neve 14; meals €25; ☺closed Mon & dinner Sun) Snugly tucked away in a *centro storico* side street, Edoardo's Kitchen is one of those cheap, scrumptious finds any local *buongustaio* (foodie) will direct you to. The focus is on tasty, regional grub, with stand out dishes including the *antipasto misto* and *zuppa di cipolle* (onion soup). Leave room for the *flan al cioccolato* (chocolate flan) and don't forget to book ahead on weekends.

Ristorante Lazzarella   TRADITIONAL ITALIAN €€
(Lungomare Trieste 92; meals €28; ☺closed Mon Sep-Jul, dinner Sun Oct-Easter & lunch Mon-Sun Aug) Bright, intimate and youthful, head here for top-tasting local dishes like *lagane e ceci* (pasta with chickpeas). Particularly fabulous is the *Lazzarella di mare,* a tasting plate of seafood specialities like *calamaro imbottito* (stuffed calamari) and *seppia in*

Salerno

0 200 m
0 0.2 miles

400 m

Piazza Sedile del Campo

Piazza Amendola

To Amalfi (26km);
Positano (42km)

Piazza Alfano

Cathedral 1

Via del Canali 4

Vico della Neve

5

Via Mercanti

Via S Michele

Via Duomo

6

2

Museo
Pinacoteca
Provinciale

Piazza
Matteotti

Via Iannelli

Via San Benedetto

Via Vella

Via Roma

Via Volpe

Via Nizza

Piazza XXIV
Maggio

Corso Vittorio Emanuele II

Via Cilento

Via Diaz

Il

Lungomare Trieste

Corso Garibaldi

Bar Cioffi for
SITA Buses
to Naples

Piazza
Giuseppe
Mazzini

CSTP Bus
Stop

3

Piazza Vittorio
Veneto

Via Torrione

Lungomare Guglielmo Marconi

Piazza della
Concordia

Porto Turistico Ferry
& Hydrofoil Terminal

Gulf of Salerno
(Golfo di Salerno)

Molo
Manfredi

Porto Commerciale Ferry
& Hydrofoil Terminal

To A3
(Southbound): Paestum
(36km)

Via Dalmazia

Salerno

agrodolce (cuttlefish with sautéed onion). The dish can be upsized from three to five *assaggi* (tastings) on request.

Pasticceria Pantaleone   PASTRIES & CAKES €
(Via Mercanti 75; pastries from €1.50; ⊘closed Tue) Where better to commit dietray sins than in a deconsecrated church? It's now home to Salerno's finest pastry shop, best known for inventing the *scazzetta,* a pastry of *pan di spagna* sponge, fresh berries and chantilly cream, soaked in Strega liqeur and finished with a strawberry glace. Wash away the guilt with a glass of the house liqueur, *Elisir,* made with aromatic herbs and orange.

ⓘ **Information**
Ospedale Ruggi D'Aragona (☎089 67 11 11; Via San Leonardo)
Post office (Corso Garibaldi 203)
Tourist infopoint (Corso Vittorio Emanuele 193; ⊘9.30am-1.30pm & 4.30-8.30pm Mon-Sat) Inside the Galleria Capitol Cinema shopping centre; has brochures, bus and ferry timetables and accommodation information.
Tourist office (Piazza Vittorio Veneto 1; ⊘9am-1pm & 3.15-7.15pm Mon-Sat)

ⓘ **Getting There & Away**

BOAT

Gescab-Alicost (☎089 87 14 83; www.alicost. it, in Italian) Operates one daily ferry and one daily hydrofoil from Salerno to Amalfi (€7/9), Positano (€11/13) and Capri (€18.50/20) from mid-April to October.
Gescab-Linee Marittime Partenopee (☎081 704 19 11; www.consorziolmp.it, in Italian) Runs hydrofoils and fast ferries from Salerno to Capri (€20/€18.50, one each daily) from April to October.
TraVelMar (☎089 87 29 50; www.travelmar.it, in Italian) Runs ferries from Salerno to Amalfi (€7, six daily) and Positano (€11, six daily) from April to October.
Metrò del Mare (☎199 600700; www.metro delmare.net, in Italian) Operates regular ferries to/from Naples and Sorrento. The service was suspended temporarily at the time of writing, so check the website for updates.

Departures are from the Porto Turistico, 200m down the pier from Piazza della Concordia. You can buy tickets from the booths by the embarkation point.

Departures for Capri leave from Molo Manfredi at the Porto Commerciale.

BUS

SITA buses for Amalfi (€2.10, 1¼ hours, at least hourly) depart from Piazza Vittorio Veneto, beside the train station, stopping en route at Vietri sul Mare, Cetara, Maiori and Minori. The Naples service, however, departs from Piazza G Mazzini, 50 metres east of **Bar Cioffi** (Corso Garibaldi 134), where you buy your €4 ticket. Tickets are also available inside the train station.

CSTP (☎800 016 659; www.cstp.it, in Italian) bus 4 runs from Piazza Vittorio Veneto to Pompeii (€2.10, one hour, 17 daily) from Monday to Saturday. On Sunday, bus 4 will get you there in 90 minutes. For Paestum (€3.30, one hour, hourly) take bus 34 from Piazza della Concordia.

Buonotourist (☎089 79 50 68; www.buono tourist.it) runs daily services (excluding Sunday and public holidays) to Naples' Capodichino airport, departing from the train station. Tickets (€7) can be bought on board; journey time is one hour.

CAR & MOTORCYCLE

Salerno is on the A3 between Naples and Reggio di Calabria, which is toll-free from Salerno southwards.

TRAIN

Salerno is a major stop on southbound routes to Calabria and the Ionian and Adriatic coasts. From the station in Piazza Vittorio Veneto there are regular trains to Naples (IC €7.50, 40 minutes, 44 services daily), Rome (Eurostar €39, 2½ hours, hourly), and Reggio di Calabria (IC €36.50, 4½ hours, nine daily).

ⓘ **Getting Around**
Walking is the most sensible option; from the train station it's a 1.2km walk along Corso Vittorio Emanuele II to the historic centre.

For car hire there's a **Europcar** (☎089 258 07 75; www.europcar.com; Via Clemente Mauro 18) agency not far from the train station.

PAESTUM

Paestum's Unesco-listed temples are among the best-preserved monuments of Magna Graecia, the Greek colony that once covered much of southern Italy. An easy day trip from Salerno or Agropoli, they are one of the region's most iconic sights and absolutely unmissable.

Paestum, or Poseidonia as the city was originally called (in honour of Poseidon, the Greek god of the sea), was founded in the 6th century BC by Greek settlers and fell under Roman control in 273 BC. It became an important trading port and remained so until the fall of the Roman Empire, when periodic outbreaks of malaria and savage Saracen raids led its weakened citizens to abandon the town.

Its temples were rediscovered in the late 18th century by road builders – who proceeded to plough their way right through the ruins. However, the road did little to alter the state of the surrounding area, which remained full of malarial swamps, teeming with snakes and scorpions, until well into the 20th century.

The **tourist office** (www.infopaestum.it; Via Magna Grecia 887; ⊙9am-1pm & 2-4pm) has practical information on Paestum and the Costiera Cilentana.

⊙ Sights

Ruins of Paestum   RUINS
(☑0828 81 10 23; admission €4, incl museum €6.50; ⊙8.45am-2 hours before sunset) Tickets to the ruins are sold at the main entry point, near the tourist office, or, in winter, from the museum, where you can also hire an audioguide (€5).

The 6th-century-BC **Tempio di Cerere** (Temple of Ceres) is the first temple you encounter from the main entrance. The smallest of the three temples, it served for a time as a Christian church.

Heading south, you pass the **agorà** (piazza), which contained the city's most important monument, a shrine to Poseidon known as the **heroon**. Nearby, a sunken area marks where a public **swimming pool** once stood, part of a larger sports campus.

The grassy rectangular area south of the pool is the **foro**, the heart of the Roman city. Among the partially standing buildings are a vast domestic housing area, an Italic temple, the Bouleuterion (where the Roman senate used to meet) and, further south, the amphitheatre.

The **Tempio di Nettuno** (Temple of Neptune), dating from about 450 BC, is the largest and best preserved of the three temples; only parts of its inside walls and roof are missing. Although originally attributed to Neptune, recent studies have claimed that it was, in fact, dedicated to Apollo.

Next door, the **basilica** (in reality, a temple to the goddess Hera) is Paestum's oldest surviving monument. Dating to the middle of the 6th century BC, and with nine columns across and 18 along the sides, it's a majestic building. Just to its east you can, with a touch of imagination, make out remains of the temple's sacrificial altar.

In its time the city was ringed by an impressive 4.7km of walls, subsequently built and rebuilt by both Lucanians and Romans. The most intact section is south of the ruins themselves.

Just east of the ruins, the **museum** (☑0828 81 10 23; admission €4, incl ruins €6.50; ⊙8.30am-7.30pm, last entry 6.45pm, closed 1st & 3rd Mon of month) houses a collection of much-weathered metopes (bas-relief friezes), including 33 of the original 36 from the **Tempio di Argiva Hera** (Temple of Argive Hera), 9km north of Paestum, of which virtually nothing else remains. The star exhibit is the 5th-century-BC Tomba del Truffatore (Tomb of the Diver); its depiction of a diver in mid-air reputedly represents the passage of life to death.

🍽 Sleeping & Eating

TOP CHOICE **Casale Giancesare**   B&B €
(☑0828 72 80 61, 333 189 77 37; www.casale-gianc esare.it; Via Giancesare 8; s €45-75, d €65-120, apt per wk €600-1300; P✳@🛜🏊🎿) A converted 19th-century farmhouse, this charming stone-clad B&B is 2.5km from Paestum. Surrounded by vineyards and olive and mulberry trees, the views are stunning, particularly from the swimming pool. Delightful owners Anna, Enzo and son Antonino are passionate about food, producing (and selling) their own olives, jams, *limoncello* and wine. Beware of road signs advertising another bed and breakfast, called Residence Giancesere.

Nonna Sceppa   TRADITIONAL ITALIAN €€
(Via Laura 53, località Laura; meals €39; ⊙lunch & dinner Easter-Sep, lunch Fri-Wed & dinner Sat rest of year) Worth seeking out as an alternative to the mediocre, overpriced on-site restaurants. Dishes are robust, strictly seasonal and, during the summer, concentrate on fresh sea-

food like the refreshingly simple grilled fish with lemon. The risotto with courgettes and artichokes is equally inspired.

❶ Getting There & Away

The best way to get to Paestum by public transport is to take **CSTP** (☑800 016 659; www.cstp. it, in Italian) bus 34 from Piazza della Concordia in Salerno (€3.30, one hour 20 minutes, 12 daily) or, if approaching from the south, the same bus from Agropoli (€1.20, 15 minutes, 12 daily).

If you're driving you could take the A3 from Salerno and exit for the SS18 at Battipaglia. Better, and altogether more pleasant, is the Litoranea, the minor road that hugs the coast. From the A3 take the earlier exit for Pontecagnano and follow the signs for Agropoli and Paestum.

COSTIERA CILENTANA

Southeast of the Gulf of Salerno, the coastal plains begin to give way to wilder, jagged cliffs and unspoilt scenery, a taste of what lies further on in the stark hills of Basilicata and the wooded peaks of Calabria. Inland, dark mountains loom over the remote highlands of the Parco Nazionale del Cilento e Vallo di Diano, one of Campania's best-kept secrets.

On the coast 75km south of Salerno, the Greek settlement of Elea (now Velia), was founded in the 6th century BC and later became a popular resort for wealthy Romans. The **ruins** (☑0974 97 23 96; Contrada Piana di Velia; admission €2; ☺9am to 1hr before sunset), topped by a tower visible for miles around, are not in great nick but merit a quick look if you're passing through.

Several destinations on the Cilento coast are served by the main rail route from Naples to Reggio di Calabria. Check **Trenitalia** (www.trenitalia.it) for fares and information.

By car take the SS18, which connects Agropoli with Velia via the inland route, or the SS267, which hugs the coast.

Agropoli

POP 21,035

The main town on the southern stretch of the coast, Agropoli makes a good base for Paestum and the beaches to the northwest. Popular with holidaying Italians, it's an otherwise tranquil place with a ramshackle medieval core on a promontory overlooking the sea.

The **tourist office** (☑0974 82 74 19; Piazza della Repubblica 3; ☺9am-1pm Mon-Fri, also 3-6pm Tue & Thu) can provide you with a city map.

🛏 Sleeping & Eating

Anna   B&B €

(☑0974 82 37 63; www.bbanna.it; Via S Marco 28-32; s €35-50, d €50-70; ✳) Across from Agropoli's sweeping sandy beach, Anna has bright, cheerful rooms with white walls, smart striped fabrics and balconies; request a sea view. Sunbeds and bicycles are available for a minimal price, and the popular downstairs restaurant (pizzas from €3, meals €18) serves gluten-free meals.

Ostello La Lanterna   HOSTEL €

(☑0974 83 83 64; lanterna@cilento.it; Via Lanterna 8; dm €18-19, d with bathroom €40-50, tr €58-65, q €80-85; ☺mid-Mar–Oct) Agropoli's friendly hostel offers dorms, doubles and four-bed family rooms, as well as a garden and optional evening meals (€10). The beach is a two-minute walk away.

U'Sghiz   TRADITIONAL ITALIAN, PIZZERIA €

(Piazza Umberto I; pizzas from €3, meals €22; ☺closed Tue Oct-May) In a 17th-century building on the headland, U'Sghiz specialises in seafood dishes like *spaghetti a vongole* (with mussels), and also has an extensive pizza menu. We suggest you ditch the quarter carafe of house red wine (€2) for one of the marginally more expensive drops.

Parco Nazionale del Cilento e Vallo di Diano

Stretching from the coast up to Campania's highest peak, Monte Cervati (1900m), and beyond to the regional border with Basilicata, the Parco Nazionale del Cilento e Vallo di Diano is Italy's second-largest national park. A little-explored area of barren heights and empty valleys, it's the perfect antidote to the holiday mayhem on the coast. To get the best out of it, you will, however, need a car – either that or unlimited patience and a masterful grasp of local bus timetables.

For further information stop by the tourist office in Paestum. For guided hiking opportunities, contact **Gruppo Escursionistico Trekking** (☑0975 7 25 86; www.getval lodidiano.it; Via Provinciale 29, Sassano) or **Associazione Trekking Cilento** (☑0974 84 33 45; www.trekkingcilento.it, in Italian; Via Cannetiello 6, Agropoli).

About 25km northeast of Paestum, the WWF **Oasi Naturalistica di Persano** (☑0828 97 46 84; persano@wwf.it; ☺9am-5pm Wed, Sat & Sun Jun-Sep, 10am-3pm Wed, Sat & Sun Oct-May) covers 110 hectares of wetlands on the river Sele. A favourite of ornithologists, it's home to a wide variety of birds, both resident and seasonal. Signs direct you there from the SS18. Visits should be booked a day in advance. Guided tours should be booked two days ahead.

There are also two cave systems worth exploring. Located about 20km northeast of Paestum, the **Grotte di Castelcivita** (☑0828 77 23 97; www.grottedicastelcivita. com; Castelcivita; admission €10; ☺tours 6 daily mid-Mar–Sep, 4 daily Oct–mid-Mar) complex is where Spartacus is said to have taken refuge following his slave rebellion in 71 BC. There are longer 3½ hour tours (€25) between June and September, when the water deep within the cave complex has dried up. Hard hats and a certain level of fitness and mobility are required. Visits should be booked a day in advance.

There is a **De Rosa** (☑0828 94 10 65) bus that departs from Capaccio (6km east of Paestum) at 9.20am and a return service departing Castelcivita at 3.20pm, Monday to Saturday. A one-way ticket costs €2.50.

By car take the SS18 from Paestum towards Salerno and follow the signs.

On the eastern edge of the park, the **Grotte dell'Angelo Pertosa** (☑0975 39 70 37; www.grottedipertosa.it; Pertosa; tours €10; ☺9am-7pm Mar-Oct, 10am-4pm Nov-Feb) is a 2.5km-long system bristling with stalactites and stalagmites. Although SITA buses from Salerno to Pertosa (€5) run Monday to Saturday, their inconvenient running times make the possibility of a day trip redundant. By car take the A3 southbound from Salerno, exit at Petina and follow the SS19 for 9km.

Continuing south on the A3 autostrada, **Padula** harbours one of the region's hidden jewels, the magnificent **Certosa di San Lorenzo** (☑0975 7 77 45; Viale Certosa, Padula; admission €4; ☺9am-7pm Wed-Mon). Also known as the Certosa di Padula, this is one of Europe's biggest monasteries, with a huge central courtyard, wood-panelled library and sumptuously frescoed chapels. Begun in the 14th century and modified over time, it was abandoned in the 19th century, then suffered further degradation as a children's holiday home and later a concentration camp.

Lamanna (☑0975 52 04 26) buses run four to six times daily from Salerno to Padula.

Puglia, Basilicata & Calabria

Best Places to Stay

» Sotto Le Cummerse (p109)

» Palazzo Rollo (p115)

» Locanda delle Donne Manache (p134)

» Truddhi (p109)

Best Places to Eat

» Cucina Casareccia (p116)

» La Locanda di Federico (p96)

» Il Frantoio (p112)

» Taverna Al Cantinone (p103)

Why Go?

Southern Italy is the Mezzogiorno (the land of the midday sun), which sums up the Mediterranean climate and the languid pace of life. From the heel to the toe of Italy's boot, the landscape reflects the individuality of its people. Puglia is the sophisticate of the south, with charming seaside villages along its 800km of coastline, lush flat farmlands, thick forests and olive groves. Basilicata is a crush of mountains and rolling hills with a dazzling stretch of coastline. Calabria is Italy's wildest area, with fine beaches and a mountainous landscape with many peaks crowned by ruined castles. The south's violent history of successive invasions and economic hardship has forged a fiercely proud people and influenced its distinctive culture and cuisine. A hotter, edgier place than the urbane north of Italy, this is an area that still feels like it has secret places to explore, although you will need your own wheels (and some Italian) if you plan to seriously sidestep from the beaten track.

When to Go

Bari

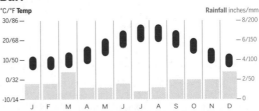

Apr-Jun Spring wildflowers are blooming: the perfect time for hiking in the mountains.

Jul & Aug Summer is beach weather and party time, with festivals, concerts and events.

Sep & Oct No crowds, mild weather and wild mushrooms galore.

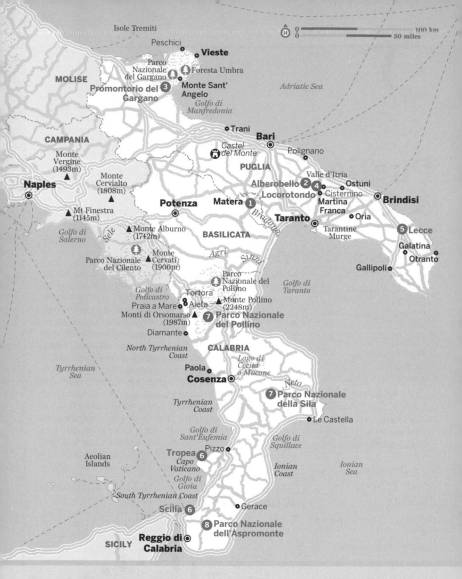

Puglia, Basilicata & Calabria Highlights

1 Marvel at the otherworldly *sassi* (former cave dwellings) of **Matera** (p127)

2 Dip into the Disney-style scenario of the gnome-size *trulli* dwellings in **Alberobello** (p108)

3 Hike in shady forests and swim in aqua blue seas in the **Promontorio del Gargano** (p102)

4 Stroll through the old centre of **Locorotondo** (p109), one of Puglia's prettiest towns

5 Wonder at ornate baroque facades in **Lecce** (p113)

6 Discover Calabria's picturesque seaside villages of **Tropea** (p146) and **Scilla** (p146)

7 Vanish into the vast hills of the **Parco Nazionale della Sila** (p140) or the **Parco Nazionale del Pollino** (p138)

8 Drive or trek into the wilds of the mysterious **Parco Nazionale dell'Aspromonte** (p142)

PUGLIA

Puglia is sun-bleached landscapes, silver olive groves, seascapes, and hilltop and coastal towns. It is a lush, largely flat farming region, skirted by a long coast that alternates between glittering limestone precipices and long sandy beaches. The heel of Italy juts into the Adriatic and Ionian Seas and the waters of both are stunningly beautiful, sometimes a translucent emerald green and sometimes a dusky powder blue. Its extensive coastline bears the marks of many conquering invaders: the Normans, the Spanish, the Turks, the Swabians and the Greeks. Yet, despite its diverse influences, Puglia is authentic.

In a land where the cuisine is all-important, Puglia's *cucina povera* (poor man's cuisine) is legendary. Olive oil, grapes, tomatoes, eggplants, artichokes, peppers, salami, mushrooms, olives and fresh seafood strain its table. Although it boasts some of Italy's best food and wines, in some places it's rare to hear a foreign voice. But in July and August Puglia becomes a huge party, with *sagre* (festivals, usually involving food), concerts and events, and thousands of Italian tourists heading down here for their annual break.

History

At times Puglia feels Greek – and for good reason. This tangible legacy dates from when the Greeks founded a string of settlements along the Ionian coast in the 8th century BC. A form of Greek dialect (Griko) is still spoken in some towns southeast of Lecce. Historically, their major city was Taras (Taranto), settled by Spartan exiles who dominated until they were defeated by the Romans in 272 BC.

The long coastline made the region vulnerable to conquest. The Normans left their fine Romanesque churches, the Swabians their fortifications and the Spanish their flamboyant baroque buildings. No one, however, knows exactly the origins of the extraordinary 16th-century, conical-roofed stone houses, the *trulli*, unique to Puglia.

Apart from invaders and pirates, malaria was long the greatest scourge of the south, forcing many towns to build away from the coast and into the hills. After Mussolini's seizure of power in 1922, the south became the frontline in his 'Battle for Wheat'. This initiative was aimed at making Italy self-sufficient when it came to food, following the sanctions imposed on the country after its conquest of Ethiopia. Puglia is now covered in wheat fields, olive groves and fruit arbours.

Bari

POP 320,150

Once regarded as the Bronx of southern Italy, Bari's reputation has gradually improved and the city, Puglia's capital and one of the south's most prosperous, deserves more than a cursory glance. Spruced up and rejuvenated, Bari Vecchia, the historic old town, is an interesting and atmospheric warren of streets. In the evenings the piazzas buzz with trendy restaurants and bars, but there are still parts of the old town that carry a gritty undertone.

Dangers & Annoyances

Petty crime can be a problem, so take all the usual precautions: don't leave anything in your car; don't display money or valuables; and watch out for bag-snatchers on scooters. Be careful in Bari Vecchia's dark streets at night.

◉ Sights

Most sights are in or near atmospheric Bari Vecchia, a medieval labyrinth of tight alleyways and graceful piazzas, which fills a small peninsula between the new port to the west and the old port to the southeast; it crams in 40 churches and more than 120 shrines.

Castello Svevo   CASTLE
(Swabian Castle; ☑083 184 00 09; Piazza Federico II di Svevia; admission adult/reduced €2/1; ⊗8.30am-7.30pm Thu-Tue) The Normans originally built over the ruins of a Roman fort, then Frederick II built over the Norman castle, incorporating it into his design – the two towers of the Norman structure still stand. The bastions, with corner towers overhanging the moat, were added in the 16th century during Spanish rule, when the castle was a magnificent residence.

Basilica di San Nicola   BASILICA
(Piazza San Nicola; www.basilicasannicola.it; ⊗7am-1pm & 4-7pm Mon-Sat, 7am-1pm & 4-9pm Sun) One of the south's first Norman churches, the basilica is a splendid example of Puglian-Romanesque style, built to house the relics of St Nicholas (better known as Father Christmas), which were

Puglia

100 km
50 miles

Ionian Sea

Otranto

Lecce
Galatina
Gallipoli
Santa Maria di Leuca

Brindisi

Ostuni
Martina Franca
Oria
Taranto
SS7
Tarantine Murge
Reserva Marina Porto Cesareo

SS379
Cisternino
Metaponto
Golfo di Taranto

Adriatic Sea

Castellana Grotte
Valle d'Itria
Alberobello
Locorotondo
SS100
SS106
SS7
SS599
Matera
SS407
Bradano
Basento
Carone
Parco Nazionale del Pollino

Polignano a Mare
SS16 a Mare
Grotte di Castellana
SS596
Bari
A14
PUGLIA
Castel del Monte
Venosa
Sauro
Agri
BASILICATA
SS598
Potenza
Sinni
Monti di Orsomarso (1987m)

Trani
Golfo di Manfredonia
Manfredonia
Monte Sant' Angelo

Rodi
Garganico Peschici La Salata
Vieste
Villaggio Umbra
Parco Nazionale del Gargano

Isole Tremiti

Foggia
SS655
Cervaro
A14
SS16
San Severo
Lucera
SS17
A16
Carapelle

Sapri
Golfo di Policastro
SS18
Parco Nazionale del Cilento e Vallo di Diano
A3
Sale
CAMPANIA

Fortore
Cigno
Parco Nazionale della Majella
MOLISE
SS87
Campobasso
SS647
SS587
Benevento
SS587
SS7
Caserta
Naples
Golfo di Napoli
Amalfi Coast
Salerno
Golfo di Salerno
Tyrrhenian Sea

Trigno
Passo San Leonardo
Parco Nazionale d'Abruzzo, Lazio e Molise
Santo
Isernia
SS650
SS647
ABRUZZO
Sulmona
LAZIO
Volturno

Golfo di Gaeta

Ferries to Civitavecchia & Naples

stolen from Turkey in 1087 by local fishermen. His remains are said to emanate a miraculous manna liquid with special powers. For this reason – and because he is also the patron saint of prisoners and children – the basilica remains an important place of pilgrimage. The interior is huge and simple with a decorative 17th-century wooden ceiling. The magnificent 13th-century ciborium over the altar is Puglia's oldest. The shrine in the crypt, lit by hanging lamps, is beautiful.

Cathedral CATHEDRAL
(Piazza Odegitria; ⊘8am-12.30pm & 4-7.30pm Mon-Fri, 8am-12.30pm & 5-8.30pm Sat & Sun). Built over the original Byzantine church, the 11th-century Romanesque cathedral retains its basilica plan and Eastern-style cupola. The plain walls are punctuated with deep arcades and the eastern window is a tangle of plant and animal motifs.

Piazza Mercantile PIAZZA
This beautiful piazza is fronted by the **Sedile**, the headquarters of Bari's Council of Nobles. In the square's northeast corner is the **Colonna della Giustizia** (Column of Justice), where debtors were once tied and whipped.

✿✿ Festivals

Festa di San Nicola RELIGIOUS
The Festival of St Nicholas, held around 7 to 9 May, is Bari's biggest annual shindig, celebrating the 11th-century arrival of St Nicholas' relics from Turkey. On the first evening a procession leaves Castello Svevo for the Basilica di San Nicola. The next day a fleet of boats carries the statue of St Nicholas along the coast and the evening ends with a massive fireworks competition.

🛏 Sleeping

Accommodation here tends to be bland and overpriced, aimed at business clientele.

B&B Casa Pimpolini B&B €
(☑080 521 99 38; www.casapimpolini.com; Via Calefati 249; s/d €60/80; ✳ @) This lovely B&B in the new town is within easy walking distance to shops, restaurants and Bari Vecchia. The rooms are warm and welcoming, and the home-made breakfast a treat. Great value.

Hotel Adria HOTEL €€
(☑080 524 66 99; www.adriahotelbari.com; Via Zuppetta 10; s/d €70/110; P✳@) A dusky-pink building fronted by wrought-iron balconies, this is a good choice near the train station. Rooms are comfortable, bright and modern.

PUGLIA, BASILICATA & CALABRIA BARI

PUGLIA ON YOUR PLATE

Puglia is home to Italy's most uncorrupted, brawniest, least-known vernacular cuisine. It has evolved from *cucina povera* – literally 'cooking of the poor' or peasant cooking: think of pasta made without eggs and dishes prepared with wild greens gathered from the fields.

Most of Italy's fish is caught off the Puglian coast, 80% of Europe's pasta is produced here and 80% of Italy's olive oil originates in Puglia and Calabria. Tomatoes, broccoli, chicory, fennel, figs, melons, cherries and grapes are all plentiful in season and taste better than anywhere else. Almonds, grown near Ruvo di Puglia, are packed into many traditional cakes and pastries, which used to be eaten only by the privileged.

Like their Greek forebears, the Pugliese eat *agnello* (lamb) and *capretto* (kid). *Cavallo* (horse) has only recently galloped to the table, while *trippa* (tripe) is another mainstay. Meat is usually roasted or grilled with aromatic herbs or served in tomato-based sauces.

Raw fish (such as anchovies or baby squid) are marinated in olive oil and lemon juice. *Cozze* (mussels) are prepared in multitudinous ways, with garlic and breadcrumbs, or as *riso cozze patata*, baked with rice and potatoes – every area has its variations on this dish.

Bread and pasta are close to the Pugliese heart, with per-capita consumption at least double that of the USA. You'll find *orecchiette* (small ear-shaped pasta, often accompanied by a small rod-shaped variety, called *strascinati* or *cavatelli*), served with broccoli or *ragù* (meat and tomato sauce), generally topped by the pungent local cheese *ricotta forte*.

Previously known for quantity rather than quality, Pugliese wines are now developing apace. The best are produced in Salento (the Salice Salentino is one of the finest reds), in the *trulli* (conical houses) area around Locorotondo (famous for its white wine), around Cisternino (home of the fashionable heavy red Primitivo) and in the plains around Foggia and Lucera.

Palace Hotel HOTEL €€€
(☎080 521 65 51; www.dominahotels.com; Via Lombardi 13; s/d €195/260; Ⓟ✳@☎) A large, impersonal hotel, the Palace has classical rooms and a renowned rooftop restaurant, the Murat.

✗ Eating

TOP CHOICE **La Locanda di Federico** TRATTORIA €€
(☎080 522 77 05; www.lalocandadifederico.com; Piazza Mercantile 63-64; meals €30; ⓒlunch & dinner) With domed ceilings, archways and medieval-style artwork on the walls, this restaurant oozes atmosphere. The menu is typical Pugliese, the food delicious and the price reasonable. *Orecchiette con le cime di rape* ('little ears' pasta with turnip greens) is highly recommended.

Vini e Cucina OSTERIA €
(☎338 212 03 91; Strada Vallisa 23; meals €10; ⓒlunch & dinner) Run by the same family for more than a century, this boisterous *osteria* chalks up its daily specials of well-prepared and filling Pugliese dishes. Grab a seat in the brick-flanked tunnel of a dining room and wait (and wait) to be served by the one impressively indefatigable waiter.

Caffè Borghese CAFE €
(☎080 524 21 56; Corso Vittorio Emanuele II 22; dishes €6-10; ⓒ8am-2am Tue-Sun) You'll experience genuine hospitality and friendly service in this small cafe. Its understated charm and simple dishes will have you returning for breakfast, lunch and *aperitivi*.

Alberosole TRADITIONAL ITALIAN €€€
(☎080 523 54 46; www.alberosole.com; Corso Vittorio Emanuele II 13; meals €40; ⓒTue-Sun) Dine alongside bankers in Brioni suits at this elegant restaurant. The contemporary menu is complemented by a traditional dining room, complete with an old stone floor and cathedral ceiling. Highly recommended by locals.

▮ Drinking

Barcollo BAR
(☎080 521 38 89; Piazza Mercantile 69/70; cocktails €7; ⓒ8am-3am) Lounge on brilliant-red banquettes or sit outside on the twinkling square supping a cocktail and nibbling work-of-art hors d'oeuvres.

Ferrarese BAR
(☎392 074 44 74; Piazza Ferrarese 1) Overlooking the harbour on Piazza Ferrarese, this is a popular hang-out for university students.

▤ Shopping

Designer shops and the main Italian chains line Via Sparano da Bari, while delis and gourmet food shops are located throughout the city.

Il Salumaio FOOD
(☎080 521 93 45; www.ilsalumaio.it; Via Piccinni 168; ⓒ8.30am-2pm & 5.30-9.30pm Mon-Sat) Stop and savour the delicious scents of fine regional produce at this venerable delicatessen.

Enoteca de Pasquale WINE
(☎080 521 31 92; Via Marchese di Montrone 87; ⓒ8am-2pm & 4-8.30pm Mon-Sat) Stock up on Puglian wines.

❶ Information

From Piazza Aldo Moro, in front of the main train station, streets heading north will take you to Corso Vittorio Emanuele II, which separates the old and new parts of the city.

CTS (☎080 521 88 73; Via Garriba 65-67) Good for student travel and discount flights.

Hospital (☎080 559 11 11; Piazza Cesare)

Information kiosk (ⓒ9am-7pm May-Sep) In front of the train station in Piazza Aldo Moro.

Morfimare Travel Agency (☎080 578 98 26; www.morfimare.it; Corso de Tullio 36-40) Ferry bookings.

Police station (☎080 529 11 11; Via Murat 4)

Post office (Piazza Umberto 33/8)

Tourist office (☎080 990 93 41; www.viaggia reinpuglia.it; 1st fl, Piazza Moro 33a; ⓒ8.30am-1pm & 3-6pm Mon-Fri, 10am-1pm Sat)

❶ Getting There & Away

Air

Bari's Palese **airport** (☎080 580 03 58; www.aeroportidipuglia.it) is served by a host of international and budget airlines, including British Airways, Alitalia and Ryanair.

Pugliairbus (☎080 580 03 58; http://pugli airbus.aeroportidipuglia.it) connects the airports of Bari, Brindisi, Taranto and Foggia. It also has a service from Bari airport to Matera (€5, 1¼ hours, four daily), and to Vieste (€20, 3½ hours, four daily May to September).

Boat

Ferries run from Bari to Albania, Croatia, Greece and Montenegro. All boat companies have offices at the ferry terminal, accessible on bus 20 from the main train station. Fares vary considerably between companies and it's easier to book with a travel agent such as **Morfimare** (☎080 578 98 26; ☎ booking office 080 578 98 11; www.morfimare.it; Corso de Tullio 36-40).

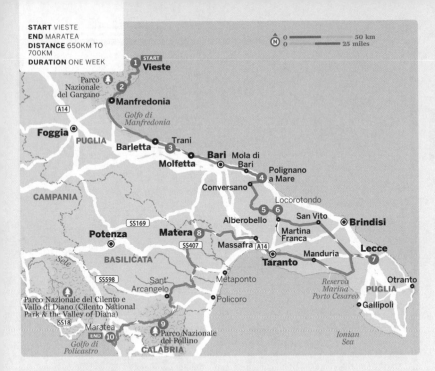

START VIESTE
END MARATEA
DISTANCE 650KM TO
700KM
DURATION ONE WEEK

Driving Tour
Italy's Authentic South

❯ Consider a gentle start in lovely, laid-back ① **Vieste** with its white sandy beaches and medieval backstreets, but set aside half a day to hike or bike in the lush green forests of the ② **Parco Nazionale del Gargano**. Follow the coast road past dramatic cliffs, salt lakes and flat farming land to ③ **Trani** with its impressive seafront cathedral and picturesque port. The next day, dip into pretty ④ **Polignano a Mare** with its dramatic location above the pounding surf before heading to ⑤ **Alberobello**, home to a dense neighbourhood of extraordinary cone-shaped stone homes called *trulli*. Shake your head in wonder and consider an overnight *trulli* stay.

Stroll around one of the most picturesque *centro storicos* (historic centres) in southern Italy at ⑥ **Locorotondo**. Hit the road and cruise on to a delightful gem of a city,

⑦ **Lecce**, where you can easily spend a full day exploring the sights, the shops and the flamboyant *palazzi* (mansions) and churches, including the **Basilica di Santa Croce**.

Day five will be one to remember. Nothing can prepare you for Basilicata's ⑧ **Matera**, where the *sassi* (former cave dwellings) are a dramatic, albeit harrowing, reminder of the town's poverty-stricken past. After days of pasta, *fave* beans and *cornetti* (Italian croissants), it's high time you laced up those hiking boots and checked out the trails and activities on offer in the spectacular ⑨ **Parco Nazionale del Pollino**. Finally, wind up the trip and soothe those aching muscles with a dip in the sea at postcard-pretty ⑩ **Maratea** with its surrounding seaside resorts, medieval village and cosmopolitan harbour offset by a thickly forested and mountainous interior.

Bari

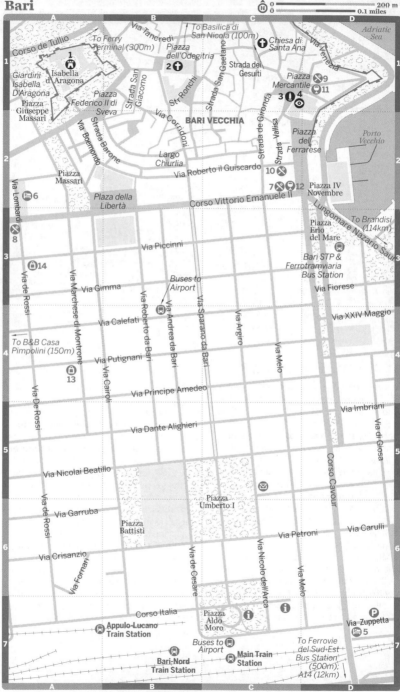

Bari

The main companies and their routes are as follows:

Agoudimos Lines (www.agoudimos-lines.com) To Cephalonia, Corfu and Igoumenista in Greece.

Jardolinija (www.jardolinija.hr) To Dubrovnik in Croatia.

Montenegro Lines (☎382 3031 1164; www.montenegrolines.net) To Bar in Montenegro; Cephalonia, Corfu and Igoumenista in Greece; and Durrës in Albania.

Superfast (☎080 528 28 28; www.superfast.com) To Corfu, Igoumenitsa and Patras in Greece. Departures at 7pm or 8pm depending on the route.

Ventouris Ferries (☎for Greece 080 521 76 99, for Albania 521 27 56; www.ventouris.gr) Regular ferries to Corfu and Igoumenitsa (Greece) and daily ferries to Durrës (Albania).

Bus

Intercity buses leave from three main locations. From Via Capruzzi, south of the main train station, **SITA** (☎080 579 01 11; www.sitabus.it, in Italian) covers local destinations. **Ferrovie Appulo-Lucane** (☎080 572 52 29; www.fal-srl.it, in Italian) buses serving Matera also depart from here, as do **Marozzi** (☎080 556 24 46; www.marozzivt.it) buses for Rome (€35, eight hours, eight daily; note that the overnight bus departs from Piazza Moro) and other long-distance destinations.

Piazza Eroi del Mare is the terminal for **STP** (☎080 505 82 80; www.stpspa.it) buses

serving Trani (€2.95, 45 minutes, frequent). **Ferrotramviaria** (☎080 529 93 52; www.ferrovienordbarese.it) runs frequent buses to Andria (€3.90, one hour) and Ruvo di Puglia (€2.60, 40 minutes).

Buses operated by **Ferrovie del Sud-Est** (FSE; ☎080 546 21 11; www.fseonline.it in Italian) leave from Largo Ciaia, south of Piazza Aldo Moro.

Alberobello €3.90, 1¼ hours; continues to Locorotondo and Martina Franca

Brindisi €7.70, 23 to 24 hours, four daily Monday to Saturday

Grotte di Castellana €2.90, one hour, five daily

Ostuni €5.20, two hours, four daily

Taranto €5.80, 1¾ to 2¼ hours, frequent

Train

A web of train lines spreads out from Bari. Note that there are fewer services on the weekend.

From the **main train station** (☎080 524 43 86) trains go to Puglia and beyond:

Brindisi From €15, one hour

Foggia From €18, one hour

Milan From €85, about eight hours

Rome From €51, four hours

Ferrovie Appulo-Lucane (☎080 572 52 29; www.fal-srl.it) serves two main destinations:

Matera €4.50, 1½ hours, 12 daily

Potenza €9.70, four hours, four daily

FSE trains (☎080 546 21 11; www.fseonline.it, in Italian) leave from the station in Via Oberdan: cross under the train tracks south of Piazza Luigi di Savoia and head east along Via Capruzzi for about 500m. They serve the following towns:

Alberobello €4.50, 1½ hours, hourly

Martina Franca €5.20, two hours, hourly

Taranto From €7.70, 2½ hours, nine daily

ⓘ Getting Around

Central Bari is compact – a 15-minute walk will take you from Piazza Aldo Moro to the old town. For the ferry terminal take bus 20 from Piazza Moro (€1.50).

To/From the Airport

For the airport, take the Tempesta shuttle bus (€4.14, 30 minutes, hourly) from the main train station, with pick-ups at Piazza Garibaldi and the corner of Via Andrea da Bari and Via Calefati. A taxi trip from the airport to town costs around €24.

Ferrovia Bari-Nord (☎080 529 93 52; www.ferrovianordbarese.it) has frequent train services to the airport (€1.10, 10 minutes).

ⓘ TRAVELLING EAST

Puglia is the main jumping-off point for onward travel to Greece, Croatia and Albania. The two main ports are Bari and Brindisi, from where you catch ferries to Vlore in Albania, Bar in Montenegro, and Cephalonia, Corfu, Igoumenista and Patras in Greece. Fares from Bari to Greece are generally more expensive than those from Brindisi. Taxes are usually from €9 to €12 per person and car. High season is generally the months of July and August, with reduced services in low season. Tariffs can be up to one-third cheaper in low season.

Car & Motorcycle

Street parking is migraine inducing. There's a large parking area (€1) south of the main port entrance; otherwise, there's a large multistorey car park between the main train station and the FSE station. Another car park is on Via Zuppetta opposite Hotel Adria.

Around Bari

TRANI
POP 53,860

The Terra di Bari, or (land of Bari) surrounding the capital is rich in olive groves and orchards, and the region has an impressive architectural history with some magnificent cathedrals, an extensive network of castles along its coastline, charming seaside towns like Trani and Polignano a Mare, and the mysterious inland Castel del Monte.

Known as the 'Pearl of Puglia', beautiful Trani has a sophisticated feel, particularly in summer when well-heeled visitors pack the diminutive array of marina-side bars. The marina is the place to promenade and watch the white yachts and fishing boats in the harbour, while the historic centre, with its medieval churches, glossy limestone streets and faded yet charming *palazzo* is an enchanting area to explore. But it's the cathedral, white against the deep blue sea, that is the town's most arresting sight.

◉ Sights

Cathedral CATHEDRAL
(Piazza del Duomo; ◈9am-12.30pm & 3-6.30pm) The dramatic seafront cathedral is dedicated to St Nicholas the Pilgrim, famous for being foolish. The Greek Christian wandered through Puglia, crying '*Kyrie eleison*' (Greek

for 'Lord, have mercy'). First thought to be a simpleton, he was revered after his death (aged 19) after several miracles attributed to him occurred. The cathedral was started in 1097 on the site of a Byzantine church and completed in the 13th century. The magnificent original bronze doors (now displayed inside) were cast by Barisano da Trani, an accomplished 12th-century artisan.

The interior of the cathedral reflects typical Norman simplicity and is lined by colonnades. Near the main altar are the remains of a 12th-century floor mosaic, stylistically similar to that in Otranto. Below the church is the crypt, a forest of ancient columns where the bones of St Nicholas are kept beneath the altar. You can also visit the **campanile** (admission €3).

Castle CASTLE
(☎0883 50 66 03; www.castelloditrani.beniculturali.it; Piazza Manfredi 16; admission €2; ◈8.30am-7.30pm) Two hundred metres north of the cathedral is Trani's other major landmark, the vast, almost modernist Swabian castle built by Frederick II in 1233. Charles V later strengthened the fortifications; it was used as a prison from 1844 to 1974.

Ognissanti Church CHURCH
(Via Ognissanti; ◈hours vary) Built by the Knights Templar in the 12th century, it was here that Norman knights swore allegiance to Bohemond I of Antioch, their leader, before setting off on the First Crusade.

Scolanova Church CHURCH
(☎0883 48 17 99; Via Scolanova 23; ◈hours vary) This church was one of four former synagogues in the ancient Jewish quarter, all of which were converted to churches in the 14th century. Inside is a beautiful Byzantine painting of Madonna dei Martiri.

⛌ Sleeping

Albergo Lucy HOTEL €
(☎0883 48 10 22; www.albergolucy.com; Piazza Plebiscito 11; d/tr/q €65/85/105; ✿) In a restored 17th-century *palazzo* overlooking a leafy square and close to the shimmering port, this family-run place oozes charm. Bike hire and guided tours available. Great value.

B&B Centro Storico Trani B&B €
(☎0883 50 61 76; www.bbtrani.it; Via Leopardi 28; s €35-50, d €50-70) This old-fashioned B&B in an old backstreet monastery is run by an elderly couple. It's basic, but rooms are large and 'Mama' makes a mean *crostata* (jam tart).

Hotel Regia
HOTEL €€

(☑0883 58 44 44; www.hotelregia.it; Piazza del Duomo 2; s €120-130, d €130-150; ✱🖥🌐) A lone building facing the cathedral, the understated grandeur of 18th-century Palazzo Filisio houses a charming hotel. Rooms are sober and stylish.

✖️ Eating

U'Vrascir
TRATTORIA €

(☑0883 49 18 40; www.uvrascir.it; Piazza Cesare Battisti 9; meals €25; ⊘Wed-Mon) With a cosy atmosphere, friendly service, and a menu written in dialect, this inviting trattoria and pizzeria is sure to satisfy. Good value.

Corteinfiore
SEAFOOD €€

(☑0883 50 84 02; www.corteinfiore.it; Via Ognissanti 18; meals €30; ⊘Tue-Sun) Romantic, urbane, and refined. The wooden decking, buttercup-yellow tablecloths and marquee-conservatory setting is refreshing. The wines are excellent and the cooking delicious.

La Darsena
SEAFOOD €€

(☑0883 48 73 33; Via Statuti Marittimi 98; meals €30; ⊘Tue-Sun) Renowned for its seafood, La Darsena is housed in a waterfront *palazzo*. Outside tables overlook the port while inside photos of old Puglia cover the walls beneath a huge wrought-iron dragon chandelier.

❶ Information

From the train station, Via Cavour leads through Piazza della Repubblica to Piazza Plebiscito and the public gardens. Turn left for the harbour and cathedral.

The **tourist office** (☑0883 58 88 30; www.traniweb.it; 1st fl, Palazzo Palmieri, Piazza Trieste 10; ⊘8.30am-1.30pm Mon-Fri, plus 3.30-5.30pm Tue & Thu) is 200m south of the cathedral.

❶ Getting There & Away

STP (☑0883 49 18 00; www.stpspa.it) has frequent services to Bari (€2.95, 45 minutes). Services depart from **Bar Stazione** (Piazza XX Settembre 23), which also has timetables and tickets.

Trani is on the main train line between Bari (€4.40, 40 to 60 minutes, frequent) and Foggia (€9.50, one hour, frequent).

CASTEL DEL MONTE

You'll see **Castel del Monte** (☑0883 56 99 97; www.casteldelmonte.beniculturali.it; admission adult/reduced €5/2.50; ⊘9am-6pm Oct-Feb, 10.15am-7.45pm Mar-Sep), an unearthly geometric shape on a hilltop, from miles away. Mysterious and perfectly octagonal, it's one

of southern Italy's most talked-about landmarks and a Unesco World Heritage Site.

No-one knows why Frederick II built it. Nobody has ever lived here – note the lack of kitchens – and there's no nearby town or strategic crossroads. It was not built to defend anything, as it has no moat or drawbridge, no arrow slits, and no trapdoors for pouring boiling oil on invaders.

Some theories claim that, according to mid-13th-century beliefs in geometric symbolism, the octagon represented the union of the circle and square, of God-perfection (the infinite) and human-perfection (the finite). The castle was therefore nothing less than a celebration of the relationship between humanity and God.

The castle has eight octagonal towers. Its interconnecting rooms have decorative marble columns and fireplaces, and the doorways and windows are framed in coral-lite stone. Many of the towers have washing rooms – Frederick II, like the Arab world he admired, set great store by cleanliness.

It's difficult to get here by public transport. By car, it's about 35km from Trani.

POLIGNANO A MARE

Dip into this spectacularly positioned small town if you can. Located around 34km south of Bari on the S16 coastal road, Polignano a Mare is built on the edge of a craggy ravine pockmarked with caves.

On Sunday the *logge* (balconies) are crowded with day trippers from Bari who come here to view the crashing waves, visit the caves and crowd out the *cornetterias* (shops specialising in Italian croissants) in the atmospheric *centro storico*. The town is thought to be one of the most important ancient settlements in Puglia and was later inhabited by successive invaders ranging from the Huns to the Normans. There are several baroque churches, an imposing Norman monastery and the medieval **Porta Grande**, the only access to the historic centre until the 18th century. You can still see the holes that activated the heavy drawbridge and the openings from where boiling oil was poured onto any unwelcome visitors to town.

Several operators organise boat trips to the grottoes, including **Dorino** (☑329 646 59 04), costing around €20 per person.

La Balconata (☑080 424 17 12; Vico Lapergola 10; meals €16; ⊘lunch & dinner) has the best position on a balcony overlooking the sea. It's a restaurant, pizzeria, sandwich bar and gelateria all in one.

LUCERA

Lovely Lucera has one of Puglia's most impressive castles, a handsome old town centre with mellow sand-coloured brick and stone work, and chic shops lining wide, shiny stone streets. Founded by the Romans in the 4th century BC, it was abandoned by the 13th century. Following excommunication by Pope Gregory IX, Frederick II decided to bolster his support base in Puglia by importing 20,000 Sicilian Arabs, simultaneously diminishing the headache Arab bandits were causing him in Sicily. It was an extraordinary move by the Christian monarch, even more so because Frederick allowed Lucera's new Muslim inhabitants the freedom to build mosques and practise their religion a mere 290km from Rome. History, however, was less kind; when the town was taken by the rabidly Christian Angevins in 1269, every Muslim who failed to convert was slaughtered.

Frederick II's enormous **castle** (admission free; ⊙9am-2pm year-round & 3-7pm Apr-Sep), shows just what a big fish Lucera once was in the Puglian pond. Built in 1233, it's 14km northwest of the town on a rocky hillock surrounded by a perfect 1km pentagonal wall, guarded by 24 towers.

On the site of Lucera's Great Mosque, Puglia's only Gothic **cathedral** (⊙8am-noon & 4-7pm May-Sep, 5-8pm Oct-Apr) was built in 1301 by Charles II of Anjou. The altar was once the castle banqueting table.

Dominated by a huge rose window, the contemporaneous Gothic **Chiesa di San Francesco** (⊙8am-noon & 4-7pm) incorporates recycled materials from Lucera's 1st-century-BC **Roman amphitheatre** (admission free; ⊙9am-2pm & 3.15-6.45pm Tue-Sun Apr-Sep). The amphitheatre was built for gladiatorial combat and accommodated up to 18,000 people.

The **tourist office** (⊘0881 52 27 62; ⊙9am-2pm & 3-8pm Tue-Sun Apr-Sep, 9am-2pm Oct-Mar) is near the cathedral.

Ferrovie del Gargano trains run to Lucera from Foggia (€1.30, 20 minutes, three daily), which is on the east coast train line between Bari and Pescara.

Although there is a twice-daily bus service from Bari, your own car is the best way to reach Polignano.

Promontorio del Gargano

The coast surrounding the promontory seems permanently bathed in a pink-hued, pearly light, providing a painterly contrast to the sea, which softens from intense to powder blue as the evening draws in. It's one of Italy's most beautiful areas, encompassing white limestone cliffs, fairy-tale grottoes, sparkling sea, ancient forests and tangled, fragrant maquis. Once connected to what is now Dalmatia (in Croatia), the 'spur' of the Italian boot has more in common with the land mass across the sea than with the rest of Italy. Creeping urbanisation was halted in 1991 by the creation of the **Parco Nazionale del Gargano**. Aside from its magnificent national park, the Gargano is home to pilgrimage sites and the lovely seaside towns of Vieste and Peschici.

Along the coast you'll spot strange cat's-cradle wood-and-rope arrangements, unique to the area. These are *trabucchi,* ancient fishing traps (possibly Phoenician in origin) from which fishermen cast their nets, 'walk the plank', and haul in their catch.

VIESTE
POP 13,890

Vieste is an attractive whitewashed town jutting off the Gargano's easternmost promontory into the Adriatic Sea. It's the Gargano capital and sits above the area's most spectacular beach, a gleaming wide strip backed by sheer white cliffs and overshadowed by the towering rock monolith, Scoglio di Pizzomunno. It's packed in summer and ghostly quiet in winter.

⊙ Sights

Vieste is primarily a beach resort. The **castle** built by Frederick II is occupied by the military and closed to the public.

Chianca Amara
HISTORICAL SITE

(Bitter Stone; Via Cimaglia) Vieste's most gruesome sight is this stone where thousands were beheaded when Turks sacked Vieste in the 16th century.

FREE **Museo Malacologico**
MUSEUM

(☎0884 70 76 88; Via Pola 8; ⊙9.30am-12.30pm & 4.30-9pm) This impressive shell museum has four rooms of fossils and molluscs, some enormous and all beautifully patterned and coloured.

Cathedral
CATHEDRAL

(Via Duomo) Built by the Normans on the ruins of a Vesta temple, the cathedral is in Puglian-Romanesque style with a fanciful tower that resembles a cardinal's hat. It was rebuilt in 1800.

La Salata
HISTORICAL SITE

(admission adult/child €4/free; ⊙5.30-6.15pm Jun-Aug, 4-4.45pm Sep, Oct-May on request) Dating from the 4th to 6th centuries AD, this paleo-Christian graveyard is 9km out of town. Inside the cave, tier upon tier of narrow tombs are cut into the rock wall; others form shallow niches in the cave floor. Guided tours are essential. Book with **Agenzia Sinergie** (☎338 840 62 15; www.agenziasinergie.it), which can also arrange customised tours of the Gargano.

Activities

Superb sandy beaches surround the town: in the south are Spiaggia del Castello, Cala San Felice and Cala Sanguinaria; due north, head for the area known as La Salata. Diving is popular around the promontory's rocky coastline, which is filled with marine grottoes.

From May to September fast boats zoom to the Isole Tremiti.

Boat hire and tours can be arranged at the port.

Centro Ormeggi e Sub
BOATING

(☎0884 70 79 83) Offers diving courses and rents out sailing boats and motorboats.

Tours

Agenzia Sol (☎0884 70 15 58; www.solvieste.it; Via Trepiccioni 5; ⊙9.20am-1.15pm & 5-9pm winter, to midnight in summer) organises hiking, cycling and jeep tours in the Foresta Umbra, as well as boat tours around the Gargano and gastronomic tours and small group tours into Puglia. It also sells bus tickets and ferry tickets for the Isole Tremiti.

Leonarda Motobarche
BOAT

(☎0884 70 13 17; www.motobarcheleonarda.it; per person €15; ⊙Apr-Sep) Boat tours of marine caves.

Sleeping

B&B Rocca sul Mare
B&B €

(☎0884 70 27 19; www.roccasul mare.it; Via Mafrolla 32; per person €25-70; ☎) In a former convent in the old quarter, this popular place has charm, with large, comfortable, high-ceilinged rooms. There's a vast rooftop terrace that offers panoramic views and a suite with a steam bath. Meals and bike hire available.

Hotel Seggio
HOTEL €€

(☎0884 70 81 23; www.hotelseggio.it; Via Veste 7; d €80-150; ⊙Apr-Oct; P🅿✳@🛜🏊) A butter-coloured *palazzo* in the town's historic centre with steps that spiral down to a pool and sunbathing terrace with a backdrop of the sea. The rooms are modern and plain but it's family run.

Campeggio Capo Vieste
CAMPGROUND €

(☎0884 70 63 26; www.capovieste.it; Litoranea Vieste–Peschici Km 8; camping 2 people, car & tent €33, 1-bedroom bungalows €77-164; ⊙Mar-Oct; 🏊) This tree-shaded campground is right by a sandy beach at La Salata, around 8km from Vieste and accessible by bus. Activities include tennis and a sailing school.

Eating

TOP CHOICE **Taverna Al Cantinone**
TRADITIONAL ITALIAN €€

(☎0884 70 77 53; Via Mafrolla 26; meals €25-30; ⊙lunch & dinner Wed-Mon) Run by a charming Italian-Spanish couple who have a passion for cooking; the food is exceptional and exquisitely presented. The menu changes with the seasons.

Osteria Al Duomo
OSTERIA €

(☎0884 70 82 43; www.osterialduomo.it; Via Alessandro III 23; meals €25; ⊙lunch & dinner Mar-Nov) Tucked away in a narrow alley in the heart of the old town, this *osteria* has a cosy cave interior and outdoor seating under a shady arbour. Homemade pastas with seafood sauces feature prominently.

Enoteca Vesta
TRADITIONAL ITALIAN €€

(☎0884 70 64 11; Via Duomo 14; meals €30-35) Housed in a cool vaulted cave, this place has a magnificent selection of Puglian wines to accompany the innovative seafood dishes on offer.

Information

Post office (Via Vittorio Veneto)

Tourist office (☎0884 70 88 06; Piazza Kennedy; ☺8am-8pm Jun-Sep, 8am-1.30pm Mon-Fri & 4-7pm Tue-Thu Oct-May)

Getting There & Around

BOAT Vieste's port is to the north, a five-minute walk from the tourist office. In summer, several companies, including **Navigazione Libera del Golfo** (☎0884 70 74 89; www.navlib.it), head to the Isole Tremiti. Tickets can be bought portside and there are several daily boats (€16.50 to €20, 1½ hours).

Several companies also offer tours of the caves which pock the Gargano coast – a three-hour tour costs around €13.

BUS From Piazzale Manzoni, where intercity buses terminate, a 10-minute walk east along Viale XXIV Maggio, which becomes Corso Fazzini, brings you into the old town and the Marina Piccola's attractive promenade. In summer, buses terminate at Via Verdi.

SITA (☎0881 35 20 11; www.sitabus.it) buses run between Vieste and Foggia (€6.50, 2¾ hours, four daily) via Manfredonia. There are also services to Monte Sant'Angelo (€4.90) via Manfredonia but **Ferrovie del Gargano** (☎0881 58 72 11; www.ferroviedelgargano.com) buses have a direct daily service to Monte Sant'Angelo (€5.80, two hours), and frequent services to Peschici (€1.60, 35 minutes).

From May to September, **Pugliairbus** (☎080 580 03 58; pugliairbus.aeroportidipuglia.it) runs a service to the Promontorio del Gargano, including Vieste, from Bari airport (€20, 3½ hours, four daily).

MONTE SANT'ANGELO
POP 13,250 / ELEV 796M

One of Europe's most important pilgrimage sites, this isolated mountaintop has an extraordinary atmosphere. Pilgrims have been coming here for centuries – and so have the hustlers, pushing everything from religious kitsch to parking spaces.

The object of devotion is the Santuario di San Michele. Here, in AD 490, St Michael the Archangel is said to have appeared in a grotto to the Bishop of Siponto. He left behind his scarlet cloak and instructions not to consecrate the site as he had already done so.

During the Middle Ages, the sanctuary marked the end of the Route of the Angel, which began in Mont St-Michel (in Normandy) and passed through Rome. In 999 the Holy Roman Emperor Otto III made a pilgrimage to the sanctuary to pray that prophecies about the end of the world in the year 1000 would not be fulfilled. His prayers were answered, the world staggered on and the sanctuary's fame grew.

Sights

The town's serpentine alleys and jumbled houses are perfect for a little aimless ambling. Look out for the different shaped *cappelletti* (chimney stacks) on top of the neat whitewashed houses.

PADRE PIO: SAINT OF THE GARGANO

Pilgrims flock to **San Giovanni Rotondo**, home of Padre Pio, a humble and pious Capuchin priest 'blessed' with the stigmata and a legendary ability to heal the sick. Pio (1887–1968) was canonised in 2002 and immortalised in the vast numbers of prefabricated statues to be found throughout the Gargano. There's even a statue of Pio beneath the waters off the Isole Tremiti.

The ailing Capuchin priest arrived in San Giovanni Rotondo, then a tiny isolated medieval village, in 1916. As Pio's fame grew, the town too underwent a miraculous transformation. These days it's a mass of functional hotels and restaurants catering to eight million pilgrims a year. It's all overlooked by the palatial Home for the Relief of Suffering, one of Italy's premier hospitals (established by Pio in 1947).

The **Convent of the Minor Capuchin Friars** (☎0882 41 71; www.conventopadrepio. com; Piazza Santa Maria delle Grazie) includes Padre Pio's **cell** (☺7am-7pm summer, 7.30am-6.30pm winter), a simple room containing mementoes such as his blood-stained socks. The **old church**, where he used to say Mass, dates from the 16th century. The spectacular **new church**, designed by Genovese Renzo Piano (who also designed Paris' Pompidou Centre), resembles a huge futuristic seashell, with an interior of bony vaulting. Padre Pio's body now lies in the geometric perfection of the semicircular crypt.

SITA buses run daily to San Giovanni Rotondo from Monte Sant'Angelo (€1.90, 50 minutes) and Vieste (€5.80, 2½ hours).

FREE Santuario di San Michele

RELIGIOUS SITE

(Via Reale Basilica; ⊙7.30am-7.30pm Jul-Sep, 7.30am-12.30pm & 2.30-7pm Apr-Jun & Oct, to 5pm Nov-Mar) Look for the 17th-century pilgrim's graffiti as you descend the steps. St Michael is said to have left a footprint in stone inside the grotto, so it became customary for pilgrims to carve outlines of their feet and hands. Etched Byzantine bronze and silver doors, cast in Constantinople in 1076, open into the grotto itself. Inside, a 16th-century statue of the archangel covers the site of St Michael's footprint.

Tomba di Rotari

HISTORICAL SITE

(admission €0.60; ⊙10am-1pm & 3-7pm Apr-Oct) A short flight of stairs opposite the sanctuary leads not to a tomb, but to a 12th-century baptistry with a deep sunken basin for total immersion. You enter the baptistry through the facade of the **Chiesa di San Pietro** with its intricate rose window squirming with serpents – all that remains of the church, destroyed in a 19th-century earthquake. The Romanesque portal of the adjacent 11th-century **Chiesa di Santa Maria Maggiore** has some fine bas-reliefs.

Castle

CASTLE

(Largo Roberto Giuscardo 2; admission €2; ⊙9.30am-1pm & 2.30-7pm) At the highest point is this rugged bijou, Norman castle with Swabian and Aragonese additions as well as panoramic views.

🛌 Sleeping & Eating

Hotel Michael

HOTEL €

(☑0884 56 55 19; www.hotelmichael.com; Via Basilica 86; s €50-60, d €70-80; 🖝) A small hotel with shuttered windows on the main street, across from the sanctuary, this traditional place has spacious rooms with extremely pink bedspreads. Ask for a room with a view.

Casa li Jalantuúmene

TRATTORIA €€

(☑0884 56 54 84; www.li-jalantuumene.it, in Italian; Piazza de Galganis 5; meals €40; ⊙lunch only Wed-Mon Feb-Dec) This renowned restaurant has an entertaining and eccentric chef, Gegè Mangano, and serves excellent fare. It's intimate, there's a select wine list and, in summer, tables spill into the piazza. Accommodation (doubles €80 to €110), decorated in traditional Pugliese-style, were soon to be available at the time of writing.

ⓘ Getting There & Away

SITA (☑0881 35 20 11; www.sitabus.it, in Italian) buses run from Foggia (€4.50, 1¾ hours, four daily) and Vieste via Manfredonia; Ferrovie del Gargano has a direct service from Vieste (€5.80, two hours, five daily). Buy your tickets from Bar Esperia next to the sanctuary.

PESCHICI

POP 4400

Perched above a turquoise sea and tempting beach, Peschici clings to the hilly, wooded coastline. It's a pretty resort area with a tight-knit old walled town of Arabesque whitewashed houses. The small town gets crammed in summer, so book in advance. Boats zip across to the Isole Tremiti in high season.

🛌 Sleeping & Eating

Locanda al Castello

B&B €

(☑0884 96 40 38; Via Castello 29; s €35-70, d €70-100; P❄🖝) Staying here is like entering a large, welcoming family home. It's by the cliffs with fantastic views. Enjoy hearty home cooking in the restaurant (meals €18).

Baia San Nicola

CAMPGROUND €

(☑0884 96 42 31; www.baiasannicola.it; camping €21.50-36.50, 2-person bungalow per week €320-360; ⊙mid-May–mid-Oct) The best campground in the area, 2km south of Peschici towards Vieste, Baia San Nicola is on a pine-shaded beach, offering camping, bungalows, apartments and myriad amenities.

Porto di Basso

SEAFOOD €€

(☑0884 91 53 64; www.portodibasso.it; Via Colombo 38; meals €30-40; ⊙Fri-Wed) Superb views of the ocean drop away from the floor-length windows beside the intimate alcove tables in this elegant clifftop restaurant. The menu of fresh local seafood changes daily. Close to the restaurant, two stylish suites with fantastic sea views were under construction at time of writing. When ready they should be the pick of Peschici's accommodation choices.

Il Trabucco da Mimi

SEAFOOD €€

(0884 96 25 56; Localita Punta San Nicola; meals €30-40; ⊙lunch & dinner Easter-Oct) For the ultimate in fresh fish you can't beat eating in a *trabucco,* the traditional wooden fishing platforms lining the coast. Watch the process in operation and dine on the catch. The decor is simple and rustic and you'll pay for the experience – but it's worth it.

CAMPING IN STYLE

If your experience of camping is the Boy Scout version of flapping tents, freezing nights and eating cold baked beans out of a tin, you will be delighted at the five-star quality of the typical campgrounds in this southern region of Italy. They are also prolific, particularly in and around the national parks. In the Gargano region alone there are an astonishing 100 campgrounds, compared to the relatively modest number of *pensioni* and hotels. If you don't fancy sleeping under canvas (or need a plug for those heated rollers) then consider a bungalow rental.

Virtually all these camping *villaggios* (villages) include well-furnished and equipped bungalows. This means you can really economise on eating out, as well as having the advantages of the campground facilities, which often include tennis courts, a swimming pool, a children's playground and small supermarket. Bungalows (normally only available for weeklong rentals) start from around €200/500 (low/high season) for a two-person bungalow or mobile-home rental. Traditional under-canvas campers can expect to pay a daily rate of approximately (low/high season) €15/25, which includes camping for two people, tent and car-parking space.

Check the following websites for more information and camping listings: www.camping.it; www.camping-italy.net and www.caravanandcampsites.eu.

ⓘ Information

Tourist office (☏0884 91 53 62; Via Magenta 3; ⊘8am-2pm & 5-9pm Mon-Fri summer, 8am-2pm Mon-Fri, 9am-noon & 4-7pm Sat winter).

ⓘ Getting There & Away

The bus terminal is beside the sportsground, uphill from the main street, Corso Garibaldi.

Ferrovie del Gargano (☏0881 58 72 11; www.ferroviedelgargano.com, in Italian) buses run frequent daily services between Peschici and Vieste (€1.60, 35 minutes).

From April to September, ferry companies including **MS&G Societá di Navigazione** (☏0884 96 27 32; www.msgnavigazioni.it; Corso Umberto I 20) and **Navigare SRL** (☏0884 96 42 34; Corso Garibaldi 30) serve the Isole Tremiti (adult €28 to €32, child €16 to €20, one to 1½ hours).

FORESTA UMBRA

The 'Forest of Shadows' is the Gargano's enchanted interior – thickets of tall, epic trees interspersed with picnic spots bathed in dappled light. It's the last remnant of Puglia's ancient forests: Aleppo pines, oaks, yews and beech trees shade the mountainous terrain. More than 65 different types of orchid have been discovered here; the wildlife includes roe deer, wild boar, foxes, badgers and the increasingly rare wild cat. Walkers and mountain bikers will find plenty of well-marked trails within the forest's 5790 sq km.

The small visitors centre in the middle of the forest houses a **museum and nature centre** (www.ecogargano.it; €1.20; ⊘9am-7pm mid-Apr–mid-Oct) with fossils, photographs and stuffed animals and birds. Half-day guided hikes (per person €10), bike hire (per hour/day €5/25) and walking maps (€2.50) are available.

Specialist tour operators organise hiking, biking and jeep excursions in the park. These include **Agenzia Sol** (☏0884 70 15 58; www.solvieste.it; Via Trepiccioni 5) and **Explora Gargano** (☏0884 70 22 37; www.exploragargano.it) in Vieste, and **Soc Cooperative Ecogargano** (☏0884 56 54 44) in Monte Sant'Angelo.

La Chiusa delle More (☏330 54 37 66; www.lachiusadellemore.it; Vallo dello Schiaffo; B&B per person €80-100; ⊘May-Sep; ⓟ❋⑈⑉) offers an escape from the cramped coast. An attractive stone-built *agriturismo* (farm stay) only 1.5km from Peschici, it's set in a huge olive grove. You can dine on home-grown produce, borrow mountain bikes and enjoy panoramic views from your poolside lounger. Note there is a three-night minimum stay.

Isole Tremiti

POP 500

This beautiful archipelago of three islands, 36km offshore, is a picturesque sight of raggedy cliffs, sandy coves and thick pine woods, surrounded by the glittering dark-blue sea.

Unfortunately the islands are no secret, and in July and August some 100,000 holidaymakers descend on the archipelago. At this time it's noisy, loud and hot. If you want to savour the islands' tranquillity visit during the shoulder season. In the low season most tourist facilities close down and the few permanent residents resume their quiet and isolated lives.

The islands' main facilities are on San Domino, the largest and lushest island, which was formerly used to grow crops. It's ringed by alternating sandy beaches and limestone cliffs, while the inland is covered in thick maquis flecked with rosemary and foxglove. The centre harbours a nondescript small town with several hotels.

Easily defended, the small San Nicola island is the traditional administrative centre – a castlelike cluster of medieval buildings rises up from the rocks. The third island, Capraia, is uninhabited.

Most boats arrive at San Domino. Small boats regularly make the brief crossing to San Nicola (€6 return) in high season; from October to March a single boat makes the trip after meeting the boat from the mainland.

◎ Sights & Activities

Head to **San Domino** for walks, grottoes and coves. It has a pristine, marvellous coastline and the islands' only sandy beach, **Cala delle Arene**. Alongside the beach is the small cove **Grotta dell'Arene**, with calm clear waters for swimming. You can also take a boat trip (€12 to €15 from the port) around the island to explore the grottoes: the largest, **Grotta del Bue Marino**, is 70m long. A tour around all three islands costs €15 to €17. Diving in the translucent sea is another option with **Tremiti Diving Center** (☑337 64 89 17; www.tremitidivingcenter.com; Via Federico 2, San Domino).

There's an undemanding, but enchanting, walking track around the island, starting at the far end of the village. Alternatively, you could hire wheels from **Jimmy Bike** (☑338 897 09 09; www.jimmybike.com; bicycle/scooter per day €20/50) at Piazzetta San Domino.

Medieval buildings thrust out of the rocky shores of **San Nicola**, the same pale-sand colour as the barren cliffs. In 1010, Benedictine monks founded the **Abbazia e Chiesa di Santa Maria** here; for the next 700 years the islands were ruled by a series of abbots who accumulated great wealth. Although the church retains a weather-worn Renaissance portal and a fine 11th-century floor mosaic, its other treasures have been stolen or destroyed throughout its troubled history. The only exceptions are a painted wooden

Byzantine crucifix brought to the island in AD 747 and a black Madonna, probably transported here from Constantinople in the Middle Ages.

There's no organised transport to **Capraia** (named after the wild caper plant), but trips can be negotiated with local fishermen. Birdlife is plentiful, with impressive flocks of seagulls.

🛌 Sleeping & Eating

In summer you'll need to book well ahead and many hotels insist on full board. Camping is forbidden.

La Casa di Gino   B&B €€
(☑0882 46 34 10; www.hotel-gabbiano.com; San Nicola; r €100-180; ✳) A tranquil accommodation choice on San Nicola, away from the frenzy of San Domino, this newly-opened B&B run by the Hotel Gabbiano has stylish white-on-white rooms.

Hotel Gabbiano   HOTEL €€
(☑0882 46 34 10; www.hotel-gabbiano.com; Piazza Belvedere, San Domino; s €45-105, d €90-210, incl breakfast; ✳🖥) An established icon on the island and run for more than 30 years by a Neapolitan family, this smart hotel has pastel-coloured rooms with balconies overlooking San Nicola and the sea. It also has a seafood restaurant.

Architiello   SEAFOOD €€
(☑0882 46 30 54; San Nicola; meals €25; ⊙Apr-Oct) A class act with a sea-view terrace, this specialises in – what else? – fresh fish.

❶ Getting There & Away

Boats for the Isole Tremiti depart from several points on the Italian mainland: Manfredonia, Vieste and Peschici in summer, and Termoli in nearby Molise year-round.

Valle d'Itria

Between the Ionian and Adriatic coasts rises the great limestone plateau of the Murgia (473m). It has a strange karst geology; the landscape is riddled with holes and ravines through which small streams and rivers gurgle, creating what is, in effect, a giant sponge. At the heart of the Murgia lies the idyllic Valle d'Itria. Here you will begin to spot curious circular stone-built houses dotting the countryside, their roofs tapering up to a stubby and endearing point. These are *trulli,* Puglia's unique rural architecture.

It's unclear why the architecture developed in this way; one popular story says that it was so the dry-stone constructions could be quickly dismantled, to avoid payment of building taxes.

The rolling green valley is criss-crossed by dry-stone walls, vineyards, almond and olive groves and winding country lanes. This is the part of Puglia that is most visited by foreign tourists and it is also the best served by hotels and luxury *masserias* (working farms). Around here are you will also find many of Puglia's self-catering villas; to find them, try websites such as www.tuscanynow.com, www.ownersdirect.co.uk, www.holidayhomesinitaly.co.uk and www.trulliland.com.

GROTTE DI CASTELLANA

Don't miss these spectacular limestone caves (☑800 231976, 080 499 82 11; www.grotte dicastellana.it; Piazzale Anelli; ☺9.30am-7pm Apr-Oct, to 12.30pm Nov-Mar), 40km southeast of Bari and Italy's longest natural subterranean network. The interlinked galleries, first discovered in 1938, contain an incredible range of underground landscapes, from extraordinary stalactite and stalagmite formations – look out for the jellyfish, the bacon and the stocking. The highlight is the Grotta Bianca (White Grotto), an eerie white alabaster cavern hung with stiletto-thin stalactites.

There are two tours in English: a 1km, 50-minute tour that doesn't include the Grotta Bianca (€10, on the half-hour); and a 3km, two-hour tour (€15, on the hour) that does include it. The temperature inside the cave averages 18°C so take a light jacket. Visit, too, the **Museo Speleologico Franco Anelli** (☑080 499 82 30; admission free; ☺9.30am-1pm & 3.30-6.30pm mid-Mar–Oct, 10am-1pm Nov–mid-Mar) or the **Osservatorio Astronomico Sirio** (☑080 499 82 11; admission €3), with its telescope and solar filters allowing for maximum solar-system visibility. Guided visits only with advance notification.

The grotto can be reached by rail from Bari on the FSE Bari-Taranto train line but not all trains stop at Grotte di Castellana. However, all services stop at Castellana Grotte (€2.90, 50 minutes, roughly hourly), 2km before the grotto, from where you can catch a local bus (€1) from the station to the caves.

ALBEROBELLO
POP 11,000

Unesco World Heritage site Alberobello resembles a mini urban sprawl – for gnomes. The Zona dei Trulli on the western hill of town is a dense mass of 1500 beehive-shaped houses, white-tipped as if dusted by snow. These dry-stone buildings are made from local limestone; none are older than the 14th century. Inhabitants do not wear pointy hats, but they do sell anything a visitor might want, from miniature *trulli* to woollen shawls.

The town is named after the primitive oak forest Arboris Belli (beautiful trees) that once covered this area. It's an amazing area, but is also something of a tourist trap – from May to October busloads of tourists pile into *trullo* homes, drink in *trullo* bars and shop in *trullo* shops.

◉ Sights

Alberobello spreads across two hills. The new town is perched on the eastern hilltop; the Zona dei Trulli lies on the western hill and consists of two adjacent neighbourhoods, the Rione Monti and the Rione Aia Piccola.

Sightseeing in Alberobello mainly consists of wandering around admiring its eccentricity. Within the old town quarter of **Rione Monti** over 1000 *trulli* cascade down the hillside, most of which are now souvenir shops. To its east, on the other side of Via Indipendenza, is **Rione Aia Piccola**. This neighbourhood is much less commercialised, with 400 *trulli,* many still used as family dwellings. You can climb up for a rooftop view at many shops, although most do have a strategically located basket for a donation.

In the modern part of town, the 18th-century **Trullo Sovrano** (☑080 432 60 30; www.trullosovrano.it; Piazza Sacramento; admission €1.50; ☺10am-6pm) is the only two-floor *trullo,* built by a wealthy priest's family. It's a small museum giving something of the atmosphere of *trullo* life, with sweet, rounded rooms which include a re-created bakery, bedroom and kitchen. The souvenir shop here has a wealth of literature on the town and surrounding area.

🛏 Sleeping

It's a unique experience to stay in your own *trullo,* though some people might find Alberobello too touristy to use as a base.

Trullidea
APARTMENT €€

(☎080 432 38 60; www.trullidea.it; Via Monte San Gabriele 1; 2-person trulli €63-149) A series of 15 renovated *trulli* in Alberobello's Zona dei Trulli, these are quaint, cosy and atmospheric. They're available on a self-catering, B&B, or half- or full-board basis.

Camping dei Trulli
CAMPGROUND €

(☎080 432 36 99; www.campingdeitrulli.com; Via Castellana Grotte, Km 1.5; camping 2 people, car & tent €30-40; ℗@⚕) This campground is 1.5km out of town and has some nice tent sites. It has a restaurant, market, two swimming pools, tennis courts and bicycle hire and you can also rent *trulli* off the grounds.

✖ Eating

Trattoria Amatulli
TRATTORIA €

(☎080 432 29 79; Via Garibaldi 13; meals €16; ⊙Tue-Sun) Excellent trattoria with a cheerily cluttered interior papered with photos of smiley diners, plus superb down-to-earth dishes like *orecchiette scure con cacioricotta pomodoro e rucola* ('little ears' pasta with cheese, tomato and rucola). Wash it down with the surprisingly drinkable house wine, costing the lordly sum of €4 a litre.

La Cantina
TRADITIONAL ITALIAN €

(☎080 432 34 73; www.ilristorantelacantina.it; cnr Corso Vittorio Emanuele & Vico Lippolis; meals €25; ⊙Wed-Mon) Although tourists have discovered this place, it has maintained the high standards established back in 1958. There are just seven tables and one frenetic waiter serving delicious meals made with fresh seasonal produce.

Il Poeta Contadino
TRADITIONAL ITALIAN €€€

(☎080 432 19 17; www.ilpoetacontadino.it; Via Indipendenza 21; meals €65; ⊙Tue-Sun Feb-Dec) The dining room here has a medieval banquet feel with its sumptuous decor and chandeliers. Dine on a poetic menu including the signature dish, fava bean purée with *cavatelli* (small rod-shaped pasta) and seafood.

❶ Information

If you park in Lago Martellotta, follow the steps up to the Piazza del Popolo where Belvedere Trulli offers fabulous views over the whole higgledy-piggledy picture. The **tourist office** (☎080 432 51 71; Via Garibaldi; ⊙8am-1pm Mon-Fri, plus 3-6pm Tue & Thu) is just off the main square. In the Zona dei Trulli is another **tourist information office** (☎080 432 28 22; www.prolocoalberobello.it; Monte Nero 1; ⊙9am-7.30pm).

❶ Getting There & Away

Alberobello is easily accessible from Bari (€4.10, 1½ hours, hourly) on the FSE Bari-Taranto train line. From the station, walk straight ahead along Via Mazzini, which becomes Via Garibaldi, to reach Piazza del Popolo.

LOCOROTONDO
POP 14,200

Locorotondo has an extraordinarily beautiful and whisper-quiet *centro storico,* where everything is shimmering white aside from the blood-red geraniums tumbling from the window boxes. Situated on a hilltop on the Murge Plateau, it's a *borghi più belli d'Italia* – that is, it's rated as one of the most beautiful towns in Italy (see www.borghitalia.it). The streets are paved with smooth ivory-coloured stones, with the church of **Santa Maria della Graecia** their sunbaked centrepiece.

From **Villa Comunale**, a public garden, you can enjoy panoramic views of the surrounding valley. You enter the historic quarter directly across from here.

Not only is this deepest *trulli* country, but it's also the liquid heart of the Puglian wine region. Sample some of the local Spumante at **Cantina del Locorotondo** (☎080 431 16 44; www.locorotondodoc.com; Via Madonna della Catena 99; ⊙9am-1pm & 3-7pm).

🛌 Sleeping

🔝TOP Sotto le Cummerse
APARTMENT €€

(☎080 431 32 98; www.sottolecummerse.it; Via Vittorio Veneto 138; apt €82-230 incl breakfast; ❄) As an *albergo diffuso* (diffused hotel), you stay in tastefully furnished apartments scattered throughout the *centro storico*. The apartments are traditional buildings that have been beautifully restored and furnished. Excellent value and a great base for exploring the region.

Truddhi
APARTMENT €€

(☎080 443 13 26; www.trulliresidence.it; C da Trito 292; d €65-80, apt €100-150, per week €450-741; ℗⚕) This charming cluster of 10 self-catering *trulli* in the hamlet of Trito near Locorotondo is surrounded by olive groves and vineyards. It's a tranquil place and you can take cooking courses (per day €80) with Mino, a lecturer in gastronomy.

✖ Eating

🔝TOP Quanto Basta
PIZZERIA €

(☎080 431 28 55; Via Morelli 12; pizza €6-7; ⊙dinner Tue-Sun) With its wooden tables, soft lighting and stone floors, this pizzeria is cosy and welcoming. The pizzas are delicious and the beer list extensive.

La Taverna del Duca TRATTORIA €€
(☑080 431 30 07; Via Papadotero 3; meals €35; ⓐlunch & dinner, closed Sun night in winter), In a narrow side street next to an ancient tunnel, this well-regarded trattoria serves local classics such as *orecchiette* with various vegetable sidekicks.

ⓘ Information
Tourist office (☑080 431 30 99; www.proloco locorotondo.it; Piazza Vittorio Emanuele 27; ⓐ10am-1pm & 3-6pm Mon-Fri, 10am-1pm Sat)

ⓘ Getting There & Away
Locorotondo is easily accessible via frequent trains from Bari (€4.50, 1½ to two hours) on the FSE Bari-Taranto train line.

CISTERNINO
POP 12,000
An appealing, whitewashed hilltop town, slow-paced Cisternino has a charming *centro storico* beyond its bland modern outskirts. Beside its 13th-century **Chiesa Matrice** and **Torre Civica** there's a pretty communal garden with rural views. If you take Via Basilioni next to the tower, you can amble along an elegant route right to the central piazza, Vittorio Emanuele.

Just outside the historic centre, the **tourist office** (☑080 444 66 61; www.prolococis ternino.it; Via San Quirico 18 ⓐ10.15am-12.15pm & 4.30-7.30pm Mon-Sat) can advise on B&Bs in the historic centre, but it's not always open.

Cisternino has a grand tradition of *fornello pronto* (ready-to-go roast or grilled meat) and in numerous butchers' shops and trattorias you can select a cut of meat, which is then promptly cooked on the spot. Try it under rustic whitewashed arches at **Trattoria La Botte** (☑080 444 78 50; Via Santa Lucia 47; meals €20; ⓐlunch & dinner, closed Thu in winter), which also serves up Pugliese favourites such as *fave e verdura* (beans and greens).

Cisternino is accessible by regular trains from Bari (€4.50, 45 minutes).

MARTINA FRANCA
POP 49,800
The old quarter of this town is a picturesque scene of winding alleys, blinding white houses and blood-red geraniums. There are graceful baroque and rococo buildings here too, plus airy piazzas and curlicue iron-work balconies that almost touch above the narrow streets. This town is the highest in the Murgia, and was founded in the 10th cen-

OUR TOP FIVE CENTRO STORICOS (HISTORIC CENTRES) IN PUGLIA
» Locorotondo (p109)
» Ostuni (p111)
» Vieste (p102)
» Martina Franca (p110)
» Lecce (p113)

tury by refugees fleeing the Arab invasion of Taranto. It only started to flourish in the 14th century when Philip of Anjou granted tax exemptions (*franchigie*, hence Franca); the town became so wealthy that a castle and defensive walls complete with 24 solid bastions were built.

ⓞ Sights & Activities
The beauty of Martina Franca is to wander around the *centro storico*'s narrow lanes and alleyways.

Passing under the baroque **Arco di Sant'Antonio** at the western end of pedestrianised Piazza XX Settembre, you emerge into Piazza Roma, dominated by the imposing, elegant 17th-century **Palazzo Ducale**, built over an ancient castle and now used as municipal offices.

From Piazza Roma, follow the fine Corso Vittorio Emanuele, with baroque town houses, to reach Piazza Plebiscito, the centre's baroque heart. The piazza is overlooked by the 18th-century **Basilica di San Martino**, its centrepiece city patron, St Martin, swinging a sword and sharing his cloak with a beggar.

Walkers can ask for the *Carta dei Sentieri del Bosco delle Pianelle* (free) from the tourist office, which maps out 10 walks in the nearby **Bosco delle Pianelle** (around 10km west of town). This lush woodland is part of the larger 1206-hectare **Riserva Naturale Regionale Orientata**, populated with lofty trees, wild orchids and a rich and varied birdlife with kestrels, owls, buzzards, hoopoe and sparrow hawks.

⚑ Festivals & Events
Festival della Valle d'Itria is an annual music festival (late July to early August) featuring international performances of opera, classical and jazz. For information, contact the **Centro Artistico Musicale Paolo Grassi** (☑080 480 51 00; www.festivaldella valleditria.it; ⓐ10am-1pm Mon-Fri) in the Palazzo Ducale.

Sleeping

Villaggio In APARTMENT €€
(☑080 480 59 11; www.villaggioin.it; Via Arco Grassi 8; apt per night €75-170, per week €335-1030) These charming arched apartments are located in original *centro storico* homes. The rooms are large, painted in pastel colours and decorated with antiques and country frills. A variety of apartments are on offer, sleeping from two to six people.

B&B San Martino B&B €
(☑080 48 56 01; xoomer.virgilio.it/bed-and-breakfast-sanmartino; Via Abate Fighera 32; d €40-120; ✳) A stylish B&B in a historic palace with rooms overlooking gracious Piazza XX Settembre. The apartments have exposed stone walls, shiny parquet floors, wrought-iron beds and small kitchenettes.

Eating

Il Ritrovo degli Amici TRADITIONAL ITALIAN €€
(☑080 483 92 49; www.ilritrovodegliamici.it; Corso Messapia 8; meals €35; ⊙lunch & dinner Tue-Sat, lunch Sun Mar-Jan) This excellent restaurant, with stone walls and vaulting, has a convivial atmosphere oiled by the region's Spumante. Dishes are traditional, with salamis and sausages the specialities.

Ciacco TRADITIONAL ITALIAN €€
(☑080 480 04 72; Via Conte Ugolino; meals €30; ⊙lunch & dinner Tue-Sun) Dive into the historic centre to find Ciacco, a traditional restaurant with white-clad tables and a cosy fireplace, serving up Puglian cuisine in a modern key. It's tucked down a narrow pedestrian lane a couple of streets in from the Chiesa del Carmine.

La Piazzetta Garibaldi OSTERIA €€
(☑080 430 49 00; Piazza Garibaldi; meals €20-30; ⊙lunch & dinner Thu-Tue) This is a highly recommended *osteria* in the *centro storico*. Delicious aromas entice you into the cavernous interior and the menu doesn't disappoint. Worthy of a long lunch.

Information

The **tourist office** (☑080 480 57 02; Piazza Roma 37; ⊙9am-1pm Mon-Sat, 4.30-7pm Tue & Thu, 9am-12.30pm Sat) is within Palazzo Ducale (part of the Bibliotece Comunal).

Getting There & Around

FSE buses run to Alberobello (€1.50, 30 minutes, five daily, Monday to Saturday).

The FSE train station is downhill from the historic centre. Go right along Viale della Stazione, continuing along Via Alessandro Fighera

to Corso Italia; continue to the left along Corso Italia to Piazza XX Settembre.

FSE (☑080 546 21 11) trains run to/from the following destinations:

Bari €5.20, two hours, hourly
Lecce €7.10, two hours, five daily
Taranto €2.40, 50 minutes, frequent

OSTUNI
POP 32,500

Ostuni shines like a pearly white tiara, extending across three hills with the magnificent gem of a cathedral as its sparkling centrepiece. It's the end of the *trulli* region and the beginning of the hot, dry Salento. Chic, with some excellent restaurants, stylish bars and swish yet intimate places to stay, it's packed in summer.

Sights

Ostuni is surrounded by olive groves, so this is the place to buy some of the region's DOC 'Collina di Brindisi' olive oil – either delicate, medium or strong – direct from producers.

Cathedral CATHEDRAL
(Via Cattedrale) This dramatic 15th-century cathedral has an unusual Gothic-Romanesque facade with a frilly rose window and an inverted gable.

FREE Museo di Città
Preclassiche della Murgia MUSEUM
(☑0831 33 63 83; Via Cattedrale 15) Located in the Convento delle Monacelle, the museum's most famous exhibit is the 25,000-year-old star of the show: Delia. She was pregnant at the time of her death and her well-preserved skeleton was found in a local cave. Many of the finds here come from the Palaeolithic burial ground, now the **Parco Archeologico e Naturale di Arignano** (☑0831 30 39 73), which can be visited by appointment. The museum was closed for restoration at time of writing. Check with the tourist office for the opening hours.

Activities

The surrounding countryside is perfect for cycling. **Ciclovagando** (☑330 98 52 55; www.ciclovagando.com; Via di Savoia 19, Mesagne; half-/full day €30/40) organises guided tours. Each tour covers approximately 20km and departs daily from various towns in the district, including Ostuni and Brindisi. For an extra €15 you can sample typical Apulian foods on the tour.

MASSERIAS: LUXURY ON THE FARM

Masserie (or *masserias*) are unique to southern Italy. Modelled on the classical Roman villa, these fortified farmhouses – equipped with oil mills, cellars, chapels, storehouses and accommodation for workers and livestock – were built to function as self-sufficient communities. These days, they still produce the bulk of Italy's olive oil, but many have been converted into luxurious hotels, *agriturismi* (farm-stay accommodation), holiday apartments or restaurants. Staying in a *masseria* is a unique experience, especially when you can dine on local home-grown produce.

The following masserias are recommended:

Il Frantoio (🖉0831 33 02 76; www.trecolline.it; SS16, Km 874; d €139-259, apt €319-350; P@) Stay in a charming, whitewashed farmhouse, where the owners still live and work, producing high-quality organic olive oil. (Or else book yourself in for one of the marathon eight-course lunches; the food is superb.) Armando takes guests for a tour of the farm each evening in his 1949 Fiat. Il Frantoio lies 5km outside Ostuni along the SS16 in the direction of Fasano. You'll see the sign on your left-hand side when you reach the Km 874 sign.

Masseria Torre Coccaro (🖉080 482 93 10; www.masseriatorrecoccaro.com; Contrada Coccaro 8, Savelletri di Fasano; d €278-1339; ❄@🌐▨) For pure luxury, stay in this superchic yet countrified *masseria*. There's a glorious spa set in a cave, a beach-style swimming pool, cooking courses on offer and a restaurant (meals €90) dishing up home-grown produce.

Masseria Maizza (www.masseriatorremaizza.com; €278-1493; ❄@🌐▨) Next door to Masseria Torre Coccaro and run by the same people, so you know luxury is assured. The two *masserias* share a balmy beach club (about 4km away) and a neighbouring golf course.

Borgo San Marco (🖉080 439 57 57; www.borgosanmarco.it; Contrada Sant'Angelo 33; s €130-140, d €180-230; P❄🌐▨) Once a *borgo* (small village), this *masseria* has 16 rooms, a jacuzzi in the orchard and is traditional with a bohemian edge. Nearby are some frescoed rock churches. It's 8km from Ostuni; to get here take the SS379 in the direction of Bari, exiting at the sign that says SC San Marco–Zona Industriale Sud Fasano, then follow the signs. Note that there's a one-week minimum stay in August.

✵ Festivals & Events

La Cavalcata   RELIGIOUS
Ostuni's annual feast day is held on 26 August, when processions of horsemen dressed in glittering red-and-white uniforms (resembling Indian grooms on their way to be wed) follow the statue of Sant'Oronzo around town.

🛏 Sleeping

La Terra   HOTEL €€
(🖉0831 33 66 51; www.laterrahotel.it; Via Petrarolo; d €130-170; P❄🌐) This former 13th-century palace offers atmospheric and stylish accommodation with original niches, dark-wood beams and furniture, and contrasting light stonework and whitewash. The result is a cool contemporary look. The bar is as cavernous as they come – it's tunnelled out of a cave.

Le Sole Blu   B&B €
(🖉0831 30 38 56; www.webalice.it/solebluostuni; Corso Vittorio Emanuele II 16; s €30-40, s €50, d

€60-80) Located in the 18th-century (rather than medieval) part of town, Le Sole Blu only has one room available: it's large and has a separate entrance, but the bathroom is tiny. However, the two self-catering apartments (doubles €60 to €80) nearby are excellent value.

🍴 Eating

Osteria Piazzetta Cattedrale   OSTERIA €€
(🖉0831 33 50 26; www.piazzettacattedrale.it; Via Arcidiacono Trinchera 7; meals €25-30; ☺Wed-Mon) Just beyond the arch opposite Ostuni's cathedral is this tiny little *osteria* serving up magical food in an atmospheric setting. The menu includes plenty of vegetarian options.

Osteria del Tempo Perso   OSTERIA €€
(🖉0831 30 33 20; www.osteriadeltempoperso.com; Gaetano Tanzarella Vitale 47; meals €30; ☺Tue-Sun) A sophisticated rustic restaurant in a former bakery, this laid-back place serves great Pugliese food, specialising in roasted meats. To get here, face the cathedral's south wall and

turn right through two archways into Largo Giuseppe Spennati, then follow the signs to the restaurant.

Porta Nova
TRADITIONAL ITALIAN €€€

(☑0831 33 89 83; www.ristoranteportanova.com; Via G Petrarolo 38; meals €45) This restaurant has a wonderful location on the old city wall. Revel in the rolling views from the terrace or relax in the elegant interior while you feast on top-notch local cuisine, with fish and seafood the speciality.

ⓘ Information
Tourist office (☑0831 30 12 68; Corso Mazzini 8; ☺9am-1pm & 5-9pm Mon-Fri, 5.30-8.30pm Sat & Sun) Located off Piazza della Libertà; can organise guided visits of the town in summer and bike rental.

ⓘ Getting There & Around
STP buses run to Brindisi (€2.90, 50 minutes, six daily) and to Martina Franca (€2, 45 minutes, three daily), leaving from Piazza Italia in the newer part of Ostuni.

Trains run frequently to Brindisi (€4, 25 minutes) and Bari (€9, 50 minutes). A half-hourly local bus covers the 2.5km between the station and town.

Lecce & Salento

The Penisola Salentina, better known simply as Salento, is hot, dry and remote, retaining a flavour of its Greek past. It stretches across Italy's heel from Brindisi to Taranto and down to Santa Maria di Leuca. Here the lush greenery of Valle d'Itria gives way to flat, ochre-coloured fields, hazy with wildflowers in spring, and endless olive groves. Lecce is the cultural heart of the region and a great base from which to savour Salento's endless sunshine, sandy beaches and some of Puglia's (and perhaps, Italy's) finest wines.

LECCE
POP 95,000

Historic Lecce is a beautiful baroque town; a glorious architectural confection of palaces and churches intricately sculpted from the soft local sandstone. It is a city full of surprises: one minute you are perusing sleek designer fashions from Milan, the next you are faced with a church, dizzyingly decorated with asparagus column tops, decorative dodos and cavorting gremlins. Swooning 18th-century traveller Thomas Ashe thought it 'the most beautiful city in Italy', but the less-impressed Marchese Grimaldi said the facade of Santa Croce made him think a lunatic was having a nightmare.

Either way, it's a lively, graceful university town packed with upmarket boutiques, antique shops, restaurants and bars. Both the Adriatic and Ionian Seas are within easy access and it's a great location from which to explore the Salento.

⊙ Sights
Lecce has more than 40 churches and at least as many *palazzi,* all built or renovated between the 17th and 18th centuries, giving the city an extraordinary cohesion. Two of the main proponents of *barocco leccese* (Lecce baroque – the craziest, most lavish decoration imaginable) were brothers Antonio and Giuseppe Zimbalo, who both had a hand in the fantastical Basilica di Santa Croce.

TOP CHOICE **Basilica di Santa Croce** CHURCH

(☑0832 24 19 57; www.basilicasantacroce.eu; Via Umberto I; ☺9am-noon & 5-8pm) It seems that hallucinating stonemasons have been at work on the basilica. Sheep, dodos, cherubs and beasties writhe across the facade, a swirling magnificent allegorical feast. Throughout the 17th and 18th centuries, a team of artists under Giuseppe Zimbalo laboured to work the building up to this pitch. Look for Zimbalo's profile on the facade.

The interior is more conventionally Renaissance and deserves a look, once you've finished swooning outside. Zimbalo also left his mark in the former Convento dei Celestini, just north of the basilica, which is now the **Palazzo del Governo**, the local government headquarters.

Piazza del Duomo
PIAZZA

Piazza del Duomo is a baroque feast, the city's focal point and a sudden open space amid the surrounding enclosed lanes. During times of invasion the inhabitants of Lecce would barricade themselves in the square, which has conveniently narrow entrances. The **cathedral** (☺8.30am-noon & 4-6.30pm), first built in the 12th century, is one of Giuseppe Zimbalo's finest works – he was also responsible for the towering 68m-high bell tower. The cathedral is unusual in that it has two facades, one on the western end and the other, more ornate, facing the piazza. It's framed by the 15th-century **Palazzo Vescovile** (Episcopal Palace) and the 18th-century **Seminario** (☺exhibitions only), designed by Giuseppe Cino.

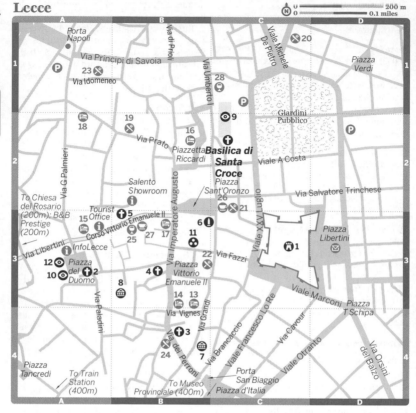

Museo Faggiano
MUSEUM

(☑360 72 24 48; www.museofaggiano.it; Via Grandi 56/58; admission €3; ⊘9.30am-1pm & 4-8pm) Breaking the floor to replace sewer pipes led the owner of this private home to the chance discovery of an archaeological treasure trove. Layers of history are revealed beneath the floors and in the walls. Look out for what appears to be the Knights Templar symbol in the rooftop tower.

FREE Museo Provinciale
MUSEUM

(☑0832 68 35 03; Via Gallipoli 28; ⊘8.30am-7.30pm Mon-Sat, to 1.30pm Sun) The museum stylishly covers 10,000 years of history, from Palaeolithic and Neolithic bits and bobs to a handsome display of Greek and Roman jewels, weaponry and ornaments. The stars of the show are the Messapians, who were making jaunty jugs and bowls centuries before the Greeks arrived to give them any pottery lessons.

Roman Amphitheatre
HISTORICAL SITE

(Piazza Sant'Oronzo; adult/reduced €2/1; ⊘10am-noon & 5-7pm May-Sep) Below the ground level of the piazza is this restored 2nd-century-AD amphitheatre, discovered in 1901 by construction workers. It was excavated in the 1930s to reveal a perfect horseshoe with seating for 15,000.

Colonna di Sant'Oronzo
MONUMENT

(Piazza Sant'Oronzo) A statue of Lecce's patron saint perches precariously on a column in the piazza. The column, originally from Brindisi, marked the end of the Via Appia – the Roman road that stretched from Rome to Brindisi.

Museo Teatro Romano
HISTORICAL SITE

(☑0832 27 91 96; Via Ammirati; adult/reduced €3/2; ⊘9.30am-1.30pm Mon-Sat, 5-7.30pm Mon-Fri) Uncovered in the 1930s, this small Roman theatre has well-preserved russet-coloured Roman mosaics and frescoes.

FREE **Castello di Carlo V**   CASTLE
(☎0832 24 65 17; ⊙9am-1pm & 5-9pm) This 16th-century castle was built around a 12th-century Norman tower to the orders of Charles V and consists of two concentric trapezoidal structures. It's been used as a prison, a court and military headquarters; now you can wander around the baronial spaces and visit the occasional art exhibition.

OTHER CHURCHES

On Corso Vittorio Emanuele II, the interior of 17th-century **Chiesa di Sant'Irene** contains a magnificent pair of mirror-image baroque altarpieces, facing each other across the transept. Other notable baroque churches include **Chiesa di Santa Chiara** (Piazza Vittorio Emanuele II; ⊙9.30-11.30am daily, 4.30-6.30pm Mon-Sat), with every niche a swirl of twisting columns and ornate statuary; the **Chiesa di San Matteo** (Via dei Perroni 29; ⊙7.30am-11am & 4-6pm), 200m to its south; and the last work of Giuseppe Zimbalo, **Chiesa del Rosario** (Via Libertini). Instead of the intended dome roof, it ended up with a quick-fix wooden one following Zimbalo's death before the building was completed. The **Chiesa dei SS Nicolò e Cataldo** (Via San Nicola; ⊙9am-noon Sep-Apr), near **Porta Napoli**, was built by the Normans in 1180. It got caught up in the city's baroque frenzy and was revamped in 1716 by the prolific Cino, who retained the Romanesque rose window and portal.

⚑ Courses

Awaiting Table   COOKING COURSE
(www.awaitingtable.com; day/weeklong course €300/1995) Silvestro Silvestori's splendid culinary and wine school provides day or weeklong courses with tours, tastings and noteworthy lecturers. Book well in advance as courses fill up rapidly.

⊨ Sleeping

Risorgimento Resort   HOTEL €€€
(☎0832 24 63 11; www.risorgimentoresort.it; Via Imperatore Augusto 19; d €145-165, ste €190-290; P⊗@☎) A warm welcome awaits at this stylish five-star hotel in the centre of Lecce. The rooms are spacious and refined with high ceilings, modern furniture and contemporary details reflecting the colours of the Salento. The bathrooms are enormous. There's a restaurant, wine bar and rooftop garden.

Palazzo Rollo   B&B €€
(☎0832 30 71 52; www.palazzorollo.it; Via Vittorio Emanuele II; 14; d €90-120, 4-person studio €100; P⊗@) Stay in a 17th-century palace – the family seat for over 200 years. The three grand B&B suites (with kitchenettes) have high curved ceilings and chandeliers. Downstairs, contemporary-chic studios open onto an ivy-hung courtyard. The rooftop garden has wonderful views.

LECCE IN ...

One Day

Start the day with a cappuccino and *pasticciotto* (custard-filled pastry) at **Caffè Alvino** on Piazza Sant'Oronzo. All that sugar and froth should be good preparation for the fanciful **Basilica di Santa Croce**, worth at least an hour of your time.

To get a sense of Lecce's history visit the fascinating **Museo Faggiano**, then come back to the present with a spot of window-shopping and browsing through the entertaining mix of shops on Corso Vittorio Emanuele II. Be sure to stop for a campari and soda at one of the many bars in town before lunching on typical Pugliese fare at firmly traditional **Alle due Corti**.

Walk off the pasta and beans by heading across town to the excellent **Museo Provinciale**. Or, for more fancy facades, Lecce's baroque feast of *palazzi*- (mansion-) flanked streets (like Via Palmieri), **churches** and the **cathedral** will keep you simpering happily till dinnertime. Crown your day with a meal at **Cucina Casareccia**, where you'll feel like one of the family. Stroll back to your hotel via the Basilica, which is spectacularly lit up at night.

Suite 68 BOUTIQUE HOTEL €€
(☑0832 30 35 06; www.kalekora.it; Via Prato; s €60-80, d €80-120; ✳) Strong colours, abstract canvases and vividly patterned rugs in the large, bright rooms give this place a contemporary feel. It's simple and stylish. Bikes available.

B&B Prestige B&B €
(☑349 775 12 90; www.bbprestige-lecce.it; Giuseppe Libertini 7; s €60-70, d €70-90; P@☎) On the corner of Via Santa Maria del Paradiso in the historic centre, the rooms in this lovely B&B are light, airy and beautifully finished. The communal sun-trap terrace has views over San Giovanni Battista church. There's also an apartment downstairs.

Patria Palace Hotel HOTEL €€
(☑0832 24 51 11; www.patriapalacelecce.com; Piazzetta Riccardi 13; s €106-210, d €165-350; P✳@☎) This sumptuous hotel is traditionally Italian with large mirrors, dark-wood furniture and wistful murals. The location is wonderful, the bar gloriously art deco with a magnificent carved ceiling, and the shady roof terrace has views over the Basilica di Santa Croce.

Casa Elisabetta B&B €
(☑0832 30 70 52; www.beb-lecce.com; Via Vignes 15; s €30-45, d €50-80; ✳☎) An elegant mansion that's centred on a graceful courtyard close to Piazza Vittorio Emanuele II, this B&B has a warren of corridors and plain functional rooms.

Centro Storico B&B B&B €
(☑338 588 12 65; www.bedandbreakfast.lecce. it; Via Vignes 2b; s €35-40, d €70-100; P✳☎)

Recently refurbished, this B&B has big rooms, double-glazed windows and coffee- and tea-making facilities. The rooftop terrace has sunloungers and views.

✕ Eating

TOP CHOICE **Cucina Casareccia** TRATTORIA €€
(☑0832 24 51 78; Viale Costadura 19; meals €20-25; ⊙lunch Tue-Sun, dinner Tue-Sat) Ring the bell to gain entry into a place that feels like a private home, with its patterned cement floor tiles, desk piled high with papers, and charming owner Carmela Perrone. In fact, it's known locally as *le Zie* (the aunts). Here you'll taste the true *cucina povera*, including horsemeat done in a *salsa piccante* (spicy sauce). Booking is a must.

Trattoria di Nonna Tetti TRATTORIA €
(☑0832 24 60 36; Piazzetta Regina Maria 28; meals €15-20; ⊙lunch & dinner daily) A warmly inviting restaurant, popular with all ages and budgets, this trattoria serves a wide choice of traditional dishes. Try the most emblematic Pugliese dish here – braised wild chicory with a purée of boiled dried fava beans, along with *contorni* (side dishes) like *patate casarecce* (homemade thinly sliced fries).

Alle due Corti TRATTORIA €
(☑0832 24 22 23; www.alleduecorti.com; Via Prato 42; meals €22; ⊙lunch & dinner daily) For a taste of sunny Salento, check out this no-frills, fiercely traditional restaurant. The seasonal menu is classic Pugliese, written in a dialect that even some Italians struggle with. Go for the real deal with a dish of *ciceri e tria* (crisply fried pasta with chickpeas).

Picton

TRADITIONAL ITALIAN €€

(☎0832 33 23 83; www.acena.it/picton; Via Idomeneo 14; meals €35-40; ☺Mon-Sat) This elegant backstreet restaurant in an old *palazzo* has a cool barrel-vaulted interior and an internal garden. The cuisine is traditional with a twist.

Mamma Lupa

OSTERIA €

(☎340 783 27 65; Via Acaja 12; meals €20-25; ☺lunch Sun-Fri, dinner daily) Looking and tasting suitably rustic, this *osteria* serves proper peasant food – such as roast tomatoes, potatoes and artichokes, or horse meatballs – in snug surroundings with just a few tables surrounded by dark ochre walls.

Gelateria Natale

GELATERIA €

(Via Trinchese 7a) Lecce's best ice cream parlour also has an array of fabulous confectionery.

🍺 Drinking

Via Imperatore Augusto is full of bars, and on a summer's night it feels like one long party. Wander along to find somewhere to settle.

All'Ombra del Barocco

CAFE, WINE BAR

(www.allombradelbarocco.it; Corte dei Cicala 9; ☺8am-1am) Next door to Il Caffè di Liberrima, this cool restaurant-cafe-wine bar has a range of teas, cocktails and *aperitivi*. It's open for breakfast and also hosts musical events.

Caffè Alvino

CAFE

(Piazza Sant'Oronzo; ☺Wed-Mon) Treat yourself to good coffee and *pasticciotto* at this iconic cafe in Lecce's main square.

Il Caffè di Liberrima

CAFE

(Corte dei Cicala) Tables fill the little square next to the bookshop and *enoteca* (wine bar) on the central pedestrianised strip – an ideal place to watch the world amble past.

Shui 13 Wine Bar

WINE BAR

(Via Umberto I 21; ☺10am-late summer, 10am-3pm & 6pm-midnight winter) A popular and atmospheric bar with a range of Pugliese wines.

ℹ️ Information

The train station is 1km southwest of Lecce's historic centre. The centre's twin main squares are Piazza Sant'Oronzo and Piazza del Duomo, linked by pedestrianised Corso Vittorio Emanuele II.

CTS (☎0832 30 18 62; Via Palmieri 89; ☺9am-1pm daily & 4-7.30pm Sun-Mon) Good for student travel.

Hospital (☎0832 66 11 11; Via San Cesario) About 2km south of the centre on the Gallipoli road.

InfoLecce (☎0832 52 18 77; www.infolecce.it; Piazza Duomo 2; ☺9.30am-1.30pm & 3.30-7.30pm Mon-Sat, from 10am Sun) Independent and helpful tourist information office. Has guided tours and bike rental (per hour/day €3/15).

Police station (☎0832 69 11 11; Viale Otranto 1)

Post office (Piazza Libertini)

Salento Showroom (☎0832 17 90 357; www.salentotime.it; Via Revina Isabella 22; ☺9.30am-1.30pm & 3.30-7.30pm Mon-Sat, from 10am Sun) Independent tourist office which can provide help with accommodation and car hire. Has internet access (per hour €3).

The Puglia (www.thepuglia.com) Voted the most popular blog on Puglia in Italy, this informative site run by Fabio Ingrosso covers culture, history, food, wine and accommodation and travel in Puglia.

Tourist office (☎0832 24 80 92; www.viaggiareinpuglia.it; Corso Vittorio Emanuele II 24; ☺9am-1pm Mon-Sat, 4-7pm Mon-Thu)

🚌 Getting There & Away

BUS

STP (☎0832 35 91 42) runs buses to Brindisi (€6, 35 minutes, nine daily) and throughout Puglia from the STP bus station.

FSE (☎0832 66 81 11) runs buses to Gallipoli (€3.50, one hour, four daily), Otranto (€2.60, 1½ hours, two daily) and Brindisi (€3.30, 45 minutes, two daily), leaving from Largo Vittime del Terrorismo.

Pugliairbus (http://pugliairbus.aeroportidi puglia.it) runs to Brindisi airport (€7, 40 minutes, nine daily). SITA also has buses to Brindisi airport (€6, 45 minutes, nine daily), leaving from Viale Porte d'Europa.

TRAIN

The main train station runs frequent services to the following destinations:

Bari From €14.50, 1½ to two hours

Bologna From €75, 7½ to 9½ hours

Brindisi From €9.40, 30 minutes

Naples From €62, 5½ hours (transfer in Caserta)

Rome From €63, 5½ to nine hours

FSE trains head to Otranto and Martina Franca.

BRINDISI

POP 89,800

Like all ports, Brindisi has its seamy side, but it's also surprisingly slow-paced and balmy, particularly the palm-lined Corso Garibaldi linking the port to the train station and the promenade stretching along the interesting seafront.

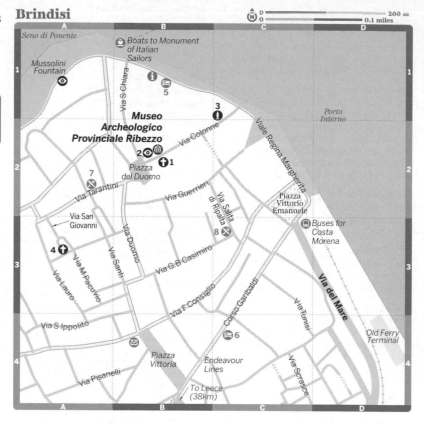

The town was the end of the ancient Roman road Via Appia, down the weary length of which trudged legionnaires and pilgrims, crusaders and traders, all heading to Greece and the Near East. These days little has changed except that Brindisi's pilgrims are sun-seekers rather than soul-seekers.

Sights & Activities

TOP CHOICE Museo Archeologico Provinciale Ribezzo   MUSEUM

(☑0831 56 55 08; Piazza del Duomo 8; admission free; ⊙9.30am-1.30pm Tue-Sat, 3.30-6.30pm Tue, Thu & Sat) This superb museum covers several floors with well-documented exhibits (in English) including some 3000 bronze sculptures and fragments in Hellenistic Greek style, terracotta figurines from the 7th century, underwater archeological finds, and Roman statues and heads (not always together).

Chiesa di Santa Maria del Casale   CHURCH

(☑0831 41 85 45; Via Ruggero de Simone; ⊙8am-8pm) Located 4km north of town towards the airport, this church was built by Prince Philip of Taranto around 1300. The church mixes up Puglian Romanesque, Gothic and Byzantine styles, with a Byzantine banquet of interior frescoes. The immense *Last Judgement* on the entrance wall, full of blood and thunder, is the work of Rinaldo di Taranto.

Roman Column   MONUMENT

(Via Colonne) The gleaming white column above a sweeping set of sun-whitened stairs leading to the waterfront promenade marks the imperial Via Appia terminus at Brindisi. Originally there were two, but one was presented to the town of Lecce back in 1666 as thanks to Sant'Oronzo for having relieved Brindisi of the plague.

Brindisi

⊙ Top Sights
Museo Archeologico Provinciale
Ribezzo...B2

⊙ Sights
1 Cathedral..B2
2 Porta dei Cavalieri Templari.................B2
3 Roman Column.................................C1
4 Tempio di San Giovanni al
   Sepolcro..A3

⊜ Sleeping
5 Grande Albergo Internazionale...........B1
6 Hotel Orientale.................................C4

⊗ Eating
7 Il Giardino......................................A2
8 Trattoria Pantagruele........................C3

Cathedral   CATHEDRAL
(Piazza del Duomo; ⊙8am-9pm Mon-Fri & Sun, to
noon Sat) This 11th-century cathedral was
substantially remodelled about 700 years
later. You can see how it may have looked
from the nearby **Porta dei Cavalieri Templari**, a fanciful portico with pointy arches
– all that remains of the Knights Templar's
main church.

**Tempio di San Giovanni
al Sepolcro**   CHURCH
(Via San Giovanni) The Knights Templar's other
church is a square brown bulk of Norman
stone conforming to the circular plan the
Templars so loved.

Monument to Italian Sailors   MONUMENT
For a wonderful view of Brindisi's waterfront, take one of the regular **boats** (return
ticket €1.80) from Viale Regina Margherita
across the harbour to the monument erected by Mussolini in 1933.

⊨ Sleeping

Hotel Orientale   HOTEL €€
(⊡0831 56 84 51; www.hotelorientale.it; Corso
Garibaldi 40; s/d €99/130; P🅿❄🛜) This sleek,
modern hotel overlooks the long palm-lined
corso. Rooms are pleasant, the location is
good and it has a small fitness centre, private
car park and (rare) cooked breakfast option.

Grande Albergo Internazionale   HOTEL €€€
(⊡0831 52 34 73; www.albergointernazionale.
it; Viale Regina Margherita 23; s/d €100/250;
P🅿❄🛜) Built in 1870 for English merchants

en route to Bombay and the Raj, the hotel
is proud of its distinguished past. It has   **119**
great harbour views, large rooms with
grandly draped curtains and an ideal location across the street from the waterfront
promenade.

✗ Eating

Trattoria Pantagruele   TRATTORIA €€
(⊡0831 56 06 05; Via Salita di Ripalta 1; meals €30;
⊙lunch & dinner Mon-Fri, dinner Sat) Named after French writer François Rabelais' satiri-
cal character, this charming trattoria three
blocks from the waterfront serves up excellent fish and grilled meats.

Il Giardino   TRADITIONAL ITALIAN €€
(⊡0831 56 40 26; Via Tarantini 14-18; meals €30;
⊙lunch & dinner Tue-Sat, lunch Sun) Established
more than 40 years ago in a restored 15th-
century *palazzo*, sophisticated Il Giardino
serves refined seafood and meat dishes in a
delightful garden setting.

ⓘ Information
The new port is east of town, across the Seno di
Levante at Costa Morena, in a bleak industrial
wilderness.

The old port is about 1km from the train station along Corso Umberto I, which leads into
Corso Garibaldi where there are numerous cafes, shops, ferry companies and travel agencies.
Ferries (www.ferries.gr) Details of ferry fares
and timetables to Greek destinations.
Hospital (⊡0831 53 71 11; SS7 for Mesagne)
Police station (⊡0831 54 31 11; Via Perrino 1)
Post office (Piazza Vittoria)
Tourist office (⊡0831 52 30 72; www.viag
giareinpuglia.it; Viale Regina Margherita 44;
⊙9am-1pm & 2-8pm Mon-Sat summer, 8.30am-
2pm Mon-Sat & 3.30-7pm Mon-Fri winter)

ⓘ Getting There & Away

AIR

From **Papola Casale** (BDS; www.aeroportidipug
lia.it), Brindisi's small airport, there are domestic flights to Rome, Naples and Milan. Airlines
include Alitalia, AirOne and easyJet. There are
also direct flights from London Stansted with
Ryanair.

Major and local car-hire firms are represented
at the airport and there are regular SITA buses
to Lecce (€6, 45 minutes, nine daily) and STP
buses to central Brindisi (€1.50, 15 to 30 minutes, every 30 minutes).

Pugliairbus (pugliairbus.aeroportidipuglia.it)
has services to Bari airport (€8, 1¾ hours) and
Lecce (€7, 40 minutes).

PUGLIA, BASILICATA & CALABRIA LECCE & SALENTO

BOAT

Ferries, all of which take vehicles, leave Brindisi for Greece and Albania. For more information see the Travelling East box on p100.

Ferry companies have offices at Costa Morena (the newer port); the major ones also have offices in town.

Companies include:

Agoudimos Lines (www.agoudimos-lines. com) To Corfu, Igoumenista and Cephalonia in Greece; to Vlore in Albania.

Endeavour Lines (☑0831 52 85 31; www.hml. it; Corso Garibaldi 8) To Igoumenitsa, Patras, Corfu and Cephalonia in Greece.

Red Star Ferries (☑0831 57 52 89; www. redstarferries.com) To Vlore in Albania.

BUS

Buses operated by **STP** (☑0831 54 92 45) go to Ostuni (€2.90, 50 minutes, six daily) and Lecce (€3.30, 45 minutes, two daily), as well as towns throughout the Salento. Most leave from Via Bastioni Carlo V, in front of the train station. Ferrovie del Sud-Est buses serving local towns also leave from here.

Marozzi (☑0831 52 16 84) runs to Rome's Stazione Tiburtina (€37.50 to €40, six to seven hours, four daily) from Viale Arno.

TRAIN

The train station has regular services to the following destinations:

Bari From €15, one hour

Lecce From €9.40, 30 minutes

Milan From €92, 8½ to 11 hours

Rome From €58, five to seven hours

Taranto From €5.10, 1¼ hours

❶ Getting Around

To reach the airport take the STP-run Cotrap bus from Via Bastioni Carlo V.

A free minibus connects the train station and old ferry terminal with Costa Morena. It departs two hours before boat departures. You'll need a valid ferry ticket.

ORIA

POP 15,400

The multicoloured dome of Oria's cathedral can be seen for miles around, surrounded by the narrow streets of this appealing medieval town. An intriguing, if ghoulish, sight is the cathedral's **Cripta delle Mummie** (Crypt of the Mummies), where 11 mummified corpses of former monks are still preserved. Surmounting the town, the Frederick II **castle**, built in a triangular shape, has been carefully restored. It is privately owned.

Dating back to Frederick II's reign, **Il Torneo dei Rioni** is the annual battle between the town's quarters. It takes the form of a spectacular *palio* (horse race) and is held every mid-August.

Borgo di Oria (☑329 2307506; www.borgo dioria.it; ste €70-75; ﹡) is a delightful *albergo diffuso* (scattered hotel) run by the charismatic and well-travelled Francesco Pipino. The self-catering apartments are large, comfortable and tastefully furnished. Reception is at Bar Kenya in Piazza Manfredi.

Waiters in medieval costume welcome you at **Alle Corte di Hyria** (☑329 662 45 07; www.allecortedihyria.com; Via Milizia 146; meals €20-25; ⊙Thu-Tue), an atmospheric restaurant in a stone-walled cavern.

Oria is on the main Trenitalia line and there are frequent services from both Brindisi and Taranto. You can also connect with Ostuni and change at Francavilla Fontana for Alberobello and Martina Franca.

GALATINA

POP 27,320

With a charming historic centre, Galatina – 18km south of Lecce – is at the core of the Salentine Peninsula's Greek past. It is almost the only place where the ritual *tarantismi* is still practised. The tarantella folk dance evolved from this ritual, and each year on the feast day of St Peter and St Paul (29 June), it is performed at the (now deconsecrated) church.

However, most people come to Galatina see the incredible 14th-century **Basilica di Santa Caterina d'Alessandria** (⊙8am-12.30pm & 4.30-6.45pm Apr-Sep, 8am-12.30pm & 3.45-5.45pm Oct-Mar), its interior a kaleidoscope of fresco. It was built by the Franciscans, whose patroness was the Frenchwoman Marie d'Enghien de Brienne. Married to Raimondello Orsini del Balzo, the Salentine's wealthiest noble, she had plenty of cash to splash on interior decoration. The gruesome story goes that Raimondello (who is buried here) climbed Mt Sinai to visit relics of Santa Caterina (St Catherine). Kissing the dead saint's hand, he bit off a finger and brought it back as a holy relic.

The church is absolutely beautiful, with a pure-white altarpiece set against the frenzy of frescoes. It is not clear who the artists Marie employed really were; they could have been itinerant painters down from Le Marche and Emilia, or southerners who'd absorbed the latest Renaissance innovations on trips north. Bring a torch.

Soothe the soul further with a stay at nearby **Samadhi** (☑0836 60 02 84; www.agri

colasamadhi.com; Via Stazione 116; per person from €40, per week from €390-995; ✳🛜🖥), located around 7km east of here in tiny Zollino. It's on a 10-hectare organic farm and the owners are multilingual. As well as ayurvedic treatments and yoga courses, there's a vegan restaurant offering organic meals. Check the website for upcoming retreats and courses.

There are frequent FSE trains between Lecce and Galatina (€1.90, 30 minutes), and Zollino (€1.30, 20 minutes).

OTRANTO
POP 5540

Otranto overlooks a pretty harbour on the blue Adriatic coast. In the historic centre, looming golden walls guard narrow car-free lanes, protecting countless pretty little shops selling touristic odds and ends. In July and August it's one of Puglia's most vibrant towns.

Otranto was Italy's main port to the East for 1000 years and suffered a brutal history. There are fanciful tales that King Minos was here and St Peter is supposed to have celebrated the first Western Mass here.

A more definite historical event is the Sack of Otranto in 1480, when 18,000 Turks led by Ahmet Pasha besieged the town. The townsfolk were able to hold the Turks at bay for 15 days before capitulating. Eight hundred survivors were subsequently led up the nearby Minerva hill and beheaded for refusing to convert.

Today the only fright you'll get is the summer crush on Otranto's scenic beaches and in its narrow streets.

◎ Sights

TOP CHOICE **Cathedral** CATHEDRAL
(✆0836 80 27 20; Piazza Basilica; ⊗8am-noon daily, 3-6pm Apr-Sep, 3-5pm Oct-Mar) This cathedral was built by the Normans in the 11th century, though it's been given a few facelifts since. On the floor is a vast 12th-century mosaic of a stupendous tree of life balanced on the back of two elephants. It was created by a young monk called Pantaleone (who had obviously never seen an elephant), whose vision of heaven and hell encompassed an amazing (con)fusion of the classics, religion and plain old superstition, including Adam and Eve, Diana the huntress, Hercules, King Arthur, Alexander the Great, and a menagerie of monkeys, snakes and sea monsters. Don't forget to look up; the cathedral also boasts a beautiful wooden coffered ceiling.

It's amazing that the cathedral survived at all, as the Turks stabled their horses here

SPIDER MUSIC

In August, one of Salento's biggest festivals is a frenzied night of *pizzica* dancing at **La Notte della Taranta** (www.lanottedellataranta.it) in Melpignano, about 30km south of Lecce. *Pizzica* developed from the ritual *tarantismi*, a dance meant to rid the body of tarantula-bite poison. It's more likely the hysterical dancing was symbolic of a deeper societal psychosis and an outlet for individuals living in bleak, repressed conditions to express their pent-up desires, hopes and unresolved grief. Nowadays, *pizzica* (which can be quite a sensual dance) means party, with all-night dances in various Salento towns throughout summer, leading up to Melpignano's humdinger affair.

when they beheaded the martyrs of Otranto on a stone preserved in the altar of the chapel (to the right of the main altar). This **Cappella Mortiri** (Chapel of the Dead) is a ghoulishly fascinating sight, with the skulls and bones of the martyrs arranged in neat patterns in seven tall glass cases.

Castle CASTLE
(www.castelloaragoneseotranto.it; Piazza Castello; adult/child €2/free; ⊗10am-1pm & 3-5pm Oct-Mar, 10am-1pm & 3-7pm Apr-May, 10am-1pm & 3-10pm Jun & Sep, 10am-midnight Aug) This squat thick-walled fort, with the Charles V coat of arms above the entrance, has great views from the ramparts. There are some faded original murals and original canon balls on display.

Chiesa di San Pietro CHURCH
(Via San Pietro; ⊗10am-noon & 3-6pm) Vivid Byzantine frescoes decorate the interior of this church. If it's closed, ask for the key at the cathedral.

🏊 Activities

There are some great beaches north of Otranto, especially **Baia dei Turchi**, with its translucent blue water. South of Otranto a spectacular rocky coastline makes for an impressive drive down to Castro (see the boxed text, p122). To see what goes on underwater, **Scuba Diving Otranto** (✆0836 80 27 40; www.scubadiving.it; Via Francesco di Paola 43) offers day or night dives as well as introductory courses and diving courses.

🛏 Sleeping

TOP CHOICE Palazzo Papaleo HOTEL €€

(☑0836 80 21 08; www.hotelpalazzopapaleo.com; Via Rondachi 1; r €119-490; Ⓟ✳@⑀) Located next to the cathedral, this sumptuous hotel was the first to earn the EU Eco-label in Puglia. Aside from its ecological convictions, the hotel has magnificent rooms with original frescoes, exquisitely carved antique furniture and walls washed in soft greys, ochres and yellows. Soak in the panoramic views while enjoying the rooftop jacuzzi. The staff are exceptionally friendly.

Balconcino d'Oriente B&B €

(☑0836 80 15 29; www.balconcinodoriente.com; Via San Francesco da Paola 71; s €40-70, d €60-110; Ⓟ✳) This B&B has an African-cum-Middle Eastern theme throughout with colourful bed linens, African prints, Moroccan lamps, and orange colour washes on the walls. The downstairs restaurant serves traditional Italian meals.

Palazzo de Mori BOUTIQUE HOTEL €€

(☑0836 80 10 88; www.palazzodemori.it; Bastione dei Pelasgi; r €120-150; ☺Apr-Oct; ✳@) In Otranto's historic centre, this charming B&B serves breakfast on the sun terrace overlooking the port. The rooms are decorated in soothing white-on-white.

✕ Eating

La Bella Idrusa PIZZERIA €

(☑0836 80 14 75; Via Lungomare degli Eroi; pizza €5; ☺dinner Thu-Tue) You can't miss this pizzeria right by the huge Porta Terra in the historic centre. Outdoor seating is great for people-watching while indoors is atmospheric and romantic. And it's not just pizzas on offer.

Laltro Baffo SEAFOOD €€

(☑0836 80 16 36; www.laltrobaffo.com; Cenobio Basiliano 23; meals €30-35; ☺Tue-Sun) This elegant modern restaurant near the castle dishes up seafood with a contemporary twist. Try the *polipo alla pignata* (octopus stew).

Acmet Pasica TRADITIONAL ITALIAN €€

(☑0836 80 12 82; Via Lungomare degli Eroi; meals €40; ☺Tue-Sun) Trading on Otranto's macabre history with the Turks, this restaurant is in a prime position overlooking the sea. As well as a large selection of seafood, there are other traditional meals on the menu.

COASTAL HIGHLIGHT

For a scenic road trip, the drive south from **Otranto** to **Castro** takes you along a wild and beautiful coastline. The coast here is rocky and dramatic, with cliffs falling down into the sparkling, azure sea. When the wind is up you can see why it is largely treeless. Many of the towns here started life as Greek settlements, although there are few monuments to be seen. Further south, the resort town of **Santa Maria di Leuca** is the tip of Italy's stiletto and the dividing line between the Adriatic and Ionian Seas.

🍷 Drinking

A number of bars along the city wall overlook the sea, including the popular **Il Covo dei Mori** (☑0836 80 20 33; Via Leon Dari).

ℹ Information

Ellade Viaggi (☑0836 80 15 78; www.ellade viaggi.it, in Italian; Via del Porto) For travel information and reservations, at the port.

Tourist office (☑0836 80 14 36; Piazza Castello; ☺9am-1pm & 3-8pm Mon-Fri Jun-Sep, 9am-1pm Mon-Fri Oct-May) Faces the castle.

ℹ Getting There & Away

Otranto can be reached from Lecce by FSE train (€2.60, 1½ hours) or bus (€2.60, 1½ hours). **Marozzi** (☑0836 80 15 78) has daily bus services to Rome (€47, 10 hours, three daily).

GALLIPOLI
POP 21,040

The old medieval centre of Gallipoli (meaning 'beautiful town' in Greek) fills an island in the Ionian Sea and is connected by a bridge to the mainland and modern city. It's a picturesque town surrounded by high walls which were built to protect it against attacks from the sea. An important fishing centre, it feels like a working Italian town, unlike more seasonal coastal places. In the summer, bars and restaurants make the most of the island's ramparts, looking out to sea.

◉ Sights & Activities

Gallipoli has some fine beaches, including the **Baia Verde**, just south of town, while nature enthusiasts will want to take a day trip about 20km north to **Parco Regionale Porto Selvaggio**, – a protected area of wild coastline with walking trails amid the trees and diving off the rocky shore.

Cattedrale di Sant'Agata
CATHEDRAL

(Via Antonietta de Pace; ⊗hours vary) In the centre, on the highest point of the island, is this 17th-century baroque cathedral, lined with paintings by local artists. Zimbalo, who imprinted Lecce with his crazy baroque styles, also worked on the facade.

Frantoio Ipogeo
HISTORICAL SITE

(☑338 136 30 63; Via Antonietta de Pace 87; ⊗10am-12.30pm & 4-6.30pm Jun-Sep, to midnight Jun & Jul) This is only one of some 35 olive presses buried in the tufa rock below the town. It's here that they pressed Gallipoli's olive oil, which was then stored in one of the 2000 cisterns carved out beneath the old town.

Museo Civico
MUSEUM

(☑0833 26 42 24; Via Antonietta de Pace 108; adult €3; ⊗9am-1pm & 4-9pm Mon-Fri, 10am-1pm Sat) Founded in 1878, the museum is a 19th-century time capsule featuring fish heads, ancient sculptures, a 3rd-century-BC sarcophagus and other weird stuff.

Farmacia Provenzana
HISTORICAL BUILDING

(Via Antonietta de Pace; ⊗8.30am-12.30pm & 4.30-8.30pm Sun-Fri) A beautifully decorated pharmacy dating from 1814.

🛏 Sleeping

La Casa del Mare
B&B €

(☑333 474 57 54; www.lacasadelmare.com; Piazza de Amicis 14; d €60-110; ✳@🎧) This butter-coloured 16th-century building on a little square in the town centre is a great choice. Helpful and friendly Federico has also restored a beautiful 18th-century palazzo nearby, **Palazzo Flora** (www.palazzoflora.com; Via d'Ospina 19; d €65-120, house €150-300), which sleeps four to six and has fantastic views, especially from the rooftop terrace. During the summer Federico cooks a sumptuous buffet feast for his guests every Friday night (per person €35).

Insula
B&B €

(☑366 346 83 57; www.bbinsulagallipoli.it; Via de Pace 56; d €60-120; ⊗Apr-Oct; ✳@) A magnificent 15th-century building houses this memorable B&B. The five rooms are all different but share the same princely atmosphere with exquisite antiques, vaulted high ceilings and cool pastel paintwork.

Relais Corte Palmieri
HOTEL €€

(☑0833 26 53 18; www.relaiscortepalmieri.it; Corte Palmieri 3; s €130-185, d €165-195; ✳🎧) This cream-coloured, well-kept hotel in the historic centre has elegant rooms accentuated by traditional painted furniture, wrought-iron bedheads and crisp red-and-white linen.

🍴 Eating

La Puritate
TRATTORIA €€€

(☑0833 26 42 05; Via S Elia 18; meals €40-45; ⊗Thu-Tue) A great place for fish in the old town, with picture windows and sea views. Follow the excellent antipasti with delicious *primi* (first courses) such as seafood spaghetti, then see what's been caught that day – the swordfish is usually a good bet.

Al Pescatore
SEAFOOD €€

(☑0833 26 36 56; Riviera Colombo 39; meals €25-30; ⊗Tue-Sun) In a hotel of the same name, this restaurant has no views but is recommended by locals for its good seafood dishes at reasonable prices.

ℹ Information

Tourist office (☑0833 26 25 29; Via Antonietta de Pace 86; ⊗8am-9pm summer, 8am-1pm & 4-9pm Mon-Sat winter) Near the cathedral in the old town.

ℹ Getting There & Away

FSE buses and trains head to Lecce (€3.90, one hour, four daily).

TARANTO
POP 193,140

According to legend, the city was founded by Taras, son of Poseidon, who arrived on the back of a dolphin (as you do). Less romantically, the city was actually founded in the 7th century BC by exiles from Sparta, becoming one of the wealthiest and most important colonies of Magna Graecia. The fun finished, however, in the 3rd century BC when the Romans marched in, changed its name to Tarentum and set off a two-millennia decline in fortunes. Its cultural heyday may be over but Taranto still remains an important naval base, second only to La Spezia.

Once a Roman citadel, the collapsing historic medieval centre is gritty and dirty but has a lovely seaside promenade. However, the mainland industrial centre, with Italy's largest steel plant, dominates the skyline.

👁 Sights

Although Taranto's medieval town centre is rundown and has a gritty undertone, it's gradually being tastefully renovated. It is perched on the small island dividing the Mar Piccolo (Small Sea; an enclosed lagoon) and the Mar Grande (Big Sea). This peculiar geography means that blue sea and sky surround you wherever you go.

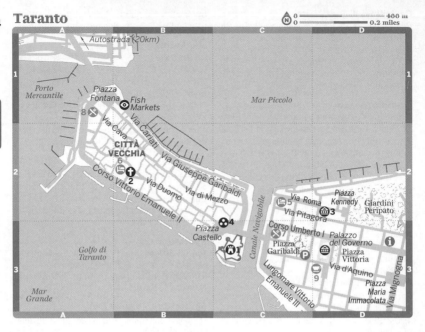

Taranto

⊙ Sights
1 Castello Aragonese C3
2 Cathedral B2
3 Museo Nazionale Archeologico D2
4 Temple of Poseidon............................C3

🛏 Sleeping
5 Europa Hotel...C2
6 Hotel Akropolis....................................B2

⊗ Eating
7 Balzi Blu C3
8 Trattoria da Ugo...................................A1

⊜ Drinking
9 Caffè Italiano D3

Museo Nazionale Archeologico MUSEUM
(⌨099 453 21 12; www.museotaranto.it, in Italian;
Via Cavour 10; adult/child €5/free; ⊙8.30am-
7.30pm) In the new town is one of Italy's
most important archaeological museums. It
houses, among other ancient artefacts, the
largest collection of Greek terracotta figures
in the world. Also on exhibit are fine collections of 1st-century-BC glassware, classic
black-and-red Attic vases and stunning jew-

ellery such as a 4th-century-BC bronze and
terracotta crown.

Cathedral CATHEDRAL
(Via del Duomo) The 11th-century cathedral is
one of Puglia's oldest Romanesque buildings
and an extravagant treat. It's dedicated to
San Cataldo; the Capella di San Cataldo is
a baroque riot of frescoes and polychrome
marble inlay.

Castello Aragonese CASTLE
(Piazza Castello; ⌨099 775 34 38; ⊙by appointment 9am-noon Mon-Fri) Guarding the swing
bridge that joins the old and new parts of
town, this impressive 15th-century structure
was once a prison and is currently occupied
by the Italian navy. Opposite are the remaining columns of Taranto's ancient **Temple of
Poseidon**.

⚑ Festivals & Events
Le Feste di Pasqua RELIGIOUS
Taranto is famous for its Holy Week celebrations – the biggest in the region – when
bearers in Ku Klux Klan–style robes carry
icons around the town. There are three processions: the Perdoni, celebrating pilgrims;
the Addolorata (which lasts 12 hours but
covers only 4km); and the Misteri (even
slower at 14 hours to cover 2km).

Sleeping

Hotel Akropolis HOTEL €€
(☎099 470 41 10; www.hotelakropolis.it; Vico I Seminario 3; s/d €105/145; ❄@) A converted medieval *palazzo* in the crumbling old town, this luxurious hotel sits grandly beside the cathedral. There are 13 stylish cream-and-white rooms, original majolica-tiled floors and tremendous views from the rooftop terrace. The downstairs bar and restaurant is enclosed in stone, wood and glass and has atmospheric curtained alcoves.

Europa Hotel HOTEL €€
(☎099 452 59 94; www.hoteleuropaonline.it; Via Roma 2; s €80-105, d €135-190; ❄🖥) On the seafront next to the swing bridge, this hotel has comfortable rooms (some with kitchenettes) overlooking the old town. A good choice.

Eating & Drinking

Trattoria da Ugo TRATTORIA €€
(☎329 141 58 50; cnr Via Cataldo de Tulio & Via Fontana; meals €18-25; ⊙lunch & dinner Mon-Fri, lunch Sat) This deeply traditional Tarantine trattoria is known for its seafood, which includes grilled mussels, octopus with lemon and olive oil, and fried prawns and squid.

Balzi Blu PIZZERIA €
(☎347 465 32 11; Corso Due Mari 22; pizza from €6.50, meals €15; ⊙Wed-Mon) A local favourite on the *corso,* serving excellent pizza with an exceptional crust made from 13 different types of flour. There are great views of the old city from the summer terrace.

Caffè Italiano CAFE
(Via D'Aquino 86a; ⊙5am-2am) Swish as you might wish, this is a Taranto hot spot, with outside seating on the pedestrianised street. Great for an evening aperitif.

ⓘ Information

Taranto splits neatly into three. The old town is on a tiny island, lodged between the northwest port and train station and the new city to the southeast. Italy's largest steel plant occupies the city's entire western half. The grid-patterned new city contains the banks, most hotels and restaurants and the **tourist office** (☎099 453 23 97; Corso Umberto I 113; ⊙9am-1pm & 4.30-6.30pm Mon-Fri, 9am-noon Sat).

ⓘ Getting There & Around

BUS

Buses heading north and west depart from Porto Mercantile. FSE buses go to Bari (€5.80, 1¾ to 2¼ hours, frequent). Infrequent **SITA** (☎899 32 52 04; www.sitabus.it) buses leave for Matera

(€5.20, 1¾ hours, one daily). STP and FSE buses go to Lecce (€7.70, two hours, five daily).

Marozzi (☎080 579 90 111) has express services serving Rome's Stazione Tiburtina (€41.50, six hours, three daily). **Autolinee Miccolis** (☎099 470 44 51) serves Naples (€19, four hours, three daily) via Potenza (€10.50, two hours).

The bus **ticket office** (⊙6am-1pm & 2-7pm) is at Porto Mercantile.

TRAIN

Trenitalia and FSE trains go to the following destinations:

Bari €7.40, 2½ hours, frequent

Brindisi €5.10, 1¼ hours, frequent

Rome From €41, six to 7½ hours, five daily

AMAT (☎099 4 52 67 32) buses run between the train station and the new city.

BASILICATA

Basilicata has an otherworldly landscape of tremendous mountain ranges, dark forested valleys and villages so melded with the rockface that they seem to have grown there. Its isolated yet strategic location on routes linking ancient Rome to the eastern Byzantine empire has seen it successively invaded, pillaged, plundered, abandoned and neglected.

In the north the landscape is a fertile zone of gentle hills and deep valleys – once covered in thick forests, now cleared and cultivated with wheat, olives and grapes. The purple-hued mountains of the interior are impossibly grand and a wonderful destination for hikers and naturalists, particularly the soaring peaks of the Lucanian Apennines and the Parco Nazionale del Pollino.

On the coast, Maratea is one of Italy's most chic seaside resorts. However, Matera is Basilicata's star attraction, the famous *sassi* of the cave city presiding over a rugged landscape of ravines and caves. Its ancient cave dwellings tell a tale of poverty, hardship and struggle, its history best immortalized in writer Carlo Levi's superb book *Christ stopped at Eboli* – a title suggesting Basilicata was beyond the hand of God, a place where pagan magic still existed and thrived.

Today Basilicata is attracting a slow but steadily increasing trickle of tourists. For those wanting to experience a raw and unspoilt region of Italy, Basilicata's remote atmosphere and wild landscape will appeal.

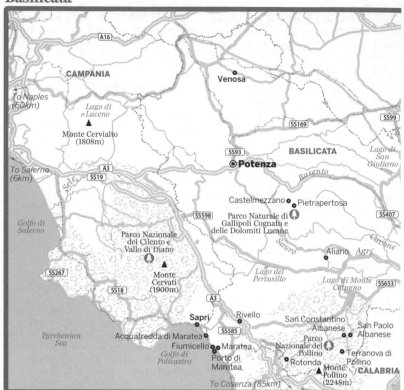

History

Basilicata spans Italy's instep with slivers of coastline touching the Tyrrhenian and Ionian Seas. It was known to the Greeks and Romans as Lucania (a name still heard today) after the Lucani tribe who lived here as far back as the 5th century BC. The Greeks also prospered, settling along the coastline at Metapontum and Erakleia, but things started to go wrong under the Romans, when Hannibal, the ferocious Carthaginian general, rampaged through the region.

In the 10th century, the Byzantine Emperor Basilikòs (976–1025) renamed the area, overthrowing the Saracens in Sicily and the south and reintroducing Christianity. The pattern of war and overthrow continued throughout the Middle Ages as the Normans, Hohenstaufens, Angevins and Bourbons constantly tussled over its strategic location, right up until the 19th century. As talk of the Italian unification began to gain ground,

Bourbon-sponsored loyalists took to Basilicata's mountains to oppose political change. Ultimately, they became the much-feared bandits of local lore who make scary appearances in writings from the late 19th and early 20th centuries. In the 1930s, Basilicata was used as a kind of open prison for political dissidents – most famously Carlo Levi – sent into exile to remote villages by the fascists.

Matera

POP 60,530 / ELEV 405M

Approach Matera from virtually any direction and your first glimpse of its famous *sassi* (stone houses carved out of the caves and cliffs) is sure to be etched in your memory forever. Haunting and beautiful, the *sassi* sprawl below the rim of a yawning ravine like a giant nativity scene. The old town is simply unique and warrants at least a day of exploration and aimless wandering. Al-

By the 1950s over half of Matera's population lived in the *sassi,* a typical cave sheltering an average of six children. The infant mortality rate was 50%. In his book *Christ Stopped at Eboli,* Carlo Levi describes how children would beg passers-by for quinine to stave off deadly malaria. Such publicity finally galvanised the authorities into action and in the late 1950s about 15,000 inhabitants were forcibly relocated to new government housing schemes. In 1993 the *sassi* were declared a Unesco World Heritage Site. Ironically, the town's history of outrageous misery has transformed it into Basilicata's leading tourist attraction.

◉ Sights

There are two *sasso* districts: the more restored, northwest-facing Sasso Barisano and the more impoverished, northeast-facing Sasso Caveoso. Both are extraordinary, riddled with serpentine alleyways and staircases, and dotted with frescoed *chiese rupestri* (cave churches) created between the 8th and 13th centuries. Matera contains some 3000 habitable caves.

The *sassi* are accessible from several points. There's an entrance off Piazza Vittorio Veneto, or take Via delle Beccherie to Piazza del Duomo and follow the tourist itinerary signs to enter either Barisano or Caveoso. Sasso Caveoso is also accessible from Via Ridola.

For a great photograph, head out of town for about 3km on the Taranto-Laterza road and follow signs for the *chiese rupestri.* This takes you up on the Murgia Plateau to the **Belvedere**, the location of the crucifixion in Mel Gibson's 2004 film, *The Passion of the Christ,* from where you have fantastic views of the plunging ravine and Matera.

Sasso Barisano

Chiesa di Madonna delle Virtù & Chiesa di San Nicola dei Greci   CHURCH
(Via Madonna delle Virtù; ⊙10am-7pm Sat & Sun) This monastic complex is one of the most important monuments in Matera and is composed of dozens of caves spread over two floors. The church of the Chiesa Madonna delle Virtù was built in the 10th or 11th century and restored in the 17th century. Above it, the simple church of Chiesa di San Nicola dei Greci is rich in frescoes. The complex was used in 1213 by Benedictine monks of Palestinian origin.

though many buildings are crumbling and abandoned, many have been restored and transformed into cosy abodes, restaurants and swish cave-hotels. On the cliff top, the new town is a lively place, with its elegant churches, *palazzi* and especially the pedestrianised Piazza Vittorio Veneto.

History

Matera is said to be one of the world's oldest towns, inhabited since the Paleolithic Age. The simple natural grottoes that dotted the gorge were adapted to become homes, and an ingenious system of canals regulated the flow of water and sewage. The prosperous town became the capital of Basilicata in 1663, a position it held until 1806 when the power moved to Potenza. In the decades that followed, an unsustainable increase in population led to the habitation of unsuitable grottoes – originally intended as animal stalls – even lacking running water.

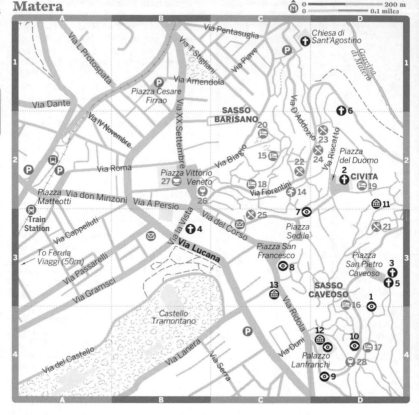

Sasso Caveoso

Chiesa di San Pietro Caveoso   CHURCH
(Piazza San Pietro Caveoso) The only church in the *sassi* not dug into the tufa rock, it was originally built in 1300 and has a 17th-century Romanesque-baroque facade.

Chiesa di Santa Maria d'Idris   CHURCH
(Piazza San Pietro Caveoso; admission adult/reduced €3/2; ⊘10am-1pm & 2.30-7pm Tue-Sun Apr-Oct, 10.30am-1.30pm Nov-Mar Tue-Sun) Dug into the Idris rock, this church has an unprepossessing facade, but the narrow corridor communicating with the recessed church of San Giovanni in Monterrone is richly decorated with 12th- to 17th-century frescoes. Purchase a joint ticket for this site and Chiesa di Santa Lucia alle Malve for €5/3.50.

Chiesa di Santa Lucia alle Malve   CHURCH
(Via la Vista; admission adult/reduced €3/2; ⊘10am-1pm & 2.30-7pm Apr-Oct, 10.30am-1.30pm Tue-Sun Nov-Mar) Built in the 8th century to

house a Benedictine convent, this church has an ornate entrance door and a number of 12th-century frescoes.

La Raccolta delle Acque   HISTORICAL SITE
(☑340 665 91 07; www.laraccoltadelleacque matera.it; Via Bruno Buozzi 67; admission €2.50; ⊘9.30am-1pm & 2-7pm Apr-Oct, 9.30am-1pm Nov-Mar) Matera's fascinating water-storage system can be better understood when you visit this ancient complex of underground cisterns and canals which was used to collect rainwater from roofs, streets and houses in the vicinity. The largest cistern is nearly 15m deep and 5m long.

Casa-Grotta di Vico Solitario   HISTORICAL SITE
(admission €1.50) For a glimpse of life in old Matera visit this refurbished *sasso* off Via Bruno Buozzi. There's a bed in the kitchen, a room for manure and a section for a pig and a donkey.

Museo della Scultura Contemporanea   MUSEUM

(MUSMA; ☎366 935 77 68; www.musma.it; via San Giacomo; ⊙10am-2pm Tue-Sun plus 4-8pm Sat & Sun; adult/reduced €5/3.50) Housed in Palazzo Pomarici, MUSMA is a fabulous contemporary sculpture museum. Some of the exhibits are artfully displayed in atmospherically lit caves. You can also book a tour to visit the **Cripta del Peccato Originale** (the Crypt of Original Sin), which has well-preserved frescoes from the late 8th century. It's known as the Sistine Chapel of the cave churches, with frescoes of dramatic Old Testament scenes.

The New Town

The focus of the town is Piazza Vittorio Veneto, an excellent, bustling meeting point for an evening *passeggiata* (stroll). It's surrounded by elegant churches and richly adorned *palazzi,* with their backs to the *sassi;* an attempt by the bourgeois to block out the shameful poverty the *sassi* once represented. Further excavations here have yielded more ruins of Byzantine Matera, including a rock church, a castle, a large cistern and numerous houses. You can gaze down to the site from the piazza.

Museo Nazionale d'Arte Medievale e Moderna della Basilicata   MUSEUM

(☎0835 31 42 35; Palazzo Lanfranchi; adult/reduced €2/1; ⊙9am-8pm Thu-Tue) The stars of the show are Levi's paintings, including the enormous mural *Lucania '61*, depicting peasant life in biblical technicolour.

Cathedral   CATHEDRAL

(Piazza del Duomo; ⊙closed for renovation) Set high up in town, the subdued, graceful exterior of the 13th-century Puglian-Romanesque cathedral makes the interior's neobaroque excess – ornate capitals, sumptuous chapels and tons of gilding – all the more surprising. Pediments mounted on its altars came from the temples at Metaponto. Matera's patron saint, the Madonna della Bruna, is hidden within the older church, **Santa Maria di Costantinopoli**, which can be accessed from the cathedral if it's open.

Museo Nazionale Ridola   MUSEUM

(☎0835 31 00 58; Via Ridola 24; adult/reduced €2.50/1.25; ⊙9am-8pm Tue-Sun, 2-8pm Mon) The impressive collection includes some remarkable Greek pottery, such as the *Craterea Mascheroni,* a huge urn over 1m high.

☞ Tours

There are plenty of official guides for the *sassi* – try www.sassiweb.it. Or, contact the **Cooperativa Amici del Turista** (☎0835 33 03 01; www.amicidelturista.it; Via Fiorentini 28-30) or English-speaking guide **Amy Weideman** (☎339 282 3618; half-day tour for 2 people €40).

MATERA IN...

One Day

Zip out to the **Belvedere** for a photo of the *sassi* before any heat haze sets in. Back in the *sassi*, approach Sasso Barisano via Via Fiorentini and wind your way to the monastic complex of **Chiesa di Madonna delle Virtù & Chiesa di San Nicola del Greci** with its original frescoes. Then head for more frescoes in Sasso Caveoso's rock churches of **San Pietro Caveoso**, **Santa Maria d'Idris** and **Santa Lucia alle Malve**. Wander through the *sassi*, imagining life in a cave, stopping to learn about Matera's fascinating system of underground cisterns at **La Raccolta delle Acque**. Early evening, enjoy a cocktail in lively Piazza Vittorio Veneto at **Caffe Tripoli** followed by dinner at **Ristorante Il Cantuccio**.

Two Days

On day two, allow a couple of hours to visit the **Cripta del Peccato Originale**, with its magnificent frescoes. Then either spend the rest of the day hiking in the **gorge** or squeeze in a few museums in town including the **Museo Nazionale d'Arte Moderna**, which showcases Carlo Levi's bold *Lucania '61*. In the heart of Sasso Caveoso the **Casa-Grotte di Vico Solitario** may sound a tad contrived but really *does* provide a vivid picture of former living conditions here. For contemporary sculptures, visit the **Museo della Scultura Contemporanea**. Finish off with dinner in a cave at stylish **Baccanti**.

For excellent guided visits, **Ferula Viaggi** (☑0835 33 65 72; www.matera turismo.it; Via Cappelluti 34) has tours of the *sassi*, classic tours, underground tours, tours that include tastings or cookery courses, longer trips to the Pollino or into Puglia, and various hiking and cycling tours. For a detailed list of walks see **Walk Basilicata** (www.walkbasilicata. it). Ferula Viaggi also runs **Bike Basilicata** (www.bikebasilicata.it), which rents bikes and helmets and supplies a road book and map so you can head off on your own; guided bike tours include a seven-night 500km odyssey across Puglia and Basilicata.

✯ Festivals & Events

Sagra della Madonna
della Bruna   RELIGIOUS
On 2 July the colourful Procession of Shepherds parades ornately decorated papier-mâché floats around town. The finale is the *assalto al carro*, when the crowd descends on the main cart and tears it to pieces.

Gezziamoci   MUSIC
(☑0835 33 02 00; www.gezziamociamatera.onyx jazzclub.it) This jazz festival in the *sassi* and surrounding Murgia park kicks off in the last week of August.

🛏 Sleeping

TOP CHOICE Hotel in Pietra   BOUTIQUE HOTEL €€
(☑0835 34 40 40; www.hotelinpietra.it; Via San Giovanni Vecchio 22; Barisano; s €70, d €110-150,

ste 220; ✳@) The lobby is set in a former 13th-century chapel complete with soaring arches, while the eight rooms combine soft golden stone with the natural cave interior. Furnishings are Zen-style with low beds, while the bathrooms are superstylish and include vast sunken tubs.

Locanda di San Martino   HOTEL €€
(☑0835 25 66 00; www.locandadisanmartino.it; Via Fiorentini 71; d €89-200; ✳🛜🖥) A sumptuous hotel where you can swim in a cave – in a subterranean underground swimming pool. The cave accommodation, complete with niches and rustic brick floors, is set around a warren of cobbled paths and courtyards.

La Dolce Vita B&B   B&B €
(☑0835 31 03 24; www.ladolcevitamatera.it; Rione Malve 51; s €40-60, d €60-80; 🛜) This delightful ecofriendly B&B in Sasso Caveoso has self-contained apartments with solar panels and recycled rainwater for plumbing. They're cool, comfortable and homey. Vincenzo is passionate about Matera and is a mine of information on the *sassi*.

Palazzo Viceconte   HOTEL €€
(☑0835 33 06 99; www.palazzoviceconte.it; Via San Potito 7; d €95-140, ste €139-350; ✳@) Rooms in this 15th-century *palazzo* near the cathedral have superb views of the *sassi* and gorge. The hotel is elegantly furnished and the rooftop terrace has panoramic views.

Il Vicinato
B&B €

(☎0835 31 26 72; www.ilvicinato.com; Piazzetta San Pietro Caveoso 7; s/d €60/70; ❀🛜) This B&B enjoys a great, easy-to-find location. Rooms are decorated in clean modern lines, with views across to Idris rock and the Murgia Plateau. There's a room with a balcony and a small apartment, each with independent entrances.

Sassi Hotel
HOTEL €

(☎0835 33 10 09; www.hotelsassi.it; Via San Giovanni Vecchio 89; s/d incl breakfast €70/90; ❀@) The first hotel in the *sassi* is set in an 18th-century rambling edifice in Sasso Barisano with some rooms in caves and some not. Singles are small but doubles are gracefully furnished. The balconies have superb views of the cathedral.

✖ Eating

TOP CHOICE Ristorante Il Cantuccio
TRATTORIA €€

(☎0835 33 20 90; Via delle Becchiere 33; meals €25; ⊙Tue-Sun) This quaint, homey trattoria near Piazza Vittorio Veneto is as welcoming as its chef and owner, Michael Lella. The menu is seasonal and the dishes traditional and delicious.

Baccanti
TRADITIONAL ITALIAN €€€

(☎0835 33 37 04; www.baccantiristorante.com; Via Sant'Angelo 58-61; meals €50; ⊙lunch & dinner Tue-Sat, lunch Sun) As classy as a cave can be. The design is simple glamour against the low arches of the cavern; the dishes are delicate and complex, using local ingredients. This is where stars go to twinkle when in town.

Oi Marì
PIZZERIA €

(☎0835 34 61 21; Via Fiorentini 66; pizzas from €6.50; ⊙dinner nightly, lunch Sat & Sun) In Sasso Barisano, this big convivial cavern is styled as a Neapolitan pizzeria – and has a great cheery atmosphere and excellent substantial pizzas to match.

La Talpa
TRADITIONAL ITALIAN €

(☎0835 33 50 86; Via Fiorentini 167; meals €15-20; ⊙Wed-Mon) Down the road from Oi Marì, the cavernous dining rooms here are moodily lit and atmospheric. A popular spot for romancing couples.

Le Botteghe
TRADITIONAL ITALIAN €€

(☎0835 34 40 72; Piazza San Pietro Barisano; meals €40; ⊙lunch & dinner Mon-Sat, lunch Sun) In Sasso Barisano, this is a classy but informal restaurant in arched whitewashed rooms. Try delicious local specialities like *fusilli mollica e crusco* (pasta and fried bread with local sweet peppers).

🍷 Drinking

Caffe Tripoli
CAFE

(Piazza Vittorio Veneto; ⊙Tue-Sun) This is a good people-watching spot for morning coffee or evening aperitifs.

19a Buca Winery?
WINE BAR

(☎0835 33 35 92; www.diciannovesimabuca.com; Via Lombardi 3; ⊙11am-midnight Tue-Sun) The question mark says it all – 13m below Piazza Vittorio Veneto the past takes a futuristic twist. This ultrachic wine bar-restaurant-cafe-lounge has white space-pod chairs, a 19-hole indoor golf course surrounding an ancient cistern and an impressive wine cellar and degustation menu (meals €30).

Morgan Pub
PUB

(www.morganpub.com; Via Buozzi 2; ⊙Wed-Mon) A hip and cavernous cellar pub with outside tables in the summer.

ⓘ Information

The maps *Carta Turistica di Matera* and *Matera: Percorsi Turistici* (€1.50), available from various travel agencies, bookstores and hotels around town, describe a number of itineraries through the *sassi* and the gorge.

Basilicata Turistica (www.aptbasilicata.it) Official tourist website with useful information on history, culture, attractions and sights.

Ferula Viaggi (☎0835 33 65 72; www.materaturismo.it; Via Cappelluti 34; ⊙9am-1.30pm & 3.30-7pm Mon-Sat) Excellent information

---

DON'T MISS

EXPLORING THE GORGE

In the picturesque landscape of the Murgia Plateau, the Matera Gravina cuts a rough gouge in the Earth, a 200m-deep canyon pockmarked with abandoned caves and villages. You can hike from the *sassi* (former cave dwellings) into the gorge and then up to the Belvedere in one to two hours, but a hike along the canyon rim gives you a better appreciation of the termitelike network of caves that gave rise to the *sassi*. **Ferula Viaggi** (www.ferulaviaggi.it) offers excellent guided hikes into the gorge, as well as hiking and cycling tours through Basilicata and Puglia.

centre and travel agency. Runs walking tours (www.walkbasilicata.it), cycling tours (www.bikebasilicata.it), cooking courses, and other great tours through Basilicata and Puglia.

Hospital (☑0835 25 31 11; Via Montescaglioso) About 1km southeast of the centre.

Internet point (☑0835 34 41 66; Via San Biagio 9; per hr €3; ☺10am-1pm & 3.30-8.30pm)

Maruel Viaggi (☑0835 33 31 35; www.maruel viaggi.com; Via Dante; ☺9am-1.30pm & 4-8pm) Private travel agency and information centre with good information on buses. Can organise tours.

Parco Archeologico Storico Naturale delle Chiese Rupestri del Materano (☑0835 33 61 66; www.parcomurgia.it; Via Sette Dolori) For info on the Murgia park.

Police station (☑0835 37 81; Via Gattini)

Post office (Via Passerelli; ☺8am-6.30pm Mon-Fri, to 12.30pm Sat)

Sassiweb (www.sassiweb.it) Informative website on Matera.

ⓘ Getting There & Away

Bus

The bus station is north of Piazza Matteotti, near the train station. **SITA** (☑0835 38 50 07; www.sitabus.it) goes to Taranto (€5.50, two hours, six daily) and Metaponto (€2.70, one hour, up to

five daily) and many small towns in the province. Buy tickets from newspaper kiosks on Piazza Matteotti.

Grassani (☑0835 72 14 43) serves Potenza (€5.30, 1½ hours, four daily). Buy tickets on the bus.

Marozzi (☑06 225 21 47; www.marozzivt.it) runs three daily buses to Rome (€34, 6½ hours). A joint SITA and Marozzi service leaves daily for Siena, Florence and Pisa, via Potenza. Advance booking is essential.

Pugliairbus (☑080 580 03 58; pugliairbus. aeroportidipuglia.it) operates a service to Bari airport (€5, 1¼ hours, four daily).

Train

Ferrovie Appulo-Lucane (FAL; ☑0835 33 28 61; www.fal-srl.it) runs regular trains (€4.50, 1½ hours, 12 daily) and buses (€4.50, 1½ hours, 6 daily) to Bari. For Potenza, take a FAL bus to Ferrandina and connect with a Trenitalia train, or head to Altamura to link up with FAL's Bari–Potenza run.

Potenza

POP 68,600 / ELEV 819M

Basilicata's regional capital Potenza has been ravaged by earthquakes (the last in 1980) and also has some brutal housing blocks. If

---

WORTH A TRIP

MAGNA GRAECIA MUSEUMS OF THE IONIAN COAST

In stark contrast to the dramatic Tyrrhenian coast, the Ionian coast is a listless, flat affair dotted with large tourist resorts. However, the Greek ruins at **Metaponto** and **Policoro**, with their accompanying museums, bring alive the enormous influence of Magna Graecia in southern Italy.

Metaponto's Greek ruins are a rare site where archaeologists have managed to map the entire ancient urban plan. Settled by Greeks in the 8th and 7th centuries BC, Metapontum's most famous resident was Pythagoras, who founded a school here after being banished from Crotone (in Calabria) in the 6th century BC. After Pythagoras died, his house and school were incorporated into the Temple of Hera. The remains of the temple – 15 columns and sections of pavement – are Metaponto's most impressive sight. They're known as the **Tavole Palatine** (Palatine Tables), since knights, or paladins, are said to have gathered here before heading to the Crusades. It's 3km north of town, just off the highway – to find it follow the slip road for Taranto onto the SS106.

In town, the **Museo Archeologico Nazionale** (☑0835 74 53 27; Via Aristea 21; admission €2.50; ☺9am-8pm Tue-Sun, 2-8pm Mon) houses artefacts from Metapontum and other sights, while in the **Parco Archeologico** (admission free), 2km northeast of the train station, are the remains of a **Greek theatre** and the Doric **Tempio di Apollo Licio**.

In Policoro, 21km southwest of Matera, the **Museo della Siritide** (☑0835 97 21 54; Via Colombo 8; admission €2.50; ☺9am-8pm Wed-Mon, 2-8pm Tue) has a fabulous display of artefacts from 7000 BC through to Lucanian ornaments, Greek mirrors and Roman spears and javelins.

SITA buses run from Matera to Metaponto (€2.70, one hour, up to five daily) and on to Policoro. Metaponto is on the Taranto-Reggio line; trains connect with Potenza, Salerno and occasionally Naples.

that wasn't enough, as the highest town in the land, it broils in summer and shivers in winter. You may find yourself here, however, as it's a major transport hub.

The centre straddles east to west across a high ridge. To the south lie the main Trenitalia and Ferrovie Appulo-Lucane train stations, connected to the centre by buses 1 and 10.

Potenza's few sights are in the old centre, at the top of the hill. To get there, take the elevators from Piazza Vittorio Emanuele II. The ecclesiastical highlight is the **cathedral**, erected in the 12th century and rebuilt in the 18th. The elegant Via Pretoria, flanked by a boutique or two, makes a pleasant traffic-free stroll, especially during the *passeggiata*.

In central Potenza, **Al Convento** (☑097 12 55 91; www.alconvento.eu; Largo San Michele Arcangelo 21; s €50-55, d €80-90; ✱◐) is a great accommodation choice housing a mix of polished antiques and design classics.

Grassani (☑0835 72 14 43) has buses to Matera (€5.30, 1½ hours, four daily). **SITA** (☑0971 50 68 11; www.sitabus.it) has daily buses to Melfi, Venosa and Maratca. Buses leave from Via Appia 185 and also stop near the Scalo Inferiore Trenitalia train station. **Liscio** (☑097 15 46 73) buses serve cities including Rome (€23, 4½ hours, three daily), Naples (€7.40, two hours, four daily) and Salerno (€5.30, 1½ hours, four daily).

There are regular train services from Potenza to Foggia (from €6, 2¼ hours), Salerno (from €6, two hours) and Taranto (from €8.50, two hours). For Bari (from €14, three to four hours, four daily), use **Ferrovie Appulo-Lucane** (☑0971 41 15 61) at Potenza Superiore station.

wrote his dazzling *Christ Stopped at Eboli,* which laid bare the boredom, poverty and hypocrisy of village life. The **Pinacoteca Carlo Levi** (☑0835 56 83 15; Piazza Garibaldi; admission €3; ⊙10am-1pm & 4-7.30pm summer, 10am-12.30pm & 3.30-6.30pm Thu-Tue winter) also houses the **Museo Storico di Carlo Levi**, featuring his papers, documents and paintings. Admission to the *pinacoteca* (art gallery) includes a tour of Levi's house and entry to the museum.

More spectacular than Aliano are the two mountaintop villages of **Castelmezzano** (elevation 985m) and **Pietrapertosa** (elevation 1088m), ringed by the Lucanian Dolomites. They are Basilicata's highest villages and are often swathed in cloud, making you wonder why anyone would build here, in territory best suited to goats. Castelmezzano is surely one of Italy's most dramatic villages; the houses huddle along an impossibly narrow ledge that falls away in gorges to the Caperrino river. Pietrapertosa is even more amazing: the Saracen fortress at its pinnacle is difficult to spot as it is carved out of the mountain.

You can spend an eerie night in Pietrapertosa at a delightful B&B, **La Casa di Penelope e Cirene** (☑0971 98 30 13; Via Garibaldi 32; d from €70). Dine at the authentic Lucano restaurant, **Al Becco della Civetta** (☑097198 62 49; www.beccodellacivetta.it; Vicolo I Maglietta 7; meals €25; ⊙Wed-Mon) in Castelmezzano, which also offers accommodation in traditionally furnished, simple whitewashed rooms (doubles €80).

Aliano is accessible by SITA bus (€5.40) from Potenza. You'll need your own vehicle to visit Castelmezzano and Pietrapertosa.

Appennino Lucano

The Appenino Lucano (Lucanian Apennines) bite Basilicata in half like a row of jagged teeth. Sharply rearing up south of Potenza, they protect the lush Tyrrhenian Coast and leave the Ionian shores gasping in the semi-arid heat. Careering along its hair-raising roads through the broken spine of mountains can be arduous, but if you're looking for drama, the drive could be the highlight of your trip.

The fascists exiled writer and political activist Carlo Levi to this isolated region in 1935. He lived and is buried in the tiny hilltop town of **Aliano**, where remarkably little seems to have changed since he

Tyrrhenian Coast

Resembling a mini-Amalfi, Basilicata's Tyrrhenian coast is short (about 20km) but sweet. Squeezed between Calabria and Campania's Cilento peninsula, it shares the same beguiling characteristics: hidden coves and pewter sandy beaches backed by majestic coastal cliffs. The SS18 threads a spectacular route along the mountains to the coast's star attraction, the charming seaside settlements of Maratea.

MARATEA
POP 5220

Maratea is a charming, if confusing, place at first, being comprised of several distinct localities ranging from a medieval village to a

WORTH A TRIP

POETIC VENOSA

About 70km north of Potenza, pretty Venosa used to be a thriving Roman colony, owing much of its prosperity to being a stop on the Appian Way. It was also the birthplace of the poet Horace in 65 BC. The main reason to come here is to see the remains of Basilicata's largest monastic complex.

Venosa's main square, Piazza Umberto I, is dominated by a 15th-century Aragonese castle with a small **Museo Archeologico** (☎0972 3 60 95; Piazza Umberto I; admission €2.50; ☺9am-8pm Wed-Mon, 2-8pm Tue) that houses finds from Roman Venusia and human bone fragments dating back 300,000 years.

Admission to the museum also gets you into the ruins of the **Roman settlement** (☺9am-1hr before dusk Wed-Mon, 2pm-1hr before dusk Tue) and the graceful later ruins of **Abbazia della Santissima Trinità** (☎0972 3 42 11). At the northeastern end of town, the *abbazia* (abbey) was erected above the Roman temple around 1046 by the Benedictines and predates the Norman invasions. Within the complex is a pair of churches, one unfinished. The earlier church contains the tomb of Robert Guiscard, a Norman crusader, and his fearsome half-brother Drogo. The other unfinished church was begun in the 11th century using materials from the neighbouring Roman amphitheatre. A little way south are some Jewish and Christian catacombs.

Hotel Orazio (☎0972 3 11 35; www.hotelorazio.it; Vittorio Emanuele II 142; s/d €50/65) is a 17th-century palace complete with antique majolica tiles and marble floors, and is overseen by a pair of grandmotherly ladies.

Venosa can be reached by taking the S658 north from Potenza and exiting at Barile onto the S93. Buses run Monday to Saturday from Potenza (€3.10, two hours, two daily).

stylish harbour. The setting is lush and dramatic, with a coastal road (narrower even than the infamous Amalfi Coast road!) that dips and winds past the cliffs and pocket-size beaches that line the sparkling Golfo di Policastro. Studded with elegant hotels, Maratea's attraction is no secret and you can expect tailback traffic and fully booked hotels in July and August. Conversely, many hotels and restaurants close from October to March.

◉ Sights & Activities

Your first port of call should be the pretty **Porto di Maratea**, a harbour where sleek yachts and bright-blue fishing boats bob in the water, overlooked by bars and restaurants. Then there's the enchanting 13th-century medieval *borgo* (small town) of **Maratea Inferiore**, with pint-sized piazzas, wriggling alleys and interlocking houses, offering startling coastal views. It's all overlooked by a 21m-high, gleaming white statue of **Christ the Redeemer** – if you have your own transport, don't miss the rollercoaster road and stupendous views from the statue-mounted summit – below which lie the ruins of **Maratea Superiore**, all that remains of the original 8th-century-BC Greek colony.

The deep green hillsides that encircle this tumbling conurbation offer excellent walk-ing trails and there are a number of easy day trips to the surrounding hamlets of **Acqua-fredda di Maratea** and **Fiumicello**, with its small sandy beach. The **tourist office** (☎0973 87 69 08; Piazza Gesù 40; ☺8am-2pm & 5-8pm Mon-Fri, 9am-1pm & 5-8pm Sat & Sun Jul & Aug, 8am-2pm Sep-Jun) is in Fiumicello.

Centro Sub Maratea (☎0973 87 00 13; www.web.tiscali.it/csmaratea; Via Santa Caterina 28) offers diving courses and boat tours that include visits to surrounding grottoes and coves.

A worthwhile day trip via car is to pretty **Rivello** (elevation 479m). Perched on a ridge and framed by the southern Apennines, it is a centre for arts and crafts and has long been known for its exquisite working of gold and copper. Rivella's interesting Byzantine history is evident in the tiny tiled cupolas and frescoes of its gorgeous churches.

⌂ Sleeping

Locanda delle Donne Monache   HOTEL €€ (☎0973 87 74 87; www.locandamonache.com; Via Mazzei 4; r €130-310; ☺Apr-Oct; P✳@☎☒) Overlooking the medieval *borgo,* this exclusive hotel is in a converted 18th-century convent with a suitably lofty setting. It's a hotchpotch of vaulted corridors, terraces and gardens fringed with bougainvillea and lemon trees. The rooms are elegantly decorated in pastel shades, while the Sacello restaurant prepares delicate dishes drawing on the regional flavours of Lucania.

B&B Nefer
B&B €

(☎0973 87 18 28; www.bbnefer.it; Via Cersuta; r €60-90; P✳@) This B&B set in a small hamlet 5km northwest of Maratea has four rooms decorated in sea greens, blues and pinks. Rooms open onto a lush green lawn complete with deckchairs for contemplating the distant sea view. There's a simple outdoor kitchen area for guest use and a small beach a short walk away along narrow seaside paths.

Hotel Villa Cheta Elite
HOTEL €€

(☎0973 87 81 34; www.villacheta.it; Via Timpone 46; r €140-264; ⊙Apr-Oct; P✳🛜) A charming art nouveau villa at the entrance to the hamlet of Acquafredda, this hotel has a broad terrace with spectacular views, a fabulous restaurant and large rooms decorated with antiques.

✖ Eating

Taverna Rovita
TRADITIONAL ITALIAN €€

(☎0973 87 65 88; www.tavernarovitamaratea.it; Via Rovita 13; meals €35; ⊙Mar-Oct) This tavern is just off Maratea Inferiore's main piazza. Rovita is excellent value and specialises in hearty local fare, with Lucanian specialities involving stuffed peppers, game birds, local salami and fine seafood.

Lanterna Rossa
SEAFOOD €€

(☎0973 87 63 52; Maratea Porto; meals €40; ⊙Feb-Dec Wed-Mon, Jul & Aug daily) Head for the terrace overlooking the port to dine on exquisite seafood. Highly recommended here is the signature dish *zuppa di pesce* (fish soup).

La Caffetteria
CAFE €

(☎Piazza Buraglia; panini from €3; ⊙7.30am-2am summer, to 10pm winter) The outdoor seating at this delightful cafe in Maratea's central piazza is ideal for dedicated people-watching.

❶ Getting There & Away

SITA (☎0971 50 68 11; www.sitabus.it) operates a comprehensive network of routes including up the coast to Sapri in Campania (€1.60, 50 minutes, six daily). Local buses (€1) connect the coastal towns and Maratea train station with Maratea Inferiore, running frequently in summer. InterCity and regional trains on the Rome-Reggio line stop at Maratea train station, below the town.

Tell a non-Calabrese Italian that you're going to Calabria and you will probably elicit some surprise, inevitably followed by stories of the 'Ndrangheta – the Calabrian Mafia – notorious for smuggling and kidnapping wealthy northerners and keeping them hidden in the mountains.

But Calabria contains startling natural beauty and spectacular towns that seem to grow out of the craggy mountaintops. It has three national parks: the Pollino in the north, the Sila in the centre and the Aspromonte in the south. It's around 90% hills, but skirted by some 780km of Italy's finest coast (ignore the bits devoured by unappealing holiday camps). Bergamot grows here, and it's the only place in the world where the plants are of sufficient quality to produce the essential oil used in many perfumes and to flavour Earl Grey tea. As in Puglia, there are hundreds of music and food festivals here year-round, reaching a fever pitch in July and August.

Admittedly, you sometimes feel as if you have stepped into a 1970s postcard, as its towns, destroyed by repeated earthquakes, are often surrounded by brutal breeze-block suburbs. The region has suffered from the unhealthy miscegenation between European and government subsidies (aimed to develop the south) and dark Mafia opportunism. Half-finished houses often mask well-furnished flats where families live happily, untroubled by invasive house taxes.

This is where to head for an adventure into the unknown.

History

Traces of Neanderthal, Palaeolithic and Neolithic life have been found in Calabria, but the region only became internationally important with the arrival of the Greeks in the 8th century BC. They founded a colony at what is now Reggio di Calabria. Remnants of this colonisation, which spread along the Ionian coast with Sibari and Crotone as the star settlements, are still visible. However, the fun didn't last for the Greeks and in 202 BC the cities of Magna Graecia all came under Roman control. Destroying the countryside's handsome forests, the Romans did irreparable geological damage. Navigable rivers became fearsome *fiumare* (torrents) dwindling to wide, dry, drought-stricken riverbeds in high summer.

Calabria's fortified hilltop communities weathered successive invasions by the Normans, Swabians, Aragonese and Bourbons, and remained largely undeveloped. Although the 18th-century Napoleonic incursion and the arrival of Garibaldi and Italian unification inspired hope for change, Calabria remained a disappointed feudal region and, like the rest of the south, was racked by malaria.

A by-product of this tragic history was the growth of banditry and organised crime. The 'Ndrangheta (from the Greek for heroism/virtue) inspires fear in the local community, but tourists are rarely the target of its aggression. For many, the only answer has been to get out and, for at least a century, Calabria has seen its young people emigrate in search of work.

Northern Tyrrhenian Coast

The good, the bad and the ugly line the region's western seashore.

The Autostrada del Sole (A3) is one of Italy's great coastal drives. It twists and turns through mountains, past huge swaths of dark-green forest and flashes of cerulean-blue sea. But the Italian penchant for cheap summer resorts has taken its toll here and certain stretches are blighted by shoddy hotels and soulless stacks of flats.

In the low season most places close. In summer many hotels are full, but you should have an easier time with the campgrounds.

PRAIA A MARE
POP 6820
Praia a Mare lies just short of Basilicata, the start of a stretch of wide, pebbly beach that continues south for about 30km to Cirella and Diamante. This flat, leafy grid of a town sits on a wide pale-grey beach, looking out to an intriguing rocky chunk off the coast: the Isola di Dino.

Just off the seafront is the **tourist office** (☑0985 7 25 85; Via Amerigo Vespucci 6; ☺8am-1pm) with information on the **Isola di Dino**, famed for its sea caves. To visit the caves expect to pay around €5 for a guided tour from the old boys who operate off the beach. Alternatively, ask at the tourist office.

Autolinee Preite (☑0984 41 30 01) operates buses to Cosenza (€5.20, two hours, 10 daily). **SITA** (☑0971 50 68 11; www.sitabus.it, in Italian) goes north to Maratea and Potenza.

Regular trains also pass through for Paola and Reggio di Calabria.

AIETA & TORTORA
Precariously perched, otherworldly Aieta and Tortora must have been difficult to reach pre-asphalt. **Rocco** (☑0973 22 943; www.roccosrl.it) buses serve both villages, 6km and 12km from Praia respectively. Aieta is higher than Tortora and the journey constitutes much of the reward. When you arrive, walk up to the 16th-century **Palazzo Spinello** at the end of the road and take a look into the ravine behind it – it's a stunning view.

DIAMANTE
POP 5400
This fashionable seaside town, with its long promenade, is central to Calabria's famous *peperoncino* – the conversation-stalling spice that so characterises its cuisine. In early September a hugely popular chilli-eating competition takes place. Diamante is also famed for the bright murals that contemporary local and foreign artists have painted on the facades of the old buildings. For the best seafood restaurants head for the seafront at Spiaggia Piccola.

Autolinee Preite (☑0984 41 30 01) buses between Cosenza and Praia a Mare stop at Diamante.

PAOLA
POP 16.900
Paola is worth a stop to see its holy shrine. The large pilgrimage complex is above a sprawling small town where the dress of choice is a tracksuit and the main activity is hanging about on street corners. The 80km of coast south from here to Pizzo is mostly overdeveloped and ugly. Paola is the main train hub for Cosenza, about 25km inland.

Watched over by a crumbling castle, the **Santuario di San Francesco di Paola** (☑0982 58 25 18; admission free; ☺6am-1pm & 2-6pm) is a curious, empty cave with tremendous significance to the devout. St Francis of Paola lived and died here in the 15th century and the sanctuary that he and his followers carved out of the bare rock has attracted pilgrims for centuries. The cloister is surrounded by naive wall paintings depicting the saint's truly incredible miracles. The original church contains an ornate reliquary of the saint. Also within the complex is a modern basilica, built to mark the second millennium. Black-clad monks hurry about.

PARCO NAZIONALE DEL POLLINO

Italy's largest national park, the **Pollino National Park** (www.parcopollino.it), straddles Basilicata and Calabria and covers 1960 sq km. It acts like a rocky curtain separating the region from the rest of Italy and has the richest repository of flora and fauna in the south.

The park's most spectacular areas are Monte Pollino (2248m), Monti di Orsomarso (1987m), and the canyon of the Gole del Raganello. The mountains, often snowbound, are blanketed by forests of oak, alder, maple, beech, pine and fir. The park is most famous, however, for its ancient *pino loricato* trees, which are only found here and in the Balkans. The oldest specimens reach 40m in height.

The park has a varied landscape, from deep river canyons to alpine meadows, and is home to rare stocks of roe deer, wild cats, wolves, birds of prey (including the golden eagle and Egyptian vulture) and the endangered otter, *Lutra lutra*.

In Basilicata, the park's main centre is **Rotonda** (elevation 626m) and is home to the official park office, **Ente Parco Nazionale del Pollino** (☎0973 66 93 11; Via delle Frecce Tricolori 6; ⊗8am-2pm Mon-Fri, 3-5.30pm Mon & Wed). Interesting villages to explore include the unique Albanian villages of **San Paolo Albanese** and **San Costantino Albanese**. These isolated and unspoilt communities fiercely maintain their mountain culture and the Greek liturgy is retained in the main churches. For local handicrafts visit **Terranova di Pollino** for wooden crafts, **Latronico** for alabaster and **Sant'Arcangelo** for wrought iron.

In Calabria, **Civita** was founded by Albanian refugees in 1746. Other towns worth visiting are **Castrovillari**, with its well-preserved 15th-century Aragonese castle, and **Morano Calabro** – look up the beautiful MC Escher woodcut of this town. Naturalists should also check out the wildlife museum **Centro Il Nibbio** (☎0981 3 07 45; Vico II Annunziata 11; admission €4; ⊗10am-1pm & 4-8pm summer, 10am-1pm & 3-6pm winter) in Morano, which explains the Pollino ecosystem.

Good hiking maps are scarce. The *Carta Excursionistica del Pollino Lucano* (scale 1:50,000), produced by the Basilicata tourist board, is a useful driving map. The largescale *Parco Nazionale del Pollino* map shows all the main routes and includes some useful information on the park, its flora and fauna and the park communities. Both maps are free and can be found in local tourist offices.

For an English-speaking guide, contact Giuseppe Cosenza from Asklepios (below), who arranges trekking, mountain biking and rafting trips in the Pollino and throughout Basilicata. Ferula Viaggi in Matera also runs mountain-bike excursions and treks into the Pollino. For guided trips in Calabria visit www.guidapollino.it.

White-water rafting down the spectacular Lao river is popular in the Calabrian Pollino. **Centro Lao Action Raft** (☎0985 2 14 76; www.laoraft.com; Via Lauro 8) in Scalea can arrange rafting trips as well as canyoning, trekking and mountain-biking trips.

The park has a number of *agriturismi* (farm-stay accommodation). **Agriturismo Colloreto** (☎347 323 69 14; www.colloreto.it; Fratelli Coscia; s/d €28/56), near Morano Calabro, is in a remote rural setting, gorgeous amid rolling hills. Rooms are comfortable and old-fashioned with polished wood and flagstone floors. Also in Calabria, **Locanda di Alia** (☎0981 4 63 70; www.alia.it; Via Ietticelle 55; s/d €90/120; P✳☒), in Castrovillari, offers bungalow-style accommodation in a lush green garden.

In Basilicata, **Asklepios** (☎0973 66 92 90, 347 2631462; www.asklepios.it; Contrada Barone 9, Rotonda; s/d €30/50) has basic accommodation but is the place to stay for walkers as it's run by hiking guide Giuseppe Cosenza. Otherwise, the chalet-style **Picchio Nero** (☎0973 9 31 70; www.picchionero.com; Via Mulino 1; s/d incl breakfast €60/73; P) in Terranova di Pollino, with its Austrian-style wooden balconies and recommended restaurant, is a popular hotel for hikers.

Two highly recommended restaurants include **Luna Rossa** (☎0973 9 32 54; Via Marconi 18; meals €35; ⊗Thu-Tue) in Terranova di Pollino, and **Da Peppe** (☎0973 66 12 51; Corso Garibaldi 13; meals €25-35; ⊗lunch & dinner Tue-Sun) in Rotonda.

You'll need your own vehicle to visit the Pollino.

There are several hotels near the station, but you'll be better off staying in towns further north along the coast.

Cosenza

POP 69,800 / ELEV 238M

Cosenza's medieval core is Calabria's best-preserved historic centre, the one piece of history that has mostly managed to escape the constant earthquakes that have levelled almost everything else in the region. It rises above the confluence of the Crati and Busento rivers, its narrow lanes winding ever upwards to the hilltop castle. Legend states that Alaric, a Visigoth king, was killed and buried at the confluence of the two rivers.

In the past Cosenza was a sophisticated and lively city but nowadays there's a gritty feel to the old town with its dark streets and fading, once-elegant *palazzi*. It's the gateway to La Sila's mountains, home to Calabria's most important university and a major transport hub – but there's not much to see or do here.

◉ Sights

In the new town, pedestrianised Corso Mazzini provides a pleasant respite from the chaotic traffic and incessant car honking. There are a number of sculptures lining the *corso*.

In the old town, head up the winding, charmingly dilapidated Corso Telesio, which has a raw Neapolitan feel to it and is lined with ancient hung-with-washing tenements, antiquated shopfronts and a worrying number of funeral parlours. At the top, the 12th-century **cathedral** (Piazza del Duomo; ☺8am-noon & 3-7.30pm) has been rebuilt in restrained baroque style in the 18th century. In a chapel off the north aisle is a copy of an exquisite 13th-century Byzantine Madonna.

From the cathedral, you can walk up Via del Seggio through a little medieval quarter before turning right to reach the 13th-century **Convento di San Francesco d'Assisi**. Otherwise head along the *corso* to Piazza XV Marzo, an appealing square fronted by the Palazzo del Governo and the handsome neoclassical **Teatro Rendano**.

South of the piazza stretches the lovely **Villa Vecchia** park with lofty mature trees providing welcome shade.

From Piazza XV Marzo, follow Via Paradiso, then Via Antonio Siniscalchi for the route to the down-at-heel Norman **castle** (Piazza Frederico II), left in disarray by several earthquakes. It's closed for restoration, but the view merits the steep ascent.

🛏 Sleeping

B&B Via dell'Astrologo   B&B €
(☎338 920 53 94; www.viadellastrologo.com; Via Rutilio Benincasa 16; s €35-40, d €60-70, tr €90; ⊛) A gem in the historic centre, this small B&B is tastefully decorated with polished wooden floors, white bedspreads and good-quality artwork. Brothers Mario and Marco are a mine of information on Cosenza and Calabria in general.

Royal Hotel   HOTEL €€
(☎0984 41 21 65; www.hotelroyalsas.it; Via Molinella 24; €100; P❄@⊛) One of the few decent options in town, the Royal is a short stroll from Corso Mazzini. Rooms are impersonal but comfortable. Stay in the new section of the hotel, around the corner from its older sister.

✖ Eating

Gran Caffè Renzelli   CAFE €
(Corso Telesio 46) This venerable cafe behind the duomo has been run by the same family since 1803, when the founder arrived from Naples and began baking gooey cakes and desserts (cakes start at around €1.20). Sink your teeth into *torroncino torrefacto* (a confection of sugar, spices and hazelnuts) or *torta telesio* (made from almonds, cherries, apricot jam and lupins).

Ristorante Calabria Bella   TRADITIONAL ITALIAN €€
(☎0984 79 35 31; www.ristorantecalabriabella.it; Piazza del Duomo; meals €25; ☺noon-3pm & 7pm-midnight) Traditional Calabrian cuisine, such as *grigliata mista di carne* (mixed grilled meats), is regularly dished up in this cosy restaurant in the old town.

Per... Bacco!!   TRATTORIA €€
(☎0984 79 55 69; www.perbaccowinebar.it; Piazza dei Valdesi; meals €25) This smart yet informal restaurant has windows onto the square. Inside are exposed stone walls, vines and heavy beams. The reassuringly brief menu includes a generous and tasty antipasto (€8).

❶ Information

The main drag, Corso Mazzini, runs south from Piazza Bilotti (formerly known as Piazza Fera), near the bus station, and intersects Viale Trieste before meeting Piazza dei Bruzi. Head further south and cross the Busento river to reach the old town.

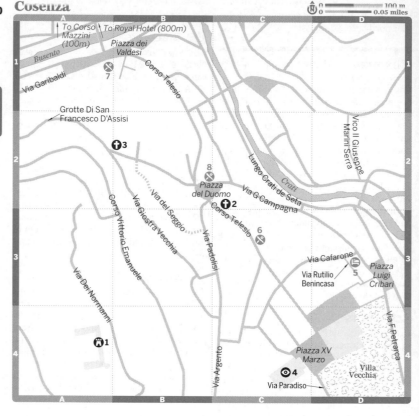

ℹ Getting There & Around

Air

Lamezia Terme airport (Sant'Eufemia Lamezia, SUF; ☎0968 41 43 33; www.sacal.it), 63km south of Cosenza, at the junction of the A3 and SS280 motorways, links the region with major Italian cities. The airport is also served by Ryanair, easyJet and charters from northern Europe. A shuttle leaves the airport every 20 minutes for the airport train station where there are frequent trains to Cosenza (€4.60, one hour).

Bus

The main **bus station** (☎0984 41 31 24) is northeast of Piazza Bilotti. Services leave for Catanzaro (€4.60, 1¾ hours, eight daily) and towns throughout La Sila. **Autolinee Preite** (☎0984 41 30 01) has buses heading daily along the north Tyrrhenian coast; **Autolinee Romano** (☎0962 2 17 09) serves Crotone as well as Rome and Milan.

Train

Stazione Nuova (☎0984 2 70 59) is about 2km northeast of the centre. Regular trains go to Reggio di Calabria (from €11.60, three hours) and Rome (from €44, four to six hours), both usually with a change at Paola, and Naples (from €26.40, three to four hours), as well as most destinations around the Calabrian coast.

Amaco (☎0984 30 80 11) bus 27 links the centre and Stazione Nuova, the main train station.

Parco Nazionale della Sila

'La Sila' is a big landscape, where wooded hills create endless rolling views. It's dotted with small villages and cut through with looping roads that make driving a test of your digestion.

Covering 130 sq km, it's divided into three areas: the Sila Grande, with the highest mountains; the strongly Albanian Sila Greca

Cosenza

⊙ **Sights**

(to the north); and the Sila Piccola (near Catanzaro), with vast forested hills.

The highest peaks, covered with tall Corsican pines, reach 2000m – high enough for thick snow in winter. This makes it a popular skiing destination. In summer the climate is coolly alpine, spring sees carpets of wildflowers and there's mushroom hunting in autumn. At its peak is the Bosco di Gallopani (Forest of Gallopani). There are several beautiful lakes, the largest of which is Lago di Cecita o Mucone near Camigliatello Silano. There is also plenty of wildlife here, including the light grey Apennine wolf, a protected species.

Good-quality information in English is scarce. You can try the national park **visitors centre** (☏0984 53 71 09) at Cupone, 10km from Camigliatello, or the **Pro Loco tourist office** (☏0984 57 81 59; Via Roma; ⏰9.30am-12.30pm & 3.30-6.30pm Wed-Mon) in Camigliatello. A useful internet resource is the official park website: www.parcosila.it. The people who run B&B Calabria in the park are very knowledgeable and helpful.

For maps, you can use *Carta del Parco Nazionale della Sila* (€8) which has walking trails (in Italian). *The Sila for 4* is a miniguide in English which outlines a number of walking trails in the park. The booklet is available in tourist offices and from the privately run **New Sila Tourist Service Agency** (☏0984 57 81 25; Via Roma 16, Camigliatello) – a good source of information on the park.

Valli Cupe (☏333 6988835, 333 8643601; www.vallicupe.it) runs hiking trips in the area around Sersale (in the southeast), where there are myriad waterfalls and the dramatic Canyon Valli Cupe. Trips cost only €8 per person per day. Specialising in botany, the guides (who speak Italian and French) also visit remote monasteries and churches. Stay in their rustic accommodation in the town.

During August, **Sila in Festa** takes place, featuring traditional music. Autumn is mushroom season, when you'll be able to frequent mushroom festivals including the **Sagra del Fungo** in Camigliatello.

⊙ Sights & Activities

La Sila's main town, **San Giovanni in Fiore** (1049m), is named after the founder of its beautiful medieval **abbey**. The town has an attractive old centre, once you've battled through the suffocating suburbs, and is famous for its Armenian-style hand-loomed carpets and tapestry. You can visit the studio and shop of **Domenico Caruso** (☏0984 99 27 24; www.scuolatappeti.it), but ring ahead.

A popular ski-resort town, with 6km of slopes, **Camigliatello Silano** (1272m) looks much better under snow. A few lifts operate on Monte Curcio, about 3km to the south. Around 5.5km of slopes and a 1500m lift can be found near **Lorica** (1370m), on gloriously pretty Lago Arvo – the best place to camp in summer.

Scigliano (620m), in Sila Piccola, is a small hilltop town and has a superb B&B; from **Sersale** (739m), further south, you can go trekking with Valli Cupe guides.

🛏 Sleeping

TOP CHOICE **B&B Calabria**   B&B €

(☏349 878 18 94; Via Roma 9, Frazione Diano, Scigliano; www.bedandbreakfastcalabria.it; s/d €40/60; ⏰Apr-Nov) In the mountains, this B&B has five comfortable rooms, all with separate entrances. Raffaele is a great source of information on the region and can recommend places to eat, visit and go hiking. Rooms have character and clean modern lines and there's a wonderful terrace overlooking endless forested vistas. Mountain bikes available.

Hotel Aquila & Edelweiss   HOTEL €

(☏0984 57 80 44; www.hotelaquilaedelweiss.com; Viale Stazione 15, Camigliatello; s €60-80, d €80-100; P✳@) This three-star hotel in Camigliatello has a stark and anonymous exterior but it's in a good location and the rooms are cosy and comfortable.

Valli Cupe
B&B €

(☎333 6988835; Sersale; www.vallicupe.it; per person €20) Valli Cupe can arrange a stay in a charming rustic cottage in Sersale, complete with an open fireplace (good for roasting chestnuts) and kitchen. All bookings via its website.

Park Hotel 108
HOTEL €€

(☎0521 64 81 08; www.hotelpark108.it; Via Nazionale 86, Lorica; r €90-130; P🖤) Situated on the hilly banks of Lago Arvo, surrounded by dark-green pines, the rooms here are decorated in classic bland hotel style – but who cares about decor with views like this!

Camping del Lago Arvo
CAMPGROUND €

(☎0984 53 70 60; camping 2 people, tent & car €10-14, bungalows €40-60) Lorica's lakeside is a particularly great place to camp. Try this large comfortable spot, near the Calabrian National Park office.

🛍 Shopping

La Sila's forests yield wondrous wild mushrooms, both edible and poisonous. Sniff around the **Antica Salumeria Campanaro** (Piazza Misasi 5) in Camigliatello Silano; it's a temple to fungi, as well as an emporium of fine meats, cheeses, pickles and wines.

ℹ Getting There & Away

You can reach Camigliatello Silano and San Giovanni in Fiore via regular Ferrovie della Calabria buses along the SS107, which links Cosenza and Crotone.

Ionian Coast

With its flat coastline and wide sandy beaches, the Ionian coast has some fascinating stops from Sibari to Santa Severina, with some of the best beaches on the coast around Soverato. However, the coast has borne the brunt of some ugly development and is mainly a long, uninterrupted string of resorts, crowded in the summer months and shut down from October to May.

It's worth taking a trip inland to visit **Santa Severina**, a spectacular mountaintop town, 26km northwest of Crotone. The town is dominated by a Norman castle and is home to a beautiful Byzantine church.

LE CASTELLA

The town is named for its impressive 16th-century Aragonese **castle** (admission €3; ⊙ 9am-midnight summer, 9am-1pm & 3-6pm winter),

a vast edifice linked to the mainland by a short causeway. The philosopher Pliny said that Hannibal constructed the first tower. Evidence shows it was begun in the 4th century BC, designed to protect Crotone in the wars against Pyrrhus.

Le Castella is south of a rare protected area (Capo Rizzuto) along this coast, rich not only in nature but also in Greek history. For further information on the park try www.riservamarinacaporizzuto.it.

With around 15 campgrounds near Isola di Capo Rizzuto to the north, this is the Ionian coast's prime camping area. Try **La Fattoria** (☎0962 79 11 65; Via del Faro; camping 2 people, car & tent €23, bungalows €60; ⊙Jun-Sep), 1.5km from the sea, with bungalows also available. Otherwise, **Da Annibale** (☎0962 79 50 04; Via Duomo 35; s/d €50/70; P🌸@🖤) is a pleasant hotel in town with a splendid fish restaurant (meals €30, open lunch and dinner).

For expansive sea views dine at bright and airy **Ristorante Micomare** (☎0962 79 50 82; Via Vittoria 7; meals €20-25; ⊙lunch & dinner).

GERACE
POP 2830

A spectacular medieval hill town, Gerace is worth a detour for the views alone – on one side the Ionian Sea, on the other dark interior mountains. About 10km inland from Locri on the SS111, it has Calabria's largest Romanesque **cathedral**. Dating from 1045, later alterations have robbed it of none of its majesty.

For a taste of traditional Calabrian cooking, the modest and welcoming **Ristorante a Squella** (☎0964 35 60 86; Viale della Resistenza 8; meals €20) makes for a great lunchtime stop. It serves reliably good dishes, specialising in seafood and pizzas. Afterwards you can wander down the road and admire the views.

Further inland is **Canolo**, a small village seemingly untouched by the 20th century. Buses connect Gerace with Locri and also Canolo with Siderno, both of which link to the main coastal railway line.

Parco Nazionale dell'Aspromonte

Most Italians think of the **Parco Nazionale dell'Aspromonte** (www.parcoaspromonte. it, in Italian) as a hiding place used by Calabrian kidnappers in the 1970s and '80s. It's still rumoured to contain 'Ndrangheta strongholds, but as a tourist you're unlikely to encounter any murky business. The national park, Calabria's second largest, is startlingly dramatic, rising sharply inland from Reggio. Its highest peak, **Montalto** (1955m), is dominated by a huge bronze statue of Christ and offers sweeping views across to Sicily.

Subject to frequent mudslides and carved up by torrential rivers, the mountains are nonetheless awesomely beautiful. Underwater rivers keep the peaks covered in coniferous forests and ablaze with flowers in spring. It's wonderful walking country and the park has several colour-coded trails.

Extremes of weather and geography have resulted in some extraordinary villages, such as **Pentidàttilo** and **Roghudi**, clinging limpetlike to the craggy, rearing rocks and now all but deserted. It's worth the drive to explore these eagle-nest villages. Another mountain eyrie with a photogenic ruined castle is **Bova**, perched at 900m above sea level. The drive up the steep, dizzying road to Bova is not for the faint-hearted, but the views are stupendous.

Maps are scarce. Try the **national park office** (☑0965 74 30 60; www.parcoaspromonte. it; Via Aurora; ☉9am-1pm Mon-Fri, 3-5pm Tue & Thu) in **Gambarie**, the Aspromonte's main town and the easiest approach to the park. The roads are good and many activities are organised from here – you can ski and it's also the place to hire a 4WD; ask around in the town.

It's also possible to approach from the south, but the roads aren't as good. The co-operative **Naturaliter** (☑347 3046799; www. naturaliterweb.it), based in **Condofuri**, is an excellent source of information, and can help arrange walking and donkey treks and place you in B&Bs throughout the region. **Co-operativa San Leo** (☑347 304 67 99), based in Bova also provides guided tours and accommodation. In Reggio di Calabria, you can book treks and tours with **Misafumera** (☑0965 67 70 21; www.misafumera.it; Via Nazionale 306d).

Stay on a bergamot farm at **Azienda Agrituristica Il Bergamotto** (☑347 601 23 38; Via Amendolea, Condofuri; per person €25) where Ugo Sergi can also arrange excursions. Hiking trails pass nearby so it's a good hiking base. The rooms are simple but it's in a lovely rural location and the food is delicious.

To reach Gambarie, take ATAM city bus 127 from Reggio di Calabria (€1, 1½ hours,

up to six daily). Most of the roads inland from Reggio eventually hit the SS183 road that runs north to the town.

Reggio di Calabria

POP 185,900

Reggio is the main launching point for ferries to Sicily, which sparkles temptingly across the Strait of Messina. It is also home to the spectacular Bronzi di Riace and has a long, impressive seafront promenade – packed during the evening *passeggiata*. Otherwise, the city's grid system of dusty streets has the slightly dissolute feel shared by most ports.

Beyond the seafront, the centre gives way to urban sprawl. Ravaged by earthquakes, the most recent in 1908, this once-proud ancient Greek city has plenty of other woes. As a port and the largest town close to the 'Ndrangheta strongholds of Aspromonte, organised crime is a major problem, with the associated corrosive social effect.

On a lighter note, there are plenty of festivals in Reggio – early August sees the **Festival dello Stretto** (www.festivaldellostretto.it), featuring the traditional music of the south.

◉ Sights

Museo Nazionale della Magna Grecia   MUSEUM

(☑0965 81 22 55; www.museonazionalerc.it; Piazza de Nava 26; adult/child €7/3, ☉9am-7.30pm Tue-Sun) The museum's pride are the world's finest examples of ancient Greek sculpture: the **Bronzi di Riace**, two exquisite bronze statues discovered on the seabed near Riace in 1972. Larger than life, they depict the Greek obsession with the body: inscrutable, determined and fierce, their perfect form more godlike than human. No-one knows who they are – whether man or god – and even their provenance is a mystery. They date from around 450 BC; it's believed they're the work of two artists.

Aside from the bronzes, there are other magnificent ancient exhibits. Look out for the 5th-century-BC bronze *Philosopher's Head,* the oldest known Greek portrait in existence.

🛏 Sleeping

Finding a room should be easy, even in summer, since most visitors pass straight through en route to Sicily.

Reggio di Calabria

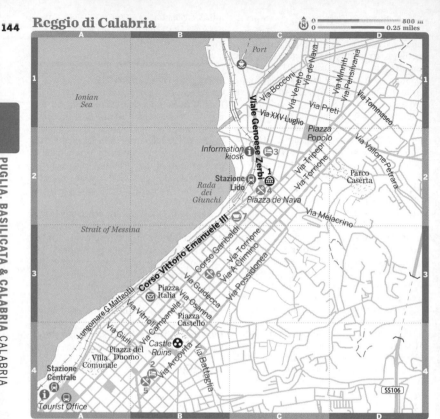

Reggio di Calabria

⊚ Sights
1 Museo Nazionale della Magna
   Grecia C2

🛏 Sleeping
2 B&B Casa Blanca B4
3 Hotel Lungomare C2

🍽 Eating
4 Cèsare C2
5 La Cantina del Macellaio B4
6 Le Rose al Bicchiere B3

🍷 Drinking
7 Caffe Matteoti C2

B&B Casa Blanca B&B €
(☎347 9459210; www.bbcasablanca.it; Via Arcovito 24; s €40-50, d €65-80; ✳🅰) A little gem in Reggio's heart, this 19th-century *palazzo* has spacious rooms gracefully furnished with romantic white-on-white decor. There's a self-serve breakfast nook, a small breakfast table in each room and two apartments available. Great choice.

Hotel Lungomare HOTEL €€
(☎0965 2 04 86; www.hotellungomare.rc.it; Viale Genoese Zerbi 13; s/d €85/130; 🅿✳@🅰) The ornate wedding-cake exterior is a welcome reprise from Reggio's faceless modern blocks. Rooms are plain and nothing special, but the staff are friendly and courteous. Ask for a room with a sea view.

✕ Eating & Drinking

Le Rose al Bicchiere TRADITIONAL ITALIAN €€
(☎0965 2 29 56; Via Demetrio Tripepi 118; meals €30; ☺lunch Mon-Fri, dinner Mon-Sat Oct-Jun) A wine bar with some delicious, fresh local and organic produce on offer to accompany wines so inviting you'll have to pour yourself onto the ferry. The local cheeses and desserts are particularly good.

La Cantina del Macellaio TRATTORIA €€
(☎0965 2 39 32; www.lacantinadelmacellaio.it; Via Arcovito 26; meals €25; ☺dinner nightly, lunch Sun) This popular trattoria, recommended by locals, dishes up typical Calabrian cuisine with an emphasis on meat dishes. The wine cellar is extensive and impressive.

Caffe Matteotti CAFE €
(www.caffematteotti.it; Corso Vittorio Emanuele 39; ☺7am-2am Tue-Sun) The tables along the corso offer sea views with your *aperitivi* and it's a prime spot for people watching.

Cèsare GELATERIA €
(Piazza Indipendenza; ☺6am-1am) The most popular gelateria in town is in a green kiosk at the end of the *lungomare* (seafront).

ⓘ Information

Stazione Centrale, the main train station, is at the town's southern edge. Walk northeast along Corso Garibaldi for the tourist office, shopping and other services. The *corso* has long been a de-facto pedestrian zone during the ritual *passeggiata*.

Hospital (☎0965 39 71 11; Via Melacrino)
Police station (☎0965 41 11 11; Corso Garibaldi 442)
Post office (Via Miraglia 14)
Tourist information kiosk (Viale Genovese Zerbi ☺9am-noon & 4-7pm); **airport** (☎0965 64 32 91); **Stazione Centrale** (☎0965 2 71 20)

ⓘ Getting There & Away
Air
Reggio's **airport** (REG; www.aeroportodellostretto.it; ☎0965 64 05 17) is at Ravagnese, about 5km south.

Boat
Boats for Messina (Sicily) leave from the port (just north of Stazione Lido), where there are three adjacent ferry terminals. In high season there are up to 20 hydrofoils daily; in low season there are as few as two. Some boats continue to the Aeolian Islands.

Services are run by various companies, including **Meridiano** (☎0965 81 04 14; www. meridianolines.it). Prices for cars are €12 one way and for foot passengers €1.50 to €2.80. The crossing takes 20 minutes.

Bus
Most buses terminate at Piazza Garibaldi, in front of Stazione Centrale. Several different companies operate to towns in Calabria and beyond. **ATAM** (☎800 43 33 10; www.atam-rc. it) serves the Aspromonte Massif, with bus 127 to Gambarie (€1, 1½ hours, six daily). **Lirosi** (☎0966 5 79 01) serves Rome (€46, eight hours, two daily). Regional trains are more convenient than bus services to Scilla and Tropea.

Car & Motorcycle
The A3 ends at Reggio. If you are continuing south, the SS106 hugs the coast round the 'toe', then heads north along the Ionian Sea. Reggio has a weirdly complex parking system – buy a parking permit (€0.50 per hour) from newspaper kiosks or from a parking representative, if you can find one.

Train
Trains stop at **Stazione Centrale** (☎0965 89 20 21) and less frequently at Stazione Lido, near the museum. There are frequent trains to Milan (from €140, 9½ to 11½ hours), Rome (from €69, 7½ hours) and Naples (from €56, 4½ to 5½ hours). Regional services run along the coast to Scilla and Tropea, and also to Catanzaro and less frequently to Cosenza and Bari.

ⓘ Getting Around
Orange local buses run by **ATAM** (☎800 43 33 10; www.atam-rc.it) cover most of the city. For the port, take bus 13 or 125 from Piazza Garibaldi outside Stazione Centrale. The Porto-Aeroporto bus (125) runs from the port via Piazza Garibaldi to the airport and vice versa (25 minutes, hourly). Buy your ticket at ATAM offices, tobacconists or newsstands.

Southern Tyrrhenian Coast

North of Reggio, along the coast-hugging Autostrada del Sole (A3), the scenery rocks and rolls to become increasingly beautiful and dramatic, if you ignore the shoddy holiday camps and unattractive developments that sometimes scar the land. Like the northern part of the coast, it's mostly closed in winter and packed in summer.

SCILLA
POP 5160

In Scilla, cream-, ochre- and earth-coloured houses cling on for dear life to the jagged promontory, ascending in jumbled ranks to the hill's summit, which is crowned by a castle and, just below, the dazzling white confection of the Chiesa Arcipretale Maria Immacolata. Lively in summer and serene in low season, the town is split in two by the tiny port. The fishing district of Scilla Chianalea, to the north, harbours small hotels and restaurants off narrow lanes, lapped by the sea. It can only be visited on foot.

Scilla's high point is a rock at the northern end, said to be the lair of Scylla, the mythical six-headed sea monster who drowned sailors as they tried to navigate the Strait of Messina. Swimming and fishing off the town's glorious white sandy beach is somewhat safer today. Head for Lido Paradiso from where you can squint up at the castle while sunbathing on the sand.

◎ Sights

Castello Ruffo CASTLE
(☑0956 70 42 07; admission €1.50; ☺8.30am-7.30pm) An imposing hilltop fortress, the castle has at times been a lighthouse and a monastery. It houses a *luntre,* the original black boat used for swordfishing, and on which the modern-day *passarelle* is based.

🛏 Sleeping

Le Piccole Grotte B&B €
(☑338 209 67 27; www.lepiccolegrotte.it; Via Grotte 10; d €90-120; ❋) In the picturesque Chianalea district, this B&B is housed in a 19th-century fishermen's house beside steps leading to the crystal-clear sea. Rooms have small balconies facing the cobbled alleyway or the sea.

La Locandiera B&B €
(☑0965 75 48 81; www.lalocandiera.org; Via Zagari 27; d €60-100; ❋🖤) Run by the same people who own Le Piccole Grotte, this B&B is just as picturesque with large, comfortable rooms and views over the sea.

✕ Eating & Drinking

Bleu de Toi SEAFOOD €€
(☑0965 79 05 85; www.bleudetoi.it; Via Grotte 40; meals €30-35; ☺Wed-Mon) Soak up the Chianalea atmosphere at this little restaurant. It has a terrace over the water and excellent seafood dishes including Scilla's renowned swordfish.

Dali City Pub DAR
(Via Porto) On the beach in Scilla town, this popular bar has a Beatles tribute corner (appropriately named The Cavern) and has been going since 1972.

CAPO VATICANO

There are spectacular views from this rocky cape, with its beaches, ravines and limestone sea cliffs. Birdwatchers' spirits should soar. Around 7km south of Tropea, Capo Vaticano has a lighthouse, built in 1885, which is close to a short footpath from where you can see as far as the Aeolian Islands. Capo Vaticano beach is one of the balmiest along this coast.

TROPEA
POP 6780

Tropea, a puzzle of lanes and piazzas, is famed for its captivating prettiness, dramatic position and sunsets the colour of amethyst. It sits on the Promontorio di Tropea, which stretches from Nicotera in the south to Pizzo in the north. The coast alternates between dramatic cliffs and icing-sugar-soft sandy beaches, all edged by translucent sea. Unsurprisingly, hundreds of Italian holidaymakers descend here in summer. If you hear English being spoken, it is probably from Americans visiting relatives: enormous numbers left the region for America in the early 20th century.

Despite the mooted theory that Hercules founded the town, it seems this area has been settled as far back as Neolithic times. Tropea has been occupied by the Arabs, Normans, Swabians, Anjous and Aragonese, as well as attacked by Turkish pirates. Perhaps they were after the town's famous sweet red onions.

◎ Sights

The town overlooks **Santa Maria dell'Isola**, a medieval church with a Renaissance makeover, which sits on its own island, although centuries of silt have joined it to the mainland.

The beautiful Norman **cathedral** (☺6.30-11.30am & 4-7pm) has two undetonated WWII bombs near the door: it's believed they didn't explode due to the protection of the town's patron saint, Our Lady of Romania.

🛏 Sleeping

Donnaciccina B&B €€
(☑0963 6 21 80; www.donnaciccina.com; Via Pelliccia 9; s €40-75, d €80-150; ❋@) Overlooking the main *corso,* this delightful B&B has retained

a tangible sense of history with its carefully selected antiques, canopy beds and exposed stone walls. There's also a self-catering apartment perfectly positioned on the cliff overlooking the sea.

Residence il Barone
B&B €€

(☎0963 60 71 81; Largo Barone; www.residenceilbarone.com; r €70-180; @※🖨) This graceful *palazzo* has six suites decorated in masculine neutrals and tobacco browns, with dramatic modern paintings by the owner's brother adding pizazz to the walls. There's a computer in each suite and you can breakfast on the small roof terrace with views over the old city and out to sea.

✕ Eating

Al Pinturicchio
TRADITIONAL ITALIAN €

(☎0963 60 34 52; www.ristorantiitaliani-it/pinturicchio; Via Dardona, cnr Largo Duomo; meals €16-22) Recommended by the locals, this restaurant in the old town has a romantic ambience, candlelit tables and a menu of imaginative dishes.

Osteria del Pescatore
SEAFOOD €

(☎0963 60 30 18; Via del Monte 7; meals €20-25; ☺dinner Thu-Tue) Swordfish rates highly on the menu at this simple seafood place tucked away in the backstreets.

ⓘ Information

CST Tropea (☎0963 6 11 78; www.csttropea.it; Largo San Michele 7; ☺9am-1pm & 4-7.30pm, to 10pm Jul & Aug) Helpful tourist office at the entrance to the old town. Can organize trekking, mountain biking, diving and cultural tours.
Tourist office (☎0963 6 14 75; Piazza Ercole; ☺9am-1pm & 4-8pm) In the old town centre.

ⓘ Getting There & Away

Trains run to Pizzo (30 minutes), Scilla (one hour 20 minutes) and Reggio (two hours). **SAV** (☎0963 6 11 29) buses connect with other towns on the coast.

Stacked high up on a sea cliff, pretty little Pizzo is the place to go for *tartufo*, a death-by-chocolate ice-cream ball, and to see an extraordinary rock-carved grotto church. It's a popular tourist stop. Piazza della Repubblica is the epicentre, set high above the sea with great views. Settle here at one of the many gelateria terraces for an ice-cream fix.

A kilometre north, the **Chiesa di Piedigrotta** (admission €2.50; ☺9am-1pm & 3-7.30pm) is an underground cave full of carved stone statues. It was carved into the tufa rock by Neapolitan shipwreck survivors in the 17th century. Other sculptors added to it and it was eventually turned into a church. Later statues include the less-godly figures of Fidel Castro and JFK. It's a bizarre, one-of-a-kind mixture of mysticism, mystery and kitsch.

In town, the 16th-century **Chiesa Matrice di San Giorgio** (Via Marconi), with its dressed-up Madonnas, houses the tomb of Joachim Murat, brother-in-law of Napoleon and one-time king of Naples. Although he was the architect of enlightened reforms, the locals showed no great concern when Murat was imprisoned and executed here. At the neat little 15th-century **Castello Murat** (☎0963 53 25 23; adult/reduced €2.50/1.50; ☺9am-1pm & 3pm-midnight Jun-Sep, 9am-1pm & 3-7pm Oct-May), south of Piazza della Repubblica, you can see Murat's cell. His last days and death by firing squad are graphically illustrated by waxworks.

Good accommodation is hard to find. **Armonia B&B** (☎0963 53 33 37; www.casa-armonia.com; Via Armonia 9; d without bathroom €50-75; @), run by the charismatic Franco, has a number of rooms (with shared bathroom). Eat at **Pizzeria Ruota** (☎0963 53 24 27; Piazza della Repubblica 36; pizzas from €4-6; ☺11am-3.30pm & 7.30pm-midnight Thu-Tue), which has splendid, big pizzas.

Sicily

POPULATION: 5 MILLION

Best Places to Eat

» Trattoria Ai Cascinari (p158)

» Quattro Gatti (p193)

» Il Liberty (p191)

» Il Gallo e l'Innamorata (p200)

» Vittorio (p200)

» Trattoria di De Fiore (p181)

Best Places to Stay

» Isoco Guest House (p175)

» Pensione Tranchina (p205)

» Villa Athena (p197)

» Villa Quartarella (p192)

Why Go?

More of a sugar-spiked espresso than a milky cappuccino, Sicily rewards visitors with an intense bittersweet experience rather than anything lightweight and frothy. Here it seems the sun shines brighter, the shadows are darker, and life is lived full-on and for the moment. Overloaded with art treasures and natural beauty, undersupplied with infrastructure and continuously struggling against Mafia-driven corruption, Sicily's complexities sometimes seem unfathomable. To really appreciate this place, come with an open mind – and a healthy appetite. Despite the island's contradictions one factor remains constant: the uncompromising quality of the cuisine.

After 25 centuries of foreign domination, Sicilians are heirs to an impressive cultural legacy, from the refined architecture of Magna Graecia to the Byzantine splendour and Arab craftsmanship of the island's Norman cathedrals and palaces. This cultural richness is matched by a startlingly diverse landscape that includes bucolic farmland, smouldering volcanoes and kilometres of island-studded aquamarine coastline.

When to Go
Palermo

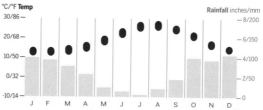

Feb Almond blossoms flower during Agrigento's Sagra del Mandorlo.

Easter Sicily's most colourful season.

May Spring weather, wildflowers and fewer crowds: a dreamy time for coastal walking.

History

Sicily's most deeply ingrained cultural influences originate from its first inhabitants – the Sicani from North Africa, the Siculi from Latium (Italy) and the Elymni from Greece. The subsequent colonisation of the island by the Carthaginians (also from North Africa) and the Greeks, in the 8th and 6th centuries BC respectively, compounded this cultural divide through decades of war when powerful opposing cities, such as Palermo and Catania, struggled to dominate the island.

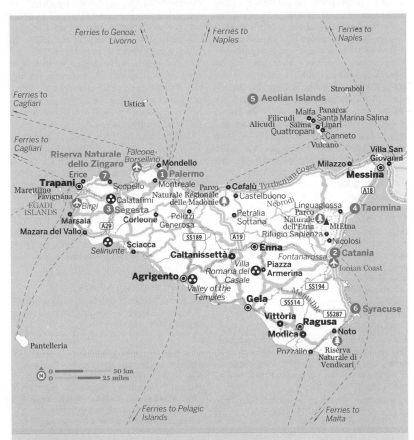

Sicily Highlights

❶ Join the ranks of impeccably dressed opera-goers at elegant **Teatro Massimo** (p159) in Palermo

❷ Bargain with the fish vendors at dawn, climb Europe's most active volcano in the afternoon and enjoy Sicily's best nightlife in constantly buzzing **Catania** (p177)

❸ Marvel at the majesty of **Segesta** (p205), whose Greek temple and amphitheatre sit in splendid isolation on a windswept hillside

❹ Shop till you drop in **Taormina** (p172), or ply the turquoise waters in the sparkling coves below

❺ Soak up the sun, watch Stromboli's volcanic fireworks and hike to your heart's content on the stunningly scenic **Aeolian Islands** (p164)

❻ Wander aimlessly in Ortygia's atmospheric alleys before settling in for an evening of classical drama at the fabled Greek theatre in **Syracuse** (p187)

❼ Hike the rugged, undeveloped coastline and scan the sky for eagles at **Riserva Naturale dello Zingaro** (p205)

Although inevitably part of the Roman Empire, it was not until the Arab invasions of AD 831 that Sicily truly came into its own. Trade, farming and mining were all fostered under Arab influence and Sicily soon became an enviable prize for European opportunists. The Normans, desperate for a piece of the pie, invaded in 1061 and made Palermo the centre of their expanding empire and the finest city in the Mediterranean.

Impressed by the cultured Arab lifestyle, King Roger squandered vast sums on ostentatious palaces and churches and encouraged a hedonistic atmosphere in his court. But such prosperity – and decadence (Roger's grandson, William II, even had a harem) – inevitably gave rise to envy and resentment and, after 400 years of pleasure and profit, the Norman line was extinguished and the kingdom passed to the austere German House of Hohenstaufen with little opposition from the seriously eroded and weakened Norman occupation. In the centuries that followed, Sicily passed to the Holy Roman Emperors, Angevins (French), Aragonese (Spanish) and Austrians in a turmoil of rebellion and revolution that continued until the Spanish Bourbons united Sicily with Naples in 1734 as the Kingdom of the Two Sicilies. Little more than a century later, on 11 May 1860, Giuseppe Garibaldi planned his daring and dramatic unification of Italy from Marsala.

Reeling from this catalogue of colonisers, Sicilians struggled in poverty-stricken conditions. Unified with Italy, but no better off, nearly one million men and women emigrated to the USA between 1871 and 1914 before the outbreak of WWI.

Ironically, the Allies (seeking Mafia help in America for the reinvasion of Italy) helped in establishing the Mafia's stranglehold on Sicily. In the absence of suitable administrators, they invited the undesirable *mafioso* (Mafia boss) Don Calógero Vizzini to do the job. When Sicily became a semi-autonomous region in 1948, Mafia control extended right to the heart of politics and the region plunged into a 50-year silent civil war. It only started to emerge from this after the anti-Mafia maxi-trials of the 1980s, in which Sicily's revered magistrates Giovanni Falcone and Paolo Borsellino hauled hundreds of Mafia members into court, leading to important prosecutions against members of the massive heroin and cocaine network between Palermo and New York, known as the 'pizza connection'.

Today most Sicilians remain less than enthralled by an organisation that continues to grow rich on money from the illegal drugs trade, human trafficking and – that old, ubiquitous cash-flow booster – extortion and protection which, experts say, many businesses in Sicily still pay. At least the thuggery and violence of the 1980s has diminished and there have been some important arrests, serving as encouragement for those who would speak out against Mafia influence.

ⓘ Getting There & Away

For additional transport details and local telephone contacts, see the Getting There & Away sections under individual cities.

AIR

An increasing number of airlines fly direct to Sicily's three international airports – Palermo (PMO), Catania (CTA) and Trapani (TPS) – although many still require a transfer in Rome or Milan. **Alitalia** (www.alitalia.com) is the main Italian carrier, while **Ryanair** (www.ryanair.com) is the leading low-cost airline carrier serving Sicily.

SICILY FERRY CROSSINGS

ROUTE	COST € (HIGH SEASON ADULT FARE)	DURATION (HOURS)
Genoa–Palermo	117	20
Malta–Catania	108	3
Naples–Catania	60	11
Naples–Palermo	55	11
Naples–Trapani	90	7
Reggio di Calabria–Messina	2	35 min
Tunis–Palermo	69	10

BOAT

Regular car and passenger ferries cross the strait between Villa San Giovanni (Calabria) and Messina, while hydrofoils connect Messina with Reggio di Calabria.

Sicily is also accessible by ferry from Naples, Civitavecchia, Livorno, Genoa, Cagliari, Malta and Tunisia. Prices rise between June and September, when advanced bookings may also be required.

BUS

SAIS (☎091 617 11 41; www.saistrasporti.it) runs long-haul services to Sicily from Rome and Naples.

TRAIN

Direct trains run from Milan, Florence, Rome, Naples and Reggio di Calabria to Messina and on to Palermo, Catania and other provincial capitals; the trains are transported from the mainland by ferry from Villa San Giovanni.

For travellers originating in Rome and points south, InterCity trains cover the distance from mainland Italy to Sicily in the least possible time, without a change of train. If coming from Milano, Bologna or Florence, your fastest option is to take the ultra-high-speed Frecciarossa as far as Naples, then change to an InterCity train for the rest of the journey.

If saving money is your top priority, Espresso or InterCity night trains will still get you to Sicily relatively fast, and won't take such a big bite out of your budget.

❶ Getting Around

AIR

Regular domestic flights serve the offshore islands of Pantelleria and Lampedusa. Local carriers include Alitalia, Meridiana and Air One.

BUS

Bus services within Sicily are provided by a variety of companies. Buses are usually faster if your destination involves travel through the island's interior; trains tend to be cheaper (and sometimes faster) on the major coastal routes. In small towns and villages tickets are often sold in bars or on the bus.

CAR & MOTORCYCLE

Having your own vehicle is advantageous in the interior, where public transit is often slow and limited. Roads are generally good and autostradas connect most major cities. There's a cheap and worthwhile toll road running along the Ionian coast. Drive defensively; the Sicilians are some of Italy's most aggressive drivers, with a penchant for overtaking on blind corners, holding a mobile phone in one hand while gesticulating wildly with the other!

TRAIN

The coastal train service is very efficient. Services to towns in the interior tend be infrequent and slow, although if you have the time the routes can be very picturesque. IC trains are the fastest and most expensive, while the *regionale* is the slowest.

PALERMO

POP 656,000

Palermo is a city of decay and of splendour and – provided you can handle its raw energy, deranged driving and chaos – has plenty of appeal. Unlike those of Florence or Rome, many of the city's treasures are hidden, rather than scrubbed up for endless streams of tourists. This giant treasure trove of palaces, castles and churches has a unique architectural fusion of Byzantine, Arab, Norman, Renaissance and baroque gems.

While some of the crumbling *palazzi* that were bombed in WWII are being restored, others remain dilapidated; turned into shabby apartments, the faded glory of their ornate facades is just visible behind strings of brightly coloured washing. The evocative history of the city remains very much part of the daily life of its inhabitants, and the dusty web of backstreet markets in the old quarter has a tangible Middle Eastern feel.

The flip side is the modern city, a mere 15-minute stroll away, parts of which could be neatly jigsawed and slotted into Paris with its grid system of wide avenues lined by seductive shops and handsome 19th-century apartments.

At one time an Arab emirate and seat of a Norman kingdom, Palermo became Europe's grandest city in the 12th century, but in more recent years the city's fame (or its notoriety) has originated from the Mafia's pervasive influence. Many judges here require 24-hour police surveillance and, despite a growing campaign of public resistance, protection pay-offs remain commonplace.

◎ Sights

Via Maqueda is the main street, running north from the train station, changing names to Via Ruggero Settimo as it passes the landmark Teatro Massimo, then finally widening into leafy Viale della Libertà north of Piazza Castelnuovo, the beginning of the city's modern district.

Palermo

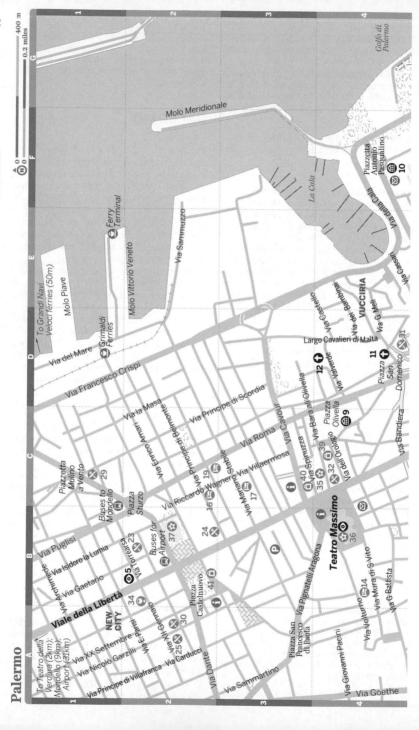

N
0   400 m
0   0.2 miles

To Teatro della
Verdura (2km);
Mondello (9km);
Airport (31km)

To Grandi Navi
Veloci Ferries (50m)

**NEW
CITY**

Molo Piave

Molo Vittorio Veneto

Ferry
Terminal

Grimaldi
Ferries

Molo Meridionale

La Cala

Golfo di
Palermo

Piazzetta
Antonio
Pasqualino

10

VUCCIRIA

Largo Cavalieri di Malta

Largo Castello

Piazza
San
Domenico

11

12

Via Valverde

Piazza
Olivella

9

Piazza
Sturzo

Piazzetta
Mulino
a Vento

29

Buses to
Mondello

Via del Mare

Via Francesco Crispi

Via la Masa

Via Enrico Amari

Via Principe di Belmonte

Via Principe di Scordia

Via Roma

Via Cavour

Via Bara all'Olivella

Via Spinuzza

Via dell'Orologio

40

35

39

32

Via Mariano Stabile

Via Villaermosa

16

19

17

Via Riccardo Wagner

24

37

Buses for
Airport

Piazza
Castelnuovo

41

30

25

5

23

34

Via Torrearsa

Via Puglisi

Via Archimede

Via Isidoro la Lumia

Via Gaetano

Viale della Libertà

Via XX Settembre

Via Nicolò Garzilli

Via E. Parisi

Via XII Gennaio

Via Dante

Via Carducci

Via Principe di Villafranca

Via Sammartino

Piazza San
Francesco
di Paola

Via Pignatelli Aragona

Teatro Massimo

36

Via Volturno

Via Mura di S Vito

14

Via G Battista

Via Giovanni Pacini

Via Goethe

Via Sammuzzo

Via delle Cale

Via Cessari

Via G. Meli

Via dei Bambinai

Via Bandiera

31

SICILY

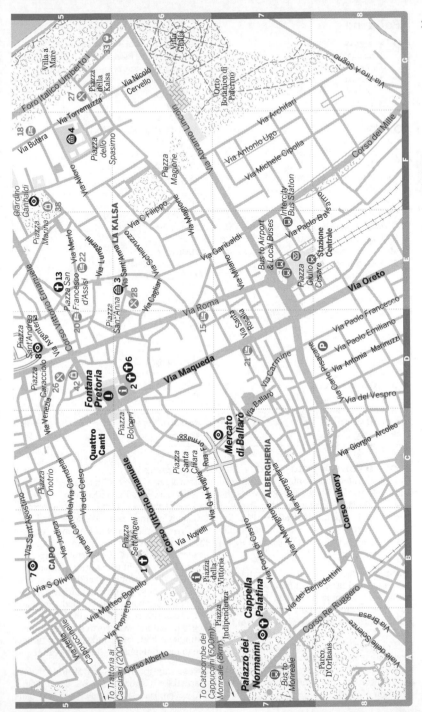

Palermo

AROUND THE QUATTRO CANTI

The busy intersection of Corso Vittorio Emanuele and Via Maqueda is known as the **Quattro Canti**. Forming the civic heart of Palermo, this crossroads neatly divides the historic nucleus into four traditional quarters – Albergheria, Capo, Vucciria and La Kalsa.

Fontana Pretoria   FOUNTAIN

This huge and ornate fountain, with tiered basins and sculptures rippling in concentric circles, forms the centrepiece of **Piazza Pretoria**, a spacious square just south of the Quattro Canti. The city bought the fountain in 1573; however, the flagrant nudity of the provocative nymphs proved too much for Sicilian church-goers attending Mass next door, and they prudishly dubbed it the Fountain of Shame.

La Martorana   CHURCH

(Chiesa di Santa Maria dell'Ammiraglio; Piazza Bellini 3; ⊙8.30am-1pm & 3.30-5.30pm Mon-Sat, 8.30am-1pm Sun) This lovely 12th-century church was originally planned as a mosque by King Roger's Syrian Emir, George of Antioch. In 1433 the church was donated to an aesthetically challenged order of Benedictine nuns who demolished most of the stunning mosaics executed by Greek craftsmen and replaced them with gaudy baroque ornamentation. The few remaining original mosaics include two magnificent portraits of George of Antioch and Roger II that are well worth seeking out; unfortunately both were indefinitely off-limits due to restoration at the time of research.

Chiesa Capitolare di San Cataldo   CHURCH

(Piazza Bellini 3; admission €2; ⊙9.30am-1.30pm & 3.30-5.30pm Mon-Sat, 9.30am-1.30pm Sun) This

12th-century church in Arab-Norman style is one of Palermo's most striking buildings, with its dusky-pink bijoux domes, solid square shape, blind arcading and delicate tracery. Disappointingly, it's almost bare inside.

ALBERGHERIA

Southwest of the Quattro Canti is Albergheria, a rather shabby, run-down district once inhabited by Norman court officials, now home to a growing number of immigrants who are attempting to revitalise its dusty backstreets.

Palazzo dei Normanni   PALAZZO, CHAPEL

(Palazzo Reale; ✆091 626 28 33; www.federico secondo.org; Piazza Indipendenza 1; Cappella Palatina only adult/reduced €7/5, combined ticket incl palace rooms & Cappella Palatina adult/reduced €8.50/6.50) This austere fortified palace was once the centre of a magnificent medieval court. Today it remains in regular use as the seat of the Sicilian parliament. Four days a week government officials vacate the building, allowing visitors access to the **parliamentary chambers and royal apartments** (◷8.15am-5pm Fri, Sat & Mon, 8.15am-12.15pm Sun), including the sumptuous **Sala di Ruggero II**, the king's former bedroom, which is decorated with stunning mosaics of Persian peacocks, palm trees and leopards.

Cappella Palatina

(Palatine Chapel; ◷8.15am-5pm Mon-Sat, 8.15-9.45am & 11.15am-12.15pm Sun) On the middle level of the palace's three-tiered loggia is Palermo's premier tourist attraction. This mosaic-clad jewel of a chapel, designed by Roger II in 1130, has been returned to its original splendour thanks to restoration work completed in 2008. Swarming with figures in glittering, dreamy gold, these exquisite mosaics recount tales of the Old and New Testaments, capturing expression, detail and movement with extraordinary grace. The harmony of the chapel's decoration is further enhanced by the inlaid marble floors and the wooden *muqarnas* ceiling, a masterpiece of honeycomb carving in Arabic style that reflects the cultural complexity of Norman Sicily.

Mercato di Ballarò   MARKET

Snaking for several city blocks southeast of Palazzo dei Normanni is Palermo's busiest street market, which throbs with activity well into the early evening. It's a fascinating mix of noises, smells and street life, and the cheapest place for everything from Chinese padded bras to fresh produce, fish, meat, olives and cheese – smile nicely for a taste.

CAPO

Northwest of Quattro Canti is the Capo neighbourhood, another densely packed web of interconnected streets and blind alleys.

Cattedrale   CATHEDRAL

(www.cattedrale.palermo.it; Corso Vittorio Emanuele; ◷8am-5.30pm Mon-Sat, 7am-1pm & 4-7pm Sun) A feast of geometric patterns, ziggurat crenulations, majolica cupolas and blind arches, Palermo's cathedral is a prime example of the extraordinary Arab-Norman style unique to Sicily. The interior, although impressive in scale, is a marble shell, a sadly un-exotic resting place for the royal Norman tombs. The **crypt** and **treasury** (adult/reduced €3/1.50; ◷9.30am-5.30pm Mon-Sat) contain various jewels belonging to Queen Costanza of Aragón, a bejewelled Norman crown and a tooth extracted from Santa Rosalia, Palermo's patron saint.

Mercato del Capo   MARKET

Capo's street market, running the length of Via Sant'Agostino, is a seething mass of colourful activity during the day, with vendors selling fruit, vegetables, meat, fish, cheese and household goods of every description.

VUCCIRIA

Museo Archeologico Regionale   MUSEUM

(✆091 611 68 05; www.regione.sicilia.it/benicultur ali/salinas; Piazza Olivella 24; adult/reduced €4/2; ◷8.30am-1.30pm & 3-6.30pm Tue-Fri, 8.30am-1.30pm Sat & Sun) In a Renaissance monastery surrounding a gracious courtyard, this wheelchair-accessible museum displays some of Sicily's most valuable Greek and Roman artefacts. Chief among its treasures is the series of decorative friezes from the temples at Selinunte. At the time of research, the museum was closing indefinitely for renovations; check the website or Palermo's tourist office for status updates.

Oratories   ORATORIES

Vucciria's most noteworthy architectural gems are its three baroque oratories: **Oratorio di San Lorenzo** (Via dell'Immacolatella 5; adult/reduced €2.50/1.50; ◷10am-6pm), **Oratorio del Rosario di Santa Zita** (Via Valverde) and **Oratorio del Rosario di San Domenico** (Via dei Bambinai 2). The latter two are known collectively as the **Tesori della Loggia** (combined ticket €5; ◷9am-1pm Mon-Sat) and can be visited on a single ticket, together with a cluster of nearby churches: covered in ornate stuccowork, these former social clubs for the celebs of their time are ostentatious displays of 17th-century status and wealth.

Mercato della Vucciria   MARKET
(Piazza Caracciolo) The market here was once a notorious den of Mafia activity but is a muted affair today, compared to the spirited Ballarò and Capo markets.

LA KALSA
Due to its proximity to the port, La Kalsa was subjected to carpet bombing during WWII, leaving it derelict and rundown. Mother Teresa considered it akin to the shanty towns of Calcutta and established a mission here. Thankfully, this galvanised embarrassed authorities into action and the quarter is now undergoing extensive restoration.

Galleria d'Arte Moderna   ART GALLERY
(☎091 843 16 05; www.galleriadartemodernapalermo.it, in Italian; Via Sant'Anna 21; adult/reduced €7/5; ☉9.30am-6.30pm Tue-Sun, to 11pm Fri & Sat) This lovely museum is housed in a 15th-century *palazzo* (mansion), which in the 17th century metamorphosed into a convent. The wide-ranging collection of 19th- and 20th-century Sicilian art is beautifully displayed, and there's a regular program of modern-art exhibitions here, as well as an excellent bookshop and gift shop.

Galleria Regionale della Sicilia   ART GALLERY
(☎091 623 00 11; www.regione.sicilia.it/beniculturali/palazzoabatellis; Via Alloro 4; adult/reduced €8/4; ☉9am-5.30pm Tue-Fri, 9am-1pm Sat & Sun) Tucked down a side street in the stately 15th-century Palazzo Abatellis, this recently reopened museum has a wide-ranging collection featuring works by Sicilian artists from the Middle Ages to the 18th century.

Museo Internazionale
delle Marionette   PUPPET MUSEUM
(☎091 32 80 60; www.museomarionettepalermo.it, in Italian; Piazzetta Antonio Pasqualino 5; adult/reduced €5/3; ☉9am-1pm & 2.30-6.30pm Mon-Sat, 10am-1pm Sun) Housing over 3500 puppets and marionettes from Italy, Japan, southeast Asia, Africa, China and India, this whimsical museum also stages delightful puppet shows most Tuesdays and Fridays at 5.30pm from October through June. For more on Sicily's famous puppet tradition, see the boxed text, p160.

19TH-CENTURY PALERMO
North of Piazza Giuseppe Verdi, Palermo elegantly slips into cosmopolitan mode. Here you'll find fabulous neoclassical and art-nouveau buildings hailing from the last golden age of Sicilian architecture, along with the late-19th-century mansion blocks that line the broad boulevard of Viale della Libertà.

Teatro Massimo   OPERA HOUSE
(☎tour reservations 091 605 32 67; www.teatro massimo.it; Piazza Giuseppe Verdi; guided tours adult/reduced €7/5; ☉10am-2.30pm Tue-Sun) An iconic Palermo landmark, this grand neoclassical opera house took more than 20 years to complete and has become a symbol of the triumph and tragedy of the city. Appropriately, the closing scene of *The Godfather: Part III,* with its visually stunning juxtaposition of high culture, low crime, drama and death, was filmed here.

Teatro Politeama Garibaldi   THEATRE
(Piazza Ruggero Settimo) Designed by architect Giuseppe Damiani Almeyda between 1867 and 1874, Palermo's second theatre has the same imposing circular layout as the Teatro Massimo and features a striking facade resembling a triumphal arch topped by a huge bronze chariot.

Hammam   BATHHOUSE
(☎091 32 07 83; www.hammam.pa.it; Via Torrearsa 17d; admission €40; ☉women only 2-9pm Mon & Wed & 11am-9pm Fri, men only 2-9pm Tue & Thu & 10am-8pm Sat) For a sybaritic experience, head to this luxurious marble-lined Moorish bathhouse, where you can indulge in a vigorous scrub-down, a steamy sauna and many different types of massages and therapies. There's a one-off charge (€10) for slippers and a hand glove.

OUTSIDE CITY CENTRE
Catacombe dei Cappuccini   CATACOMB
(☎091 21 21 17; Piazza Cappuccini; admission €3; ☉9am-1pm & 3-6pm) These catacombs house the mummified bodies and skeletons of some 8000 Palermitans who died between the 17th and 19th centuries. Earthly power, gender, religion and professional status are still rigidly distinguished down here, with men and women occupying separate corridors, and a first-class section set aside for virgins. From Piazza Independanza, it's a 15-minute walk.

✿ Festivals & Events

Settimana Santa   HOLY WEEK
Holy Week (the week leading up to Easter) is the year's major religious festival, celebrated all over the island. In Palermo there are Greek Orthodox celebrations at La Martorana (p154).

U Fistinu   RELIGIOUS
From 10 to 15 July, Palermo's biggest annual festival celebrates the patron saint of the city, Santa Rosalia, with fireworks, parades and four days of partying.

Festa di Morgana   PUPPET
(www.museomarionettepalermo.it, in Italian) In November, puppeteers from all over the world gather at Museo Internazionale delle Marionette.

🛏 Sleeping

Most budget options can be found around Via Maqueda and Via Roma in the vicinity of the train station. Midrange and top-end hotels are concentrated further north. Parking usually costs an extra €10 to €15 per day.

Butera 28   APARTMENT €
(☑333 316 54 32; www.butera28.it; Via Butera 28; 2-/4-/8-person apt per day from €50/100/150; ❄🅰) Delightful bilingual owner Nicoletta offers 11 well-equipped and comfortable apartments in her elegant old *palazzo* near Piazza della Kalsa. Units range in size from 30 to 180 square metres, most sleeping a family of four or more. Four apartments face the sea (No. 9 is especially nice), and all have CD and DVD players, plus kitchens stocked with basic essentials. Nicoletta also offers cooking classes in her gorgeous blue-and-white-tiled kitchen. Per week 2-/4-/8-person apartments cost €300/650/950.

A Casa di Amici   HOSTEL €
(☑091 58 48 84; www.acasadiamici.com; Via Volturno 6; dm €17-23, s €30-45, d €50-72, tr €60-96; ❄@🅰) In a renovated 19th-century *palazzo* with high ceilings and decorative tile floors, this artsy, hostel-type place behind Teatro Massimo has four colourful rooms sleeping two to four, with shared bathrooms and a guest kitchen. The annexe across the street, ideal for families or anyone seeking more peace and quiet, has four additional rooms, including one with private bath and terrace. Multilingual owner Claudia and her staff provide helpful maps and informational displays, plus friendly advice to help newcomers navigate the city.

San Francesco   B&B €
(☑091 888 83 91, 328 551 62 42; www.sanfrancescopalermo.it; Via Merlo 30; s €50-60, d €80-90; ❄🅰) On a side street near Piazza Marina is this lovingly restored old house with stone walls, beamed ceilings and only three rooms, run by the friendly young couple Vanessa and Filippo. The quiet, central location and the breakfast win rave reviews from guests.

B&B Amélie   B&B €
(☑091 33 59 20; www.bb-amelie.it; Via Prinicipe di Belmonte 94; s €40-60, d €60-80, tr €90-100; ❄@🅰) In an unbeatable new city location on a pedestrianised street a stone's throw from Teatro Politeama, the affable, multilingual Angela has converted her grandmother's spacious sixth floor flat into a cheery B&B. Rooms are colourfully decorated, and the corner triple has a sunny terrace. Angela, a native Palermitan, generously shares her wealth of local knowledge. People with allergies needn't worry about the cat on the logo; the place is spotless, with no pets or fur in sight!

Hotel Orientale   HOTEL €
(☑091 616 57 27; www.albergoorientale.191.it; Via Maqueda 26; s €30-50, d €45-70; ❄🅰) This *palazzo's* grand marble stairway and arcaded courtyard, complete with rusty bicycles, stray cats and strung-up washing, is an evocative introduction to an atmospheric if faded hotel. Rooms have wrought-iron beds, tall windows and heavy wooden furniture; the cheapest come with shared bathrooms. Breakfast is served under the lovely frescoed ceiling in the library. Rooms 8 and 9 overlook the tail end of the Ballaró market, close enough to hear the vendors singing in the morning.

B&B Maxim   B&B €€
(☑091 976 54 71; www.bbmaxim.it; Via Mariano Stabile 136a; s €80-90, d €110-130, ste €160-190; ❄🅰) Owner Massimo has spared no expense in creating this tony little B&B with restrained tones of cream, beige and brown. Perks include ambient sound, chromotherapy lighting in the showers, and state-of-the art designer fixtures throughout. It's on the sixth floor, high above the surrounding urban bustle, yet only a five-minute walk from Teatro Massimo and Teatro Politeama.

Grand Hotel Piazza Borsa
HOTEL €€

(☎091 32 00 75; www.piazzaborsa.com; Via dei Cartari 18; s €115-181, d €154-208, ste €340-569; P✻@🖳) This grand new 4-star opened in 2010 in Palermo's former stock exchange. Three separate buildings house the 127 rooms; the nicest ones are the high-ceilinged suites with Jaccuzi tubs and windows facing Piazza San Francesco. Internet access costs €10 extra.

Grand Hotel et des Palmes
HOTEL €€€

(☎091 602 81 11; www.hotel-despalmes.it; Via Roma 398; r €230-265; P✻@🖳) Dating from 1874, this is one of Palermo's most historically fascinating hotels. Like a royal court, it has been the scene of intrigue, liaisons and double-dealings. The grand salons still impress with their chandeliers and gigantic mirrors, while the rooms are regally luxurious. The official rates listed above are often slashed in half during slow periods; look online for special deals.

B&B 900
B&B €

(☎091 976 11 94; www.novecentopalermo.com; Via Roma 62; s €30-60, d €50-100; ✻🖳) Convenient to the train station, this welcoming B&B on the fifth-floor of a Via Roma *palazzo* wins guests over with owners Elisa and Dario's warm hospitality and a breakfast emphasizing organic ingredients.

✗ Eating

Sicily's ancient cuisine is a mixture of spicy and sweet flavours, epitomised in the ubiquitous eggplant-based *caponata* and the Palermitan classic *bucatini con le sarde* (hollow tube-shaped noodles with sardines, wild fennel, raisins, pine nuts and breadcrumbs). Cakes, marzipan confections and pastries are all works of art – try the *cannoli* (tubes of pastry filled with sweetened ricotta).

Restaurants rarely start to fill up until 9.30pm. For cheap eats, visit Palermo's markets, wander the tangle of alleys east and south of Teatro Massimo, or spend a Saturday evening snacking with locals on grilled sausages, *stigghiola*, *panelle* and *crocchè* at the outdoor food carts in Piazza Caracciolo in the Vucciria district.

TOP CHOICE Trattoria Ai Cascinari
SICILIAN €

(☎091 651 98 04; Via d'Ossuna 43/45; meals €20-23; ☺lunch Tue-Sun, dinner Wed-Sat) Friendly service, simple straw chairs and blue-and-white-checked tablecloths set the relaxed tone at this Slow Food–recommended neighbourhood trattoria, 1km north of the Cappella Palatina. Locals pack the labyrinth of back rooms, while waiters perambulate non-stop with plates of scrumptious seasonal antipasti and divine main dishes. Save room for homemade ice cream and outstanding desserts brought in from Palermo's beloved Pasticceria Cappello.

Piccolo Napoli
SEAFOOD €€

(☎091 32 04 31; Piazzetta Mulino a Vento 4; meals €25-35; ☺lunch Mon-Sat, dinner Thu-Sat) Known throughout Palermo for its fresh seafood, this Slow Food–recommended eatery is another hotspot for serious foodies. Nibble on toothsome sesame bread and plump olives while perusing the menu for a pasta dish that takes your fancy, then head to the seafood display (often still wriggling) to choose a second course. The atmosphere is bustling and the genial owner greets his many regular customers by name.

Trattoria Basile
TRATTORIA €

(☎091 33 56 28; Via Bara all'Olivella 76; meals €9-13; ☺noon-3.30pm Mon-Sat) This unpretentious trattoria offers an unforgettable, authentic Palermitan eating experience. Pay first, take a number at the window for your pasta (€2.50 to €4) or main course (€3.50 to €5), then side over to the antipasti bar and choose three items for €2 or six items for €4. While enjoying your appetisers, listen for your number – they'll bellow it out (in Italian) when the rest of your food is ready. Avoid the busy period between 1pm and 2pm when every workman in town is elbowing in for his plate of pasta.

Osteria dei Vespri
GASTRONOMIC €€€

(☎091 617 16 31; www.osteriadeivespri.it; Piazza Croce dei Vespri 6; meals €55-70, tasting menu €80; ☺lunch & dinner Mon-Sat) This sophisticated Michelin-star restaurant has a stone-vaulted ceiling and intimate dining space. In the summer, sit out under the shadow of the *palazzo* and tuck into dishes such as pasta with fennel and red prawns or spicy tuna with nutmeg-potato croquettes and mint-flavoured rice. Top it all off with a hazelnut waffle, lemon-scented ricotta and kiwis in red fruit-and-wine jam.

Ferro di Cavallo
TRATTORIA €

(☎091 33 18 35; Via Venezia 20; meals €18-20; ☺lunch Mon-Sat, dinner Thu-Sat) Religious portraits beam down from bright red walls upon the bustling crowd of tourists and locals at this cheerful trattoria near the Quattro Canti. Nothing costs more than €8 on the straightforward à la carte menu of Sicilian classics, but hungry diners can still 'splurge' on the fixed-price menu for €19, including drinks.

Sant'Andrea   MODERN SICILIAN €€
(☎091 33 49 99; www.ristorantesantandrea.eu; Piazza Sant'Andrea 4; meals €30-35; ⊙dinner Mon-Sat) Tucked into the corner of a ruined church in a shabby piazza, Sant'Andrea's location doesn't inspire much confidence, but its superbly creative Sicilian dishes and congenial high-ceilinged dining room keep well-heeled customers picking their way across the broken flagstones nightly.

Cappello   PASTRIES & CAKES €
(Via Nicolò Garzilli 10; cake slices €2.50) Famous for the *setteveli* (seven-layer chocolate cake) that was invented here – and has long since been copied all over Palermo – this hole-in-the-wall creates splendid desserts of all kinds. Not to be missed is the dreamy *delizia di pistacchio*, a granular pistachio cake topped with creamy icing and a chocolate medallion.

Antico Caffè Spinnato   CAFE €
(☎091 32 92 20; Via Principe di Belmonte 107-15; snacks €4-8) At this sophisticated cafe dating back to 1860, Palermitans throng the sidewalk tables daily to enjoy afternoon piano music, coffee, cocktails, ice cream, sumptuous cakes and snacks.

Friggitoria Chiluzzo   SANDWICH SHOP €
(Piazza della Kalsa; sandwiches €1.50; ⊙lunch Mon-Sat) This beloved street vendor makes some of Palermo's best *pane, panelle e crocchè* (sesame bread with chickpea fritters and potato croquettes). Add fried eggplant and a squeeze of lemon and call it lunch!

Pizzeria Biondo   PIZZERIA €
(☎091 58 36 62; Via Nicolò Garzilli 27; pizzas €5-14; ⊙dinner Thu-Tue) Made with super-fresh *mozzarella di bufala* (buffalo-milk mozzarella), Biondo's pizza is often recognised as the best in Palermo. An animated crowd fills the sidewalk tables and inside rooms every night.

Acanto   MODERN SICILIAN €€
(☎091 32 04 44; Via Torrearsa 10; meals €30-35; ⊙dinner Tue-Sun) New-town elegance together with inventive cooking make this one of the most fashionable restaurants among the designer-chic crowd. In the summer tables are set out on the romantic back patio.

🍷 Drinking

Palermo's liveliest cluster of bars can be found in the Champagneria district east of Teatro Massimo, centred on Piazza Olivella, Via Spinuzza, and Via Patania. Other hot spots include Via Alessandro Paternostro in the Kalsa neighbourhood and Via dei Candelai, a short stagger of a street flanked by pubs, bars and discos catering to a younger, rowdier crowd. Higher end bars and dance venues are concentrated in the newer part of Palermo. In summer, many Palermitans decamp to Mondello by the sea.

TOP CHOICE **Kursaal Kalhesa**   BAR
(☎091 616 00 50; www.kursaalkalhesa.it, in Italian; Foro Umberto I 21; ⊙noon-3pm & 6pm-1am Tue-Sun) Recline on plump sofas with silk cushions and sip a cocktail beneath the high vaulted ceilings. There's a roaring fire in winter, plus art exhibits and a bookstore with foreign newspapers. A lively unpretentious crowd is attracted by the good program of music and literary events. Meals (from €30) are served upstairs on the leafy patio flanked by 15th-century walls.

Pizzo & Pizzo   WINE BAR
(☎091 601 45 44; www.pizzoepizzo.com; Via XII Gennaio 5; ⊙closed Sun) Sure, this sophisticated wine bar is a great place for aperitivi, but the buzzing atmosphere and the tempting array of cheeses, cured meats, and smoked fish may just convince you to stick around for dinner.

☆ Entertainment

The daily paper *Il Giornale di Sicilia* has a listing of what's on. The tourist office and information booths also have programs and listings.

Teatro Massimo   OPERA HOUSE
(☎091 605 35 80; www.teatromassimo.it; Piazza Verdi 9) Ernesto Basile's art-nouveau masterpiece stages opera, ballet and music concerts. The theatre's program runs from October to May.

Teatro Politeama Garibaldi   THEATRE
(☎091 637 37 43; www.amicidellamusicapalermo.it; Piazza Ruggero Settimo) Another grandiose theatre for opera, ballet and classical music, staging afternoon and evening concerts from November through May.

Teatro della Verdura   OPEN-AIR THEATRE
(☎091 688 41 37; Viale del Fante) A summer-only program of ballet and music in the lovely gardens of the Villa Castelnuovo.

IL TEATRO DEI PUPI

Since the 18th century the traditional Sicilian puppet theatre has been enthralling adults and children alike. The shows are a mini theatrical performance with some puppets standing 1.5m high – a completely different breed from the Pooh Bear–style of glove puppet popular in the West. These characters are intricately carved from beech, olive or lemon wood with realistic-looking glass eyes and distinct features. And, to make sure that they will have no problem swinging their swords or beheading dragons, their joints have flexible wire.

Effectively the soap operas of their day, Sicilian puppet shows expounded the deepest sentiments of life – unrequited love, treachery, thirst for justice and the anger and frustration of the oppressed. The swashbuckling tales centre on the legends of Charlemagne's heroic knights, Orlando and Rinaldo, with an extended cast including the fair Angelica, the treacherous Gano di Magonza and forbidding Saracen warriors. Good puppeteers are judged on the dramatic effect they can create – lots of stamping feet and a gripping running commentary – and on their speed and skill in directing the battle scenes.

Cuticchio Mimmo PUPPET THEATRE
(☎091 32 34 00; www.figlidartecuticchio.com; Via Bara all'Olivella 95; ⊗6.30pm Sat & Sun Sep-Jul) This theatre is a charming low-tech choice for children (and adults), staging traditional shows with fabulous handcrafted puppets.

Shopping

Via Bara all'Olivella is good for arts and crafts. Check out the puppet workshop of the Cuticchio family, **Il Laboratorio Teatrale** (Via Bara all'Olivella 48-50).

For ceramics and pottery (albeit at higher prices than you'd find in Sicily's hinterland) stop by **Le Ceramiche di Caltagirone** (caltagironeceramiche@alice.it; Via Cavour 114) or **Mercurio** (www.casamerlo.it; Corso Vittorio Emanuele 231).

For edible souvenirs with a dollop of social consciousness, consider buying some wine, olive oil or pasta – all grown on land confiscated from the Mafia – at **Libera Terra** (www.liberapalermo.org; Piazza Castelnuovo 13), an organization actively working to resist the Mafia's influence in Sicilian society.

On Sundays, there's a good **antiques market** on Piazza Marina south of the port.

Information

Emergency
Ambulance (☎118)
Police station (☎091 21 01 11; Piazza della Vittoria) For reporting theft and other petty crimes.

Internet Access
There are countless internet points in the old centre, particularly around Via Maqueda where they double as phone centres for the city's immigrant population.

Aboriginal Café (☎091 662 22 29; www.aboriginalcafe.com; Via Spinuzza 51; per hr €3.50; ⊗9am-3am) A lively Australian-style bar and internet cafe.

Medical Services
Farmacia Inglese (☎091 33 44 82; Via Mariano Stabile 177; ⊗4.30pm-1pm Mon-Fri, 8pm-8.30am Sat & Sun) All-night pharmacy service, seven days a week.
Ospedale Civico (☎091 666 11 11; www.ospedalecivicopa.org; Via Carmelo Lazzaro) Emergency facilities.

Money
ATMs are plentiful. There are exchange offices open outside normal banking hours at the airport.

Post
Main post office (Via Roma 322) Smaller branch offices can be found at the train station and on Piazza Verdi.

Tourist Information
CIT tourist information booths (☎091 611 78 87; www.comune.palermo.it/comune/asses sorato_turismo, in Italian; ⊗9am-1pm & 3-7pm) At several locations throughout town, including Piazza Bellini, the port, Via Cavour and Piazza della Vittoria.
Tourist office (www.palermotourism.com) airport (☎091 59 16 98; ⊗8.30am-7.30pm Mon-Sat); city centre (☎091 605 83 51; Piazza Castelnuovo 34; ⊗8.30am-2pm & 2.30-6pm Mon-Fri) Has friendly, multilingual staff and abundant brochures.

Getting There & Away

Air
Falcone-Borsellino airport (PMO; ☎091 702 01 11; www.gesap.it) is at Punta Raisi, 31km west of Palermo.

Several no-frills airlines operate between major European cities and Palermo. Falcone-Borsellino is also the hub airport for regular domestic flights to the islands of Pantelleria and Lampedusa.

Boat

The ferry terminal is located off Via Francesco Crispi. Ferries depart regularly from Molo Vittorio Veneto for Cagliari and Naples. Ferries for Genoa leave from Molo S Lucia.

Grandi Navi Veloci (☎091 58 74 04; www.gnv.it; Calata Marinai d'Italia) Ferries from Palermo to Civitavecchia (€78-95, 12 hours, three weekly), Naples (€45-64, 12 hours, daily), Tunis (€37-42, 10 hours, weekly), Livorno (€72-92, 18 hours, three weekly), Malta (€62, 10 hours, weekly) and Genoa (€83-117, 20 hours, daily).

Grimaldi Ferries (☎091 611 36 91; www.grimaldi-lines.com; Via Emerico Amari 8) Ferries from Palermo to Tunis (€69, 10 hours, twice weekly).

Siremar (☎091 749 31 11; www.siremar.it, in Italian; Via Francesco Crispi 118) Ferries (€16.55, 2½ hours, daily) and summer-only hydrofoils (€22.95, 1¼ hours, two daily) from Palermo to Ustica.

SNAV (☎091 601 42 11; www.snav.it; Calata Marinai d'Italia) Overnight service to Naples (€55, 10½ hours, daily). The office is located at the port to the left of the main entrance.

Tirrenia (☎091 976 07 73; www.tirrenia.it; Calata Marinai d'Italia) Services from Palermo to Cagliari (€55, 13 hours, weekly) and an overnight ferry to Naples (€50, 10 hours, daily). The office is located at the port to the right of the main entrance.

Ustica Lines (☎0923 87 38 13; www.ustica lines.it) Summer-only hydrofoil service to Lipari (€39.30, 4½ hours, two daily) and other points on the Aeolian Islands.

Bus

The main intercity bus station is on Via Paolo Balsamo, one block east of the train station. Several bus companies maintain independent offices here.

Azienda Siciliana Trasporti (AST; ☎091 680 00 32; www.aziendasicilianatrasporti.it; Via Rosario Gregorio 46) Services to southeastern destinations including Ragusa (€12.80, four hours, four daily Monday to Saturday, two on Sunday).

Cuffaro (☎091 616 15 10; www.cuffaro.info; Via Paolo Balsamo 13) Services to Agrigento (€8.10, two hours, three to nine daily).

SAIS (☎091 616 60 28, 091 617 11 41; www.saisautolinee.it, www.saistrasporti.it; Via Paolo Balsamo 16) Services to Catania (€14.20, 2¾ hours, at least nine daily), Messina (€15.10, 2¾ hours, three to seven daily), Naples (€37.50, 10

hours, nightly) and Rome (€45.50, 10½ hours, nightly).

Segesta (☎091 616 90 39; www.segesta.it; Via Paolo Balsamo 26) Services to Trapani (€8.60, two hours, at least 10 daily). Also sells Interbus tickets to Syracuse (€11, 3¼ hours, two to three daily).

Car & Motorcycle

Palermo is accessible on the A20-E90 toll road from Messina and the A19-E932 from Catania via Enna. Trapani and Marsala are also easily accessible from Palermo by motorway (A29), while Agrigento and Palermo are linked by the SS121, a good state road through the island's interior.

Car hire is not cheap in Sicily. Renting onsite will typically set you back €250 to €500 per week. It's often more economical to book your rental online before leaving home. One dependable low-budget choice in downtown Palermo is **Auto Europa** (☎091 58 10 45; www.autoeuropa.it; Via Mariano Stabile 6a). **Avis** (www.avis.com) airport (☎091 59 16 84); port (☎091 58 69 40; Via Francesco Crispi 250) also has a downtown branch and is among the many larger car-hire companies represented at the airport.

Train

From Palermo Centrale station, just south of the centre at the foot of Via Roma, regular trains leave for Messina (€11.60 to €27.50, three to 3½ hours, nine to 15 daily), Agrigento (€8.10, 2¼ hours, seven to 12 daily) and Cefalù (€5, one hour, 10 to 19 daily). There are also InterCity trains to Reggio di Calabria, Naples and Rome.

For Catania or Syracuse, you're generally better off taking the bus. There's only one direct train to Catania (€12.30, three hours, weekday mornings only); all the others require a time-consuming change at Messina.

🚗 Getting Around

To/From the Airport

Prestia e Comandè (☎091 58 63 51; www.prestiaecomande.it) runs a half-hourly bus service from the airport to the centre of town (€5.80), with stops outside Teatro Politeama Garibaldi (30 minutes) and Palermo Centrale train station (45 minutes). Buses are parked to the right as you exit the arrivals hall. Buy tickets on the bus. Return journeys to the airport run with similar frequency, picking up at the same points.

The Trinacria Express train (€5.80, one hour) from the airport (Punta Raisi station) to Palermo takes longer and runs less frequently than the bus. At the time of research, due to track work, trains were only running as far as Notarbartolo station 3km northwest of downtown Palermo, making this an even less appealing option.

A taxi from the airport to downtown Palermo costs €45.

Bus

Palermo's orange, white and blue **city buses** (AMAT; ☑848 80 08 17; www.amat.pa.it, in Italian) are frequent but often crowded and slow. The free map handed out at Palermo tourist offices details all the major bus lines; most stop at the train station. Tickets (per 1½ hours €1.30, per day €3.50) must be purchased before you get on the bus, from *tabacchi* (tobacconists) or AMAT booths at major transfer points.

Three small buses – Linea Gialla, Linea Verde and Linea Rossa (€0.52 for 24-hour ticket) – operate in the narrow streets of the *centro storico* (historic centre) and can be useful if you're moving between tourist sights.

Car & Motorcycle

Driving is frenetic in the city and best avoided, if possible. Theft of, and from, vehicles is also a problem; use one of the attended car parks around town (€12 to €20 per day) if your hotel lacks parking.

Around Palermo

Just outside Palermo's city limits, the beach town of Mondello and the dazzling cathedral of Monreale are both worthwhile day trips. Just offshore, Ustica makes a great overnight or weekend getaway.

Mondello became fashionable for its long, sandy beach in the 19th century, when people came to the seaside in their carriages, prompting the construction of the huge art-nouveau pier that still graces the waterfront. Most of the beaches near the pier are private (two sun lounges and an umbrella cost €10 to €20); however, there's a wide swath of public beach opposite the centre of town with all the prerequisite pedaloes and jet skis for hire. Given its easygoing seaside feel, Mondello is an excellent base for families. To get here, take bus 806 (€1.30, 30 minutes) from Piazza Sturzo in Palermo.

Monreale's cathedral (☑091 640 44 03; Piazza del Duomo; ⊗8am-6pm), 8km southwest of Palermo, is considered the finest example of Norman architecture in Sicily, incorporating Norman, Arab, Byzantine and classical elements. Inspired by a vision of the Virgin, it was built by William II in an effort to outdo his grandfather Roger II, who was responsible for the cathedral in Cefalù and the Cappella Palatina in Palermo. The interior, completed in 1184 and executed in shimmering mosaics, depicts 42 Old Testament stories. Outside the cathedral, the **cloister** (admission €6; ⊗9am-7pm) is a tranquil courtyard with a tangible oriental feel. Surrounding the perimeter, elegant Romanesque arches are supported by an exquisite array of slender columns alternately decorated with mosaics. To reach Monreale take bus 389 (€1.30, 35 minutes, half-hourly) from Piazza Indipendenza in Palermo.

The 8.7 sq km island of **Ustica** was declared Italy's first marine reserve in 1986. The surrounding waters are a feast of fish and coral, ideal for snorkelling, diving and underwater photography. In July the island hosts the **Rassegna Internazionale di Attività Subacquee** (International Festival of Underwater Activities), drawing divers from around the world. To enjoy Ustica's wild coastline and dazzling grottoes without the crowds, try visiting in June or September. **Profondo Blu** (☑091 844 96 09; www.ustica-diving.it) is among the better established dive centres on the island, and also offers accommodation. To get here from Palermo, take the daily car ferry (€18.35, 2½ hours) operated by **Siremar** (☑091 844 90 02; www.siremar.it); or the faster hydrofoils (€23.55, 1½ hours) operated by both Siremar and **Ustica Lines** (☑091 844 90 02; www.usticalines.it).

TYRRHENIAN COAST

The coast between Palermo and Milazzo is studded with popular tourist resorts attracting a steady stream of holiday-makers, particularly between June and September. The best of these include the two massive natural parks of the Madonie and Nebrodi mountains, the sweeping beaches around Capo d'Orlando and Capo Tindari, and Cefalù, a resort second only to Taormina in popularity.

Cefalù

POP 13,800

This popular holiday resort wedged between a dramatic mountain peak and sweeping stretch of sand has the lot: a great beach; a truly lovely historic centre with a grandiose cathedral; and winding medieval streets lined with restaurants and boutiques. Avoid the height of summer when prices soar, beaches are jam-packed and the charm of the place is tainted by bad-tempered drivers trying to find parking.

From the train station, turn right into Via Moro to reach Via Matteotti and the old town. If heading for the beach, turn left and walk along Via Gramsci, which in turn becomes Via V Martoglio.

Sights

Duomo
DUOMO
(Piazza del Duomo; ⊙8am-5.30pm winter, to 7.30pm summer) Cefalù's imposing cathedral is the final jewel in the Arab-Norman crown alongside the Cappella Palatina and Monreale. Inside, a towering figure of Christ Pantocrator is the focal point of the elaborate 12th-century Byzantine mosaics. Framed by the steep cliff, the twin pyramid towers of the cathedral stand out above the magnificent **Piazza del Duomo**, which swarms with camera-snapping tourists among the pavement cafes and restaurants.

La Rocca
VIEWPOINT
Looming over the town, the craggy mass of La Rocca appears a suitable home for the race of giants that are said to have been Sicily's first inhabitants. It was here that the Arabs built their citadel, occupying it until the Norman conquest in 1061 forced the locals down from the mountain to the port below. An enormous staircase, the **Salita Saraceno**, winds up through three tiers of city walls, a 30-minute climb nearly to the summit. There are stunning views of the town below and the ruined 4th-century **Tempio di Diana** provides a quiet and romantic getaway for young lovers.

Activities

Cefalù's crescent-shaped beach, just west of the medieval centre, is lovely, but in the summer get here early to find a patch for your brolly and towel. You can escape with a boat tour along the coast or to the Aeolian Islands (from €60) during the summer months with several agencies located along Corso Ruggero.

Sicilia Divers
DIVING
(☑347 685 30 51; www.sicilia-divers.com; Hotel Kalura, Via Vincenzo Cavallaro 13; dives from €45, courses from €60) Organises dives and courses for all ages.

Scooter for Rent
BIKE RENTAL
(☑0921 42 04 96; www.scooterforrent.it; Via Vittorio Emanuele 57) Rents out bicycles (€10 per day) and scooters (from €35 per day).

Sleeping

Cheap accommodation is generally scarce year-round. Bookings are essential.

B&B Casanova
B&B €
(☑0921 92 30 65; www.casanovabb.it; Via Porpora 3; s €35-55, d €50-100, q €70-140; ❋☎) This B&B on the waterfront has rooms of varying size, from a cramped single with one minuscule window to the Ruggero room, a palatial space sleeping up to four, with a vaulted frescoed ceiling, decorative tile floors and French doors offering grand views of Cefalù's medieval centre. All guests share access to a small terrace overlooking the sea.

Hotel Kalura
HOTEL €€
(☑0921 42 13 54; www.hotel-kalura.com; Via Vincenzo Cavallaro 13; d €89-159; ℗❋@☎) East of town on a rocky outcrop, this German-run, family-oriented hotel has its own pebbly beach, restaurant and fabulous pool. Most rooms

---

WORTH A TRIP

CEFALÙ'S BACKYARD PLAYGROUND

Due south of Cefalù, the 40,000-hectare **Parco Naturale Regionale delle Madonie** incorporates some of Sicily's highest peaks, including the imposing Pizzo Carbonara (1979m). The park's wild, wooded slopes are home to wolves, wildcats, eagles and the near-extinct ancient Nebrodi fir trees that have survived since the last ice age. Ideal for hiking, cycling and horse trekking, the park is also home to several handsome mountain towns, including **Castelbuono**, **Petralia Soprana** and **Petralia Sottana**.

The region's distinctive rural cuisine includes roasted lamb and goat, cheeses, grilled mushrooms and aromatic pasta with *sugo* (meat sauce). A great place to sample these specialities is **Nangalarruni** (☑0921 67 14 28; Via delle Confraternite 5/7, Castelbuono; meals €25-45) in Castelbuono.

For park information, contact the **Ente Parco delle Madonie** (www.parcodellemadonie.it, in Italian) in Cefalù (☑0921 92 33 27; Corso Ruggero 116; ⊙8am-8pm) or Petralia Sottana (☑0921 68 40 11; Corso Paolo Agliata 16).

Bus service to the park's main towns is limited; to fully appreciate the Madonie, you're better off hiring a car for a couple of days.

have sea views, and the hotel arranges loads of activities, including mountain biking, hiking, canoeing, pedaloes, diving and dance nights. It's a 20-minute walk into town.

La Plumeria
HOTEL €€

(☎0921 92 58 97; www.laplumeriahotel.it; Corso Ruggero 185; s €70-180, d €90-220; P✳@🛜) Newly opened in 2010, this hotel's big selling point is its perfect location between the *duomo* and the waterfront, with free parking a few minutes away. Rooms are unexceptional, but clean and well-appointed. The single on the top floor is the sweetest of the lot, a cosy eyrie with checkerboard tile floors and a small terrace looking up to the *duomo*.

B&B Dolce Vita
B&B €

(☎0921 92 31 51; www.dolcevitabb.it; Via Bordonaro 8; r €60-120; ✳@🛜) This popular B&B has a lovely terrace with deck chairs overlooking the sea and a barbecue for warm summer evenings. Rooms are airy and light, with comfy beds, but the staff's lackadaisical attitude can detract from the charm. Breakfast is via a voucher system at a nearby cafe.

✖ Eating & Drinking

There are dozens of restaurants, but the food can be surprisingly mundane and the ubiquitous tourist menus can quickly pall.

Al Porticciolo
SEAFOOD, PIZZERIA €€

(☎0921 92 19 81; Via Carlo Ortolani di Bordonaro 66/86/90; pizzas €5-12, meals €20-35; ⊙closed Wed Oct-Apr) Dine in a five-star setting without shifting your credit card into overdrive at this popular waterfront eatery; in summer everyone piles out onto the ample outdoor terrace. There's pizza day and night, and fixed-price menus start at €20.

La Brace
INTERNATIONAL €€

(☎0921 42 35 70; Via XXV Novembre 10; meals €20-30; ⊙lunch Wed-Sun, dinner Tue-Sun) This Dutch-Indonesian-run eatery has won a following over the past several decades for its eclectic, reasonably priced menu, where Italian classics rub elbows with international favourites like chile con carne, *shashlik* (marinated skewers of chicken) and roast rabbit with chestnuts.

La Galleria
BAR, FUSION €€

(☎0921 42 02 11; www.lagalleriacefalu.it; Via Mandralisca 23; cocktails €5, meals €30-40; ⊙noon-3pm & 7pm-midnight Fri-Wed) Here you'll find a literary cafe, sophisticated cocktail bar, and tasteful art gallery combined into one supercool

venue. Start or end your evening here, or stick around for dinner on the outdoor patio.

 Information

ATMs are concentrated along Corso Ruggero.

Hospital (☎0921 92 01 11; Contrada Pietrapollastra) On the main road out of town in the direction of Palermo.

La Galleria (☎0921 42 02 11; Via Mandralisca 23; internet per hr €6; ⊙noon-3pm & 7pm-midnight Fri-Wed) Cocktail bar with two fast internet computers and free wi-fi.

Police station (☎0921 92 60 11; Via Roma 15)

Post office (Via Vazzana 2) Just in from the lungomare (seafront promenade).

Tourist office (☎0921 42 10 50; strcefalu@ regione.sicilia.it; Corso Ruggero 77; ⊙9am-1pm & 3-7.30pm Mon-Sat) English-speaking staff, lots of leaflets and good maps.

🛈 Getting There & Away

BOAT From June to September, **Ustica Lines** (www.usticalines.it) runs daily hydrofoils at 8.15am from Cefalù to the Aeolian Islands; destinations include Alicudi (€20.25, 1¼ hours), Filicudi (€23.40, 1¾ hours), Salina (€25.70, 2¾ hours) and Lipari (€29.10, 3¼ hours).

TRAIN The best way of getting to and from Cefalù is by rail. Hourly trains link Cefalù with Palermo (€5, one hour) and other towns along the Tyrrhenian coast.

AEOLIAN ISLANDS

The Aeolian Islands are a little piece of paradise. Stunning cobalt sea, splendid beaches, some of the best hiking you'll find in Italy, and an awe-inspiring volcanic landscape are just part of the appeal. The islands also have a fascinating human and mythological history that goes back several millennia; the Aeolians figured prominently in Homer's *Odyssey,* and evidence of the distant past can be seen everywhere, most notably in Lipari's excellent archaeological museum.

The seven islands of Lipari, Vulcano, Salina, Panarea, Stromboli, Alicudi and Filicudi are part of a huge 200km volcanic ridge that runs between the smoking stack of Mt Etna and the threatening mass of Vesuvius above Naples. Collectively, the islands exhibit a unique range of volcanic characteristics, which earned them a place on Unesco's World Heritage list in 2000. The islands are mobbed with visitors in July and August but out of season things remain remarkably tranquil.

DESTINATION	COST (€) HYDROFOIL/FERRY	DURATION HYDROFOIL/FERRY
Alicudi	18.85/13.95	2/4hr
Filicudi	15.80/12.40	1¼/2¾hr
Panarea	10.40/7.50	1/2hr
Salina (Rinella)	9.60/7.30	40min/1½hr
Salina (Santa Marina)	8.80/6.70	25/45min
Stromboli	17.80/12.40	1¾/4hr
Vulcano	5.80/4.70	10/25min

ⓘ Getting There & Away

In summer, ferries and hydrofoils leave regularly from Milazzo and Messina, the two mainland cities closest to the islands. Peak season is from June to September with winter services much reduced and sometimes cancelled due to heavy seas. All of the following prices are one-way high-season fares.

Ferry

Siremar (www.siremar.it) and **NGI Traghetti** (☑ 090 928 40 91; www.ngi-spa.it) both run car ferries from Milazzo to the islands; they're slightly cheaper, but slower and less regular than the summer hydrofoils.

Hydrofoil

Both **Ustica Lines** (www.usticalines.it) and Siremar run hydrofoils from Milazzo to Lipari (€16.80, one hour), and then on to the other islands. From 1 June to 30 September hydrofoils depart every hour or two for Lipari, stopping en route at Vulcano (€16, 45 minutes) and continuing onward to Santa Marina or Rinella (€17.55, 1½ to two hours) on Salina island. Beyond Salina, boats either branch off east to Panarea (€18.80, 2¼ hours) and Stromboli (€21.95, three hours), or west to Filicudi (€23.25, 2½ hours) and Alicudi (€28.70, 3¼ hours).

Ustica Lines also operates year-round hydrofoils to Lipari departing from Messina (€23.90, 1½ to 3½ hours, one to five daily) and Reggio di Calabria (€24.90, 1½ to 3½ hours, one to four daily).

In summer, Ustica Lines adds service to Lipari from Cefalù (€29.10, 3¼ hours, one daily) and Palermo (€39.30, four hours, two daily).

ⓘ Getting Around

Boat

Regular hydrofoil and ferry services operate between the Aeolian Islands. On Lipari all hydrofoil and ferry services arrive at and depart from Marina Lunga, where the companies Siremar and Ustica Lines both have ticket offices. On the other islands, you will find ticket offices at or close to the docks. Timetables are posted at all offices.

Car & Scooter

You can take your car to Lipari, Vulcano or Salina by ferry, or you can garage it on the mainland from €12 per day. The islands are small, with narrow, winding roads. You'll often save money (and headaches) by hiring a scooter onsite, or better yet, exploring the islands on foot.

Lipari

POP 11,300 / ELEV 602M

Lipari is the Aeolians' thriving hub, both geographically and functionally, with regular ferry and hydrofoil connections to all other islands. Lipari town, the largest urban centre in the archipelago, is home to the islands' only tourist office and most dependable banking services, along with enough restaurants, bars and year-round residents to offer a bit of cosmopolitan buzz. Meanwhile, the island's rugged shoreline offers excellent opportunities for hiking, boating and swimming.

Lipari has been inhabited for some 6000 years. The island was settled in the 4th millennium BC by Sicily's first known inhabitants, the Stentillenians, who developed a flourishing economy based on obsidian, a glassy volcanic rock. Commerce subsequently attracted the Greeks, who used the islands as ports on the east–west trade route, and pirates such as Barbarossa (or Redbeard), who coveted Lipari's lucrative obsidian and pumice mines.

Today trade is still flourishing. Lipari's two harbours, Marina Lunga (where ferries and hydrofoils dock) and Marina Corta (700m south, used by smaller boats) are linked by a bustling main street, Corso Vittorio Emanuele, flanked by shops, restaurants and bars. Overlooking the colourful snake of day-trippers is Lipari's grand dame of a clifftop citadel, surrounded by 16th-century walls.

◉ Sights

Museo Archeologico Eoliano   MUSEUM
(☏090 988 01 74; www.regione.sicilia.it/beniculturali/museolipari; Castello di Lipari; adult/reduced €6/3; ◷9am-1pm & 3-6pm Mon-Sat, 9am-1pm Sun) Within the citadel's fortifications is one of Sicily's best museums, tracing the volcanic and human history of the islands. It is divided into three sections: an archaeological section devoted to artefacts from the Neolithic period and Bronze Age to the Roman era; a classical section with finds from Lipari's necropolis (including the most complete collection of miniature Greek theatrical masks in the world); and a section on vulcanology and finds from the other islands.

⚐ Activities

Beaches   BEACHES
On the island's western side, **Spiaggia Valle i Muria** is a secluded rocky beach with gorgeous views south to Vulcano. Closed for a time following an August 2010 earthquake, it has since reopened. The most scenic way to get here is by boat, passing the dramatic *faraglioni* (rock towers) and stone arches along Lipari's southwestern shore. Call **Barni** (☏349 183 95 55) to arrange boat transport (€5/10 one way/return). Alternatively, catch the bus from Marina Lunga towards Quattropani, get off at Quattrochi and walk 15 minutes steeply down towards the water.

On Lipari's eastern shore, sunbathers and swimmers head for Canneto, a few kilometres north of Lipari town, to bask on the pebbly **Spiaggia Bianca**. Further north are the **pumice mines** of Pomiciazzo and Porticello, where there's another beach, **Spiaggia della Papesca**, dusted white by the fine pumice that gives the sea its limpid turquoise colour.

Coastal Hikes   WALKING
Lipari's rugged northwestern coastline offers excellent walking opportunities. Most accessible is the pleasant hour-long stroll from Quattropani to Acquacalda along Lipari's north shore, which affords spectacular views of Salina and a distant Stromboli. Take the bus to Quattropani (€1.90), then simply proceed downhill on the main road 5km to Acquacalda, where you can catch the bus (€1.55) back to Lipari.

More strenuous, but equally rewarding in terms of scenery, is the three- to four-hour hike descending steeply from Pianoconte, down past the old Roman baths of Terme di San Calogero to the western shoreline, then skirting the clifftops along a flat stretch before climbing steeply back to the town of Quattropani.

Diving Center La Gorgonia   DIVING
(☏090 981 26 16; www.lagorgoniadiving.it; Salita San Giuseppe, Marina Corta; dive/night dive/beginner course €30/40/55) Offers courses, boat transport and equipment hire for scuba diving and snorkelling in Lipari's crystal-clear waters.

☞ Tours

You can take boat tours to the surrounding islands (€15 to €45), or arrange a day trip to hike up Stromboli (€80) with agencies throughout town, including the following friendly, English-speaking organisations:

AvventurIsole   BOAT
(☏090 988 02 74; www.avventurisole.com, in Italian; Via Maurolico 10)

Da Massimo/Dolce Vita   BOAT
(☏090 981 30 86; www.damassimo.it; Via Maurolico 2)

Popolo Giallo   BOAT
(☏090 981 12 10; www.popologiallo.it; Salita San Giuseppe)

⌂ Sleeping

Lipari is the Aeolians' best-equipped base for island-hopping, with plenty of places to stay, eat and drink. Touts besiege arriving passengers at the port, and the tourist office can sometimes help arrange accommodation in private homes. Note that prices soar in summer; avoid August if possible.

Diana Brown   B&B €
(☏090 981 25 84; www.dianabrown.it; Vico Himera 3; s €30-90, d €40-100; ✳❋) Tucked down a narrow alley, South African Diana has delightful rooms decorated in contemporary style with tile floors, abundant hot water, bright colours and welcome extras such as kettles, fridges, clothes drying racks and satellite TV. Darker rooms downstairs are compensated for by built-in kitchenettes. There's a sunny breakfast terrace and solarium with deck chairs, plus book exchange and laun-

dry service. Optional breakfast per person is €5 extra.

Villa Diana
HOTEL €€

(☎090 981 14 03; www.villadiana.com; Via Tufo 1; s €43-80, d €76-145; P🅿❄🛜) Swiss artist Edwin Hunziker converted this Aeolian house into a bohemian-spirited hotel in the 1950s. It stands above Lipari town in a garden of citrus trees and olives and offers panoramic views from the terrace. Amenities include free wi-fi (in the reception area only) and use of the tennis court.

Hotel Oriente
HOTEL €

(☎090 981 14 93; www.hotelorientelipari.com; Via Marconi 35; s €40-60, d €60-95; P❄🛜) You'll either love this place for its quirkiness or hate it for its clutter. Just 100m west of the centre, its rooms are rather bland and faded, but the common spaces drip with character, from the spacious citrus-filled courtyard, to the eclectically decorated breakfast room and bar, to the in-house museum of Sicilian antique paraphernalia. Breakfast goes above and beyond the norm, with marinated veggies and cheese supplementing the usual bread and coffee.

Enzo Il Negro
GUESTHOUSE €

(☎090 981 31 63; www.enzoilnegro.com; Via Garibaldi 29; s €40-50, d €60-90; ❄) Run by an older couple, this simple guesthouse near Marina Corta sports spacious, tiled, pine-furnished rooms with fridges. Two panoramic terraces overlook the rooftops, the harbour and the castle walls.

✖ Eating & Drinking

Fish abound in the waters of the archipelago and include tuna, mullet, cuttlefish and sole, all of which end up on local menus. Try *pasta all'eoliana,* a simple blend of the island's excellent capers with olive oil, anchovies and basil.

Bars are concentrated along Corso Vittorio Emanuele and down by Marina Corta. In peak season everything stays open into the wee hours.

E Pulera
MODERN SICILIAN €€

(☎090 981 11 58; Via Isabella Vainicher Conti; meals €30-45; ☾dinner May-Oct) With its serene garden setting, low lighting, artsy tile-topped tables and exquisite food, E Pulera makes an upscale but relaxed choice for a romantic dinner. Start with a carpaccio of tuna with blood oranges and capers, choose from a vast array of Aeolian and Sicilian meat and

fish dishes, then finish it all off with *cassata* or biscotti and sweet Malvasia wine.

Kasbah
MODERN SICILIAN €€

(☎090 981 10 75; Via Maurolico 25; pizzas €6-9, meals €30-35; ☾dinner, closed Wed Oct-Mar) Choose the environment that suits you best: the sleek, contemporary interior dining room or the vine-covered, candlelit garden out back. The food is superb, including delicious pizzas and seafood delicacies (order from the menu or select your fish from the display case).

Bar Pasticceria Subba
PASTRIES & CAKES €

(☎090 981 13 52; Corso Vittorio Emanuele 92; pastries from €1; ☾7am-10pm) Feed your sweet tooth with fabulous pastries at this long-established bakery (since 1930) on Lipari's main drag.

La Piazzetta
PIZZERIA €

(☎090 981 25 22; pizzas €5.50-9.50; ☾dinner, closed Thu Sep-Jun) A lively pizzeria with vine-draped outdoor seating that has served the likes of Audrey Hepburn. It's off Corso Vittorio Emanuele, behind Pasticceria Subba.

🛍 Shopping

You simply can't leave these islands without a small pot of capers and a bottle of sweet Malvasia wine. You can get both, along with tuna, meats, cheeses and other delicious goodies at **La Formagella** (Corso Vittorio Emanuele 250) or **Fratelli Laise** (www.fratelli laise.com; Corso Vittorio Emanuele 118).

ℹ Information

Corso Vittorio Emanuele is lined with ATMs. The other islands have few facilities, so sort out your finances here before moving on.

Internet Point (Corso Vittorio Emanuele 185; per hr €5; ☾9.30am-1pm & 5-8.30pm Mon-Sat winter, 9am-1pm & 5.30pm-midnight summer)

Ospedale Civile (☎090 988 51 11; Via Sant'Anna) Operates a first-aid service.

Police (☎090 981 13 33; Via Gugliemo Marconi)

Post office (Corso Vittorio Emanuele 207)

Tourist office (☎090 988 00 95; www.aas teolie.191.it, in Italian; Corso Vittorio Emanuele 202; ☾9am-1pm & 4.30-7pm Mon-Fri year-round, 9am-1pm Sat summer) Lipari's office provides information covering all the islands.

ℹ Getting There & Around

BUS Autobus Guglielmo Urso (☎090 981 10 26; www.ursobus.com) runs frequent buses around the island from Marina Lunga (€1.55

to €1.90 depending on destination). One main route serves the island's eastern shore, from Canneto to Acquacalda, while the other serves the western highland settlements of Quattrochi, Pianoconte and Quattropani. Multi-ride booklets (six/10/20 rides €7/10.50/20.50) will save you money if you're here for several days.

BOAT See p165 for ferry and hydrofoil details.

CAR & MOTORCYCLE Several places around town rent scooters (€15-30) and cars (€30-50), including **Da Luigi** ([☑]090 988 05 40; Marina Lunga) down at the ferry dock.

Vulcano

POP 720 / 500M

Vulcano is a memorable island, not least because of the vile smell of sulphurous gases. Once you escape the drab and dated tourist centre, Porto di Levante, there's a delightfully tranquil, unspoilt quality to the landscape. Following the well-marked trail to the looming Fossa di Vulcano, the landscape gives way to rural simplicity with vineyards, birdsong and a surprising amount of greenery. The island is worshipped by Italians for its therapeutic mud baths and hot springs, and its black beaches and weird steaming landscape make for an interesting day trip.

Boats dock at Porto di Levante. To the right, as you face the island, are the mud baths and the small Vulcanello peninsula, to the left is the volcano. Straight ahead is Porto di Ponente, 700m west, where you will find the Spiaggia Sabbia Nera (Black Sand Beach).

🏃 Activities

Fossa di Vulcano   WALKING
(admission €3) The island's top attraction is the trek up its 391m volcano, easily manageable without a guide. Start early in the day if possible and don't forget a hat, sunscreen and water. Follow the signs south along Strada Provinciale, then turn left onto the zigzag gravel track that leads to the summit. It's about an hour's scramble to the lowest point of the crater's edge (290m). From here, the sight of the steaming crater encrusted with red and yellow crystals is reward enough, but it's well worth lingering up top for a while. You can descend steeply to the crater floor, or better yet, continue climbing around the rim for stunning views of all the islands lined up to the north.

Laghetto di Fanghi   BATHS
(admission €2) Vulcano's large harbourside pit of thick, smelly, sulphurous gloop has long been considered an excellent treatment for arthritis, rheumatism and skin disorders. Don't wear your designer swimsuit (you'll never get the smell out), keep the mud away from your eyes (it burns!), and be sure to leave your gold chains behind (they will tarnish). Afterwards, you can hop into the water at the adjacent beach where *acque calde* (hot springs) create a natural jacuzzi effect.

Beaches   BEACHES
At Porto di Ponente, on the far side of the peninsula from Porto di Levante, the dramatic and only mildly commercialised black sand beach of **Spiaggia Sabbia Nera** curves around a pretty bay. It is one of the few sandy beaches in the archipelago. A smaller, quieter black sand beach, **Spiaggia dell'Asina**, can be found on the island's southern side, near Gelso.

🛌 Sleeping & Eating

Unless you're here for the walking and the mud baths, Vulcano is not a great place for an extended stay; the town is pretty soulless, the hotels are expensive and the mud baths really do smell. If you do stay, the best hotels are situated around Spiaggia Sabbia Nera.

La Forgia Maurizio   SICILIAN, INDIAN €€
([☑]339 137 91 07; Strada Provinciale 45; meals €25-30) The owner of this devilishly good restaurant spent 20 winters in Goa, India; eastern influences sneak into a menu of Sicilian specialities, all prepared and presented with flair. Don't miss the *liquore di kumquat e cardamom,* Maurizio's home-made answer to *limoncello.* The tasting menu is an excellent deal at €25 including wine and dessert.

Trattoria Maniaci Pina   SEAFOOD €€
([☑]368 66 85 55; Gelso; meals €25-35; ⊗May–mid-Oct) On the south side of the island, beside a black-sand beach, this atmospheric, down-to-earth trattoria serves hefty portions of fresh-caught fish at affordable prices. Two local men do the fishing, and their mothers do the cooking.

❶ Getting There & Around

BOAT Vulcano is an intermediate stop between Milazzo and Lipari; both Siremar and Ustica Lines run multiple vessels in both directions throughout the day. See p165 for more details.

You can hire boats locally at **Centro Nautico Baia di Levante** (☑339 337 27 95; www.baialevante.it; ☺Apr-Oct), in a shed on the beach to the left of the hydrofoil dock.

CAR & MOTORCYCLE Scooters (per day €15 to €40), bicycles (€5 to €10) and small cars (€25 to €78) can be rented from **Sprint** (☑090 985 22 08), well signposted near the hydrofoil dock. Friendly multilingual owners Luigi and Nidra also offer helpful tourist Info and rent out an apartment in Vulcano's tranquil interior.

Salina

POP 2300 / ELEV 962M

In stark contrast to Vulcano's barren landscape, Salina's twin craters of Monte dei Porri and Monte Fossa delle Felci are lushly wooded, a result of the numerous freshwater springs on the island. Wild flowers, thick yellow gorse bushes and serried ranks of grapevines carpet the hillsides in vibrant colours and cool greens, while its high coastal cliffs plunge dramatically towards beaches. The famous Aeolian capers grow plentifully here, as do the grapes used for making Malvasia wine.

◉ Sights & Activities

Fossa delle Felci   VIEWPOINT

For jaw-dropping views of Salina and the surrounding islands, climb to Salina's highest point (962m). The trail starts at Valdichiesa, in the valley that separates Salina's two volcanoes, at the **Santuario della Madonna del Terzito**, a popular pilgrimage site. From the church, follow the track (signposted) up through a nature reserve all the way to the peak (about two hours), where you'll have unparalleled views of the entire archipelago. To get to the trailhead, take the bus from Santa Marina Salina to Malfa, then change for a Rinella-bound bus and ask the driver to let you off at Valdichiesa.

Pollara   BEACH

Don't miss a trip to Pollara, sandwiched dramatically between the sea and the steep slopes of an extinct volcanic crater on Salina's western edge. The gorgeous beach here was used as a location in the 1994 film *Il Postino*. Although the land access route to the beach has since been closed due to landslide danger, you can still descend the steep stone steps at the northwest end of town and swim across, or simply admire the spectacular view, with its backdrop of volcanic cliffs.

Nautica Levante   BOATING

(☑090 984 30 83; www.nauticalevante.it, in Italian; Via Lungomare, Santa Marina Salina; ☺Easter-Sep) Boat hire (from €65).

🛏 Sleeping & Eating

The island remains relatively undisturbed by mass tourism, yet still offers some fine hotels and restaurants. Accommodation can be found in Salina's three main towns: Santa Marina Salina on the east shore, Malfa on the north shore and Rinella on the south shore, as well as in Lingua, a village adjoining ancient salt ponds 2km south of Santa Marina.

Capo Faro   BOUTIQUE HOTEL €€€

(☑090 984 43 30; www.capofaro.it; Via Faro 3; d €150-380; ☺Apr-Sep; ✳@🕏🌊) Immerse yourself in luxury at this five-star boutique resort halfway between Santa Marina and Malfa, surrounded by well-tended Malvasia vineyards and a picturesque lighthouse. The 20 rooms all have sharp white decor and terraces looking straight out to smoking Stromboli. Tennis courts, poolside massages, wine tasting, vineyard visits and occasional cooking courses complete this perfect vision of island chic.

Signum   BOUTIQUE HOTEL €€€

(☑090 984 42 22; www.hotelsignum.it; Via Scalo 15, Malfa; d €130-280; ☺mid-Mar–early Nov; ✳🕏🌊) Hidden in the hillside lanes of Malfa is this alluring labyrinth of antique-clad rooms, peach-coloured stucco walls, tall blue windows, and vine-covered terraces. There's a lovely pool, a wellness centre complete with natural spa baths and one of the island's best-regarded restaurants onsite (meals €35 to €50). Check the website for offers.

Hotel Mamma Santina   BOUTIQUE HOTEL €€

(☑090 984 30 54; www.mammasantina.it; Via Sanità 40, Santa Marina Salina; d €110-190; ☺Apr-Oct; ✳@🕏🌊) A labour of love for its architect owner, this boutique hotel has inviting rooms decorated with pretty tiles in traditional Aeolian designs. Many of the sea-view terraces come equipped with hammocks, and on warm evenings the attached restaurant has outdoor seating overlooking the glowing blue pool and landscaped garden.

Campeggio Eolie   CAMPGROUND €

(☑090 980 90 52; www.campeggioeolie.it; Rinella; campsite per person €9-14; ☺late Jun–mid-Sep) This campground has lovely terraced sites amid olive and eucalyptus trees overlooking the sea, plus a mini-market, bar and pizzeria. It's a five-minute walk from Rinella's hydrofoil dock.

TOP CHOICE **Da Alfredo**   SANDWICH SHOP €
(Piazza Marina Garibaldi, Lingua; granite €2.50, sandwiches €7-10) The most atmospheric place on Salina for an affordable snack, Alfredo's place is renowned all over Sicily for its *granite:* ices made with coffee, fresh fruit or locally grown pistachios and almonds. It's also worth a visit for its *pane cunzato* – open-faced sandwiches piled high with tuna, ricotta, eggplant, tomatoes, capers and olives; split one with a friend – they're huge!

Porto Bello   SEAFOOD €€
(☑090 984 31 25; Via Bianchi 1, Santa Marina Salina; meals €30-45; ☺Tue-Sun) This award-winning seafood restaurant with a terrace overlooking the harbour dates back to 1978 with the same family at the helm. Aside from fish, it's famous for its *pasta al fuoco* (fiery pasta with hot peppers).

Al Cappero   SICILIAN €
(☑090 984 41 33; www.alcappero.it; Pollara; meals €20-25; ☺lunch May, lunch & dinner Jun–mid-Sep) This family-run place specialises in old-fashioned Sicilian home-cooking, including several vegetarian options. It also sells home-grown capers and rents out simple rooms down the street (€20 to €35 per person).

'nni Lausta   MODERN ITALIAN €€
(☑090 984 34 86; Via Risorgimento, Santa Marina Salina; meals €35-40) This stylish modern eatery with its cute lobster logo serves superb food based on fresh local ingredients. The downstairs bar is popular for *aperitivi* and late-night drinking.

ⓘ Information

Banco di Sicilia (Via Risorgimento, Santa Marina Salina) ATM on Santa Marina's main pedestrian street.

Post office (Via Risorgimento, Santa Maria Salina)

ⓘ Getting There & Around

BOAT Hydrofoils and ferries service Santa Marina Salina and Rinella from Lipari. You'll find ticket offices in both places.

BUS CITIS (☑090 984 41 50) buses run roughly half-hourly (every 90 minutes in low season) from Santa Marina Salina to Lingua, Malfa, Rinella, Pollara, Valdichiesa and Leni (€1.70 to €2.40 depending on destination). Timetables are posted at the ports and bus stops.

CAR & MOTORCYCLE Above Santa Marina Salina's port, **Antonio Bongiorno** (☑090 984 34 09; Via Risorgimento 240) rents bikes (per day from €8), scooters (from €26) and cars (from €50). Several agencies in Rinella offer similar services – look for signs at the ferry dock.

Stromboli

POP 400 / ELEV 924M

Stromboli's perfect triangle of a volcano juts dramatically out of the sea. It's the only island whose smouldering cone is permanently active, thus attracting both experts and amateurs, like moths to a massive flame. Volcanic activity has scarred and blackened one side of the island, while the eastern side is untamed, ruggedly green and dotted with low-rise whitewashed houses. A youngster among the Aeolians, Stromboli was formed a mere 40,000 years ago and its gases continue to send up an almost constant spray of liquid magma. The most recent major eruptions took place in February 2007 when two new craters opened on the volcano's summit, producing two scalding lava flows. Although seismic activity, including rock falls, continued for several days, fortunately no mass evacuation was deemed necessary.

Boats arrive at Porto Scari-San Vincenzo, downhill from the town. Most accommodation, as well as the meeting point for guided hikes up the volcano, is a short walk up the Scalo Scari to Via Roma.

🏃 Activities

Volcano   WALKING
Note that you're legally required to hire a guide to climb higher than 400m on the volcano.

The path to the summit (920m) is a demanding three-hour climb (rest stops every 40 minutes), but the atmosphere is charged and you will be rewarded with tremendous views of the **Sciara del Fuoco** (Trail of Fire) and the constantly smoking crater. Fiery explosions usually occur every 20 minutes or so and are preceded by a loud belly-roar as gases force the magma into the air. Departure times for organised treks vary from 3.30pm to 6pm, depending on the season; treks are always timed so you can observe sunset from the mountaintop, then ooh and aah over the crater's fireworks for about 45 minutes as night falls.

Sicily is an island lover's paradise, with more than a dozen smaller islands scattered in the seas surrounding the main island. Beyond the major islands of Lipari, Vulcano, Stromboli and Salina, covered in detail here, you can detour to the less visited Aeolian islands of **Panarea**, **Filicudi** and **Alicudi**. Off Sicily's western coast are the slow-paced **Egadi Islands** (see p201) and the remote, rugged volcanic island of **Pantelleria** (see p203). South of Agrigento, the sand-sprinkled **Pelagic Islands** of Lampedusa, Linosa and Lampione offer some fantastic beaches but are temporarily off limits to tourists because of an influx of refugees fleeing the conflicts in North Africa – check locally to see if trips have resumed. **Ustica Lines** (www.usticalines.it) and **Siremar** (www.siremar.it) provide hydrofoil and/or ferry service to all of the islands listed above; see the websites for details.

To undertake the climb you'll need heavy shoes; clothing for cold, wet weather; a torch (flashlight); a backpack that allows free movement of both arms; and a good supply of water. **Totem Trekking** (☎090 986 57 52; Piazza San Vincenzo 4) hires out all the necessary equipment, including headlamps (€3), trekking boots (€6) and windbreakers (€5).

Two other great ways to see the volcano, with less huffing and puffing, are the hike up to L'Osservatorio pizzeria and the nightly boat tours to Sciara del Fuoco. To reach the pizzeria, follow the waterfront 2km west from the hydrofoil dock to the community of Piscità, then climb the gradual, winding path 1km further, following the signs.

Beaches

BEACH

The most accessible swimming and sunbathing is at **Ficogrande**, a beach of rocks and black volcanic sand 10 minutes by foot from the hydrofoil dock. Further-flung beaches worth exploring are at **Piscità** to the west and **Forgia Vecchia** to the south.

La Sirenetta Diving Club (☎347 596 14 99; www.lasirenettadiving.it; Via Marina 33; ☺Jun–mid-Sep) offers diving courses and accompanied dives.

Tours

Magmatrek (☎090 986 57 68; www.magmatrek.it; Via Vittorio Emanuele) has experienced, multilingual vulcanological guides that lead regular treks (maximum group size 20) up to the crater every afternoon (per person €28). It can also put together tailor-made treks for individual groups. Other agencies charging identical prices include **Il Vulcano a Piedi** (☎090 98 61 44; www.stromboliguide.it; Via Roma) and **Stromboli Adventures** (☎090 98 62 64; www.stromboliadventures.it, in Italian; Via Vittorio Emanuele).

Società Navigazione Pippo (☎090 98 61 35; pipponav.stromboli@libero.it) and **Antonio Caccetta** (☎090 98 60 23) are among the numerous boat companies at Porto Scari offering daytime circuits of the island and sunset excursions to watch the Sciara del Fuoco from the sea (each €20 per person).

Sleeping & Eating

Over a dozen places offer accommodation, including B&Bs, guesthouses and full-fledged hotels.

TOP CHOICE **Casa del Sole** GUESTHOUSE €
(☎090 98 63 00; www.casadelsolestromboli.it; Via Domenico Cincotta; dm €25-30, s €30-50, d €60-100) This cheerful Aeolian-style guesthouse is only 100m from a sweet black-sand beach in Piscità, the tranquil neighbourhood at the far end of town. Dorms, private doubles and a guest kitchen all surround a sunny patio, overhung with vines, fragrant with lemon blossoms, and decorated with the masks and stone carvings of sculptor-owner Tano Russo. Call for free pickup (low season only) or take a taxi (€10) from the port 2km away.

Il Giardino Segreto B&B €
(☎090 98 62 11; www.giardinosegretobb.it; Via Francesco Natoli; d €60-120) In a 'secret garden' framed by picturesque rows of cypresses, this sweet little B&B offers stylishly decorated rooms and a rooftop terrace five minutes' walk above the church on the way to the volcano.

L'Osservatorio PIZZERIA €
(☎090 98 63 60; pizzas €6.50-10.50; ☺lunch & dinner) Sure, you could eat a pizza in town, but come on – you're on Stromboli! Make the 45-minute uphill trek to this pizzeria and you'll be rewarded with exceptional volcano views, best after sundown.

La Bottega del Marano GROCERY €
(Via Vittorio Emanuele; snacks from €1.50; ⊙8.30am-1pm & 4.30-7.30pm Mon-Sat) The perfect source for volcano-climbing provisions or a self-catering lunch, this reasonably priced neighbourhood grocery, five minutes west of the trekking agency offices, has a well-stocked deli, shelves full of wine and awesomely tasty mini-focaccias (€1.50).

Locanda del Barbablù SICILIAN €€€
(☑090 98 61 18; www.barbablu.it; Via Vittorio Emanuele 17; tasting menus excl drinks €40-56; ⊙dinner Apr-Oct) This dusky-pink Aeolian inn houses the island's classiest restaurant, serving multicourse tasting menus of traditional Sicilian recipes, with a strong emphasis on fresh-caught seafood.

ℹ Information

Bring enough cash for your stay on Stromboli. Many businesses don't accept credit cards, and the village's lone ATM is often out of service. Internet access is virtually non-existent.
Police station (☑090 98 60 21; Via Picone) Just on the left as you walk up from the port.
Post office (Via Roma)

ℹ Getting There & Away

It takes four hours to reach the island from Lipari by ferry, or 1½ to two hours by hydrofoil. Ticket offices for **Ustica Lines** (☑090 98 60 03) and **Siremar** (☑090 98 60 16) are at the port.

IONIAN COAST

Magnificent, overdeveloped, crowded – and exquisitely beautiful – the Ionian coast is Sicily's most popular tourist destination and home to 20% of the island's population. Moneyed entrepreneurs have built their villas and hotels up and down the coastline, eager to bag a spot on Sicily's version of the Amalfi Coast. Above it all towers the muscular peak of Mt Etna (3330m), puffs of smoke billowing from its snow-covered cone.

Taormina

POP 11,100 / ELEV 204M

Spectacularly situated on a terrace of Monte Tauro, with views westwards to Mt Etna, Taormina is a beautiful small town, reminiscent of Capri or an Amalfi coastal resort. Over the centuries, Taormina has seduced an exhaustive line of writers and artists, aristocrats and royalty, and these days it's host to a summer arts festival that packs the town with international visitors.

Perched on its eyrie, Taormina is sophisticated, chic and comfortably cushioned by some serious wealth – very far removed from the banal economic realities of other Sicilian towns. But the charm is not manufactured. The capital of Byzantine Sicily in the 9th century, Taormina is an almost perfectly preserved medieval town, and if you can tear yourself away from the shopping and sunbathing, it has a wealth of small but perfect tourist sites. Taormina is also a popular resort with gay men.

Be warned that in July and August the town and its surrounding beaches are swarming with tourists.

◉ Sights

A short walk uphill from the bus station brings you to Corso Umberto I (abbreviated below as Corso Umberto), a pedestrianised thoroughfare that traverses the length of the medieval town and connects its two historic town gates, Porta Messina and Porta Catania.

Teatro Greco AMPHITHEATRE
(☑0942 2 32 20; Via Teatro Greco; adult/reduced €8/4; ⊙9am-1hr before sunset) Taormina's premier attraction is this perfect horseshoe-shaped theatre, suspended between sea and sky, with Mt Etna looming on the southern horizon. Built in the 3rd century BC, it's the most dramatically situated Greek theatre in the world and the second largest in Sicily (after Syracuse). In summer the theatre is used as the venue for international arts and film festivals. In peak season the site is best explored early in the morning to avoid the crowds.

Corso Umberto PROMENADE
One of the chief delights of Taormina is wandering along its pedestrian-friendly medieval main avenue, Corso Umberto I, lined with antique and jewellery shops, delis and designer boutiques. Midway down, pause to revel in the stunning panoramic views of Mt Etna and the seacoast from **Piazza IX Aprile** and pop your head into the charming rococo church, **Chiesa San Giuseppe** (Piazza IX Aprile; ⊙9am-7pm). Continue west through the 12th-century clock tower, **Torre dell'Orologio**, into the Borgo Medievale, the oldest quarter of town. A few blocks further along is **Piazza del Duomo**, where teenagers congregate around the ornate **baroque fountain** (built 1635), which sports a two-

Taormina

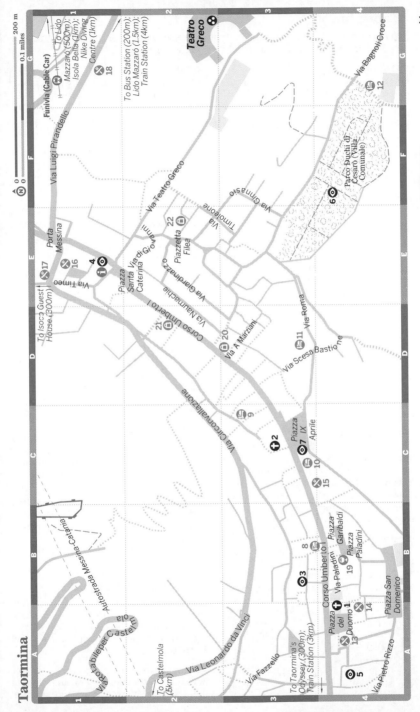

Teatro Greco

To Lido
Mazzaro (500m);
Lido Mazzarò (1.5km);
Train Station (4km)

To Lido
Mazzaro (500m):
Isola Bella (1km):
Nike Diving
Centre (1km)

Funivia (Cable Car)

Via Luigi Pirandello

Via Bagnoli Croce

Parco Duchi di
Cesarò (Villa
Comunale)

Porta
Messina

Via Teatro Greco

Via
Timoleone

Via Ginnasio

Via Timeo

Piazza
Santa
Caterina

Via di Giovanni

Piazzetta
Filea

To Isoco Guest
House (300m)

Corso Umberto I

Via Naumachie

Via Giardinazzo

Via A Marziani

Via Roma

Via Scesa Bastione

Via Circonvallazione

Piazza
IX
Aprile

Via Pietro Rizzo

Via Fazzello

Corso Umberto I

Piazza
del
Duomo

Piazza
Palladini

Piazza
Garibaldi

Piazza
Palladini

Piazza San
Domenico

To Castelmola
(5km)

Via Roma per Castelmola

Autostrada Messina-Catania

Via Leonardo da Vinci

To Taormina's
Odyssey (300m);
Train Station (3km)

0   200 m
0   0.1 miles

Taormina

legged centaur with the bust of an angel, the symbol of Taormina. On the eastern side of this piazza is the 13th-century **cathedral** (Piazza del Duomo; ☺9am-8pm). It survived much of the Renaissance-style remodelling undertaken throughout the town by the Spanish aristocracy in the 15th century. The Renaissance influence is better illustrated in various palaces along the Corso, including **Palazzo Duca di Santo Stefano** with its Norman-Gothic windows, **Palazzo Corvaja** (the tourist office) and **Palazzo Ciampoli** (now the Hotel El Jebel).

Villa Comunale   PARK
(Parco Duchi di Cesarò; Via Bagnoli Croce; ☺9am-midnight summer, 9am-10pm winter) To escape the crowds, wander down to these stunningly sited public gardens. Created by Englishwoman Florence Trevelyan, they're a lush paradise of tropical plants and delicate flowers. There's also a children's play area.

Castelmola   HILLTOP VILLAGE
For eye-popping views of the coastline, head 5km up Via Leonardo da Vinci to this hilltop village crowned by a ruined castle. The walk will take you around an hour along a well-paved route. Alternatively, Interbus runs an hourly service (one-way/return €1.70/2.80) up the hill.

🏃 Activities

Lido Mazzarò   BEACH
Many visitors to Taormina come only for the beach scene. To reach Lido Mazzarò, directly beneath Taormina, take the **cable car** (Via Luigi Pirandello; one-way/return €2/3.50; ☺8.45am-1am, every 15 min). This beach is well serviced with bars and restaurants; private operators charge a fee for umbrellas and deck chairs (€10 per person per day, discountable at some hotels).

Isola Bella   NATURE RESERVE
Southwest of the beach is the minuscule Isola Bella, set in a stunning cove with fishing boats. You can walk here in a few minutes but it's more fun to rent a small boat from Mazzarò and paddle round Capo Sant'Andrea.

Nike Diving Centre   DIVING
(☎339 196 15 59; www.diveniketaormina.com; dive from €35) Opposite Isola Bella, this dive centre offers a wide range of courses for children and adults.

Gole dell'Alcàntara   SWIMMING
Perfect for cooling off on a hot summer day, this series of vertiginous lava gorges with swirling rapids is 20km west of town; take Interbus from Taormina (€4.60 return, one hour).

🎊 Festivals & Events

Taormina FilmFest   FILM
(www.taorminafilmfest.it) Hollywood big shots arrive in mid-June for a week of film screenings, premieres and press conferences at the Teatro Greco.

Taormina Arte   ARTS
(www.taormina-arte.com) In July and August, this festival features opera, dance, theatre

and music concerts from an impressive list of international names.

Giuseppe Sinopoli Festival   MUSIC
(www.sinopolifestival.it) First held in 2005, this three-day classical music festival attracts important Italian orchestras and enthusiastic audiences in early October. Concerts are held in Palazzo Corvaja and the Teatro Greco.

🛌 Sleeping

Taormina has plenty of luxurious accommodation; the following represents a range of what's available, including some less expensive places. Many hotels offer discounted pricing (from €10) at Taormina's two public parking lots.

TOP CHOICE Isoco Guest House   B&B €
(☑0942 2 36 79; www.isoco.it; Via Salita Branco 2; s €65-120, d €85-120; ⊙Mar-Nov; P☀@) Every room in this exceptionally welcoming, gay-friendly B&B is dedicated to an artist – from Botticelli to the sculpted buttocks and pant-popping thighs on the walls of the Herb Ritts room. The excellent breakfast, free internet access, sundecks and outdoor jacuzzi are great as well. Multi-course dinners available on the terrace (€25 per person including drinks) in summer. German and English spoken.

B&B Le Sibille   B&B €
(☑349 726 28 62; www.lesibille.net; Corso Umberto 187a; d €60-100, apt per week without breakfast €400-600; ⊙Apr-Oct; @☎) This B&B wins points for its prime location on Taormina's pedestrian thoroughfare, its rooftop breakfast terrace and its cheerful, artistically tiled self-catering apartments were newly added in 2011. Light sleepers beware: Corso Umberto can get noisy with holidaymakers! English spoken.

Villa Belvedere   HOTEL €€
(☑0942 2 37 91; www.villabelvedere.it; Via Bagnoli Croce 79; d with inland view €124-184, with sea view €144-236; ⊙Mar-Nov; P☀@☎☒) Built in 1902, adjacent to the Villa Comunale, the jaw-droppingly pretty Villa Belvedere oozes class. Rooms are simple but refined with cream linens and terracotta floors, and the luxurious garden commands majestic sea views. There's even a swimming pool with a 100-year-old palm tree rising from a small island in the middle. Wi-fi costs extra.

Casa Turchetti   B&B €€€
(☑0942 62 50 13; www.casaturchetti.com; Salita dei Gracchi 18/20; d €200-250, jr ste €350; ☀☎) Every detail is perfect in this painstakingly restored former music school, recently converted to a luxurious B&B on a back alley just above Corso Umberto. Vintage furniture and fixtures, handcrafted woodwork, fine homespun sheets and modern bathrooms all contribute to the elegant feel; the spacious rooftop terrace is just icing on the cake.

Hotel Villa Schuler   HOTEL €€
(☑0942 2 34 81; www.hotelvillaschuler.com; Via Roma, Piazzetta Bastione; s €128, d €142-202; P☀@☎) Surrounded by shady terraced gardens and with views of Mt Etna, the rose-pink Villa Schuler has been run by the same family for over a century (longer than any other Taormina hotel) and preserves a homely atmosphere. A lovely breakfast is served on the panoramic terrace.

Hotel Metropole   LUXURY HOTEL €€€
(☑0942 62 54 17; www.hotelmetropoletaormina. it; Corso Umberto 154; d/ste €374/770; ☀@☎☎) In a lavishly renovated *palazzo* that incorporates ancient Roman columns and 14th-century monastery walls, Taormina's newest hotel offers a unparalleled combination of amenities, including a pool, a spa, a prime location just off Piazza IX Aprile and a restaurant and bar with full-on views of Mt Etna and the sea. The eight rooms and 15 suites are filled with designer furniture and top-of-the-line amenities, as reflected in the prices.

Taormina's Odyssey   GUESTHOUSE €
(☑0942 2 45 33, 349 810 77 33; www.taormina odyssey.com; Via Paternò di Biscari 13; dm €20, d €50-70; @☎) This family-run hostel and guesthouse offers two small dorms and three doubles (one with private bath) five minutes uphill from Porta Catania. There's a nice guest kitchen and internet area downstairs, and the dorm rate is as affordable a sleep as you'll find anywhere in Taormina.

🍴 Eating

Eating out in Taormina goes hand in hand with posing. It's essential to make a reservation at the more exclusive choices. Be aware that Taormina's cafes charge extraordinarily high prices, even for coffee.

Licchio's   SEAFOOD €€
(☑0942 62 53 27; Via Patricio 10; meals €30-40; ⊙lunch & dinner, closed Thu Nov-Mar) The seafood antipasti at this classy little eatery are

delicious and varied enough to constitute a meal in themselves, but the menu's full of other enticements: tempura-fried zucchini flowers, fabulously fresh spinach-ricotta gnocchi and divine desserts. Angelo also offers cooking classes (€80 including meal and drinks).

Trattoria Da Nino TRATTORIA €€
(☑0942 2 12 65; Via Luigi Pirandello 37; meals €27-34; ☺lunch & dinner) Bright and bustling after a recent remodel, this place has been in business under the same family ownership for 50 years. Locals and tourists alike flock here for straightforward, reasonably priced Sicilian home cooking, including an excellent *caponata* plus fresh local fish served grilled, steamed, fried, stewed or rolled up in *involtini* (roulades).

Tiramisù MODERN ITALIAN €€
(☑0942 2 48 03; Via Cappuccini1; pizzas €7-10, meals €30-45; ☺closed Tue) This stylish place near Porta Messina makes fabulous meals, from *linguine cozze, menta e zucchine* (pasta with mussels, mint and courgettes) to old favourites like *scaloppine al limone e panna* (veal escalope in lemon cream sauce). When dessert rolls around, don't miss the trademark tiramisu, a perfect ending to any meal here.

Al Duomo SICILIAN €€
(☑0942 62 56 56; Vico Ebrei 11; meals €40-45; ☺lunch & dinner, closed Mon Nov-Mar) This highly acclaimed restaurant with a romantic terrace overlooking the cathedral puts a modern spin on Sicilian classics like *pesce alla messinese* (fish fillets with tomatoes, capers and olives) and *agnello n'grassatu* (lamb stew with potatoes). For a splurge, indulge in the chef's six-course tasting menu (€60).

Casa Grugno GASTRONOMIC €€€
(☑0942 2 12 08; www.casagrugno.it; Via Santa Maria dei Greci; meals €70-80; ☺dinner Mon-Sat) With a walled-in terrace surrounded by plants, Taormina's most fashionable restaurant specialises in sublime modern Sicilian cuisine, under the direction of new chef David Tamburini. Multilingual waiters describe the origins of each ultra-fresh local ingredient as they serve up dishes such as red mullet fillets with grilled fennel, orange and saffron or risotto with green peas, candied ginger and marjoram.

Granduca PIZZERIA €
(☑0942 2 49 83; Corso Umberto 172; pizzas €7-11; ☺dinner) Forget the staid, typically pricey Taormina restaurant upstairs; the best reason to visit Granduca is for pizza on a summer evening, served on a vast outdoor terrace overlooking Mt Etna and the sea – an unbeatable combination of view, quality and price!

Drinking

Shatulle BAR
(Piazza Paladini 4; ☺closed Mon) An intimate square just off Corso Umberto, Piazza Paladini is a perennial favourite with Taormina's young, well-dressed night owls. One of the best, and most popular of the square-side bars is this hip, gay-friendly spot with outdoor seating, an inviting vibe and a fine selection of cocktails (from €5.50).

Bar Turrisi BAR
(Castelmola; ☺9am-2am) A few kilometres outside Taormina, in the hilltop community of Castelmola, this whimsical bar is built on four levels overlooking the church square. Its decor is an eclectic tangle of Sicilian influences, with everything from painted carts to a giant stone *minchia* (you'll need no translation once you see it). Sip a glass of almond wine, enjoy the view, and don't forget to check out the bathrooms on the way out!

Shopping
Taormina is a shopper's paradise. The quality in most places is high but don't expect any bargains.

Carlo Mirella Panarello CERAMIC ART
(Via Antonio Marziani)

Managò & Figlie CERAMIC ART
(www.manago.it; Via Santa Domenica)

La Torinese FOOD, WINE
(Corso Umberto 59) Olive oil, capers, jam and wine.

Information
There are plenty of banks with ATMs along Corso Umberto.

British Pharmacy (Corso Umberto 152; ☺8.30am-8pm) One of two pharmacies along Corso Umberto offering emergency night call-out service.

Gustosi Momenti (Salita Alexander Humboldt; internet per 20 min €2; ☺10am-9pm Tue-Sun Nov-Mar, 10.30am-midnight Apr-Oct) A slick internet bar with several fast computers, wi-fi and a choice of cocktails.

Ospedale San Vincenzo (☑0942 57 92 97; Contrada Sirina) Downhill and 2km southwest of the centre. Call the same number for an ambulance.

Police station (☑0942 61 02 01; Corso Umberto 219)

Post office (Piazza Sant'Antonio Abate)

Tourist office (☑0942 2 32 43; www.gate 2taormina.com; Palazzo Corvaja, Corso Umberto; ⏱8.30am-2.15pm & 3.30-6.45pm Mon-Fri, 9am-12.45pm & 4-6.15pm Sat) Busy, well-staffed tourist office.

❶ Getting There & Around

Bus

The bus is the easiest way to reach Taormina. **Interbus** (☑0942 62 53 01; Via Luigi Pirandello) services leave daily for Messina (€3.90, 55 minutes to 1¾ hours, 10 daily Monday to Saturday, two on Sunday) and Catania (€4.70, 1¼ hours, seven to 11 daily), the latter continuing to Catania's Fontanarossa airport (€7, 1½ hours).

Car & Motorcycle

Taormina is on the A18 autostrada and the SS114 between Messina and Catania. Driving near the historic centre is a complete nightmare and Corso Umberto is closed to traffic. The most convenient place to leave your car is the **Porta Catania car park** (per 24hr €15), at the western end of Corso Umberto. The **Lumbi car park** north of the centre charges the same rates, but from here you'll have to walk five minutes or take the free yellow shuttle bus to get to Porta Messina (at the eastern end of Corso Umberto).

California (☑0942 2 37 69; Via Bagnoli Croce86; Vespa per day/week €30/189, Fiat Panda €60/296) Rents out cars and scooters, just across from the Villa Comunale.

Train

There are regular trains to and from Messina (€3.80, 40 to 75 minutes, hourly) and Catania (€3.80, 40 to 50 minutes, hourly), but the awkward location of Taormina's station (a steep 4km below town) is a strong disincentive. If you arrive this way, catch a taxi (€15) or an Interbus coach (€1.70) up to the town. Buses run roughly every 30 to 90 minutes (less frequently on Sunday).

Catania

POP 296.000

Catania is a true city of the volcano. Much of it is constructed from the lava that poured down the mountain and engulfed the city in the 1669 eruption in which nearly 12,000 people lost their lives. It is also lava-black in colour, as if a fine dusting of soot permanently covers its elegant buildings, most of which are the work of baroque master Giovanni Vaccarini. Vaccarini almost single-handedly rebuilt the civic centre into an elegant, modern city of spacious boulevards and set-piece piazzas.

Catania is Sicily's second commercial city, a thriving, entrepreneurial centre with a large university and a tough, resilient local population that adheres strongly to the motto of *carpe diem* (seize the day).

◉ Sights

Catania's sights are concentrated within a few blocks of Piazza del Duomo.

Piazza del Duomo   CENTRAL SQUARE

A Unesco World Heritage Site, Catania's central square is a set piece of sinuous buildings and a grand cathedral, all built in the unique local baroque style, with its contrasting lava and limestone. In the centre of the piazza is Catania's most memorable monument, and a symbol of the city, the smiling **Fontana dell'Elefante** (built in 1736). The statue is crowned by a naive black-lava elephant, dating from the Roman period, surmounted by an improbable Egyptian obelisk. Legend has it that it belonged to the 8th-century magician Eliodorus, who reputedly made his living by turning men into animals. The obelisk is believed to possess magical powers that help to calm Mt Etna's restless activity. At the piazza's southwest corner, the **Fontana dell'Amenano** fountain marks the entrance to Catania's fish market and commemorates the Amenano River, which once ran overground and on whose banks the Greeks first founded the city of Katáne.

Duomo   DUOMO

(☑095 32 00 44; Piazza del Duomo; ⏱8am-noon & 4-7pm) Catania's other defence against Mt Etna is St Agata's cathedral, with its impressive marble facade. Inside the cool, vaulted interior lie the remains of the city's patron saint, the young virgin Agata, who resisted the advances of the nefarious Quintian (AD 250) and was horribly mutilated. The saint's jewel-drenched effigy is ecstatically venerated on 5 February in one of Sicily's largest *feste* (see p179).

La Pescheria   FISH MARKET

(Via Pardo; ⏱7am-2pm) The best show in Catania is this bustling fish market, where vendors raucously hawk their wares in Sicilian dialect, while decapitated swordfish cast sidelong glances at you across silvery heaps of sardines on ice. Equally colourful is the adjoining **food market** (Via Naumachia;

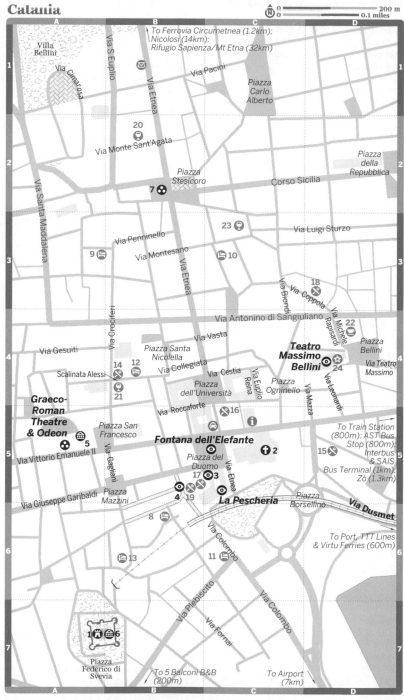

N 0 200 m
0 0.1 miles

To Ferrovia Circumetnea (1.2km);
Nicolosi (14km);
Rifugio Sapienza/Mt Etna (32km)

Villa
Bellini

Via S Euplio

Via Cimarosa

Via Etnea

Via Pacini

Piazza
Carlo
Alberto

20

Via Monte Sant'Agata

Via Santa Maddalena

Piazza
Stesicoro

7

Corso Sicilia

Piazza
della
Repubblica

Via Penninello

23

Via Luigi Sturzo

9

Via Montesano

Via Etnea

10

18

Via Coppola

Via Biondi

22

Via Antonino di Sangiuliano

Via Michele Rapisardi

Piazza
Bellini

Via Crociferi

Via Gesuiti

Via Vasta

Piazza Santa
Nicolella

Via Collegiata

Teatro
Massimo
Bellini

24

Via Teatro
Massimo

14 12

Scalinata Alessi

Via Cestia

21

Piazza
dell'Università

Via Euplio Reina

Piazza
Ogninello

Via Leonardi

Graeco-
Roman
Theatre
& Odeon

Piazza San
Francesco

Via Roccaforte

16

Via Mazza

To Train Station
(800m); AST Bus
Stop (800m);
Interbus
& SAIS
Bus Terminal (1km);
Zó (1.3km)

5

Via Vittorio Emanuele II

Fontana dell'Elefante

2

Via Gagliani

Piazza del
Duomo

15

Via Giuseppe Garibaldi

Piazza
Mazzini

17 3

Via Etnea

Piazza
Borsellino

Via Dusmet

4 19

La Pescheria

8

To Port, TTT Lines
& Virtu Ferries (600m)

13

11

Via Colombo

Via Colombo

Via Plebiscito

1 6

Via Fornai

Piazza
Federico di
Svevia

To 5 Balconi B&B
(200m)

To Airport
(7km)

Catania

◎7am-3pm), with carcasses of meat, skinned sheep's heads, strings of sausages, huge wheels of cheese and piles of luscious fruits and vegetables all rolled together in a few noisy, jam-packed alleyways.

Graeco-Roman Theatre & Odeon RUINS
(Via Vittorio Emanuele II 262; adult/reduced €4/2; ◎9am-1pm & 2.30pm-1hr before sunset Tue-Sun) These twin theatres west of Piazza del Duomo are the most impressive Graeco-Roman remains in Catania. Both are picturesquely sited in the thick of a crumbling residential neighbourhood, with laundry flapping on the rooftops of vine-covered buildings that appear to have sprouted organically from the half-submerged stage. Adjacent to the main theatre is the **Casa Liberti** (same admission and opening hours as theatres), an elegantly restored 19th-century palazzo with tiled floors and red wallpaper that now houses two millennia worth of artefacts discovered during excavation of the theatres.

Teatro Massimo Bellini OPERA HOUSE
(☎095 730 61 11; www.teatromassimobellini.it; Via Perrotta 12; guided tours €2; ◎tours 9.30 & 10.30 Tue, Thu & Sat) A few blocks northeast of the *duomo*, this gorgeous opera house forms the centrepiece of elegant Piazza Bellini. Square and opera house alike were named after composer Vincenzo Bellini, the father of Catania's vibrant modern musical scene.

FREE **Museo Belliniano** MUSEUM
(☎095 715 05 35; Piazza San Francesco 3; ◎9am-1pm Mon-Sat) This small museum houses a collection of memorabilia from the composer's life.

Museo Civico MUSEUM
(☎095 34 58 30; Piazza Federico II di Svevia; ◎9am-1pm & 3-7pm Mon-Sat, 8.30am-1.30pm Sun) Housed in the grim-looking 13th-century Castello Ursino, Catania's civic museum houses the valuable Biscari archaeological collection, an extensive exhibition of paintings, vases and sculpture, and an impressive coin collection.

Villa Bellini PARK
(◎8am-8pm) Escape the madding crowd and enjoy the fine views of Mt Etna from these lovely gardens along Via Etnea.

Roman amphitheatre AMPHITHEATRE
The modest ruins of this Roman theatre, below street level in Piazza Stesicoro, are worth a quick look.

✷ Festivals & Events

Festa di Sant'Agata RELIGIOUS
In Catania's biggest religious festival (3 to 5 February), one million Catanians follow the Fercolo (a silver reliquary bust of Saint Agata) along the main street of the city accompanied by spectacular fireworks.

Carnevale di Acireale CARNIVAL
(www.carnevalediacireale.it) Nearby Acireale hosts Sicily's most flamboyant carnival for two weeks every winter. Streets in this baroque coastal resort come alive with gargantuan papier mâché puppets, flowery allegorical floats, confetti and fireworks.

Etnafest ARTS
From July through December, this arts festival brings classical music, puppet shows and a varied program of rock, pop, blues, reggae and jazz concerts to Le Ciminiere.

🛌 Sleeping

Catania is served by a good range of reasonably priced accommodations, making it an excellent base for exploring the Ionian coast and Etna.

Palazzu Stidda APARTMENT €
(☏095 34 88 26; www.palazzo-stella.com; Vicolo della Lanterna 5; d €70-100, q €120-140;🖙🖳) A great option for families, these three delightful apartments on a peaceful dead-end alley have all the comforts of home plus a host of whimsical touches. Apartments 2 and 3 each come with a washing machine, kitchen, high chair and stroller, and ample space for a family of four. Apartment 1 is smaller and costs €10 to €20 less. Each has a flowery mini-balcony, and all are decorated with the owners' artwork, handmade furniture, family heirlooms and vintage finds from local antiques markets. French and English spoken.

B&B Crociferi B&B €
(☏095 715 22 66; www.bbcrociferi.it; Via Crociferi 81; s/d/tr €65/85/110; 🖙🖳) Affording easy access to the animated nightlife of Catania's historic centre, this B&B in a beautifully decorated family home is one of Catania's most delightful places to stay. With only three rooms, it fills up fast, so book ahead. Rooms are spacious, with high ceilings, antique tiles, frescoes and artistic accoutrements from the owners' travels in India. Each room has its own private bathroom across the hall. Mario (who speaks French) offers tours of the coastline in his private boat, while Teresa (who speaks German and English) makes a delicious, varied breakfast.

5 Balconi B&B B&B €
(☏095 723 45 34; www.5balconi.it; Via Plebiscito 133; s €30-35, d €50-65, tr €70-75; 🖙🖳) You won't find a nicer low-end option than

this lovingly remodelled antique *palazzo* in a workaday neighbourhood just south of Castello Ursino. The friendly owners offer three high-ceilinged rooms with a pair of shared bathrooms down the hall, plus a breakfast featuring local organic bread and fresh fruit (delivered to your room upon request). The street out front gets a lot of traffic, but there are views of the castle and Etna in the distance.

BAD B&B €
(☏095 34 69 03; www.badcatania.com; Via C Colombo 24; s €40-55, d €60-80, apt €90-140; 🖙🖳) An uninhibitedly colourful, modern sense of style prevails at this trendy B&B. All rooms feature local artwork and TVs with DVD players. The two-level upstairs apartment with full kitchen and private terrace is a fab option for self-caterers, especially since the fish and vegetable markets are right around the corner. Staff is great about suggesting cultural goings-on about town.

Il Principe HOTEL €€
(☏095 250 03 45; www.ilprincipehotel.com; Via Alessi 24; d €109-189, ste €129-209; 🖙🌐🖳) This boutique-style hotel in an 18th-century building features luxurious rooms on one of the liveliest nightlife streets in town (thank goodness for double glazing!). Perks include international cable TV, free wi-fi and fluffy bathrobes to wear on your way to the Turkish steam bath. Check online for regularly updated special rates. More expensive suites have marble bathrooms with Jaccuzis and spiral staircases leading to a second level.

B&B Faro B&B €
(☏349 457 88 56; www.bebfaro.it; Via San Michele 26; s €50, d €70-80, tr €100; 🖙🌐) A stylish B&B with five upstairs rooms incorporating polished wood floors, double-glazed windows, modern bathroom fixtures, antique tiles and bold colours. The two suites are especially nice, and during slower periods can be booked for the price of a double. Additional perks include free cable internet and bikes for guests' use. There's also a studio downstairs where visiting artists are invited to come and paint.

Agorà Hostel HOSTEL €
(☏095 723 30 10; www.agorahostel.com; Piazza Currò 6; dm €18-21, s €25-30, d €50-55; 🌐🖳) The six- to 10-bed dorms can get loud, and the bathrooms are pretty scuzzy, but the free wi-fi, affordable laundry facilities (€3.50 per

wash) and super-cool subterranean bar may still be enough to win over budget-minded solo travellers. Self-caterers will appreciate the location near La Pescheria and the larger guest kitchen under construction at research time.

✕ Eating

Popular street snacks in Catania include *arancini* (fried rice balls filled with meat, cheese, tomatoes and/or peas) and *seltz* (fizzy water with fresh-squeezed lemon juice and natural fruit syrup). Don't leave town without trying *pasta alla Norma* (pasta with basil, eggplant and ricotta), a dish that originated here.

The **food market** adjacent to La Pescheria is a fantastic place to shop for fruit, cheese, and sandwich fixings (don't let those staring swordfish intimidate you!).

TOP CHOICE Trattoria di De Fiore TRATTORIA €
(☑095 31 62 83; Via Coppola 24/26; meals €15-25; ⊘closed Mon) This neighbourhood trattoria is presided over by septuagenarian chef Mamma Rosanna, who uses organic flour and fresh, local ingredients to recreate her great-grandmother's recipes, including the best *pasta alla Norma* you'll taste in Sicily. (Rosanna says her grandmother called this dish *Mungibeddu* – Sicilian dialect for Mt Etna – in honour of Catania's famous volcano: tomatoes were the red lava, eggplant the black cinders, ricotta the snow and basil leaves the mountain vegetation.) Service is slow and the door doesn't always open promptly at 1pm, but food like this is well worth waiting for. Be sure not to miss the *zeppoline di ricotta* (sweet ricotta fritters dusted with powdered sugar), a dessert that was invented by Rosanna herself.

Fiaschetteria Biscari SICILIAN €€
(☑095 093 27 61; Via Museo Biscari 8; meals €35-45; ⊘closed 1 variable day per week) In the former stables of Palazzo Biscari, this wonderfully atmospheric wine bar and restaurant places a high value on quality; the menu is built around ultra-fresh ingredients from the nearby fish and produce markets.

Osteria Antica Marina SEAFOOD €€
(☑095 34 81 97; Via Pardo 29; meals €35-45; ⊘closed Wed) This rustic but classy trattoria located behind the fish market is *the* place to come for seafood. A variety of tasting menus showcases everything from

swordfish to scampi, cuttlefish to calamari. Decor-wise think solid wooden tables and rough stone walls. Reservations are essential.

Trattoria La Paglia TRATTORIA €
(☑095 34 68 38; Via Pardo 23; meals €15-25; ⊘closed Sun) Lacking the lustre as well as the higher prices of its next-door neighbour, this simple trattoria offers dependably fresh seafood and an in-your-face view of the action around La Pescheria market.

Al Cortile Alessi PIZZERIA €
(☑095 31 54 44; Via Alessi 28; pizzas €6-9; ⊘8pm-1am Tue-Sun) Catanians of all ages – but especially students – flock here on weekend evenings, drawn by the excellent pizzas, draft beer, relaxed atmosphere and outdoor courtyard overhung with banana trees.

Grand Cafè Tabbacco PASTRIES & CAKES €
(Via Etnea 28; ⊘7am-midnight) Perfect for people-watching during the *passeggiata* (evening stroll), this old-style *pasticceria* (pastry shop) has sumptuous display cases and outdoor seating on lively Via Etnea, just north of Piazza del Duomo.

🍸 Drinking

Not surprisingly for a busy university town, Catania has a reputation for its effervescent nightlife. Fun streets for bar-hopping include (from west to east) Via Alessi, Via Collegiata, Via Vasta, Via Mancini, Via Montesano, Piazza Spirito Santo and Via Teatro Massimo.

Tertulia CAFE
(☑095 715 26 03; Via Michele Rapisardi 1-3; ⊘10am-1am Mon-Sat, 5pm-1am Sun) This bookshop-cafe with a stylish tea-house atmosphere hosts occasional live music, plus literary evenings and book presentations.

Agorá Bar BAR
(www.agorahostel.com; Piazza Curró 6) This super-atmospheric bar occupies a neon-lit cave 18m below ground, complete with its own subterranean river. The Romans used it as a spa; nowadays a cosmopolitan crowd lingers over late-night drinks.

Nievski Pub PUB
(Scalinata Alessi 15; ⊘8pm-2am Tue-Sun) Popular with Catania's alternative crowd, this place serves affordable food and alcohol with a slightly arch attitude. At night the beer flows freely as students gather on the steps outside.

Energie Cafe DAR CAFE

(Via Monte Sant'Agata 10) A slick urban cafe with kaleidoscopic '70s-inspired decor, streetside seating and laid-back jazz-infused tunes.

Waxy O'Connor's PUB

(Piazza Spirito Santo 1) One of two Irish pubs on this street, where revellers down pints of Guinness on the sidewalk while listening to occasional live music.

☆ Entertainment

Pick up a copy of *Lapis,* a free bi-weekly program of music, theatre and art available throughout the city.

Teatro Massimo Bellini OPERA HOUSE

(☏095 730 61 11; www.teatromassimobellini.it; Via Perrotta 12; ☺Oct-May) Ernesto Basile's gorgeous art-nouveau theatre stages opera, ballet and music concerts.

Zò CULTURAL CENTRE

(☏095 53 38 71; www.zoculture.it; Piazzale Asia 6) Catania's renovated former sulphur works, Le Ciminiere, now house this very cool cultural centre featuring films, live music, dancing, and a bar-cafe-restaurant serving good food.

❶ Information

Banks with ATMs are concentrated around Piazza del Duomo and along Via Etnea.

Internetteria (Via Penninello 44; per hr €2; ☺9am-11pm Mon-Fri, 5-10pm Sat, 4-10pm Sun) Fast internet, wi-fi and a great little bar-cafe.

Municipal tourist office (☏095 742 55 73; bureau.turismo@comune.catania.it; Via Vittorio Emanuele 172; ☺8.15am-1pm & 2-7pm Mon-Sat)

Ospedale Vittorio Emanuele (☏091 743 54 52; Via Plebiscito 628) Has a 24-hour emergency doctor.

Police station (☏095 736 71 11; Piazza Santa Nicolella)

Post office (Via Etnea 215)

❶ Getting There & Away

Air

Catania's airport, **Fontanarossa** (☏095 723 91 11; www.aeroporto.catania.it), is 7km southwest of the city centre. To get there, take the special Alibus 457 (€1, 30 minutes, every 20 minutes) from outside the train station. **Etna Trasporti/Interbus** (☏095 53 03 96; www.interbus.it) also runs a regular shuttle from the airport to Taormina (€7, 1½ hours, six to

11 daily). All the main car-hire companies are represented here.

Boat

The ferry terminal is located southwest of the train station along Via VI Aprile.

Virtu Ferries (☏095 53 57 11; www.virtu ferries.com) runs direct ferries from Catania to Malta (passenger €50 to €108, car €59 to €117, three hours) every Saturday from May through September, with more frequent service to Malta via the southern port of Pozzallo (four hours including connecting coach from Catania to Pozzallo). Fares quoted above are one-way; substantial discounts are offered for return travel.

TTT Lines (☏800 91 53 65, 095 34 85 86; www.tttlines.it) runs nightly ferries from Catania to Naples (seat €38 to €60, cabin per person €52 to €165, car €75 to €115, 11 hours).

Bus

All intercity buses terminate in the area just north of Catania's train station. AST buses leave from Piazza Giovanni XXIII; buy tickets at Bar Terminal on the west side of the square. Interbus/Etna and SAIS leave from a terminal one block further north, with their ticket offices diagonally across the street on Via d'Amico.

Interbus (☏095 53 03 96; www.interbus.it; Via d'Amico 187) runs bus services to Taormina (€4.70, 1¼ to two hours, eight to 17 daily), Syracuse (€5.70, 1½ hours, hourly Monday to Friday, fewer on weekends) and Ragusa (€7.50, two hours, five to 10 daily).

SAIS (☏095 53 61 68; www.saisautolinee.it, www.saistrasporti.it; Via d'Amico 181) also runs services to Palermo (€14.20, 2¾ hours, hourly Monday to Saturday, nine on Sunday), Agrigento (€12.40, three hours, nine to 15 daily), Messina (€7.70, 1½ hours, hourly Monday to Saturday, nine on Sunday) and an overnight service to Rome (€47, 11 hours).

AST (☏095 723 05 35; www.aziendasiciliana trasporti.it; Via Luigi Sturzo 230) runs to many smaller towns around Catania, including Nicolosi (€2.20, 50 to 80 minutes, hourly) at the foot of Mt Etna.

Car & Motorcycle

Catania is easily reached from Messina on the A18 autostrada and from Palermo on the A19. From the autostrada, signs for the centre of Catania will bring you to Via Etnea.

Train

The private Ferrovia Circumetnea train circles Mt Etna, stopping at towns and villages on the volcano's slopes.

From Catania Centrale station on Piazza Papa Giovanni XXIII there are frequent trains to destinations including Messina (€6.80, 1¾ hours, hourly), Syracuse (€6.20, 1¼ hours, nine daily), Agrigento (€10.20, 3¾ hours, two direct daily) and Palermo (€12.30, three hours, one direct daily).

ℹ Getting Around

Several useful **AMT city buses** (☎095 751 96 11; www.amt.ct.it, in Italian) terminate in front of the train station, including buses 1-4 and 4-7 (both running from the station to Via Etnea every half hour or so) and Alibus 457 (station to airport every 20 minutes). A 90-minute ticket costs €1. From mid-June to mid-September, a special service (bus D-Est) runs from Piazza Raffaello Sanzio to the local beaches.

For drivers, some words of warning: there are complicated one-way systems around the city and the centre has now been pedestrianised, which means parking is scarce.

Catania's one-line metro currently has six stops, with more under construction. For tourists, it's mainly useful as a way to get from the central train station to the Circumetnea train that goes around Mt Etna. Tickets cost €1.

For a taxi, call **Radio Taxi Catania** (☎095 33 09 66).

Mt Etna

ELEV 3329M

Dominating the landscape of eastern Sicily and visible from the moon (if you happen to be there), Mt Etna is Europe's largest volcano and one of the world's most active. Eruptions occur frequently, both from the volcano's four summit craters and from its slopes, which are littered with fissures and old craters. The volcano's most devastating eruptions occurred in 1669 and lasted 122 days. Lava poured down Etna's southern slope, engulfing much of Catania and dramatically altering the landscape. More recently, in 2002, lava flows from Mt Etna caused an explosion in Sapienza, destroying two buildings and temporarily halting cable car services. Less destructive eruptions have continued to occur regularly over the past decade, with 2011 seeing several dramatic instances of lava fountaining – vertical jets of lava spewing from the mountain's southeastern flank. Locals understandably keep a close eye on the smouldering peak.

The volcano is surrounded by the huge Parco dell'Etna, the largest unspoilt wilderness remaining in Sicily. The park encompasses a remarkable variety of environments, from the severe almost surreal summit to deserts of lava and alpine forests.

◎ Sights & Activities

The southern approach to Mt Etna presents the easier ascent to the craters. The AST bus from Catania drops you off at **Rifugio Sapienza** (1923m) from where **Funivia dell'Etna** (☎095 91 41 41; www.funiviaetna.com; cable car one-way/return €14.50/27, incl bus & guide €51; ☺9am-4.30pm) runs a cable car up the mountain to 2500m. From the upper cable car station it's a 3½-hour return trip up the winding track to the authorised crater zone (2920m). Make sure you leave yourself enough time to get up *and* down before the last cable car leaves at 4.45pm. Alternatively, you can pay the extra €24 for a guided 4WD tour to take you up from the cable car to the crater zone.

An alternative ascent is from **Piano Provenzano** (1800m) on Etna's northern flank. This area was severely damaged during the 2002 eruptions, as still evidenced by the bleached skeletons of the surrounding pine trees. Regular 4WD excursions climb to the summit from here (around €40 per person). To reach Piano Provenzano you'll need a car, as there's no public transport beyond Linguaglossa, 16km away.

☞ Tours

Several companies offer private excursions up the mountain.

Volcano Trek   CLIMBING TOURS
(☎333 209 66 04; www.volcanotrek.com) Run by expert geologists.

Siciltrek   CLIMBING TOURS
(☎095 96 88 82; www.siciltrek.it, in German) Run by multilingual Swiss guide Andrea Ercolani.

Gruppo Guide Alpine Etna Sud   CLIMBING TOURS
(☎095 791 47 55; www.etnaguide.com, in Italian) The official guide service on Etna's southern flank, with an office just below Rifugio Sapienza.

Gruppo Guide Alpine Etna Nord   CLIMBING TOURS
(☎095 777 45 02; www.guidetnanord.com) Offers similar service from Linguaglossa on Etna's northern flank.

🛌 Sleeping & Eating

There's plenty of B&B accommodation around Mt Etna, particularly in the small, pretty town of Nicolosi. Contact Nicolosi's tourist information office for a full list.

Rifugio Sapienza MOUNTAIN CHALET €€
(☑095 91 53 21; www.rifugiosapienza.com; Piazzale Funivia; per person B&B/half-board/full board €55/75/90) As close to the summit as you can get, this place adjacent to the cable car offers comfortable accommodation with a good restaurant.

ⓘ Information

Catania's downtown tourist office provides information about Etna, as several offices on the mountain itself.

Etna Sud tourist office (☑095 91 63 56; ⊗9am-4pm) Near the summit at Rifugio Sapienza.

Parco dell'Etna (☑095 82 11 11; www.parco etna.ct.it, in Italian; Via del Convento 45; ⊗9am-2pm & 4-7.30pm) In Nicolosi, on Etna's southern side.

Proloco Linguaglossa (☑095 64 30 94; www.prolocolinguaglossa.it, in Italian; Piazza Annunziata 5; ⊗9am-1pm & 4-7pm Mon-Sat, 9am-noon Sun) In Linguaglossa, on Etna's northern side.

ⓘ Getting There & Away

Bus

AST (☑095 723 05 35) runs daily buses from Catania to Rifugio Sapienza (one-way/return €3.40/5.60, one hour). Buses leave from the car park opposite Catania's train station at 8.15am, travelling via Nicolosi, and return at 4.45pm.

Train

You can circle Etna on the private **Ferrovia Circumetnea** (FCE; ☑095 54 12 50; www.circum etnea.it; Via Caronda 352a) train line. Catch the metro from Catania's main train station to the FCE station at Via Caronda (metro stop Borgo) or take bus 429 or 432 going up Via Etnea and ask to be let off at the Borgo metro stop.

The train follows a 114km trail around the base of the volcano, providing fabulous views. It also passes through many of Etna's unique towns such as Adrano, Bronte and Randazzo (one-way/return €4.85/7.80, two hours).

SYRACUSE & THE SOUTHEAST

This is a region of river valleys, fields of olive, almond and citrus trees and magnificent ruins. Within the evocative stone-walled checkerboard lies a series of handsome towns: Ragusa, Modica and Noto. Shattered by a devastating earthquake in 1693, they were rebuilt in the ornate and much-lauded Sicilian baroque style that lends the region a honey-coloured cohesion and collective beauty. Writer Gesualdo Bufalino described the southeast as an 'island within an island' and, certainly, this pocket of Sicily has a remote, genteel air – a legacy of its glorious Greek heritage.

Syracuse

POP 123.800

A dense tapestry of overlapping cultures and civilisations, Syracuse is one of Sicily's most visited cities. Boosted by EU funding, derelict landmarks and ancient buildings lining the slender streets are being aesthetically restored. Settled by colonists from Corinth in 734 BC, Syracuse was considered to be the most beautiful city of the ancient world, rivalling Athens in power and prestige. Under the demagogue Dionysius the Elder, the city reached its zenith, attracting luminaries such as Livy, Plato, Aeschylus and Archimedes, and cultivating the sophisticated urban culture that was to see the birth of comic Greek theatre.

As the sun set on Ancient Greece, Syracuse became a Roman colony and was looted of its treasures. While modern-day Syracuse lacks the drama of Palermo and the energy of Catania, the ancient island neighbourhood of Ortygia continues to seduce visitors with its atmospheric squares, narrow alleyways and lovely waterfront, while the Parco Archaeologico della Neapolis, 2km across town, remains one of Sicily's great classical treasures.

Syracuse's train and bus stations are a block apart from each other, halfway between Ortygia and the archaeological park.

◉ Sights

ORTYGIA

Duomo DUOMO
(Map p186; Piazza del Duomo; ⊗8am-7pm)
Despite its baroque veneer, the Greek essence of Syracuse is everywhere in evidence, from the formal civility of the people to disguised architectural relics. The most obvious of these is Syracuse's cathedral, a Greek temple that was converted into a church when the island was evangelised by St Paul. The sumptuous baroque facade, designed by Andrea Palma, barely hides the Temple of Athena skeleton beneath, and the huge 5th-century-BC Doric columns are still visible both inside and out.

Syracuse

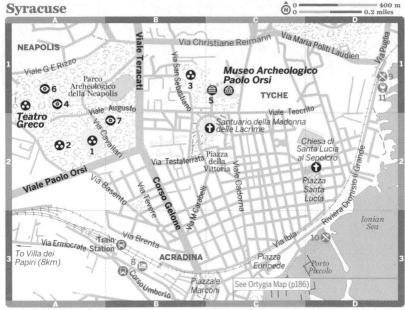

Syracuse

Fontana Aretusa ANCIENT SPRING
(Map p186) Down the winding main street from the cathedral is this ancient spring, where fresh water still bubbles up just as it did in ancient times when it was the city's main water supply. Legend has it that the goddess Artemis transformed her beautiful handmaiden Aretusa into the spring to protect her from the unwelcome attention of the river god Alpheus. Now populated by ducks, grey mullet and papyrus plants, the fountain is the place to hang out on summer evenings.

**Galleria Regionale
di Palazzo Bellomo** ART GALLERY
(Map p186; ☎0931 6 95 11; www.regione.sicilia. it/beniculturali/palazzobellomo; Via Capodieci 16; adult/reduced €8/4; ⊙9am-7pm Tue-Sat, 9am-1pm Sun) Just up Via Capodieci from the fountain is this art museum, housed in a 13th-century Catalan-Gothic palace. The eclectic collection ranges from early Byzantine and Norman stonework to 19th-century Caltagirone ceramics; in between, there's a good range of medieval religious paintings and sculpture.

Ortygia

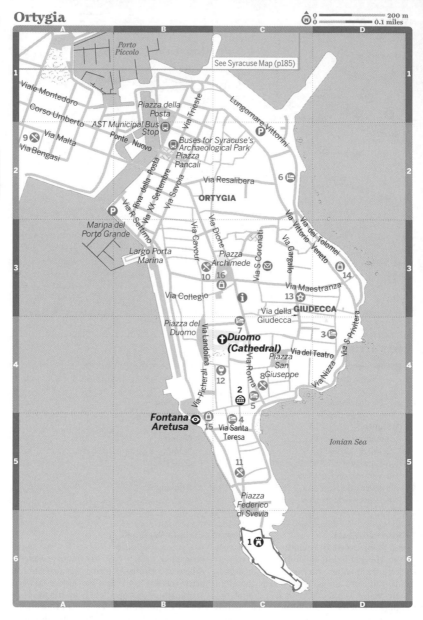

See Syracuse Map (p185)

Castello Maniace CASTLE
(off Map p186; ☑0931 46 44 20; adult/reduced
€4/2; ☺9.30am-1pm Tue-Sun) Guarding the island's southern tip, Ortygia's 13th-century
castle is a lovely place to wander, gaze out
over the water and contemplate Syracuse's
past glories. It also hosts occasional rotating
exhibitions.

La Giudecca NEIGHBOURHOOD
(Map p186) Simply walking through Ortygia's tangled maze of alleys is an atmo-

spheric experience, especially down the narrow lanes of **Via Maestranza**, the heart of the old guild quarter, and the crumbling Jewish ghetto of **Via della Giudecca**. At the Alla Giudecca hotel you can visit an ancient Jewish **miqwe** (ritual bath; Map p186; ☑0931 2 22 55; Via Alagona 52; hourly tours €5; ⊙tours 11am, noon, 4pm, 5pm & 6pm Mon-Sat, 11am & noon Sun) some 20m below ground level. Blocked up in 1492 when the Jewish community was expelled from Ortygia, the baths were rediscovered during renovation work at the hotel.

MAINLAND SYRACUSE

Parco Archaeologico della Neapolis   ARCHAEOLOGICAL SITE
(Map p185; ☑0931 6 50 68; Viale Paradis; adult/reduced €9/4.50; ⊙9am-1hr before sunset, to 4.30pm during theatre festival) For the classicist, Syracuse's real attraction is this archaeological park, with its pearly white, 5th-century-BC **Teatro Greco**, hewn out of the rock above the city. This theatre saw the last tragedies of Aeschylus (including *The Persians*), which were first performed here in his presence. In summer it is brought to life again with an annual season of classical theatre (see p188).

Just beside the theatre is the mysterious **Latomia del Paradiso** (Map p185), deep, precipitous limestone quarries out of which the stone for the ancient city was extracted. These quarries, which are riddled with catacombs and filled with citrus and magnolia trees, are where the 7000 survivors of the war between Syracuse and Athens in 413 BC were imprisoned. The

Orecchio di Dionisio (Map p185; Ear of Dionysius), a grotto 23m by 3m deep, was named by Caravaggio after the tyrant, who is said to have used the almost perfect acoustics of the quarry to eavesdrop on his prisoners.

Back outside this area you'll find the entrance to the 2nd-century AD **Anfiteatro Romano** (Map p185), originally used for gladiatorial combats and horse races. The Spaniards, little interested in archaeology, largely destroyed the site in the 16th century, using it as a quarry to build Ortygia's city walls. West of the amphitheatre is the 3rd-century BC **Ara di Gerone II** (Map p185), a monolithic sacrificial altar to Heron II where up to 450 oxen could be killed at one time.

To reach the park, take bus 1, 3 or 12 from Ortygia's Piazza Pancali and get off at the corner of Corso Gelone and Viale Teocrito. Alternatively, the walk from Ortygia will take about 30 minutes. If driving, you can park along Viale Augusto (tickets available at the nearby souvenir kiosks).

Museo Archeologico Paolo Orsi   MUSEUM
(Map p185; ☑0931 46 40 22; Viale Teocrito; adult/reduced €8/4; ⊙9am-6pm Tue-Sat, 9am-1pm Sun) In the grounds of Villa Landolina, about 500m east of the archaeological park, the wheelchair accessible museum contains one of Sicily's largest, best organised and most interesting archaeological collections. Allow plenty of time to get through the museum's four distinct sectors; serious archaeology buffs may even want to consider splitting their visit into two days.

FREE Museo del Papiro   MUSEUM
(Map p185; ☎0931 6 16 16; museodelpapiro.it; Viale Teocrito 66; ⊙9am-1pm Tue-Sun) This small museum includes papyrus documents and products, boats and an English-language film about the history of papyrus. The plant grows in abundance around the Ciane River, near Syracuse, and was used to make paper in the 18th century.

Catacombe di San Giovanni   CATACOMB
(Map p185; ☎0931 6 46 94; adult/reduced €6/4; ⊙half-hourly tours 9.30am-12.30pm & 2.30-5.30pm) A block north of the archaeological museum, this vast labyrinth of 10,000 underground tombs dates back to Roman times. A 30-minute guided tour ushers visitors through the catacombs as well as the atmospheric ruins of the Basilica di San Giovanni, Syracuse's earliest cathedral.

🏃 Activities

Beaches   BEACHES
In midsummer, when Ortygia steams like a cauldron, people flock to the beaches south of town at **Arenella** (take bus 23 from Piazza della Posta) and **Fontane Bianche** (bus 21 or 22); note that there are charges on certain sections. From mid-June to September, there's also great sunbathing (for a fee) and diving off the rocks – but no sand to lay your towel on – adjacent to Bar Zen (p189), 2km north of Ortygia.

🎊 Festivals & Events

Ciclo di Rappresentazioni Classiche   THEATRE FESTIVAL
(Festival of Greek Theatre; www.indafondazione.org) Syracuse boasts the only school of classical Greek drama outside Athens, and in May and June it hosts live performances of Greek plays (in Italian) at the Teatro Greco, attracting Italy's finest performers. Tickets (€26 to €62) are available online, from the Via Cavour office in Ortygia or at the ticket booth outside the theatre.

Festa di Santa Lucia   RELIGIOUS
On 13 December, the enormous silver statue of the city's patron saint wends its way from the cathedral to Piazza Santa Lucia accompanied by fireworks.

🛏 Sleeping

Stay on Ortygia for atmosphere. Cheaper accommodations are located around the train station.

Villa dei Papiri   AGRITURISMO €€
(☎0931 72 13 21; www.villadeipapiri.it; Contrada Cozzo Pantano, Fonte Ciane; d €70-132, 2-person ste €105-154, 4-person ste €140-208; P🅿❄@🛜) Immersed in an Eden of orange groves and papyrus reeds 8km outside Syracuse, this lovely *agriturismo* sits next to the Fonte Ciana spring immortalised in Ovid's Metamorphosis. Eight family suites are housed in a beautifully converted 19th-century farmhouse, with double rooms dotted around the lush grounds. Breakfast is served in a baronial stone-walled hall, and there are plenty of other perks to keep guests in a holiday mood, including river excursions, bike rentals and an open-door policy towards pets.

B&B dei Viaggiatori, Viandanti e Sognatori   B&B €
(Map p186; ☎0931 2 47 81; www.bedandbreakfast sicily.it; Via Roma 156; s €35-50, d €55-70; ❄🛜) An old *palazzo* at the end of Via Roma cradles this lovely B&B. Rooms are colourfully and stylishly decorated, with super-comfy beds. The sunny roof terrace with sweeping sea views makes a perfect breakfast spot.

Alla Giudecca   HOTEL €€
(Map p186; ☎0931 2 22 55; www.allagiudecca.it; Via Alagona 52; s €60-100, d €80-120; ❄@🛜) Located in the old Jewish quarter, this charming hotel boasts 23 suites with warm terracotta-tiled floors, exposed wood beams and lashings of heavy white linen. The communal areas are a warren of vaulted rooms full of museum-quality antiques and enormous tapestries, and feature cosy sofas gathered around huge fireplaces.

Hotel Gutkowski   HOTEL €€
(Map p186; ☎0931 46 58 61; www.guthotel.it; Lungomare Vittorini 26; s €80-90, d €110; ❄@🛜) Book well in advance for one of the seven sea-view rooms at this charming and friendly hotel on the Ortygia waterfront. Rooms in the original hotel have pretty tiled floors, colourful walls, and retain the building's historic character, while those in the annexe down the street have a more modern feel. There's a nice rooftop sun terrace with sea views, and a cosy internet area with fireplace.

LOL Hostel   HOSTEL €
(Map p185; ☎0931 46 50 88; www.lolhostel.com; Via Francesco Crispi 94; dm €20-26, d €60-75; ❄@🛜) Around the corner from the train station, this modern, well-kept hostel with

its variable-sized dorms and two doubles is a good bet for solo travellers. The pleasant common spaces include an open, airy guest kitchen, an outdoor patio and a sprawling lounge and bar area with four guest computers. It's 10 minutes on foot to Ortygia, or five minutes with one of the hostel's rental bikes.

B&B Aretusa
APARTMENTS €

(Map p186; ☑0931 48 34 84; www.aretusava canze.com; Vicolo Zuccalà 1; d €67-86, tr €82-115, q €105-140; P✳@☎) This great budget option, elbowed into a tiny pedestrian street, has large rooms and apartments with kitchenettes, computers, satellite TV and small balconies.

Hotel Roma
HOTEL €€

(Map p186; ☑0931 46 56 26; www.hotelroma siracusa.it; Via Roma 66; s €75-105, d €105-149; P✳@☎) Within steps of Piazza del Duomo, this restored *palazzo* has rooms with parquet floors, oriental rugs, wood-beam ceilings and tasteful artwork, plus free bike use, a gym and a sauna.

✗ Eating

Ortygia is teeming with atmospheric eateries, although many are touristy and over-priced; you'll generally find better value on the mainland.

Le Vin de l'Assassin
FRENCH €€

(Map p186; ☑0931 6 61 59; Via Roma 115; snacks €7-15, meals €25-35; ⊙dinner Tue-Sat, lunch & dinner Sun) This gay-friendly French-run bistrot provides a classy break from standard Sicilian fare. Offerings scrawled on the chalkboard include French classics like *quiche lorraine* and *croque monsieur*, Breton oysters, salads with impeccable vinaigrette dressing, a host of meat and fish mains and a splendid *millefoglie* of eggplant and sweet red peppers. It's also a perfect late night stop for wine by the glass or one of the home-made, over-the-top creamy and chocolatey desserts.

Red Moon
SEAFOOD €

(Map p185; ☑0931 6 03 56; Riva Porto Lachio 36; meals €25; ⊙lunch & dinner Thu-Tue) Serving some of the best seafood in Syracuse under its tented octagonal roof, this reasonably priced family-run place on the mainland makes a pleasant refuge from Ortygia's well-worn tourist track. Start with *spaghetti ai ricci* (spaghetti with sea urchin roe), move on to *fritto misto* (fried shrimp and squid)

or grilled fish from the case, then finish with a refreshing lemon sorbet.

Taberna Sveva
SICILIAN €€

(Map p186; ☑0931 2 46 63; Piazza Federico di Svevia; meals €25-35; ⊙closed Wed) This charming tavern has a cosy terrace on a peaceful cobblestoned square, down near the castle at Ortygia's southern tip. Food is top-notch, from primi like *gnocchi al pistacchio* (with olive oil, parmesan, pepper, garlic and grated pistachios) to a delicious tiramisu to wrap things up.

Jonico-a Rutta 'e Ciauli
SICILIAN €€

(Map p185; ☑0931 6 55 40; Riviera Dionisio il Grande 194; pizzas €4-7, meals €25-35; ⊙closed Tue Oct-May) Inconveniently located but worth the trek or taxi ride on a sunny afternoon, Jonico's open-air terrace has spectacular views of blue-green sea and sandstone cliffs, while the all-Sicilian menu features pizza at night plus seafood mains such as *orata c'aranci* (gilthead with orange juice, orange peel and black pepper).

Sicilia in Tavola
SICILIAN €

(Map p186; ☑392 461 08 89; Via Cavour 28; pasta €7-12; ⊙closed Mon) This tiny place with a dozen tables specialises in seafood appetisers and fresh pasta dishes. For dessert, try their *bicchierino* (a sinfully delicious blend of ricotta, chocolate, pistachios and almonds).

Piano B
PIZZERIA €€

(Map p186; ☑0931 6 68 51; Via Cairoli 18; pizza €5-9.50, salads €5.50-15, grilled meat €15-22; ⊙closed Mon) Brisk, friendly service complements the trendy, casual atmosphere at this new eatery just west of Ortygia. It's popular with young Syracusans for its pizzas, grilled meat and extensive salad menu.

🍸 Drinking & Entertainment

Syracuse is a vibrant university town, which means plenty of life on the streets after nightfall.

Bar San Rocco
BAR

(Map p186; Piazzetta San Rocco) Heaving till the wee hours, this is the most popular of a cluster of bars with tables sprawled across bustling Piazzetta San Rocco, just south of Piazza del Duomo.

Bar Zen
BAR

(Map p185; ⊙9am-midnight mid-Jun–Sep) At this seaside bar affiliated with Jonico restaurant, you can plunge off the rocks and sunbathe all day, then retire to the outdoor deck for evening drinks and live music.

Piccolo Teatro dei Pupi PUPPET THEATRE
(Map p186; ✆0931 46 55 40; www.pupari.com; Via della Giudecca 17) Syracuse's thriving puppet theatre hosts regular performances; see the website for a calendar. You can also buy puppets at the workshop next door.

Shopping

Ortygia is full of quirky little shops.

Circo Fortuna CERAMICS
(Map p186; www.circofortuna.it; Via dei Tolomei 20) Produces whimsical ceramics.

Massimo Izzo JEWELLERY
(Map p186; www.massimoizzo.com; Piazza Archimede 25) Specialising in jewellery handcrafted from Sciacca coral and gold.

Galleria Bellomo CARDS
(Map p186; www.bellomogalleria.com; Via Capodieci 15) For a more affordable souvenir, check out the hand-painted cards made from local papyrus.

Information

There are numerous banks with ATMs throughout the city.

Biblios Café (Map p186; Via del Consiglio Reginale 11; internet per hr €3, unlimited wireless €2; ⊗10am-1.30pm & 5-9pm, closed Wed & Sun mornings) One internet computer, plus wireless access at this comfortable bookstore-cafe.

Ospedale Umberto I (Map p185; ✆0931 72 40 33; Via Testaferrata 1)

Police station (Map p186; ✆0931 6 51 76; Piazza S Giuseppe)

Post office (Map p186; Via dei Santi Coronati 22)

Tourist office (Map p186; ✆0800 05 55 00; infoturismo@provsr.it; Via Roma 31, Ortygia; ⊗9am-7pm) English-speaking staff, city maps and lots of good information.

Getting There & Away

Bus

Long-distance buses operate from the bus stop (Map p185) along Corso Umberto, just east of Syracuse's train station. **Interbus** (✆0931 6 67 10; www.interbus.it) runs buses to Catania (€5.70, 1½ hours, 19 daily Monday to Saturday, eight on Sunday) and its airport, and Palermo (€11, 3¼ hours, two to three daily).

AST (✆0931 46 27 11; www.aziendasiciliana trasporti.it) offers services to Noto (€3.20,

55 minutes, 10 daily Monday to Saturday, two on Sunday) and Ragusa (€6.60, 2¾ hours, seven daily Monday to Saturday, one on Sunday).

Car & Motorcycle

The modern A18 and SS114 highways connect Syracuse with Catania and points north. Arriving by car, exit onto the eastbound SS124 and follow signs to Syracuse and Ortygia.

Traffic on Ortygia is restricted; you're better off parking and walking once you arrive on the island. The large Talete parking garage on Ortygia's north side is a bargain – free between 5am and 9pm, and only €1 for overnight parking.

Train

From Syracuse's **train station** (Map p185; Via Francesco Crispi), several trains depart daily for Messina (InterCity/regional train €16.50/9.50, 2½ to 3¼ hours) via Catania (€8.50/6.20, 1¼ hours). Some go on to Rome, Turin and Milan as well as other long-distance destinations. For Palermo, the bus is a better option. There are also local trains from Syracuse to Noto (€3.30, 30 minutes) and Ragusa (€7.50, 2¼ hours).

Getting Around

For travel between the bus and train stations and Ortygia, catch the free AST shuttle bus 20 (every 20 to 60 minutes). To reach Parco Archeologico della Neapolis from Ortygia, take AST city bus 1, 3 or 12 (two-hour ticket €1.10), departing from Ortygia's Piazza Pancali.

Noto

POP 23,900 / ELEV 160M

Flattened in 1693 by an earthquake, Noto was grandly rebuilt by its nobles. The town's complex of golden-hued sandstone buildings is now a Unesco World Heritage Site and the finest baroque town in Sicily, especially impressive at night when illuminations accentuate the beauty of its intricately carved facades. The baroque masterpiece is the work of Rosario Gagliardi and his assistant, Vincenzo Sinatra, local architects who also worked in Ragusa and Modica.

On 16 March 1996 the town was horrified when the roof and dome of the cathedral collapsed during a thunderstorm – luckily it was 10.30pm and the cathedral was empty. In 2007 the cathedral finally reopened after lengthy reconstruction.

Sights

San Nicoló Cathedral stands in the centre of Noto's most graceful square, Piazza Municipio, surrounded by elegant town houses such as Palazzo Ducezio (Town Hall) and Palazzo Landolina, once home to Noto's oldest noble family.

Recently restored to its former glory and open to visitors is the **Palazzo Nicolaci di Villadorata** (☑320 556 80 38; www.palazzonico laci.it, in Italian; Via Nicolaci; adult/reduced €4/2; ☺10am-1pm & 3-7.30pm), where wrought-iron balconies are supported by a swirling pantomime of grotesque figures. Although empty of furnishings, its richly brocaded walls and frescoed ceilings give an idea of the sumptuous lifestyle of Sicilian nobles.

Two other piazzas break up the long Corso Vittorio Emanuele: Piazza dell'Immacolata to the east and Piazza XVI Maggio to the west. The latter is overlooked by the beautiful **Chiesa di San Domenico** and the adjacent Dominican monastery, both designed by Rosario Gagliardi. On the same square, Noto's elegant 19th-century **Teatro Comunale** is worth a look, as is the Sala degli Specchi (Hall of Mirrors), opposite the *duomo* in the **Palazzo Ducezio** (admission to either €2, combined ticket €3; ☺9.30am-1.30pm & 2.30-6.30pm). For sweeping rooftop views of Noto's baroque splendour, climb the *campanile* (bell tower) at **Chiesa di San Carlo al Corso** (admission €2; ☺9am-12.30pm & 4-7pm) or **Chiesa di Santa Chiara** (admission €1.50; ☺9.30am-1pm & 3-7pm).

✷✷ Festivals & Events

Noto's colourful two-week-long flower festival, **Infiorata**, is celebrated in mid to late May with parades, historical re-enactments and a public art project in which artists decorate the length of Via Corrada Nicolaci with designs made entirely of flower petals.

🛏 Sleeping

B&Bs are plentiful in Noto; the tourist office keeps a detailed list.

La Corte del Sole RURAL INN €€
(☑320 82 02 10; www.lacortedelsole.it; Contrada Bucachemi; d €84-206; P❋@☎🐾) A few kilometres downhill from Noto, overlooking the Vendicari bird sanctuary is this lovely rural retreat set around a central courtyard. The best of the 34 ceramic-clad, wood-beamed rooms overlook the pool and cost only €8 extra. Other amenities include an in-house restaurant, a lovely breakfast area built around an ancient olive oil press, bike hire, cooking courses and a shuttle bus to the nearby beach.

Hotel della Ferla HOTEL €€
(☑0931 57 60 07; www.hoteldellaferla.it; Via A Gramsci; s €48-78, d €84-120; P❋☎) This friendly family-run hotel in a residential area near the train station offers large, bright rooms with pine furnishings and small balconies, plus free parking.

Ostello Il Castello HOSTEL €
(☑320 838 88 69; www.ostellodinoto.it; Via Fratelli Bandiera 1; dm €16) Directly uphill from the centre, this old-school hostel with eight- to 16-bed dorms commands fabulous views over the *duomo* and offers great value for money, despite lacking a guest kitchen.

🍴 Eating

The people of Noto are serious about their food, so take time to enjoy a meal and follow it up with a visit to one of the town's excellent ice-cream shops.

TOP CHOICE **Il Liberty** MODERN SICILIAN €€
(☑0931 57 32 26; Via Cavour 40; meals €27-35;☺closed Mon) The vaulted dining room at this brand new eatery makes an atmospheric place to sample Milan-trained Chef Giuseppe Angelino's contemporary spin on Sicilian cookery. An excellent local wine list supplements the inspired menu, which moves from superb appetisers like *millefoglie* – wafer-thin layers of crusty cheese and ground pistachios layered with minty sweet-and-sour vegetables – through to desserts like warm cinnamon-ricotta cake with homemade orange compote.

TOP CHOICE **Caffè Sicilia** GELATERIA €
(☑0931 83 50 13; Corso Vittorio Emanuele 125; desserts from €2) Dating from 1892 and especially renowned for its *granite*, this beloved place vies with its next-door neighbour, Dolceria Corrado Costanzo, for the honours of Noto's best dessert shop. Frozen desserts are made with the freshest seasonal ingredients (wild strawberries in springtime, for example) while the delicious *torrone* (nougat) bursts with the flavours of local honey and almonds.

Ristorante Il Cantuccio MODERN SICILIAN €€
(☑0931 83 74 64; Via Cavour 12; meals €30-35; ☺dinner Tue-Sun, lunch Sun) Chef Valentina presents a seasonally changing menu that combines familiar Sicilian ingredients in exciting new ways. Try her exquisite *gnocchi al pesto del Cantuccio* (ricotta-potato

dumplings with basil, parsley, mint, capers, almonds and cherry tomatoes), then move on to memorable main courses such as lemon-stuffed bass with orange-fennel salad.

Trattoria del Crocifisso TRATTORIA €€
(☑0931 57 11 51; Via Principe Umberto 48; meals €25-35) This Slow Food–acclaimed trattoria with an extensive wine list is another Noto favourite.

**Dolceria Corrado
Costanzo** PASTRIES & CAKES €
(☑0931 83 52 43; Via Silvio Spaventa 9) Just around the corner from Caffè Sicilia, Costanzo is famous for its gelati, *torrone*, *dolci di mandorla* (almond sweets) and *cassata* (with ricotta, chocolate and candied fruit).

❶ Information

Tourist office (☑0931 57 37 79; www.comune.noto.sr.it; Piazza XVI Maggio; ☺9am-1pm & 3-8pm) An excellent and busy information office with multilingual staff and free maps.

❶ Getting There & Around

BUS From the Giardini Pubblici just east of Noto's historic centre, AST and Interbus serve Catania (€7.70, 1½ to 2½ hours, 11 to 17 Monday to Saturday, six on Sunday) and Syracuse (€3.20, one hour, 16 to 19 Monday to Saturday, four on Sunday).

TRAIN There's frequent service to Syracuse (€3.30, 30 minutes, 10 daily except Sunday), but Noto's station is inconveniently located 1km downhill from the centre.

Modica

POP 55,000 / 296M

A powerhouse in Grecian times, Modica may have lost its pre-eminent position to Ragusa, but it remains a superbly atmospheric town with its ancient medieval buildings climbing steeply up either side of a deep gorge.

The multilayered town is divided into Modica Alta (Upper Modica) and Modica Bassa (Lower Modica). A devastating flood in 1902 resulted in the wide avenues of Corso Umberto and Via Giarrantana (the river was dammed and diverted), which remain the main axes of the town, lined by *palazzi* and tiled stone houses.

◉ Sights

Aside from simply wandering the streets and absorbing the atmosphere, a visit to the extraordinary **Chiesa di San Giorgio** (Modica Alta; ☺9am-noon & 4-7pm) is a highlight. This church, Gagliardi's masterpiece, is a vision of pure rococo splendour, a butter-coloured confection perched on a majestic 250-step staircase. Its counterpoint in Modica Bassa is the **Cattedrale di San Pietro** (Corso Umberto I), another impressive church atop a rippling staircase lined with life-sized statues of the Apostles.

🛏 Sleeping & Eating

The quality-to-price ratio tends to be excellent, making Modica a top destination for discerning travellers.

TOP CHOICE Villa Quartarella AGRITURISMO €
(☑360 65 48 29; www.quartarella.com; Contrada Quartarella; s €40, d €70-80) Spacious rooms and welcoming hosts make this converted villa in the countryside south of Modica the obvious choice for anyone travelling by car. Owners Francesco and Francesca are generous in sharing their love and encyclopaedic knowledge of local history, flora and fauna and can suggest a multitude of driving itineraries in the surrounding area. The ample breakfasts include everything from home-raised eggs to intriguing Modican sweets.

B&B Il Cavaliere B&B €
(☑0932 94 72 19; www.palazzoilcavaliere.it; Corso Umberto I 259; d €70-80, ste €100-120; ❋@) Stay in aristocratic style at this classy B&B in a 19th-century *palazzo*, just down from the bus station on Modica's main strip. Standard rooms have less character than the beautiful front suite and the large, high-ceilinged common rooms, which retain original tiled floors and frescoed ceilings. The elegant breakfast room has lovely views of San Giorgio church.

Albergo I Tetti di Siciliando GUESTHOUSE €
(☑0932 94 28 43; www.siciliando.it; Via Cannata 24; s €35-40, d €50-70; ❋🅢) A friendly guesthouse just uphill from Corso Umberto, with bright, artistically decorated rooms and balconies with views.

Taverna Nicastro SICILIAN €
(☑0932 94 58 84; Via S Antonino 28, Modica Alta; meals €14-20; ☺dinner Tue-Sat) With over 60 years of history and a Slow Food recommendation, this is one of the upper town's most authentic and atmospheric restaurants, and a bargain to boot. The carnivore-friendly menu includes grilled meat, boiled veal,

lamb stew and pasta specialities such as ricotta ravioli with pork *ragù* (meat sauce).

Dolceria Bonajuto
CHOCOLATE €

(☎0932 94 12 25; www.bonajuto.it; Corso Umberto I 159; ⊗9am-1.30pm & 4.30-8.30pm Mon-Sat, 4.30-8.30pm Sun) Sicily's oldest chocolate factory is the perfect place to taste Modica's famous chocolate. Flavoured with cinnamon, vanilla, orange peel and even hot peppers, it's a legacy of the town's Spanish overlords who imported cocoa from their South American colonies.

Osteria dei Sapori Perduti
SICILIAN €

(☎0932 94 42 47; Corso Umberto I 228-230; meals €15-21; ⊗closed Tue) On Modica's main drag, this attractive restaurant mixes rustic decor, elegantly dressed waiters, and very reasonable prices on Sicilian specialities like *cunigghju â stimpirata* (sweet and sour rabbit).

❶ Getting There & Away

BUS Frequent buses run Monday through Saturday from Piazzale Falcone-Borsellino at the top of Corso Umberto I to Syracuse (€6, eight daily), Noto (€3.90, 10 daily) and Ragusa (€2.40, 16 daily); on Sunday, service is limited to two buses in each direction.

TRAIN From Modica's station, 600m southwest of the centre, there are three trains daily (one on Sunday) to Syracuse (€6.80, 1¾ hours) and six (one on Sunday) to Ragusa (€2.10, 25 minutes).

Ragusa

POP 73,300 / ELEV 502M

Like a grand old dame, Ragusa is a dignified and well-aged provincial town. Like every other town in the region, Ragusa collapsed after the 1693 earthquake; a new town called Ragusa Superiore was built on a high plateau above the original settlement. But the old aristocracy were loath to leave their tottering *palazzi* and rebuilt Ragusa Ibla on the original site. The two towns were only merged in 1927.

Ragusa Ibla remains the heart and soul of the town, and has all the best restaurants and the majority of sights. A sinuous bus ride or some very steep and scenic steps connect the lower town to its modern sister up the hill.

◉ Sights

Grand churches and *palazzi* line the twisting, narrow streets of Ragusa Ibla, interspersed with *gelaterie* and delightful piazzas where the local youth stroll and the elderly gather on benches. Palm-planted Piazza del Duomo, the centre of town, is dominated by the 18th-century **Cattedrale di San Giorgio** (⊗10am-12.30pm & 4-6.30pm), with its magnificent neoclassical dome and stained-glass windows.

At the eastern end of the old town is the **Giardino Ibleo** (⊗8am-8pm), a pleasant public garden laid out in the 19th century that is perfect for a picnic lunch.

🛏 Sleeping

All places listed here are in Ragusa Ibla, the picturesque lower town.

Risveglio Ibleo
GUESTHOUSE €

(☎0932 24 78 11; www.risveglioibleo.com; Largo Camerina 3; r per person €35-45; ℗ 🛜) This welcoming place, which is housed in an 18th-century Liberty-style villa, has spacious, high-ceilinged rooms, walls hung with family portraits and a flower-flanked terrace overlooking the rooftops. The older couple who run the place go out of their way to share local culture, including their own home-made culinary delights.

Locanda Don Serafino
INN €€

(☎0932 22 00 65; www.locandadonserafino.it; Via XI Febbraio 15; s €80-138, d €90-168; ✳@) This historic inn near the *duomo* has beautiful rooms, some with original vaulted stone ceilings, plus a well-regarded restaurant nearby. For €9 extra, guests get access to the Lido Azzurro beach at Marina di Ragusa, 25km away.

L'Orto Sul Tetto
B&B €

(☎0932 24 77 85; www.lortosultetto.it; Via Tenente Distefano 56; s €45-59, d €70-100; ✳🛜) This sweet little B&B behind Ragusa's Duomo offers an intimate experience, with just three rooms and a lovely roof terrace where breakfast is served.

🍴 Eating

TOP CHOICE ⟩ **Quattro Gatti**
SICILIAN €

(☎0932 24 56 12; Via Valverde 95; meals €18; ⊗dinner, closed Mon Oct-May & Sun Jun-Sep) This fabulous Sicilian-Slovak–run eatery near the Giardini Iblei serves an amazing four-course fixed-price menu bursting with fresh, local flavours. The antipasti spread is especially memorable, as are the seasonally changing specials scribbled on the blackboard up front. Slovak-inspired offerings such as goulash and apple strudel round out a menu of Sicilian classics. The stone-vaulted rooms make a supremely cosy spot to pass away an evening.

Il Barocco TRADITIONAL ITALIAN €
(☑0932 65 23 97; Via Orfanotrofio 29; meals €17-30) This beloved traditional restaurant has an evocative setting in an old stable block, the troughs now filled with wine bottles instead of water. At the *enoteca* (wine bar) next door, you can taste cheeses and olive oils and purchase other exquisite Sicilian edibles.

Gelati DiVini ICE CREAM €
(☑0932 22 89 89; www.gelatidivini.it; Piazza Duomo 20; ice cream from €2; ⊙10am-midnight) This exceptional *gelateria* makes wine-flavoured ice creams like marsala and muscat, plus unconventional offerings including rose, fennel, wild mint and the surprisingly tasty *gocce verdi*, made with local olive oil.

Ristorante Duomo GASTRONOMIC €€€
(☑0932 65 12 65; Via Capitano Bocchieri 31; meals €90-100, tasting menus €135-140) Hailed by some as Sicily's best restaurant, Duomo serves nouvelle Sicilian cuisine in a quintet of small rooms outfitted like private parlours, ensuring a suitably romantic atmosphere.

❶ Information

Tourist office (☑0932 68 47 80; Piazza della Repubblica; ⊙10am-1pm & 3.30-6.30pm) At the western edge of the lower town.

❶ Getting There & Around

BUS Long-distance and municipal buses share a terminal on Via Zama in the upper town. Buy tickets at the Interbus/Etna kiosk in the main lot or at cafes around the corner. **Interbus** (www.interbus.it) runs to Catania (€7.50, two hours, six to 10 daily). **AST** (☑0932 68 18 18; www.aziendasicilianatrasporti.it) serves Syracuse (€6.60, three hours, eight daily Monday to Saturday, two on Sunday) via Modica (€2.40, 30 minutes) and Noto (€4.80, 2¼ hours).

City bus 33 (€1.10) runs hourly between the bus terminal and the lower town of Ragusa Ibla. From the train station, bus 11 (bus 1 on Sundays) makes a similar circuit.

TRAIN There are four daily trains to Syracuse (€7.50, two hours) via Noto (€5.60, 1½ hours).

CENTRAL SICILY & THE MEDITERRANEAN COAST

Central Sicily is a land of vast panoramas, undulating fields, severe mountain ridges and hilltop towns not yet sanitised for tourists. Moving towards the Mediterranean, the perspective changes, as ancient temples jostle for position with modern high-rise apartments outside Agrigento, Sicily's most lauded classical site and also one of its busier modern cities.

Agrigento

POP 59,200 / ELEV 230M

Agrigento does not make a good first impression. Seen from a distance, the modern city's rows of unsightly apartment blocks loom incongruously on the hillside, distracting attention from the splendid Valley of the Temples below, where the ancient Greeks once built their great city of Akragas. Never fear: once you get down among the ruins, their monumentality becomes apparent, and it's easy to understand how this remarkable complex of temples became Sicily's pre-eminent travel destination, first put on the tourist map by Goethe in the 18th century.

Three kilometres uphill from the temples, Agrigento's medieval core is a pleasant place to pass the evening after a day exploring the ruins. The intercity bus and train stations are both in the upper town, within a few blocks of Via Atenea, the main street of the medieval city.

⊙ Sights

VALLE DEI TEMPLI

Parco Archeologico ARCHAEOLOGICAL SITE
(☑0922 49 72 26; adult/reduced/child €8/4/free, incl archaeological museum €10/5/free; ⊙9am-11.30pm Jul & Aug, 9am-7pm Tue-Sat, 9am-1pm Sun & Mon Sep-Jun) Agrigento's Valley of the Temples is one of Sicily's premier attractions. A Unesco World Heritage Site, it incorporates a complex of temples and old city walls from the ancient Greek city of Akragas. Despite the name, the five Doric temples stand along a ridge, designed as a beacon to homecoming sailors. The ruins are divided into two main sections, known as the eastern and western zones. Although in varying states of decay, the temples give a tantalising glimpse of what must truly have been one of the most luxurious cities in Magna Graecia.

SICILY'S BEST-PRESERVED ROMAN MOSAICS

Near the town of Piazza Armerina in central Sicily is the stunning 3rd-century Roman **Villa Romana del Casale** (☎0935 68 00 36; museo.villacasale@regione.sicilia.it; adult/reduced €10/5; ☺9am-6pm), a Unesco World Heritage Site and one of the few remaining sites of Roman Sicily. This sumptuous hunting lodge is thought to have belonged to Diocletian's co-emperor Marcus Aurelius Maximianus. Buried under mud in a 12th-century flood, it remained hidden for 700 years before its magnificent floor mosaics were discovered in the 1950s. Visit out of season or early in the day to avoid the hordes of motor coach tourists.

The mosaics cover almost the entire floor (3500 sq metres) of the villa and are considered unique for their narrative style, the range of subject matter and variety of colour – many are clearly influenced by African themes. Along the eastern end of the internal courtyard is the wonderful **Corridor of the Great Hunt**, vividly depicting chariots, rhinos, cheetahs, lions and the voluptuously beautiful Queen of Sheba. Across the corridor is a series of apartments, where floor illustrations reproduce scenes from Homer. But perhaps the most captivating of the mosaics is the so-called **Room of the Ten Girls in Bikinis**, with depictions of sporty girls in scanty bikinis throwing a discus, using weights and throwing a ball; they would blend in well on a Malibu beach. These most famous of Piazza Armerina's mosaics were off-limits to the public due to restoration work as of late 2011, but were scheduled to reopen sometime in 2012.

Travelling by car from Piazza Armerina, follow signs south of town to the SP15, then continue 5km to reach the villa.

Getting here without a car is more challenging. Intercity buses run from Catania (Interbus, €8.30, 1¾ hours) and Enna (SAIS, €3.20, 40 minutes) to Piazza Armerina; from here catch a local bus (€0.70, 30 minutes, summer only) or a taxi (€20) the remaining 5km. For an overnight stay that's convenient to public transit, Piazza Armerina's **Ostello del Borgo** (☎0935 68 70 19; www.ostellodelborgo.it; Largo San Giovanni 6; dm/s/d €17/25/40; ☎) offers good value accommodation in a converted monastery.

The most scenic time to come is from February to March when the valley is awash with almond blossom. The main entrance to the Valley of the Temples is at Piazzale dei Templi which also has a large car park. There's a second entrance and ticket office, west of here, at the intersection of Viadotto Akragas and Via Panoramica dei Templi.

Eastern Zone

East of Via dei Templi are the most spectacular temples, the first of which is the **Tempio di Ercole** (Temple of Hercules), built towards the end of the 6th century BC and believed to be the oldest of the temples. Eight of its 38 columns were raised in 1924 to reveal a structure that was roughly the same size as the Parthenon. The magnificent **Tempio della Concordia** (Temple of Concord) is the only temple to survive relatively intact. Built around 440 BC, it was transformed into a Christian church in the 6th century. The **Tempio di Giunone** (Temple of Juno) stands high on the edge of the ridge, a five minute walk to the east. Part of its colonnade remains and there's an impressive sacrificial altar.

Western Zone

Across Via dei Templi, to the west, is what remains of the massive **Tempio di Giove** (Temple of Jupiter), never actually completed and now totally in ruins, allowing you to appreciate the sheer size of the rocks. It covered an area of 112m by 56m with columns 20m high. Between the columns stood *telamoni* (colossal statues), one of which was reconstructed and is now in the Museo Archeologico. A copy lies on the ground among the ruins and gives an idea of the immense size of the structure. Work began on the temple around 480 BC and it was probably destroyed during the Carthaginian invasion in 406 BC. The nearby **Tempio di Castore e Polluce** (Temple of Castor and Pollux) was partly reconstructed in the 19th century, although probably using pieces from other constructions.

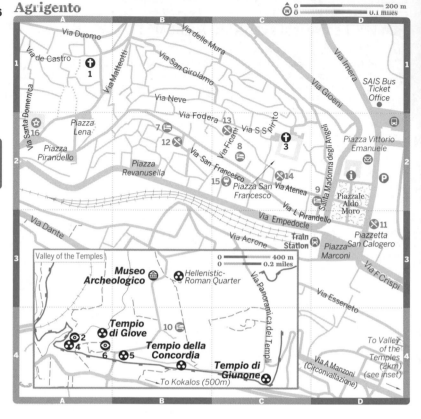

Tucked into a natural cleft at the far edge of the western zone is the **Giardino della Kolymbetra** (adult/reduced €2/1; ⊙10am-6pm Apr-Jun, 10am-7pm Jul-Sep), a lush garden with more than 300 labelled species of plants and some welcome picnic tables. It's a lovely spot for a break, but note that the climb back up is steep and tiring in hot weather.

All the temples are atmospherically lit up at night.

Museo Archeologico   MUSEUM
(☑0922 4 01 11; Contrada San Nicola; adult/reduced €6/3; ⊙9am-7pm Tue-Sat, 9am-1pm Sun & Mon) North of the temples, this wheelchair-accessible museum is one of Sicily's finest, with a huge collection of clearly labelled artefacts from the excavated site. Especially noteworthy are the dazzling displays of Greek painted ceramics and the awe-inspiring reconstructed *telamone*, a colossal statue recovered from the nearby Tempio di Giove.

MEDIEVAL AGRIGENTO
Roaming the town's lively, winding streets is relaxing after a day among the temples.

Chiesa di Santa Maria dei Greci   CHURCH
(Salita Santa Maria dei Greci; ⊙9am-12.30pm & 4-6pm Mon-Sat) Uphill from Via Atenea is this 11th-century Norman church built on the site of a 5th-century-BC temple to Athena. Glass floor panels reveal the temple's foundations, while a narrow passageway left of the church allows you to see the ancient Greek columns.

Monastero del Santo Spirito   CONVENT
This hillside convent was founded by Cistercian nuns at the end of the 13th century. Ring the buzzer at the door marked No 8, and their modern-day counterparts will sell you a tray of delicious cakes and pastries (€11), including *dolci di mandorla, cuscusu* (couscous made of almonds and pistachio) and – at Christmastime – *bucellati* (rolled sweet dough with figs).

Tours

The tourist office maintains a list of multi-lingual guides. The official rate is €140 for a half-day tour, although discounts can be negotiated.

Michele Gallo (☏0922 40 22 57, 360 39 79 30) is an excellent English-speaking guide offering individual and group itineraries, including a €90, two-hour tour of the temples and a €130, half-day tour of the temples and archaeological museum.

Festivals & Events

Sagra del Mandorlo in Fiore   ALMOND
A huge folk festival held on the first Sunday in February, when the Valley of the Temples is cloaked in almond blossom.

Festa di San Calògero   RELIGIOUS
During this week-long festival centred on the first Sunday in July, the statue of St Calògero (who saved Agrigento from the plague) is carried through the town while spectators throw spiced loaves at it.

Sleeping

The places listed below all offer good value for money.

TOP CHOICE **Villa Athena**   LUXURY HOTEL €€€
(☏0922 59 62 88; www.hotelvillaathena.it; Via Passeggiata Archeologica 33; d €190-350, jr ste €260-370, ste €300-890; P✳@🕏🌊) With the Tempio della Concordia lit up in the near distance and palm trees lending an exotic Arabian-nights feel, the views from this his-toric five-star are magnificent. Housed in an aristocratic 18th-century villa, the hotel's interior, gleaming after a recent makeover, is a picture of white, ceramic cool. The Villa Suite, with two cavernous rooms floored in antique tiles, a freestanding Jaccuzi tub and a vast terrace looking straight at the temples, vies for the title of coolest hotel room in Sicily.

Camere a Sud   B&B €
(☏349 638 44 24; www.camereasud.it; Via Ficani 6; r €60-70; ✳@🕏) Run by a friendly Agri-gentan couple, this extremely cute, comfort-able and well-signposted B&B has cheerful rooms and a tiny roof terrace.

Atenea 191 B&B   B&B €
(☏349 59 55 94; www.atenea191.com; Via Atenea 191; s €35-55, d €50-85) The gregarious, mul-tilingual and well-travelled Sonia runs this B&B on Agrigento's main shopping thor-oughfare. The breakfast terrace has sweep-ing views over the valley, as do some rooms. Sonia is a great source of local travel tips and an entertaining storyteller.

PortAtenea   B&B €
(☏349 093 74 92; www.portatenea.com; cnr Via Atenea & Via C Battisti; s €35-50, d €55-70; ✳🕏) Five minutes from the train and bus sta-tions at the entrance to Agrigento's main pedestrian thoroughfare, this B&B wins points for its large roof terrace overlooking the Valley of the Temples. The three doubles and two triple rooms are spacious and well-appointed, with hair dryers and cheerful decor.

✕ Eating

Kalòs MODERN SICILIAN €€
(☎0922 2 63 89; Piazzetta San Calogero; meals €25-40; ☺closed Mon) This stylish eatery compensates for bland decor by focusing full attention on its well-prepared fish, meat and pasta dishes. The scrumptious offerings include fettucine with prawns and artichokes, grilled lamb chops, citrus shrimp and pear tart with chocolate and hazelnuts.

Kokalos PIZZERIA €
(☎0922 60 64 27; Via Magazzeni 3; pizzas €5-11, meals €17-30; ☺lunch & dinner) This eatery, resembling a Wild West ranch, is the perfect place to enjoy wood-fired pizza on the summer terrace while gazing out over the temples. You'll need a car to get here – it's up a dusty track a couple of kilometres southeast of town.

Trattoria Concordia TRATTORIA €
(☎0922 2 26 68; Via Porcello 8; meals €18-30; ☺lunch & dinner) Tucked up a side alley, this rustic trattoria with exposed stone and stucco walls specialises in grilled fish along with traditional Sicilian *primi* like *casarecce con pesce spada, melanzane e menta* (pasta with swordfish, eggplant and mint).

Ristorante Per Bacco SICILIAN €
(☎0922 55 33 69; Vicolo Lo Presti 2; meals from €17; ☺dinner Tue-Sun) The food may not quite live up to the charm of the setting – under stone and brick arches and beamed ceilings – but the service is friendly, and the set menus for under €20 are good value at this restaurant just above Via Atenea.

L'Ambasciata di Sicilia SICILIAN €€
(☎0922 2 05 26; Via Giambertoni 2; meals €22-33; ☺Mon-Sat) At the 'Sicilian Embassy', they do everything they can to improve foreign relations, plying tourists with tasty plates of traditional Sicilian fare. Try to get a table on the small outdoor terrace, which has splendid views.

🍸 Drinking & Entertainment

Mojo Wine Bar WINE BAR
(☎0922 46 30 13; Piazza San Francesco 11-13; ☺Mon-Sat) A trendy *enoteca* (wine bar) in a pretty piazza. Enjoy a cool white Inzolia, and munch on olives and spicy salami as you listen to laid-back jazz.

Teatro Pirandello THEATRE
(☎0922 2 50 19; www.teatroluigipirandello.it, in Italian; Piazza Pirandello; tickets €18-23) This city-run theatre is Sicily's third largest, after Palermo's Teatro Massimo and Catania's Teatro Massimo Bellini. Works by local hero Luigi Pirandello figure prominently in the program, which runs from November to April.

ℹ Information

There are banks on Piazza Vittorio Emanuele I and Via Atenea.

Internet Point (Cortile Contarini 7; wi-fi/computer access per hr €2/3.20; ☺9.15am-1.15pm & 3.30-9pm Mon-Sat) Internet and international phone service.

Ospedale San Giovanni di Dio (☎0922 44 21 11; Contrada da Consolida) North of the centre.

Police station (☎112; Piazzale Aldo Moro 2)

Post office (Piazza Vittorio Emanuele I)

Provincial tourist office (☎0922 59 36 50, 800 23 68 37; www.provincia.agrigento.it) train station (☺9am-1pm Mon-Fri); Piazzale Aldo Moro (☺8am-2pm Mon-Sat, 2.30-7pm Mon-Fri) Provides both local and regional information.

ℹ Getting There & Away

Bus

The intercity bus station and ticket booths are located on Piazza Rosselli. **Autoservizi Camilleri** (☎0922 2 91 36; www.camilleriar gentoelattuca.it) runs buses to Palermo (€8.10, two hours) five times Monday to Saturday and twice on Sunday; **Cuffaro** (☎091 616 15 10; www.cuffaro.info) offers more frequent Palermo service – nine departures Monday to Saturday, three on Sunday. **Lumia** (☎0922 2 91 36; www.autolineelumia.it) has departures to Trapani (€11.30, 3½ to four hours, three daily Monday to Saturday, one on Sunday); and **SAIS** (☎0922 2 93 24; www.saistrasporti.it) runs buses to Catania (€12.40, three hours, 10 to 15 daily).

Car & Motorcycle

The SS189 links Agrigento with Palermo, while the SS115 runs along the coast, northwest towards Trapani and southeast to Syracuse.

Driving in the medieval town is near impossible due to all the pedestrianised streets. There's metered parking at the train station and free parking along Via Esseneto just below.

Train

From Agrigento Centrale station (Piazza Marconi), trains run regularly to Palermo (€8.10, 2¼ hours, eight to 11 daily) and three times daily to Catania (€10.20, 3¾ hours). For other destinations, you're better off taking the bus.

ℹ Getting Around

TUA (Trasporti Urbani Agrigento; ☎0922 41 20 24; www.trasportiurbaniagrigento.it) buses run down to the Valley of the Temples from the

In AD 830 it was conquered by the Arabs, who gave it its current name, Marsa Allah (Port of God).

It was here in 1860 that Giuseppe Garibaldi, leader of the movement for Italian unification, landed in his rickety old boats with his 1000-strong army – a claim to fame that finds its way into every tourist brochure.

◎ Sights & Activities

For a taste of local life, take a stroll at sunset around pretty **Piazza della Repubblica**, heart of the historic centre.

Cantine Florio   WINERY

(☑0923 78 11 11; www.cantineflorio.it; Lungomare Florio; tours €7; ☉wine shop 9am-1pm & 3-6pm Mon-Fri, 9am-1pm Sat, English-language tours 11am & 4.30pm Mon-Fri, 10.30am Sat) Tipplers shouldn't miss these venerable wine cellars on the road to Mazara del Vallo (bus 16 from Piazza del Popolo). Florio opens its doors to visitors to explain the fascinating history of local viticulture, the process of making Marsala wine and to give you a taste of the goods. Pellegrino, Donnafugata, Rallo, Mavis and Intorcia are other producers in the same area. Booking is recommended.

Museo Archeologico
Baglio Anselmi   MUSEUM

(☑0923 95 25 35; Lungomare Boeo; admission €4; ☉9am-7pm Tue-Sun, 9am-1.30pm Mon) Marsala's finest treasure is the partially reconstructed remains of a Carthaginian *liburna* (warship) sunk off the Egadi Islands during the first of the Punic Wars nearly 3000 years ago. Displayed alongside other regional archaeological artefacts, the ship's bare bones provide the only remaining physical evidence of the Phoenicians' seafaring superiority in the 3rd century BC; and offer a glimpse of a civilisation that was extinguished by the Romans.

Whitaker Museum   MUSEUM

(☑0923 71 25 98; adult/reduced €9/5; ☉9.30am-1.30pm & 2.30-6.30pm Mar-Sep) On tiny San Pantaleo island, 5km north of Marsala and connected to the mainland by a submerged Phoenician road, this museum houses a unique collection of Phoenician artefacts assembled over decades by amateur archaeologist Joseph Whitaker. The museum's greatest treasure is *Il Giovinetto di Mozia,* a marble statue of a young man in a pleated robe suggesting Carthaginian influences. The fields around the museum are strewn with ruins from the ancient Phoenician

---

LOST AND FOUND: THE VENUS OF MORGANTINA

In May 2011, Sicilian art lovers were thrilled to welcome the long-lost **Dea di Morgantina**, an ancient statue of Venus, back to its rightful home in central Sicily. For over two decades, the statue had been on display at the Getty Museum in Los Angeles, California, but when authorities discovered that the Getty's unscrupulous curator had actually smuggled it out of Italy with help from grave robbers, the Italian government initiated moves to repatriate it.

The statue is now proudly back on display in a special gallery at the **Museo Archeologico di Aidone** (☑0935 8 73 07; www.regione.sicilia.it/beniculturali/deadimorgantina, in Italian; adult/reduced €6/3; ☉9am-7pm), in Aidone, just outside Piazza Armerina.

Piazza Rosselli bus station, stopping in front of the train station en route. Take bus 1, 2 or 3 (€1.10) and get off at either the museum or the Piazzale dei Templi. Bus 1 continues to Porto Empedocle and bus 2 continues to San Leone. The Linea Verde (Green Line) bus runs hourly from the train station to the cathedral.

WESTERN SICILY

Directly across the water from North Africa and still retaining vestiges of the Arab, Phoenician, and Greek cultures that once prevailed here, western Sicily has a bit of the Wild West about it. There's plenty to stir the senses, from Trapani's savoury fish couscous, to the dazzling views from hilltop Erice, to the wild coastal beauty of Riserva Naturale dello Zingaro.

Marsala

POP 82,500

Best known for its sweet dessert wines, Marsala is an elegant town of stately baroque buildings within a perfect square of walls.

The city was originally founded by Phoenician escapees from the Roman onslaught at nearby Mozia. Not wanting to risk a second attack, they fortified their new home with 7m-thick walls, ensuring that it was the last Punic settlement to fall to the Romans.

settlement of Mozia. Visitors can wander at will around the island to explore these, following a network of trails punctuated with helpful maps and informational displays. The island is accessible by private boat (€5 return, every 25 minutes) from a pier along the SS115 coast road. The surrounding landscape is quite lovely, with shallow *saline* (salty pools) and softly shimmering heaps of salt presided over by picturesque windmills. The salt from these pans is considered the best in Italy and has been big business since the 12th century.

🛏 Sleeping & Eating

Marsala has few hotels within the historic centre.

Hotel Carmine   HOTEL €€
(☑0923 71 19 07; www.hotelcarmine.it; Piazza Carmine 16; s €70-90, d €100-125; P✳@🛜) This lovely hotel in a 16th-century monastery has elegant rooms (especially numbers 7 and 30), with original blue-and-gold majolica tiles, stone walls, antique furniture and lofty beamed ceilings. Enjoy your cornflakes in the baronial-style breakfast room with its historic frescoes and over-the-top chandelier, or sip your drink by the roaring fireplace in winter. Modern perks include a rooftop solarium.

TOP CHOICE Il Gallo e l'Innamorata   MODERN SICILIAN €
(☑0923 195 44 46; Via Bilardello 18; meals €25; ⊙lunch & dinner) Warm orange walls and arched stone doorways lend an artsy, convivial atmosphere to this Slow Food–acclaimed eatery with its superb fixed price menu (€25 including appetisers, pasta, main course, fruit, dessert, water and wine). The à la carte menu is short and sweet, featuring a few well-chosen dishes each day, including the classic *scaloppine* (veal cooked with Marsala wine and lemon).

ℹ Information

Tourist office (☑0923 71 40 97; ufficioturistico.proloco@comune.marsala.tp.it; Via XI Maggio 100; ⊙8.30am-1.30pm & 3-8pm Mon-Sat, 9am-1pm Sun) A friendly tourist office with good maps and brochures.

ℹ Getting There & Away

From Marsala, bus operators include **Lumia** (www.autolineelumia.it) to Agrigento (€9.40, 2½ to three hours, one to three daily); and **Salemi**

(☑0923 98 11 20; www.autoservizisalemi.it) to Palermo (€8.80, 2¼ hours, at least nine daily).

The train is the best way to get to Trapani (€3.30, 30 minutes, 14 daily, five on Sunday).

Selinunte

The ruins of Selinunte are the most impressively sited in Sicily. The huge city was built in 628 BC on a promontory overlooking the sea, and over two and a half centuries became one of the richest and most powerful in the world. It was destroyed by the Carthaginians in 409 BC and finally fell to the Romans in about 350 BC, at which time it went into rapid decline and disappeared from historical accounts.

The city's past is so remote that the names of the various temples have been forgotten and they are now identified by the letters A to G, M and O. The most impressive, **Temple E**, has been partially rebuilt, its columns pieced together from their fragments with part of its tympanum. Many of the carvings, particularly from **Temple C**, are now in the archaeological museum in Palermo (see p155). The quality is on a par with the Parthenon marbles and clearly demonstrates the high cultural levels reached by many Greek colonies in Sicily.

The **ticket office** (☑0924 4 65 40; adult/reduced €6/3; ⊙9am-1hr before sunset) is located near the eastern temples. Try to visit in spring when the surroundings are ablaze with wild flowers.

TOP CHOICE Vittorio (☑0925 7 83 81; www.ristorantevittorio.it; meals €25-45), 15km east of Selinunte on the beach at Porto Palo, is a perfect place to end your day if travelling by car. In business for over 40 years, it's earned a reputation as one of Sicily's best seafood eateries, serving hefty portions of the freshest fish and shellfish around. Come here at sunset and dine to the sound of crashing breakers. Rooms (single/double €60/80) are available upstairs for anyone too stuffed to drive home.

Selinunte is midway between Agrigento and Trapani, about 10km south of the junction of the A29 and SS115 near Castelvetrano. **Autoservizi Salemi** (☑0924 8 18 26; www.autoservizisalemi.it) runs five buses daily from Selinunte to Castelvetrano (€2.55, 20 minutes), where you can make onward bus connections to Agrigento, or train connections to Trapani (€5.60, 1¼ hours) and Palermo (€7.50, 2½ hours).

Trapani

POP 70,700

The lively port city of Trapani makes a convenient base for exploring Sicily's western tip. Its historic centre is filled with atmospheric pedestrian streets and some lovely churches and baroque buildings, although the heavily developed outskirts are rather bleak. The surrounding countryside is beautiful, ranging from the watery vastness of the coastal salt ponds to the rugged mountainous shoreline north of town.

Once situated at the heart of a powerful trading network that stretched from Carthage to Venice, Trapani's sickle-shaped spit of land hugs the precious harbour, nowadays busy with a steady stream of tourists and traffic to and from Tunisia, Pantelleria and the Egadi Islands.

◉ Sights

The narrow network of streets in Trapani's historic centre remains a Moorish labyrinth, although it takes much of its character from the fabulous 18th-century baroque of the Spanish period – a catalogue of examples can be found down the pedestrianised **Via Garibaldi**. The best time to walk down here is in the early evening (around 7pm) when the *passeggiata* is in full swing.

Trapani's other main street is Corso Vittorio Emanuele, punctuated by the huge **Cattedrale di San Lorenzo** (Corso Vittorio Emanuele; ⊙8am-4pm), with its baroque facade and stuccoed interior. Facing off the east end of the corso is another baroque confection, the **Palazzo Senatorio**.

Chiesa del Purgatorio   CHURCH
(☑0923 56 28 82; Via San Francesco d'Assisi; ⊙4-6.30pm) Just off the corso, south along Via Generale Dom Giglio, is the Chiesa del Purgatorio, which houses the impressive 18th-century *Misteri,* 20 life-sized wooden effigies depicting the story of Christ's Passion (used in I Misteri).

Santuario dell'Annunziata   CHURCH
(Via Conte Agostino Pepoli 179; ⊙8am-noon & 4-7pm) Trapani's major sight is the 14th-century Santuario dell'Annunziata, 4km east of the centre. The Cappella della Madonna, behind the high altar, contains the venerated *Madonna di Trapani,* thought to have been carved by Nino Pisano.

Museo Nazionale Pepoli   MUSEUM
(☑0923 55 32 69; Via Conte Pepoli 200; adult/reduced €6/3; ⊙9am-1.30pm Mon-Sat, 9am-12.30pm Sun, 3-7pm Wed, Fri & Sat) Adjacent to the Santuario dell'Annunziata, in a former Carmelite monastery, the museum houses the collection of Conte Pepoli, who made it his business to salvage much of Trapani's local arts and crafts, not least the garish coral carvings – once all the rage in Europe before the banks of coral off Trapani were decimated. The museum also has a good collection of Gagini sculptures, silverwork, archaeological artefacts and religious artwork.

Egadi Islands   ISLANDS
The islands of Levanzo, Favignana and Marettimo make a pleasant day trip from Trapani. For centuries the lucrative tuna industry formed the basis of the islands' economy, but overfishing of the surrounding waters means that the Egadi survives primarily on income from tourists who come to cycle, dive or simply enjoy the relaxed pace of life. The best range of meals and accommodation can be found on Favignana, while the islands' single greatest tourist attraction is Grotta del Genovese on Levanzo, a cave decorated with Mesolithic and Neolithic artwork, including a famous image of a prehistoric tuna. Siremar and Ustica Lines (see p204) both run year-round hydrofoil services to the islands.

⭐ Festivals & Events

I Misteri   EASTER
(www.processionemisteritp.it, in Italian, Spanish & French) Sicily's most venerated Easter procession is a four-day festival of extraordinary religious fervour. Nightly processions, bearing life-sized wooden effigies, make their way through the old quarter to a specially erected chapel in Piazza Lucatelli. The high point is on Good Friday when the celebrations reach fever pitch.

Couscous Fest   FOOD
(www.couscousfest.it, in Italian) In San Vito Lo Capo, 40km north of Trapani, this late September festival celebrates Sicilian multiculturalism with world music concerts and international couscous cookoffs.

🛏 Sleeping

The most convenient – and nicest – place to stay, is in Trapani's pedestrianised historic centre, just north of the port.

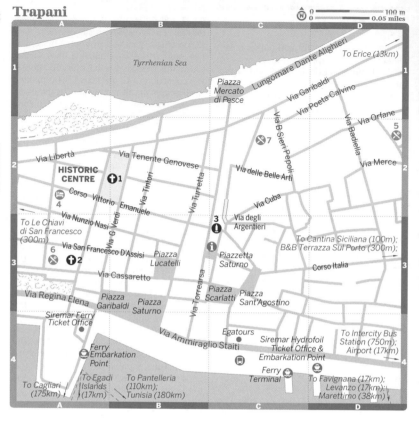

Trapani

⊙ **Sights**

B&B Terrazza Sul Porto B&B €

(☑ 0923 194 15 36; www.laterrazzasulporto.it; Via Camporeale 2; s €35-45, d €45-75; ❈🅢) For a cheap sleep with friendly hosts, clean tiled rooms and a convenient location, this five-room B&B near the ferry docks is a great option. Breakfast is served on the upstairs terrace with views of the port. There's a kitchen for guests' use, plus laundry facilities if you're staying for longer than four days.

Le Chiavi di San Francesco HOTEL €

(☑ 0923 43 80 13; www.lechiavidisanfrancesco. com; Via Tartaglia 18; d €80-105; ❈🅢) Opposite the Chiesa di San Francesco this popular hotel has 16 rooms featuring cheerful colour schemes and small but clean bathrooms. Angle for one of the superior rooms up front, which offer more space, better light and optional kitchen facilities.

Ai Lumi B&B B&B €

(☑ 0923 54 09 22; www.ailumi.it; Corso Vittorio Emanuele 71; s €40-70, d €70-100; ❈🅢) Housed in an 18th-century *palazzo*, Ai Lumi's greatest asset is its central location. Rooms vary in size and comfort; the best are the small apartments furnished with wrought-iron beds, kitchenettes and balconies overlooking Trapani's most elegant pedestrian street. Guests get a 15% discount at the hotel's atmospheric restaurant next door.

Eating

Sicily's Arab heritage and Trapani's unique position on the sea route to Tunisia have made couscous ('*cuscus*' or '*kuscus*' as they spell it around here) a local speciality.

 Osteria La Bettolaccia SICILIAN €€
(☑0923 2 16 95; Via Generale Enrico Fardella 25; meals €30-40; ⊗closed Sat lunch & Sun) This Slow Food–recommended restaurant is unwaveringly authentic, and the perfect place to try *cous cous con zuppa di mare* (couscous with mixed seafood in a spicy fish sauce flavoured with tomatoes, garlic and parsley).

Tentazioni di Gusto MODERN SICILIAN €€
(☑0923 54 81 65; www.tentazionidigusto.it; Via Badia Nuova 27/29; meals €25-35; ⊗closed Wed Nov-Mar) Young proprietors Piero and Vicenzo have created an instant sensation at this trendy new restaurant-bar, which features a mix of traditional and innovative cuisine, ample outdoor seating on the cobblestones and a newly expanded interior with stone arches and sleek wood floors.

Cantina Siciliana SICILIAN €€
(☑347 690 10 10; Via Giudecca 32; meals €25-35; ⊗lunch & dinner) The reasonably priced regional specialities here are enticing, as are the pretty blue-tiled front rooms. Unfortunately service can range from lacklustre to borderline rude, as owner Pino tends to regale his Italian friends to the exclusion of other guests. Still, it's one of Trapani's better regarded eateries and worth a visit if you're willing to focus on the food.

La Rinascente PASTRIES & CAKES €
(Via Gatti 3; cannoli €1.60; ⊗9am-1pm & 3-7pm, closed Sun afternoon & Wed) When you enter this bakery through the side door, you'll feel like you've barged into someone's kitchen – and you have! Thankfully, owner Signor Costadura's broad smile will quickly put you at ease, coupled with some of the best cannoli on the planet, which you can watch being created on the spot.

ⓘ Information

Trapani has dozens of banks with ATMs.
Ospedale Sant'Antonio Abate (☑0923 80 91 11; Via Cosenza 82)
Police station (☑0923 59 81 11; Piazza Vittoria Veneto)
Post office (Piazza Vittoria Veneto)
Torrepali web cafe (Via Ammiraglio Staiti 69; per hr €3; ⊗8am-2am) Across from the port; six computers with comfortable upstairs seating and bar service.

WORTH A TRIP

PANTELLERIA

Halfway between Trapani and Tunisia, this volcanic outcrop is the largest island off Sicily. Buffeted year-round by winds, Pantelleria is characterised by jagged lava stone, low-slung caper bushes, dwarf vines, steaming fumaroles and mudbaths. There are no true beaches, but Pantelleria's gorgeous, secluded coves – including **Cala Tramontana**, **Cala Levante** and **Balata dei Turchi** – are perfect for snorkelling, diving. and boat excursions.

The island has excellent hiking trails, along the coast and in the high vineyard country of **Piana di Ghirlanda**. Near **Mursia** on the west coast, there are signposted but poorly maintained remnants of *sesi* (Bronze Age funerary monuments). Throughout the island you'll also find Pantelleria's famous *dammusi* (houses with thick, white-washed walls and shallow cupolas). The island's exotic and remote atmosphere has long made it popular with celebrities, including Truman Capote, Sting, Madonna and Giorgio Armani.

Meridiana (www.meridiana.it) and **Alitalia** (www.alitalia.com) offer regular flights to Pantelleria from Palermo and Trapani. **Siremar** (www.siremar.it) runs one ferry daily between Trapani and Pantelleria (low/high season €31/35).

For further information about Pantelleria see www.pantelleria.com.

Tourist office (☎0923 54 45 33; point@stradadelvinoericedoc.it; Piazzetta Saturno; ☺9am-1pm & 3-7pm Mon-Sat) Provides free maps and info about Trapani and local wine routes.

❶ Getting There & Around

For bus, plane and ferry tickets, try **Egatours** (☎0923 2 17 54; www.egatourviaggi.it; Via Ammiraglio Staiti 13), a travel agency located opposite the port.

Air

Trapani's small **Vincenzo Florio Airport** (TPS; www.airgest.it) is 17km south of town at Birgi. **Ryanair** (www.ryanair.com) offers direct flights to London Luton and a dozen other European cities; **Meridiana** (www.meridiana.it) serves the Mediterranean island of Pantelleria. AST buses connect Trapani's port and bus station with the airport (€4.50, 45 minutes, hourly).

Boat

Ferry ticket offices are inside Trapani's ferry terminal, opposite Piazza Garibaldi.

For Ustica Lines and Siremar hydrofoils, the ticket office and embarkation point is 150m further east along Via Ammiraglio Staiti.

Grimaldi Lines (www.grimaldi-ferries.com) runs weekly services to Tunisia (€95, 7½ hours) and Civitavecchia (€120, 14½ hours).

Tirrenia (☎0923 52 18 96; www.tirrenia.it) runs a weekly service to Cagliari (€52, 10 hours).

Ustica Lines (☎0923 87 38 13; www.usticalines.it; Via Ammiraglio Staiti) and **Siremar** (☎0923 54 54 55; www.siremar.it; Via Ammiraglio Staiti) both operate hydrofoils year-round to the Egadi Islands. Ustica Lines also offers thrice-weekly summer-only services to Naples (€89.40, seven hours) and Ustica (€26.40, 2½ hours), while Siremar offers nightly ferry service to Pantelleria (€39.50, six hours).

Bus

Intercity buses arrive and depart from the new City Terminal 1km east of the centre (just southeast of the train station).

Segesta (☎0923 2 17 27; www.segesta.it) runs express buses to Palermo (€8.60, two hours, hourly). Board at the bus stop across the street from Egatours or at the bus station.

Lumia (www.autolineelumia.it) buses serve Agrigento (€11.30, three to four hours, one to three daily).

Two free city buses (No 1 and 2) operated by **ATM** (☎0923 55 95 75; www.atmtrapani.it) do circular trips through Trapani, connecting the bus station, the train station and the port.

Car & Motorcyle

To bypass Trapani's vast suburbs and avoid the narrow streets of the city centre, follow signs from the A29 autostrada directly to the port, where you'll find abundant paid parking along the broad waterside avenue Via Ammiraglio Staiti, within walking distance of most attractions.

Train

From Trapani's station on Piazza Umberto I, there are rail links to Palermo (€7.50, 2¼ to 3½ hours, three to six daily) and Marsala (€3.30, 30 minutes, six to 12 daily). At the time of research Palermo-bound trains were only going as far as Notarbartolo station, 3km northwest of downtown Palermo, due to track work between Notarbartolo and Palermo Centrale. Until this work is finished, the bus is a better option.

Erice

POP 28,500 / ELEV 751M

One of Italy's most spectacular hill towns, Erice combines medieval charm with astounding 360-degree views. Erice sits on the legendary Mt Eryx (750m); on a clear day, you can see all the way to Cape Bon in Tunisia. Wander the medieval tangle of streets interspersed by churches, forts and tiny cobbled piazzas. The town has a seductive history as a centre for the cult of Venus. Settled by the mysterious Elymians, Erice was an obvious abode for the goddess of love, and the town followed the peculiar ritual of sacred prostitution, with the prostitutes themselves accommodated in the Temple of Venus. Despite countless invasions, the temple remained intact – no guesses why.

Erice's tourist infrastructure is excellent. Posted throughout town, you'll find bilingual (Italian-English) informational displays along with town maps displaying suggested walking routes.

◉ Sights

The best views can be had from **Giardino del Balio**, which overlooks the rugged turrets and wooded hillsides down to the saltpans of Trapani and the sea. Adjacent to the gardens is the Norman **Castello di Venere** (Via Castello di Venere), built in the 12th and 13th centuries over the Temple of Venus.

There are several churches and monuments in the small, quiet town and you can purchase a €5 ticket to visit the lot. Especially lovely are the 14th-century **Chiesa Matrice** (Via Vito Carvini; admission €2; ☺10am-8pm May-Sep, 10am-6pm Oct-Apr), just inside Porta Trapani, and its adjacent bell tower, **Torre di Re Federico** (admission €2), where climbing the 110 steps rewards you with fabulous views.

SICILY'S OLDEST NATURE RESERVE

Saved from development and road projects by local protests, the tranquil **Riserva Naturale dello Zingaro** (☎0924 3 51 08; www.riservazingaro.it; adult/reduced €3/2; ⏱7am-8pm Apr-Sep, 8am-4pm Oct-Mar) is the star attraction on the Golfo di Castellammare, halfway between Palermo and Trapani. Celebrating its 30th anniversary in 2011, this was Sicily's first nature reserve. Zingaro's wild coastline is a haven for the rare Bonelli's eagle along with 40 other species of bird. Mediterranean flora dusts the hillsides with wild carob and bright yellow euphorbia, and hidden coves, such as Capreria and Marinella Bays, provide tranquil swimming spots. The main entrance to the park is 2km north of the village of Scopello. Several walking trails are detailed on maps available free at the entrance or downloadable from the park website (in Italian only). The main 7km trail along the coast passes by the visitor centre and five museums documenting everything from local flora and fauna to traditional fishing methods.

Once home to tuna fishers, Scopello now mainly hosts tourists, although outside of peak summer season it retains some of its sleepy village atmosphere. Its port, 1km below town, has a picturesque rust-red *tonnara* (tuna processing plant) and dramatic *faraglioni* (rock towers) rising from the water.

Pensione Tranchina (☎0924 54 10 99; www.pensionetranchina.com; Via Diaz 7; B&B per person €36-46, half-board per person €55-72; ✦🖭) is the nicest of several places to stay and eat clustered around the cobblestoned courtyard at Scopello's village centre. Super-friendly hosts Marisin and Salvatore offer comfortable rooms, a roaring fire on chilly evenings and delicious home-cooked meals featuring local fish and home-grown fruit and olive oil. Next door, **La Tavernetta** (☎0924 54 11 29; www.albergolatavernetta.it; Via Diaz 3; s €55-70, d €70-96; 🅿✦@🖭) is another good choice.

🛏 Sleeping & Eating

Hotels, many with their own restaurants, are scattered along Via Vittorio Emanuele, Erice's main street. After the tourists have left, the town assumes a beguiling medieval air.

Hotel Elimo HOTEL €€
(☎0923 86 93 77; www.hotelelimo.it; Via Vittorio Emanuele 23; s €80-110, d €90-130, ste €170; 🅿@🖭) Communal spaces at this atmospheric historic house are filled with tiled beams, marble fireplaces, intriguing art, knick-knacks and antiques. The bedrooms are more mainstream, although many – along with the hotel terrace and restaurant – have breathtaking vistas.

Erice has a tradition of *dolci ericini* (Erice sweets) made by the local nuns. There are numerous pastry shops in town, the most famous being **Maria Grammatico** (☎0923 86 93 90; www.mariagrammatico.it; Via Vittorio Emanuele 14), revered for its *frutta martorana* (marzipan fruit) and almond pastries.

❶ Information

The **tourist office** (☎0923 86 93 88; strerice@ regione.sicilia.it; Via Tommaso Guarrasi 1; ⏱9am-2pm Mon-Fri) is in the centre of town.

❶ Getting There & Away

Regular AST buses run to and from Trapani (one-way/return €2.40/3.70, 45 minutes). A **funicular** (☎0923 56 93 06; www.funiviaerice.it; one-way/return €3.80/6.50; ⏱12.30-9pm Mon, 9.30am-9pm Tue-Sun, to midnight Sat) also connects Trapani with Erice. To reach Trapani's funicular terminal, near the corner of Via Manzoni and Via Capua, take AST bus 21 or 23 (€1) eastbound from Trapani's historic centre. The funicular climbs from here to Erice, dropping you opposite the car park at the foot of Erice's Via Vittorio Emanuele.

Segesta

ELEV 304M

Set on the edge of a deep canyon in the midst of wild, desolate mountains, this huge 5th-century-BC temple is a magical site. On windy days its 36 giant columns are said to act like an organ, producing mysterious notes.

The city, founded by the ancient Elymi- ans, was in constant conflict with Selinunte in the south, whose destruction it sought with dogged determination and singular success. Time, however, has done to Segesta what violence inflicted on Selinunte; little remains now, save the **theatre** and the never-completed **Doric temple** (☎0924 95 23 56; adult/reduced €6/3; ⊙9am-1hr before sun- set), the latter dating from around 430 BC and remarkably well preserved. A shuttle bus (€1.50) runs every 30 minutes from the temple entrance 1.5km uphill to the theatre.

In July and August, performances of Greek plays are staged in the theatre during the **Festival Calatafimi Segesta** (www.festi valsegesta.com).

Tarantola (☎0924 3 10 20; www.tarantolabus. com, in Italian) runs three buses daily from Trapani (one-way/return €3.60/6.10, 35 to 50 minutes), plus a single morning bus from Palermo's train station (one-way/return €6.40/10.20, 90 minutes); drivers stop just outside the archaeological site upon request. Alternatively, catch a train from Trapani (€3.30, 30 minutes, three daily) to Segesta Tempio station. Exiting the station, turn left under the double underpass, then climb 1.5km (20 minutes) to the site.

Understand
❯ Southern Italy

population per sq km

NAPLES   LOS ANGELES   ITALY

♦ ≈ 201 people

Southern Italy Today

Environmental Woes

Southern Italy's predisposition to earthquakes, landslides and volcanic eruptions is not the region's only environmental concern. The Italian government's record on environmental issues has been consistently inconsistent and the Mezzogiorno (land of the midday sun) faces some serious challenges. One of the biggest is Naples' on-again, off-again waste-disposal crisis. After humiliating bouts in 2003, 2006 and 2008, the city's streets were once again submerged in rubbish in early 2011 as authorities struggled to sort out the city's refuse contracts. Faced with a potential public-health crisis, the Italian government deployed 170 troops to help clear the accumulated 2,000 tonnes of litter.

Environmentalists link the problem to Campania's organised-crime syndicate, the Camorra, accused of controlling waste-disposal contracts and using landfill sites and agricultural fields to dump toxic industrial waste. The illegal importation and disposal of refuse from across Europe into southern Italy is a multi-million-euro business. Its effect on people's health is less salubrious. In 2004, the medical journal *Lancet Oncology* dubbed an area northeast of Naples the 'triangle of death' due to its higher-than-average cancer rates. In 2007, Italy's National Research Council found that the mortality rate for people living closest to Campania's illegal dumping sites was between 9% and 12% higher than the norm.

According to the Italian environmental group Legambiente, 45% of Italy's estimated 31,000 annual environmental crimes occur in Campania, Puglia, Calabria and Sicily alone. That all four regions are home to powerful Mafia syndicates is no coincidence. An estimated 290 clans make up Italy's so-called 'Eco-Mafia', which turns an annual profit of €20 billion from crimes such as illegal construction and the production of fraudulent wind farms.

» Combined population: 17.4 million (2011)

» Combined size: 83,733 sq km

» Highest point: Mt Etna, Sicily (3330m)

» Number of Unesco World Heritage Sites: 13

» Average cups of coffee per person per year: 600

Dos & Don'ts

» Italians are generally chic and quick to judge on appearances, so make an effort

» Shorts and sleeveless tops are usually banned in religious buildings

» Splitting the bill is *incivile* (uncivilised). The person who invites pays, although close friends often go Dutch

» Take official opening hours with a grain of salt

» Focus on the positives Although locals regularly lament their region's shortcomings, an outsider's jibes can offend

Top Movies

Il postino (The Postman; 1994) Michael Radford

Matrimonio all'italiana (Marriage, Italian-Style; 1964) Vittorio De Sica

Cinema Paradiso (1988) Giuseppe Tornatore

belief systems
(% of population)

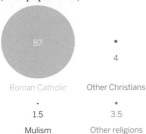

87
Roman Catholic

4
Other Christians

1.5
Mulism

3.5
Other religions

if Italy were 100 people

92 would be Italian
4 would be Albanian or Eastern European
1 would be North African
3 would be from elsewhere

Refugee Gateway

Italy's contentious immigration debate heated up in 2011 as the country replaced Greece as the main EU entry point for illegal immigrants. According to Frontex, the EU borders agency, 32,906 migrants reached Italian shores in the first quarter of 2011, mostly Tunisians and Libyans escaping political upheaval. Of these, two-thirds landed on Lampedusa, a tiny island wedged between Sicily and Tunisia.

Italy's decision to grant temporary residency permits to 30,000 of these refugees caused consternation among several EU nations, which accused Italy of trying to fob off its illegal immigrants to other Schengen Treaty countries by granting them access. On 17 April 2011, the issue escalated when France temporarily closed its border with Italy to prevent a trainload of immigrants from entering French territory.

In Italy, the issue of immigration has often been reported in the context of racial tension, occasional hate crimes or the exploitation of illegal workers on the black market. In January 2010 an air-rifle attack on African farm-workers in Rosarno, Calabria, sparked two days of race riots in the town.

Yet not all Italians are hostile to asylum seekers. Around 40 local councils in Calabria have openly welcomed the new arrivals, including the village of Riace. With many of its own people having emigrated to the New World, Riace sees the influx as an opportunity to repopulate itself. Local workshops teach new residents anything from joinery to dressmaking, and vacant homes are refurbished to offer the refugees dignified accommodation. While many of the asylum seekers ultimately move on to bigger cities, more than 200 have made the town their permanent home, injecting hope and civic pride in a once forgotten part of the country.

SOLAR POWER

Italy is Europe's third-largest producer of solar power after Germany and Spain. The country is home to more than 85,000 photovoltaic installations, turning sunlight into power at a current total capacity of around 1350MW.

Top Books

The Italians (Luigi Barzini) A revealing look at Italian culture beyond the well-worn clichés
Christ Stopped at Eboli (Carlo Levi) Bittersweet recollections from a writer exiled by Fascists to a mountain village in Basilicata

Midnight in Sicily (Peter Robb) A disturbing yet fascinating portrait of postwar Sicily
The Silent Duchess (Dacia Maraini) A feminist-flavoured historical novel set in 18th-century Palermo

Southern Playlist

Sensi e controsensi (Mia Martini; 1975)
Vai mò (Pino Daniele; 1981)
Lontano (Sud Sound System; 2003)
La banda (Banda Città Ruvo di Puglia; 1996)

History

Italy's south is frequently dismissed by refined and affluent northerners as the land of *terroni* (peasants) – the backward, static sibling to Italy's culturally savvy north. Yet the south is terribly ancient. Its history can be traced back some 8000 years; writer Carlo Levi, exiled here, sensed its dark and enduring paganism, calling it 'that other world... which no-one may enter without a magic key'. Magical it may be, but there has been plenty to regret – invasions and conquests, feudalism and lawlessness, and a scourge of malaria that lasted centuries and effectively stunted the economic and cultural development of the south. Venture into these parts and you'll learn a lot about Italy's history that will challenge your comfortable preconceptions of just what the modern country is all about.

For Archae-ological Treasure

» Museo Archeo-logico Nazionale, Naples

» Museo Archeo-logico dei Campi Flegrei, Naples

» Museo Archeo-logico Paolo Orsi, Syracuse

» Museo Archeo-logico, Agrigento

» Museo Archeo-logico Eoliano, Lipari, Aeolian Islands

The Early Years

Italy's south has been busy for a very long time. The first inhabitant we know of is the man of Altamura who's currently wedged in the karst cave of Lamalunga, Puglia, slowly becoming part of the crystal concretions that surround him. He's about 130,000 years old.

Fast forward to around 7000 BC, when the Messapians, an Illyrian-speaking people from the Balkans, were settling down in the Salento and around Foggia. Alongside them, other long-gone tribes such as the Daunii in the Gargano, the Peucetians around Taranto and the Lucanians in Basilicata were starting to develop the first settled towns – by 1700 BC there is evidence that they were beginning to trade with the Mycenaeans from mainland Greece and the Minoans in Crete.

The first evidence of an organised settlement on Sicily belongs to the Stentillenians, who came from the Middle East and settled on the island's eastern shores sometime between 4000 and 3000 BC. But it was the settlers from the middle of the second millennium BC who radically defined the island's character and whose early presence helps us under-

TIMELINE	c 200,000–9000 BC	3000–1000 BC	750–600 BC
	As long ago as 700,000 BC, Paleolithic humans like the 'man of Altamura' lived precarious lives in caves. Painted caves like the Grotta dei Cervi bear testimony to this period.	The Bronze Age reaches Italy courtesy of the Mycenaeans of Eastern Europe. The use of copper and bronze marks a leap in sophistication, accompanied by a more complex social organisation.	The Greeks begin establishing cities all over southern Italy and Sicily, including Naxos and Syracuse in Sicily, and Cumae, Sybaris, Croton, Metaponto, Eraklea and Taras in southern Italy.

stand Sicily's complexities. Thucydides (c 460–404 BC) records three major tribes: the Sicanians, who originated either in Spain or North Africa and settled in the north and west (giving these areas their Eastern flavour); the Elymians from Greece, who settled in the south; and the Siculians (or Sikels), who came from the Calabrian peninsula and spread out along the Ionian Coast.

Magna Graecia

Many say the only true civilisation of southern Italy was that of the Greeks, who founded a string of settlements along the Ionian and Tyrrhenian coasts in the 8th century BC. But that does a disservice to the local tribes of Puglia and Basilicata (the Messapians, Peucetians, Daunii and Lucanians), as well as to the Phoenicians, who had settled on the western side of Sicily in around 850 BC.

Nevertheless, the Greeks got all the good press. Following the earlier lead of the Elymians, the Chalcidians landed on Sicily's Ionian Coast in 735 BC and founded a small settlement at Naxos. They were followed a year later by the Corinthians, who built their colony on the southeastern island of Ortygia, calling it Syracoussai (Syracuse). The Chalcidians went further south from their own fort and founded a second town called Katane (Catania) in 729 BC, and the two carried on stitching towns and settlements together until three-quarters of the island was in Hellenic hands.

On the mainland, the Greeks' major city was Taras, which dominated the growing region now known as Magna Graecia (Greater Greece). They exploited its harbour well, trading with Greece, the Near East and the rich colonies in Sicily and so built up a substantial network of commerce. Their lucrative business in luxury goods soon made them rich and powerful and by the 4th century BC, the population had swelled to 300,000 and city life was cultured and civilised.

Although few monuments survive, among them the ambitious temples of Paestum in Campania and Selinunte in Sicily, the Greek era was a true golden age for the south. Art and sculpture, poetry, drama and philosophy, mathematics and science were all part of the cultural life of Magna Graecia's cities. Exiled from Crotone (Calabria), Pythagoras spent years in Metapontum and Taras; Empedocles, Zeno and Stesichorus were all home-grown talents.

But despite their shared Greekness, these city-state's deeply ingrained rivalries and parochial politics undermined their civic achievements, ultimately leading to damaging conflicts like the Peloponnesian War (431–399 BC), fought by the Athenians against the Peloponnesian League (led by Sparta). Although Syracuse fought successfully against the attacking Athenian forces, the rest of Sicily was in a constant state

---

For Graeco-Roman Awe

» Pompeii & Herculaneum, Campania

» Paestum, Campania

» Anfiteatro Flavio, Pozzuoli, Campania

» Segesta, Sicily

» Valley of the Temples, Agrigento, Sicily

Get to grips with the history, peoples and wars of Ancient Greece by logging on to www.ancient greece.com, which gives easy potted histories of all the key characters and places. It also has an online bookstore.

264–146 BC	280 BC–109	79
The Punic Wars rage between the Romans and the Carthaginians. In 216 BC Hannibal inflicts defeat on the Romans at Cannae, but the Romans go on to ultimately defeat the Carthaginians in 146 BC.	The Romans build the Via Appia and then the Via Appia Traiana. The Via Appia Traiana covered 540km and enabled travellers to journey from Rome to Brindisi in 14 days.	Mt Vesuvius showers molten rock and ash upon Pompeii and Herculaneum. Pliny the Younger later describes the eruption in letters; the towns are only rediscovered in the 18th century.

» Cast of a Pompeii victim

of civil war. In 409 BC this provided the perfect opportunity for the powerful city-state of Carthage (in modern-day Tunisia) to seek revenge for its humiliation in 480 BC, in which Carthaginian mercenaries, commanded by Hamilcar, were defeated by the crafty Greek tyrant Gelon. Led by Hamilcar's bitter but brilliant nephew Hannibal, the Carthaginians wreaked havoc in the Sicilian countryside, completely destroying Selinunte, Himera, Agrigento and Gela. The Syracusans were eventually forced to surrender everything except the city of Syracuse itself to Carthage.

During the 4th century, the mainland's Greek colonies were to come under increasing pressure from other powers with expansionist ambitions. The Etruscans began to move south towards the major port of Cumae in Campania and then the Samnites and Sabines started to capture the highlands of the Appenines in Basilicata. Unable to unite and beat off the growing threat, the Greeks had little choice but to make a Faustian pact with the Romans, long-standing admirers of the Greeks and seemingly the perfect allies. It was a partnership that was to cost them dearly; by 270 BC the whole of southern Italy was under Roman control.

Eastern Influences

Roman control of southern Italy was to set the tone for centuries to come. While they turned the Bay of Naples into a holiday hot spot for emperors, and built the Via Appia (280–264 BC) and later the Via Appia Traiana (109) – the first superhighway to the south from Rome – the Romans also stripped the southern landscape of its trees, creating just the right conditions for the malarial scourge that the region would face centuries hence. Then they parcelled up the land into huge estates (*latifondi*) that they distributed among a handful of wealthy Romans, who established a damaging agricultural mono-culture of wheat to feed the Roman army. Local peasants, meanwhile, were denied even the most basic rights of citizenship.

Despite the Romans' attempts at Latinising the region, this period actually had the effect of reinforcing Eastern influences on the south. As it was, the Romans admired and emulated Greek culture, the locals in cities like Neapolis (modern-day Naples) continued to speak Greek, and the Via Appia made Puglia the gateway to the East. In 245 when Diocletian came to power, he determined that the empire was simply too vast for good governance and split it in two. When Constantine came to power in 306, the groundwork was already established for an Eastern (Byzantine) Empire and a Western Empire – in 324 he officially declared Constantinople the capital of Nova Roma.

Situated between the Aegean and Black Sea, Constantinople was a Greek settlement; Constantine himself spoke fluent Greek. He was also

It is commonly said that there is less Italian blood running through modern Sicilian veins than there is Phoenician, Greek, Arabic, Norman, Spanish or French.

Edward Gibbon's *History of the Decline and Fall of the Roman Empire* is the acknowledged classic work on the subject of the empire's darker days. Try the abridged single-volume version.

300–337	476	827–965	1059
After a series of false starts, the Roman Empire is divided into an Eastern and Western half just east of Rome. In 330 Constantine moves the imperial capital to Byzantium and refounds it as Constantinople.	The last western Emperor, Romulus Augustulus, is deposed. Goths, Ostrogoths and Byzantines tussle over the spoils of the empire.	A Saracen army lands at Mazaradel Vallo in Sicily in 827. The island is united under Arab rule and Palermo becomes the second-largest city in the world after Constantinople.	Pope Nicholas II and Norman mercenary Robert Guiscard sign a concordat at Melfi, making Robert duke of Apulia and Calabria. Robert agrees to rid southern Italy of Saracens and Byzantines.

Bribes? *Bunga bunga* parties? Spare a thought for the ancient Romans, who suffered their fair share of eccentric leaders. We salute some of the empire's wackiest, most ruthless and downright kinkiest rulers.

Tiberius (ruled 14–37) With a steady governing hand but prone to depression, Tiberius had a difficult relationship with the Senate and withdrew in his later years to Capri, where, they say, he devoted himself to drinking, orgies and fits of paranoia.

Gaius (Caligula; ruled 37–41) 'Little Shoes' made grand-uncle Tiberius look tame. Sex, including with his sisters, and gratuitous, cruel violence were high on his agenda. He emptied the state's coffers and suggested making a horse consul before being assassinated.

Nero (ruled 54–68) Augustus' last descendant, Nero had his pushy stage mother murdered, his first wife's veins slashed, his second wife kicked to death, and his third wife's ex-husband killed. The people accused him of playing the fiddle while Rome burned to the ground in 64.

Diocletian (ruled 284–305) Dalmatian-born Diocletian had little time for the growing cult of Christianity. He ordered the burning of churches and sacred scriptures, and had Christians thrown to wild beasts in a grisly public spectacle. One of them was Naples' patron saint, San Gennaro, slaughtered in Pozzuoli's Anfiteatro Flavio.

the first emperor to legislate against the persecution of the Christians. Even today, Constantine is revered as a saint in the Eastern Orthodox Church. 'Greekness' though, it seems, was not a thing of the past at all. With southern Italy's proximity to the Balkans and the Near East, Puglia and Basilicata were exposed to a new wave of Eastern influence, bringing with it a brand-new set of Christian beliefs. This new wave of influence would officially reach Sicily in 535, when the Byzantine general Belisarius landed an army on the island's shores. Despite falling to the Visigoths in AD 470 after more than 700 years of Roman occupation, the island's population was still largely Greek, both in language and custom. The Byzantines were eager to use Sicily as a launching pad for the retaking of the lands owned by the combined forces of Arabs, Berbers and Spanish Muslims, collectively known as the Saracens, but their dreams were not to be realised.

In AD 827 the Saracen army landed at Mazara del Vallo, in Sicily. Palermo fell in 831, followed by Syracuse in 878. Under them, churches were converted to mosques and Arabic was implemented as the common language. At the same time, much-needed land reforms were introduced and trade, agriculture and mining were fostered. New crops were introduced, including citrus trees, date palms and sugar cane, and a system of

Messages could be shot around the Roman Empire in days or weeks. At wayside inns, despatch riders would have a bite and change mounts. The Romans even devised a type of odometer, a cogwheel that engaged with the wheel of a chariot or other vehicle.

1130	1215	1224	1270–1500
Norman invader Roger II is crowned king of Sicily, a century after the Normans landed in southern Italy; a united southern Italian kingdom is created.	Frederick II is crowned Holy Roman Emperor in Aachen where he symbolically re-inters Charlemagne's body in a silver and gold reliquary. He takes the cross and vows of a crusader.	The Università degli Studi di Napoli Federico II is founded in Naples. The oldest state university in the world, its alumni include Catholic theologian and philosopher Thomas Aquinas.	The French Angevins and Spanish Aragonese spend the best part of two centuries fighting over southern Italy. Instability, warfare, the Black Death and overtaxation strangle the region's economic development.

water supply and irrigation was developed. Palermo was chosen as the capital of the new emirate and, over the next 200 years, it became one of the most splendid cities in the Arab world, a haven of culture and commerce rivalled only by Córdoba in Spain.

Pilgrims & Crusaders

Ever since Puglia and Basilicata's colonisation by the Greeks, multifarious myths had established themselves in the region – many were related to the presence of therapeutic waters and the practice called *incubatio,* a rite whereby one had to sleep close to a holy place to receive revelations from a deity. In its early days, the cult of the Archangel Michael was mainly a cult of healing forces based on the saint's revelations. It started to gain currency in the early 5th century but it wasn't until the arrival of the Lombards in the 7th century that it really began to take off.

Kingdom of the Sun is John Julius Norwich's wonderful romp through the Norman invasions of the south, leading to their spectacular takeover of Sicily.

Sweeping down from the north, the Lombards found in St Michael a mirror image of their own pagan deity, Wodan. In Michael, they saw similar characteristics: the image of a medieval warrior, a leader of celestial armies. There is little doubt that their devotion to the saint was instrumental in their easy conversion to Catholicism, as they repeatedly restored and enlarged the Monte Sant'Angelo shrine, making it the most important centre of the cult in the western world.

Soon the trail of pilgrims along the Via Traiana became so great that the road was nicknamed the Via Sacra Langobardorum (Holy Road of the Lombards), and dozens of churches, hostels and monasteries were built to accommodate the pilgrims along the way. Medieval graffiti in Greek, Latin, Hebrew, Saxon and German illustrates the unrelenting devotion paid to the site. The earliest of these inscriptions dates back to the 6th century, while the rarest are written in the ancient Runic alphabet by Anglo-Saxon pilgrims.

For Arab-Norman Flavour

» Cappella Palatina, Palazzo dei Normanni, Palermo

» Chiesa Capitolare di San Cataldo, Palermo

» Cattedral, Palermo

» Duomo, Cefalù

Another group of pilgrims in this region were the Normans. A French tribe, they arrived in southern Italy in the 10th century, initially en route from Jerusalem, and later as mercenaries attracted by the money to be made fighting for the rival principalities and against the Muslim Saracens in Sicily. By 1053, after six years of mercenary activity, Robert Guiscard (c 1015–85), the Norman conquistador, had comprehensively defeated the combined forces of the Calabrian Byzantines, the Lombards and the papal forces at the Battle of Civitate. Having established his supremacy, Robert turned his attentions to expanding the territories under his control. To achieve this, he had to negotiate with the Vatican. In return for being invested with the titles of duke of Apulia and Calabria in 1059, Robert agreed to chase the Saracens out of Sicily and restore Christianity to the island. He delegated this task – and promised the island – to his younger brother Roger I (1031–1101), who

1516	1600	1647	1714
Holy Roman Emperor Charles V of Spain inherits southern Italy. The region is strategically important to Spain in its battle with France. Charles invests in defences in cities like Lecce.	Naples is Europe's biggest city, boasting a population of over 300,000. Among its growing number of residents is renegade artist Caravaggio, who arrives in 1606.	Gross mismanagement causes the southern Italian economy to collapse. In Naples, the Masaniello Revolt breaks out over heavy taxes. Revolt spreads to the provinces and peasant militias rule the countryside.	The end of the War of the Spanish Succession forces the withdrawal of Spanish forces from Lombardy. The Spanish Bourbon family establishes an independent Kingdom of the Two Sicilies.

In the late 10th century, Norman fighters began to earn a reputation across Europe as fierce and tough mercenaries. As inheritance customs left younger sons disadvantaged, younger brothers were expected to seek their fortunes elsewhere and seek they did with remarkable success.

According to one legend, Norman involvement in southern Italy began in 1013 at the shrine of St Michael at Monte Sant'Angelo, when Latin rebel Meles, chaffing under Byzantine authority, invited the Normans to serve him as mercenaries. By 1030 what had begun as an offer of service in return for booty became a series of unusually successful attempts at wresting control from local warlords.

In the forefront of the Italian conquests were the brothers Hauteville: the eldest William 'Bras de Fer' (Iron Arm; c 1009–46), who controlled Puglia, and Robert Guiscard (the Cunning; c 1015–85), who rampaged over Calabria and southern Campania. By 1053, after six years of incessant fighting, Robert had defeated the combined forces of the Calabrian Byzantines, the Lombards and the papal forces at Civitate.

Up to this point the Normans (as mercenaries) had fought both for and against the papacy as their needs had required. But Robert's relationship with the Vatican underwent a radical transformation following the Great Schism of 1054, which resulted in a complete break between the Byzantine and Latin churches. In their turn, the popes saw in the Normans a powerful potential ally, and so in 1059 Pope Nicholas II and Robert signed a concordat at Melfi, which invested Robert with the titles of duke of Apulia (including Basilicata) and Calabria. In return Robert agreed to chase the Byzantines and Saracens out of southern Italy and Sicily and restore the southern kingdom to papal rule.

Little would the pope suspect that Roger would go on to develop a territorial monarchy and become a ruler who saw himself as detached from the higher jurisdiction of both Western and Eastern Emperor – or even the pope himself.

landed his troops at Messina in 1061, capturing the port by surprise. In 1064, Roger tried to make good on his promise and take Palermo but was repulsed by a well-organised Saracen army; it wasn't until Robert arrived in 1072 with substantial reinforcements that the city fell into Norman hands. Impressed by the island's cultured Arab lifestyle, Roger shamelessly borrowed and improved on it, spending vast amounts of money on palaces and churches and encouraging a cosmopolitan atmosphere in his court.

By 1130 most of southern Italy, including Sicily, was in Norman hands and it was only a question of time before the prosperous duchy of Naples gave in to the inevitable. It did so in 1139 – the Kingdom of the Two Sicilies was thus complete.

The Arabs introduced spaghetti to Sicily; 'strings of pasta' were documented by the Arab geographer Al-Idrissi in Palermo in 1150.

» Teatro San Carlo

1737

Naples' original Teatro San Carlo is built in a swift eight months. Designed by Giovanni Antonio Medrano, it was rebuilt in 1816 after a devastating fire.

RICHARD I'ANSON/LONELY PLANET IMAGES ©

1752

Work commences on the Palazzo Reale in Caserta, north of Naples. Commissioned by Charles VII of Bourbon and designed by Luigi Vanvitelli, the palace would outsize Versailles.

1798–99

Napoleon invades Italy and occupies Rome. Ferdinand I sends an army to evict them, but his troops flee. The French counterattack and take Naples, establishing the Parthenopean Republic.

CRUSADES

The Wonder of the World

Frederick II, king of Sicily and Holy Roman Emperor, presided over one of the most glamorous periods of southern history. The fact that he came to wield such power and wear Charlemagne's crown at all is one of those unexpected quirks of history.

He inadvertently inherited the crown of Sicily and the south from his mother Constance (the posthumous daughter of Roger I) in 1208 after William II died childless; the crown to the Holy Roman Empire came to him through his father, Henry VI, the son of Frederick Barbarossa. The union of the two crowns in 1220 meant that Frederick II would rule over lands covering Germany, Austria, the Netherlands, Poland, the Czech Republic, Slovakia, southern France, southern Italy, the rich Kingdom of Sicily and the remnants of the Byzantine world.

It was a union that caused the popes much discomfort. For while they wanted and needed an emperor who would play the role of temporal sword, Frederick's wide-reaching kingdom all but encircled the Papal States and his belief in the absolute power of monarchy gave them grave cause for concern.

Like Charlemagne before him, Frederick controlled a kingdom so vast that he could realistically dream of reviving the fallen Roman Empire; and dream he did. Under his rule, Sicily was transformed into a centralised state playing a key commercial and cultural role in European affairs and Palermo gained a reputation as the continent's most important city; most of the northern Italian city-states were brought to heel. In 1225 he went on to marry Jolanda of Brienne and gained the title of king of Jerusalem, making him the first Roman emperor to bear that title. In 1228 the Crusade he launched was not only nearly bloodless but it saw the return of the shrines of Jerusalem, Nazareth and Bethlehem to the Christian fold.

As well as being a talented statesman, he was also a cultured man, and many of his biographers see in him the precursor of the Renaissance prince. Few other medieval monarchs corresponded with the sages of Judaism and Islam; he also spoke six languages and was fascinated by science, nature and architecture. He even wrote a scholarly treatise on falconry during one of the long, boring sieges of Faenza, and Dante was right to call him the father of Italian poetry.

Yet despite his brilliance, his vision for an international empire was incompatible with the ambitions of the papacy and he struggled throughout his reign to remain on good terms with increasingly aggressive popes. Finally, in 1243, Pope Innocent IV proclaimed him deposed, characterising him as a 'friend of Babylon's sultan' and a heretic. At the same time the northern Italian provinces were straining against his

Steven Runciman's *Fall of Constantinople 1453* provides a classic account of this bloody episode in Crusading history. It manages to be academically sound and highly entertaining at the same time.

1805	1814–15	1848	1860
Napoleon is proclaimed king of the newly constituted Kingdom of Italy, comprising most of the northern half of the country. A year later, he retakes the Kingdom of Naples.	After Napoleon's fall the Congress of Vienna is held to re-establish the balance of power in Europe. The result for Italy is largely a return of the old occupying powers.	European revolts spark rebellion in Italy. The Bourbons are expelled from Sicily but retake it in a rain of fire that earns Ferdinand II the epithet 'Re Bomba' (King Bomb).	In the name of Italian unity, Giuseppe Garibaldi lands with 1000 men, the Red Shirts, in Sicily. He takes the island and lands in southern Italy.

centralised control and years of war and strategising were finally taking their toll. Only in Puglia, his favourite province throughout this reign, did Frederick remain undisputed master.

In December 1250, after suffering a bout of dysentery, he died suddenly in Castel Fiorentino near Lucera. His heirs, Conrad and Manfred, would not survive him long. Conrad died of malaria four years later in Lavello in Basilicata, and Manfred was defeated at the Battle of Benevento in 1266 by Charles of Anjou, the pope's pretender to the throne. Two years later another battle took the life of Manfred's 15-year-old nephew and heir, Conradin, who was publicly beheaded in Naples.

This outright warfare between the emperor and the papacy consolidated the damaging divide between the Ghibellines (imperial supporters) and the Guelphs (who disliked central monarchy and thus supported the church), which was to cause so much civil strife over the next few centuries of Italian politics.

By 1270 the brilliant Hohenstaufen period was officially over. And while Frederick's rule marked a major stage in the transformation of Europe from a community of Latin Christians under the headship of two competing powers (pope and emperor) to a Europe of nation states, he had failed to leave any tangible legacies. The following ruling family, the Angevins, did not make the same mistake: Naples' Castel Nuovo (built by Charles of Anjou in 1279) and Castel Sant'Elmo (constructed by Robert of Anjou in the early 14th century) remain two of the city's iconic landmarks.

For a wide-ranging general site on Italian history, check out www.arcaini.com. It covers, in potted form, everything from prehistory to the postwar period, and includes a brief chronology.

Sicily's Slide from Glory

Under the Angevins, who succeeded the German Hohenstaufens, Sicily was weighed down by onerous taxes, religious persecution was the order of the day and Norman fiefdoms were removed and awarded to French aristocrats. On Easter Monday 1282, the city of Palermo exploded in rebellion. Incited by the alleged rape of a local girl by a gang of French troops, peasants lynched every French soldier they could get their hands on. The revolt spread to the countryside and was supported by the Sicilian nobility, who had formed an alliance with Peter of Aragon. Peter had landed at Trapani with a large army and was proclaimed king. For the next 20 years, the Aragonese and the Angevins were engaged in the War of the Sicilian Vespers – a war that was eventually won by the Spanish.

By the end of the 14th century, Sicily had been thoroughly marginalised. The eastern Mediterranean was sealed off by the Ottoman Turks, while the Italian mainland was off limits on account of Sicily's political ties with Spain. As a result, the Renaissance passed the island by, reinforcing the oppressive effects of poverty and ignorance. Even Spain lost

1861	1880–1915	1889
By the end of the 1859–61 Franco-Austrian War, Vittorio Emanuele II controls Lombardy, Sardinia, Sicily, southern Italy and parts of central Italy, and is proclaimed king of a newly united Italy.	People vote with their feet; millions of impoverished southerners embark on ships for the New World, causing a massive haemorrhage of the most able-bodied and hardworking southern male youths.	Raffaele Esposito invents 'pizza margherita' in honour of Queen Margherita, who takes her first bite of the Neapolitan staple on a royal visit to the city.

» Pizza margherita

PLAGUE

interest in its colony, choosing to rule through viceroys. By the end of the 15th century, the viceroy's court was a den of corruption, and the most influential body on the island became the Catholic Church (whose archbishops and bishops were mostly Spaniards). The church exercised draconian powers through a network of Holy Office tribunals, otherwise known as the Inquisition.

Reeling under the weight of state oppression, ordinary Sicilians demanded reform. Unfortunately, their Spanish monarchs were preoccupied by the wars of the Spanish succession and Sicily was subsequently passed around for decades from European power to European power like an unwanted Christmas present. Eventually the Spanish reclaimed the island in 1734, this time under the Bourbon king Charles III of Sicily (r 1734–59).

The Bourbon Paradox

Assessment of Bourbon rule in southern Italy is a controversial topic. Many historians consider it a period of exploitation and stagnation. Others, more recently, have started to re-evaluate the Kingdom of the Two Sicilies, pointing out the raft of positive reforms Charles III implemented. These included abolishing many noble and clerical privileges, curtailing the legal rights of landowners within their fiefs and restricting ecclesiastical jurisdiction at a time when the Church was reputed to own almost a third of the land within the kingdom.

Naples had already begun prospering under the rule of Spanish viceroy Don Pedro de Toledo (1532–53), whose building boom attracted some of Italy's greatest artistic talent. Under Charles, the city became one of the great capital cities of Europe, attracting hundreds of aristocratic travellers. On top of this, Charles was a great patron of architecture and the arts. During his reign Pompeii and Herculaneum (both destroyed in the AD 79 eruption of Mt Vesuvius) were discovered and the Archaeological Museum in Naples was founded. He was responsible for the Teatro San Carlo, the largest opera house in Europe, and he built the huge palaces of Capodimonte and Caserta. Some subsequent Bourbon monarchs also made positive contributions, such as Ferdinand II (1830–59), who laid the foundations for modern industry, developing southern harbours, creating a merchant fleet and building the first Italian railway line and road systems, the dramatic Amalfi drive for example.

But where Charles might rightfully claim a place among southern Italy's outstanding rulers, later Bourbon princes were some of the most eccentric and pleasure-seeking monarchs in Europe. Charles' son, Ferdinand I (1751–1825), was by contrast venal and poorly educated. He spent his time hunting and fishing, and he delighted in the company of the *lazzaroni,* the Neapolitan underclass. He much preferred to leave

Between January and August 1656, the bubonic plague wiped out about half of Naples' 300,000-plus inhabitants and much of the economy. The city would take almost two centuries to reach its pre-plague headcount again.

1908	1915	1919	1922
On the morning of 28 December, Messina and Reggio di Calabria are struck by a 7.5-magnitude earthquake and a 13m-high tsunami. More than 80,000 lives are lost.	Italy enters WWI on the side of the Allies to win Italian territories still in Austrian hands after Austria's offer to cede some of the territories is deemed insufficient.	Former socialist journalist Benito Mussolini forms a right-wing militant group, the *Fasci Italiani di Combattimento* (Italian Combat Fasces), precursor to his Fascist Party.	Mussolini and his Fascists stage a march on Rome in October. Doubting the army's loyalty, a fearful King Vittorio Emanuele III entrusts Mussolini with the formation of a government.

the business of government to his wife, the ambitious and treacherous Archduchess Maria Carolina of Austria, whose main aim was to free southern Italy from Spanish influence and secure a rapprochement with Austria and Great Britain. Her chosen administrator was the English expatriate Sir John Acton, who replaced the long-serving Tanucci, a move that was to mire court politics in damaging corruption and espionage.

When the French Revolution broke out in 1789, Maria Carolina was initially sympathetic to the movement, but when her sister Marie Antoinette was beheaded, she became fanatically Francophobe. The following French invasion of Italy in 1799, and the crowning of Napoleon as king in 1800, jolted the south out of its Bourbon slumbers. Although Napoleonic rule was to last only 14 years, this brief flirtation with republicanism was to awaken hopes of an independent Italian nation. Returning to his beloved Naples in 1815, Ferdinand, who was once so at ease with his subjects, was now terrified of popular revolution and became determined to exert his absolute authority. Changes that had been made by the Bonapartist regime were reversed, causing widespread discontent. Revolutionary agitators sprang up everywhere, and the countryside, now full of discharged soldiers, became more lawless than ever.

Try as they might, there was no putting the genii back in the box. The heavy-handed tactics of Ferdinand II only exacerbated the situation and in 1848, Sicily experienced a violent revolt which saw the expulsion of the Bourbons from the island. Although the revolt was crushed, Ferdinand's response was so heavy-handed that he earnt himself the nickname 'Re Bomba' (King Bomb) after his army mercilessly shelled Messina. From such a promising beginning, the last decades of Bourbon rule were so oppressive that they were almost universally hated throughout liberal Europe. The seeds had well and truly been sown for the Risorgimento (Resurgence), which would finally see the whole peninsula united into a modern nation state.

History of the Italian People, by Giuliano Procacci, is one of the best general histories of the country in any language. It covers the period from the early Middle Ages until 1948.

The Kingdom of Death

Although not commonly acknowledged, the widespread presence of malaria in the Italian peninsula during the 19th and 20th centuries is one of the most significant factors in the social and economic development (or lack of it) of the modern country. An endemic as well as an epidemic disease, it was so enmeshed in Italian rural society that it was widely regarded as the Italian national disease. Even the word itself, malaria, comes from the Italian *mal aria* (bad air), as it was originally thought that the disease was caused by a poisoning of the air as wet earth dried out during the heat of summer.

1927	1934	1940	1943
A study released by the Italian government puts the number of Italian citizens living abroad at around 9.2 million. Southern Italians make up over 60% of the Italian diaspora.	Screen siren Sophia Loren is born, and spends her childhood living in Pozzuoli and Naples. Her break would come in 1951, as an extra in Mervyn LeRoy's film *Quo Vadis*.	Italy enters WWII on Nazi Germany's side and invades Greece in October. Greek forces counterattack and enter southern Albania. Germany saves Italy in March-April 1941 by overrunning Yugoslavia and Greece.	King Vittorio Emanuele III sacks Mussolini. He is replaced by Marshall Badoglio, who surrenders after Allied landings in southern Italy. German forces free Mussolini.

The scale of the problem came to light in the decades following Italian unification in 1861. Out of 69 provinces only two were found to be free of malaria; and in a population of 25 million people, at least 11 million were permanently at risk of the disease. Most famously, Giuseppe Garibaldi, one of the founding fathers of modern Italy, lost both his wife, Anita, and a large number of troops to the disease. Thus stricken, Garibaldi urged the newly united nation to place the fight against malaria high on its list of priorities.

In the dawning era of global competition, Italian farming was dangerously backward. As a predominantly grain-producing economy, it was tragically ironic that all of Italy's most fertile land was in precisely the zones – coastal plains and river valleys – where malaria was most intense. To survive, farm workers had to expose themselves to the disease. Unfortunately, disease in turn entailed suffering, days of absence and low productivity.

Between 1944 and 1946 the German Wehrmacht systematically sabotaged the pumping systems that drained Italy's marshes and confiscated quinine from the Department of Health. The ensuing malaria epidemic was one of the worst the country has ever seen and is one of the great unacknowledged war crimes of WWII.

More significantly, although malaria ravaged the whole peninsula, it was pre-eminently an affliction of the south, as well as the provinces of Rome and Grosseto in the centre. Of all the provinces, six were especially afflicted – Abruzzi, Basilicata, Calabria, Lazio, Puglia and Sardinia – earning the south the lugubrious epithet 'the kingdom of death'. Furthermore, Giovanni Battista Grassi (the man who discovered that mosquitos transmit malaria) estimated that the danger of infection in the south was 10 times greater than in northern Italy.

No issue illustrates the divide between the north and south of the country quite so vividly as the malaria crisis. The World Health Organisation defines malaria in the modern world as a disease of poverty that distorts and 'slows a country's economic growth'. In the case of the Italian south, malaria was a significant factor in the underdevelopment of the region at a critical time in its history. Malarial fever thrives on exploitative working conditions, substandard housing and diet, illiteracy, war and ecological degradation, and Italy's south had certainly had its fair share by the early 20th century. As late as 1918, the Ministry of Agriculture reported that 'malaria is the key to all the economic problems of the South'. Against this background of regional inequality, the fever became an important metaphor deployed by *meridionalisti* (southern spokesmen) such as Giustino Fortunato (1848-1932) and Francesco Nitti (1868-1953) to describe the plight of the south and to demand redress. Nitti attributed the entirety of southern backwardness to this single factor.

Between 1900 and 1907, the Italian parliament passed a series of laws establishing a national campaign – the first of its kind in the world – to eradicate or at least control the disease. But it was to take the best part of half a century to bring malaria under control, as two world wars and the Fascist seizure of power in 1922 were to overwhelm domestic policies,

1944	1946	1950	1950s–60s
Mt Vesuvius explodes back into action on 18 March. The eruption is captured on film by United States Army Air Forces personnel stationed nearby.	Italians vote in a national referendum in June to abolish the monarchy (by about 12.7 million votes to 10.7 million) and create a republic. The south is the only region to vote against the republic.	The *Cassa per il Mezzogiorno* is established to help fund public works and infrastructure in the south. Poor management and corruption sees at least one third of the money squandered.	Soaring unemployment causes another mass migration of about two million people from the south to the factories of northern Italy, Europe and Australia.

HISTORY ON SCREEN

» *Il Gattopardo* (The Leopard; Luchino Visconti; 1963) A Sicilian aristocrat grapples with the political and social changes heralded by the 19th century Risorgimento (reunification period).

» *Le quattro giornate di Napoli* (The Four Days of Naples; Nanni Loy; 1962) Neapolitan courage shines through in this film about the famous popular uprisings against the Nazis in September 1943.

» *Il resto di niente* (The Remains of Nothing; Antonietta De Lillo; 2003) Eleonora Pimental de Fonesca, heroine of the ill-fated Neapolitan revolution of 1799, is the protagonist in this tale.

» *Salvatore Giuliano* (Francesco Rosi; 1963) A neorealist classic about the murder of Sicily's very own modern Robin Hood.

causing the program to stall and then collapse entirely amid military defeat and occupation.

Final victory against the disease was only achieved following the end of WWII, when the government was able to re-establish public-health infrastructures and implement a five-year plan which included the use of a new pesticide, DDT, to eradicate malaria. The designation of 'malarial zone' was only officially lifted from the entire peninsula in 1969.

Denis Mack Smith, the most prominent English-language historian of modern Italy, argued that the eradication of malaria was the most significant fact in modern Italian history. This is because the antimalarial campaign had lasting impacts beyond just the elimination of the disease. From the outset, the antimalarial warriors recognised that education and civil rights have great effects on health. The campaign also played a major role in the promotion of women's rights, the labour movement and the achievement of universal literacy; additionally, it made a major contribution towards awakening a consciousness of southern conditions and towards mobilising opinion to redress southern grievances.

The Southern Question

The unification of Italy meant sudden and dramatic changes for all the southern provinces. The huge upsurge in *brigantaggio* (banditry) and social unrest throughout the last decades of the 19th century was caused by widespread disillusionment about the unification project. It does have to be said that it was never Cavour's intention to unify the whole country, and even later during his premiership, he favoured an expanded Piedmont rather than a unified Italy.

The Nazis took Naples in 1943, but were quickly forced out during the *quattro giornate di Napoli* (four days of Naples), a series of popular uprisings between 26 and 30 September. These paved the way for the Allies to enter the city on 1 October.

1980	1999	2003	2003
At 7.34pm on 25 November, a 6.8 Richter scale earthquake strikes Campania. The quake kills almost 3000 people and causes widespread damage; the city of Naples also suffers damage.	Brindisi becomes a strategic base for the Office of the UN and the World Food Organisation. The disused military airport's hangars are converted into storage space for humanitarian aid.	Sicilian mafioso Salvatore 'Totò' Riina is arrested in Palermo. Nicknamed 'The Beast', the 'boss of bosses' had ordered the bombing death of antimafia magistrates Giovanni Falcone and Paolo Borsellino.	The Campania government launches Progetto Vesuvia in an attempt to clear Mt Vesuvius' heavily populated lower slopes. The €30,000 offered to relocate is rejected by most in the danger zone.

For southerners, it was difficult to see the benefits of being part of this new nation state. Naples was stripped of its capital-city status (a heavy cultural and political blow); the new government carried away huge cash reserves from the rich southern Italian banks; taxes went up and factories closed as new tariff policies, dictated by northern interests, caused a steep decline in the southern economy. Culturally, southerners were also made to feel inferior; to be southern or 'Bourbon' was to be backward, vulgar and uncivilised. From holding centre stage alongside cities like London, Paris and Vienna, the south was dramatically relegated to the political third division.

After WWI the south fared a little better, experiencing slow progress in terms of infrastructure projects like the construction of the Puglian aqueduct, the extension of the railways and the improvement of civic centres like Bari and Taranto. But Mussolini's 'Battle for Wheat' – the drive to make Italy self-sufficient in food – compounded many of the southern problems. It destroyed even more valuable pastureland by turning it over to the monoculture of wheat, while reinforcing the parlous state of the southern peasantry, who remained uneducated, disenfranchised, landless and at high risk of malaria. To escape such a hopeless future, many of them packed their bags and migrated to North America, northern Europe and Australia, starting a trend that was to become one of the main features of post-WWII Italy.

In the 1946 referendum that established the Italian Republic, the south was the only region to vote no. In Naples, 80% voted to keep the monarchy. Still, change moved on apace. After the wreckage of WWII was cleared – especially that caused by Allied air raids in Sicily and Naples – the *Cassa per il Mezzogiorno* reconstruction fund was established in order to bring the south into the 20th century with massive, cheap housing schemes and big industrial projects like the steel plant in Taranto and the Fiat factory in Basilicata. However, the disappearance of large amounts of cash eventually led the central government to scrap the fund in 1992.

In the same year, the huge *Tangentopoli* (Bribesville) scandal (the institutionalisation of kickbacks and bribes, which had been the country's modus operandi since WWII) made headline news. Although it was largely focused on the industrial north of Italy, the repercussions of the widespread investigation into graft (known as *Mani Pulite*, or Clean Hands) were inevitably felt in southern regions like Sicily and Campania, where politics, business and organised crime (see p230) were long-time bedfellows.

Denis Mack Smith produced one of the most penetrating works on Italy's dictator with his *Mussolini*. Along with Mussolini's career it assesses his impact on the greater evil of the time, Hitler.

The exodus of southern Italians to North and South America between 1880 and WWI is one of the great mass movements of a population in modern times. By 1927, 20% of the Italian population had emigrated.

2004–05	2005	2010	2010
Tension between rival Camorra clans explodes on the streets of suburban Naples. In only four months, almost 50 people are gunned down in retribution attacks.	Nichi Vendola, representing the Communist Refoundation Party, is elected president of Puglia. He is the first gay communist to be elected president of a southern Italian region.	Local youths in Rosarno, Calabria, shoot air rifles at African migrants returning from work in January. Around 2000 migrants subsequently clash with locals in two days of violent rioting.	In July Italian police mount one of the biggest swoops on Calabria's 'Ndrangheta mafia, arresting 300 members and seizing assets worth millions of euros. The Italian senate applauds the arrests.

Something in the Air

Despite the ongoing burden of high unemployment and corruption, the winds of change are blowing throughout southern Italy. The 2005 election of openly gay environmentalist Nichi Vendola as Puglia's president shook the region's conservative reputation. The first Communist Refoundation Party member to ever be elected as president of an Italian region, he was re-elected as president in 2010, but this time as leader of the fledgling Left Ecology Party.

In May 2011 Naples served Silvio Berlusconi's centre-right coalition a major blow by voting in the young, centrist Luigi de Magistris as its mayor. To many Neapolitans, de Magistris' background as an anti-Mafia prosecutor offers hope in a city plagued by Camorra-related crime. The so-called 'Scampia feud' of late 2004 and early 2005 – a deadly turf battle fought out by rival Camorra clans – saw up to 47 people gunned down on Neapolitan streets in four months alone. In 2008 a Camorra death squad gunned down seven men in Castel Volturno, northwest of Naples. That six of the dead were West African migrants was read as a warning to Nigerian criminal clans muscling in on the city's lucrative drugs market.

Locals also hope that de Magistris' will resolve Naples' rubbish crisis (see p208) as promised. While only time will tell, his election has at least stirred a rare sense of civic responsibility. In June 2011, 50 volunteers joined forces to clean up the city's showcase, Piazza del Plebiscito. The following weekend, a Facebook group called Cleanap organised a guerrilla gardening session in Piazza Bellini. Adding to the fledgling optimism is Naples' upcoming role as the host of Unesco's 2013 Universal Forum of Cultures.

Although much has happened since it was written, Paul Ginsborg's *A History of Contemporary Italy: Society and Politics 1943-1988* remains one of the single most readable and insightful books on postwar Italy.

HISTORY SOMETHING IN THE AIR

2011	2011	2011	2013
Thousands of boat people fleeing the revolutionary chaos in northern Africa land on the island of Lampedusa. Italy grants 30,000 refugees temporary visas, creating tension with France.	In May Silvio Berlusconi's centre-right coalition loses control of Naples and Milan in local elections, with Neapolitans voting in former public prosecutor Luigi de Magistris as their new mayor.	Best-selling Neapolitan author Roberto Saviano wins the PEN/Pinter International writer of courage award for his mafia exposé *Gomorra*. Saviano is unable to collect the prize in person for security reasons.	Naples plays host to the 4th Universal Forum of Cultures. The 101-day event sees further rejuvenation of the industrial Coroglio area between Naples and Pozzuoli.

The Southern Way of Life

Through Southern Eyes

Meet Alessio – a 30-something Sicilian expat. Born into a close-knit family near Catania, he studied physics in Florence before moving to Bonn to complete a PhD in astrophysics...and to start a career as a culinary consultant. Every Easter and Christmas, he makes the 2276km journey back home to catch up with family and friends, and to sink his teeth into a steaming *arancino* (a deep-fried, stuffed rice ball; his favourite homeland snack). Alessio's story is not unusual in a part of Italy so bittersweetly defined by emigration, nostalgia and tradition. Alessio muses: 'A deep part of my personality and feelings are based in the south. Even though I am happy and grateful for what I have obtained abroad, I often feel homesick. The bucolic life spent enjoying the sun with family and friends, eating, drinking and singing, Sicilian hills in the background, is an image that haunts me. I think this is true for many expats.'

Perhaps more uniquely southern is the love/hate dynamic underlying this relationship. As Alessio explains: 'In Germany, there's a sense of personal civic responsibility. In southern Italy, suspicion of strangers has stifled this collective feeling from developing.' The other obstacle is a stubborn sense of personal pride and vanity. 'Too often in the south, doing something that's civic minded – like picking rubbish off the street or not using your car to help reduce pollution – leave you open to mockery from others, who see your action as a sign of weakness.' There is genuine regret in Alessio's voice: 'It's frustrating to think that a society so rich in culture and traditions, so warm-hearted, could do much more for itself if it only learned to trust and cooperate.'

Yet, things are changing. Both the internet and travel are helping to shape a generation more aware of, and open to, foreign ideas. Online communities are allowing people once socially or ideologically isolated to connect with others, to share experiences and develop new ways of tackling old problems. Alessio is hopeful: 'Words like "integration" and "openness" are becoming more meaningful in the south. Slowly, people are becoming more aware of the common ground they share. With this awareness, we can hopefully build a brighter, collectively minded future.'

Dreams & Diasporas

Emigration to Immigration

Alessio's move abroad echoes that of millions of *meridionali* (southern Italians). Severe economic problems in the south following Italy's unification and after each of the world wars led to massive emigration as people searched for a better life in northern Italy, northern Europe,

A one-man 'Abbott & Costello', Antonio de Curtis (1898–1967), aka Totò, famously depicted the Neapolitan *furbizia* (cunning). Appearing in over 100 films, including *Miseria e Nobiltà* (Misery & Nobility; 1954), his roles as a hustler living on nothing but his quick wits would guarantee him cult status in Naples.

North and South America, and Australia. Between 1880 and 1910, over 1.5 million Sicilians alone left for the US, and in 1900 the island was the world's main area of emigration. In Campania, a staggering 2.7 million people left the motherland between 1876 and 1976.

Today, huge numbers of young southerners – often the most educated – continue to move abroad. This brain-drain epidemic is fuelled by a scandalously high youth unemployment rate – 29.4% in early 2011. Adding insult to injury is Italy's entrenched system of patronage and nepotism, which commonly makes landing a job more about who you know than what you know. According to Alessio, the standard of education available is another contributing factor: 'There's a common belief that southern universities aren't the best, so parents who can afford it send their kids north or overseas to complete their studies. Some return after completing their master's degree but many get accustomed to the freedom and opportunities found in the bigger cities and tend to stay.'

Yet, southern Italy has itself become a destination for people searching for a better life. Political and economic upheavals in the 1980s brought new arrivals from central Europe, Latin America and North Africa, including Italy's former colonies in Tunisia, Somalia and Ethiopia. More recently, waves of Chinese, Filipino and Sri Lankan immigrants have given Italian streetscapes an Asian twist.

While immigrants account for just 7.1% of Italy's population today, the number is growing. From a purely economic angle, these new arrivals are vital for the country's economic health. Without immigrant workers

Today, people of Italian origin account for more than 40% of the population in Argentina and Uruguay, more than 10% in Brazil, more than 5% in Switzerland and the US, and more than 4% in Australia, Venezuela and Canada.

THE SOUTHERN WAY OF LIFE DREAMS & DIASPORAS

LIFE IN A SOUTHERN TOWN

It's just 4.30am and the first of the town's bars open for farmers and insomniacs. The barman serves his first *caffé* of the day. He likes his job, but earns a modest €800 per month. He's hoping for funding from Sviluppo Italia (Develop Italy), the government development agency for the south, to launch a business selling beauty products.

By 8am the barber's bicycle is outside his shop. He'll stay open until 11am – he's past retirement age but keeps the shop going. He'd like to talk but he hasn't time today; he's going to see his son in the north.

At 9am the main road is blocked with cars. Locals are commuting from one end of the town to the other. Youths with big sunglasses and high-maintenance hair (and that's just the men) pop into the bar for a cappuccino before heading to the beach.

At 9.15am a car drives slowly around the streets, making its recorded announcement through a rooftop megaphone, 'blade sharpening, kitchen gas repairs'. There's a queue at the shop selling mozzarella (the *burrata* – cheese made from mozzarella and cream – sells out quickly). In fields outside the town, brightly dressed workers – all women – are toiling, picking tomatoes.

An Albanian woman hurries on her way to the shops. She's looking after an elderly resident in his museumlike home. The €500 she earns each month goes further at home, but it's lonely work.

At 11am the church bell tolls in remembrance for a local gentleman. His death is announced, like the others in town, by black-bordered notices plastered around the town centre.

At 1pm shopkeepers shut for lunch. The main street is deserted. Houses are shuttered. Lunch is sacred.

The town begins to stir at 5pm. Shops reopen and *nonni* (grandfathers) pedal slowly down the main street. The sun has moved, so they transfer their allegiance to the bar on the opposite side of the street.

As evening settles, dressed-up denizens hit the seafront for their ritual *passeggiata* (evening stroll), bumping into friends and relatives, checking out the talent and stopping for gelato. After midnight, the town settles in for the night... *Buona notte.*

to fill the gaps left in the labour market by pickier locals, Italy would be sorely lacking in tomato sauce and shoes. From hotel maids on the Amalfi Coast to fruit pickers on Calabrian farms, it is often immigrants who take the low-paid service jobs that keep Italy's economy afloat. Unfortunately, their vulnerability has sometimes led to exploitation, with several reported cases of farmhands being paid below-minimum wages for back-breaking work.

The North/South Divide

In his film *Ricomincio da tre* (I'm Starting from Three; 1980), acting great Massimo Troisi comically tackles the problems faced by southern Italians forced to head north for work. Laughs aside, the film reveals Italy's very real north/south divide.

From the Industrial Revolution to the 1960s, millions of southern Italians fled to the industrialised northern cities for factory jobs. As the saying goes, *'Ogni vero Milanese ha un nonno Pugliese'* (Every true Milanese has a Pugliese grandparent). For many of these domestic migrants, the welcome north of Rome was anything but warm. Disparagingly nicknamed *terroni* (peasants), many faced discrimination on a daily basis, from everyone from landlords to baristas. While such overt discrimination is now practically nonexistent, historical prejudices linger. Many northerners resent their taxes being used to 'subsidise' the 'lazy', 'corrupt' south – a sentiment well exploited by the right-wing, Veneto-based Lega Nord (Northern League) party.

Yet negative attitudes can work both ways. Many southerners view their northern compatriots as just a little *freddi* (cold) and uptight. As Raffaella, a 30-something employee at Lecce University, comments: 'Many friends of mine are desperate to return after a few years spent in northern Italy or abroad. They find life too isolated and anonymous. People don't know their neighbours.' Her friend, Deborah, a business consultant, agrees: 'People who live in the south are different from those living in the north. Here, family and friends are important, more important than work.'

The Southern Psyche

Beautiful Family, Beautiful Image

Family is the bedrock of southern Italian life, and loyalty to family and friends is usually non-negotiable. As Luigi Barzini (1908–84), author of *The Italians,* noted, 'A happy private life helps tolerate an appalling public life.' This chasm between the private arena and the public one is a noticeable aspect of the southern mentality, and has evolved over years of intrusive foreign domination. Some locals mightn't think twice about littering their street, but step inside their home and you'll get floors clean enough to eat from. After all, you'd never want someone dropping in and thinking you're a *zingaro* (gypsy), right?

Maintaining a *bella figura* (beautiful image) is very important to the average southerner, and how you and your family appear to the outside world is a matter of honour, respectability and pride. As Alessio explains: 'In the south, you are better than your neighbour if you own more and better things. This mentality is rooted in the past, when you really did need to own lots of things to attain certain social roles, and ultimately sustain your family.' Yet *fare bella figura* (making a good impression) goes beyond a well-kept house, extending to dressing well, behaving modestly, performing religious and social duties and fulfilling all essential family obligations. In the context of the extended family, where gossip is rife, a good image protects one's privacy.

Nice work, if you can get it: about 30% of Italians have landed a job through family connections, and in highly paid professions that number rises as high as 40% to 50%.

John Turturro's film *Passione* (2010) is a *Buena Vista Social Club*–style exploration of Naples' rich and eclectic musical traditions. Spanning everything from folk songs to contemporary tunes, it offers a fascinating insight into the city's complex soul.

A Woman's Place

'In Sicily, women are more dangerous than shotguns', said Fabrizio (Angelo Infanti) in *The Godfather*. 'A woman at the window is a woman to be shunned', proclaimed the writer Giovanni Verga in the 19th century. And 'Women are too stupid to be involved in the complex world of finance', decided a judge when faced with a female Mafia suspect in the 1990s. As in many places in the Mediterranean, a woman's position in southern Italy has always been a difficult one. In the domestic sphere, a mother and wife commands the utmost respect within the home. She is considered the moral and emotional compass for her family. As Alessio reveals: 'The mother is the spine of a family, hence southern men are often called *mammoni* (mummy's boys). The mum is always the mum, an omnipresent role model and the nightmare of newly wedded wives.'

But times are also changing. According to Luca, a young Pugliese: 'It's only two generations ago that men and women were almost segregated. Women only used to go out on Saturdays, and they had separate beaches for men and women.' His father Marcello adds: 'When my father met my mother, he saw her walking along the street and tried to speak to her. Her brother said to him: "You speak to me first." When he was permitted to visit, my aunt sat between them and my grandmother was a chaperone.'

These days, more and more unmarried southern women live with their partners, especially in the cities. Improvements in educational opportunities and more liberal attitudes mean that the number of women with successful careers is growing. Italian women represent 65% of college graduates, and are more likely than men to pursue higher education (53% to 45%).

Despite this progress, true gender equality is still a long way off. According to a recent report by the Uomini Casalinghi (The Italian Association of Househusbands), 70% of Italian men have never used a stove, while 95% have never turned on a washing machine. A survey released by the Organisation for Economic Co-operation and Development (OECD) in 2010 found that Italian men enjoy almost 80 more minutes of leisure time daily than their female counterparts. In the same year, a Global Gender Gap Index published by the World Economic Forum ranked Italy 87th worldwide in terms of female labour participation, 121st in wage parity and 74th overall for its treatment of women.

MINE VAGANTI

Turkish-Italian director Ferzan Özpetek explores the clash of southern tradition and modernity in his film *Mine vaganti* (Loose Cannons; 2010), a situation comedy about two gay brothers and their conservative Pugliese family.

THE SOUTHERN WAY OF LIFE THE SOUTHERN PSYCHE

THE OLD PROVERBIAL

They might be old clichés, but proverbs can be quite the cultural revelation. Here are six of the south's well-worn best:

» *Cu si marita, sta cuntentu nu jornu, Cu' ammazza nu porcu, sta cuntentu n'annu* (Sicilian). Whoever gets married remains happy for a day, whoever butchers a pig remains happy for a year.

» *Aprili fa li ciuri e li biddizzi, l'onuri l'avi lu misi ri maju* (Sicilian). April makes the flowers and the beauty, but May gets all the credit.

» *A chi troppo s'acàla 'o culo se vede* (Neapolitan). He who kowtows too low bares his arse.

» *Cu va 'n Palermu e 'un viri Murriali, sinni parti sceccu e tonna armali* (Sicilian). Whoever goes to Palermo and doesn't see Monreale goes there a jackass and returns a fool.

» *Quannu la pulice se vitte a la farina, disse ca era capu mulinaru* (Pugliese). When the flea found itself in the flour, it said it was the master miller.

» *Lu mericu piatusu fa a chiaja virminusa* (Sicilian). A compassionate doctor makes the wound infected.

CALCIO (FOOTBALL): THE OTHER RELIGION

Catholicism may be Italy's official faith, but its true religion is *calcio*. On any given weekend from September through to May, you'll find millions of *tifosi* (football fans) at the *stadio* (stadium), glued to the TV, or checking the score on their mobile phone. In Naples' Piazzetta Nilo, you'll even find an altar to Argentine football star Diego Maradona, who elevated the city's Napoli team to its most successful era in the 1980s and early 1990s.

It's no coincidence that in Italian *tifoso* means both 'football fan' and 'typhus patient'. When the ball ricochets off the post and slips fatefully through the goalie's hands, when half the stadium is swearing while the other half is euphorically shouting 'Goooooooooooooooool!', 'fever pitch' is the term that comes to mind.

Indeed, nothing quite stirs Italian blood like a good (or a bad) game. Nine months after Neapolitan Fabio Cannavaro led Italy to victory in the 2006 World Cup, hospitals in northern Italy reported a baby boom. In February the following year, rioting at a Palermo–Catania match in Catania left one policeman dead and around 100 injured. Blamed on the Ultras (a minority group of hardcore football fans), the violence shocked both Italy and the world, leading to a temporary ban of all matches in Italy, and increased stadium security.

Yet, the same game that divides also unites. You might be a Juventus-loathing Bari supporter on any given day, but when national team *Azzurri* (the Blues) bag the World Cup, you are nothing but a heart-on-your-sleeve *italiano*. In his book *The 100 Things Everyone Needs to Know About Italy,* Australian journalist David Dale writes that Italy's 1982 World Cup win 'finally united twenty regions which, until then, had barely acknowledged that they were part of the one country'.

The Sacred & the Profane

While most young southerners call themselves Catholic, chances are they haven't stepped into a church since their cousin's baptism the other month. According to a 2007 Church study, only 15% of Italy's population regularly attends Sunday mass. That said, *La Famiglia Cristiana* (The Christian Family) remains Italy's most popular weekly magazine and the church remains stronger in the south than in northern Italy. Indeed, even the more cosmopolitan, secular sections of southern society maintain an air of respect for the church.

Any self-respecting Italian bookshelf features one or more Roman rhetoricians. To *fare la bella figura* (make a good impression) among academics, trot out a phrase from Cicero or Horace (Horatio), such as 'Where there is life there is hope' or 'Whatever advice you give, be brief'.

Every town has its own saint's day, celebrated with music, special events, food and wine. These religious festivals are one of the best ways into the culture of the south. Cream of the crop is Easter, with lavish weeklong events to mark Holy Week. People pay handsomely for the privilege and prestige of carrying the various back-breaking decorations around the town – the processions are usually solemnly, excruciatingly slow.

Pilgrimages and a belief in miracles remain a central part of the religious experience. You will see representations of Padre Pio – the Gargano saint who was canonised for his role in several miraculous recoveries – in churches, village squares, pizzerias and private homes everywhere. Around eight million pilgrims visit his shrine every year. Three times a year, thousands cram into Naples' Duomo to witness their patron saint San Gennaro's blood miraculously liquefy in the phial that contains it. When the blood liquefies, the city is considered safe from disaster.

In *Christ Stopped at Eboli,* his book about his stay in rural Basilicata in the 1930s, writer-painter-doctor Carlo Levi wrote: 'The air over this desolate land and among the peasant huts is filled with spirits. Not all of them are mischievous and capricious gnomes or evil demons. There are also good spirits in the guise of guardian angels.'

While the mystical, half-pagan world Levi describes may no longer be recognisable, there is often a fine line between the sacred and the profane in the south. Here, curse-deterring amulets are as plentiful as crucifix pendants, the most famous of which is the iconic, horn-shaped *corno*. Adorning everything from necklines to rear-view mirrors, this lucky charm's evil-busting powers are said to lie in its representation of the bull and its sexual vigour. A rarer, but by no means extinct custom, is that of Naples' 'o Scartellat. Usually an elderly man, he'll occasionally be spotted him burning incense through the city's older neighbourhoods, clearing the streets of bad vibes and inviting good fortune. The title itself is Neapolitan for 'hunchback', as the task was once the domain of posture-challenged figures. According to Neapolitan lore, touching a hunchback's hump brings good luck...which beats some of the other options, among them stepping in dog poop and having wine spilt on you accidentally.

The Mafia

To many outside Italy, the Mafia means Sicily's Cosa Nostra, seared into popular culture thanks to Francis Ford Coppola's film classic, *The Godfather*. In fact, there are three more partners in crime: Campania's Camorra, Calabria's 'Ndrangheta and Puglia's Sacra Corona Unita. Together, they form a veritable cancer, trafficking drugs, people and arms, stifling regional development through kickbacks, and making a bundle along the way.

Origins

The concept of 'the *mafioso*' dates back to the late 15th century, when Sicily's rent-collecting *gabellotti* (bailiffs) employed small gangs of armed peasants to help them solve 'problems'. Soon robbing large estates, the bandits struck fear and admiration into the peasantry, who were happy to support efforts to destabilise the feudal system. They became willing accomplices, protecting the outlaws, and although it was another 400 years before crime became 'organised', the 16th and 17th centuries witnessed a substantial increase in the activities of brigand bands. The peasants' loyalty to their own people resulted in the name Cosa Nostra (Our Thing). The early Mafia's way of protecting itself from prosecution was to become the modern Mafia's most important weapon: the code of silence, or *omertà*.

In the 1860s, a band of Sicilians exiled to Calabria began forming their own organised gangs, planting the seeds for the 'Ndrangheta. For almost a century, these gangs remained a local menace, known for extortion, racketeering and rural banditry. But it was the murder of a local godfather in 1975 that sparked a bloody gang war, transforming the organisation and creating a rebellious faction infamous for holding northern Italian businessmen to ransom. With its profits invested in narcotics, the 'Ndrangheta would transform itself into Italy's most powerful Mafia entity.

The powerful Camorra reputedly emerged from the criminal gangs operating among the poor in late 18th-century Naples. The organisation had

In 2011, police seized an adult tiger from the estate of murdered Sacra Corona Unita boss Lucio Vetrugno. Kept in a cage for 16 years, the giant feline had come in handy for intimidating Vetrugno's enemies. The tiger was subsequently transferred to an animal park in Bologna.

THE MAFIA ON SCREEN

» **Gomorra** (Matteo Garrone; 2009) A shocking, award-winning Camorra exposé based on Roberto Saviano's best-selling book.

» **The Godfather Trilogy** (Francis Ford Coppola; 1972-90) Marlon Brando plays an old-school mobster in this Oscar-winning saga.

» **Il camorrista** (The Camorrista; Giuseppe Tornatore; 1986) Camorra battles and betrayals inspired by real-life *capo* (boss) Raffaele 'Il Professore' Cutolo.

» **Mi manda Picone** (Picone Sent Me; Nanni Loy; 1983) A cult comedy about a small-time hustler embroiled in Naples' seedy underworld.

» **In nome della legge** (In the Name of the Law; Pietro Germi; 1949) A young judge is sent to a Mafia-riddled Sicilian town in this neorealist film, cowritten by Federico Fellini.

its first big break after the failed revolution of 1848. Desperate to overthrow Ferdinand II, pro-constitutional liberals turned to *camorristi* to help garner the support of the masses – the Camorra's political influence was sealed. Dealt a serious blow by Mussolini, the organisation would get its second wind from the invading Allied forces of 1943, which turned to the flourishing underworld as the best way to get things done. The black market thrived and the Camorra slowly began to spread its roots again.

In turn, the Camorra would give birth to the Sacra Corona Unita (Sacred United Crown), created by Camorra boss Raffaele Cutolo in the 1970s to gain access to Puglia's seaports. Originally named the Nuova Grande Camorra Pugliese, it gained its current name in the early 1980s after its Pugliese members cut ties with Campania and strengthened their bond with Eastern Europe's criminal networks.

The Value of Vice

Today's Mafia means serious business. The combined annual earnings of Italy's organised crime networks – estimated at €10 billion – account for approximately 10% of Italy's GDP. This is a far cry from the days of roguish characters bullying shopkeepers into paying the *pizzo* (protection money). As journalist Roberto Saviano writes in his Camorra exposè *Gomorra:* 'Only beggar Camorra clans inept at business and desperate to survive still practice the kind of monthly extortions seen in Nanni Loy's film *Mi manda Picone*'.

The top money-spinner is drugs and king of the trade is the 'Ndrangheta. The Calabrian mafia is the main player in Transatlantic cocaine trafficking, overseeing its shipment from Latin America to Europe via West Africa in a business worth a staggering €43 million a year.

Another trafficked 'product' is people, with an estimated 5000 refugees, including Iraqis, Pakistanis and Afghans, smuggled annually into Puglia alone. Many illegal African arrivals are hired out as farmhands by their Mafia handlers, demanding a percentage of the labourers' below-minimum wages. Most workers receive no more than €25 for up to two weeks' work on southern farms.

The recent Global Financial Crisis (GFC) has proven another boon. With liquidity in short supply, a growing number of hard pressed companies have turned to dirty money. Mafia-affiliated loan sharks commonly offer cash with an average interest rate of 10%. In Naples alone, an estimated 50% of shops are run with Camorra money. Mafia profits are also reinvested in legitimate real estate, credit markets and businesses, from London property to Sydney fashion stores. Critics call this 'the Invisible Mafia'.

Backlash of the Brave

Despite the Mafia's ever-expanding reach, the war against it is alive and kicking. Recent blows include the 2011 prosecutions of Gaetano Riina (the brother of convicted Cosa Nostra 'boss of bosses' Salvatore 'Totò' Riina) and former Sicilian governor Salvatore Cuffaro, the latter convicted of leaking information about anti-Mafia investigations. In 2010, almost 300 members of the notoriously impenetrable 'Ndrangheta were arrested in one of the biggest ever operations against the Calabrian clans.

The assassination of Sicilian anti-Mafia judges Giovanni Falcone and Paolo Borsellino in 1992 sparked particularly intense anti-Mafia sentiment throughout Italy. In 1994, Paolo Borsellino's sister Rita cofounded the group Libera (www.libera.it), whose member organisations were permitted to transform properties seized from the Mafia into agricultural cooperatives, *agriturismi* (farm-stay accommodation) and other legitimate enterprises. Equally encouraging has been the establishment of Addiopizzo (www.addiopizzo.org), a Sicilian organisation encouraging consumers to support businesses that have said 'no' to Mafia extortion.

The Camorra's weekly drug trade rates range from €100 for lookouts to €1000 for those willing to hide the drugs at home. On the tough streets of Naples' poorest neighbourhoods, the lure of quick cash proves irresistible for many, with kids as young as 12 recruited by local clans.

Arrested in 2009, Ugo Gabriele broke the mould like no other. Beefy and cunning, the then 27 year old would go down in history as Italy's first cross-dressing mobster. In between managing prostitution and drug rackets for Naples' Scissionisti clan, 'Kitty' found time to shape his eyebrows, dab on the lipstick and dye his hair platinum blonde.

The Southern Table

If you live to eat well, you've come to the right place. Blessed with sun, mineral-rich soils and the salty goodness of the Mediterranean, southern Italy was always destined for culinary fame. Its regions lay claim to many of Italy's best-known edibles, from pizza and pasta to mozzarella and cannoli. Waves of migration have flavoured the pot – the Greeks supplied the olives, the Arabs brought the pine nuts, aubergines (eggplants), almonds, raisins and honey, and the Spanish came with tomatoes. The end result is a larder bursting with buxom vegetables, glistening fish, spicy meats and decadent sweets.

Peckish? Read on for a crash course in southern gluttony. For price ranges used in this guide, turn to p253.

The Simple Things

Picture it: wood-fired bread drizzled in extra virgin olive oil, sprinkled with ripe *pomodori* (tomatoes) and fragrant *basilico* (basil). The flavours explode in your mouth. From the chargrilled crunch of the bread to the sweetness of the tomatoes, it's a perfect symphony of textures and flavours.

In many ways, *pane e pomodoro* (bread and tomatoes) captures the very soul of the southern Italian kitchen. Down here, fresh produce is the secret and simplicity is the key. Order grilled fish and chances are you'll get exactly that. No rich, overbearing sauces… just grilled fish with a wedge of lemon on the side. After all, it's the freshness of the fish you should be savouring, right?

This less-is-more approach is a testament to the south's impoverished past. Pasta made without eggs, bread made from hard durum wheat,

---

TABLE MANNERS

The southern Italian book of etiquette:

» Cardinal sins: skipping or being late for lunch.

» *Buon appetito* is what you say before eating. *Saluté!* (cheers!) is the toast used for alcoholic drinks – don't forget to make eye contact when toasting.

» Unless you have hollow legs, don't accept a second helping of that delicious *primo* – you might not have room for the *secondo, dolce, sopratavola* and fruit.

» Devour everything to the last olive and you'll be endeared to your hosts' hearts forever.

» End your meal with a short sharp *caffè* (espresso); ordering anything else is just not on.

» If invited to someone's house, bring flowers, wine or a tray of *dolcetti* from a local *pasticceria*.

wild greens scavenged from the countryside are all delicious, but their consumption was driven by necessity. The tradition of *sopratavola* (raw vegetables such as fennel or chicory eaten after a meal) arose because people could not afford fruit. That of *sottaceti* (vegetables cooked in vinegar and preserved in jars with olive oil) is part of the waste not, want not philosophy.

In the end, it was the simple goodness of this *cucina povera* (poor man's kitchen) that would make it the darling of health-conscious foodies.

Regional Highlights

In reality, southern Italian cuisine encompasses the culinary traditions of five regions: Campania, Puglia, Basilicata, Calabria and Sicily. They might share similarities, but they are all distinctly unique. Feast your eyes on our list of top regional highlights.

Campania

Everything seems to taste a little bit better in Campania – the tomatoes are juicier, the mozzarella silkier and the *caffè* richer and stronger. Is it the lush volcanic soil? The Campanian sun? Whatever it is, your tastebuds will be too high to care.

Perfect Pizza

It was in Naples that the city's most famous *pizzaiolo,* Raffaele Esposito, invented the classic pizza margherita. Esposito was summoned to fire up a treat for a peckish King Umberto I and his wife Queen Margherita on a royal visit in 1889. Determined to impress the Italian royals, Esposito based his creation of tomato, mozzarella and basil on the red, white and green flag of the newly unified Italy. The resulting topping met with the queen's approval and was subsequently named in her honour.

Pizza purists claim that you really can't top Esposito's classic combo when made by a true Neapolitan *pizzaiolo.* Not everyone is in accordance and Italians are often split between those who favour the thin-crust Roman variant, and those who go for the thicker Neapolitan version. Whatever your choice, the fact remains that the pizza they make in Naples is nothing short of superb. It's also a brilliant cheap feed – these giant discs of bubbling perfection usually start from €3. For the ultimate pizza experience, don't miss Naples' Pizzeria Gino Sorbillo (p45).

The Cult of Caffè

The Neapolitan coffee scene trades hipsters, soy and syphons for retro-vested baristas, chintzy fit-outs and un-hyped java brilliance. Here, velvety, lingering espresso is not a fashion statement – it's a birthright. In most cases, it's also a quick, unceremonious swill standing at local bars like Campania's best, Caffè Mexico (p46). But don't be fooled – the speed with which it's consumed does not diminish the importance of its quality.

According to the Neapolitans, it's the local water that makes their coffee stronger and better than any other in Italy. To drink it like a local, keep milky options like *caffè* latte and cappuccino for the morning. After lunch, espresso and *caffè maccchiato* (an espresso with a drop of milk) are the norm. For a more watered-down coffee (shame on you!) ask for a *caffè lungo* or a *caffè americano*.

Another ritual is the free *bicchiere d'acqua* (glass of water), offered either *liscia* (uncarbonated) or *frizzante* (sparkling) with your coffee. Drink it *before* your coffee to cleanse your palate. Just don't be surprised if you're not automatically offered one. After all, what would a heathen *straniero* (foreigner) know about coffee? Don't be shy – smile sweetly and ask for *un bicchiere d'acqua, per favore.*

Awaiting Table (www.awaiting table.com), Silvestro Silvestori's Lecce-based cooking school, offers short, weekend or week-long cookery courses featuring lots of visits, tastings and guest teachers.

Don't believe the hype about espresso: one diminutive cup packs less of a caffeine wallop than a large cup of French-pressed or American-brewed coffee, and leaves drinkers less jittery.

THE SOUTHERN TABLE REGIONAL HIGHLIGHTS

» **Colazione (breakfast)** A continental affair, often little more than a pre-work espresso, accompanied by a *cornetto* (Italian croissant) or brioche (breakfast pastry). In Sicily, your brioche might be filled with gelato or *granita* (flavoured crushed ice).

» **Pranzo (lunch)** A sacred time, with most businesses closing for the *la pausa* (afternoon break). Traditionally the main meal of the day, lunch usually consists of a *primo* (first course), *secondo* (second course) and *dolce*. Standard restaurant times are noon to 2.30pm, though most locals don't lunch before 1pm.

» **Aperitivo** Popular in cosmopolitan Naples, post-work drinks usually take place between 5pm and 8pm, when the price of your drink includes a buffet of tasty morsels.

» **Cena (dinner)** Traditionally a little lighter than lunch, though still a main meal. Standard restaurant times are 7.30pm to around 11pm, though many southern Italians don't sit down to dinner until 9pm or even later.

Magnificent Mozzarella

So you think the cow's milk mozzarella served in Capri's *insalata caprese* (a salad made of mozzarella, tomato, basil and olive oil) is delicious? Taste Campania's *mozzarella di bufala* (buffalo-milk mozzarella) and you'll move onto an entirely different level of deliciousness. Made on the plains surrounding Caserta and Paestum, it's best eaten when freshly made that morning – its rich, sweet flavour and luscious texture is nothing short of a revelation. You'll find it served in *trattorie* (informal restaurants) and restaurants across the region. Sorrento even has a dedicated mozzarella eatery, Inn Bufalito (p74). Bought fresh from *latterie* (dairies), it comes lukewarm in a plastic bag filled with a slightly cloudy liquid, the run-off from the mozzarella making. As for that irresistible taste, its the high fat content and buffalo milk protein that give the cheese the distinctive, pungent flavour so often absent in the versions sold abroad.

Fifty years ago, Italy's *Domus* magazine dispatched journalists nationwide to collect Italy's best regional recipes. The result is Italy's food bible, *The Silver Spoon*, now available in English from Phaidon (2005).

Even more decadent is *burrata,* a mozzarella filled with a wickedly buttery cream. *Burrata* itself was invented in Puglia, the swampy fields around Foggia also famed for their buffalo-milk goodness.

Puglia, Basilicata & Calabria

The heartland of *cucina povera,* Italy's deep south delivers back-to-basics brilliance. In Puglia, fields of wheat produce Italy's finest olive oils, pasta and breads. To the west, Basilicata and Calabria serve up succulent sausages and wild, seasonal mountain treats.

The Beauty of Bread

Eating a meal in Puglia and Basilicata without bread is like playing tennis without a racquet – it is essential for wiping up the sauce (a practise fondly called *fare scarpetta,* 'to make a little shoe'). Puglia's wood-fired bread is the stuff of legend, usually made from hard durum wheat (like pasta), with a russet-brown crust, an eggy-golden interior and a distinctively fine flavour. The best comes from Altamura, where it's thrice-risen, getting even better with time.

Many regional recipes call for breadcrumbs, such as summery spaghetti with oven-roasted tomatoes, breadcrumbs and garlic. The breadcrumbs themselves are made from stale bread – in Italian, it's *pane rafferme* (firmed-up bread), which is a much more glass-half-full way of looking at it.

Another carbolicious staple is *friselli,* dried bagel-shaped rolls born out of practicality, ideal for labourers on the move. Douse them in water to soften and then dress with tomatoes, olive oil and oregano. Just leave a little room for bagel-shaped *taralli,* hard little savoury biscuits that make for a tasty snack. In Bari they're traditionally plain, in Taranto they're sprinkled with fennel seeds, and in Lecce they're sexed-up with a touch of chilli.

Italy's Busiest Virgin

Campania and Sicily may produce a few impressive olive oils, but southern Italy's *olio* heavyweight is Puglia. Most of the country's olive oil comes from the region's north, some of its countless gnarled, silver-green trees said to be thousands of years old. Pugliese oil is usually made up of two types of olives: *coratina* (from Corato) are faintly bitter, while *ogliarola* (from around Cima di Bitonto) produce a sweet, fat oil.

The best oil is made from olives that are picked and rushed to the mill, as olives that are left for too long after harvesting quickly become acidic. Pugliese farmers traditionally harvest the easy way: by letting the olives drop into nets, rather than paying for labour-intensive harvesting by hand. This means the olives are too acidic and the oil has to be refined, often taken north to mix with higher quality, costlier oils. That said, more and more places in the south produce stunning oils at low prices; you can buy it at local farms such as organic Il Frantoio (p112).

A recent medical study suggests that older people who use olive oil in their cooking and on their salads may have a lower risk of suffering a stroke. Other clinical trials suggest that olive oil also helps reduce the risk of heart disease.

Where the Wild Things Grow

Rugged terrain calls for hearty flavours, and that's just what you'll get in Basilicata and Calabria. Despite having little room for grazing, these regions are masters of salami and sausages – pigs here are prized and fed on natural foods such as acorns. Basilicata's star sausage is *lucanica* or *lucanega.* The ancient Romans ate it and Apicio, Cicero, Marziale and Varrone remarked on it: seasoned with fennel, pepper, *peperoncino* and salt, and eaten fresh – roasted on a coal fire – or dried, or preserved in olive oil. The drooling continues with *soppressata,* the pork sausage from Rivello made from finely chopped pork grazed in pastures, dried and

THE BIG FORK MANIFESTO

The year was 1987. McDonald's had just begun their expansion into Italy, and lunch outside the bun seemed to be fading into fond memory. Enter Carlo Petrini and a handful of other journalists from the small Piedmontese town of Bra, in northern Italy. Determined to buck the trend, these *neoforchettoni* ('big forks', or foodies) created a manifesto. Published in the like-minded culinary magazine *Gambero Rosso,* the manifesto declared that a meal should be judged not by its speed, but by the pure pleasure it offers.

The organisation they founded would soon become known worldwide as **Slow Food** (www.slowfood.com). Its mission: to reconnect artisanal producers with enthusiastic, educated consumers. The movement has taken root, with more than 100,000 members in 150 countries – not to mention Slow Food *agriturismi,* restaurants, farms, wineries, cheesemakers and revitalised farmers markets across Italy.

While traditions in the south remain stronger than in Italy's north, the Slow Food Movement does its bit to prevent their disappearance and to promote interest in food, taste and the way things are produced. For more information, see www.slowfoodpuglia.it and www.slowfoodcampania.com (both in Italian), or you can look up the main website at www.slowfood.com (in English).

REGIONAL SPECIALTIES

pressed and kept in extra-virgin olive oil, and *pezzenta* ('beggars' – probably a reference to their peasant origins) made from pork scraps and spicy Senise peppers.

Across the border, the Calabrians are equally resourceful, turning pig's fat, organ meats and hot *peperoncino* into one of their most iconic creations... spicy, cured *'nduja* sausage.

It's not all carnivorous feasting though. In August, look out for red aubergines, unique to Rotonda, Basilicata, and originally from Africa. Spicy and bitter, they're often dried, pickled or preserved in oil and served as antipasti. Come autumn and the mountains yield delicious *funghi* (mushrooms) of all shapes and sizes. A favourite of the ancient Romans was the small, wild umbel oyster, eaten fried with garlic and parsley or accompanying lamb or vegetables.

One of the best spots for a little mushroom hunting is Calabria's Parco Nazionale della Sila (p140), which even hosts a *fungo*-focussed *sagra* (local festival).

Sicily

Sicily's enviable pantry has been filled over centuries by a string of foreign settlers. It's a luscious, mouthwatering feast of succulent citrus and seafood, decadent street snacks and almond-laced sweets. Gluttons, welcome to the Promised Land.

The Art of Snacking

Sicily's repertoire of finger-licking *buffitieri* (hot street snacks) is unrivalled in breadth and flavour. One easy-to-find gut-filler is *sfincione*, a local style of pizza made with tomatoes, onions and sometimes anchovies. Another variation on pizza is calzone, a pocket of pizza-like dough baked with ham, cheese or other stuffings. Other doughy favourites include *impanata* (bread-dough snacks stuffed with meat, vegetables or cheese) and *scaccie* (discs of bread dough spread with a filling and rolled up into a crêpe).

And it doesn't stop there. Head to any street stall or *friggitoria* (a small shop selling fried snacks) and give in to *arancini* (rice balls stuffed with meat or cheese, coated with breadcrumbs and fried), *crocchè* (fried potato dumplings made with cheese, parsley and eggs) or Palermo's iconic *pane e panelle* (fried chickpea-flour fritters, often served in a roll).

Peckish thrill-seekers are catered for too, with a range of extreme snacks for the most intrepid of foodies.

For extensive descriptions of regional specialities and recipes, see www.italianmade.com.

DARE TO TRY

Consider yourself an intrepid gastronome, do you? We dare you to push the culinary envelope with the following southern extremes:

» **sanguinaccio** A hearty pig's blood sausage, particularly popular in Calabria and Basilicata.

» **cavallo** Puglia's Salento region is famous for its horse meat. Taste it in dishes like *pezzetti di cavallo* (horse meat casserole with tomato, celery, carrot and bay leaf).

» **pani ca meusa** A classic Palermo sandwich of beef spleen and lungs dipped in boiling lard.

» **stigghiola** A classic Sicilian dish of grilled sheep's or goat's intestines stuffed with onions and parsley, and seasoned with salt or lemon.

» **'mpanatigghiu** A traditional Sicilian pastry from Modica, filled with minced meat, almonds and the town's famous chocolate.

Only Naples' Mercato di Porta Nolana (p36) and La Pignasecca (p37) can rival the sheer theatricality and gut-rumbling brilliance of Sicily's *mercati* (markets). Loud, crowded and exhilarating, these alfresco larders are a technicolour testament to the importance of fresh produce in daily life. To watch the hard-to-please hagglers bullying vendors into giving them precisely what they want is to understand that quality really matters here. And it's these people, the *nonne* (grandmothers) and *casalinghe* (homemakers), who keep the region's culinary traditions alive.

Two of the most atmospheric markets are Palermo's Mercato del Capo (p155) and Catania's La Pescheria (p177), their souk-like laneways crammed with glistening tuna and swordfish, swaying sausages and tubs of olives and pungent cheeses. Look out for pistachios from Bronte; almonds from Noto; and *caciocavallo,* one of southern Italy's most renowned cheeses. Don't panic: despite the name 'horse cheese', it's made from cow's milk. It has a distinctive gourd-shaped, pale-mustard exterior, and the name is thought to have arisen either because it was once made from mare's milk, or because it would be hung from the horse's back when transported. When it's young, it tastes *dolce* (sweet); after two month's aging, it's *piccante* (spicy) or *affumicato* (smoked).

Another must for cheese buffs is sheep's-milk *pecorino;* the most distinctive Sicilian *pecorini* come from the Madonie and Nebrodi Mountains.

La Dolce Vita

Sicilians have a way with sugar that verges on the pornographic. Down here, *pasticcerie* (pastry shops) are culinary sex shops, leading tastebuds into temptation. Relax, you're not alone – Sicilians normally migrate from restaurant tables to the nearest pastry shop for a coffee and cake at the bar.

The queen of Sicilian desserts, the *cassata,* is made with ricotta, sugar, vanilla, diced chocolate and candied fruits; in Palermo, they describe a woman as 'lovely as a *cassata'.* In the west, you'll find *cuccia,* an Arab cake made with grain, honey and ricotta. The famous *cannoli,* pastry tubes filled with sweetened ricotta and (sometimes) candied fruit or chocolate pieces, are ubiquitous across the island. Also look out for *pasta di mandorle* (almond cookies) and *pasta paradiso* (melting moments).

But wait, there's more, including *gelso di melone* (watermelon jelly), *buccellati* (little pies filled with minced fruit), and *biscotti regina* (sesame-coated biscuits). If you are in Palermo around late October, before the festival of *Ognissanti* (All Souls' Day), you will see plenty of stalls selling the famous *frutti della Martorana,* named after the church that first began producing them. These marzipan biscuits, shaped to resemble fruits (or whatever takes the creator's fancy), are part of a Sicilian tradition that dates back to the Middle Ages.

The Arabs first started the Sicilian mania for all things icy – *granita* (flavoured crushed ice), *cassata* ice cream, *gelato* (ice cream) and *semifreddo* (literally 'semifrozen'; a cold, creamy dessert). Homemade *gelato* (*gelato artiginale*) is sold at cafes and bars across the island, and is truly delicious. *Granite* are sometimes topped with fresh whipped cream, or you could try it like a Sicilian – first thing in the morning in a brioche! Favourite flavours include coffee and almond, though lemon is heavenly in summer.

During spring, summer and early autumn, towns across southern Italy celebrate *sagre,* the festivals of local foods in season. Scan www.prodottitipici.com/sagre (in Italian) for a lip-smacking list.

For an excellent food and travel portal, visit www.deliciousitaly.com, which also lists courses and wine tours.

THE SOUTHERN TABLE REGIONAL HIGHLIGHTS

Southern Staples

Pasta: Fuel of the South

In the 1954 cult film *Un Americano a Roma* (An American in Rome), a US-obsessed Alberto Sordi snubs a plate of pasta in favour of an unappetising 'American-style' concoction. It only takes a few mouthfuls before Sordi thinks better of it, plunging into the pasta with unbridled passion. It's hard not to follow Sordi's lead.

A standard *primo* (first course) on menus across the south, pasta is not only delicious, it's often a filling meal in itself. Your waiter will understand and there is usually no pressure to order a *secondo* (second course).

So what exactly is on the menu? In Campania, chances are you'll be filling up on *pasta e fagioli* (with beans), *spaghetti alle vongole* (with clams and cherry tomatoes), and *gnocchi alla sorrentina* (with tomato sauce and mozzarella). Naples' Bourbon court cuisine shines through in elaborate *timballi di pasta* (pasta pies) and the ridiculously rich *pasta al forno* (baked pasta), a mouth-watering combo of maccheroni, tomato sauce, mozzarella and, depending on the recipe, hard-boiled egg, meatballs and sausage.

More humble but no less delicious is Calabria's *pasta aru tonnu* (with tuna and salted anchovies), while Sicily's *al dente* musts include *pasta con le sarde* (with sardines, wild mountain fennel, onions, pine nuts and raisins) and *pasta alla Norma* (with tomatoes, aubergines and salted ricotta).

Sicily's pasta prowess is hardly surprising given that it was here that pasta first hit Italy, introduced by Arab merchants in the Middle Ages. It was to be a perfect match. Southern Italy's sunny, windy disposition was just right for producing *pasta secca* (dry pasta), while the foodstuff's affordability and easy storage made it handy in the face of hardship. It's no coincidence that *pasta fresca* (fresh pasta) has, traditionally, been more prevalent in Italy's more affluent north.

Not that the south is without its fresh pasta icons. The best known is Puglia's *orecchiette* (meaning 'little ears'), best savoured in dishes like *orecchiette con cime di rapa* (with turnip tops) and *orecchiette con pomodori e ricotta forte* (with tomato sauce and strong ricotta).

Puglia produces around 80% of Europe's pasta, and per-capita consumption of bread and pasta is at least double that of the USA. It's also said that there are 50 million olive trees in Puglia, equivalent to the Italian population, and the region is the sixth-biggest wine-making region in the world.

Eat Your Greens... Purples, Reds and Yellows

Vegetables across the world must loathe their southern Italian counterparts. Not only do they often look more beautiful, they're prepared with a know-how that turns them into culinary protagonists. Take the humble *melanzana* (aubergine), glammed up in the punchy *melanzane ripiene al forno* (baked aubergine stuffed with olives, capers and tomatoes) and decadent *parmigiana melanzane* (batter-fried aubergine layered with parmesan, mozzarella, ham and tomato sauce). Another version, simply named *parmigiana,* does the same for *carciofi* (globe artichokes).

Southern Italians also have a way with *peperoni* (peppers). In Puglia, don't miss eating them pan-roasted and served with almonds. Across the south, antipasto platters are often adorned with silky *peperoni sottaceto* (marinated pickled peppers). A favourite Sicilian dish involving red, green and yellow peppers is *peperonata in agridolce,* where the peppers are stewed with onions, pine nuts, raisins and capers.

Legumes feel the love in Puglia's broad bean and chicory puree, described 'as a dish to die for' by celebrity chef/restaurateur/food writer Antonio Carluccio. Equally addictive is the region's *calzone pugliese* (onion pie) and its summertime *cocomeri* – stubby fat cucumbers that are startlingly crisp and sweet, and sublime eaten alongside a salty pecorino cheese.

The word *melanzane* (aubergine) comes from 'mela insane', meaning crazy apple. In Latin it was called *solanum insanum* as it was thought to cause madness.

» **Ristorante** Crisp linen, formal service and refined dishes make restaurants the obvious choice for special occasions.

» **Trattoria** A family-owned version of restaurants, with cheaper prices, more relaxed service, and classic regional specialities. Avoid places offering tourist menus.

» **Osteria** Intimate and relaxed, this is usually a small trattoria or a wine bar offering a handful of dishes from a verbal menu.

» **Enoteca** Perfect for a little *vino* downtime, wine bars often serve snacks to accompany your tipple.

» **Agriturismo** A working farm offering accommodation, as well as food made with farm-grown produce. Some allow guests to participate in farm activities. In the south, some *agriturismi* are set in fortified farmhouses called *masserie* (see the boxed text on p112).

» **Pizzeria** A top place for a cheap feed, cold beer and a buzzing, convivial vibe; the best pizzerias are often crowded. Be patient.

» **Tavola calda** Literally a 'hot table', these cafeteria-style options peddle cheap, prepared food like self-service pasta, roast meats and *pizza al taglio* (pizza by the slice).

» **Mercato** The market is an integral part of southern Italian life and a great place to pick up picnic provisions like crunchy bread, local cheeses, salami, antipasti, fruit and vegetables.

Campania isn't short of herbivorous highs either, among them *friarelli* – a bitter broccoli-like vegetable *saltata in padella* (pan-fried), spiked with *peperoncino* (red chilli) and often served with diced *salsiccie di maiale* (pork sausages). Top billing, however, goes to Campania's *pomodoro San Marzano* (San Marzano plum tomato). Grown in the shadow of Mt Vesuvius, its low acidity and intense, sweet flavour makes a perfect *conserva di pomodoro* (tomato concentrate). It's this sauce that adorns so many of Naples' signature pasta dishes, including the colourfully named *spaghetti alla puttanesca* (whore's spaghetti), which blend tomatoes, black olives, capers, anchovies and (in some cases) a provocative dash of *peperoncino*.

Off The Boat

Aside from sustaining local economies, the sea has played a defining role in southern culture. Take the pastel hues of Procida's fishing villages for example, painted so that the *pescatori* (fisherman) could pinpoint their homes while out at sea. Ponder the thought over a plate of *volamarina* (moonfish) tripe with tomato, chilli and anchovy-stuffed squid – one of the island's most famous dishes.

Fishing continues to pay in tiny Cetara, the only Amalfi Coast town to still have a fishing fleet. The star turn here are *alici* (anchovies), best savoured fresh at Al Convento (p84), or taken home in a bottle of *colatura di alici,* an intense anchovy essence for which Cetara is famous.

Sicily's own aquatic staples include sardines, tuna, and mackerel. In Palermo, look out for *sarde a beccafi co alla Palermitana* (sardines stuffed with anchovies, pine nuts, currants and parsley). On the Egadi Islands, give in to *tonno 'nfurnatu* (oven-baked tuna with tomatoes, capers and green olives) and *alalunga di Favignana al ragù* (fried albacore served in a spicy sauce of tomatoes, red chilli peppers and garlic). Top of the list, however, is Messina's legendary *pesce spada* (swordfish), best savoured in the classic *agghiotta di pesce spada* (also called *pesce spada alla Messinese*), flavoured with pine nuts, sultanas, garlic, basil and tomatoes.

Antonio Carluccio's *Southern Italian Feast: More Than 100 Recipes Inspired by the Flavour of Southern Italy,* is a splendid collection to inspire you to get cooking.

Puglia also has its seafood gems, amongst them *zuppa di pesce* (fish soup), regional darling *riso cozze e patate* (baked rice, mussels and potatoes) and the obscenely flavoursome *polpo in umido* or *alla pignata* (steamed octopus teamed with garlic, onion, tomatoes, parsley, olive oil, black pepper, bay leaves and cinnamon).

Altogether more exotic (and trickier to eat) are its spiky *ricci di mare* (sea urchins) caught south of Bari in spring and autumn. They might be a challenge to crack open, but once you've dipped your bread into the delicate, dark-red roe, chances are you'll be glad that you persisted.

In Matera, Ferula Viaggi (www.ferulaviaggi.it) is an excellent agency offering food-themed tours and tastings, where you can, for example, see mozzarella being made and taste local wines.

The Vine Revival

Winemaking in the south dates back to the Phoenicians. The Greeks introduced Campania to its now-famous Greco (Greek) grape, and dubbed the south 'Enotria' (Wineland). Yet, despite this ancient viticulture, oenophiles had often dismissed local *vini* (wines) as little more than 'here for a good time, not a long time' drops. A case in point is wine critic Burton Anderson, who in his 1990 *Wine Atlas of Italy* wrote that Campania's noteworthy winemakers could be 'counted on one's fingers'.

Anderson would need a few more hands these days. In little more than two decades, southern Italy has transformed itself into one of the world's hottest in-the-know wine regions, with renewed pride in native varieties and stricter, more modern winemaking practices.

Campania

Campanian producers such as Feudi di San Gregorio, Mastroberardino, Terredora di Paolo and Mustilli have returned to their roots, cultivating ancient grape varieties like the red Aglianico (thought to be the oldest cultivated grape in Italy) and the whites Falanghino, Fiano and Greco (all were growing long before Mt Vesuvius erupted in AD 79). Taurasi, a full-bodied Aglianico wine, sometimes known as the Barolo of the south, is one of southern Italy's finest labels. One of only three in the region to carry Italy's top quality rating, DOCG (*Denominazione di Origine Controllata e Garantita*; Controlled & Guaranteed Denomination of Origin), it goes perfectly with barbequed and boiled meats. The other two wines boasting the DOCG honour are the fresh, fragrant Fiano di Avellino and the dry, bright Greco di Tufo, both seafood-friendly whites and, like Taurasi, from the Avellino area.

Although some producers find these official Italian classifications unduly costly and creatively constraining, the DOCG (*Denominazione di Origine Controllata e Garantita*) and DOC (*Denominazione di Origine Controllata*) designations are awarded to wines that meet regional quality-control standards.

Campania's other wine-producing areas include the Campi Flegrei (home to spicy Piedirosso and tangy Falanghina vines), Ischia (whose wines were the first to receive Denominazione di Origine Controllata status) and the Cilento, home to the Cilento bianco (Cilento white) and to the Aglianico Paestum. Mt Vesuvius' most famous drop is the dry Lacryma Christi (Tears of Christ), a blend of locally grown Falanghina, Piedirosso and Coda di Volpe grapes.

Puglia & Basilicata

The different characteristics of these regions' wines reflect their diverse topography and terroir. In Puglia, there are vast, flat acreages of vineyards, while Basilicata's vineyards tend to be steep and volcanic.

It's the Pugliese reds that gain most plaudits. The main grapes grown are the Primitivo (a clone of the Zindanfel grape), Negroamaro, Nero di Troia and Malvasia. The best Primitivi are found around Manduria, while Negroamaro reaches its peak in the Salento, particularly around Salice, Guagnano and Copertino. The two grapes are often blended to derive the best from the sweetness of Primitivo and the slightly bitter, wilder edge of Negroamaro.

Almost all Puglia reds work perfectly with pasta, pizza, meats and cheeses. Puglia whites have less cachet; however, those grown on the

Murge, particularly Locorotondo and Martina, are good, clean, fresh-tasting wines, while those from Gravina are a little weightier. They are all excellent with fish.

In Basilicata, the red wine of choice is made from the Aglianico grape, the best being produced in the Vulture region. It is the volcanic terroir that makes these wines so unique and splendid. Basilicata, like Puglia, has seen a renaissance in recent years with much inward investment, such as that of oenologist Donato d'Angelo at his eponymous winery at Rionero in Vulture.

Sicily

Sicily is the second-largest wine-producing region in Italy, yet few Sicilian wines are well known beyond the island.

The most common varietal is Nero d'Avola, a robust red similar to Syrah or Shiraz. Vintages are produced by numerous Sicilian wineries, and some of the finest include Planeta's Plumbago and Santa Cecilia labels, and Donnafugata's Mille e una Notte.

Local Cabernet Sauvignons are less common but also worth sampling; the version produced by Tasca d'Almerita at its Regaleali estate in Caltanissetta province is particularly highly regarded (the estate also produces an excellent Nero d'Avola under its Rosso del Conte label).

The Sangiovese-like Nerello Mascalese and Nerello Cappuccio are used in the popular Etna Rosso, a dark-fruited, medium-bodied wine that pares perfectly with lamb and goat milk cheeses.

There is only one Sicilian DOCG, Cerasuolo di Vittoria, a blend of Nero d'Avola and Frappato grapes. Look for vintages from Planeta and COS.

While Sicily's *vini rossi* (red wines) are good, the region's real forte are its *bianchi* (whites). Common white varietals include Carricante, Chardonnay, Grillo, Inzolia, Cataratto, Inzolia, Cataratto, Grecanico and Corinto. Some of the best include Tasca d'Almerita's Nozze d'Oro Inzolia blend, Fazio's Catarratto Chardonnay, and Abbazia Santa Anastasia's chardonnay blends.

Equally impressive are Sicily's dessert wines. Top billing goes to Marsala's sweet wine; the best (and most widely known) labels are Florio and Pellegrino. Italy's most famous Moscato (Muscat) is the amber-hued Passito di Pantelleria, its taste an extraordinary mélange of apricots and vanilla.

The annual *Italian Wine Guide*, produced by the Gambero Rosso, is considered to be the bible of Italian wines, offering plenty of information about southern wines and wineries. You can buy it online at www.gambero-rosso.it.

Art & Architecture

Southern Italy is Western Europe's cultural attic – a dusty repository filled to the rafters with ancient temples and statues, exotic mosaics, brooding castles, vainglorious frescoes and innovative installations. It's an overwhelming heap, so why not start with the undisputed highlights?

Art

Classical Splendour

The Greeks had settled many parts of Sicily and southern Italy as early as the 8th century BC, naming it Magna Graecia and building great cities such as Syracuse and Taranto. These cities were famous for their magnificent temples, many of which were decorated with sculptures modelled on, or inspired by, masterpieces by Praxiteles, Lysippus and Phidias.

The Greek colonisers were equally deft at ceramics, adorning vases with painted scenes from daily life, mythology and Greek theatre. Some of the most vivid examples are the 4th-century-BC phylax vases, with larger-than-life characters and costumes that depict scenes from phylax plays, a type of ancient southern-Italian farce.

In art, as in so many other realms, the Romans looked to the Greeks for examples of best practice, and sculpture, architecture and painting flourished during their reign. Yet, the art produced in Rome was different in many ways from the Greek art that influenced it. Essentially secular, it focused less on harmony and form and more on accurate representation, mainly in the form of sculptural portraits. Innumerable versions of Pompey, Titus and Augustus all show a similar visage, proving that the artists were seeking verisimilitude in their representations, and not just glorification.

Wealthy Roman citizens also dabbled in the arts, building palatial villas and adorning them with statues looted from the Greek world or copied from Hellenic originals. You'll find many fine examples in Syracuse's Museo Archeologico Paolo Orsi, including the celebrated *Venere Anadiomene,* a 1st century Roman copy depicting a voluptuous goddess of love. Status-conscious Romans didn't stop there, lavishing floors with mosaics and walls with vivid frescoes. Outstanding mosaics live on at Sicily's Villa Romana del Casale, Pompeii, Herculaneum and Naples' Museo Archeologico Nazionale. Pompeii itself claims the world's largest ancient wall fresco, hidden inside the Villa dei Misteri.

Click on to www. exibart.com (mostly in Italian) for up-to-date listings of art exhibitions throughout Italy, as well as exhibition reviews, articles and interviews.

The Glitter of Byzantine

In 330, Emperor Constantine, a convert to Christianity, made the ancient city of Byzantium his capital and renamed it Constantinople. The city became the great cultural and artistic centre of Christianity and it remained so up to the time of the Renaissance, though its influence on the art of that period was never as fundamental as the art of ancient Rome.

Artistically, the Byzantine period was notable for its extraordinary mosaic work and – to a lesser extent – its painting. Its art was influenced by the decoration of the Roman catacombs and the early Christian churches, as well as by the Oriental Greek style, with its love of rich decoration and luminous colour.

As a major transit point on the route between Constantinople and Rome, Puglia and Basilicata were exposed to Byzantine's Eastern aesthetics. Indeed, the art that most encapsulates these regions is its 10th- and 11th-century Byzantine frescoes, hidden away in locked chapels dotted across their expanse. There is an incredible concentration in Matera, Basilicata, the most fantastic of which are the monastic complex of Chiesa di Madonna delle Virtù & Chiesa di San Nicola del Greci. In Puglia, the town of Mottola is home to the Cripta di San Nicola (nicknamed the Sistine Chapel of the south), while in Brindisi, the Chiesa di Santa Maria del Casale serves up a dazzling array of exotic tiling.

In Sicily, Byzantine, Norman and Saracen influences fused to create a distinct regional style showcased in the mosaic-encrusted splendour of Palermo's Cappella Palatina inside the Palazzo dei Normanni, not to mention the cathedrals of Monreale and Cefalù.

We regularly consulted EH Gombrich's seminal work *The Story of Art* when writing this chapter. First published in 1950, it gives a wonderful overview of the history of Italian art.

Giotto & the 'Rebirth' of Italian Art

Italy's Byzantine painters were apt with light and shade, but it would take Florentine painter Giotto di Bondone (c 1266-1337) to break the spell of conservatism and venture into a new world of naturalism. Best known for his frescoes in Padua and Assisi, faded fragments of his work survive in Naples' Castel Nuovo and Basilica di Santa Chiara.

Giotto and the painters of the Sienese School introduced many innovations in art: the exploration of perspective and proportion, a new interest in realistic portraiture, and the beginnings of a new tradition of landscape painting. The influx of eastern scholars fleeing Constantinople in the wake of its fall to the Ottoman Turkish Muslims in 1453 prompted a renewed interest in classical learning and humanist philosophy. Coupled with the increasingly ambitious, competitive nature of northern Italy's city states, these developments would culminate in the Renaissance.

Centred in Florence in the 15th century, and Rome and Venice in the 16th century, the Renaissance was slower to catch on in southern Italy, which was caught up in the power struggles between its French and Spanish rulers. One of the south's few Renaissance masters was Antonello da Messina (1430–79), whose luminous works include *The Virgin Annunciate* (1474–77) in Palermo's Galleria Regionale della Sicilia and *The Annunciation* (1474) in Syracuse's Galleria Regionale di Palazzo Bellomo.

Bad Boys & the Baroque

With the advent of the baroque, it was the south's time to shine. Under 17th-century Spanish rule, Naples was transformed into Europe's biggest city. Swelling crowds and ounter-Reformation fervour sparked a building boom, with taller-than-ever *palazzi* (mansions) and showcase churches sprouting up across the city. Ready to adorn these new landmarks was a brash, arrogant and fiery league of artists, ditching Renaissance restraint for baroque exuberance.

The main influence on 17th-century Neapolitan art was Milanese-born Caravaggio (1573–1610). A controversial character, he escaped to Naples in 1606 after killing a man in Rome; although he only stayed for a year, his impact on the city was huge. Caravaggio's dramatic depiction of light and shade, his supreme draughtsmanship and his naturalist style had an

In *M: The Man Who Became Caravaggio*, Peter Robb gives a passionate personal assessment of the artist's paintings and a colourful account of Caravaggio's life, arguing he was murdered for having sex with the pageboy of a high-ranking Maltese aristocrat.

STARS OF NEAPOLITAN BAROQUE

Michelangelo Merisi da Caravaggio (1573–1610) Bridging Mannerism and the baroque, Caravaggio injected raw emotion and foreboding shadow. Two of his greatest works are *La sette opere di Misericordia* (Seven Acts of Mercy; 1607) and *Flagellazione* (Flagellation; 1607-10), appearing in Naples' Pio Monte della Misericordia and Museo di Capodimonte respectively.

Giuseppe de Ribera (1591–1652) Though Spanish born, most of this bullying painter's finest work was created in southern Italy, including his dramatic *St Jerome* (1626) and *Apollo and Marsyas* (c 1637), both in the Museo di Capodimonte.

Cosimo Fanzago (1591–1678) This revered sculptor, decorator and architect cut marble into the most whimsical forms, producing luscious, inlaid spectacles. Naples' Certosa di San Martino aside, his beautiful high altar in Naples' Chiesa di San Domenico Maggiore is not to be missed.

Mattia Preti (1613–99) Dubbed 'Il Cavaliere Calabrese' (The Calabrian Knight), Preti infused thunderous, apocalyptic scenes with a deep, affecting humanity. Seek out his *The Feast of Absalom* (c 1670) in the Museo di Capodimonte.

Luca Giordano (1632–1705) Affectionately nicknamed Luca fa presto (Luca does it quickly) for his dexterous ways with a brush. Fabulous frescoes aside, his canvassed creations include *Apollo and Marsyas* (c 1660) in the Museo di Capodimonte.

Francesco Solimena (1657–1747) Lavish and grandiose compositions define this icon's work. One of his best is the operatic fresco *Expulsion of Eliodoro from the Temple* (1725) in Naples' Chiesa del Gesù Nuovo.

Giuseppe Sanmartino (1720–93) Arguably the finest sculptor of his time, Sanmartino's ability to breathe life into his creations won him a legion of fans, including the bizarre alchemist prince, Raimondo di Sangrio. Don't miss his *Cristo Velato* (Veiled Christ) in di Sangrio's Cappella Sansevero, Naples.

electrifying effect on the city's younger artists. One look at his *Flagellazione* (Flagellation; 1607-10) in Naples' Museo di Capodimonte or his *La sette opere di Misericordia* (Seven Acts of Mercy; c 1607) in the Pio Monte della Misericordia and you'll understand why.

One of Caravaggio's greatest fans was artist Giuseppe (or Jusepe) de Ribera (1591-1652), whose combination of shadow, colour and gloomy naturalism is brilliantly executed in his masterpiece, *Pietà* (1637), which is hanging in Naples' Certosa di San Martino. Merciless to the extreme, Lo Spagnoletto (The Little Spaniard, as Ribera was known) reputedly won a commission for the Cappella del Tesoro in Naples' Duomo by poisoning his rival Domenichino (1581-1641), as well as wounding the assistant of a second competitor, Guido Reni (1575-1642). The Duomo would be adorned with the frescoes of a number of rising stars, among them Giovanni Lanfranco (1582-1647) and Luca Giordano (1632-1705).

A fledgling apprentice to Ribera, Naples-born Giordano found great inspiration in the brushstrokes of Mattia Preti (1613–99). By the second half of the 17th century, Giordano would become the single most important artist in Naples. His finest fresco, the *Triumph of Judith,* decorates the treasury ceiling of the Certosa di San Martino's church.

Architecture

Ancient Legacies

Only one word describes the buildings of ancient southern Italy: monumental. The Greeks invented the architectural orders (Doric, Ionic and Corinthian) and used them to great effect in once-mighty cities like Akragas (modern-day Agrigento), Catania and Syracuse. More than two millennia later, the soaring temples of Segesta, Selinunte, the Valley of the

Temples and Paestum confirm not only the ancient Greeks' power, but also their penchant for harmonious proportion. This skill also underscored their sweeping theatres, the finest of which still stand in Syracuse, Taormina and Segesta.

Having learned a few valuable lessons from the Greeks, the Romans refined architecture to such a degree that their building techniques, designs and mastery of harmonious proportion underpin most of the world's architecture and urban design to this day. In Brindisi, a brilliant white column marks one end of the Via Appia – the ancient cross-country road connecting Rome to east-coast Brindisi. In Pozzuoli, they erected the Anfiteatro Flavio, the empire's third-largest arena and the very spot where San Gennaro, Naples' patron saint, met a gruesome end.

Medieval Fusion

Following on from Byzantine architecture and its mosaic-encrusted churches was Romanesque, a style that found four regional forms in Italy: Lombard, Pisan, Florentine and Sicilian Norman. All displayed an emphasis on width and the horizontal lines of a building rather than height, and featured church groups with *campaniles* (bell towers) and baptisteries that were separate to the church. Surfacing in the 11th century, the Sicilian Norman style encompassed an exotic mix of Norman, Saracen, and Byzantine influences, from marble columns to Islamic-inspired pointed arches to glass tesserae detailing. Clearly visible in the two-toned masonry and 13th-century belltower of Amalfi's Cattedrale di Sant'Andrea, one of the greatest examples of the form is the cathedral of Monreale, just outside Palermo.

With the 12th and 13th centuries came the Gothic aesthetic. The Italians didn't embrace this style as enthusiastically as the French, Germans and Spanish did. Its flying buttresses, grotesque gargoyles and over-the-top decorations were just too far from the classical ideal that was (and still is) bred in the Italian bone. This said, the Gothic style did leave its mark in southern Italy, albeit in the muted version encapsulated by Naples' Chiesa di San Lorenzo Maggiore and Chiesa di San Domenico Maggiore, and Palermo's Palazzo Bellomo and Lucera's cathedral. The south's most striking Gothic icon, however, is Puglia's Castel del Monte; its Italianate windows, Islamic floor mosaics and Roman triumphal entrance attests to the south's flair for absorbing foreign influence.

Baroque: the Golden Age

Just as Renaissance restraint redefined Italy's north, the wild theatricality of 17th- and 18th-century baroque revamped the south. Encouraging the makeover was the Catholic Church, for whom baroque's awe-inducing qualities were the perfect weapon against the Reformation and its less-is-more philosophy. Deploying swirls of frescoes, gilt and polychromatic marble, churches like Naples' Chiesa del Gesù Nuovo and Chiesa di San Gregorio Armeno turned Catholicism into a no-holds-barred extravaganza.

Inlaid marble would become a dominant special effect, adorning everything from tombs and altars, to floors and entire chapel walls. The form's undisputed master was Cosimo Fanzago (1591–1678), an occasionally violent sculptor whose masterpieces would include Naples' Certosa di San Martino's church; a mesmerising kaleidoscope of colours, patterns and precision.

In Puglia's Salento region, *barocco leccese* (Lecce baroque) saw the style reach extraordinary new heights. Local limestone was carved into lavish decorative detail around porticoes, windows, balconies and loggias, themselves crowned with human and zoomorphic figures as well

One of the few well-known female artists of the Italian Renaissance was Artemisia Gentileschi (1593–1652), whose style is reminiscent of Caravaggio's. One of her most famous paintings, *Judith and Holofernes*, is in Naples' Museo di Capodimonte.

ART & ARCHITECTURE ARCHITECTURE

For a Blast of Baroque
» Lecce, Puglia
» Noto, Sicily
» Catania, Sicily
» Naples, Campania

CONTEMPORARY MOVEMENTS

Of the many movements that shaped Italy's 20th-century art scene, few match the radical innovation of Arte Povera (Poor Art). Emerging from the economic and political instability of the 1960s, its artists aimed to blur the boundary between art and life. Using everyday materials and mediums ranging from painting and photography to installations, they created works that put the viewer at the centre, triggering personal memories and associations. The movement would ultimately pave the way for contemporary installation art. Its leading practitioners included Mario Merz (1925–2003), Luciano Fabro (1936–2007) and Giovanni Anselmo (b 1934), the latter's sculptures inspired by the geological forces of Stromboli. Another icon of the scene is the Greek-born Jannis Kounellis (b 1936), whose brooding installations often focus on the disintegration of culture in the modern world. Naples' MADRE contains a fine collection of Kounellis' creations, as well as other Arte Povera works. Among the wittiest is Michelangelo Pistoletti's *Venere degli stracci* (Venus of the Rags), in which a Greek goddess contemplates a pile of modern hand-me-downs.

Reacting against Arte Povera's conceptual tendencies was the 'Transavanguardia' movement of the late 1970s and 1980s, which refocussed attention on painting and sculpture in a traditional (primarily figurative) sense. Among its leading artists are Mimmo Paladino (b 1948) and Francesco Clemente (b 1952). Both of these Campanian artists are represented in Naples' Museo del Novecento, a museum dedicated to 20th-century southern Italian art.

as a riot of gargoyles, flora, fruit, columns and cornices. The leading exponents of the style were Gabriele Riccardi (1524–82) and Francesco Antonio Zimbalo (1567–1631), but it was Francesco's grandson Giuseppe Zimbalo (1620–1710), nicknamed Lo Zingarello (The Little Gypsy), who was its most exuberant disciple. Among his greatest designs is the upper facade of Lecce's Basilica di Santa Croce.

It would take an earthquake in 1632 to seal Sicily's baroque legacy. Faced with destruction, ambitious architects set to work rebuilding the towns and cities of the island's southeast, among them Noto, Modica and Ragusa. Grid-patterned streets were laid and spacious piazzas were lined with confident, curvaceous buildings. The result was a highly idiosyncratic *barocco siciliano* (Sicilian baroque), best known for its cheeky stone *putti* (cherubs), wrought-iron balustrades and grand external staircases. Equally idiosyncratic was the use of dramatic, centrally placed church belfries, often shooting straight above the central pediment. Two of the finest examples are Ragusa's Cattedrale di San Giorgio and Modica's Chiesa di San Giorgio, both designed by the prolific Rosario Gagliardi (1698–1762).

Sicily's most celebrated baroque architect, however, would be Giovanni Battista Vaccarini (1702–68). Trained in Rome, Vaccarini would dedicate three decades of his life to rebuilding earthquake-stricken Catania, using the region's volcanic black rock to dramatic effect in Piazza del Duomo. His reputation would see him join forces with Neapolitan starchitect Luigi Vanvitelli (1700–73) in the creation of Italy's epic baroque epilogue, the Palazzo Reale in Caserta, Campania.

Survival Guide

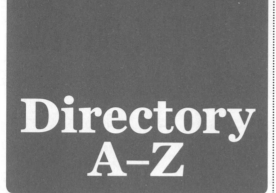

Directory A–Z

Accommodation

Accommodation in Italy's south is ever improving and increasingly varied. Hotels and *pensioni* (guesthouses) make up the bulk of the offerings, covering everything from cheap sleeps near the train station to trendy art hotels and world-renowned five star legends with dreamy ocean views. Youth hostels, camping grounds and an ever-increasing number of B&Bs are a boon for the euro-economisers, while *agriturismi* (farm stays) and *masserie* (southern Italian farms or estates) allow you to live out your bucolic Italian fantasies. Capturing the imagination still more are the options to stay in everything from castles to convents and monasteries.

Accommodation in this book is listed according to three price categories, as follows:

CATEGORY	SYMBOL	PRICE RANGE
Budget	€	under €100
Midrange	€€	€100-200
Top End	€€€	over €200

Where indicated, half-board means breakfast and either lunch or dinner; full board is breakfast, lunch and dinner.

In this book we list price ranges for accommodation: from the low-season minimum price to the high-season maximum.

Some hotels, in particular the lower-end places, barely alter their prices throughout the year. In low season there's no harm in bargaining for a discount, especially if you intend to stay for several days.

Hotels usually require that reservations be confirmed with a credit-card number. No-shows will be docked a night's accommodation.

The high season is during July and August, though prices peak again around Easter and Christmas. It's essential to book in advance during these periods. Conversely, prices drop between 30% and 50% in low season. In the winter months (November to Easter) many places, particularly on the coast, completely shut down. In the cities and larger towns accommodation tends to remain open all year. The relative lack of visitors in these down periods means you should have little trouble getting a room in those places that do stay open.

Agriturismi, Masserie & B&Bs

An *agriturismo* (*agriturismi* in the plural) is accommodation on a working farm, where you'll usually be able to sample the produce. Traditionally families simply rented out rooms in their

---

OFFBEAT ACCOMMODATION

Looking for something out of the ordinary? Italy offers a plethora of sleeping options that you won't find anywhere else in the world.

» In Naples, spend a regal night or two in the **aristocratic palazzo** of a powerful Bourbon bishop. Now the Decumani Hotel de Charme (p43), it comes complete with a sumptuous baroque salon.

» Down near Italy's heel, rent a **trullo**, one of the characteristic whitewashed conical houses of southern Puglia.

» On the island of Pantelleria, halfway between Sicily and Africa, sleep in a **dammuso** (traditional house with thick, whitewashed walls and a shallow cupola).

farmhouses; it's still possible to find this type of lodging, although many *agriturismi* have now evolved into sophisticated accommodation. There are several Italian guidebook directories devoted solely to *agriturismi*, or try www.agriturismo.it or www.agriturismo.net (also good for self-catering apartments and villas).

Unique to southern Italy, *masserie* are large farms or estates, usually built around a fortified watchtower, with plenty of surrounding accommodation to house workers and livestock. Many have been converted into luxurious hotels, *agriturismi*, or holiday apartments. A *masseria* isn't necessarily old: sometimes new buildings built around similar principles are called *masserie*. Recommended places are listed throughout this book.

B&Bs are a burgeoning sector of the southern accommodation market and can be found in both urban and rural settings. Options include everything from restored farmhouses, city *palazzi* and seaside bungalows to rooms in family houses. Tariffs per person cover a wide range, from around €25 to €75. For more information, contact **Bed & Breakfast Italia** (www.bbitalia.it).

Camping

Italians go camping with gusto and most camping facilities in Campania, Puglia, Calabria and Sicily (less so in Basilicata, where camping options are few and far between) include swimming pools, restaurants and supermarkets. With hotel prices shooting up in July and August, camping grounds can be a splendid option, especially given that many have enviable seaside locations.

Charges often vary according to the season, peaking in July and August, when accommodation should be booked well in advance. High-season prices range from €6 to €20 per adult and from €5 to €30 for a site. Many camping grounds offer the alternative of bungalows or even simple, self-contained flats. In high season, some only offer deals for stays of a week or longer.

Most camping grounds operate only in high season, roughly April to October (in many cases June to September only).

Lists of camping grounds are available from local tourist offices or online – try the following sites:

Campeggi.com (www.campeggi.com)
Camping.it (www.camping.it)
Italcamping.it (www.italcamping.it)

Major bookshops also sell the annual *Campeggi e Villaggi Turistici in Italia* (Camping and Holiday Villages in Italy, €14.90), which lists all Italian camping grounds, published by Touring Club Italiano (TCI).

Convents & Monasteries

Some convents and monasteries let out cells or rooms as a modest revenue-making exercise and happily take in tourists, while others only take in pilgrims or people on a spiritual retreat. Many impose a fairly early curfew, but prices tend to be quite reasonable.

Useful resources:

MonasteryStays.com (www.monasterystays.com) A slick and well-organised online booking centre for monastery and convent stays.

In Italy Online (www.initaly.com/agri/convents.htm) Another site well worth a look for monastery and convent accommodations. You pay US$6 to access the online newsletter with addresses.
Chiesa di Santa Susana (www.santasusanna.org/comingToRome/convents.html) This American Catholic church in Rome has searched out convent and monastery accommodation options around the country and posted a list on its website. Note that some places are simply residential accommodation run by religious orders and not necessarily big on monastic atmosphere. The church doesn't handle bookings; to request a spot, you'll need to contact each individual institution directly.

A useful, if ageing publication, is Eileen Barish's *The Guide to Lodging in Italy's Monasteries*. A more recent book on the same subject is Charles M Shelton's *Beds and Blessings in Italy: A Guide to Religious Hospitality*.

Hostels

Ostelli per la gioventù (youth hostels) are run by the **Associazione Italiana Alberghi per la Gioventù** (AIG; www.aighostels.com), affiliated with **Hostelling International** (HI; www.hihostels.com). A valid HI card is required in all associated youth hostels in Italy. You can get this in your home country or direct at many hostels.

A full list of Italian hostels, with details of prices, locations and so on, is available online or from hostels throughout the country.

BOOK YOUR STAY ONLINE

For more accommodation reviews by Lonely Planet authors, check out hotels.lonelyplanet.com/Italy. You'll find independent reviews, as well as recommendations on the best places to stay. Best of all, you can book online.

PRACTICALITIES

» Use the metric system for weights and measures.

» Since early 2005, smoking in all closed public spaces (from bars to elevators, offices to trains) has been banned... even if some locals continue to flaunt the law.

» If your Italian is up to it, try the following newspapers: *Corriere della Sera*, the country's leading daily, and its southern spin-off *Corriere del Mezzogiorno;* or *La Repubblica*, a centre-left daily with a flow of Mafia conspiracies and Vatican scoops.

» Tune into state-owned Italian RAI-1, RAI-2 and RAI-3 (www.rai.it), which broadcast all over Italy and abroad. The regions' plethora of contemporary music stations include Radio Kiss Kiss (www.kisskiss.it).

» Switch on the box to watch the state-run RAI-1, RAI-2 and RAI-3 (www.rai.it) and the main commercial stations (mostly run by Silvio Berlusconi's Mediaset company): Canale 5 (www.canale5.mediaset.it), Italia 1 (www.italia1.mediaset.it), Rete 4 (www.rete4.mediaset.it) and La 7 (www.la7.it).

Nightly rates in basic dorms vary from around €16 to €20, which usually includes a buffet breakfast. You can often get lunch or dinner for an extra €10 or so. Many hostels also offer singles/doubles (for around €30/50) and family rooms.

A few AIG hostels still have a midday lock-out period as well as a curfew from around 11pm or midnight, although these restrictions are increasingly less common.

A growing contingent of independent hostels offer alternatives to HI hostels. Many are barely distinguishable from budget hotels, with some offering sleek design and in-house perks like trendy bars and live music. One of many hostel websites is www.hostelworld.com.

Hotels & Pensioni

There is often little difference between a *pensione* (guesthouse) and an *albergo* (hotel). However, a *pensione* will generally be of one- to three-star quality and has traditionally been a family-run operation, while an *albergo* can be awarded up to five stars. *Locande* (inns) long fell into much the same category as *pensioni*, but the term has become trendy in some parts and reveals little about the quality of a place. *Affittacamere* are rooms for rent in private houses. They are generally simple affairs.

Quality can vary enormously and the official star system gives only limited clues. One-star hotels and *pensioni* tend to be basic and usually do not offer private bathrooms. Two-star places are similar but rooms will generally have a private bathroom. At three-star joints you can usually assume reasonable standards. Four- and five-star hotels offer facilities such as room service, laundry and dry-cleaning.

Prices are highest in major tourist destinations. A *camera singola* (single room) costs from around €30. A *camera doppia* (twin beds) or *camera matrimoniale* (double room with a double bed) will cost from around €50.

Tourist offices usually have booklets with local accommodation listings. Many hotels are also signing up with (steadily proliferating) online accommodation-booking services. You could start your search at any of the following:

Alberghi in Italia (www.alberghi-in-italia.it)

All Hotels in Italy (www.hotelsitalyonline.com)

Hotels web.it (www.hotelsweb.it)

In Italia (www.initalia.it)

Travel to Italy (www.travel-to-italy.com)

Business Hours

Opening times for individual businesses in this guide are only spelled out when they deviate from the standard hours outlined below.

BUSINESS TYPE	STANDARD HOURS
Banks	8.30am-1.30pm & 3-4.30pm Mon-Fri
Central post offices	8am-6pm Mon-Fri, 8.30am-1pm Sat
Smaller branch post offices	8am-1.30pm Mon-Fri, 8.30am-1pm Sat
Restaurants	noon-3pm & 7.30-11pm or midnight
Cafes	7.30am to 8pm
Bars, Pubs & Clubs	10pm-4am
Shops	9am-1pm & 3.30-7.30pm (or 4-8pm) Mon-Sat

» The opening hours of museums, galleries and archaeological sites vary enormously. As a rule, museums close on Monday, but from June to September many sights open daily.

» Exchange offices usually keep longer hours than banks, though these are hard to find outside major cities and tourist areas.

» Restaurant kitchens often shut an hour earlier than final closing time. Most places close at least one day a week; many restaurants take their holidays in August, while those in coastal resort towns usually close in the low season.

» Bars may open earlier if they have eateries on the premises; things don't get seriously shaking until after midnight.

» In larger cities, department stores and supermarkets may stay open at lunchtime or on Sundays.

Children

Throughout this book we use the child-friendly icon (⛴) to highlight places that are especially welcoming to families with children. The specific facilities you may find will vary from listing to listing, but may include family rooms or interconnecting doubles, home-like venues with animals to keep kids

entertained or a children's activity room or garden play area.

Practicalities

Italians love children but there are few special amenities for them. Always make a point of asking staff members at tourist offices if they know of any special family activities or have suggestions on hotels that cater for kids.

Book accommodation in advance whenever possible to avoid inconvenience. In hotels, some double rooms cannot accommodate an extra bed for kids, so it's always best to check ahead. If your child is small enough to share your bed, some hoteliers will let you do this for free. The website www.booking.com is good because it tells you the 'kid policy' for every hotel it lists and what extra charges you will incur.

On public transport, discounts are available for children (usually aged under the age of 12 but sometimes based on the child's height), and admission to many sites is free for children under 18.

When travelling by train, reserve seats where possible to avoid finding yourselves standing. You can hire car

seats for infants and children from most car-rental firms, but you should always book them in advance.

You can buy baby formula in powder or liquid form, as well as sterilising solutions such as Milton, at pharmacies. Disposable nappies (diapers) are available at supermarkets and pharmacies. Fresh cow's milk is sold in cartons in supermarkets and in bars with a 'Latteria' sign. UHT milk is popular and in many out-of-the-way areas the only kind available.

In most restaurants, kids are welcome but do not count on the availability of high chairs. Children's menus are uncommon but you can generally ask for a *mezzo piatto* (half plate) off the menu.

For more information and ideas, see Lonely Planet's *Travel with Children*, the superb Italy-focused website www.italiakids.com, or the more general www.travelwithyourkids.com and www.familytravelnetwork.com.

Customs Regulations

Duty-free sales within the EU no longer exist (but goods are sold tax-free in European

---

KEEPING THE KIDS HAPPY

There are plenty of sights and activities in southern Italy guaranteed to keep the kids as happy as the grown-ups. Here are a few ideas to get you started.

» Running around the ruins at ancient sites, snooping through medieval castles or prowling about Naples' mysterious underground aqueducts.

» Splashing in fountains or touring the south's booty of offshore islands on a small boat, diving off the side and sunbaking on the prow with friends.

» Dropping in on spontaneous football kick-abouts with local kids in town squares.

» Staying at *agriturismi*, particularly those with animals.

» Climbing Campania's and Sicily's surprisingly accessible volcanoes and swimming at bubbling, thermal beaches.

» Exploring the storybook *trulli* towns of Puglia and the fantastical, cave-like *sassi* of Matera.

» Eating gelato – it's the perfect mood-enhancer for the whole family, not to mention a great way to bribe your kids into better behaviour!

airports). Visitors coming into Italy from non-EU countries can import the following items duty free:

Spirits	1L (or 2L wine)
Perfume	50g
Eau de Toilette	250ml
Cigarettes	200
Other Goods	up to a total of €175

Anything over these limits must be declared on arrival and the appropriate duty paid. On leaving the EU, non-EU citizens can reclaim any Value Added Tax (VAT) on expensive purchases (see p256).

Discount Cards

Free admission to many galleries and cultural sites is available to youth under 18 and seniors over 65 years old; in addition, visitors aged between 18 and 25 often qualify for a 50% discount. In some cases, these discounts only apply to EU citizens.

If travelling to Naples and Campania, consider buying a **Campania artecard** (www.campaniaartecard.it), which offers free public transport and free or reduced admission to many museums and archaeological sites. For more information on this, see p42).

Electricity

Italy's electrical current is 220V, with a frequency of 50Hz, but older buildings may still use 125V. Wall outlets typically accommodate plugs with two or three round pins (the latter grounded, the former not).

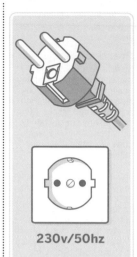

230v/50hz

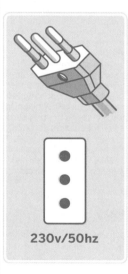

230v/50hz

Embassies & Consulates

Most countries have an embassy in Rome, where passport enquiries should be addressed. South of the capital, you'll find some honorary consulates in several major cities. For foreign embassies and consulates in Italy not listed here, look under 'Ambasciate' or 'Consolati' in the telephone directory.

Australia (☑06 85 27 21; www.italy.embassy.gov.au; Via Antonio Bosio 5, Rome)

Austria (www.austria.it) Rome (☑06 844 01 41; Via Pergolesi 3); Naples (☑081 28 77 24; Corso Umberto I 275); Bari (☑080 562 61 11; Via Bruno Buozzi 88); Palermo (☑091 682 56 96; Via Leonardo da Vinci 145)

Canada Rome (☑06 85 44 41; www.canadainternational.gc.ca/italy-italie; Via Zara 30); Naples (☑081 401 338; Via Carducci 29)

France (www.ambafrance-it.org) Rome (☑06 68 60 11; Piazza Farnese 67); Naples (☑081 598 07 11; Via Francesco Crispi 86); Bari (☑080 553 17 26; Via Giuseppe Bozzi 35); Palermo (☑091 58 34 05; Via Principe di Belmonte 101)

Germany Rome (☑06 49 21 31; www.rom.diplo.de; Via San Martino della Battaglia 4); Naples (☑081 248 85 11; www.neapel.diplo.de; Via Francesco Crispi 69); Bari (☑080 524 40 59; Piazza Umberto I 40); Palermo (☑091 34 25 75; Viale Scaduto 2D)

Ireland (☑06 697 91 21; www.ambasciata-irlanda.it; Piazza Campitelli 3, Rome)

Japan (☑06 48 79 91; www.it.emb-japan.go.jp; Via Quintino Sella 60, Rome)

Netherlands (www.olanda.it) Rome (☑06 3228 6001; Via Michele Mercati 8); Naples (☑081 551 30 03; Via Agostino Depretis 114); Bari (☑080 556 92 22; Viale Ennio Quinto 2-I); Palermo (☑091 58 15 21; Via Roma 489)

New Zealand (☑06 853 75 01; www.nzembassy.com/italy; Via Clitunno 44, Rome)

Switzerland Rome (☑06 80 95 71; www.eda.admin.ch/roma; Via Barnarba Oriani 61); Bari (☑080 524 96 97; Piazza Luigi di Savoia Duca degli Abruzzi 41a)

UK (www.ukinitaly.fco.gov.uk) Rome (☑06 4220 0001; Via XX Settembre 80a); Naples (☑081 423 89 11; Via dei Mille

YOUTH, STUDENT & TEACHER CARDS

The European Youth Card offers thousands of discounts on Italian hotels, museums, restaurants, shops and clubs, while a student, teacher or youth travel card can save you money on flights to Italy. All cards listed below are available from the **Centro Turistico Studentesco e Giovanile** (CTS; www.cts.it, in Italian), a youth travel agency with branches throughout southern Italy. The latter three cards listed below are available worldwide from student unions, hostelling organisations and youth travel agencies such as **STA Travel** (www.statravel.com).

CARD	WEBSITE	COST	ELIGIBILITY
European Youth Card (Carta Giovani)	www.europeanyouthcard.org	€11	under 30yrs
International Student Identity Card (ISIC)	www.isic.org	US$22, UK£9, €10	full-time student
International Teacher Identity Card (ITIC)	www.isic.org	US$22, UK£9, €10	full-time teacher
International Youth Travel Card (IYTC)	www.isic.org	US$22, UK£9, €10	under 26yrs

40); Bari (☑080 554 36 68; Via Dalmazia 127); Palermo (☑091 32 64 12; Via Cavour 117)

USA (www.italy.usembassy.gov) Rome (☑06 4 67 41; Via Vittorio Veneto 121); Naples (☑081 583 81 11; Piazza della Repubblica); Palermo (☑091 30 58 57; Via Vaccarini 1)

Food

In restaurant reviews throughout this book, 'meals' denotes the average price for a *primo* (first course), *secondo* (second course), *dolce* (dessert) and house wine for one person. Reviews are listed according to three budget categories as follows:

CATEGORY	SYMBOL	MEAL PRICE RANGE
Budget	€	under €25
Midrange	€€	€25-45
Top End	€€€	over €45

For more information on eating in southern Italy, see p232.

Gay & Lesbian Travellers

Although homosexuality is legal in Italy, attitudes in the south remain largely conservative and overt displays of affection by homosexual couples could attract consternation and unpleasant responses.

You'll find gay scenes in Naples, Catania and Taormina (the latter mostly in the summer), and to a lesser extent in Palermo and Bari.

Resources include:

Arcigay & Arcilesbica (www.arcigay.it) Bologna-based national organisation for gays and lesbians.

Arcigay Napoli (www.arcigaynapoli.org, in Italian) Website for Naples' main GLBTI organisation, listing special events as well as gay and gay-friendly venues in town.

Gay.it (www.gay.it, in Italian) Website listing gay venues and hotels across the country.

Gay Friendlyltalia.com (www.gayfriendlyitaly.com) English-language site produced by Gay.it, featuring information on everything from hotels to homophobia issues and the law.

Pride (www.prideonline.it) National monthly magazine of art, music, politics and gay culture.

Health

Recommended Vaccinations

No jabs are required to travel to Italy. The World Health Organization (WHO), however, recommends that all travellers should be covered for diphtheria, tetanus, the measles, mumps, rubella and polio, as well as hepatitis B.

Health Insurance

If you're an EU citizen (or from Switzerland, Norway or Iceland), a European Health Insurance Card (EHIC) covers you for most medical care in public hospitals free of charge, but not for emergency repatriation home or non-emergencies. The card is available from health centres and (in the UK) from post offices. Citizens from other countries should find out if there is a reciprocal arrangement for free medical care between their country and

Italy (Australia, for instance, has such an agreement; carry your Medicare card). If you do need health insurance, make sure you get a policy that covers you for the worst possible scenario, such as an accident requiring an emergency flight home. Find out in advance if your insurance plan will make payments directly to providers or reimburse you later for overseas health expenditures.

Availability Of Health Care

Good health care is readily available throughout southern Italy, although public hospitals tend to be less impressive the further south you travel. Pharmacists can give you valuable advice and sell over-the-counter medication for minor illnesses. They can also advise you when more specialised help is required and point you in the right direction. In major cities you are likely to find English-speaking doctors or a translator service available.

Pharmacies generally keep the same hours as other shops, closing at night and on Sundays. However, a handful remain open on a rotation basis (*farmacie di turno*) for emergency purposes. These are usually listed in newspapers, or online at www.miniportale. it (click on Farmacie di Turno and then the region you want). Closed pharmacies display a list of the nearest ones open.

If you need an ambulance anywhere in Italy, call ☎118. For emergency treatment, head straight to the *pronto soccorso* (casualty) section of a public hospital, where you can also get emergency dental treatment.

Environmental Hazards

Italian beaches are occasionally inundated with jellyfish. Their stings are painful, but not dangerous. Dousing

them in vinegar will deactivate any stingers that have not fired. Calamine lotion, antihistamines and analgesics may reduce the reaction and relieve pain.

Italy's only dangerous snake, the viper, is found throughout Puglia and Basilicata. To minimise the possibility of being bitten, always wear boots, socks and long trousers when walking through undergrowth where snakes may be present. Don't put your hands into holes and crevices, and be careful when collecting firewood. Viper bites do not cause instantaneous death and an antivenin is widely available in pharmacies. Keep the victim calm and still, wrap the bitten limb tightly, as you would for a sprained ankle, and attach a splint to immobilise it.

Always check all over your body if you have been walking through a potentially tick-infested area as ticks can cause skin infections and other more serious diseases such as Lyme disease and tick-borne encephalitis. If a tick is found attached, press down around the tick's head with tweezers, grab the head and gently pull upwards. Avoid pulling the rear of the body as this may squeeze the tick's gut contents through the attached mouth into the skin, increasing the risk of infection and disease. Lyme disease begins with the spreading of a rash at the site of the bite, accompanied by fever, headache, extreme fatigue, aching joints and muscles, and severe

neck stiffness. If untreated, symptoms usually disappear, but disorders of the nervous system, heart and joints can develop later. Treatment works best early in the illness: medical help should be sought. Symptoms of tick-borne encephalitis include blotches around the bite, which is sometimes pale in the middle, and headaches, stiffness and other flu-like symptoms (as well as extreme tiredness) appearing a week or two after the bite. Again, medical help must be sought.

Leishmaniasis is a group of parasitic diseases transmitted by sandflies and found in coastal parts of Puglia. Cutaneous leishmaniasis affects the skin and causes ulceration and disfigurement; visceral leishmaniasis affects the internal organs. Avoiding sandfly bites by covering up and using repellent is the best precaution.

Insurance

A travel-insurance policy to cover theft, loss and medical problems is a good idea. It may also cover you for cancellation or delays to your travel arrangements. Paying for your ticket with a credit card can often provide limited travel accident insurance and you may be able to reclaim the payment if the operator doesn't deliver. Ask your credit-card company what it will cover.

You can go to www.lonely planet.com/travel_services for worldwide travel insurance. You can buy, extend and claim online anytime – even if you're already on the road.

Internet Access

Throughout this guide we use the @ icon to indicate venues that offer an internet terminal (physical computer) for guests' use, and the 🛜 icon to designate places with wi-fi.

Internet access in the south has improved in the past couple of years, with an increasing number of hotels, B&Bs, hostels and even *agriturismi* now offering free wi fi. On the downside, public wi-fi hotspots and internet cafes remain thin on the ground and signal strength is variable. You'll still have to pay for access at many top-end hotels (upwards of €10 per day) and at internet cafes (€2 to €6 per hour). Certain provisions of Italy's anti-terrorism law, which required all internet users to present a photo ID and allowed the government to monitor internet usage, were rescinded in January 2011, but internet cafes will still sometimes request identification.

Legal Matters

Despite Mafia notoriety, southern Italy is relatively safe and the average tourist will only have a brush with the law if robbed by a bag-snatcher or pickpocket.

Police

Contact details for police stations, or *questure*, are given throughout this book. If you run into trouble in Italy, you're likely to end up dealing with the *polizia statale* (state police) or the *carabinieri* (military police). The former wear powder blue trousers with a fuchsia stripe and a navy blue jacket, the latter wear black uniforms with a red stripe and drive dark blue cars with a red stripe. The table below outlines Italian police organisations and their jurisdictions.

Polizia statale (state police)	thefts, visa extensions and permits
Carabinieri (military police)	general crime, public order and drug enforcement (often overlapping with the *polizia statale*)
Vigili urbani (local traffic police)	parking tickets, towed cars
Guardia di finanza	tax evasion, drug smuggling
Guardia forestale (aka *corpo forestale*)	environmental protection

For national emergency numbers, see p13.

Drugs & Alcohol

Under Italy's tough drug laws, possession of any controlled substances, including cannabis, can get you into hot water. Those caught in possession of 5g of cannabis can be considered traffickers and prosecuted as such. The same applies to tiny amounts of other drugs. Those caught with amounts below this threshold can be subject to minor penalties

The legal limit for blood-alcohol level is 0.05% and random breath tests do occur.

Your Rights

Italy still has anti-terrorism laws on its books that could make life difficult if you are detained. You should be given verbal and written notice of the charges laid against you within 24 hours by the arresting officers. You have no right to a phone call upon arrest. The prosecutor must apply to a magistrate for you to be held in preventive custody awaiting trial (depending on the seriousness of the offence) within 48 hours of arrest. You have the right not to respond to questions without the presence of a lawyer. If the magistrate orders preventive custody, you have the right to then contest this within the following 10 days.

Maps

The city maps in this book, combined with the good, free local maps available at most Italian tourist offices, will be sufficient for many travellers. For more specialised maps, browse the good selection at the national bookshop chain Feltrinelli, or consult the websites below.

Touring Club Italiano (TCI; www.touringclub.com, in Italian) Italy's largest map publisher operates shops all around Italy and publishes a decent 1:800,000 map of Italy, plus a series of 15 regional maps at 1:200,000 (€7.90 each) and an exhaustive series of walking guides with maps, co-published with the Club Alpino Italiano (CAI).

Litografia Artistica Cartografica (LAC; www.lac-cartografia.it) Produces detailed, large-scale maps, including maps of a number of Sicilian cities and Il Gargano in Puglia.

Stanfords (www.stanfords.co.uk) Excellent UK-based shop that stocks many of the maps listed above.

Omni Resources (www.omnimap.com) US-based online retailer with an impressive selection of Italian maps.

Money

The euro is Italy's currency. The seven euro notes come in denominations of €500, €200, €100, €50, €20, €10 and €5. The eight euro coins are in denominations of €2 and €1, and 50, 20, 10, five, two and one cents.

For the latest exchange rates, check out www. xe.com.

Credit & Debit Cards

Bancomats (ATM machines) are widely available throughout southern Italy and are the best way to obtain local currency. International credit and debit cards can be used in any ATM displaying the appropriate sign. Visa and MasterCard are among the most widely recognised, but others like Cirrus and Maestro are also well covered. Only some banks give cash advances over the counter, so you're better off using ATMs. Cards are also good for payment in most hotels, restaurants, shops, supermarkets and tollbooths.

Check any charges with your bank. Most banks now build a fee of around 2.75% into every foreign transaction. In addition, ATM withdrawals can attract a further fee, usually around 1.5%.

If your card is lost, stolen or swallowed by an ATM, you can telephone toll free to have an immediate stop put on its use:

Amex (☑06 7290 0347 or your national call number)
Diners Club (☑800 864064)
MasterCard (☑800 870866)
Visa (☑800 819014)

Moneychangers

You can change money in banks, at the post office or in a *cambio* (exchange office). Post offices and banks tend to offer the best rates; exchange offices keep longer hours, but watch for high commissions and inferior rates.

Taxes & Refunds

A value-added tax of around 20%, known as IVA (*Imposta di Valore Aggiunto*), is slapped onto just about everything in Italy. If you are a non-EU resident and spend more than €155 (€154.94 to be more precise!) on a purchase, you can claim a refund

when you leave. The refund only applies to purchases from affiliated retail outlets that display a 'tax free for tourists' (or similar) sign. You have to complete a form at the point of sale, then have it stamped by Italian customs as you leave. At major airports you can then get an immediate cash refund; otherwise, it will be refunded to your credit card. For information, visit **Tax Refund for Tourists** (www.taxrefund.it) or pick up a pamphlet on the scheme from participating stores.

Tipping

You are not expected to tip on top of restaurant service charges but you can leave a little extra if you feel service warrants it. If there is no service charge, consider leaving a 10% tip, but this is not obligatory. In bars, Italians often leave small change as a tip (usually €0.10 to €0.20). Tipping taxi drivers is not common practice, but you are expected to tip the porter at top-end hotels.

Post

Poste Italiane (www.poste. it, in Italian), Italy's postal system, is reasonably reliable. For post office opening hours, see p250.

Francobolli (stamps) are available at post offices and authorised tobacconists (look for the big white-on-black 'T' sign). Since letters often need to be weighed, what you get at the tobacconist for international airmail will occasionally be an approximation of the proper rate. Tobacconists keep regular shop hours (see p250).

Postal Rates & Services

The cost of sending a letter by *via aerea* (airmail) depends on its weight, size and where it is being sent. Most people use *posta prioritaria* (priority mail), Italy's most efficient mail service, guaran-

teed to deliver letters sent to Europe within three days and to the rest of the world within four to eight days. Letters up to 20g cost €0.75 within Europe, €1.60 to Africa, Asia and North and South America and €2 to Australia and New Zealand. Letters weighing 21g to 50g cost €2.40 within Europe, €3.30 to Africa, Asia and the Americas, and €4 to Australia and New Zealand.

Receiving Mail

Poste restante (general delivery) is known as *fermo posta* in Italy. Letters marked thus will be held at the counter of the same name in the main post office in the relevant town.

You'll need to pick up your letters in person and you must present your passport as ID.

Public Holidays

Most Italians take their annual holiday in August, with the busiest period occurring around August 15, known locally as Ferragosto. This means that many businesses and shops close for at least a part of that month. It also means that southern Italy's islands and coastal resorts become incredibly lively (and crowded). Settimana Santa (Easter week) is another busy holiday period for Italians.

Individual towns have public holidays to celebrate the feasts of their patron saints. National public holidays include the following:

New Year's Day (Capodanno or Anno Nuovo) 1 January
Epiphany (Epifania or Befana) 6 January
Easter Monday (Pasquetta or Lunedì dell'Angelo) March/April
Liberation Day (Giorno della Liberazione) 25 April – marks the Allied Victory in Italy, and the end of the German presence and Mussolini, in 1945.

Labour Day (Festa del Lavoro) 1 May

Republic Day (Festa della Repubblica) 2 June

Feast of the Assumption (Assunzione or Ferragosto) 15 August

All Saints' Day (Ognissanti) 1 November

Feast of the Immaculate Conception (Immaculata Concezione) 8 December

Christmas Day (Natale) 25 December

Boxing Day (Festa di Santo Stefano) 26 December

Telephone
Domestic Calls

Italian telephone area codes all begin with 0 and consist of up to four digits. The area code is followed by a number of anything from four to eight digits. The area code is an integral part of the telephone number and must always be dialled, even when calling from next door. Mobile-phone numbers begin with a three-digit prefix such as 330. Toll-free (free-phone) numbers are known as *numeri verdi* and usually start with 800. Nongeographical numbers start with 840, 841, 848, 892, 899, 163, 166 or 199. Some six-digit national rate numbers are also in use (such as those for Alitalia, rail and postal information).

As elsewhere in Europe, Italians choose from a host of providers of phone plans and rates, making it difficult to make generalisations about costs.

International Calls

The cheapest options for calling internationally are free or low-cost computer programs such as Skype, cut-rate call centres or international calling cards, which are sold at newsstands and tobacconists. Cut-price call centres can be found in the main cities, and rates can be considerably lower than from Telecom payphones for international

calls. You simply place your call from a private booth inside the centre and pay for it when you are finished. Direct international calls can also easily be made from public telephones with a phonecard. Dial ☑00 to get out of Italy, then the relevant country and area codes, followed by the telephone number.

To call Italy from abroad, dial the international access number (011 in the United States, 00 from most other countries), Italy's country code (☑39) and then the area code of the location you want, including the leading 0.

Directory Enquiries

National and international phone numbers can be requested at ☑1254 (or online at 1254.virgilio.it).

Mobile Phones

Italy uses GSM 900/1800, which is compatible with the rest of Europe and Australia but not with North American GSM 1900 or the totally different Japanese system (though some GSM 1900/900 phones do work here). If you have a GSM phone, check with your service provider about using it in Italy and beware of calls being routed internationally (very expensive for a 'local' call).

Italy has one of the highest levels of mobile-phone penetration in Europe, and you can get a temporary or prepaid account from several companies if you already own a GSM, dual- or tri-band cellular phone. You will usually need your passport to open an account. Always check with your service provider in your home country to ascertain whether your handset allows use of another SIM card. If yours does, it can cost as little as €10 to activate a local prepaid SIM card (sometimes with €10 worth of calls on the card). Alternatively, you can buy or lease an inexpensive Italian phone for the duration of your trip.

Of the main mobile phone companies, TIM (Telecom Italia Mobile), Wind and Vodafone have the densest networks of outlets across the country.

Payphones & Phonecards

Partly privatised Telecom Italia is the largest telecommunications organisation in Italy. Where Telecom offices are staffed, it is possible to make international calls and pay at the desk afterwards. Alternatively, you'll find Telecom payphones throughout the country, on the streets, in train stations and in Telecom offices. Most payphones only accept *carte/schede telefoniche* (phonecards), although some also accept credit cards. Telecom offers a wide range of prepaid cards for both domestic and international use; for a full list, see www.telecomitalia.it/tele fono/carte-telefoniche. You can buy phonecards (most commonly €3, €5 or €10) at post offices, tobacconists and newsstands.

Time

Italy is one hour ahead of GMT. Daylight savings time, when clocks are moved forward one hour, starts on the last Sunday in March. Clocks are put back an hour on the last Sunday in October. Italy operates on a 24-hour clock.

Tourist Information

The quality of tourist offices varies dramatically. One office might have enthusiastic staff, another might be indifferent. Most offices can offer you a plethora of brochures, maps and leaflets, even if they're uninterested in helping in any other way. Outside major cities and international tourist areas, it's fairly unusual for the staff to speak English.

Four tiers of tourist office exist: local, provincial, regional and national.

Local & Provincial Tourist Offices

Despite their different (and sometimes elaborate) names, provincial and local offices offer similar services and are collectively referenced with the term 'tourist office' throughout this book. All deal directly with the public, and most will respond to written and telephone requests for information. Staff can usually provide a city map, lists of hotels and information on the major sights. In larger towns and major tourist areas, staff usually have a working knowledge of at least one other language, generally English but also possibly French and German.

Main offices are generally open Monday to Friday; some also open on weekends, especially in urban areas or during peak summer season. Affiliated information booths (at train stations and airports, for example) may keep slightly different hours.

The main local and provincial tourist office categories are summarised below.

Azienda di Promozione Turistica (APT) This main provincial tourist office offers information on the town and its surrounding province.

Azienda Autonoma di Soggiorno e Turismo (AAST) These local tourist offices in larger towns and cities of the south provide town-specific information only (bus routes, museum opening times, etc).

Pro Loco These local tourist offices in smaller towns and villages offer services similar to AAST.

Regional Tourist Authorities

Regional offices are generally more concerned with planning, budgeting, marketing and promotion than with offering a public information service. However, they still maintain some useful websites, as listed below. In some cases you'll need to look for the Tourism or Turismo link within the regional site.

Basilicata (www.aptbasilicata.it)

Calabria (www.turiscalabria.it, in Italian)

Campania (www.in-campania.com)

Puglia (www.pugliaturismo.com)

Sicily (www.regione.sicilia.it/turismo)

Tourist Offices Abroad

The **Italian National Tourist Office** (ENIT; www.enit.it) maintains offices in over two dozen cities on five continents. Contact information for all offices can be found on the website.

Travellers With Disabilities

Southern Italy is not easygoing for disabled travellers. Cobbled streets, hair-raising traffic, blocked pavements and tiny lifts make life very difficult for wheelchair users, and those with sight or hearing difficulties. The Italian National Tourist Office in your country may be able to provide advice on Italian associations for the disabled and information on what help is available.

Italy's national rail company, **Trenitalia** (www.trenitalia.com), offers a national helpline for disabled passengers at ☑199 303060 (7am to 9pm daily).

For more information and help, try the following organisations:

Accessible Italy (www.accessibleitaly.com) A San Marino–based company that specialises in holiday services for the disabled, ranging from tours to the hiring of adapted transport to romantic Italian weddings. This is the best first port of call.

Consorzio Cooperative Integrate (www.coinsociale.it) This Rome-based organisation provides information on the capital (including transport and access) and is happy to share its contacts throughout Italy. Its 'Turismo per Tutti' program seeks to improve infrastructure and access for disabled tourists.

Tourism for All (www.tourismforall.org.uk) This UK-based group has information on where to hire equipment, hotels with access for disabled guests, and tour operators dealing with disabled travellers.

Visas

Italy is one of 25 member countries of the Schengen Convention, under which 22 EU countries (all but Bulgaria, Cyprus, Ireland, Romania and the UK) plus Iceland, Norway and Switzerland have abolished permanent checks at common borders.

Legal residents of one Schengen country do not require a visa for another. Residents of 28 non-EU countries, including Australia, Brazil, Canada, Israel, Japan, New Zealand and the USA, do not require visas for tourist visits of up to 90 days (this list varies for those wanting to travel to the UK and Ireland).

All non-EU and non-Schengen nationals entering Italy for more than 90 days, or for any reason other than tourism (such as study or work) may need a specific visa. For details, visit www.esteri.it/visti/home_eng.asp or contact an Italian consulate. You should also have your passport stamped on entry as, without a stamp, you could encounter problems when trying to obtain a residence permit (permesso di soggiorno). If you enter the EU via another member state, get your passport stamped there.

EU citizens do not require any permits to live or work in Italy but, after three months' residence, they are supposed to register themselves at the municipal registry office where they live and offer proof of work or sufficient funds to support themselves. Non-EU foreign citizens with five years' continuous legal residence may apply for permanent residence.

Study Visas

Non-EU citizens who want to study at a university or language school in Italy must have a study visa. These can be obtained from your nearest Italian embassy or consulate. You will normally need to show confirmation of your enrolment, proof of payment of fees and adequate funds to support yourself. The visa covers only the period of the enrolment. This type of visa is renewable within Italy but, again, only with confirmation of ongoing enrolment and proof that you are able to support yourself (bank statements are preferred).

Volunteering

Concordia International Volunteer Projects (www.concordiavolunteers.org.uk)

Short-term community-based projects covering the environment, archaeology and the arts. You might find yourself working as a volunteer on a restoration project or in a nature reserve.

European Youth Portal (europa.eu/youth/volunteering_-_exchanges/index_eu_en.html) Has various links suggesting volunteering options across Europe. Narrow down the search to Italy, where you will find more specific links on volunteering.

AFSAI (www.afsai.org) Financed by the EU, this voluntary program runs projects of six to 12 months for those aged between 16 and 25 years. Knowledge of Italian is required.

World Wide Opportunities on Organic Farms (www.wwoof.it) For a membership fee of €25 this organisation provides a list of farms looking for volunteer workers.

Women Travellers

The most common source of discomfort for solo women travellers in southern Italy is harassment. Local men are rarely shy about staring at women and this can be disconcerting,

especially if the staring is accompanied by the occasional *'ciao bella'*. In many places, local Lotharios will try it on with exasperating insistence, which can be flattering or a pain. Foreign women are particular objects of male attention. Usually, the best response to undesired advances is to ignore them. If that doesn't work, politely tell your interlocutors you're waiting for your *marito* (husband) or *fidanzato* (boyfriend) and, if necessary, walk away. Avoid becoming aggressive as this may result in an unpleasant confrontation. If all else fails, approach the nearest member of the police.

Watch out for men with wandering hands on crowded buses. Either keep your back to the wall or make a loud fuss if someone starts fondling your behind. A loud *'Che schifo!'* (How disgusting!) will usually do the trick. If a more serious incident occurs, report it to the police, who are then required to press charges.

Women travelling alone should use their common sense. Avoid solo hitchhiking or walking alone in dark streets, and look for hotels that are central (unsafe areas are noted in this book).

Transport

GETTING THERE & AWAY

A plethora of airlines link Italy to the rest of the world, and an extensive network of intra-European and domestic flights provide easy access to many southern Italian destinations. Good rail and/or bus services connect most of southern Italy's major cities and towns, while car and passenger ferries operate to ports throughout the Mediterranean.

Flights, tours and rail tickets can be booked online at www.lonelyplanet.com/bookings.

Entering The Country

European Union and Swiss citizens can travel to Italy with their national identity card alone. All other nationalities must have a valid passport and may be required to fill out a landing card (at airports).

By law you should have your passport or ID card with you at all times. You'll need one of these for police registration every time you check into accommodation.

Air

Airports & Airlines

Italy's main intercontinental gateways are Rome's **Leonardo da Vinci Airport** (Fiumicino; FCO; www.adr.it) and Milan's **Malpensa Airport** (MXP; www.sea-aeroportimilano.it). Both are served by non-stop flights from around the world.

Most direct flights into southern Italy are domestic or intra-European, so you may need to change at Rome or Milan if arriving from outside Europe.

Handy airports in southern Italy include the following:

Capodichino Airport (Naples) (NAP; www.gesac.it) Connections include London (Gatwick), Paris and Berlin. Airlines include Alitalia, British Airways, Lufthansa and EasyJet. Seasonal connections to Tel Aviv and New York (JFK).

Palese Airport (Bari) (BRI; www.aeroportidipuglia.it) Flights include London (Gatwick and Stansted), Paris (Beauvais), Madrid, Valencia, Cologne and Prague. Airlines include Alitalia, British Airways, Ryanair, Spanair, Germanwings and Wizzair.

Papoila Airport (Brindisi) (BDS; www.aeroportidipuglia.it) Destinations include London (Stansted), Paris (Orly and Beauvais), Geneva, Eindhoven, Munich and Barcelona (Girona). Airlines include Alitalia, AirOne, EasyJet, Ryanair and Air Berlin.

Lamezia Terme Airport (Sant'Eufemia Lamezia, Cosenza) (SUF; www.sacal.it, in Italian) Destinations include London (Stansted), Paris (Beauvais), and Brussels, with seasonal routes including Toronto. Airlines include Ryanair, Brussels Airlines and Air Transat.

Falcone-Borsellino Airport (Palermo) (PMO; www.gesap.it) European connections include London (Gatwick and Stansted), Marseilles, Madrid, Cologne and Stockholm. Intercontinental flights to Tunis and New York, and regular domestic flights to the islands of Pantelleria and Lampedusa.

Fontanarossa Airport (Catania) (CTA; www.aeroporto.catania.it) Destinations include London (Gatwick), Paris (Orly), Amsterdam, Copenhagen, Berlin and Cologne. Airlines include Alitalia, British Airways, Air Berlin and Cimber Sterling.

Vincenzo Florio Airport (Trapani) (TPS; www.airgest.it) Ryanair operates direct flights to several European destinations, including London (Luton), Dublin, Paris (Beauvais), Barcelona (Girona) and Stockholm (Skavsta). Meridiana serves Pantelleria.

A number of international airlines compete with the country's national carrier, **Alitalia** (www.alitalia.com), amongst them Italy's **Meridiana fly** (www.meridiana.it) and **Air One** (www.flyairone.it), as well as cut-rate big guns **Ryanair** (www.ryanair.com) and **EasyJet** (www.easyjet.com).

Tickets

The internet is the easiest way of locating and booking reasonably priced seats.

Full-time students and those under 26 may qualify for discounted fares at agencies such as **STA Travel** (www.statravel.com). Many of these fares require a valid International Student Identity Card (ISIC; see p253).

Land

Reaching southern Italy overland involves travelling the entire length of Italy, which can either be an enormous drain on your time or, if you have plenty to spare, a wonderful way of seeing the country. Buses are usually the cheapest option, but services are less frequent and considerably less comfortable than the train.

Border Crossings

The main points of entry to Italy are: the Mont Blanc Tunnel from France at Chamonix; the Grand St Bernard, Gotthard and Lötschberg Base tunnels from Switzerland; and the Brenner Pass from Austria. All are open year-round. Mountain passes are often closed in winter and sometimes even in autumn and spring, making the tunnels a more reliable option. Make sure you have snow chains if driving in winter.

Regular trains on two lines connect Italy with the main cities in Austria and into Germany, France or Eastern Europe. Trains from Milan head for Switzerland and on into France and the Netherlands. The main international train line to Slovenia crosses near Trieste.

Bus

Buses are the cheapest overland option to Italy, but services are less frequent, less comfortable and significantly slower than the train.

Eurolines (www.eurolines. com) A consortium of coach companies with offices throughout Europe. Italy-bound buses head to Milan, Venice, Florence, Siena and Rome, from where Italian train and bus services continue south.

Marozzi (www.marozzivt.it, in Italian) Offers daily services from Rome to Bari, Brindisi, Otranto and Matera.

Miccolis (www.miccolis-spa. it, in Italian) Runs several services a day from Naples to Potenza, Taranto, Brindisi and Lecce.

Marino (www.marinobus.it, in Italian) Runs daily services from Naples to Bari and Matera.

Liscio (☑0971 5 46 73) Connects Rome to several destinations, including Venosa and Potenza, and connects Basilicata with Naples and Salerno.

Lirosi (www.lirosiautoservizi.it, in Italian) Runs services from Rome to Reggio Calabria.

SAIS (www.saistrasporti.it) Operates long-haul services to Sicily from Rome and Naples.

Car & Motorcycle

CONTINENTAL EUROPE

When driving in Europe, always carry proof of vehicle ownership and evidence of third-party insurance. If driving an EU-registered vehicle, your home country insurance is sufficient. Ask your insurer for a European Accident Statement (EAS) form, which can simplify matters in the event of an accident.

A European breakdown assistance policy is a good investment and can be obtained through the Automobile Club d'Italia (see p265).

Every vehicle travelling across an international border should display a nationality plate of its country of registration.

There is an excellent network of autostrade in Italy, represented by a white A followed by a number on a green background. The main north–south link is the Autostrada del Sole, from Milan to Reggio di Calabria (called the A1 from Milan to Rome, the A2 from Rome to Naples and the A3 from Naples to Reggio di Calabria).

There's a toll to use most of Italy's autostrade. You can pay by cash or credit card as you leave the autostrada; to avoid lengthy queues, buy a prepaid card (Telepass or Viacard) from ACI offices, main motorway petrol stations and roadside Autogrill stores, and some banks, in denominations of €25, €50 or €75. These cards are valid throughout Italy. For information on road tolls and passes, contact **Autostrade per Italia** (www.autostrade.it).

Italy's scenic roads are tailor-made for motorcycle touring, and motorcyclists swarm into the country every summer. With a bike you rarely have to book ahead for ferries and can enter restricted-traffic areas in cities. Crash helmets and a motorcycle licence are compulsory. Unless you're touring, it is probably easier to rent a bike once you are at your destination.

BUS PASSES

Eurolines offers a low-season **bus pass** (www.euro lines-pass.com) valid for 15/30 days that costs €205/310 (€175/240 for under-26s and senior citizens over 60). This pass allows unlimited travel between 40 European cities, including Milan, Venice, Florence, Siena and Rome. Fares increase to €345/455 (€290/375) in midsummer.

UK

You can take your car across to France by ferry or via the Channel Tunnel on **Eurotunnel** (☏0844 335 35 35; www.eurotunnel.com). The latter runs four crossings (35 minutes) an hour between Folkestone and Calais in the high season.

For breakdown assistance, both the **AA** (☏in UK 0800 072 3279; www.theaa.com/breakdown-cover) and the **RAC** (☏in UK 0800 015 6000; www.rac.co.uk/euro-breakdown) offer comprehensive cover in Europe.

Train

The comprehensive European Rail Timetable (UK£13.99), updated monthly, is available from **Thomas Cook Publishing** (www.thomascookpublishing.com).

It is always advisable, and sometimes compulsory, to book seats on international trains to/from Italy. Some of the main international services include transport for private cars. Consider taking long journeys overnight as the €20 or so extra for a sleeper costs substantially less than Italian hotels.

Within Italy, direct trains run from Milan, Florence and Rome to Naples, Reggio di Calabria and to Messina, Sicily. Trains to Sicily are transported from the mainland by ferry from Villa San Giovanni, just north of Reggio di Calabria. From Messina, services continue on to Palermo, Catania and other provincial Sicilian capitals. For more detail on rail travel to Sicily, see p161.

Trains to Puglia and Basilicata require at least one change along Italy's main north–south route. The handiest place is Rome, although you may have to change again at Benevento, just south of Naples. From both Rome and Milan you should take an Intercity or Eurostar train to Potenza (Basilicata) and Bari (Puglia).

UK

The passenger train **Eurostar** (☏08432 186186; www.eurostar.com) travels between London and Paris, or London and Brussels. Alternatively, you can get a train ticket that includes crossing the Channel by ferry.

For the latest fare information on journeys to Italy, including the Eurostar, contact the **Rail Europe Travel Centre** (☏in UK 08448 484064; www.raileurope.co.uk) or **Rail Choice** (☏0871 231 0790; www.railchoice.com).

Sea

Multiple ferry companies connect southern Italy with countries throughout the Mediterranean. Many routes only operate in summer, when ticket prices also rise. During this period, all routes are busy and you need to book several weeks in advance. Fares to Greece are generally more expensive from Bari than those available from Brindisi, although unless you're planning on travelling in the Salento, Bari is the more convenient port of arrival and also has better onward links for bus and train travel. Prices for vehicles vary according to their size.

The helpful website www.traghettionline.com (in Italian) covers all the ferry companies in the Mediterranean. Another useful resource for

INTERNATIONAL FERRY ROUTES FROM SOUTHERN ITALY

DESTINATION COUNTRY	DESTINATION PORT(S)	ITALIAN PORT(S)	COMPANY
Albania	Durrës	Bari	Ventouris
	Vlore	Brindisi	Red Star, Agoudimos
Croatia	Dubrovnik	Bari	Jadrolinija
Greece	Cephalonia, Corfu, Igoumenitsa, Zante	Brindisi	Agoudimos
	Corfu, Igoumenitsa, Patras	Bari	Blue Star, Superfast
Malta	Valletta	Palermo	GNV, SNAV
	Valletta	Catania	Grimaldi
	Valletta	Pozzallo, Catania	Virtu
Montenegro	Bar	Bari	Montenegro Lines
Tunisia	Tunis	Palermo	GNV, SNAV
	Tunis	Palermo, Salerno, Trapani	Grimaldi

CLIMATE CHANGE & TRAVEL

Every form of transport that relies on carbon-based fuel generates CO_2, the main cause of human-induced climate change. Modern travel is dependent on aeroplanes, which might use less fuel per kilometre per person than most cars but travel much greater distances. The altitude at which aircraft emit gases (including CO_2) and particles also contributes to their climate change impact. Many websites offer 'carbon calculators' that allow people to estimate the carbon emissions generated by their journey and, for those who wish to do so, to offset the impact of the greenhouse gases emitted with contributions to portfolios of climate-friendly initiatives throughout the world. Lonely Planet offsets the carbon footprint of all staff and author travel.

ferries from Italy to Greece is www.ferries.gr.

INTERNATIONAL FERRY COMPANIES SERVING SOUTHERN ITALY

Agoudimos Lines (www.agoudimos.it)

Blue Star Ferries (www.bluestarferries.com)

GNV (Grandi Navi Veloci; www.gnv.it)

Grimaldi (www.grimaldi-ferries.com)

Jadrolinija (www.jadrolinija.hr)

Montenegro Lines (www.montenegrolines.net)

Red Star Ferries (www.redstarferries.com)

SNAV (www.snav.it)

Ventouris (www.ventouris.gr)

Virtu Ferries (www.virtuferries.com)

GETTING AROUND

Unless you're a masochist, avoid driving in larger centres such as Naples, Bari, Lecce, Palermo and Catania, where anarchic traffic and parking restrictions will quickly turn your holiday sour. Beyond these urban centres, however, having your own car is the easiest way to get around Italy's south. Buses and trains will get you to most of the main destinations, but they are run by a plethora of private companies, which makes buying tickets and finding bus stops a bit of a bind. Furthermore, the rail network in Salento is still of the narrow-gauge variety, so

trains chug along at a snail's pace.

Your own vehicle will give you the most freedom to stray off the main routes and discover out-of-the-way towns and beaches. This is particularly the case in the Parco Nazionale del Cilento e Vallo di Diano in Campania, the Pollino National Park in Basilicata, the Salento in Puglia and throughout much of rural Sicily.

This said, it's also worth considering the downside of driving. Aside from the negative environmental impact, petrol prices (see p265) are notoriously high, less-travelled roads are often poorly maintained, and popular routes (including Campania's Amalfi Coast, the SS16 connecting Bari and the Salento in Puglia, and Sicily's Ionian and Tyrrhenian coastal routes) can be heavily trafficked during holiday periods and throughout the summer.

Air

The privatised national airline, Alitalia, is the main domestic carrier. Cut-rate competitors within Italy include **Meridiana fly** (www.meridiana.it), **Air One** (www.flyairone.it), **Ryanair** (www.ryanair.com) and **EasyJet** (www.easyjet.com). A useful search engine for comparing multiple carriers' fares and purchasing low-cost domestic flights is **AZfly** (www.azfly.it).

Airport taxes are factored into the price of your ticket.

Bicycle

Cycling may be more popular in northern Italy, but it can be just as rewarding south of Rome. Cyclo-trekking is particularly popular in the Murgia and the Gargano Promontory in Puglia. Cycling is also very popular in the Salentine cities of Lecce, Galatina, Gallipoli and Otranto, with more challenging itineraries in Basilicata's Parco Nazionale del Pollino and on Sicily's hilly terrain.

Avoid hitting the pedal in large cities like Naples and Palermo, where unruly traffic makes cycling a veritable death wish. Cycling along the Amalfi Coast is another bad idea (think blind corners and sheer drops). Bikes are prohibited on the autostrade.

If you fancy seeing the south on a saddle, the following reputable organisations offer advice and/or guided tours:

Cyclists' Touring Club (www.ctc.org.uk) This UK organisation can help you plan your tour or organise a guided tour. Membership costs £37 (£23 for over-65s, £12 for under-18s).

Puglia in Bici (www.pugliainbici.com) A very good organisation offering bike rental and tailor-made itineraries throughout Puglia.

Gargano Bike Holidays (www.garganobike.com, in

Italian and German) Specialises in cultural and scenic mountain bike tours exploring the Gargano on half-day to weekly trips.

Bikes can be wheeled onto any domestic train displaying the bicycle logo. Simply purchase a separate bicycle ticket, valid for 24 hours (€3.50). Certain international trains, listed on Trenitalia's 'In treno con la bici' page, also allow transport of assembled bicycles for €12. Bikes dismantled and stored in a bag can be taken for free, even on night trains. Most ferries also allow free bicycle passage.

Bikes are available for hire in most towns. Rental costs for a city bike start from around €20 per day; mountain bikes are a bit more.

Boat

Domestic *navi* (large ferries) service Campania and Sicily, while *traghetti* (smaller ferries) and *aliscafi* (hydrofoils) service the Bay of Naples islands, the Amalfi Coast, the Isole Tremiti in Puglia, and the Aeolian Islands in Sicily. Most services are pared back between October and Easter, and some are suspended altogether during this period. Most ferries carry vehicles; hydrofoils do not.

Ferries for Sicily leave from Naples, as well as from Villa San Giovanni and Reggio Calabria. The main points of arrival in Sicily are Palermo, Catania, Trapani and Messina.

The comprehensive website **Traghettionline** (www.traghettionline.com, in Italian) includes links to multiple Italian ferry companies, allowing you to compare prices and buy tickets.

More detailed information on ferry prices and times for Campania can be found on p48, and for Sicily on p150. For other relevant destinations, see the Getting There

& Away sections of individual chapters.

On overnight ferries, travellers can book a two- to four-person cabin or a *poltrona*, which is an airline-type armchair. Deck class (which allows you to sit/sleep in lounge areas or on deck) is only available on some ferries.

Bus

Numerous companies provide bus services in southern Italy, from meandering local routes to fast and reliable intercity connections. Buses are usually priced competitively with the train and are often the only way to get to smaller towns. If your destination is not on a main train line (trains tend to be cheaper on major routes), buses are usually a faster way to get around – this is especially true for the Salento in Puglia, Basilicata and for inland Calabria and Sicily.

Services are provided by a variety of companies. While these can be frequent on weekdays, they are reduced considerably on Sundays and holidays – runs between smaller towns often fall to one or none. Keep this in mind if you depend on buses as it is easy to get stuck in smaller places, especially at the weekends.

It's usually possible to get bus timetables (*orari*) from local tourist offices and the bus companies' websites. In larger cities most of the intercity bus companies have ticket offices or sell tickets through agencies. In villages and even some good-size towns, tickets are sold in bars – just ask for *biglietti per il pullman* – or on the bus itself.

Advance booking, while not generally required, is a good idea in the high season for overnight or long-haul trips.

For destination-specific bus operators, times and prices, see the Getting There & Away sections of individual chapters.

Car & Motorcycle

Italy boasts an extensive privatised network of autostradas, represented on road signs by a white A followed by a number on a green background. The main north–south link is the Autostrada del Sole (the 'Motorway of the Sun'), which extends from Milan to Reggio di Calabria (called the A1 from Milan to Rome, the A2 from Rome to Naples, and the A3 from Naples to Reggio di Calabria). The east–west A16 links Naples to Canosa di Puglia. From here, it becomes the A14, shooting southeast to Bari and continuing south to Taranto. From Bari, the single-lane SS16 is the main arterial route to the Salento, although in summer this can be heavily trafficked.

There are tolls on most motorways, payable by cash or credit card as you exit. For information on traffic conditions, tolls and driving distances, see www.autostrade.it (in Italian).

There are several additional road categories, listed below in descending order of importance.

Strade statali (state highways) Represented on maps by 'S' or 'SS', they vary from toll-free, four-lane highways to two-lane main roads. The latter can be extremely slow, especially in mountainous regions.

Strade regionali (regional highways connecting small villages) Coded SR or R.

Strade provinciali (provincial highways) Coded SP or P.

Strade locali (local roads) Often not even paved or mapped.

Automobile Associations

The **Automobile Club d'Italia** (ACI; www.aci.it) is a driver's best resource in Italy. For 24-hour roadside emergency service, dial ☎803116 from a landline or ☎800 116800 from a mobile phone. Foreigners do not have to join but instead pay a per-incident fee.

Driving Licence

All EU member states' driving licences are fully recognised throughout Europe. In practice, many non-EU licences (such as Australian, Canadian, New Zealand and US licences) are accepted by car-hire outfits in Italy. Travellers from other countries should obtain an International Driving Permit (IDP) through their national automobile association.

Fuel & Spare Parts

Italy's petrol prices are among the highest in Europe and vary from one service station (*benzinaio, stazione di servizio*) to another. As this book went to press, lead-free gasoline (*senza piombo; 95 octane*) was averaging €1.57 per litre, with diesel (*gasolio*) costing €1.44 per litre.

Spare parts are available at many garages or via the 24-hour ACI motorist assistance number ☎803116.

Hire

Pre-booking via the internet often costs less than hiring a car in Italy. Renters must generally be aged 25 or over, with a credit card and home country driving licence or an International Driving Permit. Consider hiring a small car, which will reduce your fuel expense and help you negotiate narrow city lanes and tight parking spaces. Check with your credit-card company to see if it offers a Collision Damage Waiver, which covers you for additional damage if you use that card to pay for the car.

Multinational car rental agencies include the following:
Auto Europe (www.autoeurope.com)
Autos Abroad (www.autosabroad.com)
Avis (www.avisautonoleggio.it)
Budget (www.budgetautonoleggio.it)
Europcar (www.europcar.com)
Hertz (www.hertz.it)
Maggiore (www.maggiore.it)

All the major car-hire outlets have offices at the airports.

MOTORCYCLES

Agencies throughout Italy rent motorbikes, ranging from small Vespas to larger touring bikes. Prices start around €20/140 per day/week for a 50cc scooter, or upwards of €80/400 per day/week for a 650cc motorcycle.

A licence is not required to ride a scooter under 50cc but you should be aged 14 or over and you cannot carry passengers or ride on an autostrada. To ride a motorcycle or scooter up to 125cc, you must be aged 16 or over and have a licence (a car licence will do). For motorcycles over 125cc you need a motorcycle licence.

Do not venture onto the autostrada with a bike of less than 150cc.

Road Rules

Before getting behind the wheel, it's worth acquainting yourself with the country's road rules. Here are some of the most essential:

» Cars drive on the right side of the road and overtake on the left.
» Seat belt use (front and rear) is mandatory.
» Give way to cars entering an intersection from a road on your right, unless otherwise indicated.
» In the event of a breakdown, a warning triangle is compulsory, as is the use of an approved yellow or orange safety vest if you leave your vehicle. Recommended accessories include a first-aid kit, spare-bulb kit and fire extinguisher.
» Italy's blood-alcohol limit is 0.05%. Random breath tests take place and penalties can be severe.
» Some cities, including Naples, ban non-residents from driving in the *centro storico* (historic centre). Fines can be steep.
» Speed limits for cars are 130km/h to 150km/h on autostradas; 110km/h on other main highways; 90km/h on minor, non-urban roads; 50km/h in built-up areas.
» The speed limit for mopeds is 40km/h.
» Speeding fines follow EU standards and are proportionate with the number of kilometres that you are caught driving over the speed limit, reaching up to €2000 with possible suspension of your driving licence.
» Helmets are required on all two-wheeled transport.
» Motorbikes can enter most restricted traffic areas in Italian cities, and traffic police generally turn a blind eye to motorcycles or scooters parked on footpaths.
» Headlights are compulsory day and night for all vehicles on the autostradas, and are advisable for motorcycles, even on smaller roads.

Local Transport

Bus & Underground Trains

Every city or town of any size has an efficient *urbano* (urban) and *extraurbano* (suburban) system of buses. Services are generally limited on Sundays and holidays. Naples and Catania also have a metro system.

Purchase bus and metro tickets before boarding. Validate bus tickets onboard and metro tickets at the station turnstile. Tickets can be bought from a *tabaccaio* (tobacconist), newsstands, ticket booths or dispensing machines at bus stations and in underground stations, and usually cost around €1 to €1.50. Some cities offer good-value 24-hour or daily tourist tickets.

Taxi

You can catch a taxi at the ranks outside most train and bus stations, or simply telephone for a radio taxi. Note that radio taxi meters start running from when you've called rather than when you're picked up.

Charges vary somewhat from one region to another. Most short city journeys cost between €10 and €15. Generally, no more than four people are allowed in one taxi.

Train

Trains in Italy are relatively cheap compared with other European countries, and the better train categories are fast and comfortable.

Trenitalia (☑892021, in Italian; www.trenitalia.com) is the partially privatised, state train system that runs most services. Other private lines are noted throughout this book.

There are several types of trains. *Regionale* or *interregionale* trains stop at all or most stations. Intercity (IC) trains, and their international counterparts known as Eurocity (EC), are faster services that operate between major cities. Even faster *pendolini* (tilting trains) capable of

reaching speeds of 250 to 300km per hour are collectively known as Eurostar Italia (ES).

In late 2009, Italy's newest, fastest, most expensive trains – the Alta Velocità (high speed) services variously known as Frecciarossa, Frecciargento, AV and ESAV – began operating on the Turin–Milan–Bologna–Florence–Rome–Naples–Salerno line, revolutionising train travel on that route.

As with the bus services, there are a number of private train lines operating throughout Italy's south, including the following:

Circumvesuviana (www.vesuviana.it) Links Naples and Sorrento, stopping at Ercolano (Herculaneum) and Pompeii.

Train Routes

Map legend:
- Principal Train Lines
- Local Train Lines
- Private Train Lines

Cities and locations shown on map: ROME, Termoli, Frosinone, Cassino, Campobasso, Manfredonia, Isernia, Foggia, Formia, Barletta, Caserta, Benevento, Spinazzola, Bari, Cancello, Avellino, Fasano, Naples, Mercato S S, Potenza, Gioia, Brindisi, Gragnano, Battipaglia, Taranto, Salerno, Metaponto, Lecce, Tyrrhenian Sea, Lagonegro, Sibari, Paola, Cosenza, Crotone, Catanzaro, Lamezia Terme C., Catanzaro Lido, Tropea, Rosarno, Ionian Sea, Messina, Palermo, Messina Marittima, Reggio di Calabria, Trapani, Randazzo, Taormina, Marsala, Sicily, Termini Imerese, Alcantara, Riposto, Castelvetrano, Enna, Catania, Agrigento, Caltanissetta, Licata, Gela, Ragusa, Siracusa, MEDITERRANEAN SEA, Noto

Ferrovia Cumana (www.sepsa.it) Connects Naples to the Campi Flegrei to the west. Stops include Pozzuoli.

Ferrotramviaria (www.ferrovienordbarese.it, in Italian) Services towns in Puglia's Terra di Bari, including Bitonto, Ruvo di Puglia, Andria and Barletta. Replacement bus service operates Sunday.

Ferrovie Appulo Lucane (FAL; www.fal-srl.it) Links Bari province with Basilicata, including stops at Altamura, Matera, Gravina in Puglia and Potenza. Replacement buses on Sunday.

Ferrovie del Sud-Est (www.fseonline.it) The main network covering Puglia's Murgia towns and the Salento, servicing tourist hotspots like Castellana Grotte, Alberobello, Martina Franca, Lecce, Gallipoli and Otranto. Replacement buses on Sunday.

Ferrovia Circumetnea (www.circumetnea.it) A 114km line connecting the towns around the base of Mt Etna in Sicily. No service on Sunday.

Classes & Costs

Prices vary according to the class of service, time of travel and how far in advance you book. Most Italian trains have 1st- and 2nd-class seating; a 1st-class ticket typically costs from a third to a half more than the 2nd-class ticket.

Travel on Intercity, Eurostar and Alta Velocità (AV) trains means paying a supplement, determined by the distance you are travelling and included in the ticket price. If you have a standard ticket for a slower train and end up hopping on an IC train, you'll have to pay the difference on board. (You can only board a Eurostar or Alta Velocità train if you have a booking, so the problem does not arise in those cases.)

Validate train tickets in the yellow machines (usually found at the head of rail platforms) just before boarding. Failure to do so usually results in fines.

Reservations

Reservations are obligatory on Eurostar and Alta Velocità trains. Otherwise they're not required on other train lines and, outside of peak holiday periods, you should be fine without them. You can make reservations at railway station counters, travel agents and, when they haven't broken down, at the automated machines sprinkled around most stations. Reservations carry a small extra fee.

Language

WANT MORE?

For in-depth language information and handy phrases, check out Lonely Planet's *Italian phrasebook*. You'll find it at **shop .lonelyplanet.com**, or you can buy Lonely Planet's iPhone phrasebooks at the Apple App Store.

Standard Italian is taught and spoken throughout Italy. Regional dialects are an important part of identity in many parts of the country, but you'll have no trouble being understood anywhere if you stick to standard Italian, which we've also used in this chapter.

The sounds used in spoken Italian can all be found in English. If you read our coloured pronunciation guides as if they were English, you'll be understood. The stressed syllables are indicated with italics. Note that ai is pronounced as in 'aisle', ay as in 'say', ow as in 'how', dz as the 'ds' in 'lids', and that r is a strong and rolled sound. Keep in mind that Italian consonants can have a stronger, emphatic pronunciation – if the consonant is written as a double letter, it should be pronounced a little stronger, eg *sonno son*·no (sleep) versus *sono so*·no (I am).

BASICS

Italian has two words for 'you' – use the polite form *Lei* lay if you're talking to strangers, officials or people older than you. With people familiar to you or younger than you, you can use the informal form *tu* too.

In Italian, all nouns and adjectives are either masculine or feminine, and so are the articles *il/la* eel/la (the) and *un/una* oon/*oo*·na (a) that go with the nouns.

In this chapter the polite/informal and masculine/feminine options are included where necessary, separated with a slash and indicated with 'pol/inf' and 'm/f'.

Hello.	*Buongiorno.*	bwon·*jor*·no
Goodbye.	*Arrivederci.*	a·ree·ve·*der*·chee

Yes.	*Sì.*	see
No.	*No.*	no
Excuse me.	*Mi scusi.* (pol)	mee skoo·zee
	Scusami. (inf)	*skoo*·za·mee
Sorry.	*Mi dispiace.*	mee dees·*pya*·che
Please.	*Per favore.*	per fa·*vo*·re
Thank you.	*Grazie.*	*gra*·tsye
You're welcome.	*Prego.*	*pre*·go

How are you?
Come sta/stai? (pol/inf) ko·me sta/stai

Fine. And you?
Bene. E Lei/tu? (pol/inf) *be*·ne e lay/too

What's your name?
Come si chiama? pol   ko·me see *kya*·ma
Come ti chiami? inf   ko·me tee *kya*·mee

My name is ...
Mi chiamo ...   mee *kya*·mo ...

Do you speak English?
Parla/Parli   *par*·la/*par*·lee
inglese? (pol/inf)   een·*gle*·ze

I don't understand.
Non capisco.   non ka·*pee*·sko

ACCOMMODATION

Do you have a ... room?	*Avete una camera ...?*	a·*ve*·te *oo*·na *ka*·me·ra ...
double	*doppia con letto matrimoniale*	*do*·pya kon *le*·to ma·*tree*·mo·*nya*·le
single	*singola*	*seen*·go·la

How much is it per ...?	Quanto costa per ...?	kwan·to kos·ta per ...
night	una notte	oo·na no·te
person	persona	per·so·na

Is breakfast included?
La colazione è compresa?	la ko·la·tsyo·ne e kom·pre·sa

air-con	aria condizionata	a·rya kon·dee·tsyo·na·ta
bathroom	bagno	ba·nyo
campsite	campeggio	kam·pe·jo
guesthouse	pensione	pen·syo·ne
hotel	albergo	al·ber·go
youth hostel	ostello della gioventù	os·te·lo de·la jo·ven·too
window	finestra	fee·nes·tra

DIRECTIONS

Where's ...?
Dov'è ...?	do·ve ...

What's the address?
Qual'è l'indirizzo?	kwa·le leen·dee·ree·tso

Could you please write it down?
Può scriverlo, per favore?	pwo skree·ver·lo per fa·vo·re

Can you show me (on the map)?
Può mostrarmi (sulla pianta)?	pwo mos·trar·mee (soo·la pyan·ta)

at the corner	all'angolo	a·lan·go·lo
at the traffic lights	al semaforo	al se·ma·fo·ro
behind	dietro	dye·tro
far	lontano	lon·ta·no
in front of	davanti a	da·van·tee a
left	a sinistra	a see·nee·stra
near	vicino	vee·chee·no
next to	accanto a	a·kan·to a
opposite	di fronte a	dee fron·te a
right	a destra	a de·stra
straight ahead	sempre diritto	sem·pre dee·ree·to

EATING & DRINKING

What would you recommend?
Cosa mi consiglia?	ko·za mee kon·see·lya

What's in that dish?
Quali ingredienti ci sono in questo piatto?	kwa·li een·gre·dyen·tee chee so·no een kwe·sto pya·to

KEY PATTERNS

To get by in Italian, mix and match these simple patterns with words of your choice:

When's (the next flight)?
A che ora è (il prossimo volo)?	a ke o·ra e (eel pro·see·mo vo·lo)

Where's (the station)?
Dov'è (la stazione)?	do·ve (la sta·tsyo·ne)

I'm looking for (a hotel).
Sto cercando (un albergo).	sto cher·kan·do (oon al·ber·go)

Do you have (a map)?
Ha (una pianta)?	a (oo·na pyan·ta)

Is there (a toilet)?
C'è (un gabinetto)?	che (oon ga·bee·ne·to)

I'd like (a coffee).
Vorrei (un caffè).	vo·ray (oon ka·fe)

I'd like to (hire a car).
Vorrei (noleggiare una macchina).	vo·ray (no·le·ja·re oo·na ma·kee·na)

Can I (enter)?
Posso (entrare)?	po·so (en·tra·re)

Could you please (help me)?
Può (aiutarmi), per favore?	pwo (a·yoo·tar·mee) per fa·vo·re

Do I have to (book a seat)?
Devo (prenotare un posto)?	de·vo (pre·no·ta·re oon po·sto)

What's the local speciality?
Qual'è la specialità di questa regione?	kwa·le la spe·cha·lee·ta dee kwe·sla re·jo·ne

That was delicious!
Era squisito!	e·ra skwee·zee·to

Cheers!
Salute!	sa·loo·te

Please bring the bill.
Mi porta il conto, per favore?	mee por·ta eel kon·to per fa·vo·re

I'd like to reserve a table for ...	Vorrei prenotare un tavolo per ...	vo·ray pre·no·ta·re oon ta·vo·lo per ...
(two) people	(due) persone	(doo·e) per·so·ne
(eight) o'clock	le (otto)	le (o·to)

I don't eat ...	Non mangio ...	non man·jo ...
eggs	uova	wo·va
fish	pesce	pe·she
nuts	noci	no·chee
(red) meat	carne (rossa)	kar·ne (ro·sa)

Key Words

bar	*locale*	lo·*ka*·le
bottle	*bottiglia*	bo·*tee*·lya
breakfast	*prima colazione*	*pree*·ma ko·la·*tsyo*·ne
cafe	*bar*	bar
cold	*freddo*	*fre*·do
dinner	*cena*	*che*·na
drink list	*lista delle bevande*	*lee*·sta de·le be·*van*·de
fork	*forchetta*	for·*ke*·ta
glass	*bicchiere*	bee·*kye*·re
grocery store	*alimentari*	a·lee·men·*ta*·ree
hot	*caldo*	*kal*·do
knife	*coltello*	kol·*te*·lo
lunch	*pranzo*	*pran*·dzo
market	*mercato*	mer·*ka*·to
menu	*menù*	me·*noo*
plate	*piatto*	*pya*·to
restaurant	*ristorante*	ree·sto·*ran*·te
spicy	*piccante*	pee·*kan*·te
spoon	*cucchiaio*	koo·*kya*·yo
vegetarian (food)	*vegetariano*	ve·je·ta·*rya*·no
with	*con*	kon
without	*senza*	*sen*·tsa

Meat & Fish

beef	*manzo*	*man*·dzo
chicken	*pollo*	*po*·lo
duck	*anatra*	*a*·na·tra
fish	*pesce*	*pe*·she
herring	*aringa*	a·*reen*·ga
lamb	*agnello*	a·*nye*·lo
lobster	*aragosta*	a·ra·*gos*·ta

meat	*carne*	*kar*·ne
mussels	*cozze*	*ko*·tse
oysters	*ostriche*	o·*stree*·ke
pork	*maiale*	ma·*ya*·le
prawn	*gambero*	*gam*·be·ro
salmon	*salmone*	sal·*mo*·ne
scallops	*capasante*	ka·pa·*san*·te
seafood	*frutti di mare*	*froo*·tee dee *ma*·re
shrimp	*gambero*	*gam*·be·ro
squid	*calamari*	ka·la·*ma*·ree
trout	*trota*	*tro*·ta
tuna	*tonno*	*to*·no
turkey	*tacchino*	ta·*kee*·no
veal	*vitello*	vee·*te*·lo

Fruit & Vegetables

apple	*mela*	*me*·la
beans	*fagioli*	fa·*jo*·lee
cabbage	*cavolo*	*ka*·vo·lo
capsicum	*peperone*	pe·pe·*ro*·ne
carrot	*carota*	ka·*ro*·ta
cauliflower	*cavolfiore*	ka·vol·*fyo*·re
cucumber	*cetriolo*	che·*tree*·o·lo
fruit	*frutta*	*froo*·ta
grapes	*uva*	*oo*·va
lemon	*limone*	lee·*mo*·ne
lentils	*lenticchie*	len·*tee*·kye
mushroom	*funghi*	*foon*·gee
nuts	*noci*	*no*·chee
onions	*cipolle*	chee·*po*·le
orange	*arancia*	a·*ran*·cha
peach	*pesca*	*pe*·ska
peas	*piselli*	pee·*ze*·lee
pineapple	*ananas*	*a*·na·nas
plum	*prugna*	*proo*·nya
potatoes	*patate*	pa·*ta*·te
spinach	*spinaci*	spee·*na*·chee
tomatoes	*pomodori*	po·mo·*do*·ree
vegetables	*verdura*	ver·*doo*·ra

Other

bread	*pane*	*pa*·ne
butter	*burro*	*boo*·ro
cheese	*formaggio*	for·*ma*·jo
eggs	*uova*	*wo*·va
honey	*miele*	*mye*·le

ice	ghiaccio	gya·cho
jam	marmellata	mar·me·la·ta
noodles	pasta	pas·ta
oil	olio	o·lyo
pepper	pepe	pe·pe
rice	riso	ree·zo
salt	sale	sa·le
soup	minestra	mee·nes·tra
soy sauce	salsa di soia	sal·sa dee so·ya
sugar	zucchero	tsoo·ke·ro
vinegar	aceto	a·che·to

Drinks

beer	birra	bee·ra
coffee	caffè	ka·fe
(orange) juice	succo (d'arancia)	soo·ko (da·ran·cha)
milk	latte	la·te
red wine	vino rosso	vee·no ro·so
soft drink	bibita	bee·bee·ta
tea	tè	te
(mineral) water	acqua (minerale)	a·kwa (mee·ne·ra·le)
white wine	vino bianco	vee·no byan·ko

EMERGENCIES

Help!
Aiuto!   a·yoo·to

Leave me alone!
Lasciami in pace!   la·sha·mee een pa·che

I'm lost.
Mi sono perso/a. (m/f)   mee so·no per·so/a

There's been an accident.
C'è stato un incidente.   che sta·to oon een·chee·den·te

Call the police!
Chiami la polizia!   kya·mee la po·lee·tsee·a

Call a doctor!
Chiami un medico!   kya·mee oon me·dee·ko

Where are the toilets?
Dove sono i gabinetti?   do·ve so·no ee ga·bee·ne·tee

Question Words		
How?	Come?	ko·me
What?	Che cosa?	ke ko·za
When?	Quando?	kwan·do
Where?	Dove?	do·ve
Who?	Chi?	kee
Why?	Perché?	per·ke

I'm sick.
Mi sento male.   mee sen·to ma·le

It hurts here.
Mi fa male qui.   mee fa ma·le kwee

I'm allergic to ...
Sono allergico/a a ... (m/f)   so·no a·ler·jee·ko/a a ...

SHOPPING & SERVICES

I'd like to buy ...
Vorrei comprare ...   vo·ray kom·pra·re ...

I'm just looking.
Sto solo guardando.   sto so·lo gwar·dan·do

Can I look at it?
Posso dare un'occhiata?   po·so da·re oo·no·kya·ta

How much is this?
Quanto costa questo?   kwan·to kos·ta kwe·sto

It's too expensive.
È troppo caro/a. (m/f)   e tro·po ka·ro/a

Can you lower the price?
Può farmi lo sconto?   pwo far·mee lo skon·to

There's a mistake in the bill.
C'è un errore nel conto. che oo·ne·ro·re nel kon·to

ATM	Bancomat	ban·ko·mat
post office	ufficio postale	oo·fee·cho pos·ta·le
tourist office	ufficio del turismo	oo·fee·cho del too·reez·mo

TIME & DATES

What time is it?	Che ora è?	ke o·ra e
It's one o'clock.	È l'una.	c loo·na
It's (two) o'clock.	Sono le (due).	so·no le (doo·e)
Half past (one).	(L'una) e mezza.	(loo·na) e me·dza

in the morning	di mattina	dee ma·tee·na
in the afternoon	di pomeriggio	dee po·me·ree·jo
in the evening	di sera	dee se·ra

yesterday	ieri	ye·ree
today	oggi	o·jee
tomorrow	domani	do·ma·nee

Monday	lunedì	loo·ne·dee
Tuesday	martedì	mar·te·dee
Wednesday	mercoledì	mer·ko·le·dee
Thursday	giovedì	jo·ve·dee
Friday	venerdì	ve·ner·dee
Saturday	sabato	sa·ba·to
Sunday	domenica	do·me·nee·ka

January	gennaio	jo·na·yo
February	febbraio	fe·bra·yo
March	marzo	mar·tso
April	aprile	a·pree·le
May	maggio	ma·jo
June	giugno	joo·nyo
July	luglio	loo·lyo
August	agosto	a·gos·to
September	settembre	se·tem·bre
October	ottobre	o·to·bre
November	novembre	no·vem·bre
December	dicembre	dee·chem·bre

NUMBERS

1	uno	oo·no
2	due	doo·e
3	tre	tre
4	quattro	kwa·tro
5	cinque	cheen·kwe
6	sei	say
7	sette	se·te
8	otto	o·to
9	nove	no·ve
10	dieci	dye·chee
20	venti	ven·tee
30	trenta	tren·ta
40	quaranta	kwa·ran·ta
50	cinquanta	cheen·kwan·ta
60	sessanta	se·san·ta
70	settanta	se·tan·ta
80	ottanta	o·tan·ta
90	novanta	no·van·ta
100	cento	chen·to
1000	mille	mee·lel

TRANSPORT

Public Transport

At what time does the ... leave/arrive?	A che ora parte/ arriva ...?	a ke o·ra par·te/ a·ree·va ...
boat	la nave	la na·ve
bus	l'autobus	low·to·boos
ferry	il traghetto	eel tra·ge·to
metro	la metro-politana	la me·tro-po·lee·ta·na
plane	l'aereo	la·e·re·o
train	il treno	eel tre·no

... ticket	un biglietto ...	oon bee·lye·to
one-way	di sola andata	dee so·la an·da·ta
return	di andata e ritorno	dee an·da·ta e ree·tor·no

bus stop	fermata dell'autobus	fer·ma·ta del ow·to·boos
platform	binario	bee·na·ryo
ticket office	biglietteria	bee·lye·te·ree·a
timetable	orario	o·ra·ryo
train station	stazione ferroviaria	sta·tsyo·ne fe·ro·vyar·ya

Does it stop at ...?
Si ferma a ...?   see fer·ma a ...

Please tell me when we get to ...
Mi dica per favore   mee dee·ka per fa·vo·re
quando arriviamo a ...   kwan·do a·ree·vya·mo a ...

I want to get off here.
Voglio scendere qui.   vo·lyo shen·de·re kwee

Driving & Cycling

I'd like to hire a/an ...	Vorrei noleggiare un/una ... (m/f)	vo·ray no·le·ja·re oon/oo·na ...
4WD	fuoristrada (m)	fwo·ree·stra·da
bicycle	bicicletta (f)	bee·chee·kle·ta
car	macchina (f)	ma·kee·na
motorbike	moto (f)	mo·to

bicycle pump	pompa della bicicletta	pom·pa de·la bee·chee·kle·ta
child seat	seggiolino	se·jo·lee·no
helmet	casco	kas·ko
mechanic	meccanico	me·ka·nee·ko
petrol/gas	benzina	ben·dzee·na
service station	stazione di servizio	sta·tsyo·ne dee ser·vee·tsyo

Is this the road to ...?
Questa strada porta a ...?   kwe·sta stra·da por·ta a ...

(How long) Can I park here?
(Per quanto tempo)   (per kwan·to tem·po)
Posso parcheggiare qui?   po·so par·ke·ja·re kwee

The car/motorbike has broken down (at ...).
La macchina/moto si è   la ma·kee·na/mo·to see e
guastata (a ...).   gwas·ta·ta (a ...)

I have a flat tyre.
Ho una gomma bucata.   o oo·na go·ma boo·ka·ta

I've run out of petrol.
Ho esaurito la   o e·zow·ree·to la
benzina.   ben·dzee·na

GLOSSARY

(m) indicates masculine gender, (f) feminine gender and (pl) plural

abbazia – abbey

agriturismo – tourist accommodation on farms; farm stay

(pizza) al taglio – (pizza) by the slice

albergo – hotel

alimentari – grocery shop; delicatessen

anfiteatro – amphitheatre

aperitivo – before-evening-meal drink and snack

APT – Azienda di Promozione Turistica; local town or city tourist office

autostrada – motorway; highway

battistero – baptistry

biblioteca – library

biglietto – ticket

borgo – archaic name for a small town, village or town sector (often dating to Middle Ages)

camera – room

campo – field

cappella – chapel

carabinieri – police with military and civil duties

Carnevale – carnival period between Epiphany and Lent

casa – house

castello – castle

cattedrale – cathedral

centro storico – historic centre

certosa – monastery belonging to or founded by Carthusian monks

chiesa – church

chiostro – cloister; covered walkway, usually enclosed by columns, around a quadrangle

cima – summit

città – town; city

città alta – upper town

città bassa – lower town

colonna – column

comune – equivalent to a municipality or county; a town or city council; historically, a self-governing town or city

contrada – district

corso – boulevard

duomo – cathedral

enoteca – wine bar

espresso – short black coffee

ferrovia – railway

festa – feast day; holiday

fontana – fountain

foro – forum

funivia – cable car

gelateria – ice-cream shop

giardino – garden

golfo – gulf

grotta – cave

isola – island

lago – lake

largo – small square

lido – beach

locanda – inn; small hotel

lungomare – seafront road/promenade

mar, mare – sea

masseria – working farm

mausoleo – mausoleum; stately and magnificent tomb

mercato – market

monte – mountain

necropoli – ancient name for cemetery or burial site

nord – north

osteria – simple, trattoria-style restaurant, usually with a bar

palazzo – mansion; palace; large building of any type, including an apartment block

palio – contest

parco – park

passeggiata – traditional evening stroll

pasticceria – cake/pastry shop

pensione – guesthouse

piazza – square

piazzale – large open square

pietà – literally 'pity' or 'compassion'; sculpture, drawing or painting of the dead Christ supported by the Madonna

pinacoteca – art gallery

ponte – bridge

porta – gate; door

porto – port

reale – royal

rifugio – mountain hut

ristorante – restaurant

rocca – fortress

sala – room; hall

salumeria – delicatessen

santuario – sanctuary; 1. the part of a church above the altar; 2. an especially holy place in a temple (antiquity)

sassi – literally 'stones'; stone houses built in two ravines in Matera, Basilicata

scalinata – staircase

scavi – excavations

spiaggia – beach

stazione – station

stazione marittima – ferry terminal

strada – street; road

sud – south

superstrada – expressway; highway with divided lanes

tartufo – truffle

tavola calda – literally 'hot table'; pre-prepared meat, pasta and vegetable selection, often self-service

teatro – theatre

tempietto – small temple

tempio – temple

terme – thermal baths
tesoro – treasury
torre – tower
trattoria – simple restaurant
Trenitalia – Italian State Railways; also known as Ferrovie dello Stato (FS)
trullo – conical house

via – street; road
viale – avenue

vico – alley; alleyway
villa – town house; country house; also the park surrounding the house

behind the scenes

SEND US YOUR FEEDBACK

We love to hear from travellers – your comments keep us on our toes and help make our books better. Our well-travelled team reads every word on what you loved or loathed about this book. Although we cannot reply individually to postal submissions, we always guarantee that your feedback goes straight to the appropriate authors, in time for the next edition. Each person who sends us information is thanked in the next edition – and the most useful submissions are rewarded with a free book.

Visit **lonelyplanet.com/contact** to submit your updates and suggestions or to ask for help. Our award-winning website also features inspirational travel stories, news and discussions.

Note: We may edit, reproduce and incorporate your comments in Lonely Planet products such as guidebooks, websites and digital products, so let us know if you don't want your comments reproduced or your name acknowledged. For a copy of our privacy policy visit lonelyplanet.com/privacy.

AUTHOR THANKS

Cristian Bonetto

A heartfelt *grazie* to my *re e regina di Napoli*, Luca Coda, Valentina Vellusi, Carmine Romano, Marcantonio Colonna, Diego Nuzzo, the wonderfully hospitable Voza family, Domenico Rotella, Donatello Ciao, Luigi Mosca, Mirella Armiero, Francesco Calazzo, Carolyn Jackson, Peter Bardwell and Carlo Buono. Sincere thanks also go to Joe Bindloss for the commission, and to my talented and diligent coauthors, editors and cartographers.

Gregor Clark

Thanks to all the kind-hearted Italians who helped make this trip so memorable, especially Michele in Taormina, Angela in Palermo, Marisin and Salvatore in Scopello, Francesco in Modica, as well as fellow travellers Susan Morgan, France Soucy, Lucia Tancredi and Ross Parks. Thanks to Wes for joining me on the Aeolians and helping me renew my Stromboli obsession. Finally, warm hugs to Gaen, Meigan and Chloe, who always make returning home the happiest part of the trip.

Olivia Pozzan

Warmest thanks go to my parents, both of whom passed away during the production of this book. They came from Due Ville, near Vicenza in the Veneto, emigrating to Australia after their marriage. I thank them for many things – fostering my adventurous nature, the independence afforded by an Australian upbringing, pride in my Italian heritage and encouraging all my endeavours. Heartfelt thanks to Andrew who shared my joys and sorrows and whose patience and support carried me through difficult times.

ACKNOWLEDGMENTS

Climate map data adapted from Peel MC, Finlayson BL & McMahon TA (2007) 'Updated World Map of the Köppen-Geiger Climate Classification', *Hydrology and Earth System Sciences*, 11, 163344.

Illustration pp62–3 by Javier Zarracina.

Cover photograph: four kids in Cefalù, Sicily; Felix Oberhage, Getty Images.

Many of the images in this guide are available for licensing from Lonely Planet Images: www.lonelyplanetimages.com.

This Book

This 1st edition of Lonely Planet's *Southern Italy* guidebook was researched and written by Cristian Bonetto, Gregor Clark and Olivia Pozzan. This guidebook was commissioned in Lonely Planet's London office, and produced by the following:

Commissioning Editors Joe Bindloss, Shawn Low

Coordinating Editor Kate Whitfield

Coordinating Cartographer Valentina Kremenchutskaya

Coordinating Layout Designer Paul Iacono

Managing Editors Brigitte Ellemor, Anna Metcalfe

Managing Cartographer Amanda Sierp

Managing Layout Designer Jane Hart

Assisting Editors Carly Hall, Elizabeth Harvey, Charlotte Orr

Cover Research Naomi Parker

Internal Image Research Aude Vauconsant

Illustrator Javier Zarracina

Language Content Annelies Mertens

Thanks to Cat Craddock, Ryan Evans, Yvonne Kirk, Sophie Splatt, Gerard Walker

NOTES

index

how to use this book

These symbols will help you find the listings you want:

- ⊙ Sights
- 🐦 Beaches
- 🏃 Activities
- 🍃 Courses
- ☞ Tours
- ✦ Festivals & Events
- 🛏 Sleeping
- ✕ Eating
- 🍸 Drinking
- ☆ Entertainment
- 🛍 Shopping
- ⓘ Information/Transport

Look out for these icons:

- **TOP CHOICE** Our author's recommendation
- **FREE** No payment required
- 🌱 A green or sustainable option

Our authors have nominated these places as demonstrating a strong commitment to sustainability – for example by supporting local communities and producers, operating in an environmentally friendly way, or supporting conservation projects.

These symbols give you the vital information for each listing:

- ♩ Telephone Numbers
- ⊙ Opening Hours
- Ⓟ Parking
- ⊖ Nonsmoking
- ✳ Air-Conditioning
- @ Internet Access
- ⓐ Wi-Fi Access
- ⓢ Swimming Pool
- ⓥ Vegetarian Selection
- ⓔ English-Language Menu
- ⓕ Family-Friendly
- ⓟ Pet-Friendly
- ⌷ Bus
- ⛴ Ferry
- Ⓜ Metro
- Ⓢ Subway
- ⊖ London Tube
- ⌷ Tram
- Ⓡ Train

Reviews are organised by author preference.

Map Legend

Sights
- 🐦 Beach
- 🔺 Buddhist
- 🏰 Castle
- ✝ Christian
- 🕉 Hindu
- ☪ Islamic
- ✡ Jewish
- ❶ Monument
- 🏛 Museum/Gallery
- ⊗ Ruin
- 🍷 Winery/Vineyard
- 🐾 Zoo
- ⊙ Other Sight

Activities, Courses & Tours
- 🤿 Diving/Snorkelling
- 🛶 Canoeing/Kayaking
- ⛷ Skiing
- 🏄 Surfing
- 🏊 Swimming/Pool
- 🚶 Walking
- 🏄 Windsurfing
- ⊕ Other Activity/Course/Tour

Sleeping
- 🛏 Sleeping
- ⛺ Camping

Eating
- ✕ Eating

Drinking
- ☕ Drinking
- ☕ Cafe

Entertainment
- ☆ Entertainment

Shopping
- 🛍 Shopping

Information
- ✉ Post Office
- ⓘ Tourist Information

Transport
- ✈ Airport
- ⊗ Border Crossing
- ⌷ Bus
- Cable Car/Funicular
- Cycling
- Ferry
- Ⓜ Metro
- Monorail
- Ⓟ Parking
- Ⓢ S-Bahn
- Taxi
- Train/Railway
- Tram
- ⊖ Tube Station
- Ⓤ U-Bahn
- • Other Transport

Routes
- Tollway
- Freeway
- Primary
- Secondary
- Tertiary
- Lane
- Unsealed Road
- Plaza/Mall
- Steps
- Tunnel
- Pedestrian Overpass
- Walking Tour
- Walking Tour Detour
- Path

Boundaries
- International
- State/Province
- Disputed
- Regional/Suburb
- Marine Park
- Cliff
- Wall

Population
- ★ Capital (National)
- ◉ Capital (State/Province)
- ● City/Large Town
- ● Town/Village

Geographic
- 🏠 Hut/Shelter
- 🔦 Lighthouse
- 🔭 Lookout
- ▲ Mountain/Volcano
- 🌴 Oasis
- ❶ Park
-)(Pass
- 🌳 Picnic Area
- 💧 Waterfall

Hydrography
- River/Creek
- Intermittent River
- Swamp/Mangrove
- Reef
- Canal
- Water
- Dry/Salt/Intermittent Lake
- Glacier

Areas
- Beach/Desert
- + + + Cemetery (Christian)
- × × × Cemetery (Other)
- Park/Forest
- Sportsground
- Sight (Building)
- Top Sight (Building)

OUR STORY

A beat-up old car, a few dollars in the pocket and a sense of adventure. In 1972 that's all Tony and Maureen Wheeler needed for the trip of a lifetime – across Europe and Asia overland to Australia. It took several months, and at the end – broke but inspired – they sat at their kitchen table writing and stapling together their first travel guide, *Across Asia on the Cheap*. Within a week they'd sold 1500 copies. Lonely Planet was born.

Today, Lonely Planet has offices in Melbourne, London and Oakland, with more than 600 staff and writers. We share Tony's belief that 'a great guidebook should do three things: inform, educate and amuse'.

OUR WRITERS

Cristian Bonetto

Coordinating Author, Naples & Campania As an ex-writer of farce and TV soap, it's not surprising that Cristian clicks with Campania. The Italo-Australian writer has been hooked on the region for years, his musings on it appearing in print from Sydney to London. Cristian has contributed to a dozen Lonely Planet titles, including *Naples & the Amalfi Coast, Rome Encounter* and *Copenhagen Encounter*. When he's not putting on weight in Italy, chances are you'll find him guzzling coffee in New York, Scandinavia or his hometown, Melbourne.

Gregor Clark

Sicily Gregor caught the Italy bug at age 14 during a year in Florence in which his professor dad trundled the family off to see every fresco, mosaic and museum within a 1000km radius. He's lived in Venice and Le Marche, led northern Italian bike tours, and huffed and puffed across the Dolomites while researching Lonely Planet's *Cycling Italy*. Highlights of his latest Sicily trip include celebrating his birthday at Segesta and racing up Etna at sunset to see an unexpected eruption.

Olivia Pozzan

Puglia, Basilicata & Calabria Although born and raised in Australia, Olivia's Italian heritage continually draws her back to the 'home country'. Having contributed to Lonely Planet's *Puglia & Basilicata* guide, she was keen to revisit the region to face a delicious onslaught of pasta, pizza and red wine. As an adventurous outdoors enthusiast, she has hiked mountain ranges, led caving expeditions and worked for an Arabian prince. When not exploring the world's most exotic places she lives the Aussie beach lifestyle, and is a practising veterinarian.

Published by Lonely Planet Publications Pty Ltd
ABN 36 005 607 983
1st edition – February 2012
ISBN 978 1 74179 236 2
© Lonely Planet 2012   Photographs © as indicated 2012
10 9 8 7 6 5 4 3 2 1
Printed in Singapore